THE
HEALING
CHRONICLES
OF
HENRY JONES

Peter Stephen Shrimpton

Published by The Henry Jones Wellness Institute
PO Box 50660, West Beach, 7449
Cape Town
www.henryjoneschronicles.com | info@henryjoneschronicles.com

First edition 2019

THE HEALING CHRONICLES OF HENRY JONES
ISBN 978-0-620-67875-9

Editor: Michelle Bovey-Wood
Cover and book designer: Vanessa Wilson
Typesetting and production: Quickfox Publishing
Printed by CastleGraphics, Cape Town

THE HEALING
CHRONICLES OF
HENRY JONES

The Henry Jones Book Series:

This book, *The Healing Chronicles of Henry Jones*, is accompanied by a Workbook, Handbook and Notebook. Together, they enable you to follow the healing journey described in the novel and do all the recommended healing exercises. This complete self-healing kit is designed to help you heal yourself naturally, holistically and permanently.

THE HENRY JONES NOVEL

*The Healing Chronicles of Henry Jone*s is a self-help novel that will entertain and enlighten you. This extraordinary story reveals the secrets of self-healing. It contains a treasure-trove of knowledge and wisdom that you'll need to heal yourself: physically, mentally, emotionally and spiritually.

THE HENRY JONES WORKBOOK

The *Henry Jones Workbook* is a practical jumpstart healing program that has been designed for personal use. It includes a daily Activity Planner that spans 40 days and 40 nights, allowing you to design and manage your own personal healing plan based on the experience of the characters in the novel. The Workbook enables you to schedule healing treatments; record your experiences; monitor and evaluate your progress; set goals and create incentives for yourself. *You can't heal yourself by reading a book – you must apply what you learn!*

THE HENRY JONES HANDBOOK

The Henry Jones Handbook provides the facts without the fiction. This quick reference guide gives you direct access to the essential knowledge needed to complete the prescribed daily healing exercises and heal your body. It includes summaries, checklists, study lists and step-by-step instructions to make learning easy. The Handbook is also loaded with hard facts, sage advice, words of wisdom and power statements to inspire you to heal yourself. *Get it, study it, live it!*

THE HENRY JONES NOTEBOOK

The Henry Jones Notebook is a personal, blank book to record your answers to the questions posed to you in the prescribed healing exercises. Use it to keep a journal of your healing journey, and more. *This is important!*

I dedicate this book to my loving wife, Mandy, who has been the light in my darkest hour; my strength when I was weak; my rescuer when I was lost; and my healer when I was sick. I thank you for your unconditional love and gracious self-sacrifice during the years I spent writing this book.

Thank you for being my sounding board; for bringing clarity to my thinking; for being so patient with me; for accepting all that I do; for teaching me to open my heart and to love; and for sharing your love with me. I am truly blessed and eternally grateful.

TABLE OF CONTENTS

PART 1

MENTAL HEALING

INTRODUCTION BY LEAFLET

It was just another cold, dreary day in hospital. I had no clue that Henry Jones was about to turn my world upside down and change it forever. Shuffling restlessly in an uncomfortable chair in the jam-packed waiting room, I had little else to do but worry about my test results and glare scornfully at the hospital staff and the other patients. I made no attempt to conceal my disdain for them. The nameless faces of the others in the waiting room stared back at me, gaunt and grey. I could tell they were scared, too. We were all sick, withered creatures with good reason to be anxious. Even the wilted pot plant beside me seemed to be gasping its last breath. An old woman tried to make conversation with me in a pitiful attempt to settle her nerves, but I fobbed her off quickly and without mercy. Sick and agitated, I picked up a promotional leaflet that someone had left on the coffee table in front of me. It read:

Stop and ask yourself …
– Are you sick?
– Are you in pain?
– Are you worried about your health?
– Are you scared?
– Is there something wrong with your body?
– Are you experiencing the symptoms of disease?
– Has your doctor given you 'the bad news'?
– Are you taking medication?
– Do you have to go to hospital?
– Do you need surgery?
– Does your mind dwell on your physical problems?

Now answer this …
- Do you want to get better?
- If there was something you could do to heal your body, would you do it?
- Are you willing to try anything, but don't know where to start?
- Are you searching for answers?

Look no further! I can help you to …
- Heal your body naturally, holistically and permanently.
- Discover the natural path to perfect health.
- Bring true wellness into your life.
- Prevent sickness and disease in the future.

I will show you how to …
- Boost your immune system.
- Rid your body of poisonous toxins.
- Purify your blood.
- Cleanse your internal organs.
- Regenerate your body's cells.
- Increase your natural energy levels.
- Open your neural pathways and remove blockages.
- Connect with the natural healing power within you.

I can teach you effective techniques to …
- Relieve physical discomfort and pain.
- Stop worrying.
- Let go of your doubts and fears.
- Restore peace and harmony in your body.

Yes, you can …
- Cure your sickness, disease, ailment, affliction or pain.
- Restore your body to perfect health.
- Enjoy boundless energy.
- Look and feel terrific.
- Experience radiant health and vitality every day for the rest of your life.

Sound good? Then all you need to do is …
– Keep an open mind.
– Don't be afraid to try new things.
– Give it a go.
– Embrace change.
– Try to enjoy yourself. (No matter what!)

It's time for you to …
– Heal your body.
– Open your mind.
– Awaken your spirit.
– Free your emotions

Interested? Call me right now.
The telephone number followed.

What rubbish! I thought. I crumpled the leaflet into a tight ball and tossed it into a nearby dustbin. Disillusioned, I slumped back in my seat and sighed deeply, scowling at the stopped clock hanging above the exit sign on the door. The irony of it struck me: We were both stuck, broken and going nowhere. Heaven knows I didn't want to be in this awful situation. Hospital was the last place on Earth I wanted to be. But, I was sick. I wouldn't have admitted it at the time, but I was also sad, scared and lonely. I took another look around the waiting room. The emaciated faces of the other patients quickly reminded me that I wasn't alone. Yes, we're all sick, withered creatures, I groaned to myself. Our time was ticking away and our choices, it seemed, were limited.

CHAPTER 1

MEETING HENRY JONES

"Meet Henry Jones," said Sister Lillian, smiling from ear to ear. I wasn't in the mood to meet anyone. I had geared myself up for another dull, dreary day in hospital and certainly wasn't expecting anyone named Henry Jones. She swished back the blinds and the first rays of morning poured into my room. Blinded by the light, I grunted disapprovingly. "It's time to get up," she announced in an annoyingly cheery voice. "It's a beautiful day outside!"

I rubbed my eyes and squinted at the silhouette standing at the foot of my bed. I felt sick, tired, and depressed. I didn't want to meet any Henry Jones. I wanted to be left alone to wallow in self-pity and go back to sleep. But Sister Lillian was having none of it. She put her hand on my forehead, as if to feel my temperature. Her manner made me feel like a small child again.

"Mmmmm, much better," she said matter-of-factly and gave me a reassuring smile. I wasn't so sure. She leaned over and whispered in my ear: "Henry Jones is here to visit you. Try to be nice."

"It's hard to be nice when you feel like crap," I snarled. She broadened her smile defiantly. Over the past few months, she'd become an expert at brushing aside my belligerence.

"He's all yours," she said as she exited the room. I watched her leave. As had become her custom, she stopped in the doorway, looked back at me, smiled reassuringly, and then left the room to do her rounds. I liked Sister Lillian. She was dependable and genuinely seemed to care.

Henry Jones was a short fellow – in fact, diminutive. Probably in his mid-50s, he looked perfectly ordinary: He was the kind of person you wouldn't spare a second glance on the street. I wasn't impressed at all. But then Henry

16

Jones smiled at me and something quite extraordinary happened. Somehow, his smile transcended my worries and woes and I felt my soul flit. He had a surprisingly fabulous smile. It was wide and sunny, the kind of smile that people envied. He was instantly likable. Unfortunately, though, Henry Jones had caught me on a bad day. The moment passed as quickly as it had come, and I was once more my belligerent self.

"What do you want?" I grumbled, not feeling an ounce of guilt about the harshness of my tone.

"Why are you sick?" he asked me.

What a ridiculous question! I thought. How was I supposed to know why I was sick? I stared sulkily out the window. That stupid question doesn't warrant an answer, I told myself, fuming inside.

Henry Jones held the silence. He didn't say a word. Not a single one. He just stood there, waiting patiently for me to answer him. An awkward tension built between us. I started feeling very uncomfortable. The truth is, I didn't know the answer to his question. Throughout my treatment, I'd repeatedly been asked: "How do you feel?", "What do you feel?" and "Where do you feel it?" Nobody had ever asked me: "Why are you sick?"

"How am I supposed to know?" I finally blurted out begrudgingly.

"How, indeed?" Henry Jones replied enthusiastically, pulled up a chair and sat down beside me. "When you know the answer to this question, you can start the journey towards wellness," he said, beaming.

"What are you going on about?" I barked. Henry Jones was starting to piss me off. It was far too early in the morning for this strange conversation, and my condition made it utterly inappropriate.

"Healing," Henry Jones said, nodding excitedly. He smiled at me once more. I swear the Sun shone a bit brighter at that moment. I guess I must have looked at him strangely because he repeated himself even louder: "Healing!"

He kept nodding as if I should understand him. The way he said the word "healing" made the hairs on my forearms stand up. The man was clearly passionate about the subject.

"Go on, say it," he ordered gently.

"Say what?"

"Say the word out loud ... healing."

"Why?"

"Come on ... just say it."

"Why?" I growled.

He cocked his head to the side and asked: "Do you want to be healed?"

"Of course I do," I retorted, without much conviction. The doctors had told me everything I could expect from my disease. Henry Jones clearly remained unconvinced, but he graciously disregarded my doubt and gestured for me to say that darn word again: *Healing*.

For some peculiar reason, I found it hard to oblige him. The word stuck in my throat. I just couldn't bring myself to say it. Seconds dragged by. When I eventually spoke, I mumbled scornfully: "I'm very sorry. I've been feeling sick for a long time. It's just too hard for me to think about …" Once again, I couldn't get my tongue around the word.

"Healing," Henry Jones said, finishing my sentence.

"Yes."

"I understand," he replied. "I really do. I've interviewed hundreds, if not thousands, of sick people. A significant percentage of them struggle to embrace the concept of healing. You see, they feel like victims of disease. They expect their physicians to heal their bodies. When that fails, they feel betrayed by the healing process and become resentful and angry."

"Now that you mention it …" I was about to admit to the very same feelings when he cut me short.

"There's no point in playing the powerless patient. That won't help you to heal your body. You need to become actively involved in your healing process, my friend."

I felt irritated. What was I supposed to do? Who was this man to order me to do anything, anyway?

"I'm not prepared to have this conversation with you," I muttered.

He looked at me with great empathy and said: "I'm not surprised. No matter who you are, where you come from, or what you've done, nothing in life prepares you to cope with illness. Especially if your sickness can kill you!"

"What do you know about it?" I moaned.

"Well, my story is no different from the millions of people who get told 'the bad news' every year," he said. "I once found myself sitting opposite a specialist who took great care to draw my urinary tract on a sheet of paper and explain 'my problem', as he called it. I sat dead quiet and listened to his explanation of the disease that was ravaging my body. As if I understood a word of it! Hah! In all honesty, I didn't have a clue what my doctor was talking about. All the medical jargon went straight over my head."

I understood what Henry Jones was saying. I didn't fully understand what was happening inside my body, either. Most of the time I didn't understand my doctors. I felt the urge to interject, but I dared not disturb Henry Jones.

"Everything inside me screamed: 'This can't be happening to me.'" I tried to concentrate on the doctor's drawing, but my eyes kept drifting to the word he'd written in the top right-hand corner of the page: Terminal."

I swallowed hard.

"My doctor spoke to me about 'support groups' and 'inevitability planning'. He recommended that my wife attend our next appointment. I foolishly told him that my wife didn't need to know about 'my problem'. How dazed and confused was I?" tittered Henry Jones.

I couldn't bring myself to answer him. I'd tried to hide my sickness, too.

"What was wrong with you?" I asked instead.

"Hmmmm, that's a matter of opinion," he replied, rubbing his chin. "I had bladder cancer. There was a malignant tumor in my bladder the size of a ripe strawberry. The news devastated me. I was 52 years old, madly in love with my gorgeous wife, Isabel, and I absolutely adored my 17-year-old son, Thomas. I successfully ran my own business from lavish offices, drove fast sports cars, and lived in a beautiful house. In short, I loved my life. And I really, really didn't want to get sick and die! It all seemed surreal – like I was starring in a bad horror movie from which I couldn't escape."

"So, what happened next?" I asked, captivated.

"Well, by the time I came to my senses, I was sitting in my car in the hospital parking lot. I remember staring at my reflection in the rearview mirror for the longest time. I distinctly remember saying to myself: 'You're in big trouble, Henry Jones!'"

He kept quiet for a moment, as if lost in thought. His eyes were closed, but he appeared calm. It gave me time to study the lines on his face.

"And then?"

He sighed. "Intuitively, I knew that I was somehow responsible for this horrible health crisis. And I knew instinctively that it was my responsibility to get myself out of it! Right then and there, at that moment, I made up my mind to heal my body, no matter what!"

"How did you know what to do?" Henry Jones looked as fit as a fiddle to me. He certainly didn't look like a dying man. In fact, he radiated vitality and wellness – especially when he smiled!

"I didn't know where to begin," he confessed. "It'd been a long, painful journey to the doctor's office. I'd been urinating blood for well over a year, so I knew that something was wrong with me. I tried to convince myself that I was bleeding because of my extremely stressful work situation or intense exercise program. I hoped the problem would just go away when things eased up. But, it didn't. My physical and psychological symptoms just grew worse.

"Apparently, we're singing from the same hymn sheet," I muttered.

He flinched and then continued: "I dreaded going to the toilet. The sight of blood leaving my body and swirling in the bowl daily churned my gut. I'm sorry to give you the gory details, but you need to know where I'm coming from."

"It's okay," I added. "This is a hospital. I've seen it all here."

He nodded knowingly and then continued his story: "My thoughts and actions revolved around my dilemma with progressive intensity. Instead of using urinals, as most men do, I'd skulk into the toilet because I was afraid that someone would see I was bleeding. Blood would leak into my underpants, especially after urinating, and I was always terrified that an 'accident' would reveal my dirty little secret and I'd be humiliated. As the director of my own asset management company, it was a living nightmare for me. You see, I had 25 or so hard-nosed financial brokers working for me. I was terrified they would lose confidence in my leadership. Poor old me!" he chortled.

That was the first time I'd heard Henry Jones laugh. It was a strange laugh that seemed too deep for his small frame. It didn't last long, though – one spurt and it was over. I studied his face closely. I'd never have pegged Henry Jones as an influential stockbroker. He looked too ordinary to be a wheeler-dealer financial executive. Only his hands corroborated his story. They were soft, smooth, and refined. Henry Jones didn't swing shovels for a living, that much was certain. His engaging manner and disarming friendliness had captured my attention. Minutes earlier, I had wanted to go back to sleep, but all of a sudden, I was interested in Henry Jones. He had a story to tell and, as fate would have it, I had plenty of time to listen to it.

"It must've been a tough time for you," I responded, wondering what my cut-throat colleagues at the publishing house were thinking about me.

"It was," he said. "I could avoid urinals, but what I couldn't escape was the fear. In the back of my mind there was a constant fear that something was terribly wrong with me, and I just didn't want to face it … then the pain started," he said softly. "At first, I hoped it would just go away, but it didn't. Instead, it got worse – much worse! Weeks became months, and the worse it became, the more I resisted doing anything about it. Stupid, eh?" he said, striking a nerve.

"I've learned not to underestimate the power that fear can have over us," I mumbled, biting my bottom lip.

"Yes, fear can destroy you, if you let it," he agreed earnestly. "At the time, it consumed me. I was debilitated by it. I must confess, though, I also had personal power issues I had to face. I was working on a really big deal at the time, which I believed would make me super rich. I wanted that wealth really badly. I was so committed to the success of my new business venture that I was willing to risk my company, personal wealth, reputation, and well-being. The fabulous world I was crafting for myself needed my full attention, I told myself. I needed to be on top of things or it might all come crashing down. I literally couldn't afford to get sick, I thought," said Henry Jones. He half-smiled and then looked down, as if embarrassed by his foolishness.

"Please go on," I said.

He took a deep breath and continued his story: "I was determined to control my reality. And I didn't want to give up control for anything – especially illness! You see, from childhood I had been conditioned to regard sickness as a weakness. Ill-health wasn't tolerated in our house. When I felt poorly, my parents told me straight: 'You're not dying. Go to school.'"

"My father used to say: 'You only go to the doctor when you have a broken leg,'" I interjected.

"I've heard that one before, too," he said, amused. We shared a chuckle. It didn't last long because it really wasn't funny.

He cleared his throat and continued: "So as many people do, I clung to the ridiculous belief that sickness represents weakness and failure, and those weren't options for me at the time. Even though the little voice in my head kept telling me to get a medical examination, I chose to ignore it."

"I did the same thing," I admitted.

"That didn't work out too well for me in the long run either," said Henry Jones. "Try as I might, I couldn't ignore the symptoms of disease. Eventually, my nether region was so swollen that I thought my bladder and prostate were going to explode. I couldn't cross my legs, walk, or sleep without discomfort. It was horrible. I opened my eyes in the morning and immediately felt pain. During the day I constantly dealt with pain, and I went to sleep at night still processing that pain. No matter how I tried, I couldn't escape the pain."

Henry Jones rose and poured two glasses of water. He gulped down one glass and handed me the other. I took it without question and waited for him to continue.

"Reflecting back, I can say that the only thing worse than the pain was the fear that churned in my gut. It made me sick to my core. I was worried, scared, lonely and sore … Not a nice place to be, huh?" said Henry Jones. "Of course, my wife knew of my troubles. She constantly urged me to see a doctor, but I made a string of excuses and avoided the subject whenever possible. I didn't discuss my problem with her because I didn't want her to worry. At least, that's what I told myself. Everyone else was oblivious to my suffering. I didn't share my problem with people for fear of losing face. It was my own private hell."

"What happened next?" I asked, eager to know more.

"Well, I eventually reached the end of the line. I had a good and proper meltdown. I remember it like it was yesterday. All my suffering culminated in a single, definitive moment when I just couldn't go on any further. I was attending a critical meeting in the boardroom with my partners. They were locked in a heated debate about money, but I was lost to another cause. The pain consumed me. It had so completely eaten into the fabric of my consciousness that I could no longer tell where the pain was located in my body. It was constant, everywhere and utterly unbearable," he said. Then he closed his eyes and seemed to drift back in time once more. He sighed. "I remember tears welling in my eyes. They obscured my vision. I was afraid to blink in case they spilled down my cheeks. I just couldn't stand it anymore. I was unable to pretend a minute longer. I needed help. By the time I finally went to the doctor, I was out of options. The mere sight of my bloody urine sample made my GP's eyes pop. He immediately referred me to a urologist. After a series of tests, I was referred to the medical specialist who delivered my prognosis using a hand-drawn sketch of my urinary system."

In only a few minutes, Henry Jones had disclosed shocking and intimate details of his past. I was hooked and needed to know more. Why had he come to visit me? How did he know Sister Lillian? What did he want with me? I had so many questions that needed answers.

I didn't know it then, but Henry Jones had entered my life for a reason. He had something of immeasurable value to offer me. I was curious to know how he had become well again.

"So, what did you do after staring at your reflection in the rearview mirror?" I asked, taking him back to his story.

He didn't miss a beat. "I told myself again and again: 'You got yourself into this situation, you get yourself out of it!' After some time, I pulled myself together and drove to a lunch meeting with one of my partners. He could see I was distracted and asked what was bothering me. I couldn't stop myself from telling him. It was like the dam wall broke inside me, and I poured my heart out. I'll never forget his response. After hearing my long, sad story he said these simple words: 'Geez Henry, what are you going to do?'"

"What are you going to do?" I echoed him.

"Yes. What are YOU going to do?" Henry Jones asked, looking at me intently. Feeling intimidated, I looked away. He continued: "This confirmed for me that sickness is solely the sufferer's problem. Sure, other people can be caring, concerned, sympathetic or empathetic, but at the end of the day, your sickness isn't their problem. When you get sick, it's your problem, so you must sort it out. I knew I had to take responsibility for healing my body, but I didn't know what to do, or where to begin."

"So, what happened?" I asked.

"I wish I could tell you that I was brave from the start, but I can't," he confessed. "The truth is, I went home, sunk on to my bedroom floor, put my head in my hands, and cried like a baby for the first time in my adult life. I know we're all going to die eventually, but my hourglass had suddenly been turned upside down and I was terrified!"

I knew that my condition was different from Henry Jones's, but I shared his despair. I was sick, and I'd been unwell for a really long time.

"I'm terrified that I won't get well again," I heard myself admitting, much to my own surprise. I shuddered violently. "I'm sorry for interrupting you. Please, go on with your story," I said. Henry Jones graciously obliged me.

"At first, I was in denial. I'd always been healthy. I was the guy in the office who didn't catch any of the bugs going around. I went to gym four times a week and had done so ever since I was a teenager. No, this ghastly affliction couldn't be happening to me, I thought." He sighed loudly. "It was only when I got sick that I woke up to the fact that nothing in the world is more important than your health. Fame and fortune are useless against disease."

"Sickness is a great equalizer," I agreed.

"Yup, you can have all the money in the world, but when you get sick, you're just as mortal as the pauper lying in the hospital bed next to you. Ask me. I know," said Henry Jones. "I was scheduled for surgery within a matter of days – and I wasn't given a choice in the matter. According to my doctors, 'there wasn't anything else I could do.'"

"So, did you have surgery?" I asked.

"Yes. It was an awful experience," he said.

"How come?"

"Well, lying in the pre-surgery waiting room with the rest of the patients was dehumanizing. The beds were lined up one after the next. Nobody uttered a sound, and everyone looked scared!"

I nodded knowingly.

"There was a young girl lying beside me. She kept rubbing her head, which had obviously just been shaved for surgery. I felt profound sadness for her. The look in her eyes haunts me to this day. It said: "Help me!" Henry Jones batted his eyelids, as if to push away the memory that plagued his mind. "The staff members were professional, but they lacked love and tenderness. It was clear that we were just numbers on their daily roster. I felt like a piece of meat."

"I often feel that way, too," I said. "Like a lab rat waiting to be experimented upon."

Henry Jones didn't comment. "I tried to pray, but God felt very far away," he said, looking briefly out of the window. "After surgery, I hoped the pain would stop, but it didn't! My surgeon said it would stop once my body had recovered from the operation, but it continued. I was scheduled to see him again in three weeks to discuss 'the path forward', as he called it. During that time, I devoured books on human healing, like a drowning man gasping for air."

Talking about healing brought Henry Jones to life. He exuded passion. It was contagious and I hung on his every word.

"A new, vital driving force was slowly emerging within me. I felt compelled to understand the cause of my sickness. Common sense told me that when the cause was removed, the symptoms would disappear."

"But we don't know the cause of disease," I said bluntly.

"That's what I used to think, too," he replied. "But then I discovered that medical science is standing on the verge of a new era. A whole new approach to healing is emerging, and it's very exciting."

"What medical journals did you read?" I asked sarcastically.

"To be quite candid, reading books on modern medicine felt dis-empowering. You see, modern medicine is very clinical and cold. The books I read spoke about 'the science of medicine' and referred to human beings as 'specimens'. They didn't actively involve the individual in the healing process at all. The content revolved around what modern medicine can do for the patient, but very little about what patients can do for themselves. I'm not knocking the physicians who write these books – I'm sure they have the best intentions – it's just that I couldn't relate to those books," Henry Jones said, beating fiercely on his chest.

"Now, on the other hand, everything I read about natural and holistic healing resonated with me. The more I learned about these fascinating fields, the more motivated I became to take responsibility for healing myself – or at the very least, to start helping my body to heal itself. Each word struck a chord with me, and I grew increasingly empowered by the vast array of healing modalities and techniques that I discovered."

"You don't mean those wholewheat, sandal-wearing, candle-burning, New Age self-help guides, do you?" I asked skeptically.

"I read those, too," he chuckled. "If you really want to get well again, you've got to try everything to see what works for you."

He had a point. Why not try everything to get well again? Why have mental blocks if they're potentially preventing you from restoring your health? I hadn't thought of it like that.

"I guess so," I mumbled.

Henry Jones was on a roll. "My biggest gripe is that modern medicine is devoid of spirit. I'm not saying the essential spiritual quality of the healing process is understated, I'm saying it's left out completely. Modern medicine may be filled with marvelous science, but it's been dehumanized. No wonder so many sick people feel hopeless."

I felt hopeless, like a medical case. I was a patient more than a person and I didn't like it! Henry Jones was starting to make sense to me. I'd done absolutely nothing to heal myself except rely on my doctors and medication. I was so busy asking medical staff what they could do for me that I never stopped to ask what I could do for myself. It never occurred to me to question my role in the healing process.

"So, reading helped you?" I asked, instantly realizing it was a silly question. I needed Henry Jones to tell me more.

"Oh yes, definitely. The next time I saw my doctor, I was filled with hope," he said. "I was armed with the very latest information in the field of holistic healing. I began by asking for his medical opinion on alternative healing techniques, but he answered abruptly, saying it was 'airy-fairy, esoteric, mumbo-jumbo that offers people false hope'. I retorted by drawing his attention to recent breakthroughs in our understanding of the body-mind relationship. He didn't know what I was talking about! I went on to share with him some of the new knowledge I'd discovered, but I could see a brick wall building between us. When I mentioned chakra points, he checked his wristwatch, as if to let me know that he didn't have any more time for me. I left his office shortly afterward and never went back."

I scratched my head. Chakra points, the body-mind relationship, and holistic healing were all new concepts to me. I was accustomed to medication and surgery. I felt a fit of panic. I was so sick, tired, and depressed. I was a hospital patient, and pretty soon doctors would surround me, along with nurses and students who would push, prod, and poke me. I was a victim of disease. I hoped the doctors would heal me, but I was at their mercy. I was a lab rat. But now, Henry Jones, with his fabulous smile, was telling me something different, and I didn't know what to believe. Could Henry Jones be right? Was there an alternative path to healing? Would it work for me? I wondered.

"So, you never went back?" I asked.

"Never!"

"No check-ups or tests?"

"I had many of those. I just made sure my new doctors practised integrative medicine."

"What's that?" I asked.

He smiled. "It's a blend of the best of modern medicine and the best of alternative medicine. You see, there are myriad approaches to human healing out there and all of them are available to you: From ancient healing practices to revolutionary new breakthroughs in healing technology. You have a smorgasbord of wellness programs to choose from."

"Is that what you did?" I asked.

"Yes, exactly! I embarked on an incredible healing journey," said Henry Jones. "I made it my mission to meet many healers and to read as much as possible."

"Did they all work for you?" I quizzed him.

"Some healing techniques worked for me, others didn't. Not because they don't work, but because healing is subjective. What works for one person may not work for another. The most important thing to do is to keep practising healing techniques that you feel work for you until your body has been restored to perfect health. I wanted to get well, so I tried everything on the healing menu. That's what worked for me!"

"How long did it take?" I asked.

"I'm still doing it," he answered happily. "Healing your body and keeping it healthy is a lifestyle choice. It's not something you practise just to get well. Some people treat healing like a hangover. You know, people make all sorts of false promises about never drinking again when they feel hungover, but as soon as they feel better again, they forget their words. Right?"

"Yup, I've done that a few times," I confessed.

"I had to make permanent decisions because I wanted to heal my body permanently. I made dramatic life changes and I stuck to them. Within a few years, I'd completely reinvented myself. I changed my occupation; geographic location; diet; exercise program; value system; habits; and principles. In short, I became a whole new person. I healed myself holistically. Trust me, it's the only way."

"What do you mean 'holistically'?" I asked abruptly. I felt impatient when I had to learn new things. I abhorred ignorance, and Henry Jones had knowledge of a whole new world that I knew nothing about.

"Holistically means physically, mentally, emotionally and spiritually," he said. "It's very important to treat a patient as a whole person. You can't just treat the physical body."

That statement resonated with me. Something was missing from my treatment. When Henry Jones pointed out the gaps, I felt angry again.

"Why didn't my doctors tell me about holistic healing? Why haven't I been exposed to this information before?" I barked at Henry Jones, as if he had all the answers.

"I guess it has a lot to do with how medical practitioners are trained," he said without further explanation. Seconds ticked by.

"Go on," I demanded.

He chuckled. "Medical practitioners study within a very narrow band of medical science. The knowledge they acquire is all they know, so they tend to be skeptical and mistrusting of any information that's outside of that narrow band. I learned this the hard way. I'd restored my body to perfect health by practising natural, holistic healing techniques, and I wanted to share my new-found knowledge and experience with anyone who cared to listen. I started volunteering at a local hospital. That gave me the opportunity to meet people who either practised medicine or needed medical treatment. I can tell you that speaking to people about healing in a hospital is a real eye-opener."

"In what way?" I asked.

"Well, I usually get one of two responses," he answered. "Medical practitioners are taught to diagnose, drug and cut. They struggle to integrate new healing modalities into their treatments and are mostly dismissive of alternative ideas. On the other hand, I find most patients are very interested to know how they can relieve their suffering and pain. They want to speed up their healing process, regardless of the approach. However, most patients don't know the fundamentals of self-healing. Sick people always want to get well again, but they don't always know how to go about it."

"Like me," I said.

"Yes," he answered compassionately. "But it's okay, because I can help you find your way to perfect health. I've become completely obsessed with recording healing techniques and mapping the connections on the healing continuum. You'll be amazed at what I can teach you. Healing is a fascinating, magical, mystical thing."

When I thought of healing, I thought of doctors, hospitals, strange smells, injections, and vile-tasting medication. "Healing?"

"Yes, healing," Henry Jones said excitedly, shaking his fist in the air. "At last, I've heard you say it."

What is it about healing that gets Henry Jones so fired up? Why does he care so much for others? Is this guy for real? I wondered.

He tapped my shoulder to get my attention. "Most importantly, I've already applied this knowledge to heal my body and many others. I believe I can help you, too."

"Are you a pharmaceutical sales rep?" I asked suspiciously.

"Goodness no!" chortled Henry Jones. "Nothing like that!"

"What then?"

"Sister Lillian asked me to share my story with you because she thinks we can help each other. I can take you on an amazing, holistic healing journey and show you many wonderful techniques that will help you to heal your body," he announced.

The magnitude of his offer didn't sink in immediately.

"And what can I do for you?" I replied.

"Sister Lillian told me you're a publisher, is that right?"

"Yes," I drawled slowly.

"Here's the thing," he said. "The sick people I talk to about holistic healing often express a genuine desire to learn more. They always ask me for reading material, but I don't have anything to give them, except extracts from my notes."

"That's a shame," I said. "But surely such books are already available?"

"Yes, but it would take a reader many years to acquire the knowledge I have at my fingertips," he said, and then drew closer to me as if to reveal a great secret. "Over the years, I've seen and done things in the field of human healing that will astonish you. I've read hundreds of books on healing and countless medical journals. I've also interviewed scores of healers from all around the world. I don't claim to have developed any of these healing techniques or modalities, but I can honestly say that I've practised every single one of them. I genuinely believe they've all contributed to my healing in some way!"

"You do look very healthy."

"I am," replied Henry Jones. "I experience radiant health and vitality every day of my life. I have boundless energy and enjoy a balanced life. But most importantly, I no longer ever think about being sick."

I tried to recall what that felt like.

"You can, too," he said. "If you want to heal your body, I can show you how to do it, but you must commit to the process and apply what you learn."

"Can you promise that these techniques will work for me?" I asked.

"Of course not," he replied. "I can't promise my healing program will heal your body. Some things are beyond the control of us mere mortals. I can promise you this, however: I'll show you everything you need to know. I'll give you a roadmap to perfect health and personally escort you every step of the way. I can promise that I will do my utmost best to ensure you reach your destination. How does that sound?"

I avoided answering him. "So, you want to write your memoirs?"

"Oh no!" he exclaimed. "Luckily for us, during my healing journey I made comprehensive notes and kept important articles, insights, and quotations. I've compiled a hefty file of information about human healing. It's jam-packed with powerful healing techniques from around the world. All you need to do is consolidate and organize the material for publication."

"What kind of publication?" I inquired.

"I'm hooked on the idea of producing a book that provides readers with practical, step-by-step guidelines on how to heal themselves physically, mentally emotionally and spiritually. You see, I've read tons of fascinating books on biology; nutrition; diet, psycho-neuro-immunology; quantum physics; cellular healing; spirituality; meditation; positive thinking and alternative healing, to name but a few subjects. However, I can't think of a single book that provides all the information across all aspects of the healing continuum. That's why I've decided to produce one, and I need your help," he declared.

I rubbed my chin. My heart was beating faster. It was a compelling offer. I'd nothing to lose and everything to gain. I should've screamed: "Yes!" but I didn't. What was stopping me? Why was I so afraid? What choice did I have? My thoughts scrambled around in my head.

Sensing my hesitation, Henry Jones laid his cards on the table. "Do you want to know how to heal your body?" he whispered.

"Yes," I breathed.

"Listen up," he said. I moved closer to him. "The secret of self-healing lies in restoring the balance between your body, mind, emotions and spirit."

"That's it?" I had expected a more complex answer.

"Yes, that's it!" he affirmed. "After studying human healing for many years, I can say without a shadow of a doubt that there's an inseparable inter-connectedness between your body, mind, emotions and spirit. They all play a key role in the healing process. I promise you this: When you've brought a holistic balance back into your life, your body will be healed."

"How can you be so certain it'll work for me?" I asked.

He laughed. "This simple healing formula has helped countless sick people throughout the ages, and there's no reason it wouldn't work for you, too."

I suddenly wanted to believe Henry Jones. I wanted to believe I could get well again and enjoy a normal life. It seemed like a fair exchange. I'd help Henry Jones to compile his book and he'd help me to restore my body to perfect health. If his healing techniques worked for me, they might work for others, too.

"Tell me more about your ideas for this book," I said.

"I want to produce a book that shows people exactly what to do, and how to do it. The directions must be slap-your-forehead simple," he explained. "You shouldn't need a medical dictionary to explain the terminology, nor a degree in physiology to understand the content. It must be easy to follow and practical in application."

"Why now?" I asked curiously.

"I'm leaving for a faraway land soon, and I doubt I'll be coming back," he replied. "I feel compelled to leave behind my healing legacy."

"Where are you going?"

"I recently discovered a small island village where I wish to live out my days," he said. "I've spent the past 20 years traveling the world, researching healing and helping the sick. I've enjoyed my work and have no regrets, but I'm tired of being surrounded by sickness all the time. This modern lifestyle we lead destroys health. Sickness and disease are escalating at alarming rates."

"Tell me about it," I moaned.

"The villagers on the island are healthy, strong and deeply spiritual. They live off the land and sea, as nature intended. I've built a house on the shore, and I want to go back home."

"How old are you Henry?" I suddenly asked.

"Seventy-two," he told me proudly.

I was stunned. "You look in your mid-50s," I said in amazement.

"I get that a lot," he replied. "It's no surprise. I've been walking the natural path of health and healing for two decades."

"Have you always lived so passionately?" I asked.

"Yes," he admitted. "When I was younger, I was passionate about money and success. Since I retired 20 years ago, I've been passionate about healing and about helping sick people. Now, I want to be with healthy, happy people – people who make the right life choices. I believe my body of work is tremendously important and will deliver great value to others seeking to be healed. My work is almost done, but I need your help to compile my notes into a book. Will you help me?" he asked.

"I'd like to think it over," I said. "I'm sick, and tired, and I don't have much energy at the moment."

"Excellent!" he cried. "This gives me the perfect chance to prove myself to you. I'll help you to feel better before you know it, and then you'll have the energy you need to organize my material."

Henry Jones didn't take no for an answer. I was beginning to see why he had been a successful trader in his day. Nothing seemed to be a problem for him. He had a solution for everything. I liked that about him. He was positive, and he genuinely seemed to care, like Sister Lillian.

"You're getting out of hospital in two days, aren't you?" he asked.

"For a while," I answered begrudgingly. "I've more tests in six weeks."

"Brilliant," he exclaimed. "We've got plenty of time. In 40 days and 40 nights, I'll convince you that you have the power to heal your body – and give you the tools to do it. Come on!" he said, urging me to accept his offer. "What's the worst that can happen? If we fail, you can always come back here and be sick and miserable again, right?"

"I suppose so," I mumbled. I'm not the type of person who makes spontaneous decisions. I like to brood things over and weigh up all my options. But there was something about Henry Jones. I was captivated by his confidence and cool disposition. He was no phony. I intuitively trusted him.

"So, do we have a deal?" he asked, his hand outstretched. Before I had a chance to respond, my doctor entered the room; his entourage marching in single file behind him. Students and nurses clutched their clipboards and clicked their pens.

"Morning. How are *we* today?" my doctor asked without lifting his eyes from my chart.

"We?" I retorted. He ignored my comment. We both knew why. His eyes darted towards Henry Jones and then back to my chart.

"Henry," he sighed, acknowledging his presence with a half-hearted nod. "Doctor," Henry Jones replied in the same tone.

It was obvious they knew each other. It was also obvious that they had their differences. "Still spreading the gospel, are we?" the doctor said, smirking unnecessarily.

"It is the path to the truth and the light, isn't it?" Henry Jones taunted.

The doctor chose to ignore him.

"Roll over," he commanded. I hated this part of the morning procession. Hospital gowns are most undignified. I obeyed his instruction and felt conscious of my hairy bottom showing to all and sundry.

"What do we have here, Jenkins?" asked the doctor. The student grappled with his notes and then read aloud a long sentence labeling my disease. "Correct. And how do we treat it?" Again, the student grappled with his notes, then read aloud another long sentence detailing my medication. I looked back over my shoulder in time to see Henry Jones shaking his head from side to side as he left the room.

"Henry!" I called after him.

"I know," he shouted without looking back. "I know."

I didn't see Henry Jones over the next two days. During that time, I thought seriously about our conversation. It wasn't like I had much else to do.

Lying in a hospital bed gives one plenty of time to think. His words echoed in my mind: "I can take you on an amazing holistic healing journey," and "You have the power to heal your body. I can help you to heal yourself."

In the end, I decided to accompany Henry Jones for 40 days and 40 nights, and Sister Lillian was kind enough to make the arrangements. Sure enough, he was waiting for me on a park bench outside the hospital on the day of my release, as planned. I was pleased to be leaving the hospital. But I was apprehensive about the new journey that awaited me.

CHAPTER 2

CONVERSATION ON A PARK BENCH

"All that the human experience is about
is the journey towards wholeness."

"How do you feel?" Henry Jones asked me as I sat down beside him on the bench in the hospital courtyard.

"Weak. Nauseous. Tired," I replied, breathing heavily.

"I mean, how do you feel emotionally?" he said.

"Oh! I'm not sure," I muttered, stopping to think about it. It was an odd question. Until then, no one had bothered to ask me how I had really felt during my treatment. My body was all that seemed to matter. Nobody cared about my emotions. I slumped into a moment of silence, pretending to catch my breath. The truth was: I didn't quite know how to respond to the question.

"Let me guess, it's been a while since anyone asked about your feelings," Henry Jones said, as if reading my thoughts. His perceptiveness startled me and my curiosity was roused. "I can't say I'm surprised. Most people, especially medical practitioners, underestimate the importance of emotions in the healing process. That's a fundamental mistake. I'll explain more about that later. But for now, please tell me how you're feeling emotionally. "

"Numb," I said.

"No, that's not true," he responded abruptly. "I bet you're filled with emotions."

"I can't feel them."

"Because you don't want to feel them."

"Why wouldn't I want to feel my emotions?" I barked.

"You don't like the way they make you feel," he replied calmly. "It's a common response. People often block out their feelings, or suppress them, to spare themselves emotional pain," he said. "But I should warn you, this only works in the immediate term. It's a very dangerous, dysfunctional practice in the medium to long term."

"Why?"

"Storing negative emotions makes you sick!" Henry Jones exclaimed, looking astonished by my obvious ignorance. "Suppressing emotions seriously impairs the healing process."

How was I supposed to know that? No one had ever told me. I didn't know what Henry Jones was talking about. Sitting beside him, I felt like a fish out of water, gasping for air. I wondered: Was I making a mistake? Was I just wasting my time on a futile exercise?

I fidgeted anxiously with the strap of my bag. A part of me wanted to get up and leave. I knew I could be home in 30 minutes, sitting on my sofa, watching telly with a whiskey in my hand. I seriously considered it for a moment. But, just for a moment. There was something about Henry Jones that compelled me to stay put. I knew he had answers to important questions: Questions that I didn't even know to ask!

"You do want to heal your body, don't you?" he asked.

"Yes, of course I do."

"In that case, I'll tell you something your doctor isn't telling you: Healing your body is your responsibility. Your top question to yourself right now should be: 'What can I do to help my body heal itself as fast as possible?'"

"I'm taking medication," I mumbled feebly.

Henry Jones shook his head vigorously. "Taking medication and relying on your doctor isn't the answer. The only thing popping pills will do is suppress the symptoms of disease."

"But the doctor said they'll help me with the nausea and pain."

"Oh sure, treating the effects may provide you with temporary relief from physical discomfort, but it certainly won't go to the root of your problem, or cure it. And that is your real challenge!"

"How do I find out what is causing my sickness?"

"Good question. I should warn you in advance that you might not like what I'm about to tell you. But, the sooner you face it, the sooner you'll start to heal your body," he said. Henry Jones leaned towards me and looked into my eyes with great compassion. "Something in your life has made you sick. When you figure out what that something is and deal with it, then, and only then, will your body start to heal itself."

"You're saying I made myself sick?"

"Yes."

"… and therefore, it's my responsibility to heal my body?" I asked sarcastically.

"Precisely!" he said. "You broke it, you fix it." Then, as if absolutely satisfied that he'd made an irrefutable point, he sat back on the bench, folded his arms, gave a single, sharp nod and stared into the distance.

I didn't like the sound of that one little bit. Why would I make myself sick? How could I make myself sick? I wondered. They were difficult questions to answer. Popping pills seemed easier. Much easier!

"Are you saying I shouldn't take my medication?" I asked nervously.

"Definitely not!" he exclaimed. "Modern medicine plays an important role in the healing process. Keep taking your medication, but don't only depend on it to heal your body. There are other aspects of your being that are equally important on your healing journey."

"Like what?"

"Emotions," he said. "So, let's try again, shall we? Take a deep breath, close your eyes, and answer these simple questions. Are you ready?"

I obeyed, filling my lungs with air and exhaling slowly. It sounded like a disgruntled sigh.

"Are you *happy* to be out of hospital?" he asked.

"Yes."

"Do you *resent* being told to go back in six weeks?"

"Yes."

"Are you *angry* about being sick?"

"Yes."

"Are you *anxious* about spending the next six weeks with me?"

"Yes."

"Are you *afraid* the healing processes I'll show you won't work for you?"

"Yes."

"See!" he cried victoriously. "You're loaded with feelings. The problem is: You're just not in tune with them anymore. Don't worry, we'll fix this together. One of our key objectives in the weeks ahead will be to put you back in touch with your emotions. This is very, very important," he said, slapping his hands on the thick, brown envelope on his lap. Up until that moment, I hadn't noticed it.

It's all about attitude

"What's that?" I asked, relieved to change the subject.

"Some notes to get you started," he replied.

"What's in them?"

"Important information on essential focus areas, like attitude," said Henry Jones. "Among other things that will truly amaze you. But let's start with attitude. It's the perfect place for you to begin your healing journey."

I flinched, knowing full well that I had a bad attitude. I was angry, short-tempered, mean-spirited and resentful. I didn't know how Sister Lillian or my wife, family, and friends, for that matter, had put up with me.

"Is that where you started your journey?" I asked.

"Actually, it was," he answered. "In the beginning, I struggled to find my way. I was willing to do whatever it took to heal my body, but I didn't know where to begin. My big breakthrough came when I changed my attitude towards my physical problem."

"How did changing your attitude help your body?" I asked skeptically.

"It made a huge difference. Huge!" Henry Jones said, gesticulating widely. His animation amused me. I couldn't help being intrigued by this enigmatic character. His exuberance enthralled me.

"One day, I was sitting on a park bench, much like this one, when a lady strolled by pushing a pram. On the side of the pram was a sticker that read: 'In all adversity there's the seed of great opportunity.' The words leaped out and smacked me straight between my eyes. In that moment, my world became unstuck. Until then, I'd been bitter and resentful about my suffering. I'd felt victimized, persecuted and punished. I had shaken my fist at the heavens and shouted: 'Why me?' What I failed to realize was that I'd been so busy feeling sorry for myself that I hadn't stopped to consider the opportunity that was waiting for me. So, I printed those words of wisdom on to sheets of paper and pasted them all over my house and office. I asked myself repeatedly: What am I missing? What am I missing? What am I missing?

"People must've thought you'd lost the plot," I scoffed.

"Some did," he chortled from deep within his belly. "But I didn't care what people thought of me. I was determined to find the answers I needed to heal my body. Then, one day the penny just dropped. I remember it clearly. I was brushing my teeth when suddenly I was drawn to my reflection in the bathroom mirror. I stared at my face for ages, as if for the first time. Then, all at once, it dawned on me that being sick had irrevocably changed me."

"How come?"

"I'd become a whole different person."

"In what way?" I heard myself asking, much to my surprise.

"Well, until I became ill, I'd never thought twice about my health or about human suffering. Then, everything changed! You see, I took my life and the people in it for granted. I lived from day to day without appreciating how lucky I was to be alive and healthy. I failed to recognize how blessed I was. I was numb to the joy of living. It was only when I lost my health that I realized that life is wondrous and precious. Looking back now, I can honestly say that getting sick was the best thing that ever happened to me."

Once more, I was skeptical. "Why?"

"It gave me an opportunity to re-orient my value system. My illness made me take a long, hard look at my life, and I realized that my priorities were all wrong. Before I got sick, I had pursued my personal ambitions and dreams, but I had never done anything for anyone else but myself. I had put success and prosperity above my family and friends. I had traded love for power, and I had valued possessions over compassion. The truth is, my life was meaningless. I didn't make the world a better place, and if I had died, I don't think anyone would really have missed me."

I couldn't imagine good old Henry Jones being the ruthless person he described. The man I'd just met was kind, caring and compassionate. How could he have changed so much? What did he do to change so radically? Could I change that much, too? I wondered.

"Fortunately, destiny had other plans for me," he said with a disarming smile. "Right there, in the bathroom, I fell to the floor and cried and cried and cried. My life genuinely flashed before my eyes and, I must admit, I was ashamed to see it. There I was praying for grace and healing, but I suddenly reckoned that I wasn't worth saving."

"That's a bit harsh, isn't it?" I asked.

"Harsh, but true," he replied. "I'd been a real son-of-a-bitch for most of my life. I grew up having to fend for myself, so I didn't have much regard for others. People were a commodity to me. I used them for my own gain, and when I was done with them, I discarded them at my leisure. Don't get me wrong: I wasn't a bad person. I had never harmed anyone, but I wasn't a loving person, either," he concluded.

I felt a pang of guilt. Henry Jones and I were similar in many ways. I, too, was a bastard most of the time. As a result, my marriage was on the rocks and I had no real friends to speak of. If I died, the world wouldn't miss me, either. My life was meaningless.

I suddenly wanted to vomit, but I managed to suppress my gagging.

"Life moves on. So must we," Henry Jones said after a long pause.

"So, what happened on the bathroom floor?"

"I had an epiphany!" he replied. "It was a real light-bulb moment. In a flash, I realized that I had become sick so that I could learn how to heal my body. With this knowledge, I could help others to heal themselves. So, at my lowest point, in the midst of my suffering, fear and pain, I vowed that if I was given grace, I'd dedicate my life to serving humanity."

"Seriously?"

"Yes, totally! I knew that was my destiny."

I thought about what he had said for at least a minute, and then asked: "How did you begin?"

"Well, I intuitively knew that to make that turnaround a reality, I needed to reinvent myself completely. As I told you when you were in hospital, I needed to change everything about myself: My occupation; values; principles; habits; ways; geographic location; diet and exercise program – my whole life!"

"Jeepers," I moaned. "I'm not sure I can do all of that."

Henry Jones fired off a short spurt of laughter. "I'm not expecting you to do the same. Each person has their own healing journey to follow, and it differs from person to person. Some people need to commit to relationships to get well, while others need to end them. Some people need to heal old emotional wounds, and others need to let go and move on. There are infinite variations and unlimited possibilities. I had to reinvent myself. There's no telling yet where your healing journey will lead you. But you can be sure that the path will reveal itself soon enough."

I felt a wisp of excitement. Could it be true? Was there a path leading to my recovery? How would I find it? Once again, my gut told me Henry Jones had the answers I sought.

"What happened next?"

"I got off my knees and immediately started making plans and putting them into action", he replied.

"Was it that simple?" I asked suspiciously.

"Oh, heavens no!" he cried. "I wish I could tell you that it was easy, but I can't. Do you remember when we first met I told you that I'd invested all my money in a business venture that was supposed to make me, my partners and our investors super rich? Well, they weren't sympathetic to my suffering. Nor did they appreciate my change of heart. I'd led them to believe that we'd all get much, much richer, and they expected me to deliver on that. I had genuinely wanted to make us a fortune at that time, but after I became sick, above all else I wanted to get well again. Being rich and dead didn't appeal to me. My priorities shifted, and with it, my life's purpose changed. I knew it was the right thing to do for me, so I had to do it, regardless of the consequences."

Trust your inner voice

Henry Jones suddenly clicked his fingers, like a confident magician at the turn of a trick. It startled me. I hardly had time to come to my senses before he started up again. "Do you know the little voice inside you that tells you what you should and shouldn't do?"

"Yes."

"It's critical to listen to that little voice on your healing journey, no matter what!"

"Even if you don't like what it's telling you to do?"

"Especially then," he retorted. "That voice knows what's best for you. Believe it and trust it. Whenever I tuned into myself, the little voice screamed: 'Cut your losses and get out!' That was undoubtedly the most difficult time of my life. I couldn't just unplug the money-making machine I'd spent years creating – I had obligations. Of course, my ego was also attached to the illusion of a personal fortune, and my desire to succeed was deeply ingrained in me. But, when my focus shifted to healing my body, I was unable to feed the machine and it quickly transformed into a hungry money-shredder. Over the course of a year, my financiers withdrew their capital commitments and my investments folded, one after the other. Eventually, I lost all my money."

"You lost everything?" I gasped.

"No. Not everything. Just my money," he replied calmly.

I felt panicked. "I'm not rich, but financial security is very important to me," I told Henry Jones. "Under no circumstances do I want to lose my nest egg. My father died penniless, and I don't want to be anything like him."

"I hear you," replied Henry Jones. "Hopefully, your healing journey will be different from mine. I figured out that my true worth lay in my life, not in my will. I also realized that I couldn't take wealth with me when I die. Don't get me wrong, I didn't want to let go of my fortune, but I was willing to do so if that's what it took to heal my body. In hindsight, I think I made the right choice for me and my family."

How could I argue with Henry Jones? He was living proof that he had made the right decision. "What happened next?" I asked.

"Oh, I held on as tight as I could to the bitter end. But, when my business folded, I went down hard. My life as I knew it smashed to smithereens. As if the stress of disease wasn't enough, I had to cope with bankruptcy. All my Earthly possessions were ripped from my hands and I was forced to retire from the financial world with my business reputation in ruins," he said with a curious serenity.

"How can you be so calm about it?" I moaned.

Henry Jones just smiled. "In the weeks ahead, you'll discover the importance of overcoming ego. When you find your true-self, then you'll know why I'm at peace."

That statement went right over my head.

We sat together in silence on the park bench in the hospital courtyard. Henry Jones warmed his eyelids in the morning Sun while I pondered his words. Dull, grey buildings loomed ominously over us. It took a while for Henry Jones's life story to sink in. He had a compelling tale to tell. He'd sacrificed his successful career and dreams to become a helper and healer of others. Occasionally, I glanced across my shoulder at his face. Each time I was struck by the deep serenity on it. He seemed so content with life. I'm certain Henry Jones could've sat on that park bench for hours. He watched the birds dropping from the branches to the ground, and then flitting back up again.

After several minutes, I found something to say: "How did you cope with the stress?

"Well, it's the strangest thing," he replied, as if our conversation hadn't missed a beat. "Would you believe I saw another bumper sticker on the back of a car?"

"What did it say?"

"It said: 'Surrender and release.' I don't know who put it there or why, but I'm very grateful to them. For a long time, I felt as if I was swimming against the flow of the universe. It was hard work, not to mention futile! I nearly killed myself trying to project my will on to my reality. But the moment I surrendered my will to that of the Divine, I felt relaxed and at ease. I trusted that life would take me exactly where I needed to go on my healing journey. The instant I released my personal plans and notions, and surrendered to the process, I was able to watch the destruction around me as if it was happening to somebody else. In time, I came to realize that this was both necessary and important on my healing journey."

"It sounds a bit 'out there' to me," I said, frowning.

"Have you ever heard of the dark night of the soul?" Henry Jones asked suddenly.

"Sure," I replied. "What about it?"

"When you go through the dark night of the soul, you come out the other side a better person," he responded cheerfully. "That is the real purpose of sickness. Your body lets you know that there is something wrong with your life. It tells you there's an imbalance that must be corrected. Naturally, the greater the imbalance, the more serious your problem."

"The darker the night…" I heard myself mumble.

Henry Jones nodded, slowly but surely. "I was lucky. My wife stood by me through it all. She was my angel of light. It was my wife who taught me that love has the power to transform all things. She encouraged me to surrender and release and to follow my heart. We went through hell together, but we emerged stronger and more open to new experiences."

"You're lucky. Mine wants a divorce!" I grumbled.

"I'm sorry to hear it," he said with deep compassion.

"Apparently, she's sick and tired of me being sick and tired," I said. My attempt at being funny was a dismal failure. More importantly, I knew it wasn't true; I was to blame. I knew it was my fault she was leaving me.

Was my wife a part of my healing journey? Did I have to heal my relationship with her? Would she take me back if I got better and changed my ways? I wondered.

Henry Jones had got me thinking about others. That felt good, for once in my miserable life.

"As I said, love has the power to transform all things," he reminded me.

I had no snappy comeback. No quirky or snide remark. All I had was a sense of despair in the pit of my stomach. I'm pretty sure Henry Jones saw through me. He saw my confusion, pain and regret, but he didn't judge me. He didn't dig into my mistakes nor delve deeper into my life. He just accepted me for who I was right then and there. I was grateful to him. I appreciated his sensitivity and admired his restraint.

Time for transformation

He continued his story: "I knew I had to transform myself in order to heal my body. Transformation brings healing, and healing brings transformation. Healing without transformation will eventually result in sickness again. Only when you discover the life-lesson in your suffering and embrace it wholeheartedly will you heal your body permanently. This path will lead you to radiant health and long life."

"You make it sound so easy."

"It is easy when you know what to do," he replied. "Of course, it helps to have the right tools."

"Tools?"

"Sure. Try felling a tree with your bare hands, or digging a grave without a shovel, or climbing ice without a pick, and you'll soon realize the value and importance of tools."

"What's your point?"

"Healing techniques are the tools you need to use to heal your body."

"Can you give me an example?"

"Okay … transforming your ways means breaking old habits and forming new ones. Let me warn you that this is very difficult to do. Old habits die hard. It's not easy to break a routine or change your lifestyle. I can show you specific techniques that you can use to make and break habits. These 'tools' will come in handy when you shape your future self."

"I've got some bad habits that I can't imagine giving up," I admitted.

"Well, you'll need to make sacrifices on your healing journey. With all human endeavors, there's usually a cost, right?"

"I suppose so."

"Fortunately, you'll never be asked to sacrifice anything that's good for you. All the sacrifices you'll need to make will be related to your old, unhealthy way of living."

"It'll be hard to give up whiskey, cigars and rich food. I don't know if I can do it."

"You've got to be convinced that the benefits outweigh the sacrifices. Otherwise, don't even start your healing journey. You'll only be setting yourself up for failure. If you keep doing the same thing, you'll keep getting the same result. Right?"

"I guess so."

"It's very sad," said Henry Jones. "Most people are trapped in destructive behavioral patterns. They habitually do what is wrong for them – especially what's wrong for their bodies! They work too hard; eat too much of the wrong foods; drink too much alcohol; watch too much television; think too negatively; exercise too little and stress too much. They don't have any regard for the fragile chemical and biological universe in their bodies. As a result, most people's bodies are in a state of crisis. Their internal organs have suffered years of improper diet and incorrect living, not to mention exposure to pollution, pesticides, poisonous gases, preservatives, chemicals, and toxic urban environments."

"Is that why hospitals and clinics are always jam-packed?"

"You bet! But I'm not just talking about sickness that is localized in the body – I'm talking about the overall condition of the body. The whole body is in crisis. Sickness and disease are merely a manifestation of the problem."

I'd spent countless hours focusing on my sickness, but not two minutes thinking about the overall state of the rest of my body. I wanted to get well; I wanted my diseased organs to function normally, but I hadn't considered my body as a whole system. I felt another flush of panic. What was I thinking? How could I be so stupid? Why don't the medical fraternity and media drum this message home? I wondered.

"It's very important that we inform our readers upfront that their bodies are in a state of crisis," I said with a newfound sense of urgency.

"Odds are, if they make the time to read our book, they're probably already sick or in pain – or they know of someone who is suffering in some way. Most people only become conscious of healing when they need it. Agreed?"

"Sad, but true," I admitted.

Henry Jones scratched around in his brown envelope, pulled out a pack of Post-it notes and shuffled through them. "Keep this," he commanded. I looked down at the hand-written note.

> *"Health is not valued till sickness comes."* – Dr Thomas Fuller, British Physician (1654c–1734): *Gnomologia*, 1732.

I read the quotation several times. I was guilty as charged. I closed my eyes and wondered how I was ever going to get out of the horrible situation that I'd so carelessly created for myself. I stuffed the note in my pocket.

"What happens when something goes wrong with your body?" Henry Jones asked suddenly. "Your whole life comes to a grinding halt, doesn't it? You suddenly realize that nothing in the world is more important to you than your health, right?"

"That's for sure!" I agreed.

"I don't know anyone who would trade a million bucks for terminal cancer. Do you?"

"Nope," I responded.

"So, if you've been ignoring your body for years, then you've got a serious problem. I'll shoot straight: Your immune system has broken down – that's why you're experiencing the symptoms of disease. Your weakened immune system is failing to cope with the amount of poisonous toxins in your body. Disease and pain are your body's way of telling you that it can't go on with the way you've been treating it. Take heed, my friend. Your body is desperately trying to send you a message. It urgently needs rejuvenation and healing. You've got to start doing something about your situation immediately!" he emphasized, pounding the brown envelope on his lap.

Henry Jones had the hell-fire conviction of a Southern preacher man. His words reached the core of my being and stirred my soul. "What should I do first?"

"Good question. You need to get into the habit of giving your body exactly what it needs, when it needs it. Right now, you must put your body's needs before your own needs. Things that taste good aren't necessarily good for you. In fact, many harmful substances are put into food to make it taste better. Manufacturers are driven by profit, shelf-life, appearance and taste. Your health isn't their primary concern. You need to carefully evaluate the nutritional value of everything you put into your body."

"That would definitely mean changing my lifestyle and making sacrifices."

"Well, as I see it, you have a choice to make," Henry Jones said sternly. "You can continue your life as you did before and likely end up dead before your time, or you can change your ways, heal your body, and enjoy a long, healthy life. It's that simple."

"Okay, okay. I've already said I'll try your program."

Commit to succeeding

"Don't say, 'I'll try this program'. You're setting yourself up to fail. Can you see your escape clause? *I tried it, but …* Being committed to trying isn't the same as being committed to succeeding. You either do it, or you don't do it. There's no in-between when it comes to healing your body."

Henry Jones was deadly serious. That was my defining moment. Yes, I'd made up my mind to spend six weeks with this man and to experiment with his healing techniques, but I certainly hadn't committed to changing my whole life. I had planned to participate in the exercise to see what happened, but I hadn't fully committed to making it happen. I suddenly realized that Henry Jones wasn't going to heal my body. Only I could do that. Only I could change my ways. I had to make a shift from being a cynical observer to an enthusiastic doer. With my personality, was that even possible? Would I succeed or fail? I wondered.

"Take a moment to think about the decision you're about to make. Unless you're genuinely prepared to give up your old lifestyle and develop new, healthy habits, you may as well toss my pile of notes into the bin and brace yourself for the effects of your disease."

I sat back on the bench, pushed my bag out in front of me and stared at it. I knew I was at a crossroads. I wanted to get well again, but that would mean radical change. Did I have the strength to do it? What if I didn't do it?

I thought about the things I loved: Whiskey, cigars, junk food, parties, and stress. Yes, stress. I was a workaholic. I loved the pressure of deadlines. They gave me a reason to be demanding and an excuse to be a royal pain!

Then I thought of my family and loved ones. I recalled our togetherness, the holidays we shared, and the good times.

My conversations with Henry Jones suddenly stacked up. Everything he'd told me so far came back to me in a blinding realization of truth. My life had been leading up to that point. Being sick was my problem, and I needed to sort it out. Henry Jones could show me the way, but it was *my* healing journey to take. It was up to me. Only me. Tears welled up in my eyes.

'You're going to be okay'

A hard lump formed in my throat and I couldn't speak. I looked to the sky to stop my tears from falling. Despite my best efforts, they streamed down my cheeks.

"You're going to be okay," Henry Jones said softly. "You're going to be okay."

I buckled. My dam wall broke. I sat forward, placed my elbows on my knees, held my head in my hands and cried and cried. All I could think about was my family and how I'd let them down. I'd made them so miserable over the years. My illness had made their lives even more miserable, because I was more miserable. Why did I mess up so badly? How could I ever make it right? I wondered. Henry Jones rubbed my back and kept repeating: "You're going to be okay; you're going to be okay; you're going to be okay."

I just kept sobbing. I was so afraid. It wasn't until that moment that I realized how truly afraid I was. I was afraid I wouldn't get better; that my condition would get worse; and of more medical treatment. I was afraid of losing my job, my wife and my life. I felt very sorry for myself. More than anything in the world, I just wanted to get better, heal my body, mend my relationships, and become a better person.

"I need a second chance," I cried. "I just need a second chance. I would do everything so differently."

"You're going to be okay."

"I will do whatever it takes."

"You're going to be okay."

"Just tell me what to do and I will do it."

"You're going to be okay."

Henry Jones must have repeated himself about 50 times. The sentence had a profound impact on me. It was just what I needed to hear. I needed to know there was light at the end of the tunnel, even if I couldn't see it at the time. I needed hope and encouragement. I needed to believe. I didn't know how much I needed someone to tell me that I would be okay until I heard Henry Jones saying it, over and over again.

I believe my healing journey began in that moment. I suddenly had a new goal – something to strive for. I had a destination to work towards and a glimmer of hope. When I calmed down, I wiped away my tears and composed myself.

"I'm sorry," I said softly.

"No need to apologize."

"I don't know where those emotions came from."

"Yes, you do."

"I guess they've been building up for months."

"Perhaps years!"

"I feel lighter now."

"Good," Henry Jones said, smiling. He then folded his arms, bowed his head and closed his eyes. Except for the faint smile on his lips, it seemed as if he was about to nod off to sleep. He smiled the way mothers smile at their sick children to assure them of recovery. I took a tissue from my pocket and blew my nose hard. The sound reverberated through the hospital courtyard. I looked around me. The walls were grey and lifeless. It wasn't a place of wellness, it was a place of sickness and disease. I wanted to leave and never go back. Yes, I was very grateful to Sister Lillian and my doctors for treating me, but I knew I'd be happier if I never saw them again. I inhaled deeply, as if I was about to dive from a great height into deep water. I exhaled slowly. Absently, I slid my bag to one side. Lost in my introspection, I faintly heard Henry Jones say: "So, are you ready to start your healing journey now?"

I took a minute to gather my senses. "Yes, I am," I replied in all sincerity. What did I have to lose? Besides my health, healing, and future – not much!

"Excellent. Then let's not lose a single second. I'm certain you've heard this expression before: A journey of a thousand miles begins with a single step."

"Yes," I replied.

"So, are you certain you're ready to take your first step right now?"

"Yup," I said.

"…and you'll commit to the process all the way to the end, no matter what?"

"All the way, no matter what!"

"Okay then, I'd like you to begin by extending your right hand. Fold it backward and pat yourself on your back."

I raised my eyebrows.

"Go on, do it now. Don't be shy," he said playfully. "You must acknowledge yourself for accepting responsibility for healing your body."

All at once, I decided to go with the flow. I patted myself on the back, and it felt great. A light-hearted laughter bubbled up inside of me. It felt good to laugh again. It felt good to…let go.

Henry Jones slapped his hand firmly on my leg. "You made the right choice," he said. "I'm very proud of you."

Even though he was almost a stranger to me, it pleased me to receive Henry Jones's praise. There was a fatherly quality to him, which was foreign to me. It made me feel…better. He evidently cared, and I immediately felt indebted to him.

"You can also count on me to help you publish your book," I said.

"I never doubted it," he replied.

"So, where would you like me to start?"

"Right off the bat, the primary goal of our book should be to show readers exactly how to restore their bodies to perfect health – naturally, holistically and permanently. That's what you want, too, isn't it?" he asked me again.

"Yes, most definitely," I replied.

The basics of healing

"Good. Then let's get straight into it, shall we? You need to understand the basics of healing. When you know those fundamentals and apply them, you'll be on your way to recovery."

A pigeon flew down from the branches above and pecked at the ground near our feet. Henry Jones took a moment to enjoy the company of our feathered friend. I shuffled my feet impatiently and it flew off.

He continued: "Let me clarify two key points for you: Firstly, healing yourself naturally means using God's own natural products to help restore your body to health."

"Like fruit, vegetables, nuts, sprouts and stuff?" I asked, pulling a face. I wasn't a healthy eater. I didn't care for rabbit food, as I called it.

"Yes," Henry Jones replied. "Secondly, healing yourself holistically means treating yourself as a whole person."

"You mean physically, mentally, emotionally and spiritually, right?" I was rather proud of myself for recalling our previous conversation.

"Right! Well done. You're a quick learner."

"I've thought of little else in the past two days. You made me aware of the gaps in my treatment. I realized there are aspects of my being that aren't being treated at all. You're right! I'm more than a physical body. I'm an emotional, mental and spiritual being, too."

"You've got it!" he shouted, nearly jumping out of his seat. His passion was infectious. "It's as simple as one, two, three," he said excitedly, holding up three fingers. "One: You have a body that enables you to act. Two: You have a mind that enables you to think. Three: You have a spirit, which is the life force that enables you to think and act upon your thoughts. In short, your whole existence is nothing short of a miraculous expression of body, mind and spirit."

"Okay, that's easy enough to understand," I remarked.

"Good. Now let's take it to the next level. There's an inseparable inter-connectedness between your body, mind and spirit. These three aspects of your being influence each other, which in turn affects your overall quality of life. Got it?"

"Got it."

Henry Jones clapped his hands. He appeared to be enjoying himself. In all honesty, so was I. It was hard to believe that just a few days earlier I'd felt depressed and hopeless. Back then, I'd wanted to be left alone. I'd barked at anyone who had tried to be nice to me. In just a few minutes with Henry Jones, I'd forgotten about feeling weak, tired, and nauseous. Why had my mood lifted? Was it possible that I was feeling a bit better already? I wondered.

"Have you noticed that when your mind is stressed, your body gets sick easily and your spirits drop? And when your body is healthy, your mind is sharp, and your spirits are high?"

"Yes, that's true," I replied.

"So then, if you want to heal your body, it's imperative that you restore the natural balance between your body, mind and spirit. I can't stress enough how vital it is to do this. Unless they're in balance, you simply can't be in harmony with yourself or with the universe around you. Trying to heal your body in an unbalanced state is like chugging down the road to recovery in first gear. Your engine will most likely break down before you get to your desired destination. Make sense?"

"Definitely!"

"Good. To heal your body permanently, you must combine your medical treatment with natural and holistic healing. You must!" Henry Jones repeated forcefully.

"Okay, I've got it! What's next?"

The three brains

"Tell me once more: What do you want more than anything else in the world right now?" Henry Jones asked.

"I want to get well."

"So, you want to 'be healed'?" he said, drawing inverted commas in the air.

"Yes, of course."

"In that case, I'd better tell you about your three brains. It's crucial that you understand how they work together, or you'll never know how to heal yourself. Never!"

"Three brains?"

He nodded sincerely. "We have three brains. Not one – three. They allow us to move from thinking, to doing, to being. They're called the neocortex brain, the limbic brain, and the cerebellum. Each brain is its own individual bio-computer, with its own anatomy, chemistry, circuitry, and physiology. They even have their own history and their own sense of time and space."

I scratched my head. Where was he going with this?

"As you can imagine, I meet many sick people in my line of work. They always ask me the same question: 'How can I be healed?' They, too, want to get well, but they don't know where to start. They know for certain there's something wrong with their bodies. The symptoms they experience are real in the physical world, but they think sickness and disease are localized in the body. It's an easy mistake to make."

I did a double-take. Did he just tell me that my disease was not a physical reality? I asked myself.

Henry Jones continued. "So, I always begin the process of healing by putting sickness in its place. The first thing you need to understand is that sickness and disease do not stem from the body. They manifest in the body, but they stem from consciousness. If you want to heal your body, you must heal your consciousness. True healing happens in the realm of consciousness. When you heal the consciousness, the body heals itself."

"What does this have to do with my three brains?" I asked.

He laughed. "Everything! Thoughts are electrical impulses. They are streamed from your consciousness and decoded by your brain. There are more electrical impulses in your brain each day than in all the cellphones on Earth. The neocortex is the outer brain. It looks like a bicycle helmet. It's the newest brain and is the most evolved. It's highly specialized in human beings, and it gathers information from your five senses. It's also the seat of your conscious mind. Right now, you're listening to me using your neocortex. Your limbic brain is housed inside the neocortex. It's the size of a lemon; and is also called the chemical brain, emotional brain or mammalian brain.

It regulates internal chemical order. Your cerebellum is located at the back of the brain stem. It's also called the reptilian brain. It's the oldest brain in evolution, and it's the seat of your sub-conscious mind."

I was intrigued.

Creating neural pathways

"Now, there are about 100 billion neurons in your brain. Stack 100 billion sheets of paper and they'd be 5 000 miles high. Imagine that!"

I struggled to comprehend it.

"They each possess the unique ability to store information and communicate with one another. By learning this fact, you have just created a synaptic connection in your thinking brain, and your brain physically changed. Learning creates communities of synaptic connections. Over the next 40 days, you will learn many new and interesting things. It will be a learning neural connection experience."

"Are you saying neural connections are made when thoughts come together?"

"Precisely! The principle of neuroscience is that nerve cells that fire together, wire together. As you learn new things, you biologically wire information into your cerebral architecture. You literally upscale your brain hardware. This 'learning' is organized in your neocortex."

"But what if I forget the information?" I asked, fearing this new knowledge would go in one ear and out the other.

"Remembering is about maintaining and sustaining cerebral connections. The secret is to keep putting this new information into your brain. More communication means stronger connections. When you constantly create connections, you make neural pathways that ultimately create neural networks. That is how your brain works. Ideas; concepts; memories; beliefs; experience; skills; behaviors and actions are all neural networks in your brain. Your mind is simply your brain in action."

"So, our 50 billion neurons can be configured differently?" I stammered.

"You hit it on the head. We can choose how our brains fire and wire. Suicide bombers believe they're doing the right thing because that information is drummed into their heads. They've constructed the neural connections, pathways, and networks to facilitate this idea. Most of us may think it's crazy, but they're willing to die for it. In exactly the same way, a person who doesn't jog daily never thinks about it, but an athlete can't wait to go for a run every day. Their brains are hardwired to support their dominant thoughts."

"I don't ever think about exercising anymore," I said.

"Now you know why. To change your ways, you must change your thinking. This will change your brain architecture and facilitate a new, healthier approach to life. Here's where your limbic brain plays a key role: When you begin to understand something intellectually, theoretically or philosophically, and you start to apply what you learn, you modify your behavior. Behavior modification is simply doing something differently. This provides you with a new experience. When you do it repeatedly, your five senses report this new experience to your brain and the neurons organize themselves into patterns. The moment neurons spring into place, your limbic brain releases a chemical, which is actually a feeling or an emotion."

Get your body to understand what your brains knows

"Why is this significant?" I asked.

"Experience enriches your brain circuitry neurologically, but your limbic brain releases chemical emotions, which create a memory. Thought plus feeling equals memory. The stronger the emotion, the stronger the memory. Can you remember receiving 'the bad news' from your doctor? Can you recall the birth of your child? Can you picture your wedding day? Of course you can! Your limbic brain produced powerful chemical emotions in these situations, which enabled your body to understand the information your brain received through your five senses. Now, tell me, what did you have for supper last Tuesday?"

"I can't remember," I said.

"I'm not surprised. Routine lulls the brain to sleep. This is your wake-up call. You've fallen into the dreary habit of doing the same old, self-destructive behaviors every day. The thrill of smoking your first cigar, or getting tipsy for the first time, or losing your temper, has waned. Now, they're just a matter of routine. You're stuck in a rut; you're bored; you're sick and tired; but you don't know how to change yourself. Right?"

He had me pegged. I didn't bother to answer.

Henry Jones rocked my leg. "Let's shake things up a bit. Tell me: What do you love to eat on Sunday mornings?"

"That's a no-brainer. Eggs; bacon; sausage; fried tomato; mushrooms and ciabatta toast; washed down with percolated coffee," I grinned.

He grimaced. "You'll soon learn why that is not the best option for you. For breakfast, your body needs fruit and water. Right now, you don't agree with me. You can't agree with me because the neural networks in your brain aren't there to facilitate this new, improved way of thinking. But, in the next few weeks, you'll learn and grow as I share essential, new information with you. Through repetition, you'll strengthen these neural networks, until they start to become your dominant thoughts."

"Good luck," I muttered under my breath.

He smiled compassionately. "I realize the thought of eating fruit for breakfast creates stress in your mind and body now. Stress activates your sympathetic nervous system, which is your fight or flight response. That's why, right now, you probably want to grab your bag and get as far away from me as fast as your legs can carry you. Agreed? This response is natural, instinctive, neurological and biological. It governs you. You don't govern it."

I chewed my lip.

"Now, pay attention. Here's the problem: When you activate the stress response and you can't switch it off, you start heading for sickness and disease. What is adaptive becomes maladaptive. Your unhealthy food choice for breakfast is nothing more than a bad habit that's been neurologically programmed into your mind. The good news is, I'm going to spend the next 40 days and 40 nights filling your head with all the knowledge and wisdom you need to heal your body, and you'll get the chance to practise powerful healing techniques over and over.

"Repetition is key here. Soon, you'll begin to notice your thoughts and feelings, and observe how you are being connected to your old self. This is called metacognition. Think of it as the volume control of your thoughts. It lowers the volume of the circuits connected to your old self, which enables you to observe, instead of participate. Right now, the idea of eating a greasy, fatty, unhealthy breakfast is loud, but it will simmer down over time. I promise. You see, neurons that no longer fire together, no longer wire together."

I couldn't conceal my skepticism.

Henry Jones persisted: "When you start to think about a new way of being; when you constantly remind yourself of who you want to be; when you hold an image of yourself doing it and plan your behavior and new actions, nerve cells fire in new sequences and patterns. By doing this, you create circuits to use for an event in the future. In short, you install the neurological hardware necessary to create the new experience. This is called intention."

Planning creates intention

"Well, I have no intention of eating fruit and drinking water for breakfast," I fumed.

Henry Jones agreed. "You're absolutely 100% neurologically correct to say this. But, when you persist with new thoughts and you raise the amplitude of your new intention, the neurons of the loudest thought must eventually be forged by your brain. Your brain must make the dominant thought permanent. This is called neural adaption and adoption."

"I still have my doubts," I huffed.

"Don't fret. You'll understand all of this when you get to understand the neural growth factor. It's the glue that sticks neurons and synapses together. There is only a certain amount of neural growth factor in your brain to go around, so when a new, dominant thought is created and sustained, your neurons start to steal glue from the neighboring circuits. Old memories start to fade away. If there's no fire, there's no wire. This is how you biologically and neurologically prune away your old ways. Eventually, the only signal left will be the new, dominant thought. This is the science of changing your mind."

I had to admit that the concept was intriguing. Still, I needed to understand how this information was going to help my healing.

How to be healed

Henry Jones explained: "Creating a new you is simply the process of unhooking from your old ways and connecting to new ways. This happens every time you consciously change your thinking and behavior, because new neural pathways are formed. Once again, repetition is key. Through repetition, your cerebellum kicks in. When your behavior matches your intention; when your actions equal your thoughts; and when your mind and body work together, you teach your body emotionally what your mind understands intellectually, theoretically or philosophically. This neurological and biological transformation activates the cerebellum, and you enter a state of being. Hear these words: knowledge is for the mind what experience is for the body. To do what's truly best for you, you must embody this new knowledge. Do this, and the word becomes flesh. This is how you neurochemically condition your mind and body to make the right life choices. They become innate – a habit – a skill – an automatic behavior. No person, thing, or experience can shift you from your new ways. Your sustained level of coherence puts you in a state of being. This, my friend, is how you can 'be healed'. You have to go through the process of converting thinking to doing to being. How exciting is that?"

I stewed on this concept for a time.

"And you're going to show me how to do this?" I eventually asked.

"Definitely! I'm a great fan of Dr Joe Dispenza's work in the field of neuroscience. You should read all of his books, too. They're amazing! I developed my healing system with neuroscience in mind. It's designed to facilitate the process of moving from thinking, to doing, to being. The goal is to restore homeostasis in your body."

"Say what?"

Activate homeostasis

"Let me quickly explain how your endocrine system works: In short, your endocrine system is the collection of glands that produce hormones that regulate metabolism, growth and development; tissue function; sexual function; reproduction; sleep and mood, among other things. When you are stressed, your body produces cortisol and adrenaline. These hormones cause inflammation, which activates your sympathetic nervous system. On the other hand, when you are peaceful and calm, your parasympathetic nervous system is activated, and your body is in a state of homeostasis."

"What's that?"

"Homeostasis is your body's ability to regulate and repair itself – in other words, to heal itself. Now, here's where it gets interesting: The vagus nerve is a cranial nerve that connects your brain to your body. Among many other functions, it switches homeostasis on and off. The principle is this: When you are in a state of stress – let's say a lion is chasing you – your body thinks: 'I don't have time to heal now, I must run', and it switches off homeostasis. The problem is that many people are in a constant state of stress, so the body's ability to regulate and repair itself is grossly impaired or disabled. This is the main reason why so many people are sick. If you want to heal your body, you must activate homeostasis. I believe your body's natural ability to heal itself can destroy every disease known to man."

"So how do I do that?" I snapped.

"Isn't it obvious? Meditate; rest; sleep; eat natural food; exercise; stretch; move; breathe deeply; think positively, and be happy. These activities are essential to the healing process. They produce hormones that activate homeostasis and help to heal your body."

It can't be that simple, can it? I wondered.

CHAPTER 3

GETTING WITH THE PROGRAM

The four areas of healing

"Now, let me tell you exactly what you can do to get well – and stay well," he said. "You can start healing yourself immediately in four areas of your life."

"Wait," I cried. "Let me jot this down." I reached into my bag and took out a pen and notepad that I'd swiped from the hospital. "Okay, go for it."

He lifted his fingers into the air to count on them. "Mentally, you can get all the knowledge you need to heal your body into your head as quickly as possible. Physically, you can help your body's natural healing processes by giving your body exactly what it needs, when it needs it, to restore physical balance and harmony. Spiritually, you can become more conscious of your true-self, which will put you in touch with the natural healing energy within you. Lastly, you can identify the emotional blockages that are making you sick, and then deal with them once and for all."

"I'm going to need my dictaphone," I said, scribbling as fast as I could.

"Don't worry, my notes will provide you with everything you need to know," he said, putting the big, brown envelope on my lap. "Read them and you'll discover the natural way to bring your body, mind and spirit back into balance. I promise you this: When your body, mind and spirit are in harmony with the natural laws, you'll experience radiant health and vitality every day for the rest of your life."

"How can you be sure this approach will work for me?" I asked once again. "I've been sick for a while. Isn't it too late?"

"No," he said with confidence. "It's never too late to start healing your body naturally and holistically. You see, your body is designed to heal itself, but it needs your help. This is the wonder of it. When you embark on a healing journey, your body instantly begins to respond positively. Take action and you'll be amazed at how quickly you begin to see and feel results."

"That sounds fantastic. What's next?"

"Well, to get you started, I've divided my notes into three sections: Theory, Workbook and Handbook. The Theory section will provide you with the knowledge you need to heal your body; the Workbook will give you the chance to apply what you've learned and to record your experience; and the Handbook will provide quick reference to the facts. It also contains healing exercises for each day of your 40-day, jump-start healing program. I strongly recommend that you read the Theory section from start to finish before you start the 40-day healing program."

"Why?"

He scratched his chin. "It helps to see the picture before you build the puzzle. True?"

"True."

"Good. Now, let's go over the three sections again," Henry Jones said in a tone that reminded me of a grade school teacher I'd once had. "As I've just said, the Theory section is jam-packed with all the information you'll ever need to heal your body. The really great part is that it not only explains exactly how to balance your body, mind and spirit, but it also includes the science behind it, so you can understand how and why it works."

"Excellent," I replied, clutching the big, brown envelope a little tighter. "If I am to believe, I need the facts."

"Most people do. The Theory section also includes practical, step-by-step guidelines that make learning easy. Study them. You'll discover many new, breakthrough techniques that'll boost your immune system, speed up your healing process, restore your body to perfect health, and bring true wellness into your life. I've also included many mystical, ancient healing methods that really work. Make no mistake, they're incredible!"

"It sounds too good to be true," I said.

"Oh, it's all true," he assured me. "I can say that with absolute certainty. Of course, the notes need to be edited and organized. That is your end of our bargain, right?"

"Of course."

"Good," he said. "Next, once you've internalized the theory of healing, I recommend you tackle the Workbook. That's where you'll have to roll up your shirtsleeves and get stuck into the material yourself. If you want to see results, you need to practise the healing techniques and exercises. You can't read your way to perfect health. You must apply what you've learned. Okay?"

"Okay," I said, nodding my head. I wondered what I was getting myself into. I peeked into the big, brown envelope, but could only see a stack of papers with handwritten notes scrawled across them.

"In the Workbook, you'll also find a section called Activity Planner. It's very easy to use. You simply select the healing techniques that appeal to you in the Theory section and then, using your Activity Planner, schedule appointments with yourself to do them."

"Like managing a diary?"

"Exactly! You do what you feel like doing, when you feel like doing it. That is the beauty of this complete, holistic and natural self-healing kit. You get to decide on your own course of action. Not having to follow someone else's formula for success is liberating. Between you and me, I can't stand diets and exercise regimens that tell me what to do and when to do it. I think they are controlling and restrictive."

"Me, too."

"Think of the theory section as a buffet of healing techniques. You can help yourself to whatever appeals to you. It's a feast of wellness activators. The best part is: There's no charge, so you can indulge as much and as often as you like."

"That's neat," I said.

Plan and record

"Good," Henry Jones said with a wry smile. "You need to plan each day in advance. This is absolutely crucial on your healing journey."

"Why?"

"Because planning ahead gives you a program to follow," he replied matter-of-factly.

"Simply put, a program is a sequence of activities or events that are structured to produce a desired result. This is a very basic but crucial concept that you need to comprehend in order to succeed on a healing journey. That will be your key to success. You need to wake up each morning to a planned schedule and activities. Make sense?"

"Sure. It's not exactly rocket science."

"There's a little more to it. I've also created a space in the Workbook for you to write notes to yourself. That is also very, very important."

"Why?"

"Personal notes each day transform a diary into a journal. There's a big difference between the two. I'd like you to use your Workbook to record how each healing technique makes you feel. This is an essential part of each exercise. I promise you, you'll find great value in your notes when you look back on your healing journey. Each entry will be an experiential milestone and benchmark of your accomplishments."

"Consider it done," I stated firmly. "So, let me see if I've got this straight: My daily goal should be to go to bed at night knowing I did everything I planned to do. That includes making a journal entry and planning my activities for the next day."

"Yes, you've got it. I call that a True-Day. When you have True-Days, you'll feel a sense of achievement and fulfilment. I should know. I've been practising this system for years."

"How did you keep it up for so long?"

"It's easy to succeed when you take one day at a time. Got it?"

"Yup!"

"Excellent! I'd like you to score yourself daily. That will help you to evaluate your performance and measure your results over time. Each day in the Activity Planner includes a very simple personal and program scoring system that makes it easy for you to award yourself points each day for doing activities that promote healing and wellness."

"What's the difference between the personal and program scores?" I asked.

"Some folks are content to do the best they can without putting themselves under too much pressure. Other folks like to excel at what they do and thrive on competition and excellence."

"I'm the latter," I told him.

He nodded. "The personal scorecard enables you to identify a few key activities that you feel comfortable doing each day in the four focus areas: Physical, mental, spiritual and emotional. The program scorecard enables you to track your performance against all the activities that I recommend for natural, holistic healing.

"The Program Scorecard is more intense than the Personal scorecard. You can use both scorecards to evaluate your day's performance if you're a super-achiever, or just the Personal Scorecard, if you want to stay within your comfort zone."

"What's the maximum points I can score on your program each day?"

"One hundred points," he replied.

"So, a True-Day gets a full score?" I asked.

"No," he replied. "I must make this point clear. A True-Day refers to achieving all that you set out to achieve on the day. You don't need to score 100 points in a day to have a True Day. You must simply do everything that you planned to do. Got it?"

"Yeah."

"I'm pleased. Now, you should strive for True-Days and do your best to get the highest score possible each day and week. This means you'll have to break old habits and build new routines."

"How long will it take?"

"The Activity Planner lasts for 40 days and 40 nights, as I said, but your healing journey should continue until you've restored your body to perfect health."

"Why 40 days and 40 nights?" I asked.

"Well, it's short enough for you to stay focused and remain committed, and just long enough for you to see and feel results," he replied. "I've designed the four healing processes to run sequentially over this period, so you can plan properly, track your progress, set goals and measure your results. But don't think of this program as a quick fix. It is just a jumpstart to your healing journey – an ideal chance to change your lifestyle for the better, for good. You do want to live a long, healthy life, don't you?"

"Certainly!"

"So then, do your best to have True-Days."

Lapse, relapse and collapse

"But, what if I slip?"

"Slip?"

"You know. Backslide. Fall off the wagon. Succumb to my demons."

Henry Jones cocked his head to the side. "What is the meaning of the word 'lapse'?" he asked.

"A lapse is a small mistake or return to old habits," I replied.

"Exactly! And what is a relapse?"

"A relapse is when you go back to old habits for several days or weeks," I answered. "I know. My father was an alcoholic and drug addict."

"I'm sorry to hear it," he said. "While you're on your healing journey, you simply shouldn't allow yourself to lapse, especially during the first 40 days and 40 nights. After that initial period, you'll find lapses are inevitable! You can bet that life will throw special occasions and parties in your path, and it'll be very hard for you to keep to your program on those days."

"I haven't been going to many parties lately," I mumbled.

"That's too bad. Celebrations, reunions, special events, birthdays and office parties are some of the joys of life. When those occasions arise, follow your intuition and your heart. It's not a sin to break your healthy lifestyle on occasion. In fact, just the opposite is true. It's unhealthy to be too rigid in your ways. Flexibility is a vital attribute of a healthy mind."

"So, I can cheat occasionally after 40 days and 40 nights?" I asked.

"If you feel that it's absolutely necessary to have a Break Day, then by all means take one. But, don't abuse a Break Day. It's not an excuse to indulge in junk food or to drink excessively. The further you step off the path to perfect health, the longer it will take you to achieve your ultimate goal. You'll need to practice moderation and self-control."

"Those are not my strong points," I confessed.

"I appreciate your honesty," Henry Jones said. "But, keep this in mind: If you take a one-day-on, one-day-off approach, it'll take you 10 times longer to heal your body than if you remained committed to your program."

He pulled me closer. I cocked my ear to hear what he had to say. "Too many lapses in your program may lead to a relapse, which will result in your collapse. You don't want that to happen. So, don't bank on taking Break Days. They aren't good for you. But, if you do happen to slip, the important thing is to exercise your free will appropriately and then get right back on track the very next day. Okay?"

"Okay," I promised.

"Good. Now, this is when the scorecard comes in handy. Poor results stand out as blemishes in your Workbook. They're an indicator of how seriously you want to heal your body. If you have a less than True-Day and you're serious about healing your body, then you'll make sure you get a better score the next day, and the next. You follow?"

"What if I cheat and give myself an inaccurate score?" I asked.

"Remember, you're on a healing journey for yourself, not for anyone else. You can't cheat your way back to health."

"That makes sense," I said sheepishly.

Reward yourself

"Don't worry about scoring poorly. Just stick to your program and you'll be fine. More importantly, reward yourself for good performance. In your Workbook, you'll also find a section on Targets and Rewards, he said. "That is my favorite section."

I liked the sound of that.

"It's crucial to reward yourself for achieving your goals," said Henry Jones. "Ask experts on goal-setting and they'll confirm it. Rewards give you something to aim for. They motivate you to excel. If you really want the reward, you'll strive to achieve it. They also peg your accomplishments. You'll remember achieving the goal by the reward you receive. Interestingly, being rewarded is often more valued than the reward itself. Children will run as fast as they can to win a race; or they'll tidy their rooms; or perform in front of strangers, for a lollipop. It's not just the lollipop that drives them. It's the chance to be rewarded for their accomplishment."

"So, you're saying the rewards can be small, inexpensive items?"

"Yes. Small, big, cheap or expensive, it doesn't really matter. Rewards can even be experiences that bring you pleasure but cost nothing. What's important is that you feel rewarded by receiving or experiencing them."

"Sounds like fun."

Henry Jones chortled. "The trick is to enjoy the process, even though you're taking it seriously. But, whatever you do, don't stress out while trying to achieve True-Days. That will do you more harm than good. Making progress is more important. Take one day at a time and do your best to link one True-Day to the next."

"Because True-Days lead to true wellness …"

"Yes, success is just that simple!" Henry Jones replied.

Set a start date

"Okay, then. So, when should I start writing in the Workbook and practising the techniques?"

"I recommend you set your start date for the day after you finish reading the Theory section."

I gulped. "I had been hoping to ease into it over time."

"Why?"

"Well, I've heard people say it's better to change your ways gradually. Apparently, slow change doesn't shock your system or rock your lifestyle too much."

"Rubbish!" scoffed Henry Jones. "That might work for a fad diet, but when you're sick, it's a different story. You want to get well as soon as possible, don't you?"

"Yes."

"In that case, read the Theory section as a matter of urgency. But don't rush through it. It's important to understand and internalize the information. If you need to, read it more than once. Only when you're certain that you can begin with the end goal in mind, should you begin working through the healing exercises and writing in your Workbook. Understand?"

"Yup."

"Of course, this doesn't mean to say that you can't apply the healing principles immediately. On the contrary, if anything strikes a chord in you while reading my notes, try at once to integrate the lesson into your life. For example, you don't have to wait until you finish reading the Theory section to stop eating junk food. The slightest move towards positive change is a big step in the right direction. The sooner you start living a healthier lifestyle, the better it'll be for you. Right?"

"Yes."

"Good, now let's go back to discussing your start date. It's true to say your healing journey begins the instant you decide to take responsibility for healing your body. However, the day you actually start practising healing techniques and writing in your Workbook is the most significant."

"How come?"

"Well, firstly you can record your progress from a fixed point in time. This provides a benchmark from which to track your performance and measure the changes in your life. As time goes by, your start date will become more meaningful to you – much like alcoholics who keep vigilant records of how long they've been sober. The longer you stay on your program, the more you'll want to preserve the integrity of your start date, and the easier it'll become. I guarantee you: The further you get from your Start Date, the stronger you'll feel physically, mentally, emotionally and spiritually. But, I'm biased. I've done it before. Try it for yourself, and you'll understand what I'm talking about."

"Do you really think I can do it?

"Yes. I do."

"I hope you're right," I said.

Hope births possibility

"Good for you," replied Henry Jones. "Hope is crucial. It makes the present come alive with possibility. It's important to keep your hopes up on your healing journey. If you lose hope, you'll undoubtedly fall off your program."

"How can I avoid that?" I asked.

"The key is willpower," said Henry Jones. "Willpower is a crucial healing force that provides people the 'oomph' to see things through."

"I'll need an extra dose," I retorted.

"Fortunately for you, willpower is an unlimited natural resource, and it's absolutely free. You can use as much of it as you like and it doesn't cost a cent," he replied cheerfully. He scratched through his pile of Post-its, and then handed me this note:

> *When you apply willpower to achieve a specific goal, it becomes an extremely constructive energy.*

"So, tell me more about the Handbook," I said peering into the big, brown envelope.

He grinned from ear to ear. "The Handbook will help you to internalize the information I share with you. I've extracted the educational content from my notes, categorized it into themes, and presented it in hotlists, checklists and summaries that will make learning a breeze. Each text block has a reference number, which makes it easy to do the healing exercises found in the Handbook. Basically, you'll have all the knowledge you need at your fingertips to complete the healing exercises. All you have to do is study it and live it!"

I tapped the big, brown envelope like a man kicks the tyres of a car he is thinking about buying. "So, you really think I'll get better?"

"Natural healing works!" Henry Jones said with confidence. "Combined with other holistic healing techniques, the results are phenomenal. The only one who can fail is you – and you can only fail by quitting. So, if you want to heal your body, don't quit. It's that simple."

I sighed. What an extraordinary morning it had been. I'd spent an hour at the dispensary getting bottles and tubs of medicine. They'd told me what to take and when to take it. I'd felt disempowered and pathetic. I was grateful for the medication, and it had certainly eased my suffering in the past, but I was dependent on it. If the medicine failed, I was doomed, I thought. Then, along came Henry Jones with his big smile, Father Christmas laugh, and big brown envelope. I knew my world would never be the same again. I was no longer a victim of disease, or a powerless patient. I was the master of my own recovery. He had given me back my personal power. Even though my healing journey had just begun, I felt different inside. I closed my eyes and searched my feelings. I felt comforted … reassured … hopeful … grateful … excited … and strong!

Perhaps Henry Jones sensed that I was about to express my gratitude to him and, not needing acknowledgement, he quickly added: "By now, you must be curious about the healing processes I have planned for you?"

"Yes, I am."

A new start

"Excellent. I won't keep you waiting a minute longer. Let's walk to my car.

As I stood to my feet and swung my bag over my shoulder, I caught a glimpse of my hospital room window. I shuddered involuntarily. My plans were now set in stone: For the next 40 days and 40 nights, I'd stay with Henry Jones. That happened to suit me. My wife and I had agreed to separate when I left the hospital, so I needed a place to stay. Henry Jones had invited me to live with him while we worked on his book. This was it. My healing journey was about to begin. I turned my back on the hospital and scampered after Henry Jones with the brown envelope clutched to my chest.

Yes, I was apprehensive. I didn't have a clue what he had in store for me, but I was more concerned I'd mess up again. I'd good reason to be worried. I knew the consequences of failure all too well. My heart pounded in my chest. I was on my way at last.

"In the weeks ahead, you'll experience four simple and yet extremely effective healing processes. These short, powerful healing processes are vital steps on the path to true wellness. Each of them is an essential leg in your race to recovery."

"What do I have to do?"

"Stick to the guidelines in the Workbook I gave you," he said. "Follow the step-by-step instructions and you won't lose your way."

A solo journey

"Let me stake out the four healing processes for you. We're going to heal your body; open your mind; awaken your spirit and free your emotions."

"Sounds good," I said excitedly. Still, I had no clue what he was talking about.

"I'm very confident these physical, mental, spiritual and emotional healing processes will sort out your health problems once and for all."

"In 40 days and 40 nights?" I asked, hurrying to catch up to him.

"I can't say how long it'll take you, as I've said before. Your body will respond to the four healing processes in its own good time. Once again, think of the weeks ahead as a jumpstart program. It's the start of a new lifestyle for you. During our time together. I'll point you in the right direction and even lay out the path for you to follow, but only you can make the journey. It's up to you to accept responsibility for healing yourself. You need to remain committed every step of the way, no matter how long it takes you."

"I've a feeling this is going to be a life-changing event," I said.

"I hope so, for your sake. It's up to you now. You see, healthy living is a skill. It's applied knowledge. The ticket here is you. You've got to apply what you learn, not just in the weeks ahead, but for as long as you live," Henry Jones said as he directed me towards a white Land Rover in the distance.

"That's our ride?" I inquired.

"Yes. Why?"

"I pictured you in a luxury sedan," I remarked and then immediately regretted it. Thankfully, he just ignored me.

"I've a question for you," he said, shuffling through the set of keys in his hand. "What would life be without rules?"

"Absolute chaos," I replied confidently.

"That's right! We need rules to keep us in check, so I've instituted one rule on your healing journey. Are you going to like it? Probably not, but it's for your own good."

"Come on, let's have it then."

"If you break your program for longer than 48 hours, you've got to fast or eat fruit only for the next 48 hours."

"No food, just fruit?" I exclaimed.

"Yes. Preferably no food at all, but if you must eat, then just fruit! This is an excellent way to reboot your recovery," he said, rubbing his hands together mischievously. "This rule isn't meant to be a punishment. It's merely there to deter you from falling off your program. This single rule will also help you to take your start date seriously. If you allow yourself another Break Day after 48 hours have passed, then you should seriously question your commitment. It'll be important for you to reflect on what you've accomplished, and to then visualize your end goal. So, do the right thing. Get back on track, okay?"

"Okay. Will do," I promised.

"Good. Jump in," Henry Jones said as he hoisted my bag on to the backseat of his 4x4.

I mustered a feeble nod. It was my attempt to express my gratitude. It was all I could do. I was out of breath. You see, I hadn't done any exercise for a long time. Being sick, exercise was the furthest thing from my mind. Climbing into the Land Rover, I suddenly got the sense that I was about to embark on an adventure with Henry Jones. I was both excited and apprehensive. "Where are we going now?" I asked as he jumped into the driver's seat beside me. I was impressed by his agility. He lifted himself effortlessly. The muscles that rippled beneath the surface of his paper-thin skin momentarily amazed me.

"We're going right back to the beginning," he replied. "I've a friend who runs a fertility clinic. She's expecting us in 20 minutes."

"Are you serious?"

"Oh yes," Henry Jones chuckled with a twinkle in his eye. "You need to know where you come from in order to know where you're going."

"Really? A fertility clinic?"

"Yup! But that's just for starters. I've got lots of interesting things lined up for you to do, and loads of interesting people for you to meet. You're about to embark on a miraculous healing journey, my friend. I suggest you buckle up and enjoy the ride."

CHAPTER 4

IN THE BEGINNING

"Follow me, please," an attractive nurse requested politely.

"With pleasure," I replied, with a little too much enthusiasm in my voice.

She blushed ever so slightly. Henry Jones rolled his eyes at me and I felt rather silly. We walked down a long passage, adorned on either side by huge, framed photographs of foetuses in wombs, and mothers suckling babies. They rendered my flirtations totally inappropriate, and I felt even sillier. The nurse ushered us into a small office. A desk and two chairs made the room seem full. The cluttered desk indicated that whoever worked in that tiny space was a very busy person. The walls were filled with certificates of qualifications, merit awards, and hundreds of photos of bedraggled women clutching their newborn infants. They all looked as if they had been dragged through hell. I recalled the birth of my daughter and the awful suffering my wife had endured. It hadn't been an easy labour. The photos gave me the willies. Fortunately, we didn't have to wait long.

"They are all miracles of nature," I heard a woman with a strong German accent say from behind me. I spun around sharply, as if I'd been caught sneaking a peek at someone's private photo album. I looked straight over her head. She was that short! In front of me stood a woman I could only describe as Red Riding Hood's grandmother. Professor Kaufmann wore a small pair of round spectacles balanced on the end of her sharp nose, and pinned her grey and white hair up in a large Victorian-style bun. She held a plate of freshly-baked cookies that smelled delicious.

You're one in a billion

"Pardon," I said as I collected myself.

"Your conception was nothing short of a miracle. An inexplicable, natural miracle!" she declared. "Consider that in half a teaspoon of sperm there are enough sperm cells to impregnate half the world's population!"

"Wow!" I exclaimed.

"So, what does that tell you?" inquired Henry Jones. I shrugged my shoulders.

"You simply wouldn't be here today if it wasn't for the irrefutable fact that you're a natural-born winner!" she declared triumphantly.

"That's true!" said Henry Jones with a wink.

"You took first place in the great race for life," she said.

Henry Jones clapped: "You won!"

"Against seemingly impossible odds!" she affirmed. "You're one in a billion."

They could've been performing a well-rehearsed script.

"So, don't ever think you're not someone special, okay?" Professor Kaufmann said, offering me a cookie.

"Fortunately for you, no pictures were taken of you at the time of this miraculous achievement," added Henry Jones.

"Why?"

"Because, at the time, you looked very much like a microscopic tadpole," Professor Kaufmann sniggered, greeting Henry Jones with a kiss on each cheek. "Let me explain further. Look at this chart," she said.

On the back of her office door was the type of educational poster one finds in a grade school classroom. It showed the life cycle of a foetus. The illustrations were hand-drawn and brightly colored.

"You must pay attention now," Henry Jones said, "because you'll need to remember this information further along on your healing journey. There's an amazing emotional healing therapy session you'll discover that involves the womb. It's extremely effective."

The uniqueness of you

Professor Kaufmann turned to face the poster. "With supreme instinct and divine intelligence, you knew to penetrate the outer membrane of the egg. Once inside, your tail fell off and you were able to fuse with the egg completely. Within this single cell, genes from both of your parents combined to create an entirely new and unique life form – you."

71

"She's saying you're a unique individual, unlike any other human being who has ever lived," Henry Jones whispered to me.

"Ja, ja!" Professor Kaufmann affirmed abrasively. "The sperm and the egg each have 23 chromosomes, and when they come together, they then have the full 46 chromosomes needed to form a human being."

"How does this cocktail of ordinary chromosomes spark life?" Henry Jones asked. Once again, I suspected he already knew the answer.

"No one knows. It's a mystical wonder that the mind of man can't begin to fathom. You should just accept it and appreciate that you're an expression of nature's brilliance and divine genius. But, your life had only just begun. Your wondrous adventure really got rolling when you, the fertilized egg, journeyed down the fallopian tube to the womb. On your way, you began to divide rapidly into two cells, then four, then eight, and so on. This was the true beginning of your life. Within days, you were a cluster of about 60 cells, known as a blastocyst. You had to survive on your own energy stores, much like a self-contained space capsule. Your mission was to get to the womb in approximately 6 days before you exhausted your supply of energy!"

"Evidently, I made it!" I said smugly.

"Hooray! Good for you," she said, fixing her eyes on the chart and gesturing that I do the same. Once again, I obeyed. "Once inside the womb, you expertly docked yourself on to the wall of the womb by commissioning specific cells to grow into the womb's lining. Then, your life support system, the placenta, began to form. Once you had established your home base for the next 9 months, you had to communicate with your mother's body's immune system through the release of chemicals."

"Why?"

"So that it didn't misinterpret your arrival as an alien invasion and begin to attack and destroy you. That's why!"

"Phew! A lot of responsibility for a microscopic entity," I said jokingly.

"It's incredible!" Professor Kaufmann replied excitedly, as though she was discovering this phenomenon for the first time. She and Henry Jones shared a similar passion for their work. They were two peas in a pod.

"After six weeks, you had developed into a perfectly healthy embryo."

"Look here … that blob is you," Henry Jones joked as he pointed to a tiny spot on the poster. The Professor leaned in to examine the picture more closely.

"You'll notice that inside the womb it appears that you were floating around in a fluid-filled bubble, holding a balloon. That was a yolk sac that supplied you with vital nutrients until the placenta was fully developed. You had a blob-like head that curved down to a pointed tail. On your head, you had gill-like folds that would later develop into your facial features. On your body, you had little buds with nodules on the ends. They would ultimately grow into your arms and legs."

"Life was taking shape," mused Henry Jones.

"Ja, ja. Your heart had begun to flutter, and your internal organs had started to form. You survived on energy and protein that you received through the tiny blood vessels that were attached to the wall of your mother's womb. Of course, then, you were only one-third the size of your fingertip."

"Isn't life grand?" Henry Jones exclaimed in apparent wonderment.

"I guess so," I replied, studying the poster more carefully.

"After 9 to 12 weeks, you had quadrupled in size. You could then be called a foetus. You resembled a perfect, tiny human being. Your ears, nose, mouth and chin were visible. You had fingers; toes with nails; a four-chambered fully functioning heart; a relatively big brain that could transmit messages to your body; reproductive organs; and the outline of all your bones and joints. You even had all your teeth."

"Most importantly, you were in immaculate health," said Henry Jones.

"This is mostly because of the placenta," Professor Kaufmann said. "It's truly amazing. This is biological engineering at its best! While you were in the womb, the placenta produced hormones that were vital to your survival and enabled you to breathe, digest and excrete. It was attached to the inside wall of the womb, and you were attached to the placenta by your umbilical cord. The placenta acted as a filtering membrane to provide you with oxygen and nutrients. It also allowed you to expel carbon dioxide and waste products without ever mixing the good with the bad."

"Tell him about the umbilical cord," Henry Jones said enthusiastically.

Professor Kaufmann smacked a ruler against the poster to get my attention. "Your umbilical cord consisted of three, intertwined blood vessels. Two of the vessels took impure blood from your body to the placenta, and one vessel returned pure blood from the placenta back to your body. Through this process, you were able to purify your system and sustain perfect health for the remaining 28 weeks."

An amazing blueprint

"In that time, you continued to develop in accordance with the blueprint of God. Every stage of your growth was on schedule. Never too early, nor too late! Your consciousness and coordination were well established. You fed, slept and moved around to make yourself comfortable. You could kick, punch, nod your head, look around and even wriggle your fingers and toes. You could sense light through your closed eyes, hear noises, feel vibrations and taste and swallow. You could get a fright, so you knew fear, and you could be calm, so you knew peace. You were influenced by the emotions of your parents, especially your mother. You could also recognise both of their voices. Inside the womb, you felt totally safe and secure. It was the perfect place for you to be. Every single biological function worked towards sustaining your life and nurturing your development. Inexplicably, through umpteen million chemical processes and cellular reactions, you transformed from a flat sheet of cells into a plump, perfectly healthy baby, ready to be born, in just 40 weeks. This is truly remarkable, don't you think?" Professor Kaufmann asked.

"Yes, it's quite remarkable."

She sighed. "I'm amazed you opted to leave the womb, but I guess you knew that life had other plans for you."

"Were things about to change, or what?" chuckled Henry Jones.

The miracle of birth

"Let us revisit your birth experience now," she said, turning to the chart. "Inside the womb, you grew more uncomfortable with each passing day. You felt cramped and your movements were restricted. Occasionally, you experienced contractions that felt as though they were trying to force you out of your 'home base'. Then, one eventful day, the amniotic fluid that surrounded and protected you inside the womb suddenly drained away."

"Things would never be the same again," whispered Henry Jones.

"In that moment, you became aware of a natural force far greater than yourself. It was intent on forcing your evolution. Until then, everything had been about you. Every biological process and function had been geared towards your survival, development, nurturing and growth. Now, nature's way was taking over, pushing you towards another form of existence."

"You were about to be born," Henry Jones declared.

"Ja, ja. The onset of contractions increased in frequency and intensity. Your head pushed against your mother's cervix, causing it to soften and dilate. Distress signals flew between mother and child, adrenaline pumped, and hearts pounded. Eventually, the cervix opened. You slowly squeezed through the pelvis and down the narrow vaginal passage, towards the light."

"Birth truly is a miraculous event, isn't it?" I said breathlessly, studying the poster even more closely.

"Ja, ja. Ask anyone who has ever witnessed a birth of any kind, and they'll likely describe the experience as joyous; thrilling; awesome; incredible; humbling; reverent and spiritual. I never get used to it. It boggles my mind every time, without fail," she said.

"Birth reminds us of the wonder of nature and the miracle of life," Henry Jones said. "Unless you had unresolved karmic issues or other complications at birth, you were a completely formed, perfect, tiny human being. You were pure in body, mind and spirit."

"Ja, Ja. This is exactly so. You were made in the image of God. Perfect."

Henry Jones patted me on the back: "Welcome to existence, newcomer."

We laughed together before moving to the nursery, where mothers left their babies while they underwent their postnatal examinations. It had been many years since I had held a baby. Then, suddenly, there I was, surrounded by them. They laughed, cried, and gurgled. Their perfect little facial features and tiny fingers and toes overwhelmed me. I wished my own body radiated such health. I bottle-fed a baby boy whose deep stare seemed to penetrate my soul. "Where did you go wrong? Why are you sick? How will you restore your health?" the baby boy seemed to ask me as he stared into my eyes.

I sat with my thoughts as we drove away from the clinic, along the highway. As cars whizzed past us, I stared out of the window and watched the world flash by, one lamppost at a time. I was overcome by the stark contrast between our fast-paced modern lifestyle and the stillness of the newborn babies.

"Where are we going next?" I eventually asked Henry Jones, breaking the silence.

"The planetarium," he declared.

"Planetarium?"

"Yes. A visit to the planetarium will put your life on Earth into context in relation to the rest of space and time. I'm certain this insight will help you on your healing journey. In my notes, you'll discover many interesting facts and figures about the size and scope of the universe. I'd like you to find a novel way to include this information in our book. Our readers need to understand the basic concept of relative physics. This will help them to appreciate the enormous creative energy and power of the universe. I have a friend who works at the planetarium. He opened my eyes to the connection between heavenly bodies and physical bodies. This knowledge can help you to heal your body. I've arranged for us to meet him today. He's expecting us at 3pm sharp. We don't want to be a minute late."

"Why the tight schedule?"

"Well, let's just say he's sensitive about time arrangements. Punctuality and precision are important to him. My guess is that he needs order more than most people. Over the years, I've grown accustomed to his ways. He's quite a character, but trust me, we don't want to be late," exclaimed Henry Jones as he put his foot to the accelerator pedal. We raced towards the planetarium as fast as his shuddering Land Rover allowed.

"Get out of the way," Henry Jones cried out on more than one occasion, pounding on the hooter. But, despite his best efforts, the traffic was against us and we arrived a few minutes late for our appointment.

"It's about bloody time!" A deep, powerful voice barrelled down from the huge telescope as we entered the dome-shaped building. His rich Indian accent was unmistakeable.

"Hello, my old friend," Henry Jones said to the mountain-like figure descending down the telescope stairs in leaps and bounds.

"Don't you bloody-well call me your old friend, Henry! What bloody friend keeps someone waiting for 12 and a half bloody minutes? 3 o'clock. Bloody 3pm. That was the time we arranged to meet, and you're bloody late."

"Forgive us," he replied. "We got caught in traffic."

"Bloody unacceptable! I thought you weren't coming. Bloody forgotten me, that's what I thought. Let me tell you straight, Henry, I have better things to do with my time than to climb up and down bloody stairs when people don't show up for meetings on time. You've wasted my precious time. Have I not explained to you the importance of time?" he ranted, waving his large arms in the air like an angry protestor at a rally.

I'd frozen in my tracks. Dr Sahib was a big man – not fat, just big. He exited the room and slammed the door behind him. We were left standing alone in the empty planetarium. The night sky twinkled on the vast dome above our heads. Stupefied, I stared in wonderment at the stars. It seemed I could reach out and touch them. They appeared so bright, clear and close.

Out of the stillness, I heard Henry Jones whispering: "Three, two, one ..." and on cue the door swung open.

"Bloody unacceptable, Henry! You know better than this!" Dr Sahib yelled as he marched towards us. "Is this the guy who got himself sick?"

"This is ..." but Henry Jones wasn't given the chance to finish his sentence.

"What the bloody hell is wrong with you?" Dr Sahib shouted, pointing at me.

"We got stuck in traffic," I stammered.

"No, I mean what the bloody hell is wrong with you, buddy-boy," he said, beating his chest like an angry gorilla.

"Oh, I've got ..."

"Never mind, never mind. It makes no difference to me. One sickness is the same as another. It's only the symptoms that differ. I'm *the* Dr Sahib," he said, extending his spade-like hand. "I'm not a medical doctor. I have my PhD in astrophysics, but I will help you to heal your body."

"I appreciate you taking the time to meet with us. My name is ..."

"Never mind, never mind. It makes no difference," he snorted again. "One person's the same as another; it's only the name that differs."

He turned to Henry Jones: "You're very lucky that I don't have time to spare on being angry with you today, Henry. Time waits for no man. Give me a hug and let us put your tardiness behind us." He enveloped Henry Jones in a warm embrace that lifted him off his feet. "Tell me, my friend, has life been good to you?"

"Yes. I'm very well indeed, thank you," Henry Jones replied, sucking air back into his lungs.

"Bloody excellent! Your good fortune fills me with much happiness. I can no longer be cross with you. Come with me. I have something magnificent to show you. This will blow your bloody mind."

We followed Dr Sahib into a dark room where he presented us with a photograph of outer space. In the center of the photo was a circled speck of light that didn't seem any bigger than the other specks of light.

"What are we looking at?"

Vastness beyond comprehension

"This is a photograph of a star that's many thousand times bigger than our Sun. I took it myself at 2.16am six days ago. Look at it. Can you imagine the size of it? No, don't even try to imagine it! I know you can't. It's impossible for our teeny-weeny brains to comprehend such vastness."

"Which one is it?" teased Henry Jones.

"It's the one with the bloody circle around it, of course!"

I pointed it out. Dr Sahib nodded approvingly and slapped my back. Had I been wearing false teeth, I'm sure they'd have flown out my mouth.

"How far away is this star from Earth?" I asked, exaggerating my interest.

"Oh, my goodness! Bloody far, buddy-boy. Bloody, bloody far," he yelled. "I could tell you the exact distance, but the sheer number of miles is probably beyond your reckoning. Let's start closer to home, shall we? How far away do you think the Sun is from Earth? Go on, have a guess. You can try, but I doubt you'll even get close."

"I haven't got a clue."

"Tell us," piped up Henry Jones.

"Okay, you asked for it. But I still don't think you'll be able to get your head around it, buddy-boy. Get this: For the early morning sunbeams to give you that bloody wonderful feeling of well-being as they dance on your eyelids, they must travel a whopping 93 million miles, give or take!"

"Gosh!"

"That's nothing at all. It's just a hop, skip and jump away in relation to the rest of space. As you most probably already know, scientists use light years to measure space. Right?"

"What's a light year?" Henry Jones asked, although I once again suspected he knew the answer.

"A light year is simply the distance a beam of light travels in one year," he told me. "But how far does it travel? That is the question," said Dr Sahib.

"No idea."

"Well then, let me be the one to put an end to your bloody ignorance. We estimate it to be about 600 billion miles. Can you imagine how far that is? Not a chance, right? It's unfathomable! Now consider this: The nearest star to our planet is four and a half light years away, and the Milky Way is 100 000 light-years in cross-section."

"Is that huge, or what?" exclaimed Henry Jones.

"Pretty huge," I admitted.

"That is nothing. Our galaxy is one of several billion galaxies in the universe, and each galaxy consists of billions of stars and solar systems. On top of this, the universe is an interwoven pattern of energy systems in which time can speed up and slow down, and the same elementary particle can exist in two places at the same time. We scientists now believe that space is curved and finite, yet unending and possibly even multi-dimensional."

"Huh?"

"Bloody mind-boggling stuff, isn't it?" responded Dr Sahib. "But, by now, if you had half a bloody brain, you would be wondering to yourself: What is this dashingly handsome Indian's point?"

"What?" His remark caught me by surprise.

"What's what? The point is that it's simply impossible for the mind of man to conceive the immensity and complexity of the universe. It's just too big for our teeny-weeny brains," he said, as he strutted back into the dome-shaped building.

The presence of the Divine

"I'm not sure I understand you," I said, scurrying after him.

"Look up," he said, pointing to the roof of the planetarium. "Only a bloody fool denies the existence of a supreme intelligence. What do you think? Do you think all of this happened by accident? No bloody way! I've been studying the universe for many decades and I can tell you without hesitation there's an almighty force responsible for the creation and maintenance of everything in existence. This omnipotent energy is everywhere. It sparked the creation of the universe, solar system, Planet Earth and everything on it."

"Including you," said Henry Jones.

"Indeed!" yelled Dr Sahib.

"I'm still not sure I get your point. What are you trying to tell me?"

"Oh my gosh! We'll have to take it slow with this one, Henry," said Dr Sahib. He grabbed my shoulders, spun me around to face him, stared straight into my eyes, and said very slowly: "We're trying to tell you the Divine intelligence that created everything exists all around you, and even in you. It seems we're having difficulty getting this concept through your thick skull, buddy-boy."

"Do you mean God?"

"Oh my goodness! That's a small, man-made word for a bloody huge concept," said Dr Sahib. "You can call it whatever you like. It makes no difference to me. Or to the Divine Source, I suspect! You can say God, the supreme intelligence, the universe, energy, or even the Big G! The point is:

This creative energy exists in everything in the universe, whether we choose to believe it or not."

"Okay, I get it, but why are you telling me this?"

"Well, buddy-boy, when you accept it and believe it, you can connect with it."

"And then you'll discover an extremely powerful healing force," interjected Henry Jones.

"Healing force?"

"Indeed!" Dr Sahib yelled again. Except this time, he pretended to sucker-punch my gut. Of course, in that moment, I didn't think he was just pretending. I doubled over and groaned in anticipation of the pain. That made Dr Sahib laugh loudly and then lock my head in his thickset arm and ruffle my hair with his sausage-like fingers.

His jovial demeanor didn't help to convince me of his affections. After some time had passed, Henry Jones tapped Dr Sahib on the shoulder and motioned him to release me from his grip. He did, and I gasped for air.

"You see, healing doesn't just happen on a physical level. It happens on a spiritual level, too. I brought you to the planetarium to experience this dimension. It's important to reconnect with your spirituality when you want to heal your body," said Henry Jones.

"But I'm not religious," I mumbled as I straightened my hair and composed myself.

"You don't have to be religious," announced Dr Sahib. "Religion and spirituality are not necessarily the same thing. When you make the connection between the universe and your inner being, your spirituality awakens, regardless of your bloody religious beliefs."

We are all interconnected

"Try this experiment," Dr Sahib commanded. "Right here, right now, lift your eyes to the stars on the roof of the planetarium and sense the awesome creative energy of the universe around you. Allow your consciousness to expand into it. You'll feel how becoming aware of the universe connects you to God. When we make the connection between the heavenly bodies and our physical bodies, then we become one with the universe. This is a bloody powerful healing experience for human beings. It's awesome. Go on, give it a go, buddy-boy."

I felt awkward. Henry Jones and Dr Sahib were unusual characters, to say the least. They were an odd couple: One was short, one was tall, but they were significantly larger than life. Although the planetarium auditorium was dimly lit, I could clearly see their encouraging smiles and bobbing heads urging me to embrace the exercise. To escape my embarrassment, I looked up at the roof of the planetarium and all at once I was lost in wonderment. I transcended my self-awareness, and my spirit seemed to merge with the myriad galaxies and stars that shone brightly above me. They were truly spectacular. I felt a rush of energy through my body. In that moment, I felt alive and free, and, dare I say it, I felt a sense of oneness … of wholeness … of healing! Sadly, it didn't last long.

"Why do you think the almighty force that made everything in existence can't make you well again? What makes you so special, buddy-boy?" Dr Sahib growled.

His question brought me back to Earth with a thud. What indeed? Who was I to deny the existence of God? Why couldn't I tap into the creative universal energy within me to heal my body? I wondered. I needed to know more. I needed to know why tuning into the vastness of the universe made me feel essential, instead of insignificant. I lost myself in the night sky above my head. For an instant, I forgot I was sick. I felt a strange connection to a cosmic vitality more than the ill-effects of my disease. It was sensational. "Why do I feel this way?" I whispered.

"Why do you have to understand it? You don't have to know the bloody composition of the Sun to enjoy its warmth, do you? If healing is what you seek, then just accept that there's a magnificent, omnipotent higher power that's responsible for the creation and maintenance of everything in existence."

"And this includes you, my friend," said Henry Jones.

"But if this is so, why did God make me sick in the first place?"

"He didn't. You made yourself sick. You strayed from God's law," said Henry Jones.

"Humanity has strayed from God's law," Dr Sahib said loudly. He turned to me and prodded my chest with his enormous finger. "Everything in existence is governed by God's laws. Just as the law of gravity holds together all the stars and planets in the universe, the law of nature sustains all of life on Earth."

Newcomers to the planet

"For 4.5 billion years Mother Nature maintained the balance of all living things. Together, they lived in harmony with the Earth, and sustained their health by consuming what Mother Nature intended them to eat. Life was pristine for billions of years, and then we came along and messed everything up. If mankind didn't exist on this planet, every species would live in perfect harmony with the laws of nature. Without human beings, the natural world would remain pristine, just as it did for billions of years before we arrived."

"In the grand scheme of things, we're a new arrival to Planet Earth," Henry Jones commented.

"We've only been in existence for about 65 000 years. Modern man has only been around for a few thousand years. That is just a blink of an eye in the life cycle of Mother Earth. But, we don't respect the laws of nature. In the relatively short time we've been on Earth, our impact has been bloody devastating! Look around you. Most of the big cities in the world today didn't exist 100 years ago. Most of the diseases didn't exist, either! Is there a correlation between the two? I think so, buddy-boy. Our society is spreading like a rampant cancer on the face of the Earth. How does George-the-Surfer put it, Henry?" Dr Sahib suddenly asked.

"I believe he says: 'Modern cities spread faster than hurled eggs splatter against brick walls'," Henry Jones replied.

"George-the-Surfer?" I inquired.

"He's next on our schedule," Henry Jones said.

"Ah! Good. George will put him straight ..." They nodded at each other,

"Now, where were we ...? We've disrupted the natural order of things. Most of our natural ecosystems have long since been destroyed and concrete jungles have emerged in their place. We no longer live off the land. We live off bloody supermarkets that sell us man-made substitutes for natural food. These junk substances poison us slowly, and we carry on killing ourselves in the fast lane, trying to make the money we need to buy them. Trust me: God didn't make you sick, buddy-boy. Your lifestyle in the modern world made you sick. If you don't believe me, ask George-the-Surfer," said Dr Sahib.

I opened my mouth to speak but didn't get the chance to say a word.

Nature's enemy

"If ever you took the time to compare human behavior to that of other species, you might conclude we're alien to this planet. I often entertain this not-so-crazy idea myself. Look how we've colonized Earth. All we do is consume the natural resources, and we bloody destroy everything in our path to get our greedy hands on them."

"It's all true," said Henry Jones. "As we spread over the Earth, we encroach on nature without any regard for the natural environment. In many ways, our behavior is unnatural."

"To make matters worse, we've developed a system that enables people to profit from the pillage and plunder. We've gone bloody berserk. Our mad craving for power and control is devastating the natural environment and ruining the quality of life for every other living species on Earth. We're clearly destroying the very world that progress was supposed to improve," said Dr Sahib.

"And we'll probably keep at it until the Earth can no longer sustain us," added Henry Jones.

"It's madness, I tell you. Each year we pump 24 billion tons of carbon dioxide and other dangerous pollutants into our atmosphere. You must understand that in relation to outer space, our atmosphere is a very thin membrane. It's all that separates us from everything out there," Dr Sahib said pointing to the roof of the planetarium. "We're totally dependent on the atmosphere for our survival. The problem is that pollution can't escape our atmosphere, ever! Instead, this swirling concoction continues to accumulate and intensify in toxicity. Each breath you take has an estimated 70 000 particles of smoke, fumes, gases and solid matter, such as tars and poisonous heavy metals." He gagged and pretended to spit on the floor.

The clock is ticking

"If you live near a city, the air you breathe is putrid and foul. Extensive research has revealed that the level of pollution in most cities around the world is actually dangerous to human life."

"You may be shocked to learn that the oxygen content of air trapped in glaciers for thousands of years is 51%, while the oxygen content in our air today is about 21%," Henry Jones added.

"Exactly! Well done, Henry. Now tell this poor, ignorant soul when we'll asphyxiate and die."

"At 6%," Henry Jones said, looking impressed with himself.

Dr Sahib moaned as he slumped to the first step on the ladder leading to the telescope. He placed his head in his hands and pulled his hair. "Pollution is steadily destroying our whole biological support system. We're poisoning the air we breathe; the water we drink; the soil in which we grow our food;

and the land on which we live. It's no bloody wonder so many people are sick."

"But why do we do this to ourselves?" was all I could think to say.

"Because we're bloody selfish! Selfish, greedy and stupid, that's why!" bellowed Dr Sahib. "Human life is characterized by greed and envy. Have you noticed how much competing, controlling and conquering is going on? The culprits are selfishness and desire. People are prepared to do whatever it takes to get what they want, regardless of the consequences for themselves or others. In pursuit of personal ambitions and profit, there exists a very high probability that our species will destroy itself. Did you know that we've built enough weapons of mass destruction to blow the world up hundreds of times over?" asked Dr Sahib.

"No. I didn't."

"That should tell you something about the state of world affairs and the human condition. Whose interests do you think politicians and business leaders have at heart? Yours? It's time to open your eyes. Our society is sick. We just don't give a damn about anything that happens to our children's children. We can't see 50 years ahead. Nowadays, we can make a telescope that can see to the end of our galaxy, but we can't see that we're destroying our quality of life and our children's future."

Before I could respond, Dr Sahib leaped to his feet and started marching towards his office. "That's it, Henry my friend. Time's up," he called out, tapping his watch above his head.

"It was good to see you again. Thank you for your time," Henry Jones shouted after him. That was it. Our conversation ended abruptly. There were no niceties or fond farewells. It was simply over.

The planetarium suddenly felt very empty. I turned to Henry Jones for an explanation. He just shrugged his shoulders. "Time's up!" he said with a broad smile. I was speechless. He motioned for us to leave the room. We shuffled like penguins towards the neon exit sign that blinked in the darkness. Henry Jones followed close behind me, his hand resting gently on my shoulder. It made me aware of his age. I remembered my father being afraid of falling in his later years.

Unconsciously, I reached up and held his hand. I surprised myself. I'd not done anything nice for anyone in a long time. It felt good. I took one last look at the stars above my head, and then pushed open the planetarium hall swing doors and allowed Henry Jones to pass through them. Momentarily blinded by the daylight, we collected ourselves and headed to the carpark.

"Excuse me, sirs!" We turned to see Dr Sahib's assistant running towards us.

We stopped to allow him to catch up. The assistant needed a moment to catch his breath.

My heart skipped a beat. I didn't want our conversation with Dr Sahib to end the way it had. I wanted more. No, I needed more.

"Well, what is it?" I asked impatiently.

"Believe," he replied. I motioned for him to continue, but he just stared at me blankly.

"That's it?" I exclaimed.

"Yes."

"Nothing else?"

"No. Just believe."

"That's all Dr Sahib told you to tell me?"

"Yes," he said in a manner that was cripplingly shy.

I could see by the relief on his face that he'd delivered the message as instructed, but I couldn't hide my disappointment.

"Thank you very much," replied Henry Jones. "Please tell Dr Sahib we're grateful for his wisdom."

I didn't say anything. We climbed into the car in silence.

"You okay?" he asked.

"Fine." I replied curtly.

"How do you feel?" he inquired.

"Fine."

"Good. Have you got enough energy for one more meeting?"

"I'm a bit tired," I responded, looking out the window to avoid eye contact.

"We can skip it. I'm sure George will understand," he offered kindly.

"George-the-Surfer?"

"Yup, George-the-Surfer."

"What's his story?" I asked, somewhat sarcastically.

Henry Jones smiled from ear to ear. "You're going to learn a lot from George," he said. The Land Rover sprung to life like a lazy, old workhorse at the crack of a whip. Henry Jones revved the engine until it made a deafening roar. I did have the energy to meet George-the-Surfer, and Henry Jones knew it. I was just being difficult because Dr Sahib's message hadn't met my expectations. "So, what's it to be?" Henry Jones inquired.

"Let's go to George-the-Surfer," I huffed.

"Off we go then!" he yelled happily.

CHAPTER 5

GETTING REAL WITH GEORGE-THE-SURFER

"Let me tell you all about George's escapades as an activist for alternative healing and his many legal battles against giant pharmaceutical companies," Henry Jones chuckled.

"How does he earn a living?" I inquired abruptly. I'm not sure why I asked. Perhaps to judge him. Henry Jones didn't answer me until we'd turned on to the main road leading out of the city.

"It's funny how we perceive a person's value to be linked to the status we associate with their occupation, isn't it?" he finally replied.

The condescending tone in my voice had given away my skepticism about meeting George-the-Surfer. Apparently, he made his money online by giving health, diet and healing advice. He also gave massages using techniques he learned from healers in distant islands. Henry Jones told me that George was somewhat of an expert in this field, but he worked only to sustain his lifestyle, which mostly involved surfing waves for thrills and surfing the Internet for research. He lived in a ramshackle caravan that had not moved in 10 years. It did not even have wheels. Apparently, more often than not, there was a sign on the door that said: "Gone surfing", which could mean the point-break 200m away, or Bali, Indonesia, Hawaii, or other remote surf spots known only to George-the-Surfer and his beach buddies. We travelled for nearly an hour to reach his campsite.

"Mind my marigolds, dude!" George shouted as we pulled up next to the caravan. He leaped effortlessly from a hammock. He was the archetypal surfer: Long, blonde, shaggy hair; lean, rippling muscles; very little body fat; a deep tan; and he wore board-shorts that hung off his lanky hips. However, he was much older than I had expected. Henry Jones pulled hard on the steering wheel. The vehicle veered to the side, narrowly missing a patch of flowers growing in what seemed to me to be the middle of the driveway. We came to an abrupt halt.

"Whoa! Radical entrance, dudes!" George yelled, squatting down to check on his precious marigolds.

I couldn't remember the last time anyone had dared to call me 'dude'. Or 'buddy-boy' for that matter. I felt my blood pressure rising. I wondered if meeting George-the-Surfer was going to be a waste of my time. What would I have in common with a deadbeat, hippie surfer? Why had Henry Jones brought me to meet this layabout? What value could he offer me?

"That's a daft place to plant your flowers!" I growled as I climbed out the Land Rover, exaggerating the effort.

"Whoa! What's with the self-important vibes, bro?" George replied and stepped right up to me. His nose was literally inches from mine. His long, muscular arms extended on either side of me, as if daring me to fight him. His eyes were fearless and piercing, and his head rocked tauntingly from side to side.

I suddenly realized that I'd stupidly challenged a man who surfs 25ft waves for fun. He could've snapped me like a twig. My legs went weak, I felt a gush of nausea and took a step backwards. But George stepped forward and resumed his position. Then he pulled the meanest expression I'd ever seen and made a deep growling sound. I nearly peed in my pants.

"I'm a sick man," I whimpered, amazed at how pathetic I sounded.

"Stop teasing him, George," said Henry Jones. "He thinks you're being serious."

George growled even louder. "I could swallow you whole and use your legs to dig scraps from my teeth," he drawled slowly. It had been years since I'd connected with my inner child, but in that moment, I was once again a schoolboy about to take a beating in a brawl. Then, much to my amazement, George burst out laughing. He buckled over and slapped his leg repeatedly. "Dude!" he howled, pointing at me. "You should've seen the expression on your face. It was classic, bro. Henry, did you see it? Did you see it?"

"I missed it," Henry Jones replied graciously.

"It was awesome! No offence, dude, but your response was classic. Classic! Thank you for proving an important point: People who try to intimidate others often do so to conceal a deep-rooted insecurity within themselves. When intimidation is met with defiance and aggression, the projected image no longer serves its purpose, so it shatters into pieces, revealing the vulnerability. Pretty much like the school bully who gets punched on the nose by a weakling and then goes home crying to mommy. Right, dude?"

George-the-Surfer stood with his hands firmly on his hips and stared me down. Henry Jones was right. I would learn a lot from him. My first lesson was to not be judgmental. My second was that George-the-Surfer was nobody's fool. He lived by his own rules. He did things his way, and he was beneath no one. It was admirable.

"I'm sorry," I said, extending my arm to shake hands. "We got off on the wrong foot. It was my fault. Can we start again?"

"It's too late, bro. There's no going back after take-off. But we can always make the necessary adjustments as we go," George told me, jumping into a surfing position. I was left with my arm hanging in mid-air. George looked at my hand curiously and grinned. I evidently amused him. "There's no need to wrestle me, dude. Just give me five," he instructed. I went to slap his outstretched hand, but he moved it away. "You're too slow on the uptake, bro. You've got to be quicker than that if you want to catch George. Try again."

I tried and missed.

"Again!' he cried, but that time he purposely let me slap his hand. I felt relieved. "Well done, bro. Now that's behind us, will you kindly stop standing on my freaking marigolds?"

I looked down, and sure enough, I was standing squarely on his flowers. I leaped to one side as though I had stood on a rattlesnake. George rolled his eyes and then exchanged a complex handshake with Henry Jones. He invited us into his caravan for herbal tea, which Henry Jones accepted on our behalf.

The caravan was crammed with books and files stacked one on top of the other. Every surface was covered. It was clean, but messy. The walls were pasted with photos of George and his friends on beaches and catching waves around the world. They were all happy snaps: The kind of photos that make one feel envious. I couldn't have lived in that caravan, not even for one night, but George-the-Surfer seemed content. It wasn't long before we were in deep discussions about health and healing.

"The origin of disease is most mysterious, man. Where does it come from? We don't know for sure, right? I think the mystery will be revealed when we explore the realms of possibility that suggest there's an inseparable interconnectedness between all things," George exclaimed, as he poured herbal tea into three little cups that appeared to be of Indonesian origin.

"I know that Henry agrees with you," I interjected.

George continued rambling. "You see, man, there's a curious bond between the condition of the Earth and the condition of mankind's bodies. The sicker our planet gets from pollution, exploitation and over-population, the sicker we get from new diseases."

Sick Earth, sick people

"Think about the smallpox epidemic that broke out in America in the days of the Wild West. When small towns grew on this pristine body of land, small sores began to manifest on the bodies of man. Is that just a strange coincidence? Is there a connection between the emergence of so many blood disorders and the pollution in the rivers of the Earth? Could the great forests be Mother Nature's lungs? If so, is there a connection between deforestation, pollution, and the rise of so many new lung diseases? What about cancer? A cancer cell is a single cell that reproduces itself without regard for the survival of the cells around it, right? Since cities expand in much the same way, isn't it curious that under a microscope, cancer cells looks almost exactly like modern day cities photographed from outer space? These are interesting questions, don't you think?"

"It's a bit far out," I responded, sniffing the tea. I removed a soggy leaf from my cup and scraped it off on to Henry Jones's saucer when I thought he wasn't looking.

"Yeah man! Far out!" George replied nodding. He chuckled like a stoner. "Let me ask you this: What do you do when someone is annoying you and they just won't stop it?"

I shrugged my shoulders. "I don't know."

"Think about it. How will you ultimately respond?"

"I suppose I'll eventually hit them."

"Exactly, bro! You need to send a physical message, right? A little attitude adjuster! It's like when a grommet drops in on your wave, bro. Sometimes you just gotta smack 'em upside the head so they learn the rules. Right?"

I turned to Henry Jones for his interpretation. "A grommet is a child surfer …," he told me, "and one surfer 'drops in' on another when he catches a wave that the other surfer is already riding."

This was all new to me. "Right on, Henry, dude!" George-the-Surfer exclaimed, breaking into a quirky smile. "So now, tell me man, why wouldn't Mother Nature do the same thing to us? It's certainly worth thinking about, right? She sends disease to show us we're out of alignment with her, man." He paused. "Don't you hate it when someone answers their own questions? I do."

George-the-Surfer laughed at his joke, then pushed on. "When we hurt her, she hurts us. Sadly, we don't seem to care too much about the environmental damage we're doing to our planet, so let's focus our attention on the measurable effects on mankind. After all, we only seem to care about ourselves anyway. Right, dude?"

"I guess."

"Give him the facts," Henry Jones said, sipping slowly on his herbal tea. I could've done with a stiff cup of coffee or a cappuccino. Heck, I would've killed for a whiskey! I took a sip of the herbal tea and blatantly showed my dissatisfaction. It wasn't that it tasted bad – I just felt like something much stronger. They both ignored me.

"It's very simple," George-the-Surfer said, gulping his tea before making a long "aah" sound, as if his pleasure would compensate for my dissatisfaction and appease the tea gods. "In order to sustain our bodies, we need to eat, drink, sleep and breathe. Fortunately for us, nature provides these essential elements in abundance and free of charge. You'd think we'd be grateful and respectful, right dude? But how do we respond? I can tell you all about the pollution we pump into the Earth's atmosphere. It's disgusting, dude. Some cities have oxygen booths on every corner and the inhabitants walk around with face masks. Can you imagine that?"

"Yes, I've seen it on television."

"How sad is that, dude?" George-the-Surfer stared intensely out the window for a while. "Our air is bad, man. It's really bad, and it's getting worse every day."

Our food reflects our health

"What about the food we eat?" asked Henry Jones.

"Food is a major problem, bro. In its natural state, it is filled with all the essential life-giving elements we need to stay healthy. Mother Nature made it for us, so it's perfect. However, in our attempts to master nature, we've chosen to manufacture our own food. The key criteria are taste, appearance, shelf-life and profit. The nutritional value and effect on human health are not really considered."

I'd heard that before.

"They shouldn't be allowed to get away with it," Henry Jones commented, spurring him on. Henry Jones's tag-team style of conversation was now familiar to me. I appreciated the way he stimulated discussion and steered my learning experience.

"Right on, Henry my brother!" George-the-Surfer replied, raising his fist towards Henry Jones, who somehow knew to tap his knuckles against George's. "Would you like me to tell you how food manufacturers get away with making this junk?"

"Sure. Why not?"

"It's easy, dude. They wrap it up in bright, colorful packaging so it looks attractive. Then they dish up lots of saucy advertising, which tricks us into believing this junk is good for us. We're so dumb that we queue up in super-markets to buy it. Literally! We swallow their crap, hook, line and sinker."

"Supermarkets are convenient, though. Who has time to grow their own food?" I replied. From the look of disgust on George's face, I knew I'd said the wrong thing.

"You don't have to grow your own food, man. You just need to choose the right food to buy. In a world ruled by convenience, consumers don't think twice when they pack their shopping baskets with man-made food substitutes. They don't even take the time to read the ingredients on the packaging. Do you know what I mean?"

I took a swig of herbal tea, hoping I wouldn't have to answer.

"Well?"

"Okay, I must admit, I never read the ingredients."

"If you're anything like most shoppers, you probably don't even know what these chemicals are, or how they're made, never mind the negative effect they have on your body."

"You've got a good point," I acknowledged bashfully.

"No, it's a bad point, man. It's a very bad point! Consumers fail to realize these laboratory concoctions are devastating to human health. They contain refined sugars, highly-refined grains, highly-refined hydrogenated fats, artificial flavorings, colorings, preservatives and other chemicals and acids."

"Let's not forget the negative effects of chemically-treated soils, inorganic fertilizers and heavily chlorinated water," Henry Jones added.

For this, he was awarded another knuckle tap from George-the-Surfer.

"Have you ever stopped to consider the effects of this junk on your system? How do you think your natural body copes with all these unnatural substances, man? The impact on your well-being is devastating. This is tragic. Not just for you, bro, but for all of humanity." His words sizzled with passion.

"How come?" I heard myself asking. It was easy to get caught up in his zeal.

"I've got two words for you, bro: Nutritional deficiency. The reason you need to heal your body is most likely because of nutritional deficiency. The number one killer of human wellness is – you guessed it – nutritional deficiency. The problem is: We don't collect our food from the fields anymore. We find it in supermarkets, stuffed in cardboard boxes and wrapped in plastic, right? By then, it's been totally stripped of its natural goodness. You may as well eat the packaging, bro."

"You're being facetious, right?"

"Am I? How would you know? When last did you pick, hunt or catch your food? How often do you think urbanites spend a day on a farm? Once a year? Once every two years? How about once every five years? Try once every 15 years. If that! That's why we've lost touch with the Earth, man. Urban life has changed irrevocably in the past 200 years. Our lifestyles are radically different. Millions of people cram into a few square miles and hardly ever leave the city. Food is shipped in from hundreds, if not thousands, of miles away. The natural order of things has become perverted. Most people spend their time indoors. It's totally unnatural, dude."

"The big problem in our society is that most people have become desensitized to the potential health hazards of modern-day life," added Henry Jones.

"But what choice do we have?"

"Dude!" exclaimed George-the-Surfer. "People make choices every day. They choose to compound their problems by practising wrong living habits. They drink, smoke, take unnatural drugs and generally abuse their bodies at will. Anyone who is guilty of this behavior is making a grave mistake. Get it?" George-the-Surfer said, nodding frantically.

"I get it now, sure, but before I got sick, I didn't care about my health. Come on, how many people do you know who really pay attention to their health or understand the underlying causes of human illness?"

"Why is that?" Henry Jones asked me.

"I don't know. You tell me."

"What is more important to human beings than long-term health?"

"I know the answer to this one," George-the-Surfer yelled, putting up his hand. "Instant gratification!"

"You nailed it. In the moment, people either serve their desires or comfort their woes. This is all that seems to matter. They don't look ahead. Even if they are smart enough to know their lifestyle is bad for them, they do it anyway. Is that dumb or what?" Henry Jones said in amazement.

"Pretty dumb, man," George-the-Surfer answered. He turned towards me. "Have you heard this expression before: 'Live for today, for tomorrow we may die'?"

"Yup."

The only way is natural

"This advice only sounds cool while it appears the body is managing to resist the onslaught of unnatural, poisonous toxins it is receiving through continuous wrong living. Here's another corker for you: 'Life is short, so live for the moment.' That's short-sighted, isn't it? Following advice like that is just plain stupid, dude! Trust me, bro, people aren't nearly so zealous when their bodies break down. That's when they find themselves on bent knees before God, begging to be relieved of their suffering. Know what I mean?"

"I'm afraid I do."

"Sorry, bro. That was insensitive of me," he said apologetically.

"I guess some people have to learn the hard way."

"Learn what?" Henry Jones prompted me.

"That nothing in the world should be more important to us than striving towards perfect health," I said.

"Exacto-mondo!" yelled George-the-Surfer. To my surprise, I got a knuckle tap. "Don't be a sucker to the modern lifestyle, bro. Life is too precious. You're being deceived by greedy profiteers who exploit your ignorance and rob you of the quality, vitality and richness of life that was given to you by Almighty God. This is your wake-up call, dude. The next time you see mouth-watering packaging on man-made foodstuffs – don't swallow it! Literally! The natural way is the only way. Yeah?"

"You mean fruit and vegetables?"

"I mean if it looks like Mother Nature made it, eat it. If it looks like man made it, don't eat it. It's that simple, dude. Mother Nature is good, man is bad. Got it?"

"Trust in Mother Nature, not in Man," I said spiritedly. I raised my knuckles and got my second knuckle tap. It felt good. On some strange level, we had connected.

"Right on, man. You're okay," he said.

"Actually, I'm rather sick," I replied, looking down in shame.

"Dude! You've got to stop claiming your sickness. Every time you say you're sick, you affirm it. Hasn't Henry discussed mental healing with you?"

"Not yet," I said, looking to Henry Jones for input.

"Soon enough," he replied.

"So, what's the deal with you two? Eh?" George suddenly inquired. "Our friend Henry here is a firm believer in fair exchange. I know what he'll do for you, but what are you going to do for him?"

"We're going to write a book together," Henry Jones said enthusiastically.

"At last, bro!" George-the-Surfer said to Henry Jones and he got his third knuckle tap.

"Anything else to add to our book?" Henry Jones inquired with a whimsical smile.

A bad diet breeds disease

George-the-Surfer thought for a moment. "If your readers only learn one thing from reading your book, let it be this: Disease, sickness and pain are caused by improper diet, wrong living, unresolved emotions and negative thinking. I can't make it any clearer for them than that, can I?"

"Nope," said Henry Jones.

"I thought getting sick was just bad luck. That's what my doctor told me when he gave me my diagnosis."

"Did you honestly think disease is some terrible affliction sent by a Higher Power to punish you without reason? Sorry dude. It doesn't work like that! You'll be one step further down the path to recovery when you accept that you not only contributed to your own misery, suffering and pain, but you're solely responsible for it!"

"Ouch! That hurts," I moaned softly.

"Sorry, bro. That was insensitive of me. Again! But such is life, man. When the wave jacks up for you, you gotta ride it. So, surf's up, dude. This is your moment. Ask yourself: Why did I get sick? Why am I experiencing the symptoms of disease?"

Lessons from the past

"You tell me."

"The answer is simple, dude. Disease is nature's way of cleaning house. When you get sick, your body wants to rid itself of toxic waste, so symptoms of disease or discomfort become apparent. Disease is nature's way of starting the healing process. Put another way: It's your body's way of calling for radical change in your diet, lifestyle and mind state, man. Sickness is your soul's way of calling for transformation. In academic subjects we're clued up, but in our spirituality, we're just bumbling infants," he said with conviction.

"Are you saying healing is spiritual, too?" I asked.

"Definitely, bro. No doubt about it. Healing was considered 'spiritual in nature' for many thousands of years. The spiritual leaders of the tribes, such as the medicine men and the shamans, treated the sick and injured. They healed their patients with natural remedies."

"Even Hippocrates, who is known as the father of modern medicine, believed in the 'effort of nature'," Henry Jones said. "He insisted that disease only had natural causes, and that only nature could heal the body."

"I believe he said: 'Physicians are at best nature's helpers,' George-the-Surfer added. He turned to me: "Hippocrates was a cool dude. He treated his patients with herbs, a proper diet, fresh air, sunlight and regular exercise. He also corrected their bad habits and changed their living conditions. This was the way human beings treated disease for many thousands of years, until the emergence of the infamous medieval church during the Middle Ages. That's when things got gnarly, dude!"

"Gnarly?"

"It's a surfing term used to describe waves that are scary, threatening and powerful," Henry Jones told me.

"Thanks."

"The crusaders were bug-eyed crazy, man. In their mad craving for control and power, they mercilessly slaughtered the pagan priests and priestesses who mostly practised natural healing. Most of their herbal remedies were wiped out, dude. So then, the church priests took on the role of healers and began exploring 'alternative healing methods'. When I tell you about their techniques, your blood will curdle in your veins, bro. Check it out. In God's good name, they experimented with leeches; bleeding; beatings; penance; exorcisms; torture; and many other atrocities that are too gnarly to mention. It was a radical time to be sick, bro. Towards the end of the Middle Ages, the healing process had been perverted to such a degree that its 'spiritual nature' had been removed entirely. Now, you need to understand at that time there was tremendous conflict between the ideologies of the medieval church and the new discoveries of science."

"Give me an example."

"Well, for instance, the Church adopted a model for the universe that had been proposed by the astronomer Ptolemy in the second century AD. For mystical reasons, he felt that the Earth was the center of the universe. Go figure! He also believed that the Sun and moon revolved around the Earth. Outside of this model were, in his opinion, fixed stars. So, why did the church favor his theory?"

"I give up."

"Because the 'fixed stars' left lots of place for Heaven and Hell! How whack is that, bro? Now, at the time, challenging the approved ideologies of the Church would've cost you your life. Ask poor Nicolas Copernicus. He was burned at the stake because he believed that the Earth rotated around the Sun in a 'solar system'. Hello! Centuries later, as we know, Galileo confirmed this theory when he used a radical, new invention called a telescope to observe the heavens. What did this do for the Church's model of the universe? Thanks to technology, it was tossed out the window, along with the power base of the Church. But wait, it gets gnarlier, bro. After many decades of struggle, renaissance reformers were eventually given permission to explore worldly phenomenon without interference from the Church. At last, there was a split between science and spirituality, or should I say Christian religion. With its new-found freedom, science was only too glad to focus on the outside world. Those who studied medicine focused on finding cures for the external effects or 'symptoms of disease'. Anything to do with internal healing was considered too close to the domain of religion."

"What happened next?"

"Obviously, medical scientists were looking for something to replace the gnarly treatments practised by the priests. In 1493, Theophrastus Bombastus von Hohenheim, the son of a physician living in Switzerland, began to study the relationship between alchemy, chemistry, metallurgy and medicine. After working on a mine for a short while, Theo got the idea to research and experiment in chemically purifying the human body using minerals. Was this a good idea? Nope. Not a chance, bro. This technique may have worked on a mine, because you can purify one mineral with another, but it wasn't about to work on the human body. Believe it or not, man, poisonous minerals like mercury and arsenic were administered to patients. Often in fatal doses! The theory was that one poison would counteract the other. Hah!" George-the-Surfer yowled and slapped his knee.

"The only thing more bizarre than this theory is the fact that the concept caught on big time," Henry Jones added. "This is how physicians became known as 'quacks'."

"I don't get it."

"They administered mercury, or quack sabre, to their patients," George-the-Surfer howled. "In later years, smaller doses of minerals and other poisons were administered in powdered form, and modern medicine was born. I kid you not, bro. That's how the shit went down."

Coincidently, it was then that I noticed one of Henry Jones's Post-it notes stuck to the mirror of George-the-Surfer's caravan.

> *Half of the modern drugs could well be thrown out of the window, except that the birds might eat them." – Dr Martin Henry Fischer.*

The timing was perfect.

"Admittedly, medical science has come a long way since mercury was considered a cure-all treatment," Henry Jones offered. "Academically and technically, our physicians are far-advanced. May I have some more tea, please?"

George-the-Surfer obliged. "I must admit, dude, their diagnostic and surgical skills are outstanding. However, they still focus their attention on alleviating or suppressing the symptoms rather than curing the disease. That's a big mistake."

Listen to the warning signal

"Why?" I heard myself ask.

"What's the first thing your body does when it requires healing? It sends you a signal in the form of ailments, symptoms or pain, right?"

"I suppose so."

"Well, these discomforts are nature's warning signals, bro. In these situations, your body is doing exactly what it's supposed to do in a crisis. But what's the first thing you do when you feel poorly? You race off to the doctor so that he can prescribe medicine to help you feel better."

"Yes."

"You couldn't be more wrong, man! Sure, narcotic drugs deaden the inflamed nerves and tissue, and this temporarily relieves discomfort, but they ruthlessly disregard the real cause of your problem. Now let me ask you this: What do you think happens when you continually suppress symptoms?"

"I don't know."

"Isn't it obvious? The problem doesn't go away. It just gets suppressed, bro. Keep that up and your body eventually manifests some form of chronic illness. Then, the drugs that are prescribed for you are totally foreign to your body's natural healing processes. Nine times out of 10, the side-effects are extremely detrimental to your system as a whole."

"Give us an example," Henry Jones instructed him.

He didn't have to think about it. "Antibiotics, for instance. They may kill the troublesome bug, but they also destroy all the other bacteria and fungi which are necessary for a balanced system. The drug nukes everything! It literally takes your body months to restore itself. And that's just an antibiotic! Can you imagine the side-effects of harder, more serious drugs and treatments? Have you ever seen a chemotherapy patient? Did you know that the pills are so toxic that patients aren't allowed to touch them? What happens inside your body is another story altogether. I know many people who stopped chemo because the side-effects are so disgusting."

Embrace the best of both worlds

"Are we saying that if you have cancer, you should stop chemotherapy, or that all science and modern medicine should be tossed out of the window? Definitely not! If you have a rusty nail in your foot, don't wrap it up and practise natural healing principles in the hope that it will go away. That's just plain silly, dude. The smart thing to do is take it out immediately and get a tetanus shot. First and foremost, get rid of the problem and take medication, and then practise natural healing principles to aid your recovery, man."

"If your doctors are optimistic that they can help you with surgery or medicine, we urge you to take their advice. If they can increase your chance of survival, recovery or remission, then go for it. Why not get the best of both worlds? Let them do their best to help you, and then complement their efforts by doing your best to help yourself," Henry Jones advised.

"Exactly! But use discretion, dude. Today, there's a pill for every little ache and pain. Trust me, the man will find a way into your pocket by peddling any kind of crap you're stupid enough to buy. There are literally hundreds of thousands of different kinds of medication in the marketplace, and more emerging all the time. Aren't you sick and tired of having the wool pulled over your eyes, man?" George-the-Surfer asked me. "Doesn't it turn your stomach to know that a few fat cats are getting ridiculously rich keeping the general public ignorant?"

"What are you raging about?"

Medical money-makers

"What am I raging about? The medical industry, that's what! Global insurance, pharmaceutical and healthcare companies rake in profits of billions of dollars each year at the expense of the little guy. I'm trying to find peace in my heart on this issue, but I must confess it really makes my blood boil when I think about the unnecessary misery and suffering that so many millions of people endure each year. Do you honestly think that, with all their money, these corporations haven't commissioned medical scientists to investigate the cause of disease? Do you really think they don't know that the best way to stay vibrantly healthy is to eat fresh fruit and vegetables? They know it! You know it, and I know it. So, what are they doing about it? Not a darn thing! In comparison to their massive marketing budgets to sell drugs or policies, they're doing absolutely nothing! Zilch!"

"Why?"

"Well, this example should shed some light on the matter for you. Over 200 000 heart bypass operations are performed every year in the USA. These procedures cost a small fortune. But when you compare it to the very big fortune that's made from using these killer statistics to sell medical insurance, then the truth reveals itself. It's time to lift the veil, man. You need to start seeing things for how they really are. Sickness and suffering are big business for some corporations. It suits them to keep the public ignorant."

There's no profit in cures

"There's no ongoing profit in cures, and there's no market when people are healthy," said Henry Jones.

"If they really cared for your health, they'd be broadcasting the need for a natural diet through every media channel, every day. Governments would be using their power to banish food products that are lacking in nutrition. Instead, global media corporations sell out to the global food, pharmaceutical and financial services corporations for advertising revenue, while the governments sell out to the corporations for the taxes they get on the enormous profits made. The whole system is sick, man. It seems the powers that be are happy to turn a blind eye to human suffering if it means the right people are making a buck. The man doesn't give a shit about you, dude. You're just a dumb slave to the system."

"It's enough to make you sick, huh?" Henry Jones said, elbowing me in the side.

"I guess the smartest thing to do is to prevent yourself from getting sick in the first place," I retorted.

"Or, as in your case, once you've restored your body to perfect health, you should do whatever it takes to prevent yourself from getting sick again in the future."

"Definitely!"

"You can keep this," George-the-Surfer said, yanking a dusty Post-it note from a cupboard door.

> *"As I see it, every day you do one of two things: Build health or produce disease in yourself." – Adelle Davis*

I slid it into the top pocket of my shirt for safekeeping.

"Thanks. I'll try to include this quotation in our book. Maybe the book will be a bestseller and we'll change the world," I remarked jovially and winked at Henry Jones.

Change yourself first

"If you want to change the world, start by changing yourself. You don't have to be a victim, dude. You don't have to remain ignorant. You don't have to take it lying down – in a hospital bed – if you know what I mean. You can restore your body to health, and we're going to help you do it. You're going to be okay, dude," George-the-Surfer said in all sincerity, putting his arm around me.

I felt a strong gush of emotion. It was as if an artist had mixed an array of colors in the palette of my heart to create a totally new color that I'd never seen before. I felt excited yet fearful; happy yet sad; enthusiastic yet cautious; strong yet weak; invincible yet vulnerable; exposed yet sheltered. I felt a sense of, dare I say it, brotherhood. These strangers had found a way to open my mind. I suddenly realized that I couldn't have an open heart when I had a closed mind – and mine had been closed for far too long. I had shut out everyone who didn't conform to my standards or expectations and I'd trapped myself in 'being me'. Then, Henry Jones had come along with his band of weird and wonderful friends. Through their love for life, humanity, nature, and the Earth, they'd shown me that I wasn't the person I thought I was. I was just a sad, sick, slave to the system.

I suddenly couldn't breathe. I was having a panic attack and needed air.

"Where are you going, bro?" George-the-Surfer called after me as I scampered from the caravan. I couldn't answer him. I had no idea. I just wanted out. Out of the caravan, out of my situation, out of the system! Out, out, out!

CHAPTER 6

SOUL SEARCHING WITH SHIRLEY

I found myself plodding barefoot along the beach. Icy-cold waves washed over my feet, soaking my trousers. I didn't care. Once again, tears streamed down my cheeks. It felt wonderful to be there – in the moment. I took deep breaths. Without doubt, this had been one of the most important and memorable days of my life. I savored the seconds as they slipped by. I could've walked forever, leaving my troubles behind me, but time was marching by, as much as I wished for the clock to stop.

The Sun was setting by the time I found my way back to the beachfront, near the caravan. I paused for a moment, closed my eyes and listened carefully, hoping to hear a hiss as the golden orb of the Sun sank into the ocean far out on the horizon. Pastel pink and blue clouds streaked across the expansive sky. I watched in awe as the last fragments of golden light rippled playfully along the crashing waves. Just ahead, someone had made a fire on the beach. I assumed it was our host. Even from a distance, I could hear the flames crackling.

George and Henry Jones were talking to a woman I would soon learn was George's lover, Shirley. She was a surfer babe, or at least that was how George described her. She had long, dark-brown, matted hair that whipped from side to side, in unison with her feminine hips. Somehow the dreadlocks suited her big, round, Sun-soaked face. From her brown skin, I guessed she was native to one of the islands frequented by George-the-Surfer. Her inner beauty was luminous, and I was captivated by it. Some people just sparkle. There's an 'aliveness' in their being that makes them shimmer. Shirley was one such person. She looked radiantly healthy and happy. As she saw me approach, she jumped to her feet and skipped down the beach to meet me. Before I even had time to introduce myself, she threw her arms around my waist and squeezed me tightly.

I was taken aback. Has she been told my story? Did she pity me? I wondered, but then quickly decided that it didn't matter. On that day, in that moment, I just held her in my arms and let that strange, wonderful exchange of human energy take place. That decision marked a change in me – and I liked it! Her hug lasted a minute at most, but it seemed like ages. When she felt it was time to let go, she reached up, cupped my head in her hands, drew me towards her, and planted three gentle kisses on my face – one on each cheek and the last on my forehead. "I'm pleased to meet you," she said sincerely.

"Likewise," I replied, breaking into an awkward smile. I felt myself blushing. "Look, the Sun is setting." I pointed to the horizon, and then realized how silly of me it was to state the obvious.

"Oh, how lovely!" she said. "You came back at the perfect time."

"Why?"

"George and Henry are making plans for you to sleep here tonight. They want to know if you're up for it."

"In the caravan?" I exclaimed, failing to conceal my horror.

"No silly. Right here on the beach."

I hadn't camped out under the stars in decades. I always opted for hotels with room service, mini-bars and television.

"I'm not sure I can."

"Sure, you can. C'mon, it'll be fun."

Go with the flow

"What does Henry say?"

"It was his idea. He thinks it'll be good for you."

I hesitated, but not for long. On this weird and wonderful day, I'd go with the flow.

"Okay, what the heck!" I sighed.

"Groovy," she said, and pecked me on the cheek again. She slipped her arm around my elbow and led me up the beach towards the caravan. "Let's go fetch the sleeping bags and pillows. I also want to bring the fruit bowl and some juice I've prepared for us. You can help me carry, if you like."

I did. It was almost dark by the time we arrived at the fire with all the provisions. George and Henry Jones were engaged in a game of chess, which Henry eventually won.

I helped Shirley make a large fruit salad and turn the potatoes and corn cobs wrapped in foil on the coals. George-the-Surfer kept us all entertained with stories of the monster waves he'd surfed, and the times he'd come close to drowning. He had a wonderful sense of humor. Shirley laughed loudly at all his jokes and demonstrations, although I suspected she'd heard them a hundred times over.

She had a few amazing stories of her own. I could tell they cared very deeply for each other. After supper, the conversation about health and healing started up again.

"Dr Deepak Chopra is definitely one of my greatest heroes, dude," George-the-Surfer announced.

"Me, too," chimed in Henry Jones.

"I've never heard of him," I replied.

"We'll remedy that, I promise you," George-the-Surfer said. "He says that your body is an exquisitely balanced system. It's infinitely intelligent and it knows how to heal itself. Deepak is a world-renowned neurosurgeon who combines modern medicine with ancient Indian philosophy and mysticism. His books have changed the way we look at science, spirituality and healing forever, man. I think he deserves a Nobel Peace prize for sure."

I raised my eyebrows. "I've got a whole lot of reading to do," I thought aloud.

"Yes, you do," replied Henry Jones. "You've got to get into your head all the knowledge you need to heal your body as quickly as possible." He winked affectionately.

Your body needs your support

"Dr Deepak Chopra is dead on the money. You must read his books. He frequently emphasizes the importance of balance. Your body's natural tendency is to balance itself and remain in balance. All it needs is your support."

"You've got to help your body stay in balance, dude," drawled George-the-Surfer, pretending to surf another wave.

Henry Jones hammered home another key point: "When your body is in physical harmony, you'll be in a state of perfect health."

George-the-Surfer slapped his hand on my shoulder: "It's your natural birthright to enjoy radiant health and vitality. But, there's one, simple condition. Stay with me for a moment, dude, you're about to learn a very important life-lesson. Close your eyes and picture your car in your mind now. Can you remember how excited you felt when you first bought it? I bet you were thrilled, right?"

"Yup!"

"Cool. Now, let's take it for a quick spin around your imagination. Picture yourself driving your car. While you're doing this, think about how much you depend on your car to take you where you need to go. Your vehicle is very important to you. Isn't it?"

"Sure is!"

"Now, see yourself pouring a packet of potato chips into the tank, followed by a cheeseburger with fries and a fizzy drink. While you're at it, add chocolates, sweets, cakes, canned food, sauces and a few TV dinners into the tank. Mix it all up in your mind. Now, just imagine you did this to your car every day for the rest of your life. Imagine trying to drive around all day and night with that gunk in your engine. You wouldn't do it, would you?"

"Never," I answered and felt myself cringe.

"Why not? Because you know that your car needs gas and oil, so you make sure it gets what it needs. No other junk goes into the tank or the engine. Right?"

"Right."

"So, how come you're prepared to stuff all kinds of junk into your body, when you know that it needs healthy food to function optimally? Surely, your body is more valuable to you than your car? You can always replace your motorcar, but it's impossible to replace your body. Isn't that so?"

"Yes, that's true," I acknowledged. The point had been made.

"When you value something, you tend to look after it, right dude? How often did you wash and polish your car when you first got it?"

"Often!"

"And now that you've had it for a while and take it for granted? Tell me, do you need a dustbin bag to take out all the rubbish? Do you think that by taking out the rubbish, the engine will perform any better? To get your engine working perfectly again, you've got to clean out the tank and give it a good service, right? And to keep it working perfectly, you must look after it and service it regularly. Agreed?"

"Uh huh."

"Since you know all of this, you'll probably also know the answer to my next question: What happens when you don't ever service your engine? It eventually breaks down, right?"

"Right."

"Speak to any good mechanic and he'll confirm that when one car part stops working properly, it can easily damage the rest of the engine. I hope you can see where I'm going with this, dude?"

Your body needs proper maintenance

"Drive your point home, dude," Henry Jones jested.

"Your body needs even more attention than your motorcar. Especially now! After years of improper diet, wrong living and negative thinking, your body has had enough! It just can't cope anymore. Because of your unhealthy lifestyle, your body is clogged with gnarly, toxic waste material, dude. I know it sounds disgusting, but a thick, sticky, mucous-like substance has permeated your internal organs at a cellular level. This gunk is preventing your blood from circulating properly and your body cells from functioning effectively."

"Mucous?" I remarked skeptically.

"Definitely, dude! Mucous membranes line all the openings of your body that lead to the surface. This includes your air passages, lungs, urinary and genital organs, as well as your whole intestinal tract, from your mouth to your rectum. The mucous membrane excretes foul material and secretes useful substances when they're in a fluid state. When you eat natural foods, like fruit and vegetables, these mucous membranes are naturally cleansed. When you eat greasy, oily, fatty, fleshy food, these mucous membranes become clogged and congested. Your body has to work much harder trying to function normally, man. It also spends a great deal of energy trying to break down this mucous-like, toxic sludge. Try this now ..." he commanded as he reached over, grabbed a pillow off his sleeping bag and tossed it to me. "Put a pillow over your face and press down hard for 10 minutes. Try to breathe normally, bro. This exercise may help you to experience what your internal organs feel like all the time, smothered by stodgy mucous."

I did as he suggested but got the point in less than 10 seconds.

"Not very nice, huh?" said George-the-Surfer. I shook my head. "Now, would you want to live like that? I doubt it. Is there a better way to live? Yes. Listen up, dude. You must start treating your body like it's the most valuable thing you've got. Why? Because it is, man. It just is!" George-the-Surfer continued, clutching his chest dramatically. "It's of utmost importance that you cleanse your body, so that your blood can flow freely and all of your organs can function efficiently and effectively. Only by releasing the mucous in your system will you ever truly experience radiant health and vitality. And the only way to get rid of the mucous is to rejuvenate your body by eating natural foods."

"We're going to show you how," said Shirley, handing me a drink of some sort.

"What is this?"

"It's carrot juice with a blend of apple, ginger and celery. It's delicious and very good for your body."

"And the little, pink umbrella?" I asked, pointing to the cocktail accessory.

"That's to make it pretty for you," she answered. I would've gulped down the whole glass for her, even if it tasted terrible. But it didn't. It was surprisingly refreshing and delicious.

"We're going to help you to heal yourself, dude. Starting right now."

Make rejuvenation a priority

"What is your top priority, right now?" Henry Jones asked me.

"To heal your body, yeah?" George-the-Surfer replied on my behalf.

I nodded.

"Since you don't have a moment to spare, let me introduce you to the basic principle of rejuvenation. This is how it works: Every cell in your body stores energy, naturally. The amount of energy in your cells affects every aspect of your life. It determines your health, strength, stamina, vitality and well-being. Believe it or not, bro, it also influences your attitude, moods, thoughts and emotions. Got it?"

"Yup."

"Now, as a result of improper diet, incorrect living and negative thinking, along with pollution, pesticides, poisonous gases and toxic urban environments, yada-yada-yada, your body cells are depleted of energy. This really affects the quality of your life, dude! A lack of energy results in complacency, lethargy, moodiness, depression, sickness, and even death. Make no mistake about it!" George-the-Surfer said sternly. "Your body requires immediate rejuvenation!"

"I get it, but what can I do about it?"

"Well, you can start by restoring the natural energy in your body cells. It's so simple: Eat naturally! That's the only way to rejuvenate your body cells. Then, your cells will have all the natural energy they need to heal themselves!" said Henry Jones.

George-the-Surfer jumped in: "Luckily for you, your body is infinitely intelligent and knows how to heal itself. I know that's not the first time you've heard me quote Dr Chopra, and it won't be the last, but it's that important that you get it! The moment you take action, your body will take action. Start a cleansing program on the outside, and your body will start a cleansing program on the inside."

"The secret is to keep at it, so your body will keep at it. And it won't stop until it has restored itself to perfect health," Henry Jones added.

Escape the tiger's cage

"Excellent, now here's another question," George said. "If someone dared you to climb into a cage with a vicious, man-eating tiger, would you do it?"

"No way," I answered.

"Of course not, bro! That would be crazy, right? Now answer this question: If the tiger could only eat one person at a time, and four other people climbed into the cage with you, would you do it?"

"Not for all the money in the world."

"Good answer, dude!" he exclaimed. "Regardless of the odds on your survival, we both know that the smart thing to do would be to not get into the cage."

"What's your point?"

"My point is this, bro: Cancer kills one in four people – and the number is climbing! You see, sickness springs on you like a hungry tiger. One day you're healthy, and the next day you're not! For your own sake, you must realize that unless you eat healthily and look after your body, you'll be sitting in the tiger's cage every day for the rest of your life, just waiting for it to pounce."

"That's a scary thought," I said.

"Your life is happening right now, bro! The present moment is all you've got. Get out of the tiger's cage now, man. Eat healthily. Your life depends on it, bro."

Shirley nodded enthusiastically. "You should print it in bold letters in Henry's book: 'IF YOU DON'T EAT HEALTHILY, SICKNESS WILL INEVITABLY POUNCE ON YOU'."

George-the-Surfer broke off a slice of his orange and handed it to Shirley. She accepted it with a smile. Their loving exchange was lovely to see. He was so gentle with her and their love was palpable. Lucky George, I thought to myself.

Healing is within you

"The forces of healing are within you and within nature, dude," he said. "Pill popping isn't the answer to wellness. Whatever you do, don't make the mistake of allowing modern medicine to handicap your healing process by taking the responsibility of healing away from you. There's no law against you being your own doctor. Let nature heal you. Nature is God's physician. What's more, dude, your body is the most superior pharmacy in your universe. It naturally produces antibiotics, painkillers, sleeping pills and every other combination of healing chemicals known to man. Your own internal intelligence is far superior to anything you can try to substitute from the outside."

"It's true. Nothing can compete with your body's own ability to heal itself," said Henry Jones. "When you cut your finger, your body instantly and inexplicably commissions millions of healing processes to occur at a cellular level. What's the difference between a cut on your finger and other diseases? In terms of your body's incredible ability to heal itself, nothing! You just need to understand the healing process and work with it. Naturally!"

I glanced down at the embers. I wanted to believe it, but I was afraid it wouldn't work for me. Shirley sensed it.

"No matter how sick you are, or how much pain you're in, nature wants to heal you. No matter how much you may have abused your body in the past, nature wants to rejuvenate every single cell," she said kindly.

"It's true. Regardless of your age or physical condition, you can restore your body to perfect health and bring true wellness into your life. It's not only possible, but also probable – if you follow the right path."

"It's not hard to do. I promise," said Shirley, slurping the last of her carrot juice. She giggled at the noise.

"Yeah man. The laws that govern your body and nature are one and the same," George said earnestly. "When you eat natural foods, your body's restoring, rebuilding and rejuvenating abilities are set in motion. They automatically proceed in an orderly manner to heal your body in accordance with natural, physiological laws. When you feed your body properly, it naturally produces everything it needs to restore, rebuild and rejuvenate itself at a cellular level. The instant you provide your body with essential nutrients, it begins to purify your system. That's how it works, bro!"

Start with healthy living

"Eat natural foods, exercise regularly and practise healthy living. When you do this, you'll be employing the oldest and most powerful healing system known to man. Try it. It works, dude."

"You can bet your life on it!" said Henry Jones.

"Believe us, dude. When you accept responsibility for this healing process, nature will take care of the rest, no matter what. By rejuvenating your body, you can cure yourself and prevent yourself from ever getting sick again. The fact is: Your body already naturally renews itself. When you correct an improper diet, you enable your body to take advantage of this natural phenomenon and build clean, healthy tissue."

"Internal cleanliness is an absolute necessity for your body to heal itself," said Henry Jones.

"Cleanliness is next to godliness, my grandmother used to say," said George-the-Surfer, wagging his finger. We laughed, although I'm not sure it was meant to be funny.

George-the-surfer drummed his message home. "Every disease, ailment and affliction on Earth can be prevented and cured through proper treatment; diet; water; herbs; sunshine; fresh air; meditation; exercise and rest. Without exception! These build a powerful foundation for rejuvenation and healing. I'll tell you again and again and again: Your body is supremely intelligent and knows how to heal itself."

"Of course, it stands to reason that if you're suffering from a so-called 'terminal' disease or chronic illness, you might not expect the same quick results as someone suffering from a minor ailment. Young bodies also heal faster than old bodies. But, whatever the condition, no one should be discouraged. As long as they're patient and keep at it, they'll find their way to perfect health," Henry Jones replied.

"Trust in the power of nature," advised Shirley.

I thought for a few minutes. "I want to believe you. I want to believe I'll get well again, but I'm still afraid it won't work for me."

"Don't worry, dude. Henry will soon show you how to promote your healing process internally as well as externally."

"What are you talking about?"

Make your mind work for you

"You must learn how to get your mind to work for you instead of against you. How can you expect to get better if you don't believe it? You can't! To heal yourself naturally, you must think that you will heal yourself naturally, and believe it. This is very important, dude."

Dr Sahib's message came back to haunt me. It rang out in my mind: Believe. Believe. Believe!

George-the-Surfer continued: "You've heard of the body-mind relationship, haven't you?"

"Nope. Not really. I've heard Henry say the words but I don't know what they mean."

"I can't believe it! How long have you been in treatment, dude?"

"Almost a year."

George flapped his lips. "Extensive research has revealed startling evidence of the body-mind relationship. Simply put, your thoughts are real, tangible forces and they have the power to influence and shape your physical reality. Especially your body!"

"Are you saying that I can heal myself just by thinking about it?"

"Yes. It's a known fact that willpower and a positive outlook are powerful healing forces. Get this, man: Everything is created twice. First in thought and then in reality."

"Isn't it obvious?" said Henry Jones. "Just think about it. Negative thinking creates mental stress, which ultimately results in physical stress."

"You mean sickness and pain?"

"Yes. Likewise, healthy, positive thinking inspires well-being, vitality, energy, rejuvenation and healing. I can assure you that the natural healing process is as much mental as it's physical. Nothing is more natural than thought. Your mind lives in your body. Believe me, when you combine positive thinking with a healthy diet, it activates your internal healing energy. This is extremely powerful. Many people have performed miracles by harnessing their own internal healing energy," Henry Jones told me.

"When you set your mind to healing and take action, your body responds by restoring health. Ta da! There's your miracle, dude!" yelled George-the-Surfer.

He lay back and adjusted his pillow. Shirley snuggled closer to him for warmth. There was a chill in the air and night had descended. A cool breeze blew in from the ocean. We fell into a thoughtful silence, mesmerized by the fire's flames.

I shut my eyes and thought of my wife, who walked the dogs on the beach every weekend. I hadn't joined her in years. I was always too busy or too self-absorbed. We'd drifted further and further apart. In that moment, sitting alone, I felt her loneliness. My heart ached for her and our failed marriage. Would I ever find the humility to say I was sorry? Would I find the courage to ask her if I could walk the dog with her sometime in the future? Would she agree – after all I had and hadn't done? I wondered.

My thoughts were interrupted by George's snoring. He was out for the count. Shirley was still awake and so was Henry Jones. Someone had stacked the fire with fresh logs. I guessed it was Shirley.

"He's talked out," she whispered, breaking into a giggle.

"Amazing," I said. "I guess I'll get another earful tomorrow, huh?"

"He'll be gone by the time we wake up," whispered Henry Jones.

"How come?"

"Surfs up, bro." Shirley mimicked George.

We chortled.

I sighed. "So, do you really think I can do it?"

"Heal your body? Definitely! Just be like a postage stamp, bro. Its success comes from sticking through to the end," Henry Jones replied, imitating George-the-Surfer too.

I looked across to Shirley who had been watching us. She smiled ever so sweetly, flipped her dreadlocks over her shoulder and buried her head into George's chest. Not another word was said that night. I lay listening to the fire, and the waves. I had lots to think about. It had been a big day. I imagined myself telling my wife about my great adventures; her wrapping her arms around my waist, then kissing and squeezing me gently. For once, I imagined myself responding positively to her. Then I cried myself to sleep.

CHAPTER 7

BREAKFAST WITH BOTH OF ME

Henry Jones was right, yet again. By the time we awoke, George and Shirley were gone. Their footprints disappeared down the beach. They had resuscitated the fire and left a pot of herbal tea brewing on the grill.

I didn't appreciate the tea. Not one little bit. Strong coffee would've pleased me more. Much more! I slurped the tea, begrudgingly. Henry Jones, on the other hand, was delighted. His cheery disposition reminded me of Sister Lillian and I felt irritated. I hadn't slept well. The beach sand had been surprisingly hard. I was also hungry. The fruit salad and vegetable kebabs we had eaten for dinner hadn't filled me. I wanted a big, greasy breakfast of eggs, bacon, tomato, hash browns, sausages, syrup and toast, washed down with thick, black coffee and two teaspoons of sugar!

"That's what I need," I thought aloud.

"What's that?" Henry Jones asked, rolling up his sleeping bag with military precision. I told him.

He smiled compassionately. "That's not what you need, it's what you want! There's a huge difference."

I didn't respond. He was right, and I knew it. That made me even grumpier. I was confused. The day before, I had been repenting of my sins and promising to change my ways. Now, I was craving an unhealthy breakfast and, worst of all, behaving like a spoilt brat because I couldn't get my way. What had happened to me? Why was I so different? What's making me so angry? I wondered.

Henry Jones let me be. I clanged the dishes together, kicked sand on the burning embers, stomped on the litter, wrung out my sleeping bag and threw the pillows into a pile – all with excessive force. Henry Jones hardly batted an eyelid. I was so miserable that I even thought about tramping on George's precious marigolds on our way to the Land Rover.

I watched Henry Jones write a note for George and stick it to the window of his rickety caravan. I sat in the car, twisting the knobs on the dashboard and wiping away tiny pieces of dust and dirt from inside the door handle. "Today is going to be a great day for you," Henry Jones announced, hoisting himself into the driver's seat.

"What's so bloody special about today?" I growled.

His smile broadened. "Well, for one thing, you're going to learn the difference between your ego-mind and your true-self."

"I don't know what you're talking about."

Your true-self

"Well, then, let's get started immediately, shall we?" he said, snapping his fingers. "Have you ever jumped out of bed in the morning with plans to start a new diet, or stop smoking or drinking? Then, later the same day, you find yourself eating that left-over piece of chocolate cake in the fridge, or having a cigarette with a sundowner in your hand?"

He'd pegged me. "Yeah! Weird, huh?" I replied sarcastically.

"It's almost like you're two completely different people, isn't it? In one moment, you're totally committed to your new plan and are determined to make it happen. In the next, you go straight ahead and do the exact opposite."

"Hmmm," I grunted.

"What gives?"

"Perhaps I have a split personality, or I'm schizophrenic, or something!" I growled.

Henry Jones chuckled. "Before you race off to find a shrink, let me assure you this behavior is quite normal. There's no need to panic. We all do it, especially when we don't know any better."

"Are you saying if I knew better, I'd be able to stop doing it?"

"That's precisely what I'm saying," Henry Jones replied, turning on the car engine. The Land Rover whinnied like an old workhorse on a winter's morning.

"Fortunately for you, the notes I gave you yesterday explain exactly why people behave in this manner, and what they can do to change their ways. It's fascinating reading, and essential knowledge for anyone embarking on a healing journey!"

Understand your duality

"How come?" I asked as I glanced over to the backseat to make sure the big brown envelope was still there.

"It's simple. You need to transform your way of life in order to heal your body. But you'll never be able to do that until you understand your duality. You see, we all have two distinct sides to ourselves. I call them your ego-mind and your true-self. They are polar opposites. The one is good for you, and the other is bad for you. The one will help you to heal your body; the other will make you sick, or sicker. Pay attention: You're about to learn a life-lesson that's vital to your healing process."

The early morning traffic whizzed past us. I watched enviously as people went about their lives. I felt detached from the real world and stuck in the moment. There was no way out of my situation. My sentence had been passed and I had nowhere to go.

The ego-mind vs true-self

Henry Jones continued: "I'm going to teach you how to distinguish between your ego-mind and true-self. If you don't know the difference between them, you'll get sick over and over again."

"Go on, then. I have all day."

"Good," he replied, taking no notice of my poor attitude. "Your ego-mind causes sickness, whilst your true-self sustains health. It's essential for you to have a clear understanding of these two facets of yourself in order to identify which part of YOU is expressing itself at any given time. When you can tell the difference between the thoughts and feelings of your ego-mind, and the thoughts and feelings of your true-self, then, and only then, can you make conscious choices about your behavior."

"I have a feeling you understand me better than I understand myself," I said, thinking back to the awful tantrum I had thrown earlier.

"Well, let's just say I understand human nature. Don't forget, I've been helping people to heal themselves for decades. I've seen it all before. From my experience, I can say with confidence that when people become aware of their ego-mind and true-self, they are changed forever."

"Really?"

"Oh yes. I'm not exaggerating! You'll never be the same again. Did you ever see a film called *The Matrix* with Keanu Reeves?"

"Yes."

"Great. In that case, it should be easy for you to relate to this metaphor: Imagine you're holding two pills – one red and one blue. The blue pill is your ego-mind. The red pill is your true-self. If you swallow the blue pill, then your life will continue as it did before. But, if you take the red pill, then the veil will be lifted from your eyes and things will never be the same again. What are you going to do?"

I smiled to myself. I could tell Henry Jones was trying to cajole me out of my miserable mood. "The latter," I mumbled. What choice did I really have?

Understanding the ego-mind

"Let's look at the ego-mind. It's time to illuminate your personality and expose it for what it really is. Brace yourself: Just who do you think you are?"

"Excuse me!"

"Ah! Your defensive response indicates you've heard that question before. Right? That tells me you've taken a few ego trips in your time."

"What are you talking about?"

"Think back to those times in your life when you projected your thoughts and feelings without any regard for others. Come on, I'm sure you can recall occasions when your personality shone so brightly that it blinded you to the emotional needs of everyone else around you. Did you stop to consider how your actions made others think or feel in those moments? Probably not."

I winced. No further response was needed.

"Ask yourself: Who is it that you project to others? Where does this personality come from? How did it evolve? What's its purpose? Knowing the answers to these questions is vital. Understanding the origin and composition of your personality will shed some light on your path to perfect health. Without this knowledge, you'll be fumbling in the dark and you'll repeatedly bump your head!"

"Ouch! I don't need any more mistakes," I moaned.

Where does your personality come from?

"Firstly, your personality is a construct of your ego. It started developing in your early childhood. How old were you when you started saying: 'I', 'me', and 'mine'? Probably as soon as you could talk, right? People are all the same. We quickly learn to project ourselves and manipulate others to get what we want. Just spend some time with toddlers – 10 minutes would do the trick. You'll soon see how tenacious they are in getting their own way. Toddlers think the world revolves around them. They develop and masterfully execute a wide range of behavioral patterns to get their own way. They can be cute and adorable one moment, and little terrors the next. The thing is: We don't change as we get older. We constantly engineer our thoughts and actions to get what we want and need. The only thing that makes us different from each other is how we go about it. This is the function of the personality. Its primary purpose is for you to express yourself to get what you want. Got it?"

"I think so."

"Good. Now get this: The thoughts that support your personality are the building blocks of your ego-mind. If you want to see your ego-mind in action, just observe your thoughts. You know the little voice in your head?"

I thought about it for a split second, and then replied: "Ah huh."

"Well, that's the mouthpiece of your ego-mind."

The voice inside

In that moment, another thought entered my head: How did he know? As I focused my attention on the voice in my head, I suddenly became aware of how much I silently talked to myself.

Where does the voice come from? Who exactly am I talking to? How did I think before I learned to speak? I wondered. For the first time in my life, I thought about the origin of my thoughts.

Henry Jones cleared his throat.

I had to admit it: "The voice in my head natters constantly."

Henry Jones laughed. "You're not alone, my friend. Most people have busy minds. This is because your ego-mind wants to be in control all the time. It tells you how to think, feel and act. But, don't be fooled! It's not who you really are. It's just a cover-up. Your ego-mind is the mask you show the world. It's who you pretend to be, not who you actually are. It's who you become, it's who you think you should be, and who you want other people to think you are."

"How can I tell the difference between my ego-mind and who I actually am?" I asked.

"Good question. There are many telltale traits that expose it. For example: Your ego-mind schemes, predicts and makes assumptions. It's selfish and withholding. It likes to take charge, and it thrives on fear, guilt and conflict. Your ego-mind justifies and promotes idealism, judgment, criticism and condemnation. It also encourages doubt, skepticism and distrust. More than anything else, your ego-mind wants to control you and rule your life!"

Don't fall for the tricks

"That sounds awful. I don't want to be like that. How does it control me?"

"Oh, let me assure you, your ego-mind has many tricks. For one, it gets you to constantly anticipate the future based on your past experiences – or should I say, your perception of your experiences."

"Eh?"

"Let me explain. Information is fed into your brain through your five senses. What you see, hear, smell, taste and touch becomes your experience. But how you evaluate and interpret your experience is your perception. So, in fact, your perceptions are not external observations but rather projections of your thoughts. What you call reality is just your perception of your experience. What's more, your perception of reality isn't necessarily the truth. Truth is always relative. Two people can share the same experience but form completely different perceptions of it. Remember the old adage: Two people standing behind bars – one looks up and sees the sky, the other looks down and sees the ground."

"Sure, I do. This means some people choose to see the positive side of life, while others see the negative. Right?"

"Exactly! Is the glass half-empty or half-full? How you perceive reality, or life, is entirely up to you. Make no mistake about it, the choice is yours!"

In that brief moment, I felt the discomfort that accompanied the disease in my body. "That's all well and dandy when things are rosy, Henry Jones, but life is filled with negative experiences, too. What are we supposed to do when things go wrong for us?"

He turned his head sharply towards me and said: "You can always create a positive perception from a negative experience."

"How?"

"I'll tell you how. All experiences, good and bad, should be perceived as learning experiences. They are opportunities for personal growth."

"Even sickness?"

"Especially sickness!" exclaimed Henry Jones, slapping his knee. He leaned towards me, as if he was about to disclose an important secret: "Listen up now: When you fail to perceive the positive in negative situations, you fail the life-lessons that these situations are trying to teach you. As I'm sure you already know, sometimes the lessons can be hard and painful – especially the ones you don't want to learn. Don't be surprised when these problems or challenges keep manifesting in your life. You can expect them to keep repeating themselves in different forms until you learn the life-lessons they are trying to teach you."

"Are you suggesting that my illness is a test, and I'll continue to be tested until I successfully learn my life-lesson, or die?"

"Yup," he replied casually.

"Is this some weird, radical, new fringe approach to sickness and health?" I barked.

"Actually, it's not! Mankind has shared these views for thousands of years. Hippocrates said: 'A wise man should consider that health is the greatest of human blessings and learn how by his own thought to derive benefit from his illnesses.'"

"You're like a walking encyclopaedia of healing, Henry Jones," I marvelled.

He chuckled. "All I'm saying is this: When you learn the life-lesson your sickness is offering you, you will heal your body. You will! We'll explore the concept of 'life-lessons' in more detail further down the line. Right now, though, I must tell you: Holding on to negative perceptions of past experiences distorts your outlook on life in the present moment. This is detrimental to your well-being."

"How come?"

"Because your perception determines how you react, and your reaction determines how you feel, and your feelings determine the quality of your life. Make sense?"

"Kinda. Do you have an example?"

"Okay, let's discuss Dr Sahib's assistant. What if you misinterpreted his shyness as unfriendliness? How would you react towards him the next time you met?"

"I'd probably be indifferent and unfriendly."

Assumptions are based on perceptions

"Precisely! Your ego-mind would make an assumption based on your perception, despite the fact that your perception may be entirely wrong. That is how your ego-mind works. It keeps you trapped in your past. You become imprisoned by your perceptions and misperceptions. Your ego-mind rationalizes your present thinking and behavior by analyzing and interpreting your past perceptions. You end up thinking that your thoughts, actions, opinions and responses are 100% right all the time. Does that sound like an ego trip, or what?"

I nodded.

"In this particular case, your ego-mind will justify your indifference and subsequently deny you the chance to discover the man's true value. Now, your ego-mind is free to run amok. Can you see how this scenario will play out? Your reaction to his shyness will set in motion an unfortunate chain of misunderstandings. He'll probably respond by further withdrawing from you, which your ego-mind will interpret as more unfriendly behavior and justify your continued indifference and unfriendliness. You get the picture?"

"Yes, but how is that detrimental to my well-being. What could Dr Sahib's assistant possibly do for me?"

"How will you ever know?" asked Henry Jones. "In an infinite universe, there are unlimited possibilities. He might know someone who could help you to heal your body, or he may have access to information that could be useful to you or give you advice that could change your life for the better. Anything is possible. But, if you don't see the light within him because you're blinded by your perception, you'll never know his true value."

Henry swerved into the fast lane to overtake a tractor and trailer that was parked on the side of the road.

People reflect the state of your mind and life

"Now, try to get your head around this fact: People reflect the state of your mind and the condition of your life."

The Land Rover engine moaned as he stepped on the gas. The car shuddered violently. I double-checked my safety belt.

"Your ego-mind's viewpoint, however, is that people only exist to satisfy your needs. When your ego-mind is in the driving seat, your relationships are always conditional. When you don't think you stand to gain anything from giving of yourself, then you're less inclined to do so. You may not be conscious of it, but your ego-mind gives to get in return. Suffice to say, when you stop getting, you stop giving."

An image of my wife popped into my head, pushing aside thoughts of Dr Sahib's assistant. I couldn't ignore my conscience. "That explains why my wife left me," I mumbled.

Henry Jones sighed sympathetically. "In fact, she left your ego-mind, not you. I bet she still loves you."

"I doubt it. She told me that I'd changed too much. Apparently, I'm not the same man she married. She told me I don't meet her emotional needs and that we have irreconcilable differences."

"This makes total sense. You see, she fell in love with your true-self, but lived with your ego-mind. This is the main reason relationships fall apart. Love is an expression of the true-self, not the ego-mind. It felt wonderful when you first fell in love, right? This is because you were functioning from your true-self. But as soon as your ego-mind took control of your life, the wonderful feeling disappeared. True?"

"Yes, but why did I let it happen?"

The ego-mind sets up relationships to fail

"Well, the ego-mind knows many crafty tricks to rule you. When it comes to relationships, your ego-mind loves to create expectations, which eventually become conditions. It thrives on setting others up to fail. Failure leads to disappointment, dissatisfaction, frustration and regret. In this territory, your ego-mind is unbound. It has free reign over your mind. Why? Because it masterfully creates the conditions in which it thrives. In the right mental environment, your ego-mind naturally produces the thoughts, perceptions and expectations on which it feeds. It cultivates its own existence. So, your ego-mind will happily stretch your relationships to the limits. It will even destroy them. No problem! This breeds resentment, condemnation, self-pity, anger and remorse. Yummy! Your ego-mind loves it. You see, the last thing your ego-mind wants to do is to give up control to your true-self. When your true-self is present, your ego-mind ceases to exist in the moment. That state of mind goes against everything the ego is about. Does that make sense to you?"

"Yeah. It's becoming clear as daylight. I only wish I had known about my ego-mind a few years back, before my marriage was on the rocks. Things could be so different now."

"You still love your wife very much. I can tell. If she hasn't fallen in love with someone else, you might still be able to win her back."

"How?" I gasped.

"People are like animals. We move towards what gives us pleasure and away from what brings us pain. We experience pleasure when our expectations are met, and we experience pain when they are unmet. How strongly we feel satisfied or dissatisfied depends on the greatness of our needs or expectations. Your wife expects you to be the person with whom she fell in love. You can be that man. All of those qualities exist in your true-self. The secret to winning her back is to be your true-self."

"Tell me about the true-self now!" I commanded impulsively.

"In a moment. First, I'd like to ask you something personal. Okay?"

"Okay." I replied somewhat nervously.

"Dr Sahib's assistant is one example of how the ego-mind can create misperceptions, but let's bring it closer to home. Have you ever been betrayed by a loved one?"

I paused before answering. The hairs on the back of my neck prickled. "Yes."

"What happened?"

I looked away. A big truck roared past and I flinched. It took a moment for me to collect my thoughts. Henry Jones hung on my answer.

"I once had a fiancée who left me for someone else."

"How did that make you feel at the time?"

I felt myself growing angry. A part of me wanted to tell Henry Jones to mind his own damn business and to stop prying into my life. A part of me wanted to lash out at him, and to bark, snarl and bite, as usual. But I didn't. Instead, I bit my lip.

"Were you heartbroken?"

"I guess."

"How did you feel at the time?"

I shrugged. "Rejected. Angry. Resentful. Bitter."

"Even full of hatred?"

I nodded. "Yeah, I still hate the bitch."

He geared down. The engine groaned.

"Can I ask you something deeply personal?"

"What?"

"Do you trust your wife?"

"I don't trust women, period. Never have. Never will."

"Can you see your ego-mind at play here?" he replied. "To protect you, your ego-mind has created a perception that the opposite sex isn't to be trusted. There's a good chance that your ego-mind decided you'll never love wholeheartedly again for fear of being hurt. Now let me ask you this: Do you honestly think your wife would cheat on you?"

I'd thrown scores of jealous rages in the past, but deep down I didn't really doubt her fidelity. Being unfaithful was simply not in her nature. I shook my head.

"So, your fiancée left you for someone else, but later down the line you met your true soulmate, fell in love, got married and had a beautiful child. In hindsight, I'd say being dumped was the best thing for you."

"Why?"

"Because it made way for you to meet the right person. You found a true, loving, loyal partner with whom you could share your life."

"You make a good point."

"So, your perception about women should change. Your wife has proved to you that women can be faithful and committed life partners. However, your ego-mind still holds on to the misperception that loved ones are not to be trusted. This explains why you've withheld your love from her, doesn't it? It also explains why you've been jealous, insecure, reserved and inhibited. Make sense?"

I felt sick to my stomach. Countless times I'd heard my wife pleading with me to trust her and open up to her; to love her completely – like she loved me – like she needed to be loved. My mind raced. My ego-mind wasn't only in the driver's seat – it had driven straight over my wife repeatedly throughout our marriage. She gave and gave and gave. I took and took and took. I took until she had nothing left to give. I sat in silence, drenched in self-pity and shame. Henry Jones let me stew in my guilt.

Eventually, I announced somewhat sheepishly: "I made a rod for my own back, didn't I?"

"Don't beat yourself up, my friend. It's not your fault. You didn't know any better at the time. But now, the red pill will take effect, and your life can be totally different. Your ego-mind may have moulded your thinking and behavior in the past, but the past no longer exists. It's done. Over! Gone!"

"But I've made so many mistakes in my past that will affect my future," I moaned, rubbing my fingers in slow, round circles on my eyelids.

See mistakes as lessons

"How you interpret your past actions is your choice. Your ego-mind regards mistakes as failures. It uses these memories to bring you down with feelings of remorse, regret and shame. Your true-self regards mistakes as learnings. It uses these memories to build you up through personal growth, development and wisdom gained. If you stop and think about it, your memories are just sets of thoughts inside your head. Fortunately, you have the ability to choose your thoughts."

"Jeez, how on Earth am I going to learn all this new information? My head is already spinning."

"You don't have to know it all. There's a short cut. Observe how your thoughts make you feel. If you feel bad, or your state of mind is negative, your ego-mind is in control. If you feel good, or your state of mind is positive, your true-self is in control. Simple!"

"But how do I stop worrying about my future? I worry about not getting well again. I worry about my wife falling in love with someone else. I worry about losing my job to some healthy, young buck. These worries are real issues in my life, darn it."

"No one knows what tomorrow will bring, my friend. The future exists only in a state of pure potentiality. Be aware: Your ego-mind drives your personal ambitions for the future. It fuels your positive and negative fantasies. Along with these desires come envy, jealousy, possessiveness and competition. In these mind states, you'll never be satisfied with your lot in the present moment. Moreover, as long as you're dwelling on the past, or dreaming about the future, you can't be in the present moment."

"What's your point?"

"The past is behind you and the future is yet to unfold. The present moment is all that exists. All you have is this moment. Your point of power is now."

"Why is this so important?"

You are not a victim

"Healing occurs in the present moment. Each and every moment that slips by either brings you closer towards your healing or pushes you further away from it. The reason you need to heal your body now is because of wrong living, improper diet, unresolved emotions and negative thinking in your past, as George said. All of these traits stem from the ego-mind. The true culprit behind all energy depletion, sickness, disease and pain in the human body is the ego-mind."

"Seriously?"

"Yes. Your ego-mind would have you believe that you're a passive observer of your life – that life unfolds around you – that you're at the mercy of whatever situation comes your way. It wants you to believe that you're not responsible for your sickness. That is totally false! You're not a victim of your current life situation: You created it. At the deepest level, you choose your life-lessons, just as you choose how to perceive them. Your sickness is a blessing in disguise. It's a powerful sign that the time has come for you to learn the ultimate life-lesson. Your higher self, your true-self, wants to take back control of your life from your ego-mind. This belief is crucial to your healing process. Herein you'll find the power to heal your body. The reason you became sick and now experience pain is because your ego-mind has run amok with your life."

"Go on," I begged him.

"The really great news is this: Because your ego-mind created your physical problem, you have the power to let it go. To heal your body, you need to release your ego-mind's control over your life and give authority back to your true-self. Only once you accept responsibility for your ailment, affliction and condition, can you release it. Only when you make this decision will you start down the road to recovery. That is the only way to perfect health," Henry Jones said with great fervency. His fist pounded on the steering wheel with each sentence. His cheeks flushed bright red and his eyes glimmered like burning coals. Once again, the sheer force of his passion and conviction overwhelmed me.

"Crikey Moses, Henry! You should be a motivational speaker. I actually got goosebumps during that outburst," I spluttered, raising my forearm to show him my hairs standing on end.

Henry Jones broke into a broad smile, and the Land Rover groaned as he ground through the gears. Caught in the moment, I watched the morning Sun stream down on the valley below, illuminating patches of green grass that twinkled with glistening dewdrops.

"Let's pull in here for some breakfast," he suggested, pointing to a quaint farm stall at the side of the road. I agreed. It wasn't long before we were seated at a cosy table near a crackling fireplace. A bleary-eyed waitress took our order without much enthusiasm. I could tell that she needed black coffee and a fry-up as much as I did. Alas, I made do with a fruit salad and another darn carrot juice.

The health breakfast was awful and I resented each mouthful.

"You'd better tell me about my true-self before I snatch the bacon from the plate of the child sitting beside us," I said half-jokingly. My fist-clenched fork was ready to stab it.

Henry Jones chuckled. "I know there's a part of you that's serious, so I'll tell you right away. We wouldn't want the restaurant manager to throw us out!"

I prodded a piece of papaya with my spoon, and then pushed a slice of banana around the outer edges of my plate. The bacon smelled seriously good, as did the coffee percolating noisily nearby. Together, they mercilessly taunted my craving.

"Brace yourself," Henry Jones said in a chipper voice.

My yawn was a silent scream for coffee.

He scooped up a mouthful of mango and chewed it slowly. "You see, there's something wondrous within your being," he announced, tapping the center of his chest. "It has the power to miraculously transform your life when you reconnect with it. Trust me, you will transcend the pain, misery, fear, doubt and negativity of your ego-mind when you rediscover this essential part of you. This is probably the reason why some people refer to it as the 'higher-self'. To access it, you must rise above your lower self, which I call the ego-mind. I prefer to call your higher-self, your true-self. Why? Because it's who you truly are! It's the part of you that's spiritual, eternal and divine. It's the essence of your being – the core of your inner goodness. When you reconnect with your true-self, you feel energetic, creative, alive and full of possibility. Your true-self is ever-present and always accessible."

"How do I find it?"

"That's simple. Look within," he said, munching on his toast with great satisfaction.

"What do you mean?"

"I mean all the higher qualities that you need in order to experience a peaceful and joyous life are within you. Love; joy; happiness; contentment; appreciation; gratitude; peace and bliss come from within you. They're not created in response to external forces. They originate from within you. They're ever-present. All too often people make the mistake of allowing their external world to determine their internal world. Their thoughts and feelings are a response to their current experience. When life is good on the outside, they're happy on the inside. When life is bad on the outside, they're sad on the inside. Sound familiar?"

"Yes."

Be proactive, not reactive

"The problem with this way of living is that it's reactive and not proactive. People learn to depend on the outside world to produce their happiness and fulfilment. But this is just another trick the ego-mind plays on them to keep control. It counts on the fact that there will always be things to rob one of joy in an imperfect world."

"So, let me get this straight. You're saying I should consciously connect to my true-self, no matter what happens to me?"

"Precisely!"

"But how am I supposed to connect to 'the higher qualities' within me when life is hard, and people usually piss me off?"

Henry Jones chortled. "Once again, stay in the present. Become aware of your thoughts and how they make you feel. When you're struggling to cope in difficult times, or feel stressed out by others, then you're functioning from your ego-mind. Your true-self allows you to be patient, understanding, tolerant, caring, compassionate and forgiving. This helps you accept others more easily. You can accept yourself more easily, too."

"I'm not the problem," I retorted. "I'm fine. It's other people who put me in a bad mood."

"Listen to what you're saying, my friend. Firstly, you're admitting that you're influenced by external forces. This is an attribute of the ego-mind. Secondly, blaming others for how bad you sometimes feel doesn't make you feel any better. It brings you down. When your true-self is present, you have loving and positive thoughts, regardless of your life circumstances. This makes you feel whole, fulfilled, content and happy. This lifts you up. Can you see the pattern here? When you feel down, you're functioning from your lower self and your ego-mind is in control. When you feel up, you're functioning from your higher self, and your true-self is in control. Get it?"

"Yes, but it's natural to feel bad when things go wrong. What are we supposed to do when life sucks?"

"Trust that everything that happens to you is for your highest good. Your true-self accepts that everything happens for a reason. This gives you peace of mind, no matter what happens to you."

"I haven't felt at peace for a long, long time," I replied sincerely.

"You can only find peace and happiness when you connect with your true-self, my friend. You see, your true-self is a state of consciousness that allows you to be in harmony with the universe. It makes you feel safe, secure, and loved."

I grunted disapprovingly. "I don't feel loved or loving. I'm sick."

"That sounds like an excuse to me," said Henry Jones. "Excuses are an attribute of the ego-mind, too. Your true-self doesn't need to make excuses. Especially not for poor health."

"Why not?"

"Well, the very first place that your true-self manifests its dominion is over your body. It's a fact. You eat healthily and exercise regularly when you're living from your true-self."

"How come?"

"You know it's good for you, so you do it. No ifs or buts. You just do it."

A blob of honey dropped from his toast to the plate. He scooped it up and wiped it off on his tongue, then sucked it and swallowed. His eyes closed. He savored the taste.

I wished I, too, could live to my fullest potential, like Henry Jones.

Your true-self makes wholesome life choices

"The choices you make depend entirely on your state of mind. Your ego-mind always makes unhealthy life choices, while your true-self always makes wholesome life choices. This is most evident in the food you choose to eat. In the next few days, you'll learn about food that feeds your ego-mind and food that nourishes your true-self. This understanding is crucial, because the part of you that you feed is the part of you that grows!"

"Hold on a second. Let me get my head around this statement. Are you saying that the food I eat affects my state of mind, or my state of mind affects my choice of food?"

"Both. It's either a vicious cycle or a value circle."

"Huh?"

You are what you eat

"When your ego-mind is in control, you choose to ingest acidic, toxic substances that are bad for you, which give you toxic, acidic thoughts. They make you feel bad, which feeds the ego-mind that chooses to ingest, toxic substances, and so on. A vicious circle is created. Get it?"

"I guess."

"Now, on the other hand, when your true-self is in control, you choose to ingest healthy substances, which give you happy, healthy thoughts. They make you feel good …"

"… which feeds my true-self, which chooses to ingest healthy substances, thereby creating a value circle?"

"You've got it!" Henry Jones cried, licking the last of the honey from his fingertips. "There's more than a link between the food you eat and the state of your mind. They are one and the same. You are what you eat."

I need to eat a skinny person, I thought to myself, rubbing my fat belly.

"Next week, I'm going to introduce you to a friend of mine who is a molecular biologist. She'll explain to you how every morsel of food you eat becomes your body at an atomic level. Every thought and feeling you have becomes your body at an atomic level, too. This insight is really going to blow your mind. Cheque, please!" Henry Jones called to the waitress.

I waved my spoon in protest. I didn't want to leave yet – I wanted to talk more. I was beginning to understand myself a little better. My miserable mood swings and bad attitude were starting to make sense to me. I used to think that I had life all figured out and that my only problems were created by the people around me and the stressful situations I experienced. Could it be possible that the root cause of my unhappiness was actually me? Was I to blame for what I had become? How could I change my ways, and would that make me well again? I wondered.

Henry Jones leaned towards me. "We're out of time, I'm afraid. I've a full schedule planned for today and we must leave shortly, or we'll be late for our next appointment."

"I don't care," I retorted. "I need to know more about my true-self."

Henry Jones laughed. "I can tell you this: Your true-self not only does what is best for you, but also what is best for everyone else around you. When you act from your ego-mind, you don't care about anyone but yourself. You put your immediate needs and desires first. But, when you act from your true-self, you consider the thoughts and feelings of others."

129

"Why should I care about anyone else?"

"Here's why: Your true-self knows that you're not separate from other people. It recognizes that there's a universal oneness that binds us all. When you understand this concept, you'll understand that it's better to create happy, healthy relationships with everyone you meet. Why? Because you're creating happiness and health for yourself! Make sense?"

It did, but I still wasn't ready to leave. Fortunately, the waitress was in no hurry either. I saw her grab a packet of cigarettes from the bar counter and head out the back door of the restaurant. Henry Jones sat back and folded his arms. "You should try to finish your breakfast. You'll need the energy to get through the day ahead."

I glanced down at my half-eaten health breakfast. I was hungry but had no appetite for it. To appease Henry Jones, I picked apart a piece of pineapple and begrudgingly ate a slither. He smiled and nodded approvingly.

How could I eat when I had a gut filled with guilt? I never did what was best for others. I only did what suited me. To my surprise, I found myself telling Henry Jones about the many times I drank excessive amounts of whiskey at parties to ensure I had 'a good time', even though I drove home drunk with my wife in tears beside me. I wasn't concerned about her safety or well-being. I'd rant about my need to blow off steam and have some fun and accuse her of being a 'party pooper' and a 'square' for asking me to slow down. He listened attentively.

When I was done, he asked only one question: "Who was driving?"

I knew what he meant. "Definitely not my true-self," I answered.

"How do you know?" he asked.

"Because my true-self would've been considerate of her thoughts and feelings?"

He nodded.

"I feel like crap," I moaned, pushing my plate to the side.

Henry Jones gently slid the plate back in front of me, implying that I should finish my breakfast. I reluctantly complied.

He continued with a sympathetic smile: "If we learn and grow from our mistakes, then they're not mistakes. Right? This outlook on life stems from the true-self. You see, we're not born to be perfect. We're born to learn and to grow. Our true-self understands that mistakes are an important part of our development. It knows they help us to progress, to evolve, to expand and to live to our fullest potential."

"Nice try, but I still feel crap," I groaned. "Talking to you has made me realize that I treated my wife horribly over the years. No wonder she left me."

"Perhaps she will forgive you."

"How can I expect her to forgive me?"

"From what you've told me about your wife, she seems to be true to herself. This may bode well for you, my friend. Your true-self allows you to see your worst transgressors as your greatest teachers of forgiveness. When your true-self is present, you simply can't hold on to grudges, because they are liberated by your compassion. You know that a special lightness comes from letting go and moving on. This precious insight makes it much easier to forgive and forget."

"But, I must have hurt her so much!"

Henry Jones sighed. "Yes, that's probably true." He paused for a moment to stir his tea. The herbal tea leaves swirled in tight circles on the surface before sinking out of sight. In that time, my guilt set in. I bit my lip hard.

He continued: "Now is a good time for me to tell you that when you experience negative emotions, like hurt, sadness, disappointment and regret, and your true-self is present, you nonetheless feel very alive. You regard these moments as learning experiences and you're grateful for them."

"How on Earth can I expect my wife to be grateful for the horrible way I treated her?" I snapped.

"I'm not talking about your wife, my friend. I'm talking about you. This is your healing journey. The life-lesson is yours."

"Mine?"

"Yes. You have the chance to learn from your mistakes, to grow from them, and to move forward a better person."

I wanted to believe Henry Jones. I was tired of being belligerent. I was sick of trying to prove I was right about everything all the time, but that just seemed to be my nature. How could I change myself? What would it take to change? Was it possible for me to be a different person?

I stared at the distorted image of myself in the stainless-steel sugar bowl. It seemed to symbolize my personality, and it wasn't a pretty sight. I felt ashamed.

Your true-self boosts your self-confidence

"Don't fret," Henry Jones said. "The good news is that you develop self-respect, self-worth and self-esteem when you exercise your true-self. These qualities boost your self-confidence, and so you feel better about yourself. Consequently, the insecurities of the ego-mind are dissolved and removed."

I don't know where it came from, but a tear slipped from my left eye and down my cheek before I had the chance to wipe away the evidence. It must have been there all along, waiting for the right moment to escape.

"I'm sorry," I muttered, tucking my cheek into my shoulder.

Henry Jones was quick to respond. "That's okay. In fact, it's more than okay. It's great! You see, your true-self allows you to get in touch with your feelings and gives you the courage to express them. I'm pleased you're starting to feel something. As I've said before, allowing yourself to feel your emotions is very important on a healing journey. Recovery is impossible without releasing blocked emotions."

More tears spilled down my cheeks and I grew extremely self-conscious. "Stop it, Henry! You'll have me bawling in a minute."

He chuckled. "Oh, my sense is that we have a long way to go before you break down completely, my friend. You're a tough nut to crack. But, we'll get there. You may appear hard as nails on the outside, but I think you're as soft as marshmallow on the inside."

"My wife used to say that about me, once upon a time."

"She has you pegged. There's hope for you yet. I'm utterly convinced your true-self will eventually win the battle."

"Battle?"

"Yes. You may not be aware of it, but there's a constant battle going on between your ego-mind and your true-self. Do you have any idea what they're fighting over? Go on, have a shot."

"Me."

"You guessed it. The fight is for control of your life. Unfortunately, the ego-mind usually wins."

"How come?"

"Most times, you allow your ego-mind to be the decision-maker in your life. For instance: When you come home after a stressful day at the office, all your ego-mind wants you to do is pour a drink, order take-out food and watch television. You see, your ego-mind's quick-fix is sensory stimulation and instant gratification. Your true-self, on the other hand, knows you should exercise to loosen your muscles and increase your blood circulation; eat wholesome food to give your mind and body the nutrients they need to function more effectively; and then rest to avoid unnecessary clutter filling your head. Your true-self knows that this behavior is a long-term plan that will ultimately help you to better cope with stressful days. But, what do you do?"

"Whiskey, take-outs and TV. But, how do I change my behavior?"

"You're an adult, right? You know what's good for you and what's bad for you. You know what you should do and what you shouldn't do. Agreed?"

"Yes, but why do I make the wrong choices?"

"The answer is simple. You allow your ego-mind to govern your behavior. You let it control you, regardless of whether the outcome of your actions is good for you or not," Henry Jones said, waving to the waitress. He attempted to show her that we were ready to pay our bill and leave.

"It's not my fault," I exclaimed. "Until this morning, I didn't even know there were two sides to me. I've just been living each day as it comes. I haven't been analyzing my thoughts and feelings to establish their origins. I'm just me," I yelled, pounding my chest.

Henry Jones cocked his head to the side and widened his eyes.

"I just did it again, didn't I? I reacted from my ego-mind."

He smiled. "You're making fantastic progress, my friend. You're already starting to tell the difference between your ego-mind and your true-self. Excellent work! Most people never discover this aspect of themselves. They constantly listen to their ego-minds, and their true-selves get buried beneath massive egos. These people live their lives from their lower-selves, with their ego-minds ruling their heads. They never transcend to their higher-selves. They never reach their full potential. Never!"

"That sounds terrible. I don't want to live a half-life."

Henry Jones narrowed his eyes, as if sizing me up. His beady stare made me feel insecure and vulnerable. Was I ready to hear what he had to say? Could I handle his advice? Did I have what it took to act on his words? He looked around the restaurant furtively. I got the feeling he was about to say something meant for my ears only.

"Look closely at your current life situation and ask yourself: Has your life spun out of control? Do you feel like you've lost balance and harmony? Have you taken a wrong turn somewhere? Does your life teeter on the brink of disaster? Are you your own worst enemy? The answers to these questions will reveal what the external signs are telling you – whether or not your ego-mind is ruling your life. When you fail to interpret the external signs, the true-self has no other choice but to let you know that something is wrong with your state of mind by manifesting the problem in your body. You get sick, or you feel pain! The severity of your ailment will indicate exactly how far you've strayed from your true-self!"

I grimaced.

If you want to heal, you need to make a choice

"Here it is straight: If you want to heal your body, you've got a choice to make. You can continue to allow your ego-mind to rule your life, which will result in fear, anxiety, pain, suffering, chronic illness, and possibly early death."

"Or?"

"Or you can immediately begin to do what is good for you. Listen to your true-self. That's the way to restore your body to perfect health and bring true wellness into your life."

His words hit their mark. I had problems. The external and internal signs were communicating with me, loud and clear. I couldn't ignore them any longer. My train of thought was unexpectedly derailed when the waitress dumped the bill on our table. Henry Jones nodded appreciatively. I would've yelled at her and demanded to speak to the manager about her rude and appalling service. Not Henry Jones. Instead, he wished her a pleasant day and tipped her. I silently noted that his way involved significantly less conflict and drama than mine.

"So, all things considered, I don't really have a choice, do I?"

He shook his head. "Not if you want to enjoy radiant health and a long life, my friend."

We left the restaurant and walked to his vehicle in silence. My journey had begun.

One step at a time, I told myself. Take one step at a time.

"You're in for a real treat now," Henry Jones said as he hoisted himself into the driver's seat.

"Why? What's next?"

"You're in for a dramatic, life-changing experience. Nothing less – I can assure you of that," he drawled.

"How dramatic!"

"Very! Your life will never be the same again," Henry Jones replied, grinning mischievously.

I gulped involuntarily. What did he have in store for me? Where was he taking me next?

CHAPTER 8

ON THE ROAD TO NOWHERE

"You'd better brace yourself, my friend. We're going to teach your ego-mind an important life-lesson," Henry Jones stated confidently, firing up the engine of his Land Rover. "We're going to show your ego-mind that it's not the ultimate decision-maker in your life. It may think that it's the boss, but it's not. Your true-self is the real decision-maker in your life. That's a fact! Your ego-mind can't make decisions that your true-self can't override. To prove it, you're going to give your true-self the opportunity to demonstrate its power over your ego-mind. This is your next objective."

"How are we going to do that?" I asked timidly.

"You're going to sit in isolation on top of a mountain for three days."

"What?" I exclaimed.

"You heard me," he replied. "And I'd like you to sit in silence."

"I can't speak?"

"Not a word."

"Have you lost your mind?" I cried out.

He chortled, slapping the steering wheel repeatedly. I didn't see the humor.

"Trust me. There's no better way to evoke the authority of your true-self than to be still, rest and fast."

"Fast?"

"Yes. Did I forget to mention that you're not going to eat either?"

"You must be joking! Have you forgotten that I'm sick? I've just been released from hospital, for Pete's sake!"

"I made sure to get your doctor's approval first," he assured me. "And I've told your family that you'll be out of contact for 72 hours. Don't worry. All of the necessary preparations have been made."

I took a few minutes to comprehend the magnitude of the proposed exercise. It seemed radical. I couldn't imagine not eating for one day, never mind three. The idea terrified me. "Why make me fast?" I moaned, clutching my big tummy.

"The physical effect of fasting is astonishing, but the principle you need to understand about fasting is that it's not of the body. It's of the mind."

"Ridiculous!" I scoffed. "My body needs food. This is a terrible idea. You're making a serious mistake. There's something you need to know about me. I can't skip meals. If I don't eat when I'm hungry, I get cranky … and you don't want to see me cranky!"

Henry Jones was amused. "Cranky? You? Never!"

I saw the absurdity in his mockery, and it almost made me smile. Almost, but not quite.

"Is this exercise absolutely necessary?" I protested.

"Yes. I can assure you that the best way to kickstart a natural healing program is to fast, rest and be still. If you don't believe me, look at the animal kingdom. What do animals do when they get sick? They stop eating, lie down and wait for their bodies to heal naturally. Right? That's nature's way!"

"That's true."

Henry Jones continued: "But what do we humans do when we get sick? We race off to the doctor or pharmacy to get medication. We treat ourselves by purchasing packets of pills that cost a small fortune," he stated with disgust. "Sickness has become big business. The craziest part of all is that nature's way doesn't cost a cent."

"You mean fasting?"

Fasting is a magic formula

"Yes. Fasting is nature's oldest, best and least expensive method of healing. All you need to do is stop eating food; drink lots of water and rest. That's it! I truly believe this simple, magic formula is able to cure every known disease on the planet, without exception!"

I refrained from commenting. I wanted to believe him, but my disbelief was strong. Henry Jones detected my doubt and dived into another rant to persuade me otherwise: "I'll say it again: Your body knows how to heal itself.

Given the right opportunity, your body will immediately begin to restore, rebuild and rejuvenate your entire system at a cellular level. When you fast, all the energy that your body would normally use to digest food is redirected to problem areas. Instead of processing food, your whole body gets involved in a massive clean-up operation. It works to remove and expel impurities, toxins and disease. That is why fasting has been practised and promoted by healers throughout the ages. It's an opportunity for the human body to correct the damage caused by wrong living and improper diet. You've got to try it for yourself – your true-self. That is the only way to see and feel the amazing effect fasting can have on your body."

He sold it well, but I wasn't totally convinced.

"For how long should one fast?"

"It depends on you and your condition. If you just want to detoxify your system, then 48 to 73 hours will suffice. If your problem is more serious, you should consider a series of short fasts. I'd say five to 10 days at a time is optimal."

"What? Five to 10 days without food? You must be mad!" I bellowed.

"Oh, people fast for much longer than that," he told me.

"Would you recommend it?"

"No. I don't recommend long fasts for people who are on a healing journey. It's unnecessary and unhealthy to starve your body of vital nutrition for long periods of time. Also, the build-up of impurities released during a long fast can become very dangerous for someone in a weakened state."

"How long did you fast on your healing journey?" I inquired.

"The longest water fast I did was 21 days," he replied.

"Are you serious?" I howled. "How was that for you?"

"It was a powerful experience, but I got the best results from intermittent fasting. I'd water-fast from Monday to Friday, and eat fruit and veggies on Saturday and Sunday. Once, I repeated that cycle four times in succession."

"You did that for a whole month!" I exclaimed.

"Yes, intermittent fasting performs miracles when combined with a proper diet. Genuinely! It's the ultimate healing remedy, my friend."

"But isn't starving your body dangerous?"

"No. Intermittent fasting eliminates all risk. Your system gradually expels toxic waste materials without seriously affecting normal bodily functions, and your blood is slowly but steadily cleansed and regenerated over time. This makes it easier for you to cope with the release of poisons and toxic waste."

"That sounds awful. I don't think my body needs that right now. Wouldn't that worsen my condition?" I asked.

Henry Jones narrowed his eyes and stared intently at the road ahead. He tightened his grip on the steering wheel. "The sudden release of hardened toxins and impurities may have a negative effect on your system in the short term. It's normal to get headaches, feel nauseous, break out in sores, get aches in your joints, throw up, become dizzy, sweat profusely, smell badly and suffer from severe cramps."

"Oh no! That sounds awful."

"Doesn't it?" Henry Jones replied as he slammed into a higher gear. "But believe it or not, those are all good signs. If you feel this way, it means your body is eliminating unwanted toxins. It's much better for you to feel poorly in the short term and get rid of poisonous toxins than to have them swirling around in your system in the long term. Poisonous toxins that are not expelled make you sick and prevent healing!"

"I'm still worried about the negative side-effects of fasting on my system," I replied.

Cleansing recovers health

"The most important thing to know is that short fasts will cleanse your system while giving you the natural energy you need to function normally. That's why I highly recommend it."

"I don't like the sound of headaches, nausea, vomiting and aching," I protested.

"You should focus on the positive results, not the negatives," he advised me.

I chewed on his words. Henry Jones was very convincing.

"What exactly am I supposed to do over the next three days?"

"Fast, rest and be still."

His words hammered home. It was going to be tough.

"All I can drink is water?"

"Yes."

"And after I have completed this exercise, you expect me to continue fasting intermittently?"

"Yes. We'll do a series of short fasts in the weeks ahead. But then you can add a little lemon juice and honey to the water."

"How long do I have to do this for?"

"Two to five days, followed by a cleansing diet of fruits and green vegetables in their natural state for a slightly longer period of time. There's no fixed rule. Eat for a few days, fast for a few days. Trust me: If you continue with this cleansing program, you will recover your health." Henry Jones said confidently.

"I can't go five days without food. I can't go five hours without food," I moaned.

"You'll be surprised what you can achieve when you put your mind to it. Your goal is to heal your body, right? In this case, you must give your body the chance to cleanse itself," he said.

I tried to object further: "But I don't even like fruit."

He ignored my comment. "Fruit is essential between fasts. It helps to loosen, dissolve and remove the mucus, poisons and toxins that have been released into your system. Don't fret. Your taste buds will change as you begin to eat healthily. You'll soon be very happy to eat a big bowl of fruit."

"Do you recommend this approach for everyone?"

"No. Definitely not! It's not advisable for people who are in the last stages of a life-threatening illness to place their systems under more stress. The same applies to old people in a weakened state. Fasts should be approached sensibly. You must plan them properly. Although the methodology is very simple, fasting isn't easy to do. Eating is your strongest, oldest habit. It's not easily broken. I recommend a great deal of premeditation."

"I haven't been given adequate time to prepare physically and mentally for this fast," I bleated.

"Actually, I've been preparing you for this exercise since we first met," he told me with a reassuring smile. "Of course, there's a great deal more to learn about fasting than what I've just told you. Many excellent books have been written on this subject. I suggest you read a few of them. It would also be a good idea to engage the services of someone who specializes in assisting people through fasts. There may be professionals who operate in your area. Search for them. You'll probably find them on the Internet."

"That's unlikely to happen any time soon," I scoffed.

He smiled. "You may change your mind once you've tried it. Do one fast, and I promise you that when your body has eliminated all the junk that's clogging up your internal system, you'll feel fantastic!" At that exact moment the Land Rover backfired, and a black cloud of smoke bellowed from the exhaust. That amused Henry Jones immensely. "That reminds me, I strongly recommend starting and ending a fast with an enema."

"A what?"

"You heard me, an enema! We'll discuss the amazing benefits of enemas in the near future, but for now, all you need to know is that this treatment is necessary to wash away toxins and impurities that may be lodged in your colon. Your recovery will only begin when you've properly cleansed your system."

My day wasn't getting any better. I grunted like a water buffalo at the sight of a long plain to cross. Henry Jones grinned broadly. I knew he wasn't enjoying himself at my expense. I just assumed he knew better than me. His joy came from a place I hadn't yet discovered. Yes, I'll admit that I was intrigued. I wanted to heal my body, but the process scared me.

"Relax. It's going to be okay. You'll get through it. In fact, I bet you'll pass this exercise with flying colors," he reassured me kindly.

"How can you be so sure?"

"Because fasting naturally revitalizes your body, mind and soul. Just wait and see. It will be good for you. Plus, you will have boundless energy when you start to eat the right foods again," he said.

"How soon can one eat after a fast?"

"You should eat raw fruit and vegetables before and after a fast for as long as the fast itself."

"So, you're saying if I fast for three days, I should eat raw fruit and vegetables for three days before I start fasting, and then for another three days after I've finished fasting?"

"Precisely! That's exactly what you should do. Now, since we're talking about breaking fasts, let me give you a wonderful tip: Drink half a glass of freshly-squeezed orange juice when you come off a fast. That will gently wake your digestive system from slumber. Plus, it'll be the most delicious and memorable drink you'll ever have in your life. Your taste buds will dance with joy."

I didn't get too excited. I still had a long plain to cross. I wasn't looking forward to the days ahead.

"I can't remember the last time I didn't do anything for three days," I eventually said.

Henry Jones was quick to respond. "If you want to heal your body, you must be a human being, not a human doing."

"Huh?"

"I'm merely saying you should maintain a settled, peaceful, restful state of being during a healing journey."

"Relaxation is a luxury of time that I don't have. I'm a busy man," I tried to explain.

It didn't stick. "You may think that total, deep relaxation is a luxury, but when healing is required, it's a necessity. Complete rest is now vital for you."

I cast my eyes out the window and watched the world whizz by. How could I make him understand the pressure I was facing at work? Couldn't he guess that my sickness and treatment had caused me to fall behind on critical deadlines? How would I ever catch up my enormous workload? I contemplated.

Yes, I had committed myself to Henry Jones and his healing techniques, but that didn't mean my real-world problems had gone away. I knew they'd be waiting for me when I got back to my normal life after spending forty days with Henry Jones. I started to panic, and Henry Jones sensed it.

"Don't worry. It'll do you some good to leave the hustle and bustle of your work life behind you for a while. Breaking your routine to nurture yourself is essential. Think about it: The energy that you would normally spend running around at work can be used to repair, rebuild and restore your internal system. Make sense?"

"I guess so."

Stress aggravates disease

"Good," Henry Jones replied, patting my leg. "After all, your health is the most important thing in the world to you, right?" He winked at me.

I didn't respond.

"So, this is why you should avoid situations that cause you stress during your healing journey. Stress is detrimental to your health. It aggravates disease, if it doesn't cause it. Do you hear what I'm telling you? Disease is the result of dis-ease. Try not to evoke negative emotions, such as fear; anger; frustration; doubt; aggravation or hurt on your healing journey. Personally, I wouldn't even watch violent, suspenseful, action-orientated movies or television. They can have a negative impact on your psychology and physiology – and you don't want that! Simply rest your mind and body. Do things that bring you pleasure and calm you down. For example, take gentle walks outdoors; bathe in soft sunlight; relax in long, hot, bubble baths; or read stimulating material. You should also unleash your creative side."

Creative energy is healing

"I can't draw to save my life," I replied curtly.

"It doesn't matter. The objective is to be creative, not to be good at it. Even if you think you can't draw to save your life, give it a go. You may just surprise yourself. Paint; draw; write; build; sew; knit or decorate. Just be creative. But, remember, it's not a competition. No one is judging you. The key here is to release your creative energy – it is healing energy. Plus, we usually enjoy ourselves when we're being creative, and this has a positive effect on our attitude. Don't forget, healing requires quality of mind; the will to recover; positive thinking; and a healthy mental attitude."

"Sounds exhausting," I moaned.

Henry Jones laughed. "Don't worry. I'll make sure you get plenty of rest. After practising all the wonderful healing techniques I'll share with you in the weeks ahead, you'll be ready for bed at night. I guarantee it."

My eyes rolled in my head.

"Here's something else you should know: It's important to get a good night's sleep while on a healing journey. Your body automatically steps up its repair and cleansing operation while you're asleep. That's why you should never eat anything before going to bed. If you do this, your body will use most of its energy to digest the food instead of repairing, cleansing and rebuilding itself. To ensure peaceful sleep, eat a light meal three hours before you retire; take a warm bath 20 minutes before getting into bed; and listen to soothing music while practising relaxation techniques."

It sounded good, but my head couldn't get past the next three days that lay ahead of me. Fast, rest and be still. My stomach grumbled at the thought of it. "Are you absolutely sure I have to fast?"

"Completely and utterly," he replied swiftly.

I still didn't buy it, but I'd committed myself to the process. I sat back in my seat, crossed my arms fiercely and sulked for at least an hour. Henry Jones was unperturbed and drove along peacefully, as if he didn't have a care in the world. It wasn't that he didn't care for me; he just didn't care for egos. I don't know why, but I wondered about his wife in that moment: Where was she? What was she like? What had he told her about me? I couldn't find it in me to ask him about her.

I watched the world pass by as we traversed a long, winding mountain pass. The roads gradually narrowed into a single lane. Had another vehicle approached us from the opposite direction, one of us would've needed to reverse until space for two cars to pass could be found. Fortunately, that never happened. We found ourselves alone on that road. The exquisite, rural countryside had begun to trigger a long-forgotten sense of adventure within me.

Suddenly, and without warning, we turned sharply into a concealed driveway. Henry Jones slammed on brakes and the vehicle came to an abrupt halt in front of a rusty farm gate. I shot forward. The large sign above the gate read: "Serendipity." I was unconvinced.

CHAPTER 9

CABIN IN THE WOODS

"We're here!" Henry Jones announced excitedly. He fiddled in the glove compartment and then handed me a single, bronze key. The tag on the keyring read "Main Gate".

"You've got to be kidding me," I grumbled. We were in the middle of nowhere and there wasn't a hotel in sight. I was definitely out of my comfort zone.

"If you'd be so kind," Henry Jones said, pointing to the padlock on the gatepost. I got out and begrudgingly unlocked it. To open the gate, I had to lift it and carry it to the opposite side of the road. It was surprisingly heavy. Henry Jones revved the motor once or twice and then chugged past me. He stopped about 20m up the road. I literally ran to the car. Together, we drove a kilometer or two up a sand road until we reached a small cabin tucked away at the end of the track.

Henry Jones killed the engine.

"Come on, let me show you a sight for sore eyes," he said, leaping from the car. I followed him cautiously. Instinctively, I locked the car door and double-checked it to make certain that thieves couldn't open it. "That won't be necessary here," he commented.

"I guess not," I mumbled sheepishly, not having seen another soul for miles around. It felt good to stretch my legs after the long ride, but there was no mistaking that I felt out of place in nature. I frantically waved my mobile phone in the air, trying to find a signal for Whatsapp. I'm sure my discomfort was noticeable, but Henry Jones never let on. He knew exactly where to find the front door key. He'd clearly visited this cottage before.

"Welcome," he declared, as he opened the front door and motioned for me to enter the cabin. I did as I was instructed. The room was dimly lit. A few, misplaced slits in the closed window shutters filtered thin beams of light into the room, so I could just make out my surroundings. The cabin was just big enough to house two single beds, a table with three chairs and an open-plan kitchen area. It bore only the essentials but had a rustic charm.

"Just wait until you see this ..." Henry Jones said reverently. He unlatched and pushed open the window shutters on the opposite side of the cabin. An explosion of glorious sunlight immediately blinded me. Seconds later, I heard a door unbolt and I was hit by another blast of light. I shuffled towards the brightness.

The cabin opened on to a large balcony overlooking a range of mountains that rolled on and on as far as the eye could see. The strange, exotic colors that had been splashed against this canvas stunned me. Copper rock outcrops punctuated light shades of purple, green and blue. These pastel colors washed in and out of each other as they rolled their way down the valley to the hazy horizon in the distance. It was only when my eyes had adjusted to the sunlight that I was able to fully comprehend the beauty and splendor in front of me.

"My God!" I gasped.

"Indeed." Henry Jones stood motionless beside me. Suspended in awe, time stood still. In that moment, facing that view, I felt ... transient. I knew beyond a shadow of a doubt that my existence would come and go in a blink of an eye, but the mountains before me would remain unchanged for another 100 million years and more.

I stood there for some time, speechless. I thought about the pathetic tantrum I'd thrown earlier that morning. It now seemed so unnecessary and stupid. Henry Jones was so patient with me. I spent several minutes listening to my thoughts and wondering just who was doing the talking.

That night we made supper together and discussed the contents of the book we would write together, as well as the process that lay ahead of me in the next 72 hours.

"But how can you be certain this process will work for me?" I asked.

"It works for everyone," he assured me.

"But what if I get so hungry that I can't think straight?"

"That won't happen," he promised. "Remember, fasting is a mental exercise. Clearing your body has a way of clearing your head. You'll discover this soon enough."

"But what if I've something important to say to you?"

"Stay quiet."

I groaned loudly.

He smiled sympathetically at my animated objection. "Let's go over the details one more time, shall we? From sunrise tomorrow morning, you won't utter a sound until it sets on the third day. Three days of silence! Got it?"

"Yes," I huffed.

"We'll walk up to the viewing area at first light. There you'll make a circle of stones about one meter in diameter and force yourself to sit inside it for three days."

"I can't move out of the circle at any time?" I exclaimed.

"Well, you can leave the circle to relieve yourself and to sleep. That's all."

I made a face.

"And you can't sleep during the day! You need to be awake from sunrise to sunset. That rule shouldn't be broken. Understood?"

"Understood. But I can take drinking water and a notepad and pen, right?"

"Yes. Take lots of water. You can drink as often as you like. It's also very important to write down your most significant thoughts and feelings, especially personal realizations! These notes are essential to the process. One more thing: Don't try to manage your thoughts – just allow them to be. When you observe them in a passive state, the process takes effect."

Henry Jones leaned towards me. The candle on the table flickered in the draft and the cabin shimmered eerily. "It's an extremely powerful exercise," he stated slowly. "There's a constant battle in your head between your ego-mind and your true-self. Your ego-mind thinks it's the boss because most times you let it rule you. But when your true-self decides not to eat, speak or move for a period of time, your ego-mind will learn that there's absolutely nothing it can do about it. It can't change the situation, no matter how hard it tries. It'll eventually realize that your true-self is the ultimate decision-maker in your life."

My eyes widened.

"You can expect your ego-mind to try everything in its power to get you to move, or talk, or break the fast. Don't succumb to it. Push on with the process and you'll experience an extraordinary event. Your ego-mind will eventually break down completely, and you'll start to think about your life from the perspective of your true-self. When you learn how to still your ego-mind and listen to your true-self, your life will never be the same."

These words rang in my ears as I lay in bed that evening. I tried to sleep, but the darkness of night was a palette for my restless mind. I'd never done such a radical exercise. Yes, sickness had slowed me down a bit, but I was still busier than most people I knew. Would I cope? Would I quit? Would I find my true-self? I wondered.

I lay awake for hours, or so it seemed. I checked my watch and was surprised to discover it was only 10.33pm. It'd been another full day and I was relieved when sleep finally found me.

In the morning, we executed Henry Jones's plan for me with the precision of a Swiss watch. Extracts from my notes best tell the story:

Day One: *I've been sitting still for a few hours now. My head is very busy. Random thoughts race through my mind constantly. I'm trying to be watchful of them, but this is much harder than it sounds. I'm also trying to allow them to be, as Henry Jones suggested, but that isn't working very well. I keep trying to control their outcome.*

The little voice inside my head talks constantly about anything and everything. I'm easily distracted. I feel frustrated. If I wasn't sick, I sure as heck wouldn't be sitting here. The view is magnificent, but my bum is sore, and I'm bored.

(Break) It's late afternoon now. Time is dragging. Seriously! Each second is like a minute. This has been the longest day of my life. I think my mind is settling down. I don't think about moving, or making a noise, or food as much anymore. I just say: "NO!" There's a part of me that desperately wants to move around and talk, sing or hum, and eat. I'm very aware of it. It's part of me but separate from me (I hope this makes sense later). I know this exercise is for my own good, so I'm determined to see it through to the end.'

Day Two: *After 24 hours of solitude, silence and fasting, my mind is far less active. I've detached from my thinking (that's the best way I can describe it). I can 'see' my thoughts more clearly because I've nothing else to do but observe them. In this state, I can distinguish between the thinking patterns of my ego-mind and that of my true-self. Henry Jones was right (again!). There's a distinct difference between them. My ego-mind is frenetic and erratic. Those thoughts try to distract me and they hold no substance or value for me or anyone else. I occasionally* *catch myself thinking negatively about someone or something. These thoughts really do make me feel bad. I get it now. I understand what Henry Jones means when he says they originate from my lower-self. I know I must transcend them, or they'll keep me bogged down in complex negativity forever.*

On the other hand, the thoughts that originate from my true-self, my higher-self, are simple, yet profound. They resolve conflict and drama and make me feel happy.

(Break). After 36 hours, I've grown to appreciate the stillness around me. It has helped me to find stillness within. There's no real contest between the ego-mind and the true-self. The true-self is vastly superior in every way. A great sense of freedom has come over me. I feel very alive. I can do this! I think I'm going to be okay.

Day Three: *At last, I have found peace of mind. Truly, I have! I am at one with myself, my true-self, and it feels wonderful! There are periods of time when I don't think at all. I'm very aware of my surroundings in these moments of nothingness. I am myself. I feel at ease. I have nothing to fear. Everything is exactly as it should be (I've heard that before). Occasionally, wayward thoughts pop into my head, but I'm able to recognize them as mere distractions of my ego-mind. They offer no value and are meaningless. I push these thoughts aside easily. Every so often, 'real' thoughts surface in my mind. They are clearer, more powerful, and more significant. They are relevant to my highest good. They are never negative. These thoughts emanate from within, as if spoken by my inner voice or intuition. They are final. I don't have to dwell on them. I know at once they are the truth – a profound truth that resonates with my inner core. They take no nonsense from my ego-mind. These thoughts change me – irrevocably, completely and permanently. The realizations are simple, yet profound. They unlock the doors of perception in which my ego-mind has imprisoned me. Issues that I clung to for a long time have lost their hold over me. They have also lost their grip on my future.*

(Break) It's almost evening. The Sun is lingering on the horizon. I feel as though I have a sword of light in my hands and I'm able to cut through what is real (because my true-self accepts it as being real) and what is unreal (because it has been fabricated by my ego-mind).

For the first time, I'm able to see my reality as an intricate web of illusions – and I was caught in the middle of it. Many of these illusions are false perceptions spun by my ego-mind. I see this now. I've harboured them for too long. I realize that they don't offer me value, so I toss them aside. No negativity is spared. On the other hand, I take ownership of my intuitive thoughts, or real thoughts. I know they offer me value because they fill me with love, peace and bliss.

I'm experiencing moments of sheer bliss. I'm filled with excitement and enthusiasm for life. These thoughts are precious. My true-self rejoices in them. They fill me with great joy and lift me closer to Almighty God (quite a turn-around for a non-believer!). I know that my healing process has begun.

In my physical body, I'm aware of twitches and twinges that feel like little electric shocks. It's as though I'm a tightly wound elastic band that's slowly unraveling, knot by knot. Each time this happens, I feel a release within and I give thanks to God.

I find that by holding an empty mind, the "coming undone" sensation occurs more easily. When I meditate on this state of nothingness, surges of energy are released through my body. I imagine God touches me in these moments. By focusing on my breathing, my state of awareness is heightened and I'm able to work with the energy that's released within me. As I exhale, I consciously release the tension in my body. Then I'm able to relax so deeply that it feels like I'm no longer in my body at all. My entire being is a state of consciousness. I feel very close to God right now.

Taken out of context, my notes may seem melodramatic, but at the time, my observations were very real, powerful and moving. Henry Jones joined me just before sunset on the third and final day. I caught glimpses of him several times during the process, especially at sunrise and sunset. He watched over me like a guardian in the distance. We had a security system: He had told me to place a pebble on a nearby rock and remove it if I genuinely needed help or assistance. I never did.

Entering my campsite, he took the pebble from the rock and placed it in my hand. That was my first human contact in three days and it was warm and reassuring. I'm not sure why, but I kept the pebble as a memento. We sat in silence together and watched a red Sun steadily sink into wave-like mountains in the distance. Gold and pink clouds streaked across the sky like the tails of the galloping horses of the Gods. It was a beautiful sunset – just for the two of us – a befitting end to this powerful process.

"We did it!" I shouted at the top of my voice as the last ember of sunlight went out. The echo carried my voice through the valley below and yonder, announcing our victory to the world.

"You did it, my friend, and I'm very, very proud of you," Henry Jones said with genuine tears in his eyes.

I grabbed him in my arms, lifted him off his feet, and swayed him from side to side in a Dr Sahib-like grip. It was one of the greatest highlights of my life!

After that, I spoke a lot. I was a real chatterbox, which was so unlike me. I spoke constantly while we walked back to the cabin, made a fire, prepared dinner and did the dishes. In retrospect, Henry Jones washed up. I watched him while I spoke. Strangely, conversation was a priority over food. Sure, I was hungry. I had even contemplated eating a grasshopper that jumped within my reach on day one, but that was as close as I got to filling the hole in my stomach. A fruit salad had never tasted so good. I was on a natural high. It felt weird to feel so good, especially without medication. I hadn't taken any painkillers during the process. Yes, I had experienced moments of discomfort, but I pushed through them. I wondered if I'd broken my dependency on medication. I'd grown accustomed to carrying a little bottle of pills with me. They reminded me I was sick. It was liberating not having them with me for those three days.

"Is it mandatory for everyone to complete this process on their healing journey?" I asked.

"Nope," he replied, packing away the last of the dishes. "It's not necessary to follow the process to a tee. The point of the exercise is merely to get the ego-mind to submit to the fact that the true-self is the ultimate decision-maker and authority in one's life. To achieve this, people can stay at home and take a vow of silence; or fast; or stay in isolation while eating regularly. It doesn't really matter how they mix it up. Of course, the more they put into it, the more they'll get out of it."

"What do you recommend?" I probed.

"If the patient is able to fast, meditate and be alone, then I highly recommend the Full Monty," he said, wringing out the dishcloth.

"Like I did?"

"Yes. Exactly! Together, fasting, meditation, silence and isolation pack a powerful punch. They'll teach most egos who's boss. This exercise is essential. The healing process can only begin when power and control is returned to the true-self."

I puffed up my chest. I'd learned a valuable life-lesson and I was proud of myself. Not in an egotistical way. I could only liken it to the feeling you get when you've done something well. Only, that felt more significant.

"So, what's next?" I asked curiously.

"I suggest we sit by the fire," he replied. "It's a full moon tonight and the stars will be out."

"I meant, what's next on our healing journey?" I asked, as we carried our seats to the fire.

"I know what you meant," he chortled. "Have I unleashed a tiger, or what?"

"I'm just excited and interested to learn more," I answered back.

"That's good. Getting in touch with your true-self makes you feel alive. This 'aliveness' is the source of healing. It gives you the energy you need to feel better about yourself mentally, physically, spiritually and emotionally."

"I do feel much stronger," I told him. "I'm ready to embrace a brand-new approach to life."

"It's amazing how much better you feel when you take a break from your ego-mind, isn't it?" Henry Jones commented, throwing a log onto the fire.

The burning embers crackled like gunshots. We sat chatting beside the fire for a while. Despite my best efforts to stay alert, the flickering flames eventually hypnotized me. My thoughts were lured into the roaring coals, and I finally slipped into silence and my eyelids began to droop. There was simply no fuel left in my tank. Henry Jones, on the other hand, was wide awake. As much as I wanted to stay up and talk more, my soft mattress was calling me.

"I'm beat," I mumbled reluctantly.

He nodded. "You should get some rest. We've lots of work to do tomorrow!"

"Work?" I gasped.

"Yes, if you're up for it? I'd like to start working on our book. I'll share with you plenty of simple yet powerful techniques that will keep you in touch with your true-self."

I pointed my fingers at him like a pistol, fired off an imaginary shot, and retreated to bed. I fell asleep in seconds.

CHAPTER 10

THE SPIDER, THE DUCK AND THE FAKE SNAKE

I awoke at sunrise with Henry Jones tugging on my shoulder. "It's time to stir your soul from slumber, my friend. We have plenty of powerful healing techniques to discuss. This is your wake-up call."

"Eh, what?" I groaned, befuddled.

"I've made breakfast for us, and I'm sure you'll love it," he declared. "You'll swear your taste buds are in heaven."

"How on Earth are you always so chipper in the mornings?" I whined.

"Look!" he responded, pulling open the curtains. The dawn spilled into the room. It was light-grey outside – cloudy, almost overcast. I buried my head in my pillow.

"Leave me alone," I groaned.

"Can you see the extraordinary opportunity this day offers us? Today is the first day of the rest of our lives. It's ours for the taking."

"Enough with the clichés," I sneered. My old self was back. The fire inside me had gone out.

So soon? Is it gone for good? I wondered. Panic hit me like a bucket of cold water in the face. I jumped up and got dressed.

"All of a sudden, you look like a man who overslept and is about to miss his train," Henry Jones observed.

I didn't want to tell him how I felt inside or to disappoint him. The negative thinking was back, and I was scared.

Why can't I stay on track? Have I lost the plot? I wondered.

The breakfast was tasty, but I was too distracted to fully appreciate it. The walk afterwards made me even more pensive. A part of me wanted to run back to the viewing area, make a ring of stones and sit inside it again, but that wasn't practical. I started to worry about myself – the kind of worry that chews a hole in your gut. I was afraid I wouldn't get better and that I would never get the chance to make up with my wife. I was terrified my healing journey would be a dead-end and I'd find myself back in hospital with doctors and interns prodding me with their cold, clammy fingers. I could've stewed in my pity-filled thoughts all day long. Luckily, Henry Jones had other plans for me.

"Let's get started, my friend," he said cheerfully as he thumped his thick, brown envelope on to the small table in the cabin.

"Where do we begin?" I asked.

"I'm going to show you how to get in touch with your inner-self."

"I got in touch with my inner-self yesterday. That's the last time I use single-ply toilet paper," I joked.

The three questions

Henry Jones tried not to smile. "I'm going to ask you three questions, and I want you to think about your answers carefully. Write them down on a piece of paper. Take your time … What have you done in your past that you think was wrong?" Henry Jones paused. "What are you ashamed of? And what are you afraid of?"

"Have you got more writing paper for me?" I jested. He smiled compassionately.

"Jot down whatever springs to mind. There's usually something specific that leaps out. I say this with certainty because fear, shame and guilt lurk inside us all. They are the primary vices that the ego-mind uses to control us. The purpose of this exercise is to access the dark recesses of your mind. This is a rare chance for you to exorcize the demons that haunt your consciousness. Spew everything! Get it all out of you and on to the paper."

I was reticent at first, but got swept up in the process once I started writing down my answers. Old, painful memories came flooding back to me. I scribbled as fast as I could. It wasn't a pleasant exercise. Who wants to remember the things they've done wrong? Certainly not those of us who strive so hard to be right all the time. Who likes to admit that they're ashamed or afraid? I took all the time I needed to complete my list. Henry Jones kept himself busy. I guess an hour or two ground by. Eventually, I was ready.

"There it is! Every sordid detail of my wrong-doings! Now what?" I said, flinging the pages across the table. I'm not sure why I flung them at Henry Jones. Perhaps I wanted to be rid of them. He collected them calmly and handed them back to me.

"Now do this: Take several minutes to dwell on the issues that came to mind. Focus your complete attention on them. I want you to tune in to how these memories make you feel."

I obeyed. A few minutes passed. "Done?"

"Yes," I mumbled.

"And?"

"I don't feel good," I barked, slapping the table. My hand was stinging. "When I think about all the things I've done wrong, I don't like myself. And when I think about the things I fear, I feel anxious, worried and scared."

"Exactly! Thinking about fear, shame or guilt makes you feel under attack, doesn't it? When you think of fear, you anticipate pain, and when you think of shame and guilt, you expect punishment. These responses cause you to feel attacked. That is a classic attribute of your ego-mind. Whenever your thoughts harm you, they come from your ego-mind."

"I also feel a bit nauseous," I added.

"I'm not surprised. Fear, shame and guilt induce a physical reaction in the body. If the memory or thought is strong enough, the physical response can be violent. Have you ever experienced a terrible fright and then felt nauseous afterwards? Have you ever been consumed with guilt and felt sick to your stomach? It's important that you really understand how negative emotions affect your body. For now, it's enough to know that guilt, shame and fear make you feel sick. Accepted?"

"Yes."

"Good. Now let me ask you this: What do you think happens when you keep guilt, shame or fear locked up inside of you for a long time?"

I guessed the answer he sought, but I didn't give it to him.

He pushed on. "You told me about your ex-fiancée, but have you suppressed other negative emotions? Emotions that you just couldn't deal with at the time, or simply chose not to process at all?"

Violent memories from my childhood flashed through my mind. Inner rage instantly surged up within me. My father had been mean-spirited and cruel. He had emotionally abused my mother and me. I used to fantasize about expressing my anger towards him, but I never did, for fear he would laugh at me or beat me. I never understood why she stayed with him. As a child, I had wanted to escape his clutches, but couldn't. I was trapped by circumstance until I finally left home to join the marines at the age of 18. I never returned home and never even attended his funeral. Henry Jones read the sad expression on my face.

"Don't worry. You're not alone. We've all experienced negative emotions that we couldn't face at the time. Instead of processing these feelings in a healthy way, we attempt to block them out or bury them. As we've discussed before, it's quite normal to move away from what causes us pain. But that reaction doesn't solve the problem, does it?"

"No. I guess not," I said, sucking air between my clenched teeth, trying to cool the anger within.

"We can't avoid feeling negative emotions, my friend. They exist within us. By shelving them, we store them up. We may not notice their effects, but they weigh us down, until eventually we can't take the internal pressure any longer and something physical gives in," Henry Jones said, rubbing my back affectionately.

Suppressing your emotions makes you sick

"Suppressing your emotions is a temporary coping mechanism. It spares you from feeling bad in the moment, but it's detrimental to your health in the long run. Anyone suppressing fears of rejection, abandonment, lack of money, failure, sickness, death or any other personal issue is sitting on a time bomb – one that can explode at any second.

"Make no mistake, fear, shame and guilt spawn disease and pain. If you hold on to these negative emotions, the external attack will eventually manifest internally. Listen to me carefully, my friend. If you're holding on to fear, shame or guilt, then you must do whatever it takes to let them go. You need to identify and deal with the issues in your life that make you feel guilty, ashamed or afraid. Don't try to justify or validate these emotions. They are killers! You must deal with them."

"What should I do? Tell me, please."

"Luckily for you, my notes contain a highly effective process to release fear, shame and guilt. We must include it in our book. It's imperative that we show our readers exactly how to deal with fear, shame and guilt, once and for all."

"Can we do it now?" I asked, somewhat surprised at my own enthusiasm.

"All in good time," replied Henry Jones. "Just keep on making daily progress and we'll get to emotional healing before you know it. Right now, though, I want to discuss something else very powerful that will put you in touch with your true-self."

"What is that?"

The power of forgiveness

"Forgiveness."

The word made me cringe. I wasn't sure why.

"It's essential to forgive yourself and others, especially on a healing journey. At some point in the near future, when we get to your spiritual healing process, I'm going to introduce you to a friend of mine. I'm sure Swami G will cover this topic with you. Today, however, I just want to plant the seed in your mind. Tell me: Can you think of anyone from your past or present whom you have not forgiven for a perceived wrong?"

"Sure. Lots of people," I mumbled.

"Who stands out in your mind?"

I shrugged. "I suppose my ex-fiancée and my father. But I could probably produce a list as long as my arm, if you gave me more time."

"And how did you deal with these damaged relationships?" he asked.

"Effectively!" I replied without hesitation.

Henry Jones raised his eyebrows and cocked his head. I knew he wanted me to explain further.

"I severed my relationships with them so that they couldn't hurt me any further."

Henry Jones froze and closed his eyes. I looked away, then glanced back at him. He never said a word.

"Seriously! They're all out of my life. Gone for good. I've put them behind me."

Henry Jones eventually spoke: "A lack of forgiveness binds you to your transgressors."

It hit me like a ton of bricks.

"You may have cut ties with these individuals, but you're emotionally bound to that which you think they've done wrong. This keeps you tied up in resentment, bitterness, hatred and loathing. Of course, this is just another tactic your ego-mind uses to keep you trapped in the past. It tricks you into believing that by killing the relationship, you bury the hurtful emotions. Hah! Don't buy it! They surface the instant you think about the person. Trust me on this: You'll never be free from your ego-mind unless you're truly able to forgive those people you think have harmed you in some way. Forgiveness is a crucial part of the healing process. It enables you to let go and move on!"

Forgive yourself

"While we're on the subject of letting go and moving on, you should know that it's also vital to forgive yourself for the things you think you've done wrong."

"Me?" I asked foolishly.

"Yes, you! Are all the people on your list entirely to blame for your unhappiness, or were you at fault, too?"

I didn't have to think about my answer. "No, I've made my fair share of mistakes," I admitted.

"And can you genuinely say you've forgiven yourself?"

I had to think about this one. What did that mean? How do you forgive yourself? I couldn't recall sitting down and forgiving myself, ever. I wouldn't have known where to start the process.

"Many people find it easier to forgive others than to forgive themselves," Henry Jones said. "Self-forgiveness is different from justifying your actions or rationalizing your behavior. It's not about making excuses for yourself. It's about you coming to terms with the fact that your ego-mind has wronged your true-self. Try this exercise: Think of your true-self as another person. Think of the values, morals and principles that are important to that kind of individual. Now ask yourself: How often have you hurt, violated, offended, disappointed or embarrassed that person?"

I looked away in shame.

"Do you owe that person an apology?"

I nodded.

"Good. That is another breakthrough for you, my friend. The good news is that your true-self is quick to forgive. I strongly suggest that you put it to the test. Forgiveness unlocks and releases negative emotions that would otherwise be stored in your system! This is essential."

"If we don't release stored negative emotions, they ultimately manifest as disease," I interjected sheepishly.

"Exactly! Even trivial transgressions, if not forgiven and released, can result in disease."

"So, what should I do now?" I asked.

Take action

"If you want to heal your body, there are three things you must do." He lifted his hand and counted them down on his fingers. One: Make a list of all the people in your life that you need to forgive, and then call them or visit them to tell them you forgive them. Two: Make a list of all the people you think you've wronged, and then call them or visit them to apologize and ask for forgiveness. Three: Make a list of all the things your ego-mind has done to wrong your true-self and ask your true-self to forgive them all."

"Are you serious?"

"Yes."

"I don't think I can do that?"

"Why? What are you afraid of?"

"I'm afraid the people concerned will think I've lost my mind or that I'm weak!" I exclaimed.

"The weak can never forgive, my friend. Forgiveness is an attribute of the strong. That's what Mahatma Gandhi said," he replied.

I quickly played through a few scenarios in my mind. They gave me the heebie-jeebies. Some seemed impossible. "But what if the individuals are dead?" I asked.

"Imagine they're sitting beside you and then tell them exactly how you feel. Don't just think about it. It's important that you vocalize and then release your feelings."

"I'll definitely need to do this in a private place, or people will think I've gone crazy," I exclaimed.

Henry Jones chortled for a moment and then grew serious.

Forgiveness restores the body

He looked at me intently. "Don't put off this exercise, my friend. As hard as it seems, it's essential to forgive yourself and others. Listen closely to what I'm about to tell you. Love is the one true force that binds the universe together. You'll feel a permanent 'separateness' until forgiveness makes you whole again. Forgiveness heals. It restores peace and harmony. I promise you this: When peace and harmony are restored in your mind, then peace and harmony will be restored in your body."

I thought about the people in my life whom I needed to forgive and ask for forgiveness. Henry Jones was right again. I felt both separated from them and connected to them. I was separated from them because I'd cut them out of my life and severed my emotional ties with them, but I was connected to the pain they had caused me, and the pain I had caused them. The idea of engaging with them again terrified me. What if they rejected me? Would I be humiliated? Would I lose my sense of power over them?

In my gut, I knew that my greatest fear was that my marriage was over. I was about to lose the one person who had loved me unconditionally. I'd driven her away. I desperately wanted her back in my life again, but I couldn't face admitting to my mistakes. I clung to my personal power as though it was all I had left. Call it pride, stubbornness or stupidity, my ego-mind had me in its grip. I could feel it squeezing the life out of both me and my marriage.

"I'm afraid of rejection and humiliation." I blurted aloud, much to my horror.

Henry Jones never flinched. "There's nothing more damaging to your health and more destructive to your well-being than not confronting your fears," he said. "You've got to realize that you can't run away or hide from your fears. They exist in your head, so you take them with you wherever you go."

"But, I don't have to think about them," I retorted.

"You can't escape your fears by ignoring them. The longer you put them off, the worse they get – mostly because you worry about them – and worry is a killer!"

I knew he was right. I'd spent weeks in hospital unsuccessfully trying not to think about my failing marriage, miserable boss and ailing physical condition. But, I was afraid my marriage, job and quality of life were over. I was worried sick.

"Here's something else to keep in mind: Whatever you dwell upon grows in your experience. You'll learn more about this phenomenon when we discuss the law of attraction in due course. For now, though, I need to warn you not to obsess over your fears. What you fear most will come upon you.

Fear is a very strong emotion and therefore a powerful creative force. Until you confront your fears on your own terms, they'll manifest in your life on their terms. Your fears will haunt you until you finally deal with them – or they deal with you. Got it?"

"Yup," I gulped. My throat was dry. I needed something to quench my thirst.

Facing my worst fear

Standing on tip-toes, I reached for a glass on the top shelf and pulled it towards me. To my absolute horror, a spider dropped from the top shelf and landed on the shelf below, eye-level with me. To say that I have an unreasonable fear of spiders is a gross understatement. The sight of anything with eight legs freaks me out. It's their 'legginess' and erratic movements that disturb me. Fortunately, most spiders are small and easily squashed by a shoe. This was not one of those. It was huge! Inches from my nose, I could tell its body was furry and smooth. It had inconspicuous shades of brown and grey on its back with reddish patches over its mouthparts. Its extraordinarily long legs were twisted in such a way that they extended forward in a crab-like fashion. I was close enough to see eight eyes in two forward-facing rows – four eyes on each side. Squinting, I could tell they were staring right at me and the spider looked very, very angry.

I let out a blood-curdling scream and leaped backwards like an Olympic backstroke champion at the clap of a start gun.

"It's a huntsman spider," Henry Jones yelled excitedly.

"I don't care. I'm going to kill it," I shouted.

The spider heard me and took off with astonishing speed. I howled and jumped on to the nearest chair.

"Calm down," Henry Jones said.

"When you see an eight-legged intruder rapidly scuttling across the floor, it's a perfectly natural response to shit yourself," I barked.

Seeing the spider was a problem, but it became a bigger problem when it disappeared behind a curtain.

"Spiders are beneficial predators. They're good to have around," Henry Jones said.

I was having none of it. "Find it! Kill it!"

"Killing them should only be a last resort. I'll get rid of it by using the old jar and paper trick."

He found a transparent glass jar in the kitchen cupboard. I looked on in terror as he shook the curtain and the spider fell to the floor.

"I'll catch it now. Except if it moves, then I'm going to scream, jump and run for it, too," he told me. I climbed from the chair to the table.

He chuckled and casually placed the jar over the spider.

"Make sure the rim of the glass is flat against the ground so the spider can't crawl out," I advised from afar.

He slid a folded piece of paper under the jar and pushed it through to the other side. The spider was trapped. I insisted he ensure the makeshift prison was secure.

He flipped the jar and leaned in to admire the creature.

"Out, out, out!" I yelled, shooing him and the spider out of the cottage with a broom. He released it in the garden. The thought of it being there kept me on edge for the rest of my stay at the cottage. In fact, it still does!

"Let's put a positive spin on that experience, shall we?" Henry Jones said upon his return. "The good news is that in most cases, confronting your fears is never as bad as it seems. In fact, you feel empowered when you muster the courage to take action. Do it, and you'll see that facing your fears builds character. It makes you realize your true potential, which brings you closer to your true-self."

After the incident with the spider, I needed a lot more convincing. "So, what's the best way to overcome fear?"

Fight fear

"The first thing you need to know is that there are two kinds of fear: There's fear that you can do something about, and then there's fear that you can't do anything about. Try this: Take out the list of things of which you are afraid. Divide them into these two categories: Whatever you can do something about – do it. Wherever you can't do anything – let it go. For example, if you're fearful that you haven't got the money to pay your bills, phone your creditors immediately and explain your situation. I guarantee you'll feel better afterwards, and they'll be the ones pacing up and down. On the other hand, if you're fearful about dying in a nuclear war, let it go. There's absolutely nothing you can do about that situation, so why bother wasting your time worrying about it? Get it?"

"Yes, but I'm still worried about being rejected or humiliated."

Why worry?

Henry Jones grinned. "We tend to spend a lot of time worrying about stuff that never happens."

"I'm still worrying about that spider. What if he had a mate?" I shuddered.

Henry Jones brushed it off. "Worrying never accomplishes anything. It only drives the worrier to distraction. Worry can keep your thoughts tied up for hours – even days, months and years!"

A groan escaped my throat.

"You've allowed your thoughts to twist around every possible scenario, looking at ways for things to go wrong, haven't you?"

"Yes."

"And where did that get you?"

"Nowhere."

"Precisely! There's no point worrying. All it does is send destructive signals out into the universe without sorting anything out. Worrying is a classic attribute of your ego-mind. It's a highly effective way to keep your head busy. Worrying fuels your ego-mind, too. You can't have peace of mind when you're worrying about stuff. And, as you now know, peace of mind is an attribute of your true-self."

Stop worrying in 30 seconds

"Before I did the three-day process, I hadn't experienced peace of mind for a very long time," I admitted.

"In that case, let me show you how to stop worrying in 30 seconds. Seriously!"

"Okay, let's go," I said, egging him on.

"The principle is this: Worry is nothing more than a bad-thinking habit. Like all bad habits, it can and must be broken. Write down what is worrying you. Your problems become much clearer once you've distilled your thinking into writing. Next, write down the scenarios or outcomes that are most likely to happen. Then, choose the outcome that you most prefer and do everything in your power to make that happen."

"That seems simple."

"Yes ... but that's the beauty of it. It's that simple, and it works!"

I frowned.

"Don't knock it 'til you've tried it," said Henry Jones. "The process is highly effective. But, it gets even better. You must continue the exercise by writing down your plan of action. Ask yourself: What must I do? When must I do it? With whom must I speak? What will I say?"

Come up with an action plan

"When you've got the answers to all the key questions, then put your plan into action. The bottom line is this: You won't have time to worry because you'll be too busy working on your plan. Oh, before I forget, you must refer to your plan regularly, and tick off what you've done once you've done it, okay?"

"Okay, I can handle that. But I'm still concerned about the fears and worries I can't do anything about. For example: I can't quit my job, even though I hate it, I need the money. I can't make my wife take me back. I can't change my test results. What if I can't resolve these situations? What if they're out of my control? What if the people involved don't play ball?"

"If you truly believe you can't change these things, let go. Just let go."

"What do you mean, let go?" I barked.

"I mean let go of the outcome you think might happen."

"How do I do that?"

"It's easy. Follow these simple instructions: Fill your head with positive thoughts; hope for the best; do your best; trust that you'll get the result that's best for you; and surrender the outcome to the will of the Divine. That's the way to stop worrying and start living. There's an amazing book called exactly that: *How To Stop Worrying And Start Living*, by Dale Carnegie. Get your hands on it and read it, twice. It made a huge difference to my life, and I'm convinced it'll do the same for you, too."

"You make it sound so easy – almost child's play."

"What's wrong with that? Children are wonderful teachers. You can learn a lot from them."

"How so?"

"For one thing, they can show you how to live from your true-self. Seriously. If you want to speed up your healing process, spend more time with children. Observe their behavior closely. You'll notice that children are open and trusting. They're not afraid to be vulnerable and defenceless. They don't judge. They're curious instead of skeptical. They live in the now.

Children like to play and have fun. They get over emotions quickly. They're genuine, expansive and loving … and, most of all, they love themselves. What outstanding qualities of your true-self!"

"I find children annoying," I remarked.

"Oh dear. That's sad news," replied Henry Jones. "Someone who doesn't like children is not in touch with their own inner child."

"My what?" I huffed.

Discover your inner child

"Your inner child. We all have one. It's the part of us that never grows up. It's our connection to our younger selves – our earliest memories. We may get older and more rigid and serious, but the child within us always stays young. Connecting with your inner child is very good for you. It's very healthy to unleash your childlike qualities, especially on a healing journey. I double dare you to practise one childlike quality per day for the rest of your healing journey. You'll be amazed at the effect it'll have on you."

"Let me get this straight: I'm going through the worst time of my life and you're suggesting that I deliberately act like a child?"

"Precisely! I guarantee you'll feel younger, more energetic, lighter, and better. Go on. Give it a go. Don't be too big for your boots," Henry Jones said. Then he did the strangest thing. He put his thumbs in his ears, wriggled his fingers and pulled a face at me.

I was dumbfounded. It'd been decades since anymore had treated me like a child. Under normal circumstances, I'd have blown my top, but on this occasion, I burst out laughing. It came from deep within me. I laughed so hard that my stomach wobbled and my shoulders shook. I literally howled with laughter. Henry Jones watched in utter amazement. He never broke a smile. That made me laugh even harder. Tears ran down my cheeks. Then, without any consideration, I did the strangest thing. I stuck out my tongue at him and squinted.

That was completely out of the ordinary for me. It shattered the mould I'd made of myself, and it felt fantastic. Henry Jones caught my giggles. We enjoyed a good, long, healthy laugh together. I will always treasure that moment.

"That felt good, really good," I managed to splutter.

It's the little things in life

"Laughter is good medicine," Henry Jones stressed. "It's very important to make time for the little things in life that bring you pleasure, such as laughter. They are a great tonic for your true-self. They make life more enjoyable; rewarding; pleasing; stimulating; satisfying; worthwhile and gratifying. This is especially true when you feel poorly. If you want to feel a bit better, I've got the perfect remedy for you." He scratched around in his notes and then handed me another piece of paper with the following suggestions written on it:

> *Pick someone flowers. Play the fool. Use your imagination. Sing in the shower. Catch the sunrise. Give yourself a massage. Pamper yourself. Read a good book. Wiggle your toes. Put your feet up. Meditate daily. Give unconditionally. Run on a beach. Play with children. Make a fire. Walk in the rain. Shake a leg. Sleep under the stars. Let your hair down. Watch the Sun set. Share your smile. Be kind to a stranger. Have some fun. Work in the garden. Wish upon a star. Stamp your feet. Scream out loud. Hug a tree. Stop to smell the roses. Go on a picnic. Visit the countryside. Paint a picture. Dance like no one is watching. Walk barefoot on green grass.*

The list went on and on. I read it to the end and then remarked: "It's been a very long time since I've done any of these things."

"Read the list again and tell me how it makes you feel."

"It makes me feel good."

"Ah huh! So now, if merely reading these suggestions has a positive effect on you, just imagine how awesome you'll feel when you put them into practice. You should make time to do these exercises. I guarantee they'll lift your spirits, connect you with your true-self and remind you that it's great to be alive."

"I don't have the time," I responded abruptly. "I'm so busy with my work that I barely have time to think about anything else."

Love is a doing word

Henry Jones studied me closely. "You know what your problem is?" he asked.

"Tell me."

"You don't love yourself enough," he declared.

"What do you mean?" I barked defensively.

"I need you to tell me what love is."

"Huh?"

"What is love?"

I was taken aback. I tried to think of something clever to say, but my mind went blank. "It's just something you feel," I finally mumbled pathetically.

"No, no! That's not it at all," Henry Jones was quick to respond. "You've got it all wrong. Love is something you do. It's the practice of kindness; tenderness; patience; gentleness; compassion; consideration; understanding; affection; caring; light-heartedness, honour and respect. That's what loving is all about! When someone says they love you without showing you – by being 'loving' towards you – their words are empty and meaningless, aren't they?"

"I guess so."

"That's because love is a doing word, my friend. It must be put into action. If you don't make time to love yourself, how can you expect to love someone else? You must first fill your cup with love before it can spill over to fill the cup of others."

"But I have responsibilities. I'm time-poor. I'm a busy man," I protested.

Henry Jones shrugged that off. He literally wiped his shoulders clean. "That's your ego-mind talking, and I don't want to listen to it. Your obsession with work has robbed you of the simple joys of life. Your servitude to your self-imposed responsibilities has ruined your relationship with the ones you love. Tell me: Where has that gotten you?"

I was unable to speak.

"Now isn't the time to be timid," he snapped. "You know the answers I seek. Out with it."

"Sick and alone," I murmured.

"Is that what you want?" he shouted, attempting to provoke me.

His assertiveness startled me. "No," I yelled back.

Love yourself first

"Well then, do something about it, man. Start to love yourself!" Henry Jones pounded his chest like a bass drum. "You deserve it, damn it. I've told you before: You're a unique individual, unlike anyone who has ever lived. Your body is a miracle of nature and your life is a Divine gift. Don't cower behind the complexities of your work, responsibilities, and the pressures of your adult life. That's just your ego-mind tricking you into submission. That's not the life you want for yourself – your true-self. You want to love yourself and to be loved in return. This is the ultimate expression of a life worth living."

"Okay, okay, I get it," I conceded. "Simmer down. At your age, you'll give yourself a heart attack if you continue to go off like that."

His eyes twinkled mischievously. Henry Jones looked thoroughly pleased with the effects of his dramatic outburst. He knew he'd made his point. I was trapped in behavioral patterns that were destroying me and the ones I loved. In that moment, the penny dropped.

"I need to change my behavior if I want to get different results, don't I?"

"Yes, of course! Doing the same thing over and over expecting to get different results is madness," he replied. "You must change your ways."

Trying something new

I felt unwashed from the night before and needed to rinse the image of that darn spider from my head. I couldn't think of a better way to get clean and get some much-needed R&R than by taking a good ol' fashioned bath. I usually prefer to shower, but there was a Victorian-style bath tub at the cottage that appealed to me. It was outdoors. Hidden from the balcony by a bamboo fence on one side, but open to the spectacular view on the other, it was a perfect place to escape the world. It had been a tough morning. The gruelling conversation and gigantic spider had taken their toll on me. Working for a single second longer would have been a mighty challenge. I couldn't resist the appeal of the bathtub.

"Don't hop into that tub just yet! Let me help you to soak in the experience the right way," Henry Jones said, handing me an over-sized bottle of bubble-bath, some essential oils and a fluffy towel.

I rinsed away the dust and residue left by the natural elements and gave the tub a scrub. Then, I enthusiastically plugged the drain and turned on the hot water tap. Henry Jones advised me to begin filling the tub with lukewarm water. I didn't listen to him. I'd been listening to him all morning. Neither did I test the water with my elbow, as he'd suggested, before getting in to ensure the temperature wasn't scalding. I ran the hot water full-blast and poured in copious amounts of scented oils and bubble bath. I filled the tub three-quarters of the way and got right in!

"Ouch!" I yelped, yanking my foot out the bath like I'd stepped on a hot poker. I heard Henry Jones giggle on the balcony as I danced in circles holding my ankle.

"Nobody likes I-told-you-so,'" I reminded him. He giggled harder. I didn't wait for the water to cool down. I topped the tub up to the brim with cold water, and tried again. Once I stepped into the bath, the water level rose quickly and spilled over the sides. Fortunately, the tidal wave spillage could go everywhere because I was outside.

"If the water is too hot, it can agitate your nervous system and can cause a drop in your blood pressure. Your heart will start pumping harder, and you may feel dizzy or sick," Henry Jones called out.

I was too proud to admit that psychedelic orange and red splotches churned on the back of my eyelids. The bath was too hot for me to relax right off the bat. I lay there like a boiling lobster with my legs draped over the sides. Beads of sweat bubbled on my brow and dripped off my nose. I should listen to Henry Jones more often, I reminded myself.

Luckily, the water cooled over time and the outdoor bath transformed into a private spa. I started feeling clean, comforted, and relaxed. Henry Jones played a delightful piece of classical music on the sound system. He turned the volume up so that I could hear it clearly. I appreciated his continuous efforts to make me feel at ease.

Much to my amusement I found a little, yellow, rubber duck on the edge of the bath. That's when the fun began.

"Hey Henry! Where do ducks go when they're sick?"

"No idea!" he shouted back.

"To the ducktor."

"Don't be a wise quacker," he joked.

"Knock knock."

"Who's there?"

"Dwayne."

"Dwayne who?"

"Dwayne the bath I'm drowning," I said, submerging the rubber duck. It bobbed back to the surface.

We kept quackin' jokes until we couldn't think of anything else funny to say.

"I'm loving this bath," I announced.

Love is at the heart of healing

I heard him place a chair on the other side of the thin, bamboo fence. "Good. You need to start practising love. Love has the power to transform all things – and you need to transform yourself right now!"

I listened closely.

"It's necessary to transform yourself to heal your body. You can't first heal your body and then transform yourself. Healing doesn't work that way. You must transform yourself, then you will heal your body."

I sunk lower into deep water.

"Love yourself and love others, and you will be happy. The path to wellness is adorned with happiness. Seek happiness and you will find your way. If you are looking for the fastest way possible to get there, let love lead you. Again, what do you want to achieve right now?"

"I want to heal my body …"

"Well then, you're going to be thrilled when you hear what I'm about to tell you: No matter how sick you are, you can heal yourself through the power of love."

I stared blankly at the befuddled expression on Dwayne the duck's face. An apt name for him, I thought. A few seconds ticked by.

"Pay attention now. These will be the most profound words you'll ever hear from me: Love resides at the heart of healing. Find love within yourself and express it. Love your body. Love others. Love life. But first love yourself. That is fundamental. When you love yourself, your true-self, you will radiate vitality and well-being, your health will return to you, and your life will flourish again. It's not any more complicated than that!"

"Okay, since you're dishing out such great advice. Tell me exactly what I … er, our readers should do."

Henry Jones never said a word. I heard him scribbling on paper like a mad scientist with a brilliant idea in his head. After a minute had passed, he pushed the folded page through the bamboo fence. This is what he wrote:

> *Practise being loving towards yourself.*
> *Give yourself lots of tender, loving care.*
> *Be kind and gentle to yourself.*
> *Give yourself what you really need.*
> *Nurture and pamper your body.*
> *Be patient with yourself.*

I passed the note back to him. "There's plenty more where that came from," he said.

"I will do this," I said, recalling each line carefully. The power of the sentences didn't sink in immediately, but I could feel them drilling into my brain. Processing them would take some time. "I'll also make sure that list goes into your book."

"Good. While you're at it, be sure to tell the readers that love also produces faith and trust. Whatever you do, don't leave that out. Faith and trust are powerful healing forces, too. Faith and trust must be carefully and deliberately cultivated on a healing journey."

"How do you do that?" I asked, scooping up a handful of bubbles and putting them on Dwayne the duck's head for a hat.

"You grow them with dedication, devotion, and commitment. That's how," he replied matter-of-factly. "These qualities are the labour of love." That said, I heard Henry Jones bite into an apple. Loud crunching momentarily distracted me.

"Bombs away," he yelled, lobbing an apple over the fence. It landed with a splash. I wiped soap from my eyes and sunk my teeth into it.

Love leads to belief

"This delicious apple has given me fabulous inspiration. It's a glorious metaphor for our book. You should say this: The fruit of the labour of love is belief. It's the sweetest fruit of all! Believe it."

That statement smacked me over the head. Somehow, I just knew that in my mind I had to string together the pearls of wisdom he so casually weaved into our conversation. Abstract concepts, like faith, trust, love and belief, weren't my thing – they were intangible. I was a realist. My intellectual mind floundered. I was like a duck, calm on the surface, but paddling like crazy underneath to keep up. I knew I needed to fully comprehend what Henry Jones was telling me, and that somehow, I had to stretch my mind to embrace these illusive concepts. I had to stop the insanity of repeating the same behavior while expecting a different outcome.

I wanted to be loved, but I wasn't *loving* towards myself or my loved ones. The sad truth was that love wasn't a 'doing' word for me. I didn't practise kindness; tenderness; patience; gentleness; compassion; consideration; under-standing; affection; caring; light-heartedness, honour or respect. My head filled to the brim with heavy questions: How could I expect my wife to love me when I didn't truly love her in return? How could I expect to heal my body if I didn't treat it with love? How could I start loving myself? I asked myself.

I was doing mental gymnastics. Henry Jones worked his way through his apple while I worked my way through my thoughts. I was like a duck out of water. Neither of us said a word. I had other things on my mind.

Belief comes with practice

Dr Sahib's power word had come back to haunt me again: "Believe." The word rang in my head and echoed through my being. Believe. And then, boom, it happened! All of a sudden, I realized that belief isn't an innate quality. Neither is it some random gift from the gods. Belief is the result of practice. That is what Henry Jones was trying to tell me. Believing that you'll heal your body comes through practice. The more you practise, the stronger your belief grows. The light bulb went on in my head.

"I get it now. I get it now," I cried out to Henry Jones.

"What's that?"

"I understand how to believe. The key is practice. When you tell someone: 'I love you', they'll only believe it when you've been loving towards them. And, when you look in the mirror and say: 'I love myself,' you'll only believe it when you know that you've been loving towards yourself. Oh boy! This changes everything!" I yelled, leaping to my feet. Water sloshed onto the ground.

"Lord love a duck! I think he's got it!" Henry Jones exclaimed.

I cast my eyes towards the heavens. "And when you say to yourself: 'I can heal my body,' you'll only believe it when you've been practising healing techniques. That's it, isn't it?" I yelled, slapping my forehead. I leaped out the bath, jumped up and down and danced in circles. I was ecstatic!

"It may be common sense to you, but this realization is a profound revelation to me," I told him proudly, patting my body dry with the fluffy towel.

"Common sense isn't so common," he replied.

This made me laugh even harder. I paced up and down the bathroom excitedly. "No wonder my wife left me. I wasn't loving towards her. No wonder I'm sick. I wasn't loving towards myself – my true-self. I now get where I was going wrong. I've been tighter than a duck's arse with my emotions. I didn't demonstrate my feelings. I let my ego-mind tie me up with my self-imposed responsibilities and self-importance, anxiety, worry and stress. I tied the knots really, really tight. I could hardly move, never mind escape from the person I'd become. So, do you know what I did? I made myself sick. Sickness was a way out for me. I made myself sick!"

"Eureka!" shouted Henry Jones. "We have another breakthrough. That's the first time you've admitted you made yourself sick. This is a good day, indeed!"

Adorned in a bathrobe, I collapsed on to the chair beside Henry Jones. "I've had too much excitement for one day," I panted. Henry Jones suggested we celebrate by sharing a pot of herbal tea. I didn't flinch, grimace, or moan. "That'll be nice, thank you," I said instead. My body tingled all over.

He grinned broadly and scratched through his notes. "You should use your common sense more often," he said. "It's good for you. Using common sense is necessary on a healing journey. Here: Read this page while I put the kettle on. It's filled with good common sense.

> *Live by these simple rules and you'll enjoy a long, healthy life:*
> *Accept yourself. Don't worry. Follow your heart and not your head. Let*
> *yourself be. Don't make demands on others. Don't be manipulative. Share*
> *everything. Play fair. Live in the now. Rekindle your spirit. Don't worry,*
> *be happy. Love unconditionally. Don't try to change people. Let your*
> *heart dictate. Look within. Follow your dreams. Think big. Use your*
> *imagination. Appreciate the little things. Say thank you. Let it go. Say you're*
> *sorry. Respect your elders. Stick together. Be aware of wonder. Respond to*
> *opportunity. Never give up. Surrender to the universe. Trust in a Divine*
> *plan. Love yourself. Live your truth. Trust in your intuition. Listen to your*
> *inner voice.*

By the time Henry Jones had made tea, I had read the list several times and filed it away for safekeeping. I was bothered by the line: "Listen to your inner voice." I wondered why my inner voice had let me down. Why didn't it call out to me? How come I had never heard it before? Why hadn't it stopped me from hurting myself and others? I still had so many questions.

"A penny for your thoughts," Henry Jones said as he handed me a cup of herbal tea. The cinnamon aroma was strong and refreshing. I explained my dilemma to him. He listened without interrupting. When I was done talking, he nodded his head in silence. I took that as a cue to talk more.

Every decision starts with a choice

When I was finally done, Henry Jones spoke again: "Let's back up a bit," he said. "Every decision you ever make in your life starts by you choosing to think with your ego-mind or your true-self. Try to think of it as gears in your brain. When the ego-mind gear is engaged, you think with your head. When your true-self gear is engaged, you think from your heart. The voice you hear depends entirely on which gear you're in. Make sense?"

"Yes. I wondered if there was something wrong with me, because I seldom hear my heart speaking to me," I said.

Creating new thinking habits

"When your head is noisy, you'll never hear your heart, my friend. When you learn to still your mind, I guarantee you'll hear your heart loud and clear," he said, serenely sipping on his tea. He smacked his lips together and continued: "Please remind me to explain how to quieten your mind. Right now, though, I want to use this opportunity to tell you how to create a new thinking habit."

"Eh?"

"Let me explain. The way we think is a habit. If you're not in the habit of following your heart – your true-self – you'll have to retrain your mind to create this new thinking habit. We'll also discuss habits and mental programs in more detail later on. But, I'll give you a taste of things to come. It's a very simple process: Start by observing your thoughts. Become conscious of the two voices inside you. Listen to what they're telling you. Is there conflict? If so, favor the thinking that'll provide for your well-being and that of others in the long-term, even if this means short-term pain."

He'd mentioned this before, but it still wasn't clear to me. "What do you mean?" I asked, slightly panicked. I didn't need any more pain.

"Well, the illusions created by your ego-mind may have to come crashing down when you follow your heart. How you view yourself, others and your life situation in the past, present and future could change dramatically when you examine yourself from an entirely different point of view. I must warn you: Your ego-mind won't like that one little bit. Over the years, it has probably tricked you into believing false truths about yourself and others. Your memories may have been processed incorrectly. Who you think you are, and who you've convinced others you are might not be the real you. The building blocks of your personality are not necessarily reflective of your true-self. When this house of cards collapses, it can put enormous strain on you and on your relationships with others."

"That doesn't sound good."

"Oh, but it is! It's not only good for you, but also very necessary on a healing journey. Change is essential. You see, physical healing requires personal and spiritual transformation. Before healing can occur, there must be a dramatic shift in awareness. Simply put: You need to tune out from your ego-mind and tune in to your true-self. This step is crucial for you to take on a healing journey, no matter how much discomfort it may cause you in the short term."

"But there are some situations one just can't change!" I exclaimed.

"Such as?"

"Situations where we have responsibilities and obligations!"

Henry Jones sighed. "There you go again. Your ego-mind will always try to keep you trapped in your illusions, my friend. It spins webs with sticky strings – not least of which are the strands of responsibility and obligation. Boy oh boy, if I had a dollar for every time I've heard someone use their responsibilities or obligations as an excuse not to change their circumstance, I'd be a rich man. Count on it, your ego-mind will do its best to convince you that change isn't possible for you right now 'under the circumstances'. Hah! Don't be deceived! If something isn't right for you, then it's just not right for you. And the inner voice that comes from your heart will keep on reminding you of this fact until you finally listen to it!"

I recalled being in a relationship that was wrong for me. I told myself to break it off a 1 000 times. But, I didn't. I stayed in the relationship for all the wrong reasons. I can clearly remember my inner voice screaming: 'What the hell are you doing with this person?' The relationship eventually ended badly. I sighed heavily. "If only I knew then what I'm learning now," I said aloud.

"Better late than never," Henry Jones replied. He got up to open a window, giving me a moment to collect my thoughts. A fresh mountain breeze gushed into the cabin. "What do you see when a duck bends over?" he asked suddenly.

I shrugged.

"Its butt-quack," he laughed. "Go get dressed and then I'll tell you about the importance of long-term thinking. Hang the bath robe on the towel rack, okay?"

I'd forgotten I was still wearing it.

Think long term

Minutes later, we were at it again. "The key is to think long term. Your ego-mind prefers short-term thinking and likes to make rash, impulsive decisions. You should always give yourself as much time as you need to make decisions that are right for your ultimate well-being. Put aside your rational, deductive, analytical mind. Don't allow yourself to judge or evaluate. Instead, tune in to how you feel. I'm about to rock your world, so brace yourself for impact. Your emotions are an internal guidance system. You should always make decisions and perform actions that move you towards what makes you feel good – not physically, but emotionally. I'll say it again: When your thoughts are negative – anxious, worried, suspicious, stressed, vengeful and hateful – your ego-mind is in gear. Negative thoughts always make you feel bad, but positive thoughts make you feel good. Kindness; compassion; acceptance; tolerance; respect; forgiveness and understanding are the thoughts of your true-self. Got it?"

"Got it."

"Good. Now let me ask you this: Have you been ignoring an inner truth for a while? Is your inner voice calling out to you about a specific issue in your life right now?"

I nodded like a guilty man. There was something bothering me; something deeply personal that churned in my gut. Henry Jones saw it.

"That inner voice is compelling, right? There's no point in trying to ignore it either"

I kept nodding.

"You've got to get out of whatever situation you're in, my friend." Henry Jones placed his hand gently on my knee. His touch sent tremors through my body. I wasn't accustomed to gentleness and affection from a man. He leaned forward: "Do it. Do whatever your inner voice is telling you to do, no matter what. You won't regret it. You'll only ever regret not listening to your inner voice."

"What if I can't do it?"

"What's stopping you?" he asked, sipping on his tea.

"I'm afraid of the consequences."

"Don't fear the possible consequences. There's no use attaching yourself to an outcome. Whatever you think might happen is just an assumption.

176

Remember, in an infinite universe, there are unlimited possibilities. The actual outcome may surprise you. The only thing that's certain is that whatever happens; whatever the outcome, it can't be worse for you than not listening to your inner voice. When you listen to that voice, you follow your heart, which leads you to what is best for you."

"I want to believe you. I really do, but . . ."

Quieten your head and hear your heart

"You must still your mind, my friend," he whispered. "Let me say it another way: If your head is too busy, you won't have time to follow your heart."

"How do I quieten my mind?"

"You must deliberately make time each day to disengage from your ego-mind and connect to your true-self."

"How much time?"

"Ten minutes a day should work, for starters. Try this simple exercise: Set aside a specific time each day when you can sit quietly in a peaceful environment. Sunrise, sunset and just before you go to sleep are good times. I also recommend sitting outside in a garden or park. The fresh air and sunlight will do you good."

I scribbled down notes diligently.

"Make sure you won't be disturbed. Turn off your phone. Once you've created a quiet, calm, external space, establish that same quiet and calm within yourself."

"How?" I asked impatiently.

"Try this: Sit up and straighten your spine. Slightly lift your sternum and chin. Breathe slowly and deeply. Relax your body from top to toe. Close your eyes and observe your thoughts. Try to detach yourself, as if you were looking into the mind of someone else. Just let your thoughts come and go without judging them or trying to rationalize them. Allow this time for self-exploration. Look within."

In a few minutes I began to feel relaxed and at ease. I enjoyed letting go of the tension in my shoulders and stomach. It soothed me and I wanted more of it. Henry Jones obliged.

"Now, I'd like you to imagine that you're smiling through your eyes. Try it."

I did. It was surprisingly easy.

"For now, look upon the world around you with kindness. Feel how you soften inside. As you breathe in, invite love and peace into the very core of your being."

I thought of my wife. She has gentle, loving eyes. Fond memories carried me off.

"Next, empty your mind of thought. Still the little voice in your head. Try not to think of anything at all. It helps to focus on your solar plexus and on your breathing. If thoughts pop up, simply push them away. Don't be concerned if that happens. It's normal to lose concentration when you first learn to meditate. You'll get better with practice. No one is judging you. You're doing this exercise for yourself – your true-self."

I nodded once more. He allowed me to hold the pose for a few more minutes. I must admit, keeping my mind free of thought was a real challenge. I really had to focus on my breathing.

"You'll get a sense of serenity flowing over you," he said. "Once this happens, you're in an altered state of consciousness. This is a special state of mind in which prayer and visualization are very powerful."

I raised an eyebrow. Prayer and meditation weren't my thing either. He noted my hesitation and gestured for us to continue.

"In your mind's eye, picture yourself doing what is best for you in the long run. See yourself eating healthy food, exercising regularly and living correctly. Imagine your body naturally restoring itself to perfect health. Think happy, healthy thoughts."

We continued with the exercise for five more minutes. I let my imagination run wild. I imagined myself running on a beach and being fit and strong again. I took it even further and imagined my blood had special healing properties. As it pumped through my veins, it restored my body to perfect health. I really enjoyed the experience. Those thoughts were totally different from the self-defeating, destructive ones I'd entertained for hours, even days, in the hospital.

"Now, when you're ready, take a deep, long breath and let it out with a big sigh. Aaaaaaah! Feels good, doesn't it?"

"It sure does," I blurted out "Wow, I've never done anything like that before. It felt fantastic!"

"Keep it up," replied Henry Jones. If you practise this simple meditation exercise daily, it will help you to find true peace of mind. When your mind returns to a natural, peaceful, loving state, your body will soon follow. Take my word for it!"

It turns out, Henry Jones was right. My body did follow. I suddenly needed to go.

"Use the outhouse," he suggested, pointing to the rickety shed at the bottom of the garden. I'd wondered about the purpose of that little structure. I should've guessed it was a loo.

My head was busy with thoughts of meditation – a weird paradox, I know. I made myself comfortable and got down to business. Not two minutes later, I heard Henry Jones shout out my name in a peculiarly long drawl. It sounded like he sang it in slow motion. Something was obviously wrong! Instinctively, I reached down for the loo paper. That's when I saw it! A great, big snake at my feet! I didn't know it was possible for a grown man to grab his trousers at his ankles and bound forward several meters with a single push. I would've qualified for an Olympic sack-racing team, if there had been such an event. I only stopped hopping when I fell over my feet and rolled forward into a bush.

Henry Jones was very apologetic. Apparently, the owners left plastic snakes in the outside sheds to scare away vermin. It only dawned on him once I'd settled down to relieve myself in the loo. That explained his holler.

"Well, it's safe to say I've shat myself now, so we can move on," I grumbled. "What other tricks have you got up your sleeve?"

He tried not to laugh. "Just wait until I introduce you to Swami G. You'll never be the same again. But, I'll leave that for another day."

"Swami G?"

"Another time," he replied, waving his hand. "Alright then, what else can I do?"

Listen to the universe

He shrugged his shoulders and said: "Look out for signs."

"Huh?"

"Tune into messages from the universe."

"Are you serious?"

"Oh yes! Believe it or not, the universe is in constant communication with you. I must admit that I was skeptical when I first heard about this phenomenon. But, when I started looking for signs, the messages that were revealed to me made my eyes pop. But, don't take my word for it. Try it for yourself."

"What am I supposed to do?"

Wait for the answers

"It's very simple. Meditate on receiving the answer to a specific question. Then, look out for signs. Read signposts; bumper stickers; posters; pamphlets; advertisements and headlines. You'll be amazed at how often you get the right message at the right time. A few years back I was working on an important project. It was very challenging, and I didn't feel like I was making any progress. I was feeling disheartened and was considering quitting. I was driving to inform the people involved and I switched on the radio. The words of the song told me to 'keep on truckin'. So, I did. I stayed with the project and it worked out well in the end. Another time, I was exhausted and at my wits end. I saw an advertisement that instructed me to 'Take a break'. I didn't go out and buy the product, but I did take the advice. You get the message?"

"I think so."

"Here's a list of telltale signs to confirm messages are from the universe," he purred. This is what it said:

You'll know it's the universe talking to you when...

— *The message catches your eye (big or small).*
— *You instantly know it's meant for you.*
— *The timing is perfect.*
— *It completely resonates with your true-self.*
— *It brings you comfort and relief or gives you direction.*
— *It makes you feel lighter and elated, or peaceful and calm.*
— *You feel strange physical sensations, like goosebumps, tingles or your blood running cold.*

"You should give it a go," Henry Jones suggested. "Just think about an issue in your life (past, present or future) in which you would like to receive guidance from the universe. Ask for a sign each day. Keep your eyes open and look out for signs everywhere. Your message will pop up soon enough – often when and where you least expect it."

"Alright, I'll do it," I said. I knew immediately on which issue I would focus.

There is no such thing as a coincidence

"Now, let's discuss coincidences, shall we? You should know right up front that there's no such thing as a coincidence."

"Eh?"

"A coincidence is a synchronistic phenomenon that occurs when things are meant to be. The Indian poet, Rumi, once wrote: 'Coincidence is the thin thread that weaves the universe together.'"

"I like that," I remarked.

"Me, too," replied Henry Jones. "You should put it in our book. Our readers need to be aware of the 'strange coincidences' in their lives. They are definitely signs from the universe."

Disturbing images of a spider, a duck and a fake snake flashed in my mind. Were these coincidences? I wondered.

"So, what are we supposed to do when we take note of a coincidence?" I asked, shuddering.

"Ask yourself what message it brings. What associations can be made? What piece of the cosmic puzzle is being revealed to you?"

This concept is a couple of sandwiches short of a picnic, I told myself. But, who was I to argue with Henry Jones?

"What other signs are there?"

"Well, you should also pay attention to your dreams."

"Why?"

"You'll be surprised at how informative they can be. The next time you remember a dream, try to interpret what you think it's telling you."

"How will I know if I'm right?"

"Trust your intuition. It won't steer you wrong."

I parked dreams alongside coincidences. "Is there anything else?"

"Yes. Last but not least: Listen to your body. When you fail to take heed of the external signs, your body becomes an internal signpost: Nausea; aches; pains; lumps; bumps; cuts; scrapes; bruises; sniffles; coughs and rashes are all trying to send you a message."

"What?" I exclaimed skeptically.

"I realize this concept may seem off beat to you, but I strongly urge you to give it a chance before you dismiss it as poppycock. The principle is this: Everything that happens to you, happens for a reason. If you bump your head; stub your toe; cut your finger; bleed; bruise; break out in sores or get sick, your body is sending you a message."

"How will I know what it's trying to tell me?" I asked.

"The key to getting the message is learning to understand the language of your body. Your body talks to you in metaphors. The key to deciphering the metaphors is a blend of common sense, wisdom, discernment and intuition. Let me give you a few examples to illustrate how it works." He dived into his big, brown envelope, scratched around and then handed several papers to me. I studied them closely but wasn't sure what to make of the information they contained. Here are some examples:

- *If you get earache: What are you hearing that is hurting you?*
- *If you lose your voice: What is it you don't want to say?*
- *If you get ulcers in your mouth: What are you saying that is acidic or what are you not saying that is worrying you?*
- *If your eyes are troubling you: What are you seeing that concerns you?*
- *If your face is affected: What is affecting your self-image?*
- *If your nose is a problem area: What is concerning you about your direction in life? (i.e. follow your nose)*
- *If you bump your head: What are you doing in your life that is causing you to feel like you're bumping your head?*
- *If you stub your toe: What are you doing to yourself that is hurting you?*
- *If you burn yourself: What are you doing in your life that is causing you to feel as though you are, or could be, getting burned?*
- *If you strain your muscles: What life issue is putting you under strain?*
- *If you bleed: What issue is causing you to lose or spill your life energy?*
- *If you bruise yourself: What life issues are you bumping into?*
- *If your ears are blocked: What don't you want to hear?*

I flipped through page after page of metaphors. Each body part had been accounted for. Take your hands for example:

- *If you hurt your thumb: Do you feel like someone has you under their thumb?*
- *Your index finger: Your direction (as in pointing).*
- *Your middle finger: Sexuality.*
- *Your ring finger: Friendship, loyalty, and commitment.*
- *Your baby finger: Clinging to small details and hanging on to the last moment.*

Your internal organs also tell a story:

> — *Kidneys and bladder: Holding on to negative emotions and not releasing hurt.*
> — *Heart: Not loving or being loved.*
> — *Lungs: Feeling suffocated (especially by the ego-mind).*
> — *Bowels: Holding on to all of life's ... dare I say it ... crap, not moving on or letting go.*
> — *Stomach: Issues relating to personal power.*
> — *Liver: Not filtering the good from the bad.*
> — *Prostrate: Power issues, loss of power.*

There was more for me to get my head around:

> — *Spine: Your life's structure.*
> — *Lower spine: Financial concerns.*
> — *Joints: Flexibility.*
> — *Hips: Being too rigid and not going with the flow.*
> — *Elbows and knees: Resentment and anger.*

I found this concept intriguing. Was this really possible? Could it be that no physical affliction was random? Do our bodies constantly talk to us? I wondered. I skimmed through the notes in search of the metaphor relating to my condition.

"As you may know, energy flows from negative to positive, and time flows from the past to the future. In the human system, the left-hand side of the body is the negative and represents the past and the feminine. The right-hand side is the positive and represents the future and the masculine. So, if your problem is on the left-hand side of your body, it's past issues that are troubling you. If your problem is on the right-hand side of your body, it's your future that's troubling you."

"That sounds a bit far-fetched," I remarked.

"Before you raise an eyebrow, let me share another example with you: A yellow car smashed into a man on a bicycle, and he wound up in hospital with serious spinal injuries. The right side of his body was temporarily paralysed. His estranged father came to his aid and nursed him back to health. By the time he was back on his feet, their relationship had healed. He was no longer worried about not having a relationship with his father in the future. Would you believe the father drove a yellow car for most of the man's childhood?"

"It could be just a coincidence," I said, and then remembered our previous conversation about thin threads that weave the universe together.

"Hmmm … I think not!" Henry Jones declared. "I've been helping people heal themselves for decades and the body metaphors are seldom wrong."

Embrace your spirituality

"You'll have to be patient with me, I'm afraid. I've been a cynic far too long to instantly accept all of this New Age crap," I moaned. I didn't mean to be disrespectful – I was just speaking my mind. Oops! My ego-mind. I bit my tongue.

"You need to have faith," Henry Jones whispered.

"I'm just not into spiritual stuff."

"If you want to heal your body, then you must endeavour to become more spiritual, my friend," Henry Jones said solemnly. "Spirituality is crucial in achieving full recovery from any medical or psychological condition."

"I'm just not a spiritual person," I protested.

"In the grand scheme of things, we're all spiritual beings having a human experience, not human beings having a spiritual experience."

"Urgh! No thank you. That's not for me. I dreaded going to church as a child. The services dragged on for hours. It was like watching paint dry. The only thing that kept me from dozing off was the bats squeaking in the church rafters, and their occasional kamikaze swoops over the heads of the choir."

Henry Jones chuckled at my dismay.

"My mother's parents were devout Christians. They taught me that God is an invisible superpower who sees everything we do and punishes us for sinning by sending us to burn in hell for all eternity. But, He loves us! Is that a peculiar paradox, or what?" I asked.

"One shouldn't criticise religions of any kind, my friend. Religion gives hope to those who need it."

"Are you religious, Henry Jones?"

He paused. "There was a time in my past when I didn't have any interest in following rituals, practising ceremonies, or adhering to religious rules. I, too, wanted nothing to do with religion, spirituality or God, because I also thought they were connected. For many years, I wandered in a spiritual wasteland, searching for truth. Then, one day on my healing journey, I found myself in a contemplative mood and felt close to God. I was alerted to the spirituality within my being and how it could manifest through my thoughts, feelings and actions. I began to practise this 'alertness' as often as possible. I steadily became more conscious of myself. I became aware of an eternal watchfulness within me. I was slowly awakened to the fact that the essence of my being has existed for all time. I realized that my soul is eternal, and my spirituality has nothing to do with any man-made religion. It stems from my own self-awareness. As a conscious individual, I understand that I'm responsible for making my own reality. Yes, I'm a co-creator of my destiny through my thoughts, feelings and actions. So are you, my friend. You decide the direction of your life every second of the day. It can be a journey towards peace, harmony and bliss, or a journey towards anxiety, stress and pain. The choice is ultimately yours."

"Hold on a second. Is becoming more spiritual yet another technique to stay connected to my true-self?"

"Definitely! The essence of your higher-self is your spirit and your soul, but the essence of your lower-self is your ego and mind. If you want to heal your body, then you should get back in touch with your spirit and soul. They're pure and perfect. There's no sickness or disease in them."

"Wait a minute. I'm confused. Are you saying that I'll connect with my spirituality when I function from my true-self, or when I function from my true-self, I'll connect with my spirituality?"

"Both. That's the beauty of it. When you connect with your true-self, you quiet your ego-mind, and when you quiet your ego-mind, your spirituality grows."

It was a lot to take in. Henry Jones scrounged around in his big, brown envelope once more. I knew to expect another pearl of wisdom.

"Here it is. This is what I was looking for!" He handed me a Post-it:

> *A busy mind is a sick mind; a slow mind is a healthy mind;*
> *A still mind is a Divine mind.*

"So, now you know what you need to do, right?"

"Yes, I need to reconnect with my true-self and allow it freedom of expression in my life."

"And how will you achieve this new mission?"

185

"By practising every day the loads of powerful healing techniques that you've just given me," I said.

"Excellent answer. The key word is practice. When you make a point of integrating these principles into your life, you will connect with your true-self. But it won't happen by osmosis. Your true-self is always within you, but it takes time, effort and discipline to release it. Give it a go. I can assure you the rewards are worth it."

Your true-self knows how to heal your body

"Your true-self unleashes powerful healing forces. It knows what you must do to heal your body, and your body knows exactly how to respond to this treatment. The best doctors and specialists haven't even begun to fathom how it truly works. They're only scratching the surface of a very complex internal universe. It's far easier to prescribe medication. And if the medicine manages to heal your body without healing your mind, what will most likely happen?"

"The thoughts, perceptions or memories that are attacking me will probably manifest in my body in some other form."

"And then?"

"I'll get sick again. For my body to completely restore itself to perfect health, my mind must return to a natural, loving state. To achieve this, all I need to be is myself – my true-self."

Henry Jones smiled from ear to ear. "Well done, my friend. You've made remarkable progress."

He got up from the table and placed the empty teacups and pot in the sink. I watched him rinse the cutlery and then place them on the drying rack. My unwashed breakfast dishes were still stacked in the sink. I hated doing dishes. I had been forced to do dishes as a child and I resented it. The mere thought of doing dishes as an adult annoyed me. I didn't like being reminded of my childhood. Henry Jones proceeded to wash my dishes. I watched him clean up after me without offering to help. I had done the same the previous night. This time, though, I felt extremely uncomfortable. My inner voice told me to help him. I knew I should, but I didn't. My little voice grew louder and louder. In that moment, I realized the strength of my conscience. On that day, however, I chose not to follow my inner voice. I sat back and let Henry Jones clean up my mess, but I felt awful.

"I'm going for a walk," I blurted out. "I need a break from all this…" I didn't finish my sentence. I couldn't find the words.

I burst out of the cabin and stomped along the pathway leading to the road. I contemplated taking the Land Rover for a long drive but chose to get some exercise instead. I walked and walked, and walked, but there was nowhere to go. I was miles from civilization. Henry Jones had given me a lot to think about. The knowledge he had shared with me challenged everything I thought I knew about myself and life in general. I wasn't exactly sure what to believe anymore. Henry Jones had opened my eyes to a world of possibility that I never knew existed. I'd swallowed the red pill and I knew that my point of view had been changed irrevocably. There was no going back. I'd never be able to forget what I'd already learned.

I was, however, in a state of flux. I had one foot in the 'old me' and one foot in the 'new me'. I could see the light at the end of the tunnel as he constructed it ahead of me, but it was still so easy to slip into the darkness of my past.

One thing was certain: I wasn't thinking about my sickness. What once dominated my mind had been pushed aside by a tide of new knowledge and wisdom. I grappled with everything. Could I stay connected to my true-self for longer than a minute? I wondered. I walked through the desolate countryside, all the way to the main gate. It was a long hike – much longer than I had anticipated!

Two hours later, I found myself standing under the 'Serendipity' sign. The irony struck me. I imagined Sister Lillian, Professor Kaufman, Dr Sahib, George and Shirley pointing at me and laughing their arses off. They taunted my consciousness. I slumped on to a nearby rock and just sat there with my head in my hands.

What a sight I must've been! I was no longer the 'me' I knew. I was nowhere. All that existed was the present moment, and I was lost to the world; lost to myself; lost to my wife and daughter; lost to my work; lost to Sister Lillian; Professor Kaufman; Dr Sahib; and George and Shirley! I was a lost cause.

I sat there on that rock and breathed in and out. It was all I could do. I didn't fancy the long walk back to the cabin. I was still sick. The symptoms were ever-present in me. I could feel the discomfort, even pain. My energy was low. I'd pushed myself too hard and walked too far. The overcast morning had cleared up and the Sun was belting down. I didn't have a hat to protect me and became conscious of my growing thirst.

"I should've helped Henry Jones with the dishes. I should've listened to my inner voice. I should've followed my heart," I muttered to myself repeatedly. I vowed not to make that mistake again. Just when my situation seemed hopeless, I heard the familiar sound of the Land Rover chugging towards me. I couldn't see it, but the grinding gears were unmistakeable. Sure enough, within minutes Henry Jones had pulled up alongside me in a cloud of dust and diesel fumes.

"Howdy. I thought you might like a lift back," he said cheerfully.

I couldn't hide my delight. "Would I ever!" I yelled.

"Come on, jump in."

He didn't have to ask me twice.

"Hang on tight," Henry Jones suggested. "I'm going to give you the ride of your life."

CHAPTER 11

MIND OVER MATTER

Henry Jones and I thundered along the dirt track towards the cabin. I was grateful to him for finding me, and told him so. He grinned broadly and put foot to pedal.

It was good to be back at the cabin. Exhausted, I took a nap. When I awoke, I heard an axe cracking through wood. Henry Jones was chopping firewood. My legs were already stiff from the long walk. They hadn't felt that way in years, but it felt good. I gulped down orange juice that Henry Jones had left for me.

"Need any help?" I asked, walking out on to the balcony. The spectacular view never failed to amaze me.

"Sure I do. We have a small job to do, but it's very important."

"No problem," I shrugged.

He buried the head of the axe into a big log with astonishing force, then walked towards me.

"I'm sorry for storming out earlier and for making you fetch me," I murmured.

"Think nothing of it," he replied. "We made excellent progress this morning, and it was my pleasure to give you a lift when you needed it."

I nodded appreciatively. "We can work on your book after supper, if you'd like," I offered.

"Are you sure you're up for it?"

"Yes. I'd like that very much. Let's get started after I've done the dishes," I said.

Henry Jones paused for a split second, and then gave a little grin.

"That's marvelous," he said. "Just marvelous! Now then, do you see that wall behind you?"

I turned around and studied the back wall of the cottage.

"It needs a coat of paint, don't you think?"

I examined it more closely. "Sure, I'll get my phone and try to find a contractor in the area. If I can get reception, that is."

My effort was rejected. "I thought we could paint it now," he said.

"What?" I howled. Manual labour was not my thing, and I told him so.

"Without labour, there can be no progress," Henry Jones replied. "There's a ladder; rollers; brushes; paint; trays; two buckets and a groundsheet in the shed. Be a pal and get them for us."

His instructions were suspiciously clear and concise. I wondered if that job had been part of his master plan for me. There was no point arguing. I left in a huff.

"Watch out for fake snakes!" he hollered after me.

Ten minutes later, we were dressed in the overalls I'd found folded on the paint tins in the shed.

"Are you ready?" he asked, rolling up his sleeves.

I grumbled an incomprehensible response.

He handed me a paint scraper, but dropped it before I could take it. He picked it up and did the same thing again. "Hmmm, it's evidently time to lay down the laws," he said, placing the scraper in my hands and covering his eyes. "Drop it, please."

I did as I was told.

"I'm willing to bet you a million dollars that it fell to the floor, right?"

"That's not exactly rocket science!"

"Yes, but how was I able to predict the result?"

"You know the Law of Gravity," I answered.

"Precisely! I'm aware that there are physical laws that govern the universe. But what you may not know is that there are mental laws that govern conciousness and therefore the outcome of your life. They're just as real and effective as the physical laws of the universe. When you apply the five mental laws to healing your body, the outcome will be as predictable as the paint scraper hitting the floor."

I was intrigued. I picked up the tool and started using it on the walls. Dried flecks of paint peeled away easily. Henry Jones mixed some plaster for me to fill the cracks and then stirred a big barrel of white-wash. He whistled cheerfully. I was less thrilled.

The Law of Cause and Effect

"Here's the first mental law," he announced. "It's the Law of Cause and Effect. *For every action there's an equal and opposite reaction.* This is a fundamental law of the universe. Scientists will confirm this. In your universe, however, your thoughts are the cause and your life circumstances are the effect. I believe in a fair exchange. To aid my cause, I thought we should paint this wall for the cottage owner in return for our board and lodging. The effect will be a freshly-painted wall – and a dollop of gratitude, I bet. In the same way, your current physical condition was determined by your past thoughts. So, if you want to heal your body and keep it healthy in the future, you need to change your thinking in the present. Make sense?"

"Yup. I've got it," I said, dodging a paint chip.

The Law of Control

"Wonderful. You're doing very well indeed. The next mental law is called the Law of Control. It's quite simple. The principle is this: *Whatever you accept responsibility for in your life, you're able to control.*"

"Can you give me an example?"

"When you accept responsibility for healing yourself, you're able to take control of the healing process. Taking control of your healing journey requires that you take charge of your thoughts, feelings and actions. You decide how to think, feel and act every minute of the day. By accepting responsibility for your thoughts, feelings and actions, you determine your own destiny. Why?"

"Because they determine your reality?" I interjected.

"That's right, you guessed it. Your thoughts, feelings and actions determine your success, status and station in life. They're 100% responsible for your well-being."

"Let me see if I've got this right," I said, finding a strange satisfaction in scraping paint chips off the wall. "You're saying I should become conscious of my ego-mind. I mustn't allow it to rule my life. I have the power to control how I react to every situation, even when things go wrong. My reaction and response are always my choice."

"Well done," said Henry Jones. "Remember, too, that making the right choices in life is your responsibility."

191

"And whatever I accept responsibility for in my life, I'm able to control," I added.

"Keep this up and you'll be as fit as a fiddle in no time at all," Henry Jones said.

I beamed with pride. I must admit, I loved his encouragement. Henry Jones made me believe in myself. He built me up. Right then and there, I realized the importance of being with positive people while on a healing journey. Could it be that I was actually enjoying myself on my healing journey – doing manual labour?

The Law of Belief

"Now, let's talk about the Law of Belief. It's my favorite. *To succeed at anything in life, you must first believe that you can succeed*," said Henry Jones, applying paint to the part of the wall I'd prepared for him. "That is why Dr Sahib sent you that message. He knows that whatever you accept and believe becomes your reality. When you accept and believe you will heal your body, you will create that reality for yourself. But, if you don't believe you can heal your body, you may as well give up."

"I want to believe you," I said. "I really do. But I must admit, some of this new knowledge challenges my existing belief systems. They either go against what I was taught to believe, or they're brand-new to me. I'm not exactly sure what to believe anymore."

"Well, it's good to question your beliefs. It's possible to hold on to beliefs that are based on insufficient, inaccurate or irrational information. You've got to watch out for self-limiting belief systems, too. They'll do nothing for you except hold you back – even make you sick. Let me ask you this: What do you think are your weaknesses? What don't you like about yourself? What do you think you're not good at?"

Henry Jones rolled out these questions with strong brush strokes.

"Do you believe your answers? If so, I should warn you: Self-limiting beliefs become true to the extent that you believe in them. You see, what you believe, you begin to expect. So, whatever you expect, becomes a self-fulfilling prophecy, because you help to bring it into reality. When you expect positive results, you tend to bring about positive outcomes. When you expect negative results, you tend to bring about negative outcomes. Are you following this?"

"I think so."

"You must think about restoring your body to perfect health all the time. Don't let doubt creep into your head. That is just your ego-mind messing with you. Focus on the objectives and desires of your true-self!"

I stepped back to examine my work. I'd missed a spot.

The Law of Concentration

"This brings me neatly to the Law of Concentration: *Whatever you concentrate on grows in your experience.* Did you notice that the new motorcar you were thinking about buying suddenly appeared everywhere you went?

That's the power of the Law of Concentration. It can work to your advantage or not. If you dwell on sickness and pain, your symptoms will worsen and you'll have reason to be grumpier, if that's possible."

"One more crack like that and I'll plaster ya," I teased.

Henry Jones smiled. "To heal your body, you should concentrate on the positive outcomes you desire for yourself and those around you. Think about them constantly. By doing so, you'll steadily draw this reality into your life."

The Law of Attraction

Scraping the wall was actually fun, but I wanted to paint it too. From that activity, we saw immediate results. Henry Jones scratched an itch on his nose and left behind a swathe of paint on his cheek. I thought that was hilarious, and told him so. He attempted to wipe away the paint mark on the wrong side and left a splodge on the other cheek. I didn't have the heart to tell him.

"Once again, you have the power to choose your thoughts, and what you constantly think will usually come about," he said. "Stay focused on being positive about everything, especially your health. You will create it. Practise a healthy lifestyle and you'll increasingly attract to yourself the people; products; opportunities; benefits and rewards that go with it. This is called the Law of Attraction. It's based on the principle that like attracts like."

"Huh?"

"All I'm saying is this: You can expect to attract people and circumstances that harmonize with your current dominant thought. For instance, to find a loving, loyal partner, you must be a loving, loyal person yourself. I can't tell you how many people I know who are desperately looking for their one true love, yet they jump in and out of bed with anyone who gives them attention. Now, why would anybody who has the qualities of a 'one true love' want anything to do with someone who is promiscuous? They wouldn't, would they? They would probably run a mile from someone like that, right?"

I flinched. Henry Jones was cutting close to the bone.

"The fastest way to attract love; loyalty; devotion; affection; kindness; compassion; understanding; thoughtfulness and gentleness into your life is to display those qualities yourself. If you want to be with your soulmate, write down all the qualities you would expect this person to have, then practise them yourself. You'll be swept away by love sooner than you think. Try it. It really works."

"But how?" I had to ask.

Henry Jones rubbed his chin. That was a mistake. He was starting to look like a Navajo Indian preparing for war. "Think of your computer," he said. "All your programs and information are stored on your hard drive, right?"

"Uh huh."

"When you want to work on a specific file, you request it from the hard drive and it opens on your screen, yeah?"

"Uh huh."

"Your subconscious mind is like your hard drive, and your conscious mind is like your computer screen. In the memory of your subconscious mind is stored all the biological programs that keep your body functioning, as well as every thought, emotion and experience of your entire life. If I ask you to think of a juicy, red apple, your subconscious mind finds the file in your memory that contains this image and then opens it in your conscious mind. I bet as I'm speaking to you now, the image of a juicy, red apple was instantly uploaded and displayed in your mind's eye. Am I right?"

I couldn't deny it.

"And while this happened, your lungs breathed; your heart pumped; your eyelids blinked; and millions of other biological processes took place without you even having to think about them. That is the power of your subconscious mind. It is also able to store multimedia files, and your conscious mind can play them. If I ask you to imagine hearing yourself biting into that apple, the sound is played in your imagination, right?"

I heard it.

"Pretty amazing, huh? Now get this: Just like water takes the shape of its vessel, your subconscious mind exerts energy into your reality and thereby creates it. In his book, *Power Of Your Subconscious Mind*, Dr Joseph Murphy says: 'Habitual thinking and imagery mould, fashion and create your destiny. For as a person thinketh in his subconscious mind, so is he.' Is that electrifying, or what?"

My reading list was growing steadily. I'd become a sponge. "Are there any other books I should read on this subject?" I asked, splashing on the groundsheet we'd placed at the base of the wall.

"You'd better clean that up. If you step in it, you'll walk paint through the house."

I tip-toed towards the cloth.

Henry Jones howled with laughter. "You look like a ghoul scaring kids on Halloween."

He mimicked me and stood on his paint tray. What a mess!

Your subconscious produces your reality

We sat down to clean our shoes.

"Since Dr Joseph's groundbreaking book, many other world-renowned thinkers, such as Anthony Robbins, Stephen Covey and John Kehoe, concur that whatever information is encoded into your subconscious mind produces your reality. They have all written about this phenomenon, and their books are bestsellers because the content changes lives.

"You can create your reality through the power of your subconscious mind. It doesn't know the difference between right and wrong, true or false, good or bad. Like a computer, your subconscious mind only knows what has been programmed into it. So, if a parent repeatedly tells a child that he or she is useless, or stupid, or pathetic, the child will eventually believe this to be true because of the mental program that has been created in the child's subconscious mind. This can have a disastrous effect on their future. Instead of living up to his or her true potential, the child will most likely grow up feeling inferior, or worse – trying to prove they are superior. Do you get the idea?" Henry Jones looked at me.

"I sure do."

"Now, think how much negative programming your mind has received over the years from parents, teachers, partners, colleagues, spouses and friends. Even complete strangers can say some really mean things, can't they?"

I shuddered.

"Most of us have had the misfortune of being in at least one destructive relationship. They are soul-destroying, aren't they? Just think of all the negative things that were said to you in those circumstances."

I cringed.

Henry Jones continued: "Those harmful words are still encoded in your head. They shape your subconscious mind, whether you like it or not. If you think you've gotten over them, you're just kidding yourself. Those experiences are very real in your memories, and the pain lives somewhere in your body."

"What?"

"Don't panic! There are ways of dealing with this problem. It would be nice if you could take out the corrupt file and toss it away, but it doesn't work like that. The only way to change a mental program or belief system in your subconscious is to reprogram it."

How to reprogram your subconscious mind

"So, how do I reprogram my mind?" I asked, slipping my foot back into my shoe.

"Just like a computer, your subconscious mind accepts whatever information you program into it. And, whatever program exists in your subconscious mind becomes your reality. The worst thing you can do is constantly say: 'I'm sick'. By doing so, you're creating a mental program that reinforces your illness. When you tell yourself over and over that you're sick, you believe it, which makes it so. You should create a new mental program – one that believes you're getting well. You should be telling yourself repeatedly: 'I'm getting better. I am better.' It really works!"

"Seriously?" It was then that I remembered the scolding George-the-Surfer gave me when I claimed my sickness in his caravan a few days earlier.

"Yup. Do you know anyone who has shed a few pounds while on a diet, only to regain the weight soon after they stop dieting? Why do you think that happened?"

I shrugged.

"Their subconscious mind is programmed with their average weight of the past few years. So, as soon as they stop dieting, their subconscious mind runs the usual program, which immediately starts putting weight back on to their body. Unless they create a new mental program – one that believes they're thin – they'll spend the rest of their life dieting. Now apply this principle to healing your body: When you have a mental program that believes you're restoring your body to perfect health, that's exactly what happens. I hope you can see how valuable this information is to your healing journey," Henry Jones said.

"You bet! So, how do I program my mind?" I asked again anxiously.

Engage your five senses

"Information is programmed into your subconscious mind through your thoughts and five senses. If you want to change a negative mental program, then you must bombard your brain with new, positive information."

"What do my five senses have to do with it?"

"Well, if you had to carry a grand piano down a flight of stairs, would it be easier to carry it on your own or with the help of five good friends? Obviously, the more help you get, the easier and faster you'll achieve your objective."

"Sure thing. I wish I had five friends to help us paint this wall right now."

Henry Jones chuckled. "So, you need to employ as many of your five senses as possible to create a new program for getting well. For example: If you write down on a piece of paper: 'I'm healed', then whenever you read it, your eyes will send that message to your subconscious mind. And if you read it aloud, then your ears will send that message to your subconscious mind.

"Your subconscious mind is extremely sensitive to suggestion. It doesn't rationalize, evaluate, interrogate, analyze or compare. It just processes information as it gets it. Heck, if you tell yourself that you're getting better every time you drink a glass of water, then eventually your subconscious mind will develop a mental program that makes this association, and you'll enhance your healing process every time you drink a glass of water. Try it. Hold a glass of water in your hands for a minute or two before you drink it and imagine the water molecules purifying and healing your system. You'll be amazed at the result after just a few days."

"That's a great idea," I declared.

"I experimented with this phenomenon by repeatedly rubbing my tummy and telling myself I was feeling less pain. Do you know what happened?"

"You felt less pain?"

"Bingo. To this day, if I rub my tummy, it soothes me. Why not try it yourself?"

"How long should I do these exercises for?" I asked.

"All the experts I've consulted say it takes about 21 days of daily programming to rewrite a mental program. That's only three weeks of commitment, effort and dedication. Not bad for a whole new life, huh?"

"Not too shabby," I agreed, studying my handiwork. The wall was taking shape.

Visualize

"Great! In that case, I'll give you a few more powerful techniques to accelerate your progress. Let's start by discussing visualization. It's one of my favorite mental programming techniques. I highly recommend it!"

"Tell me more."

"In short, when you hold an image in your conscious mind, it becomes imprinted into your subconscious mind."

"How do I do that?"

"Use your imagination. It's not just for thinking of fairies and fantasylands, you know. It's an extremely powerful creative tool. Albert Einstein said: 'The imagination is more important than knowledge'. Just think about that!"

"But how does your imagination create reality?"

"Another good question. Surrounding you is a sea of energy that comprises a mind-boggling myriad quantum molecules. In this quantum soup, everything exists in a state of pure potentiality. When you hold a mental image in your mind, it's like throwing a pebble into a sea of infinite possibilities. And, as your intention ripples through this pure potentiality, the universe orchestrates itself to bring that thought into reality. Let's give it a go."

"Now?" I cried, lifting my hands for him to see my paint tray and brush.

"Why not?" replied Henry Jones. He summoned me to sit on the first step of the ladder and close my eyes. Resistance was futile.

"Picture yourself having healed your body. See yourself fit and well. Imagine all the fun and exciting things you'll do when you've restored your body to perfect health. Hold these images in your mind, making full use of your multimedia capabilities. Hear people acknowledging your accomplishment. Taste your victory meal as you celebrate your success. Smell the cologne you put on after a workout at the gym. Feel how loosely your clothes fit your body. Most of all, imagine yourself well."

We continued the exercise for a few minutes, and it felt good.

"The more senses your imagination employs, the more powerful your visualization exercises will be," he said. "You can also work with actual pictures and photographs. I once had a client who would browse through health or sports magazines, imagining her head on the bodies of all the healthy-looking women she saw in the pictures. She visualized herself healthy. This worked so well that she cut out headshots of herself in old photos and pasted them on to the bodies of healthy athletes. She literally saw herself fit and well. This image made her excited and happy, and she allowed herself to feel it. She let her emotions flow. Guess what? Her subconscious mind got the message, and today she's radiantly healthy!"

"How often should I visualize?"

Visualize throughout the day

"You can do it whenever you like. That's the beauty of it. But I recommend you do it daily. Repetition is the key. You should practise your visualization techniques throughout the day. Put your imagination to work whenever you have a moment. Use time to your advantage. For instance: Visualize while you're waiting for the kettle to boil; your bath to run; the traffic light to change; or a queue to end. You don't have to do it for hours. A few minutes here and there will take you a long way. Of course, if you visualize for 20 minutes or more, it's like healing rocket fuel. The trick is to keep visualizing."

"That's cool." I said.

Just then, a blob of paint fell on my head. I felt it running down the back of my neck and heard it hit the groundsheet. Henry Jones saw it too. He handed me a cloth without saying a word. I assumed he was more concerned about the floor than my person.

He pushed on.

Make time to reflect

"Just as important as visualization is reflection," Henry Jones said. Make time to deliberately reflect on your past. All you need to do is sit quietly and think back on your life. You'll be amazed at the memories that come to mind –memories that you thought you'd forgotten. When this happens, you need to ask yourself: 'Why did that pop up now? What's the relevance of this mcmory to my current life circumstance?'"

"How come?"

"Looking back on your life with hindsight is a fantastic opportunity to make peace with your past. Through reflection, hindsight allows you to transform your memories into opportunities for personal growth and development."

"You mean that we can reprogram our memories?"

"Exactly. How incredible would it be if we had an editing suite in our heads? Imagine that! At the end of each day, we could edit out all of our negative thoughts and emotions and save only the good stuff."

"That would be pretty neat."

"But, we don't, so the next best thing is reflection. It allows us to go back into the mental past and reprogram all of our old memories – especially the ones that have negative emotional attachments that we no longer need. This simple process is very cathartic. It's liberating and healing, too!"

"I bet it is. So, you're suggesting that I make time to reflect each day – just like I need to make time to visualize?"

"Correct. Answer this question using your common sense: Would your bathroom be cleaner if you set aside time each day to scrub it thoroughly, or if you wiped up some of the mess whenever you happened to go there?"

"It would be much better to give it a good, regular clean."

"Of course, it would! If you chose the latter, then your bathroom would be a mess most of the time, right? This is what the inside of your head looks like without reflection! Have I made my point clear?"

"You certainly have, Henry Jones."

"In that case, I'll expect you to make time for daily reflection. It's a must-do on your healing journey, okay?"

"Okay."

The power of affirmations

"Good. Now, since we're talking about things you must do, affirmations are also a must."

"Affirmations?"

"Oh yes. There's power in the spoken word. 'Life and death are in the power of the tongue'. That quote comes straight out of the Bible, Proverbs 18.21."

I wrote it down in my notepad, and left a smudge of paint on my page. That's when I noticed thousands of tiny, white paint dots on the back of my hand. It struck me: Did my face look like that, too?

"What's an affirmation exactly?" I asked, trying to see my reflection in the cottage window.

"Simply put: Affirmations are self-affirming statements that are based on positive principles. Write down a few affirmations now. Go on, take your pen and write down positive statements about yourself and your goals for the future. For instance: I am healthy; I am healed; I am fit and strong; I am well."

"But right now, those statements are untrue!" I responded awkwardly. "And I'm covered in paint!"

"It doesn't matter if they're not true yet. Your subconscious mind can't tell the difference. State your affirmations as if they are so. Your positive affirmations shouldn't be in the future tense, such as: 'I will enjoy radiant health and vitality every day of my life.' They should state: 'I enjoy radiant health and vitality every day of my life.' Got it?"

"Yes. That's easy enough to remember."

"Good. When you repeat affirmations aloud to yourself each day, your subconscious mind will eventually accept that they're true and begin working to create this reality. Even if, at first, there's evidence to the contrary, you'll gradually bring whatever you desire into your reality," he said.

I sat down and started writing down a few affirmations. Henry Jones continued working. His brush strokes were slow and elegant, unlike mine. He'd done this before, no doubt, but it was my first time.

"After reading *The Power Of Your Subconscious Mind*, I prepared a list of powerful healing affirmations and recited them daily.

He reached into his top pocket. "Ah! Here you go. Use them freely. They did the trick for me, and they'll do it for you, too."

I read the list, slowly and carefully.

> — *I am aware of the infinite intelligence and power of my subconscious mind. It holds the perfect blueprint of my body and it knows how to heal me.*
> — *My body reflects my thought life, so I project an image of wholeness, harmony, love and peace into my subconscious mind.*
> — *The infinite intelligence that created my body is now saturating every atom of my being.*
> — *Silently and quietly, all distortions in my subconscious mind are dissolved and removed.*
> — *The idea of perfect health is now filling my subconscious mind.*
> — *I am open and receptive to the healing currents that are flowing though me like a river, washing away all negative thought patterns, restoring me to perfect health.*

> - *The healing intelligence within me is now transforming every cell of my being, making me whole and perfect in accordance with the perfect pattern of all the organs lodged in my subconscious mind.*
> - *The vitality, wholeness and beauty of the life principle are made manifest in every atom of my being.*
> - *I know and decree that harmony, peace and perfect health are now being expressed in my body.*
> - *I give thanks for the healing that is taking place in my body at this time.*
> - *I am whole, perfect, strong, powerful, harmonious, happy and healed.*

My whole body tingled. "I sincerely hope they'll work for me too," I muttered to myself.

"You must build your faith in them," Henry Jones replied gently.

"As you know, I've very little faith in man or religion." I knew instantly that it was my ego-mind talking. I detected my own doubt, distrust and skepticism and I wished I could take back my words. Then I realized it was probably my ego-mind that wanted me to retract my words, in an effort to conceal itself. All at once, I felt happy that I was able to tell the difference and then learn and grow from the experience. My heart skipped a beat. Was I becoming self-aware? Could I really be changing that quickly? Was I experiencing the metacognition Henry Jones had spoken about? Was that knowledge so powerful? I pondered.

Henry Jones didn't respond at first. He finished painting a straight line between the wall and the balcony roof before slowly reaching into the other pocket of his paint jacket. He handed me a Post-it note. "This may help you," he said with a smile.

> *Faith is the substance of things hoped for, the evidence of things not yet seen.*
> *– Bible, Hebrews 11:1*

Faith is built

"Faith has eluded me all of my life," I told him.

"Nobody is born with faith, my friend. It is cultivated over time," Henry Jones said. "Think about it. People aren't born Buddhists, Christians or Hindus. They build their faith by continuously processing supportive information. Right?"

"I suppose so."

"Good. Now, did you notice that I said you must *build* faith? Why didn't I say you must *have* faith? What's the difference?" he asked.

I paused to think about it. I could see the difference between 'building a good body' and 'having a good body'. Bodybuilding requires a lot of effort. You need to train hard and practice on a regular basis. This takes dedication, devotion and commitment. The output of the input is 'having a good body'. I applied this logic to the abstract concept of faith. It fitted neatly into my breakthrough realization of the need to practise love. I joined the dots.

"I can't have faith unless I build it," I eventually replied.

Henry Jones grinned like a Cheshire cat.

"I think you're saying I must practise affirmations daily."

"And why must you repeat them aloud on a regular basis?"

"Because I'll start to believe they'll work for me, too."

"Yes! You can only build your faith by practising it. Visualizations and affirmations are awesome faith-builders. They command repeated effort, and they're loaded with intention. The fact is: The more time you invest in practising these techniques, the more faith you'll build in them. When you deliberately build your faith, you harness the awesome power of your subconscious mind, which creates your reality! Do it," urged Henry Jones. His excitement was infectious. It made my heart pound in my chest.

"Jeez, Henry! You make me emotional."

Get emotional

"Good," he shouted. "Emotions are powerful, creative forces. The more excited, enthusiastic, eager, keen, happy, joyous, thrilled and passionate you are about healing your body, the faster it's going to happen."

"Really?"

"Oh yes! It's essential to get your emotions flowing on a healing journey. Laugh, cry, scream, rage or howl at the moon. Do whatever it takes to bring your feelings to the surface."

"That isn't my strong point," I reminded him. "I've always suppressed my feelings."

"When you suppress your emotions, you suppress the essence of life. You empty the rocket fuel out of your subconscious mind's creative tank. What a waste of good energy! I suggest you put your emotions to good use. Get them to work for you in the creation process – specifically in your healing process. Muster 'em up! Feel 'em in your bones and then let them loose."

"But I like to think of myself as cool, calm and collected. I like to be in control."

"And where has this behavior got you, eh?"

I shrugged awkwardly. I had thought I was on top of my game, but actually, I was lost. I was cut off from my true-self. Would my wife have left me if I had been more in touch with my feelings? I wondered.

Henry Jones continued: "You have the power to be whoever you want to be, my friend. You can change your ways anytime you like. The old you no longer exists. The new you lives in the present moment. The here and now is a wonderful, magical place. Stop for a second and take a breath. In this moment, you can be who you want to be – who you really are. You can choose to express your emotions and live a rich and full life. How you live your life is always your choice."

I stopped painting and took a breath.

"Answer this question: Are you having fun painting this wall with me?" Henry Jones suddenly asked.

"I guess so. Yes."

"In that case, I strongly suggest you shout for joy. Let rip. Show me how much fun you're having right now."

What the heck! I thought. Why not? What's stopping me from living to my fullest potential? I leaped on to the ladder and shouted louder and longer than I'd done in many, many years. It felt awesome! I yelled until no more sound escaped my throat. I felt a tremendous unleashing of emotion, which took my breath away and echoed through the valley. With one, big gulp, I sucked delicious, thick air into my lungs, until they felt as though they might pop.

Henry Jones clapped wildly.

It took several minutes for things to simmer down. I fetched us two glasses of water and reread the list of affirmations several times.

"Something shifted in me," I told Henry Jones.

"I'm not surprised. At the most fundamental level, we decide what to think, say and do. Who we are, what we do and how we interpret and respond to our experiences is always our choice. The secret to enjoying radiant health and a successful life is to make the right decisions at the right time."

My jubilance was short-lived. I felt a pang of guilt. I knew I was sick because I'd been making the wrong life choices. Henry Jones had made that quite clear.

"But how can I be certain that I'll always make the right decisions?" I asked.

Base decisions on your principles

"That's easy," he replied. "You base your decisions on your principles."

"My principles?"

"Exactly!"

"Your principles are the key to correct decision-making. Principles are natural laws. They are the codes or ethics you live by. They define you as an individual and are central to your thoughts and deeds. I promise you, my friend, when you abide by your principles, you'll always make the right decisions for your life. That is why your principles should be extremely important to you. Sadly, most people in our modern society don't take their principles too seriously. They certainly don't live by them."

I said nothing. I used 'my principles' when it suited me. Henry Jones had me pegged.

"It seems the masses are so busy trying to survive in these overloaded, complex, modern times that they just don't have the time to instil sound principles in their children. As a result, our society is gradually becoming less principled. To make matters even worse, a lot of modern-day learning comes from watching television, where people say and do whatever it takes to get ahead. Heck, we see people lying; manipulating; deceiving; betraying; cheating and stealing – even killing – every single day."

"The problem is, we usually get away with being unprincipled," I commented.

"Oh no, my friend, you couldn't be more wrong," Henry Jones retorted.

The power of your conscience

He looked at me with an astonished expression and then stated in a firm voice: "You can't get away with it because you have a conscience – your deep, inner awareness of right and wrong."

"I have a clean conscience. I haven't used it once," I joked.

He was not amused. "When you see or do something wrong, no matter how small, it pricks your conscience. An alarm bell goes off inside of you. It can be deafeningly loud or very faint, but you always hear it. You know what I'm talking about, don't you?"

I nodded bashfully.

"You never get away with it. Never, never, ever! Every time you do something wrong and it pricks your conscience – even if you are telling a simple, white lie – you're damaging yourself!"

"That's a bit harsh, isn't it?"

Henry Jones sat down to catch his breath. He'd been working like a machine since we started painting the cottage wall. I had struggled to keep up with him. He remained deadly serious. "Your subconscious mind keeps a scorecard. It records every indiscretion you make. The penalties for continued self-abuse can be very severe indeed!"

"Are you implying they can tally up to make us sick?"

"Yes. That's it exactly! We can't change the past, my friend, but we can change the future. If you want to get well and stay well in the future, you must abide by the correct principles. You see, there are two kinds of principles, and you must know the difference between them. I'll try to make this really simple for you to understand."

"Go for it."

"There are correct principles and incorrect principles, and they're governed by natural laws. In a nutshell: When you practise correct principles, you naturally do what is right for you and those around you. When you practise incorrect principles, you do what is wrong for you and everybody else. Make sense?"

"Ah huh!"

"Good. In that case, I'll move on to my next point. The easiest way to determine if principles are correct or incorrect is to apply basic common sense. Intrinsically, you already know the difference between right and wrong. You just need to be reminded of it. In his book, *Seven Habits Of Highly Effective People*, Stephen Covey lists some of the big hitters in both categories."

Henry Jones disappeared into the cottage. I carried on painting. We were making great progress. The wall was almost done. We still needed to paint around the edges and clean up, but the impact was already visible for all to see.

"Read this list carefully," he said, re-emerging and handing me a small sheet of paper.

> *The correct principles are: Honesty; integrity; fairness; human dignity; potential; nurturance; excellence; change; patience; encouragement; acceptance and belief.*

"Wow! That's an impressive list," I responded, suppressing a giggle at the sight of the white paint on his cheeks, chin, collar, jacket, hands and feet.

"Isn't it?" he exclaimed. "Covey goes on to say: 'Consider the absurdity of attempting to live an effective life based on their opposites. I doubt anyone would seriously consider unfairness; deceit; baseness; uselessness; mediocrity or degeneration to be a solid foundation for lasting happiness and success.'"

Henry Jones's passion and love for his work were inspirational.

"Once again, this isn't rocket science. Stay away from incorrect principles. When you apply principles that are wrong for you, the outcome will always be wrong. On the other hand, when you apply principles that are good for you, the outcome will always be good for you. When you apply them, they'll work for you. This is an essential life skill."

Reaffirm your principles

"First I need to dust off my principles," I moaned, wiping dried paint and plaster from my shoulders and chest. "I'm not sure what they are."

"When last did you write them down?" Henry Jones asked.

"Never!"

"Well, there's no time like the present," he replied. "We have sufficient time now for me to show you a very simple, yet extremely effective exercise to reaffirm your principles. It'll take about 15 minutes of your time, but the exercise will change your life forever. When you're conscious of your principles, you'll live by them. They become a part of your decision-making process and therefore guide your personal conduct. By acting in accordance with your principles, you'll make great progress on your healing journey. Take a break from painting and do this now."

"Okay," I said, climbing down the ladder. I fetched my notepad and pen. Through knowledge and practise, I was becoming a different person. I wanted to learn as much as I could.

Henry Jones grinned. "To begin this exercise, I'd like you to jot down the principles you think are most important."

I referred to Stephen Covey's list of correct principles to refresh my memory.

Henry Jones added: "There are many more good principles for you to choose from, too, such as: loyalty; giving; kindness; generosity; balance; enthusiasm and commitment. The latter are very important on a healing journey."

I took all the time I needed to compile my list and select principles. I was surprised to discover that I had the capacity to practise certain principles, but seldom did. I had the capacity to be generous, but I was overcome by greed. I had the capacity to be kind, but I was often cruel. As my list took shape, I began to take shape. I saw the person I wanted to be manifesting before my eyes. I realized that I'd not been a principle-centered individual. I had no code of ethics to live by. I also realized that to truly experience the magic of this exercise, I actually had to practise it.

When I was done, I read out my list to Henry Jones. The sound of my voice was like a hammer driving home a nail. The list was important to me.

"Very good. Now, I want you to reaffirm each principle by completing the sentence: 'I am/have/strive for …' For example: I am loyal. I have integrity. I strive for excellence."

"Why?"

"Because when you state them 'as if they were so', you make them real."

Henry Jones worked on the finer details of the cottage wall. He pushed his brush into the nooks and crannies, ensuring no gaps were left unpainted. He took great care in his work and I admired his attention to detail. Once I'd done this exercise, he pushed on. "Now, I'd like you to write down the definition of each of your principles. A neat, one-liner will do nicely. If necessary, use a dictionary," Henry Jones said, pointing to the bookshelf in the cottage.

That proved to be a simple task, but profoundly rewarding. The words gathered mass and impetus as I developed a deeper understanding of them.

When I was finished, Henry Jones said: "Now, write down the benefits of applying each principle. For example: The benefits of being honest are …"

"Um … not having to fear being caught out for lying."

"And?"

"Trust and respect from others."

"And?"

"A good reputation."

208

"Yes, exactly! If you don't know the long-term benefits to your life, then you won't know why you need to stay motivated. Benefits build desire. You must have the desire to live by your principles, or you won't do it."

"So, you're saying I must know the benefits of my principles and keep them in mind to create the motivation I need to live by them?

"Eureka!" shouted Henry Jones.

"My head is usually so busy that I'm afraid I'll forget them in a day or two."

"You must internalize them, my friend. Internalization of the correct principles and their benefits is the key to healing your body naturally."

"But how do I internalize them?"

"The way to internalize information is to repeatedly download it into your head. Use your senses. Read your list of principles and their benefits aloud to yourself every day for 21 days. Follow this simple instruction and it will pay off big time. You'll become a principle-centered individual, which will change your whole life! The beauty of living by your principles is that you're able to predict the long-term results."

"That's incredible," I commented, scanning the white-washed wall from side to side.

Principles produce predictable outcomes

"Yes, it is! Live by your principles and you can plot the course of your life, just as surely as a compass points north. That's a fair exchange for your time and effort, isn't it?" Henry Jones asked.

I nodded soberly. The pieces of the puzzle had suddenly fallen into place. The benefits would become my reality because I would program them into my subconscious mind, which was responsible for creating my reality. Henry Jones had masterfully led me to that point of realization.

"I'll read my list of principles every day for 21 days," I announced loudly.

"That's music to my ears," he replied.

"I've realized that if I want to produce different results, then I've got to change my actions. I want to heal my body. I want to be well again, so I'll do whatever it takes to succeed!" I patted my list of principles with great enthusiasm. "After all, commitment is high on my list!"

Focus on your higher goals

Henry Jones took a few steps back to assess our work, and nodded approvingly. "The way to succeed is to focus on your higher goals. If you're serious about wanting to heal your body, then you should think and act from where you want to be, rather than from where you actually are. In other words, don't let your past determine your present. Let your present be determined by your desires for the future."

"That's quite a difference," I remarked.

"Indeed, it is a real paradigm shift," he replied thoughtfully. "You must live by your higher goals. Literally. The good news is that when you practise this new life approach, it soon becomes a habit."

"Why is this good news?" I asked.

Without hesitation, he scratched in the back trouser pocket of his overall. "Ah ha! Here it is," he trumpeted, handing me yet another Post-it note for my growing collection.

> *"Nothing is stronger than habit." – Ovid, Roman poet (43BC–17AD),* ArsAmatoria

I slipped it into my top pocket for safekeeping. Then, suddenly, Henry Jones's expression changed.

"I've a confession to make," he murmured. "I enjoy eating popcorn at the movies – and have done so for years. I follow the same routine whenever I go to the movies: I buy a ticket and head straight for the popcorn counter. It has become a conditioned response. I don't stop to think about it, I just do it! Do you know why that is?" he asked me.

"Nope."

"In its attempt to self-organize, the subconscious mind writes programs to predict our behavior and directs us towards it. That mental program is called a habit. There are a few things about habits you should know," he said.

"Such as?"

"Well, for starters, habits are easily formed. Whatever you repeatedly think, say or do becomes a habit. Don't underestimate their significance! They are powerful creative forces of influence on your life."

The power of habits

"How come?"

"They condition your behavior, whether you're aware of it or not."

"How does that work?"

"It's simple. Repeated behavior becomes normal practice. That is the beauty and horror of habits. They become unconscious actions. You begin to act on impulse. When this happens, your subconscious mind short circuits self-awareness, independent will and freedom of choice. It just plays the mental program over and over again. These patterns of behavior create the cycles in your life. You may think your life is unfolding in a linear fashion, but if you observe it objectively through the lens of your habits, you'll quickly realize that you're going in circles, like a hamster on a wheel.

"This is good news when the behavioral patterns are positive for you, but disastrous when they're self-destructive. For example: If your natural tendency is to avoid conflict, then (through repeated behavior) you'll most probably get into the habit of running away from your problems. That pattern will stay in your life for as long as that program exists in your head. Is this making sense?"

"Yes. You're saying I've got good habits and bad habits, and that they are deeply ingrained in my behavior. So much so that I may not think of them as habits at all. I might mistakenly think my behavior is 'me being me', when in fact it's just a mental program playing itself over and over again?"

"Precisely!"

"...and I probably won't realize this is happening because repeated behavior becomes normal?"

"Bingo! Let's put this theory to the test, shall we? Do you usually pour yourself a glass of whiskey when you get home from work?"

"Yes, I like my whiskey!"

"Every night?"

"Yes," I retorted.

"That's nothing more than a bad habit."

I grimaced. He was right, and I knew it. I could see where this was heading. "Now you're probably going to tell me the reason I'm sick is because my bad habits have got the better of me. Right?"

"Uh huh."

"... and if I want to heal my body, I've got to get rid of my bad habits and replace them with good habits. Correct?"

Break bad habits

"You guessed it. Bad habits will only bring you down."

"So, how do I break a bad habit?"

"I'll tell you if you'll help me clean up," Henry Jones said, pointing to the mess we'd left in our wake. The wall was finished. It looked fantastic. Henry Jones put his arm around me and pulled me close to him. "Breaking bad habits requires a healing process. Without a proper process to follow, you're pretty much doomed. It's very rare that people break bad habits without knowing exactly what to do and how to do it. I should warn you in advance: Breaking bad habits is not fun. I first realized this fact when I stopped eating popcorn while I was on my healing journey."

"You didn't even eat popcorn?" I exclaimed.

"No, certainly not! Processed oil and salt are unhealthy for the human system. They make you feel full for a moment but they don't give your body the nutrients it needs to build health in the long-term. Most food manufacturers know this fact and use it to their advantage because it keeps you craving their products. I only ate fruit and vegetables on my healing journey. But I can tell you this: I craved popcorn. Going to the movies just wasn't the same without it. I felt cheated. Not being able to eat popcorn when I wanted to eat it made me miserable and grumpy. I can remember feeling sorry for myself. That's when I first realized how wretched we feel when we try to break a habit. The part of us that indulges our bad habits wants to exist. It needs to exist!"

"You're talking about the ego-mind, right?"

"Yes, indeed. Now you can understand why we feel horribly deprived when we try to suppress our bad habits. The ego-mind doesn't want to give up control. It'll throw tantrums to exist through our bad habits, like a two-year-old in a candy store."

I thought back to the tantrums I'd thrown when my wife had asked me to stop drinking so much. I shook the memories from my head. I started to roll up the groundsheet, and round up the paint trays.

"So, what did you do? How did you break the popcorn habit?"

"I learned to focus on my higher purpose. I made sure I knew my goals and all of their benefits," he said, dusting paint chips from his hair. It dawned on me that I'd dropped them on him when he was working below me, and I blushed.

Understand the benefits of your goals

"Only when you're convinced of the benefits of your long-term goals can you become committed to attaining them. I knew I wanted to be well again, but that wasn't enough. I had to drill down into the benefits of being well.

That was where I found my true motivation. It gave me the staying power to succeed. You can ask thousands of sales experts: People buy benefits, not features. The trick is to stand apart from your emotions. You may not have realized it yet, but you have emotional attachments to your bad habits. We all do. For example, junk food makes some people feel satisfied. They become dependent on the instant gratification they gain from eating it. That's why they find themselves sinking their teeth into a burger whenever they feel emotionally or mentally dissatisfied."

Whiskey and cigars made me feel successful, which gave me comfort. My emotional attachment was clear.

"What other tools can I use to break my bad habits?"

Don't act impulsively

"Here's a good one: Don't act on your impulses."

"Why not?"

"Your impulses are generated by your past. You need to think and act from the future. So, you should always choose what is best for you in the long run. Impulses are also expressed in the present moment, so be aware. You may be holding on to habits that you enjoy in the moment, but that could be harming you in the future. Let's talk about smoking. Some people enjoy it, even though it kills them slowly. Take a long walk through a lung cancer ward and you'll soon see the critical importance of thinking about the long term."

"What else?" I asked.

Stand up to peer pressure

"Don't give in to peer pressure," he replied.

"Ooh! That's a tough one," I remarked, knowing how much I enjoyed knocking back a few drinks with the boys after work. What do you suggest?"

"Your friends and family are used to your old ways. They'll expect you to behave in the same way you always did. Heck, it may even suit them and help them to feel comfortable in their relationship with you because they can anticipate your behavior. But, don't let your peers or loved ones pull the strings that connect you to your past. Be aware of people who try to lead you astray, and situations that challenge your willpower. If you can't avoid them, stay strong! Exercise your independent will. This is yet another tool. You have the ability and power to act free of influences. Use it! You'll win the respect from those who fail to cajole you, and admiration from bystanders. The only way to lose is by giving in to your bad habits."

"Got it," I declared, wiping the paint brushes and rollers against the side of the bucket containing the white-wash. At that moment, I got the biggest fright. I'm not sure how it happened, but I felt a tug on my ring finger as it scraped against the rim. Confused, I lifted my hand and stared at it. Something was wrong! My wedding ring was gone! My God, my wedding ring was gone! At the height of my ego-driven days, I'd stupidly often contemplated whether or not my marriage was right for me. I'd fantasized about meeting someone else – someone more like me. Sometimes, fantasy had become reality, I'm ashamed to admit. But, the sight of my ring finger without my wedding ring instilled a great panic within me. What did it symbolize? I pushed both hands into the white paint and began scratching around frantically for my ring.

"Fuck! Fuck! Fuck!" I cried out.

Henry Jones knew something was very wrong. His hands dived into the paint bucket too.

"I've lost my wedding ring. I've lost my wife. I've lost my love," I cried. I couldn't see clearly because tears of frustration obscured my vision. An anxiety attack took hold of me and I gulped desperately for air as I fell backwards, my hands pressed against my chest.

"You're going to be okay. You're going to be okay. You're going to be okay," Henry Jones said calmly, lifting my ring from the bucket.

When I saw his pure-white, paint-covered hand holding my pure-white, paint-covered ring, I bawled my eyes out. I grabbed him and sobbed hard and long. "You're going to be okay. You're going to be okay. You're going to be okay," he repeated over and over again.

There's always a message in the mess

No, I didn't wait to wipe the paint off my wedding ring before putting it back on my ring finger. I needed to feel it where it belonged. I'd clean up my mess later. In that moment, Henry Jones's master plan made its mark. I'd been so busy labouring through his exercise that I'd failed to realize the power of the lesson. We'd brought about transformation through our labour. Our efforts to renew the wall had renewed me, too. The impact was clear!

"Thank you, thank you, thank you Henry Jones," I sobbed.

He held me in his arms, rocking me from side to side. Something about this movement shifted me too. My consciousness swayed back and forth between my ego-mind and my true-self, like slow, elegant strokes of a master's paint brush.

"'Temperance and labor are the two true physicians of man,'" he whispered. "That is one of my favorite quotations from Jean Jacques Rousseau."

No, Henry Jones didn't wait for us to finish cleaning up our mess or pack away the tools we'd used to transform the cottage wall. He got right back on track.

Follow your conscience

"Lastly, when you want to break bad habits, listen to your conscience. It's your internal security system. It will always let you know if what you're doing opposes your new goals. You'll hear the alarm bells. Obviously, your new goals need to be well defined, or your conscience will have no frame of reference in which to act. You can't just quit a bad habit – you'll need to fill the void with something else that's good for you. The good news is that habits can be formed as easily as they can be broken. All that's required is a new mental program.

"When forming a new habit – one that's good for you – the bulk of your programming must come through your actions. You can't just think about creating good habits. You've got to practise them, over and over again. This always requires planning and preparation. For instance: You could get into the habit of making a fresh fruit juice to drink after work. Stop off at the shop and buy the ingredients for a delicious non-alcoholic cocktail on your way home. This will dramatically increase your chances of actually doing it. Now, do this every day for 21 days in a row and it'll become a healthy habit."

Implement a game plan

Henry Jones softened his tone: "It's never too late to start implementing a winning game plan, my friend. I can give you a game-changer right now."

"Hold on a second. My pen has run dry," I yelled, scratching around for another one.

Henry Jones casually pointed to the spare pen I had tucked behind my ear.

"There are six spheres of human life: Physical, mental, emotional and spiritual, plus social and financial. To heal yourself holistically, you must know what your goals are in each of these six spheres, and then work towards them. Goals give your life purpose. When you know your life's purpose, then you have a reason to get well. The opposite is also true. I've seen many patients with terminal illnesses who suddenly feel they no longer serve a purpose and rapidly go downhill. Your purpose will give you the motivation to fight your problem. The more reasons you have to get better, the faster your body will heal itself."

"I've had financial goals at work, but I've never had goals in all six spheres of my life," I admitted.

Henry Jones frowned disapprovingly. "Many people focus on achieving their financial goals only. This is the reason why there are so many unhealthy, unhappy, rich people. Are they successful? Financially, yes, but in life, not. True success comes from working towards a balanced life."

"Don't you mean achieving a balanced life?"

Set goals

"Success isn't a destination – it's the journey. You become successful the instant you start working towards your goals. If you want to be successful tomorrow, you can do it. Just make sure you define your goals tonight and apply yourself to achieving them tomorrow."

It seemed so simple. Almost too simple.

"I need to be more goal orientated," I announced. "I know there are areas in my life that need attention. How would you suggest I get started, Henry Jones?"

He laughed loudly. "There isn't much to it. Goal-setting is very easy to do. Simply write down what you want to achieve; when you want to achieve it by; and how you plan to achieve it. Then make it happen. That's it! I don't think you'll ever find an easier 'formula for success'."

"Nope! That's pretty straight forward," I concurred, but couldn't help feeling that something was missing. It couldn't be that easy.

"Your first step is to write down your goals. The mechanical act of putting pen to paper is of the utmost importance. Your thoughts are intangible. When you transfer them to paper, they become tangible. As you read them, they become real."

"Writing down your goals also sets the process in motion," I added.

"Exactly! Your thoughts create your reality through the power of your subconscious mind. When you write out your goals, you give your subconscious mind a set of instructions to carry out. The more detailed these instructions, the more efficient your subconscious mind can become. Each time you write out your goals or read them, the deeper their impression is imbedded into your subconscious mind. This literally programs your mind to produce the outcomes you desire. For maximum impact, don't be satisfied with your first draft. Keep refining, rephrasing and rewording your goals. Keep them short and sharp, so that they pack a punch. Use powerful adjectives to express your emotions, then take what you read to heart."

"How often should I read my list of goals?" I asked.

"Make a point of reading them twice a week, at least. If you're really sick, read them twice a day – once in the morning and once at night."

"Gotcha."

"And read them aloud!"

"Because hearing programs our subconscious mind, right?"

"Exactly! When you hear the sound of your own voice telling you your goals, it breathes life into them. Do this, my friend, and your goals will become an unstoppable force."

"Is that it?"

Set deadlines

"Nope. There's more to it. Goals without deadlines are just dreams."

"I like that. I'll make sure it goes into our book," I promised.

"Good. But make sure your deadlines are realistic. Give yourself manageable time frames that you believe are possible to achieve. Deadlines are marvelous for creating a sense of urgency. But, there's no point in putting yourself under too much pressure. That's just silly! Driving yourself to achieve your goals shouldn't be a white-knuckle exercise – it should be enjoyable. After all, it's your life. Deadlines are goal posts. That's all!"

"What if I miss a deadline?" I asked. As a publisher, I knew all about missing deadlines.

"Don't beat yourself up. Just set a new due date – one that you can achieve. Okay?"

"Okay."

"The important thing is to persevere. Persist, persist and persist! As long as you're pushing forward in the right direction, you're bound to get there. This reminds me: If you wish to lose weight, please don't try to achieve target weights with deadlines. This idea really cooks my goose!"

"Why?"

"If you diet and watch the scale, you've got it all wrong. Dead wrong! You're striving for the wrong goal. Forget the scale. Toss it out. Your body is beautiful just the way it is. So what if you're overweight today? That's a temporary problem. Focus on your long-term well-being. Feed your body properly and forget about your weight. Your body will balance itself to its ideal weight in its own good time. Trust me! When you think about your well-being instead of fat loss, you'll be shrugging a big monkey off your back. When I think about the billions that get spent on diet shakes and weight-loss advertisements each year, it boils my blood," he fumed.

Henry Jones took a deep breath. "Now that I've got that off my chest, let's get back on track, shall we? Goals require action plans. You must have a plan of action on a healing journey. That's why I gave you a Workbook, remember?"

I reached over and patted it.

"Good. Don't lose it. Keep it close to you, always! Your Workbook is your activity planner and account of your experience. You must use it every day on your healing journey. Take a look at what you must do each day to achieve your goals. Then lay out manageable steps that lead to success. Write them into your Workbook, then work your plan daily. Got it?"

"Yeah. Convert thinking – to doing – on my way to being. I get it."

You are the key

"This practice takes self-discipline. You need to develop a new mental program for your subconscious mind. You're the key, and only you can make it happen! The power of your subconscious mind is awesome, but it needs your input. Input requires effort. You can't think your way to the top of a mountain. You can visualize all you like, but the only way to get to the top is to put in effort. To get on top of your recovery, you need to plan your route and take the appropriate action. This involves looking ahead. The upside of this approach is that you are able to predict potential obstacles in your path."

"What then?"

"Analyze them and plan how to get around them. Do this well in advance. Ask yourself: Of what future situations should I be wary? What am I going to say and do when people try to lead me astray? If you haven't worked out a strategy for success, you could quickly lose your way. One more thing: A good plan is flexible. If your plan is too rigid, any default could spell disaster. Keep your options open at crucial stages and think ahead. How are you going to respond to life's curve balls? Knowing the answers to these questions can save your life."

"Jeez, you weren't kidding when you said managing yourself isn't easy. I need to organize my life in a whole new way," I moaned.

Embrace the mind-map

"Mind-maps are your answer," Henry Jones stated. "They're a great way to organize your thinking. They're quick to draw, easy to use, and they make remembering a breeze."

"I've never heard of them."

"Tony Buzan developed this technique. Simply draw a small circle in the center of your page. Write the name of the issue with which you're dealing in the circle. For example: 'Physical Goals'. Next, take a moment to think of your first physical goal. Let's say it's to eat natural foods. Draw a spider's leg from the circle and attach another small circle on the end of it."

"I don't like the sound of that. The thought of spiders makes my eye twitch," I moaned. My eight legged friend was still out there, somewhere!

Henry Jones chortled. "In the small circle, write down 'Eat natural foods daily'. Now move onto your next goal. Draw another spider's leg and circle. In this circle write 'Get fit.' Another good goal would be 'Avoid harmful vices'. You get the picture?"

"I sure do."

"By the time you're done, your drawing should look like a spider with many legs and big, flat feet. I assure you, it really works."

"I'm sold."

Henry Jones continued: "You can then take it to the next level. Each spider's foot can become another mind-map. For example: Write: 'Avoid harmful vices' into the center circle on a new page and start the process over. On each leg, you could write down things that you know are destructive to your long-term well-being, such as coffee, refined sugar, white flour, alcohol, meat, etc. While you're at it, make a mind-map for the benefit of achieving your physical goals. Think about how much your life will change for the better. Really go into detail. When your mind-map has 10 or more spider legs, you'll have all the motivation you need to pursue your physical goals and achieve them."

"This is a great technique," I agreed. "It paints a mental picture in your mind."

When we'd finally packed away the paint equipment and finished scrubbing spilled paint off the balcony floor, I collapsed into the nearest chair. My eyes closed involuntarily. I rubbed my temples in slow circles. It had been a long day and I was dog-tired. I'd absorbed so much information that my head felt as if it was going to explode.

"We're done." I mumbled, lifting a lame arm to point at the wall.

Henry Jones stood beside me. We were a sorry sight. "Do you think there's more paint on us or the wall?"

We were covered from head to toe. I had two, white hand prints on my chest, which he thought was very funny. We laughed until it hurt.

"Before you go off to shower, tell me what you learned today," he instructed.

I turned to my notebook and flipped through the pages. My eyes scanned through the underlined headings in my notes. There were plenty of them. Some jumped out at me: *Become conscious of your actions; Change your ways; Take on new behavioral patterns; Practice healthy living daily; Adopt a new lifestyle.* Overwhelmed by it all, I pushed my notebook aside, closed my eyes and sat quietly for a minute or so.

"Well, I learned that to heal my body, I must first heal my mind. To accomplish this, I must break free from my ego-mind and get in touch with my true-self. Then, we explored plenty of effective ways to make this happen."

"Do you remember them?"

"I have them written down," I replied, reaching for my notebook again.

Avoid fear, doubt and shame.

Confront your fears.

Don't suppress your emotions.

Forgive yourself and others.

Stop worrying.

Let go.

Become childlike.

Get in touch with your inner child.

Take pleasure in little things.

Love yourself.

Be loving to others.

Have faith and trust.

Believe.

Transform yourself.

Use common sense.
Get into the right gear.
Create new thinking habits.
Embrace change.
Think long term.
Use your emotional guidance system.
Still your mind.
Listen to your inner voice.
Listen to the universe.
Look for coincidences.
Interpret your dreams.
Confront your fears.
Live in the moment.
Read your body.
Embrace your spirituality.

"Next, we explored the five mental laws: The Law of Cause and Effect; Control; Belief; Concentration and Attraction."

"What else?"

"We discussed the power of the subconscious mind. I learned powerful techniques to reprogram my subconscious mind, such as visualization and affirmation. As if that wasn't enough, you explained how we can create our own reality by using faith and emotions. We also analyzed the importance of principles and habits. And, to top it off, I learned how to do goal setting using mind-maps."

"Wow, you did have a busy day, didn't you?" Henry Jones remarked.

After watching yet another glorious sunset beside the crackling fire, night fell. Henry Jones whistled away as he prepared our meal. I emptied his big, brown envelope and sorted through some of his notes. The afternoon's lessons were still fresh in my mind – almost as fresh as the paint on the white-washed cottage wall. Our whole-foods, plant-based supper was surprisingly delicious. I kept my word and did the dishes while Henry Jones lit candles to create sufficient light for me to write notes in my Workbook and Notebook. When I was done, he invited me to step outside on to the balcony to see the effect of our labour. The white-washed wall gleamed resplendently in the firelight.

"This job showed me the error of my ways," I admitted.

Henry Jones put his loving arm around me, once more. "It's not the first time I've painted this wall," he told me with a twinkle in his eye. I had suspected as much.

"The previous time, being frugal, I had to pinch and scrape to spend the absolute minimum on materials. We were only partway through the job when we realized that we didn't have enough paint to complete the job. Not wishing to spend any more money if we absolutely didn't have to, we decided we'd just dilute the paint to make it go further. We did this a couple more times before we finished, which caused striping on the cottage wall as the paint got lighter each time it was thinned. We'd almost finished the job, when, all of a sudden, the sky darkened, and the rain started to pour down. As the paint streamed down the sides of the cottage, a voice boomed from the heavens: "Repaint, you thinners! Repaint, and thin no more!"

We burst out laughing. My body ached from head to toe. My long walk and the paint job had left me exhausted. It was time to call it a day.

"Off you go then. Sleep tight. I'm going to put a few more logs on the fire. It's our last night at the cabin and I want to enjoy it a little while longer."

Henry Jones made his way to the fireplace. He stopped in his tracks and turned around slowly. I looked at him expectantly.

"Do you remember that awesome scene in *The Matrix* when Neo realizes that he is 'the one'?" he asked.

"Sure I do."

"Well, I've got some amazing news for you. This is really big." He pointed at me and said: "In your universe, you're the one."

That made my day.

PART 2

PHYSICAL HEALING

CHAPTER 12

CLEANED OUT BY MRS MOFFET

I woke up in the early hours of the morning and I couldn't get back to sleep. The cabin was dark and eerily quiet. I looked around but couldn't see or hear anything. Dawn hadn't broken yet, so I lay in bed, motionless, processing my thoughts. I had a lot to think about. Henry Jones had turned my world upside down and inside out. My old belief systems lay strewn on the floor. Everything I thought I knew had been challenged and conquered. But, I didn't feel defeated. On the contrary, I felt rebooted. It had all been surprisingly cathartic.

Yes, technically I was sick. I could feel it in my body. An annoying ever-present pinch of pain reminded me of my disease. But, I was on a healing journey, and that understanding gave me more than a measure of comfort – it gave me a sense of purpose. I revelled in my new feelings and ideas. They kept me entertained until the silence was eventually usurped by the sounds of nature. I listened intently as flocks of birds and colonies of insects gradually came to life. The stillness of the cabin had served its purpose well.

I can't say for certain what time I surfaced, but I know it was long before sunrise. Only when I lit a candle did I notice that Henry Jones's bed was empty. Both he and his mattress were missing. That struck me as odd, but I wasn't surprised. He was full of surprises.

We'd planned to leave for the city after breakfast, so I decided to make the most of the time I had left at the cabin by taking a stroll down to the spot where I'd sat in silence for three days. I knew I'd miss that extraordinary place. Henry Jones and I had shared a very special time together. I'd never forget it. It had been life-changing. I'd rediscovered the peace of mind I had not realized I'd lost. I only knew I wanted more of it. Lots more!

I found Henry Jones asleep on the balcony beside the waning fire. He'd obviously camped out under the stars. It was the perfect time and place for it, after all. He sure knew how to suck the marrow out of life.

I couldn't help staring at his face for a moment. Asleep, he looked his age. His cheeks were sunken and his mouth drew downwards at the corners. His slow, deep breathing might've been mistaken for a snore. Without his radiant life energy in motion, he seemed to be a perfectly ordinary, elderly person. I had such great appreciation and affection for the man that it was impossible not to smile. I patted his back ever so gently and tip-toed across the creaking balcony towards the steps that led to the viewing area.

The sunrise was spectacular. Of all the mornings I'd spent at the cabin, that particular sunrise was by far the most memorable. I felt certain Mother Nature had produced it just for me. Yes, she had conjured up this extraordinary exhibition so that her limitless capacity for beauty and splendor would forever be etched in my mind. Light poured in from the shimmering sphere nestled in the saddle between two hilltops at the horizon, and then it rolled up the valley towards me. I watched in awe as the mountains and gorges gradually revealed themselves to me. I soaked up each second of the experience, until I felt the warm rays on my face and the new day had finally arrived in all its glory. It was a grand start to my day.

After sunrise, I made my way back to the cabin, where I found Henry Jones staring intently at a big, ripe strawberry. He held it in his fingers, examining it closely. Without looking up, he said: "Do you remember the scene in *The Matrix* when Neo stops the bullets mere inches from his face, and then picks one out with his fingers, looks at it, and then tosses it aside because he had no use for it?"

"Sure I do," I replied somewhat perplexed by this strange salutation.

"Do me a quick favor," he said. "Take a look at your hands. Wriggle your fingers."

I did as he asked and then stared at him quizzically.

He took his time to respond. "The most natural thing that you can do with your hands is pick fruit and vegetables and put them into your mouth. They were perfectly designed for this purpose. Unfortunately, in the matrix of modern life, people use plastic or metal instruments to feed themselves unnatural food products, so the connection to nature is lost. Worst of all, in this anaesthetized state, very little consideration is given to the effect ingested substances have on the body. People happily shovel any old good-tasting junk food into their stomachs. How detached must you be from your true-self to eat food and drink liquid that's harmful to you?"

I wasn't sure if this was a question or an exclamation. It sounded more like the latter.

"As detached as one can be is my guess."

"Terribly tragic!" he sighed. Henry Jones snatched his eyes away from the strawberry and flashed them towards me. I felt his steel gaze. "You mustn't do this anymore, my friend."

"Do what?"

Eat clean

"You mustn't put unnatural food into your body. The next time you're about to eat something, I want you to stop and consider your actions. If the food isn't useful to your body, toss it aside, no matter how good it tastes. It's time to bring out the Neo in you."

I chuckled. His metaphor amused me immensely. I got it. The ego-mind is the veil that's pulled over your eyes to blind you from the truth, but the instant you discover your true-self, the veil is lifted, and life as you know it can never be the same again.

I wanted Henry Jones to know that I'd received his message loud and clear. Impulsively, I snatched the strawberry from his hand, popped it into my mouth, and chewed it, moaning with sheer delight. His jaw dropped. He hadn't expected that response from me.

"Ha-ha-ha-ha!" he suddenly roared from his belly and repeatedly slapped his leg. Once again, his big smile filled his beautiful face. I bathed in his jubilance. Henry Jones was my tonic.

We enjoyed a fruit breakfast. Yes, I enjoyed it, too. Well, most of it anyway. Not long after, we were gunning it back down the sand road to the city. I felt sad to leave the cabin behind us and wondered if I'd ever return to that place. I imagined showing it to my wife. It was a pleasant thought.

Henry Jones put his Land Rover to the test on the dirt track. He floored it, and the vehicle responded with great enthusiasm. When we hit the smooth, tarred road, the old wagon showed her age. We chugged along while modern sedans overtook us like angry wasps on their way to war. My euphoria was about to be shattered.

"What's next?" I asked inquisitively.

"Colonic irrigation," he replied.

I gulped. I knew what that meant. Dread loomed inside of me.

"Is this absolutely necessary?" I protested.

"Yes."

I sucked in a big mouthful of air to carry my longwinded objection, but instead let it out like a deflating balloon. I sank into silence. What was the point? I knew I could not persuade Henry Jones otherwise. My healing journey felt like a rollercoaster ride.

"What kind of person sucks poo from people's bums for a living?" I eventually griped.

"You'll see soon enough," he sniggered, optimistically swerving the Land Rover into the fast lane.

I sat back in my seat, folded my arms in a huff and stared out the window. The upcoming procedure dominated my thoughts. I wasn't happy about it. Yes, I knew that the origin of my skepticism and closed-mindedness was my ego-mind, but I didn't care. In that moment, I knew that acceptance and open-mindedness would've been the appropriate response, but for some reason I just couldn't rise above my frustration. I felt conflicted. On the one hand, I wanted to live from my true-self and see the good in all things. On the other, some arbitrary stranger was about to stick a pipe up my arse. Where's the fun in that? Nope, I didn't fancy that. It sounded awful. My thoughts stewed in my head for the rest of the trip.

We arrived at the clinic without a minute to spare. Henry Jones dropped me at the entrance while he went to park the car. I rang the buzzer. The sign on the door said: Private Practice of Susan Moffet. The security door eventually clicked open. I took a deep breath and went inside.

"I'm here to see Susan," I grumbled to the person standing behind the counter.

The receptionist blew a bubble with her chewing gum until it burst. She had jet-black hair with dyed purple streaks that hung across her face, thick black eyeliner, pimples galore and studs in her lip, nose and ears. I didn't care for her type.

"You call her Mrs. Moffet," she told me in broken English with too much attitude and a strong Asian accent.

Her unprofessionalism pushed my buttons and my blood pressure shot up. This wasn't a good time for anyone to give me attitude. I was way out of my comfort zone and feeling vulnerable. My fuse was short.

"Listen," I growled. "When a customer walks into your place of business, the very least you can do is greet them properly."

My reaction was met by a deadpan stare and yet another big chewing gum bubble. My outburst hadn't perturbed her in the slightest. She pointed to the sofa. "You sit now," she shrieked.

"This service is unacceptable. I want to speak to your manager," I demanded.

"No, you take seat, fatso," she instructed.

"How dare you speak to me like that, you pimple-faced brat?" I bellowed.

"You no make trouble here! We busy here. You not only arsehole we see today."

That was it. I blew my top. I'd not had a good rant in ages and it felt really good. I told her exactly what I thought of her. I criticized and condemned her appearance, attitude, colonic irrigation, even Chinese food – I hit her with everything I had. But, it had no effect on her whatsoever. She gave me the middle finger. I thought my head was going to explode. My eyeballs bulged with anger. The only person readier for a fight than me was her. She clenched her fists and assumed an attack position.

"You wanna piece of me? I kung fu your fat arse, mister," she whined like an injured cat. Luckily, Henry Jones appeared on the scene. He was just in time, too. Things were about to get ugly! Another woman emerged hastily from an adjacent room and gripped the Asian kid at the elbows. Henry Jones pushed himself between us, but I did my best to push past him to get to her throat. It was on!

"That's enough!" shouted the woman holding back the punk kid. Her voice rang out above the chaos and hit its mark. I snapped out of my blind rage. Not the kid. She had to be dragged out of sight, kicking and screaming. Of course, I had no clue what she yelled at me in her mother tongue, but I'm pretty certain if I'd understood it, I would've wanted to wash her mouth out with soap.

"I can't leave you for a second, can I?" Henry Jones asked.

"She started it," I protested. "She …"

I never got to finish my sentence. Henry Jones closed his eyes and shook his head. He wasn't interested in my story. I suddenly realized how foolish I

CHAPTER 12 | CLEANED OUT BY MRS MOFFET

must've looked. What was I thinking? Why had I lashed out like that? What had come over me? I wondered.

The lady returned shortly. "I'm so sorry about that," she said, straightening her dress. "Lucy is an intern on a foreign exchange program. She doesn't usually manage our reception – that's my job – but I had to run an errand. Please accept my apology."

I composed myself. The actual receptionist was well-spoken and polite – absolutely professional. Normality had returned. Henry Jones gestured to me. "And?" he said in a parental way.

"I'm sorry for my bad behavior, too," I drawled somewhat sheepishly.

She nodded graciously.

"Mrs Moffet will be with you shortly," the receptionist said, pointing to the sofa in the waiting room. "Please, take a seat."

Henry Jones avoided eye contact with me. I assumed he was disappointed. I felt bad about that. We sat in silence for at least 15 minutes, which gave me a chance to cool off. The incident was over, but I still felt awkward about this appointment. The thought of a colonic irrigation gave me the willies.

I couldn't help but read and reread the only framed poster on the waiting room wall: "Clean Up Your Act." I wondered if it was a sign from the universe. It did jump out at me and the message gave me direction.

"You're absolutely certain I must do this ...?" I eventually asked Henry Jones once again.

He graciously accepted my attempt to break the ice.

"Yes. You can't have a mass of poisonous toxins floating around in your system if you want to heal your body. It's that simple," he told me quietly. "You've got to cleanse your bloodstream and activate your organs of elimination," he added in a low voice.

A few minutes went by before I spoke. "Are you sure Susan is the right person for this particular job?"

"Mrs Moffet."

"Eh?"

"Susan prefers to be called Mrs Moffet."

"Well, I think, since we're about to share such an intimate experience, we should at least be on a first-name basis."

Henry Jones cracked a hint of a smile. "Mrs Moffet prefers to keep a professional distance between herself and her clients. First names are out."

That made sense. Just then, I heard voices from down the hallway. Two women were approaching. Mrs Moffet wore a white laboratory coat and her patient had a freshly-dressed look about her. They hugged at the exit, for a long while. Mrs Moffet rubbed her patient's back affectionately. Their intimacy made me feel awkward. I stopped staring and pretended to check my fingernails instead. Then, it was my turn.

"You're up," Henry Jones said as Mrs Moffet floated towards us. His elbow jabbed my side. At that moment, I connected to my inner child. I felt like a naughty schoolboy waiting for the principal to dispense punishment. Henry Jones took to his feet and I followed him immediately. I struggled to make eye contact with her. I'm not sure why.

"Hello, Henry," Mrs Moffet said sweetly. Her voice was crystal clear. They also hugged one another. "And you must be Henry's special friend."

My nod was animated.

She shook my hand. Her touch was gentle – no, her whole being was gentle. One look at Mrs Moffet's lovely face and all my troubles seemed to melt away. She was in her mid-50s, attractive, slim and feminine. She had a pretty smile, and freckles scattered on her nose and cheeks. Most notably, Mrs Moffet sparkled and shone. I liked her instantly. In that moment, I realized my procedure would be just as unpleasant for her as it was going to be for me.

"I'm sorry for being here today," I murmured.

"Don't be a silly bumpkin," she replied softly. "I can help you to heal your body. That is the only thing that matters, right?"

It wasn't what she said that impacted on me so profoundly as the way she said it. Earlier on, I'd been raving about the kind of person who works as a colonic therapist. Now I knew: Someone who seeks to heal people; someone who cares more than most. What a fool I was! What an ego trip I'd been on! What a lesson I'd just learned!

"Please follow me. It's time to clean out your system," she said gently.

I smiled awkwardly.

"I'll wait right here," said Henry Jones.

"Oh no, you won't," she replied. "You're coming too, Henry."

He didn't argue.

Mrs Moffet flipped through my file as we walked to her consulting room. Her eyes widened. She was kind enough not to comment, but I could tell what she was thinking: I'd abused my body for years and now I was paying the price for it. I was out of shape, unfit, weak as a bird, and sick. I felt pathetic.

"Please take a seat," she said, pointing to the two visitor's chairs in front of her desk. We did exactly as she asked. Mrs Moffet didn't waste a minute. She got straight to it. "Let's begin by discussing your organs of elimination."

"What are those?" I asked flinching.

Jumpstart your organs of elimination

"Your body's organs of elimination are the skin, lungs, liver, kidneys and bowels," she said in the gentlest voice I'd ever heard. "We need to get all of these organs working for you. They're extremely effective at eliminating unwanted toxins and cleansing your system."

"How do we do that?" I asked.

"Well, the good news is that your body naturally detoxifies itself when you feed it properly and treat it well. You need a balanced diet."

"My idea of a balanced diet is a beer in each hand," I joked.

She wasn't amused. "This is your responsibility from now on. But, on top of this, I'm going to show you how you can individually activate your organs of elimination. Think of the techniques I'm about to share with you as tools that you can use to give your system a spring clean. Let's start at the bottom, shall we?" she said with a shy giggle.

I blushed.

She did, too. "As you already know, your bowels eliminate solid waste material. But what you may not know is that when food remains in your bowels for too long, it begins to rot. It's important to understand that your colon is your internal sewage system. When you eat food that's difficult to digest, you're creating a cesspool in your body. The problem is that this toxic waste doesn't remain in your colon," she added.

"Tell him where it goes," chirped Henry Jones.

"The toxic waste is absorbed into your bloodstream and then distributed throughout your entire body. Unfortunately, this weakens your whole system and sickness is spawned as a result."

"Your body literally poisons itself," Henry Jones interjected.

"He's right," she said. "I'm sad to say, all your organs of elimination have to work much harder to expel the toxins and impurities. So, your body burns vital energy trying to cleanse itself. This affects your mood, attitude, health and life," she told us.

"You don't want to lose energy on a healing journey," Henry Jones said. "You need every bit you have to heal your body. That is why you need to clean your bowels – and keep them clean."

Mrs Moffet agreed with him. She rubbed my arm encouragingly.

"So, I need colonic irrigation and a new diet. Right?" I responded in a brave voice.

"Yes. You need colonic irrigation because ingesting excessive amounts of bad food causes the toxic waste to become encrusted on the walls of your colon. This unwanted material can remain in your system until you die. I've seen autopsies where the colons are so encrusted with waste that the open channels are the width of a pencil. Can you imagine how much discomfort and pain this must've caused the poor person?"

I shuddered. "Okay, you've convinced me. Let's move on. What about my diet?"

Watch your diet

"You should stay away from refined foods, such as white sugar, white flour, white rice, processed oil and margarine. They're the main culprits of a clogged colon."

"While you're at it, you should also avoid greasy food and fleshy food," Henry Jones added.

"How come?"

Mrs Moffet whispered: "Well, for one thing, meat has no fibre in it, so it's very difficult to digest and expel."

My slow metabolism suddenly made sense. I was a big meat eater. I'd gorge myself on steak and chips at the drop of a hat. In fact, I insisted on seeing meat and potatoes on my plate every day, because I knew the meal would fill me up.

"I often feel constipated," I confessed.

"Well, you'll say goodbye to constipation when you start eating food that's rich in vitamins, minerals, fibre, bran and natural oils," she replied kindly. "Try eating fruit, fresh salads, raw or steamed vegetables, and wholegrain products for a week. You'll be astonished at how much better you feel," Mrs Moffet advised me.

"Actually, since we met, Henry Jones has insisted that I eat this way. Come to think of it, you're absolutely right. I do feel a bit better!"

"Of course you do, silly bumpkin," Mrs Moffet replied. "Eating the right food helps to keep your bowels regular. This ensures they stay clean and healthy."

I suddenly felt ashamed. I'd stuffed myself with junk food for years and I'd become a mean, old, grumpy bastard. In my defence, I never made the connection between the food I ate, my bowels and my behavior until that conversation with Mrs Moffet and Henry Jones. In that moment, I realized that I was my own worst enemy.

"Now, unfortunately I need to really gross you out," said Mrs Moffet. "I'm loath to tell you about some really low down, nasty little critters, but I must. They're the worst, foulest, meanest bacteria, and they thrive in your colon. If they're not flushed away regularly, they can cause infection. If ever you get an infection anywhere on or in your body, it's most probably because your colon is putrid and the bacteria are mounting an invasion. It's true. When you feel sick, down, depressed, or have aches and pains, it's most likely because of excess toxic waste in your body." She grimaced ever so sweetly. "For this reason, your first step to recovery should be to flush your bowels. That is why we are talking about enemas now."

"Oh dear! This is the part I've been dreading all morning," I confessed.

Start at the bottom

"You must get over it!" she answered back with surprising force. "Enemas are extremely beneficial. If you're sick and want to heal your body, then your healing process should always begin with an enema, followed by a short fast, followed by another enema, followed by the many wonderful healing techniques that Henry will undoubtedly show you, with regular enemas in between. They're that important! Whatever you do, you absolutely must break through the misconceptions you have about enemas. The best way to do that is to have an enema! Only by experiencing the amazing therapeutic effects of enemas will you come to realize their awesome power and importance in the healing process."

"I'd like to take your word for it, but that won't be enough, will it?"

"I'm afraid not. You've got to do it. But, don't panic! The procedure is uncomplicated and painless," Mrs Moffet said reassuringly.

Her effort to comfort me failed miserably. The mere thought of it terrified me. I couldn't hide the horror on my face.

Mrs Moffet turned to Henry Jones. "We've prepared a treatment room for you down the hallway, Henry. You know the procedure. You can leave us now."

Alone, she turned to me and smiled empathetically. Feeling uncomfortable and awkward, I reached for my notepad. Only when she had my undivided attention did she continue: "You have two options for enemas: You can visit a practitioner who specializes in colonic irrigation, like me, or you can purchase the proper equipment for a reasonable price from any good pharmacy and do it yourself."

"What equipment does one need?" I asked, hoping to find a way out of my predicament.

Mrs Moffet scrounged in the top draw of her desk. "Here we go," she said, handing me a small packet. "I'm feeling generous today, so you can have it. It's yours."

I wasn't sure what to say. I didn't know how to thank her. A home enema set was hardly a conventional gift.

"Open it up. Look at the contents. Enema packages usually consist of a container, a connecting hose with a clamp to control the flow, a specially made rectal tip (for easy insertion), step-by-step instructions and, if you're lucky, a lubricating gel. Otherwise just use body cream, Vaseline or soap."

"And then?"

"It's simple, really. Lie on your back with your feet in the air or resting on the toilet seat. Insert the flexible, soft, well-lubricated enema tip several inches into your rectum. Then, slowly release warm water (or a specially prescribed herbal tea) into your colon by adjusting the clamp or control mechanism. You can help to work the liquid through your colon using massage or by simply rocking from side to side. Roll on to your left side for a few minutes and then on to your right side. It may take several treatments before you'll be able to cleanse your entire colon without having to relieve yourself intermittently. Keep practising this technique. Practice is what makes perfect health possible!" she told me cheerfully.

I felt awkward just holding the packet, never mind actually using the equipment. "What about laxatives? Why can't I use laxatives instead?"

"Laxatives are great. I do recommend them. But they won't wash the entire length of your colon as effectively as an enema. This is very important!"

"What laxative do you suggest I use?" I asked, trying to change the subject.

"Oh, there are many excellent herbal products available on the shelves of supermarkets and pharmacies. Most of these products are already packaged in tea bags, so all you need to do is add hot water and allow the tea bag to soak for five to 10 minutes. Don't forget to drink them after meals. Not before!"

"My wife once gave me one of those 'poo teas' when I was constipated," I scowled. "But it gave me terrible stomach cramps."

Mrs Moffet dispensed an empathetic look. "To avoid stomach cramps, you should start by consuming small doses. If you like, I can give you the number of a good herbalist, who will provide you with the right herbs, show you how to prepare them for consumption, and advise you on quantities."

"What kind of herbs?" I asked suspiciously. Herbs didn't sound medical to me. I associated herbs with witchdoctors and people with bones through their noses.

"There are quite a few actually. Fennel seed, rhubarb root, calamus root, sage, senna, mandrake, mullein, psylla, and aloe all work well. But, I must caution you: Don't abuse herbal laxatives. Take them only when necessary. I repeat: You mustn't drink them for enjoyment. They must be consumed on occasion with the express intention of cleansing your bowels."

"Okay," I said.

"If you opt to go to an herbalist, make sure you find someone who is credible and trustworthy. Don't buy herbs from just anyone. There are a lot of snake-oil salesmen out there. While we're on the subject, there are other products that are designed to cleanse your colon, too. Go shopping. Most supermarkets, pharmacies and health stores offer a variety of other products. Many of them contain psyllium, which is very effective in aiding bowel function by providing a natural mucilaginous fibre. One or two teaspoons in a large glass of water, one hour before a meal, will usually do the trick. They don't taste great, but they work!"

"Okay, I'll give it a go."

"Excellent. Now, let's clean out your system, shall we? It's time for your enema."

I gulped loudly.

"Strip down to your underpants and then slip on this robe. I'll be expecting you in the treatment room next door."

I obliged.

"Please lie down on the bed and make yourself comfortable," Mrs Moffet whispered and crinkled her nose. She rubbed my arms tenderly. "It'll be alright, Sweetie. I've done this therapy hundreds and hundreds of times before." What followed should not be described. It wasn't fun, but it wasn't nearly as bad as I imagined it would be. It was painless. Only my ego was bruised. More importantly, the treatment washed my colon clean. I was purged.

Afterwards, Mrs Moffet and I got chatting. "Tell me, Dearie, have you ever heard the expression: 'Prevention is better than cure'?"

"Sure. Why do you ask?"

"Isn't it obvious?"

The wonders of fruit

"You can save yourself all this bother by eating lots of fruit – it's the perfect food. It's full of vitamins, minerals, proteins, essential nutrients and natural sugars. The nutrients, sugars, proteins and fats are in their simplest form, which means that fruit doesn't have to be broken down any further in your stomach. It's ready to be digested and absorbed into your system as soon as you swallow it. So, your body uses very little energy to process fruit and your body has more energy to focus on cleansing your system and restoring your health. Fruit also contain acids that help your body to eliminate toxins and other impurities. A fruit diet will disinfect your stomach and keep your system clean. Best of all, fruit leaves an alkaline residue in your bloodstream. When its alkaline and pure, your bloodstream will dissolve all poisons, bacteria and viruses and carry them away. No disease can exist in a body that has a pure bloodstream."

I pricked up my ears. Had I heard her correctly? "Eating fruit purifies your bloodstream?"

"Yes, it does. Mother Nature is a genius. She knows exactly what your body needs. I encourage you to read up on fruit. You'll discover there are three basic categories of fruit: Acidic, sub-acidic and sweet fruit. You should eat fruit from one category at a time, although sub-acidic fruits can be eaten with sweet and acidic fruits."

"Why is this important?"

"In short, acidic fruits are digested like proteins, and sweet fruits are digested like starches. I'm pretty sure Henry will tell you all about food combining in due course. I'll leave that lesson to him. What I will tell you, however, is that consuming proteins and starches together isn't good for you. When you eat fruit from the same category, your body will digest the fruit more easily and absorb more nourishing nutrients. That will give you even more energy."

I made a note to search for lists of acidic, sub-acidic and sweet fruits on the Internet. I knew I'd find all the information I needed in seconds.

"That sounds good to me. Heaven knows, I need all the energy I can get," I told her.

Liquidize your veggies

"In that case, let me introduce you to veggie juices. They're my favorite drink in the world! They're nutritious and delicious and will make you feel energetic, healthy and rejuvenated. There's no going back once you get into drinking veggie juices."

"Liquidized vegetables!" I exclaimed in horror. Henry Jones had been pumping me full of carrot juice every chance he got, but I never thought about adding other vegetables. I ate vegetables on a Sunday afternoon with roast chicken. I never drank them!

"Yes. You should try it. You'll be surprised how much natural moisture is contained in vegetables. It's quite incredible! Drinking this liquid is exceptionally good for you! Veggie juices are very powerful healers."

"Really?"

"Oh yes, Sweetie. Essentially, vegetables are composed of moisture and roughage. The moisture contains the nutrients and the roughage stimulates the intestines. When your body digests vegetables, it relies on enzymes to separate the moisture from the roughage. The moisture is absorbed into your bloodstream, and the roughage is excreted as waste. When you liquidize vegetables, all the vitamins, minerals, essential fats, proteins and carbohydrates are released into your glass. You also get a healthy dose of flavonoids, enzymes, chlorophyll and carotene, which help to protect your body. So, as you can probably imagine, drinking vegetable juices greatly assists the digestive process. By consuming the nutrients in liquid form, they're absorbed into your bloodstream and used by your body within minutes. This gives your blood a nutrient transfusion, which feeds your organs and balances your system. But most of all: The energy that your body would've used digesting the solid food can be used for rebuilding, repairing and restoring your cells. Try it. But, don't expect immediate results. Your body must first expel all the toxins and poisons from your system before your recovery process can begin. That may take a while, so be patient. Continue to nurture yourself properly, and nature will cure you in its own time and in its own way. Does this make sense to you?"

"It does, thank you," I answered, tapping my notepad with the back of my pen. I wondered what vegetable combinations would work well together. I couldn't think of any. "Where can I find recipes for veggie juices?" I asked Mrs Moffet.

"Well, you can always nip out to your local bookstore and buy a book on vegetable juices. They're bound to have more than one for you to choose from. But, I believe the best way is to experiment with different combinations for yourself. It's very easy. Use carrot juice as the primary ingredient in your vegetable juice blends. A ratio of 50/50 will do nicely. Try different combinations of celery, beetroot, ginger, green and yellow peppers, lettuce, spinach, and whatever else you can find in your fridge. Give it a go. You'll discover an amazing range of taste sensations that'll have you wiping the bottom of your glass with your finger and scooping the last morsels into your mouth. They're that tasty!"

Tips for juicing

"There are a few important points to remember," Mrs Mofett said.
"Such as?"
"Well, for one, you shouldn't mix vegetable and fruit juices."
"Why not?"
"Because fruit has an eliminating effect, while vegetables have a building effect. Plus, fruit contains water and vegetables contain oils. The two don't work well together. I'd be strict about this on a healing journey. But, if you promise not to tell anyone, I'll admit that I love the taste of carrot juice with apples and grapes and pineapples and peaches and pears and avocado, or even combinations of these fruits. Especially with crushed almond nuts! Those blends are super-yummy! Another thing: Make sure you wash the vegetables thoroughly before you liquidize them. The pesticides and preservatives used by farmers are toxic. Be careful!"

"Should I remove the skins?" I asked.

"No. Don't remove the skins. The skin is very nutritious. Your liquidizer will separate the skin from the juice. Oh, by the way, you should avoid unripe, over-ripe and wilted vegetables. Fresh vegetables are best for you, and it's best to drink the juice as soon as possible after liquidizing."

Henry Jones later explained to me that raw vegetable juices don't contain preservatives, so they can go off within a couple of hours of being liquidized.

Mrs Moffet walked over to a bar fridge and returned with a jug of juice. She poured two glasses. The juice dropped into the glasses like wet cement. It was thick and chunky. "Here we go. Try this, Sweetie," she said, handing me a spoon.

"What is it?" I asked.

"A delightful surprise!" she replied, smiling.

"It looks like baby food," I remarked, failing to conceal my revulsion.

She giggled. "Go on, try it. It's good for you."

I won't lie. I was reluctant to taste it. It was green, clumpy and dotted with white specks. But I didn't really have a choice. I took a bit on my spoon and tasted it on the tip of my tongue before putting it into my mouth. Much to my surprise, it was delicious! "That's not half bad. What's in it?" I asked.

"Mashed papaya, avocado and almond. Mashing is the key. Whenever you need to heal your body, it's a good idea to assist your digestive system by mashing fruit and vegetables into a pulp before eating them. It makes it much easier for your stomach to separate the moisture from the roughage when the food arrives soft. Don't forget this: Less energy spent in your tummy means more energy for healing. It also helps to chew your food properly because your mouth produces more saliva, which contains enzymes that help to digest certain foods. As a rule of thumb, you should only swallow when you think the food in your mouth can't be broken down any further. Alright Dearie?"

"My grandmother told me to chew my food 22 times before swallowing," I recalled.

"In principle, that's good advice. Do it. Do whatever it takes to heal your body. Now, while you're enjoying your liquid meal, let's discuss your skin."

"My skin?" I blurted. Had she not read my file? My health problem had nothing to do with my outer wrapping. It was my inner workings that weren't functioning properly.

"Have you ever heard the expression: 'Shiny, happy people'? That's because healthy people have beautiful, radiant complexions. Skin fascinates me. It's your body's biggest organ, and it breathes. It thrives on sunlight and fresh air, and it constantly purifies itself. Believe it or not, you shed at least one layer of skin a day."

"That much?"

Care for your skin

"Oh yes, Sweetie. Your skin is amazing! It has an extraordinary ability to regenerate itself. It actually has an inbuilt mechanism to clean and purify itself. In fact, your skin is porous. That is why you have to be so careful about what lotions and oils you apply. They seal your pores and suffocate your skin. Modern cosmetics are toxic – they contain chemicals and other foreign substances that are poisonous to your system. These are absorbed straight through your skin into your body. Obviously, this affects your system, no matter what the manufacturers tell you," she said, clenching her fist. "The truth is that your skin is an outward reflection of your internal condition. The only way to nourish your skin is from within."

"How do I do that?"

"You silly bumpkin. When you eat the correct food, your skin naturally produces oils that keep it looking and feeling great."

"I should've guessed."

"Your diet is the key here. You can tell at a glance if someone eats healthily. Healthy skin glows. But when you see skin that's grey, dull, dry, oily, spotty or blemished, you can bet it's because of a bad diet and poor living habits. It's honestly that simple."

"Does it have something to do with the purity of the blood?"

"Exactly! The state of your skin is determined by the state of your blood. If you want to have clean, healthy skin, then you must do whatever it takes to get clean, healthy blood. And the best way to do this is …?"

Mrs Moffet paused. She was testing me.

"Eating healthily, exercising regularly and living correctly," I answered back proudly.

"Wow! Henry is certainly working his magic on you," she teased.

We laughed. Yes, I was making progress. Had Mrs Moffet met me a month ago she would've thought I was a monster. I suddenly regretted my altercation with the intern. It had been uncalled for. She was just a pimple-faced kid after all. I felt the urge to apologize to Mrs Moffet. She listened intently as I tried to explain myself. When I was done, she just sighed.

"Lucy is a special case. She desperately needs skin treatment but couldn't afford it back home. She comes from a very poor family. They have lived on the streets of Shanghai for most of their lives. Unfortunately, her diet consisted of whatever she could scavenge. This wreaked havoc on her skin and self-image."

I suddenly knew why Lucy let her hair hang down over her face. I also realized why she had reacted so badly to me. I had called her a pimple-faced brat. The blood drained from my cheeks. I felt dreadful. Lucy was right. I was an arsehole. What the hell was wrong with me?

Right then and there, my morning lesson with Mrs Moffet and Henry Jones sunk in. I realized that I was full of crap. Literally! I shuddered to think of the state of my bowels before the enema. I bet poisonous toxins encrusted my intestines. I was grumpy, irritable, short-tempered and mean-spirited.

The morning sunrise had elevated my consciousness to a new level, yet a few short hours later, I was attacking a homeless street urchin from Shanghai. My healing journey had hit another rocky patch.

"You with me? You drifted off for a moment," she said.

"Sorry." I shook my head to clear my thoughts. "Will you be able to help Lucy?"

"Of course. The human body has a remarkable ability to recuperate and repair damage. We'll help her to purify her blood by feeding her natural foods and flushing her system regularly. The instant she embarks on a healthy lifestyle, her skin will start to heal."

"How long have you been treating her?"

"She only arrived from Shanghai a few days ago, but give her two or three months and you won't recognize her. We're hoping to find a sponsor to pay for her full treatment. With a bit of luck, by the time she goes back home, she'll be staring at her complexion in the mirror in utter amazement. Her attitude will be much better, too! Psychologically speaking, healthy skin does wonders for one's self-image. It's easy to feel great about yourself when you look good. Have you noticed that people who have poor skin tend to be very self-conscious?"

I scribbled down notes as fast as possible. Something Mrs Moffet said had given me a great idea. More about that later.

Learning how to activate my organs of elimination was making me feel empowered. "So, how else can one treat skin?"

Dry rub

"Well, cold and hot towel rubs are a great way to improve blood circulation. They're very easy to do, and only take a couple of minutes. Try this technique now," she said, handing me a rough hand towel. "Sit at the end of the bed by the basin. You can do this at home, sitting at the edge of the bath or on a stool. Wet the towel in cold water, wring it nearly dry and wrap it around your hand. Then, proceed to rub the towel vigorously up and down one body part at a time."

I did as she asked. She kept herself busy by filling a kettle with water and bringing it to the boil.

"How long must I keep this up?"

"Since you're light-skinned, do it until your skin turns pink. When you've finished rubbing a body part, use a warm towel to dry it off immediately. Pat your skin gently. Repeat this process until you've done your whole body."

"How do I get to my back?"

"Grip each end of the towel and pull it back and forth across your back."

It was surprisingly tiring and I was soon out of breath. "Shoo, this is hard work. I thought you said towel rubs were easy," I panted.

"Hmmm, the technique is simple, but practising it can be quite exhausting – especially when you're not well! So, take it easy. Relax between body parts. Catch your breath. Only move on to the next body part when you're perfectly ready."

Sure enough, my skin turned pink. I felt invigorated and could see and feel instant results.

"My skin is tingling all over," I murmured in amazement.

"I'm not surprised. The flowing blood cells are stimulating your nerve endings. They're loving it! It's not just the physical reaction to which they're responding. On another level altogether, your intention to nurture and heal your body is activating your ability to self-heal. When you apply concentration and focus to healing yourself, you harness an incredible, natural power."

"I'm enjoying this healing technique immensely," I declared excitedly.

She responded. "For really great results, give yourself a complete cold towel rub before taking a relaxing bath, either early in the morning or at night before you go to bed. Your whole body will come alive. Imagine the tingling sensation is healing energy flowing through your body. I'm certain you'll find the exercise soothing and enjoyable. It's good to pamper yourself occasionally. It's one of life's great joys."

"I'm sold on joy," I said.

Hot and cold fomentations

"Speaking of which, let me introduce you to hot and cold fomentations. They're a great way for you to pamper yourself and heal your body."

"What do fomentations do?"

"Fomentations draw blood to your skin, relieving internal congestion."

"How does that work?"

"Well, when you apply a cold-water fomentation to your skin, your blood vessels contract after a few minutes. When the fomentation is removed, your blood vessels dilate. This brings new blood to the area, stimulating improved circulation. The opposite effect happens when a hot fomentation is applied. Your blood cells will dilate when you apply the hot fomentation, and contract when you remove it. This will squeeze blood through your veins. It'll also increase your heart rate and induce perspiration, which is great for improving circulation and cleansing your pores. Because of the contraction and dilation, blood is pumped to your internal organs. Obviously, the organs closest to the fomentation are the most affected, so specific ailments can be treated directly. These treatments are very soothing and, when applied correctly, genuinely ease pain and discomfort."

"Can I do it myself?"

"Yes, but it's far more therapeutic and enjoyable to be pampered by a friend or loved one."

"What do I do exactly?" I asked with the steely tone of a solo pilot with engine trouble.

Mrs Moffet read between the lines and nodded compassionately. "Let me show you, Sweetie," she replied kindly. "These treatments require preparation. For a cold fomentation, put a couple of liters of water into the fridge or freezer a couple of hours before your treatment. For hot fomentations, boil a kettle just before you begin the process. I boiled the kettle earlier, so let's make a hot fomentation now."

"Alright, lead the way."

"When you give yourself a fomentation, you must create a comfortable environment where you can lie down and have all the necessary equipment nearby. Today, we'll use this bed. At home, you can lie on a bed or on the floor. I recommend the floor, which is grounding. But make sure that the ground beneath you isn't cold. Use a pillow for your head, and lay down a towel to absorb excess water," Mrs Moffet said. Next, she handed me a stack of towels from a nearby shelf. "To make a single fomentation, you'll need two hand towels. You might use three or four fomentations in one session. Fold one of the hand towels over to create three layers and then pour the hot or cold water over the middle of this towel until it's saturated. You must wring out the excess water, so try not to wet the ends of the towel. When it's nearly dry, unwind it back to three layers. Now, wrap it in one of the dry towels, front and back. Lie down and place a dry towel over the area that requires attention. Then, place the fomentation on top of the dry towel, which will help to protect your skin. You can put a piece of plastic over the fomentation to contain the heat or cold. For maximum effect, tuck in the plastic on the sides of the fomentation."

Mrs Moffet handed me all the items I needed. I followed her instructions to a tee. She watched my every move. I must say, the heat the fomentation generated on my skin surprised me. It started to burn.

She spotted my distress. "If the heat or cold causes you too much discomfort, slightly lift the fomentation for a moment. The relief will be instant," she said. She was right. I replaced the fomentation on a different area. It was piping hot. "Whatever you do, don't tense your body during this treatment. Hot and cold applications should be very relaxing. This is crucial. You must be able to enjoy the comfort the fomentation brings. Once again, you may feel a pleasant tingling sensation inside your body, or on your skin. That's a sure sign the treatment is working."

I could feel it. It was unmistakable.

Mrs Moffet continued her lesson. "To increase the psychological effects, breathe deeply and imagine that you're drawing each breath through the fomentation, instead of your nose or mouth. This technique creates a circular flow of energy inside your body, which is very stimulating and highly therapeutic."

Breathe through the fomentation? Is that even possible? I wondered. I tried it. To my amazement, I discovered that you can trick yourself into believing that you're breathing through the fomentation.

"It's working!" I cried.

"That's good. Very good!" she replied. "I'll leave you to treat yourself for about 10 minutes. When the temperature seems to lose its effect, remove the application, dry off your body completely and repeat the process. Okay, Sweetie?"

"How many times?" I asked.

"Three or four times will be sufficient to produce the desired effect. You hang in there. I'm off to see how Henry is doing. I'll be back to check on you soon."

I lay there, motionless, waiting for the fomentation to work its magic. Occasionally, I'd make adjustments and change positions. There wasn't anything else to do except think. Lucy took center stage. I wondered how she had got an internship with Mrs Moffet, and I wondered about her life on the streets of Shanghai and how I could make up for my bad behavior. I practised breathing through the fomentation. But focus and concentration eluded me. I'd only learn how to focus and concentrate much further down the line on my healing journey.

Mrs Moffet returned a short while later with a soft, fluffy blanket. "When you've finished your session, be sure to keep warm and relax. Wrap yourself in this blanket."

I took it and padded myself down. My skin was delightfully sensitive. "That was amazing, thank you."

She smiled. "You'll feel the effect of this simple yet powerful treatment for a few hours after each session."

"How often should I do it, Mrs Moffet?"

"During the initial stages of your healing journey, two sessions per week will suffice. If you're in pain, you can do more. No doubt, this treatment will help you tremendously. I'm certain of it. Caring for yourself is a wonderful tonic."

"Anything else?"

Salt glow

"Have you ever done a salt glow?" Mrs Moffet's question grabbed my attention.

"Nope. I don't even know what that is."

"Well, you're in for a real treat. Salt glows are fantastic, Sweetie. They make you feel alive and invigorated. I don't know anyone who has had a salt glow and not felt invigorated and uplifted afterwards," Mrs Moffet declared. "Salt glows must be experienced. It's the only way to see how effectively they open and clean out your skin's pores. I highly recommend salt glows, especially when you're sick!"

"What do I have to do?" I sighed. It wasn't that I was apathetic about trying the technique. On the contrary, I was keen to try it right then and there. I had sighed because she'd reminded me I was sick.

"Follow me," she said, leading me to a small, private bathroom. It was more homely than clinical, and someone had taken the time to decorate it nicely. I guessed it was Mrs Moffet herself, judging by the way she straightened a framed photograph of flying ducks that had been mounted to the wall at the bathroom entrance. She had the look of a proprietor.

"Now, I'd like you to run a hot bath that's ankle-deep. Then, sit on the edge of the bath with your feet in the water. Cover your shoulders with a towel to keep warm. Take a handful of this common coarse salt, dip it into the water and proceed to rub the coarse salt vigorously over your entire body. Work on one body part at a time – just as you did with the towel rub," she said. "Keep your hand cupped to contain the salt. The excess salt will fall into your bath water and dissolve. Most importantly, don't press too hard on your skin. You don't want the salt to be too abrasive. Be gentle, but firm."

"What does the salt do?" I asked.

"It removes dead skin cells and cleanses your skin pores," she replied. When you've completed the treatment, sit or lie down in the bath and gently wash the salty water over your entire body. Be loving to yourself. After bathing in the salty water, wash the salt off your skin in a warm shower. Don't use soap or apply any cream. Water is all you need."

"Got it," I assured her. It seemed simple enough to me.

"I'll be back in a minute or two. I want to see that you're doing the exercise correctly, and then I'll leave you to treat yourself for about 10 minutes," she informed me.

I gave a salute and she giggled.

"Oh, by the way, don't be surprised if your skin tingles afterwards. You can also expect it to feel very smooth and sensitive. Slight redness is normal. You won't believe how awesome your skin will look and feel within an hour or two. It's amazing! When the natural oils in your skin come to the surface, your skin will literally glow. Hence the name: Salt glow."

She exited the room and I was left alone with a packet of course salt in my hand and a stupefied expression on my face. I looked around the room. It was empty and the door was closed. No one could see me, so I did it! I gave myself a salt glow, and it was good. Really good! I followed Mrs Moffet's instructions, and they worked like a charm. She was dead right. My skin did feel and look awesome afterwards. It may have been the old me on the inside, but I felt like a new me on the outside. It's like getting your hair cut, or clipping your toenails, or walking in new shoes, only better. I had tingles all over my body, and I liked it!

After washing the salt from my body in the shower cubical, I wrapped a robe around my glistening body and waited on a bench outside the bathroom for Mrs Moffet to return. The sunlight felt delicious on my skin and face. I felt invigorated and my head was spinning. I'd never felt that good in hospital. Why hadn't I taken better care of my body? Why hadn't I frequented wellness spas? Why did I deny myself this nurturing and care? I wondered.

"What's next?" I whispered apprehensively.

CHAPTER 13

CRASH, BOOM, BANG!

Mrs Moffet glided towards me, as if on air. "Next on our agenda is a session with our chiropractor."

That's odd, I thought. I hadn't hurt my back. What was she up to now?

"Meet Kevin," Mrs Moffet said. "He's going to reset your bone structure."

"But I …" I never got in another word.

"Every healing journey should begin with a trip to a chiropractor. It's essential to restore the structural integrity of your spine and reduce pressure on the sensitive neurological tissue. This will consequently improve your health. Fifteen minutes on the table with Kevin and you'll feel like a different person. He'll align and balance the architecture of your body, so the vital force of your natural energy system can flow unencumbered through it. Lie down, Sweetie," she instructed, patting the bed.

I did as I was told. She gave Kevin a commanding nod, and he bowed his head as she left the room. I'm not sure why, but I felt awkward and vulnerable. Kevin proceeded to make my back, neck, shoulders and joints pop and crack like an angry fire. Much to my surprise, it wasn't painful at all. In fact, I rather enjoyed it. The sudden release of tension with each new position invigorated me. As it turns out, Mrs Moffet was right. After my session, I did feel like a whole, new person.

Mrs Moffet arrived precisely as my treatment with Kevin ended.

"Right, we're off to the steam bath and sauna now. Follow me, please," she announced and made off down the corridor.

Steam it out

"If you're fortunate enough to have one of these facilities in your vicinity, use it as often as possible. I recommend you have a sauna or steam bath a couple of times a month, at least! If you're on a healing journey, you need to do it twice a week or more. Do you know why?" she asked, opening the door for me.

"Let me guess," I replied. "Steam baths and saunas are excellent for opening your skin pores and getting rid of your body's waste material."

She grinned. "That's correct, Sweetie."

The inside of the building smelled like a gymnasium locker room. There was also the scent of another fragrance that I couldn't quite put my finger on. The presence of an exercise bike and treadmill was ominous.

"First of all, it's highly beneficial to exercise before taking a steam bath or sauna, even if it's just mild cardiovascular exercise, such as walking," Mrs Moffet said. "This helps to get your heart rate up. I want you to pop on to the treadmill and work up a sweat, if you can. Let's burn off 2000 calories in 20 minutes."

She must've seen the horrified look in my eyes.

"The last time I burned 2000 calories in 20 minutes, I forgot to take my wife's brownies out of the oven."

She laughed. "Don't panic, Sweetie! This exercise won't kill you. Promise."

I felt embarrassed. Twenty years ago, I would've jumped on to the treadmill and jogged five miles with ease. But, that was 20 years ago. Things had changed a lot since then.

"I don't have time to exercise much. I'm a very busy man," I tried to explain away my poor shape.

"Nonsense, Sweetie!" she answered back in an I'm-not-buying-it tone of voice. "You don't make time to exercise and you've become lazy." She told me straight without blinking or stammering. You could've knocked me over with a feather.

"Come on, jump on." Mrs Moffet coaxed me on to the treadmill. I looked down at my flabby belly in disgust. I recognized my feelings of self-loathing. She did, too. I wasn't obese – not even close. Let us just say that my middle-age spread had set in. In my mind, I wanted to be in good shape – fit and strong – like I was 20 years ago. But my present reality didn't match the image I had of myself. I felt like a failure. My ego-mind exposed itself to both of us.

"One step at a time," I quietly told myself.

As things turned out, it was a helluva lot more than one step at a time. Mrs Moffet set the treadmill to a blistering pace and left me to it. I almost had to run to keep up. I finally settled on a brisk walk. I found the right rhythm by swinging my arms like an Olympic speed walker, only with much less grace and elegance. My body jiggled like a lump of jelly on a spoon in the hand of a 90-year-old woman with a nervous disorder. To make matters worse, the sauna room was warm – much, much warmer than outside! I soon poured with sweat. It literally dripped off my nose. My desperate attempt to suck oxygen into my lungs, for fear of otherwise dying, combined with my wet, slimy skin and blubbery exterior, made me look like an alien life form that had just arrived on Earth and was struggling to adjust to our atmosphere. I wasn't a pretty sight – especially in my shorts! I know this to be true because someone had mounted life-sized mirrors on three of the four walls surrounding me. My God, I thought. Thank goodness no one can see me now. At that precise moment, the door opened and, to my absolute horror, I heard: "You no run too fast, fatso! You catch speed wobble. Then you fall off and hit the wall. Mrs Moffet no want broken wall," the crazy intern from Shanghai shrieked.

All it took was that single momentary loss of concentration and I tripped over my big feet and was sucked backwards with great force. It was calamitous, to say the least. I attempted to save myself by grabbing the rail of the treadmill as I flew by. This action not only failed dismally, but made matters considerably worse. My body swung around. The sheer velocity ripped the railing from my hand and sent me rolling towards her. I travelled in much the same way that a greased, 110kg bowling ball would glide down a smooth lane. Every second or so, I'd see her screaming face. My rolling was unstoppable. Now, I know Henry Jones had been filling my head with images from *The Matrix* all week long, but I swear at the last second before I rammed into her, the world shifted into slow motion and Lucy leaped into the air like a cat that had been thrown into a pit of bull terriers.

She missed me – not by inches, but by feet. Unfortunately for me, gravity set in and I veered to the left. I streaked through the thin table legs of the only table standing between me and the door. This table had been supporting a large bowl of lilies. I only realized that when the bowl disintegrated next to me and it started raining flowers. Things came to an abrupt halt when I crashed into the door. The hinges, as it turned out, were made of iron and the door stood fast. I, on the other hand, folded like a giant water balloon that had been blasted from a cannon.

Lucy landed on her feet like a ninja. "Now you done it, mister. You crash house. You in big trouble now," she cried out, and pointed at me accusingly. She backed towards the exit. I expected her to leave the room with a flying forward roll, but that didn't happen. She stomped her foot, as if crushing a cigarette butt, and stormed out shouting for Mrs Moffet as loudly as she could.

Henry Jones was the first to appear on the scene. He was wet and naked, except for a small, white towel clenched around his waist. Although he looked a comical sight, he was taking my accident very seriously. He was genuinely concerned for me. Coming around, I propped myself up against the wall and scanned my body for pain. My ribs hurt, but everything else seemed fine.

It was one heck of a wallop, but it wasn't a serious injury. I was fine. More than fine, actually. Henry Jones, Mrs Moffet, Lucy and the receptionist had all arrived at once and were clearly distraught.

"Don't move," Mrs Moffet yelled as she and the others scrambled to get to me.

"Don't crowd him. Give him air," Henry Jones added.

Had this bizarre incident happened to me a week ago, I would've lost my mind completely. Seriously! I'd have screamed blue murder, and probably threatened to sue them. But, good, caring people surrounded me. They didn't deserve that kind of outburst from me. They only had my best interests at heart. I knew this to be true. Besides, it was my fault. I had tripped. I was out of shape, unfit, uncoordinated and clumsy. I hadn't been paying proper attention to the exercise because I had been on an ego trip. I saw myself for what I was, and all I could do was laugh loudly. I laughed so hard that my belly and ribs hurt even more, but that didn't stop my guffaw.

"He must be hysterical," the receptionist suggested. They studied me closely with stupefied expressions on their faces.

Lucy had another viewpoint. "He hit head. He no think too clear now. Fatso confused."

"I'm fine," I insisted, wiping the tears from my eyes.

"Are you sure? Does it hurt? Is anything broken?" Mrs Moffet asked.

"No. Seriously, I'm fine."

"Try standing up. Slowly." Kevin said, lifting me carefully from behind.

"Ouch!" I moaned.

251

"Be gentle," Henry Jones added.

"He's hurt!" cried the receptionist. "I'll call a doctor."

"No, no, no," I insisted, getting to my feet. "My ribs are a bit sore, otherwise, I'm perfectly fine. Thank you for caring so much, but there's no need to be concerned. Really!"

They stepped back cautiously, although I could tell they were ready to pounce forward in case I toppled over. I offered them my friendliest smile in an effort to reassure them.

"I told you. He crazy guy. He not right in the head!" Lucy squawked, pointing at me accusingly.

Mrs Moffet naturally tried to take charge of the situation. She ushered the others out of the room.

"Boy-oh-boy, I've been a troublesome customer, huh?" I said sheepishly.

Mrs Moffet blinked repeatedly. I'd startled her. "Let's just say you're unforgettable," she said, searching for something positive to say. I appreciated her response. It'd been an unforgettable experience for me, too.

"Should we continue?" she asked.

I smiled. "There's no way back now," I replied. "I'm on a healing journey."

Crash, boom, pow! Hearing those words from my mouth hit me like a ton of bricks. It was the first time that I'd publicly proclaimed my process. I was actually doing it, and that made me feel good. I was no longer a victim of disease. I was no longer patient number 63507/2018. I was proactively helping my body to heal itself, and that was empowering. Henry Jones had given me back control of my life. He'd helped me to realize that healing my body was in my hands. It was my responsibility – and mine alone. No one else could make me live as my true-self. No one else could eat healthily for me. No one else could make me visit healing practitioners. That was all up to me. For the first time in a long time, I had a sense of hope and a goal. I was a man on a mission. I was on my way to restoring my body to perfect health. Yes, I was on my healing journey, and I liked it.

"Okay then, if you're absolutely 100% certain you're up for it …"

"I am. Believe me."

Mrs Moffet slowly slid open the shower door without taking her eyes off me for a second. "You should always take a hot shower just before you enter a steam room or sauna," she said. "This'll help to cleanse and vitalize your skin pores. But don't use soap of any kind. I repeat: Don't use soap. Water is God's own cleaning agent," Mrs Moffet instructed.

"Got it," I said.

"Then, when you're in the steam room or sauna, sit upright. You may have seen people sitting folded over or lying down. This is entirely wrong. You should sit upright and lift your sternum, so that your chest opens up and you can breathe easily. Remember, your lungs are organs of elimination, too. Work them. Take deep, slow breaths through your nose and mouth. Occasionally, rub your entire body vigorously using your fingertips. Tighten your finger muscles for deeper penetration. This'll get your circulation going and vitalize your skin. But be gentle over your ribs, okay Sweetie?"

I gave her a thumbs-up.

"Be warned: As your body releases toxins, you may feel dizzy or nauseous. If this happens, get out of the sauna or steam bath immediately and cool down by fanning yourself and taking deep breaths. Furthermore, don't stay in the steam room or sauna if the heat becomes unbearable. Did you hear me? Don't overdo it. Cleansing treatments are meant to be pleasurable, not torture. If you don't enjoy them, you won't want to do them again."

Make your shower count

"Alright," I assured her, shooing her away from the cubicle door so that I could get on with taking a shower.

"I'm not done yet, Sweetie," she responded. "After leaving the steam room or sauna, you should take another long, warm shower. I want you to shower for as long as you were in the steam room or sauna. Consider this process to be a water massage more than a shower. Once again, don't use soap. Rub your entire body vigorously with your fingertips. Allow the water to splash down on the spots that you're rubbing. This helps to wash away dead skin cells and released waste. It's also very beneficial for you to massage your kidneys with the balls of your hands. Use the back of your hands to rub your back. Your internal organs will love it."

"Is that it?" I asked over-eagerly.

"No. Another great area to massage is the top of your bum cheeks. This is where your lymph glands are situated. By stimulating your lymph glands, you help them to dispose of your body's waste material, which is their natural function."

"Jeez, I should fetch my notepad," I joked. "You take showering to a whole, new level."

She blushed. It was good to see the color come back into her cheeks. My accident had left her white as a sheet.

"I've got even more tricks up my sleeve for you," she said sweetly, tugging on the cuffs of her white lab jacket. "I want you to slowly massage your scalp and cheeks too. This is very pleasurable. You can also stroke your face. Push your fingers against your skin. This'll drive the blood through your face. Rub your ears inside and out using your forefingers and thumbs. This'll help to wash away any oily residue inside your ears. Do this, and you'll feel wonderful afterwards. I promise."

I nodded in much the same way a soldier nods to a commanding officer. "I sometimes switch off the hot water and end with a cold shower. That's okay, isn't it?" I asked.

"No. It's not! Never switch the shower water from hot to ice cold. The shock to your system is unnecessary. You must always be gentle on yourself during your healing process. Your body will respond positively to tender loving care. If you want to end off with a cold shower, which can be invigorating, adjust the water from hot to cold in stages. Make sure you feel comfortable with the new temperature before you add more cold water. Oh yes, be sure to inhale deeply each time you make the water colder. This'll help you and your body to process the change in temperature. By the time you get out of the cold shower, you should feel revitalized and very much alive. Are you ready now?"

"I sure am."

"Good. Then go for it. I'll be back in 20 minutes or so. Enjoy your shower and steam bath," Mrs Moffet said, heading for the door.

The healing power of massage

Half an hour later, I found Mrs Moffet. She'd left a note on the door, telling me to meet her in the Lavender Room when I was done. There was no sign of Henry Jones.

"Has anyone ever rubbed your shoulders after a really stressful day at work?"

"Sure," I replied.

"It feels great, doesn't it?"

"You bet."

"Massages are one of life's true pleasures," Mrs Moffet declared, beaming. "What's more, the healing qualities of massages are sensational because they stimulate your skin; tissues; muscles; joints; lymph glands; nerves and internal organs. In short: They restore health to your entire body."

The truth is, massages just weren't my thing. Stripping down to my shorts in front of strangers and then having them rub their oily hands over my body didn't ring my bell. It was too intimate for my liking. Maybe I was too self-conscious to relax and enjoy the experience. Whatever the reason, it had been my loss, as I was about to discover.

"There are different kinds of massages and they all produce positive results. Especially when you're sick! Since you're not well now, you'll know first-hand that anxiety always accompanies ill-health. The good news is that massages relieve tension, help you to relax and inspire a feeling of well-being. This will make you feel better! Remember, it's crucial for you to be in a restful, peaceful, settled state during your healing process."

"I used to think massages were just for pleasure," I remarked.

"Sweetie, massages are vital to your recovery. Lie down," Mrs Moffet suddenly commanded. I complied instantly, like a well-trained pooch. She oiled up her hands and proceeded to smear them across my back and shoulders. She spoke to me in a gentle voice as she started work on my muscles.

"The masseuse's hands act as a cleansing agent. They help to push blood through your skin and muscle tissue. This increases the red blood cells and haemoglobin in that area, which subsequently restores muscle tissue, forces out congested waste material, breaks down adhesions and promotes circulation."

"Wow! Sounds good. And feels good, too," I groaned.

Her soft hands were surprisingly firm and strong. She pressed her fingers in between my shoulder blades and pushed them up and down the sides of my spine. I couldn't help shivering with delight. My eyes closed, and my thoughts drifted away. Damn, I should've joined my wife at the spa, I thought to myself. So many times, she'd begged me to join her. I recalled the disappointment on her face every time she climbed into the car alone. What an idiot I'd been! What a fool I was! I lambasted myself. Fortunately, Mrs Moffet started up a conversation.

"If you're unable to employ the services of a professional masseuse, you should make every effort to learn how to massage yourself. It's very easy to do. Simply use your hands to stroke; knead; pat; chop; beat; shake and rub your body."

"That's it?" I drawled.

"Uh-huh. You'll soon learn what works for you and what doesn't. Just follow your intuition. Let your hands lead you. They have healing powers, you know. They'll know where to go and what to do."

I wanted the treatment to continue. "Can you give me a few more pointers?" I asked.

"Spend extra time working on your muscles. Press softly when you go over a bone, especially the spine. You can also massage your internal organs by gently pushing, prodding and kneading your fingers into your solar plexus and lower abdominal region. This technique greatly assists your body in moving waste material through your intestines, kidneys and bladder," Mrs Moffet said.

"How often should I massage myself?"

"Daily."

"For how long?"

"Not long. Take five minutes to massage your body during your day. I sometimes massage my body in the bath or shower. Soap makes it easy for my hands to slide over my skin. You should try it. You'll be doing yourself a great service on your path to recovery."

"You mean, I should do it, not try it!"

"Touché," she replied.

I was completely relaxed. Mrs Moffet's hands were sensational – especially when she pressed down on my lymph glands to cleanse them! Years of training and practice meant she knew exactly where to find them and how to treat them. I groaned and moaned and sighed and whimpered. It wasn't all pleasurable – it hurt at times – especially when she pressed down hard on a sensitive spot. I let out the occasional howl. Apparently, this is to be expected during this healing technique. Mrs Moffet ignored the weird sounds. She'd lost herself in the rhythm of her movements. Her hands conducted a symphony of pleasure over my body. Mrs Moffet was a healer. Her expert touch moved me mentally, emotionally and spiritually, too. At one point, I cried. I don't know what she did, or how she did it, but I couldn't stop the tears from running down my cheeks. I knew my tears didn't stem from sadness. It was a strange emotional release from an unknown origin.

Just then, Mrs Moffet spoke. "Can you recall becoming drowsy, irritable, dull or nauseous after being cooped up in a poorly ventilated room for too long?" she asked.

"Uh-huh," I mumbled incoherently.

"I'm not surprised. Breathing stale air is awful, isn't it? Your body eventually screams at you to go outside for a breath of fresh air, doesn't it? What happens to you when you don't get enough fresh air? You get a headache. Right? That's because your brain cells suffer most from a lack of oxygen. Do you know how bad it is for you to breathe impure air? Your lungs distribute external impurities into your entire system, so your whole body is affected. Not just your lungs! Do you know what this means? It means all your organs of elimination must mop up the toxins, over and above performing their normal duties. This is a waste of good energy. Understood?"

Silence prevailed. I guessed that was my cue. "Un-der-stood," I garbled as she pounded my back like a big bass drum.

"Okay, I'd like you to roll over on to your back, close your eyes and take a deep breath."

I obeyed. She covered my body with a towel.

"Now gently blow air out through your lips."

I did as she asked.

"Does that feel great, or what?" Mrs Moffet cried, clapping her hands together like an excited child.

"Yeah, that feels pretty good," I admitted.

Drink in oxygen

My response seemed to please her immensely. "Each and every breath we take is precious," she declared. "You see, Sweetie, our breath connects us to our life energy. If you doubt this statement, stop breathing. I dare you. You'll quickly discover that very little else is more important to you than your next breath. If you don't take another breath, you'll lose consciousness and die within a minute or two."

"Your point is well made," I murmured in total agreement.

"Good. Now, close your eyes and take a slow, deep breath. This time, drink the oxygen as it passes down the back of your throat. As you do this, feel your chest rising. When your lungs are full, hold your breath for a second or two, and then gently relax your chest cavity. Let it fall. As you do so, release the carbon dioxide from your lungs by blowing out through your lips."

I followed her instructions.

She continued: "Now, let's take a closer look at what happens inside your body. I'd like you to repeat this exercise, but this time imagine your blood flowing through your system. Picture this: As your blood returns to your heart from traveling through your body, it's low in oxygen and full of carbon dioxide and other impurities that it collects along the way. As a result, it's a dark, purplish, bluish color."

"Is that why we turn blue when we hold our breath?"

"Yes, that's correct. We turn blue because of the lack of oxygen in our blood. Now, visualize this blood as it pumps through your pulmonary arteries to your lungs. In your lungs, the pulmonary arteries branch off into smaller and smaller blood vessels, until they're the width of a single, red blood cell. These tiny blood vessels are surrounded by about 300 million air sacs in your lungs. And, as your blood cells pass these air sacs, they give off carbon dioxide and impurities that they've been carrying, then take on a fresh supply of oxygen. Your heart then pumps this oxygen-rich blood, which is bright-red, throughout your body. This cycle is repeated until you draw your last breath. Isn't it amazing?"

"Yeah. It sure is."

"Our lungs can connect us to the present moment more than any other organ in our body. This is so important. Unfortunately, most people breathe unconsciously. They breathe instinctively. In and out, in and out, all day and all night! But, when we breathe with intention and focus, a wondrous thing happens. Our world stands still for a brief, glorious moment, and we exist entirely in the present moment."

"I often struggle to breathe," I confessed. "I get a blocked nose."

"Your problem is your diet, Dearie! You ingest the wrong foods. I bet sugar or dairy are the root cause of your troubles. Don't worry about it. Your sinuses will clear up when you start to follow a whole-foods, plant-based diet. Then you'll be able to breathe freely. That'll make a huge difference to your life."

"Isn't that a bit of an exaggeration?" I asked skeptically.

"Definitely not! There's an ancient Indian proverb that says: 'A man who half breathes, half lives'. She then told me about prana, which is the life energy contained in the air we breathe. I was amazed.

"Every word is true, Dearie. Your lungs feed your entire body with life-giving air. Alas, you don't even think about breathing when you're in good health. Do you? No. It remains an unconscious action. But when you're sick, every single breath becomes important to you, doesn't it? One deep breath can make you feel a whole lot better. It can alleviate pain, relieve nausea and allay fears – even if only for a moment. That's because there's healing power in each breath – whether you know it or not. Again, please."

I did as she asked. My lungs wheezed. "I've enjoyed too many cigars, I'm afraid."

Practise your breathwork

Mrs Moffet looked at me with sympathy. "Here's the thing," she said. "It's essential for you to strengthen your lungs. You need to increase their capacity to oxygenate your blood and eliminate impurities."

That sounded reasonable enough to me. "So, what can I do to strengthen my lungs?"

"You can exercise regularly and practice special breathing techniques," she said.

That sounded easy to do. Well, easier than physical exercise at least.

"The beauty of lung exercises is that you can practice them anywhere and anytime."

"Such as?"

"I'll show you a few of my favorites to get you started right now."

Tummy Balls

"The best way to begin is by learning how to breathe into your stomach. I call this exercise Tummy Balls. To do it, place your hand on your tummy and inhale slowly through your nose. Imagine that your stomach is a basketball that's filling with air. Take in as much air as possible, hold your breath for a moment, and then use your stomach muscles to force the air out of your body. Blow out through your mouth. Try it."

I tried it and was pleasantly surprised by how good it made me feel.

"How long should I keep this up?"

"You should repeat this process seven times or more in each session," Mrs Moffet replied. She gestured to me to continue with the exercise.

Greedy Gulps

"Now try Greedy Gulps: Inhale until your lungs feel full; hold your breath for a second, and then force more air into your lungs by taking another big gulp of air. Release the air slowly. Repeat this process seven or more times in succession."

I did as she asked. That exercise made me feel calmer, and more relaxed. I liked it.

"Got any more?" I asked.

Lonely Nostrils

"Sure I do. I call my favorite breathing exercise Lonely Nostrils. Try it now: Breathe in through one nostril at a time. To do this, place your thumb and forefinger on your nose and block your nostrils. Release your forefinger and breathe in slowly through the open nostril; then block that nostril, release your thumb and exhale through the opposite nostril. Keeping this nostril open, inhale slowly. When you have sufficient air in your lungs, close this nostril with your thumb and exhale back through the opposite nostril. Try this seven times, or more."

Mrs Moffet did the exercise with me. In and out, in and out.

Deep Dive

"Holding your breath is yet another fantastic way to strengthen your lungs," Mrs Moffet said.

"I call this exercise Deep Dive. Hold your breath seven times in succession right now and experience the benefits for yourself. You can do more if you like."

It was much harder to do than it sounded. I felt like quitting after five breaths, but I didn't. Afterwards, I felt dizzy and my heart beat faster.

"Let's take a break, shall we Sweetie?" When you practise breathing techniques, it's important to rest between sessions to avoid feeling light-headed, dizzy or nauseous. Is that how you feel now?"

"Yup," I admitted. "I used to think breathing was the easiest thing in the world to do, but breathwork is tiring."

Hot Dog

"That's nothing! Your next exercise separates the men from the boys. Let me fetch you a glass of water, and then I want you to try Hot Dog. All you have to do is pant in and out quickly through your nose, like an exhausted dog, for seven minutes or longer."

"What?" I exclaimed. "That sounds ridiculous!"

"You may say that now, but you'll feel differently about it once you've tried it," she assured me. "This technique is also known as holotropic breathing. I know people who do it for hours without taking a break."

"Why on Earth would they do that?"

"It produces extreme results: Physically, mentally, emotionally and spiritually. You must experience it to know what I'm talking about. But, you will need stamina and strength for this exercise. It's not advisable to do long sessions of Hot Dog if you're very sick. You should also do long sessions in a supervised environment. You can search for holotropic breathing practitioners on the Internet. For today, I suggest you do a short session. Seven minutes is a great start. You can try a marathon session at some point in the future. Now, let me get you that glass of water. It's important. You must always have a glass of water nearby when you do this breathing exercise. Your mouth will become very dry and this could cause you to lose concentration and feel discomfort."

She left the room and returned with the water. I hadn't moved. I lay there staring at the ceiling, wondering what the heck was about to happen. True to her word, Mrs Moffet made me pant like a dog for seven whole minutes. Once again, I considered giving up a few times, but Mrs Moffet insisted I push through to the end. I'm pleased I listened to her. I accomplished what I set out to do, even though I had considered quitting several times. But, I never gave up. No, I still hadn't crossed the finish line. Mrs Moffet wasn't done yet.

Star Grabs

"Now, I want you to try Star Grabs. It's simple to do. Tuck your elbows into your sides and clench your fists at your shoulders. Then, shoot your hands up into the air while breathing in through your nose. Keep your mouth closed. Spread your fingers wide when your arms are fully extended. Then, exhale with force as you pull your arms down, so that you return to your original position with your fists clenched at your shoulders. Do this exercise seven times or more, right now."

I tried it, and I liked that, too.

"I've got one last breathing exercise to share with you. It's the most powerful of all, and you're going to love it," she told me, her eyes twinkling.

Ujjayi

"Lay it on me," I replied, trying to make my eyes sparkle, too.

"This exercise brings you into the present moment more than any other exercise I know,' she said, rubbing her chin. It's called ujjayi breathing. You pronounce it 'oo-ja-yee'. This means 'victorious'," she explained. "When done properly, ujjayi breathing should be both energizing and relaxing."

Mrs Moffet told me to make a sound by gently constricting the opening of my throat to create some resistance with the passage of air. The secret is to gently pull the breath in on inhalation and gently push the breath out on exhalation. This resistance creates a well-modulated and soothing sound, almost like a snore. The first time I tried it, I choked and spluttered.

"No, silly bumpkin. Too much effort creates a grasping quality and a grating sound. Your breath should be both long and smooth. Try it again. Only this time, focus on creating a soothing and pleasing sound that's unhurried and unforced – something like the sound of ocean waves rolling in and out."

I tried it again and did much better.

"Try to maintain the length and smoothness of your breath," she advised me. "Total relaxation is key here. Just breathe deeply. Breathe into the core of your being – your solar plexus. The mystics call this 'the seat of the soul'. Try it."

I'm not exactly sure for how long I did that breathing exercise. Minutes seemed like hours, but I remained completely in the present moment. I loved it. By focusing on the sound in my throat and my breathing, I was somehow able to transcend the past and the future. Nothing else existed but the present moment. I felt more alive than ever before. I'd discovered a way to escape my thoughts and still my mind. It was perhaps the greatest single gift anyone had ever given me. I hung there, cherishing the moment, in total relaxation. It was life-changing!

Afterwards, Mrs Moffet and I sat together on a bench in the garden and shared a pot of herbal tea. It had a strong citrus taste, and I detected cinnamon and honey. Much to my surprise, I enjoyed it. The thought of slugging back thick, black coffee loaded with sugar didn't appeal to me after all my cleansing treatments. It'd been a long day filled with activity, but I wasn't tired. I felt energized and excited. I'd learned a lot, too, and my notepad was almost full.

Find fresh air

"When you want to heal your body, you really should spend as much time as possible outdoors," said Mrs Moffet. "The fresh air will do you the world of good."

I inhaled deeply. It was good to feel the fresh air fill my lungs. I suddenly realized what I'd been missing. "I spend most of my time indoors, I'm sad to say," I blurted.

"If you must be indoors, then be sure to open all the doors and windows, so that you get lots of fresh air – weather permitting, of course."

"I've been cooped up in an air-conditioned hospital room for weeks. I wonder why it didn't occur to me to open the windows and doors," I said aloud.

She was quick to respond. "It's a travesty to see patients in dimly lit, air-conditioned hospital wards, when what they need most is sunlight and fresh air. It's a fact: Oxygen is the elixir of life. It purifies your blood, calms your nerves and helps to heal your body. You can easily see the difference between people who live indoors and those who live outdoors. People who spend too much time indoors tend to have a dull, grey, lifeless quality to their skin, while people who spend time outdoors look vibrant and healthy. Fresh air – that's the ticket!"

"Fortunately for us, nature provides it free of charge and in abundance," I added.

She grinned.

"Got anymore great advice for me?" I jested, pen in hand.

She rubbed her chin. "Here's a good tip. When you want to heal your body, you should surround yourself with living plants, because they release oxygen. You should also advise your readers not to send sick people cut flowers. They may look pretty for a day or two, but it makes no sense to give them flowers that are themselves gasping for life. A big, healthy, green pot plant – that's the tonic!"

I wrote that down. "Anything else?"

263

Embrace sunlight

Mrs Moffet was quick to respond. "Well, we should also discuss the importance of sunlight. Sunshine has healing power. It revitalizes the energy of your body. Want proof? Just spend some time working, relaxing or playing in the Sun. You'll feel a heightened sense of well-being afterwards. Guaranteed!"

"Why?"

"Your skin synthesizes vitamin D from the Sun, which provides your body with essential nutrients. As a result, you feel stronger, happier, energized and more content."

I scribbled as fast as I could. Her pistons were firing and I could hardly keep up.

"Let me caution you: This doesn't mean to say that you should bake in the Sun for hours. Definitely not! You must avoid sunburn at all costs. Your skin is very sensitive and must be protected from the Sun – especially when you have other health issues to be concerned about. You don't want to lose vital energy as your body tries to restore sun-damaged skin cells. Don't overdo it, okay?"

"Got it."

"I'm sure Henry has told you already, but you need to take it easy on a healing journey. Find a comfortable place to sit in soft sunlight each day. Close your eyes and feel the warmth of the rays on your skin. This practice calms the nerves and soothes the soul."

"How long?"

"Eh?"

"How long should one sit in the Sun?"

"Five to 10 minutes of soft sunlight each day is all you need."

"That's sounds easy enough."

Do regular exercise

"Excellent. The sunlight will recharge your batteries and give you the energy you need to do some exercise."

"What?" I exclaimed in horror.

"You know, exercise."

"Argh!"

"You simply must get into the habit of exercising regularly."

I immediately screwed up my face.

"Don't give me that look," Mrs Moffet retorted. "Exercise is very important. It builds strength, fitness and stamina; improves circulation and breathing; increases the mobility of your joints; reduces fat; tones your muscles and conditions your body. It also burns calories and boosts your metabolism. But, that's not all. Exercise also makes you stronger mentally, emotionally and even spiritually. It requires self-discipline, commitment and determination. These are important qualities that build character.

"Besides, when your heart is pumping and your lungs are expanding to their fullest, you feel very alive. This inner strength is highly beneficial to you, especially when you're in a weakened state. You see, exercise provides you with the energy you need to perk yourself up. After exercise, you feel invigorated, exhilarated and rejuvenated. That's because your blood pumps through your system faster, purifying it more quickly. Exercise ultimately makes you feel fantastic."

"Okay, okay, okay!" I conceded. "I'll start to exercise."

She clapped her hands excitedly. "I recommend you do some form of exercise for at least 20 minutes a day, three times a week. Your primary objective should be to increase your heart rate and exercise your lungs. The easiest way to achieve this goal is with mild aerobic activities such as brisk walking, dancing, swimming, jogging, cycling, climbing stairs or even jumping up and down. If going to the gym is simply not your thing, then try outdoor activities, like hiking. But, be sure to warm up and cool down when you exercise, and drink lots of water. It's important to keep your body hydrated. Once again, don't overdo it!"

"That won't be a problem," I muttered to myself.

"Don't joke," she retorted. "You have a competitive nature, I can tell. So, once you get into it, you'll most likely push yourself to the limit. But, you mustn't over-exert yourself when your body requires healing. Be sensible and listen to your body. If you become dizzy, short of breath or feel heart palpitations, then you're overdoing it. Stop, catch your breath, and only continue if you think you're up to it."

"I feel like I'm going to have a heart attack when I exercise," I remarked.

She frowned. "Exercise doesn't have to be strenuous, Sweetie. You can work your muscles to within your limits, and thoroughly enjoy yourself while doing so."

Find exercise you enjoy

"You must find a form of exercise that you enjoy doing."

"I like doing didley-squats," I joked.

Mrs Moffet giggled. "If you don't take pleasure in exercise, your ego-mind will work against you. It'll do its utmost best to dissuade you from doing it again. Trust me, if you don't enjoy the experience, you'll lack motivation and quickly lose interest."

"I like walking," I threw out, instantly regretting not walking the dogs with my wife on the beach more often. I used to do it and enjoy it, but somewhere along the way life bogged me down and, as Mrs Moffet said, I became lazy. I stopped making an effort to care for both my marriage and myself. Unfortunately for me, as fate would have it, I was now paying the price for my foolishness.

"Then start walking, Sweetie," she said encouragingly. "No one can take your body for a walk but you. Only you can make it happen."

I opened my mouth to protest, but she raised a hand to silence me.

"Don't give me that 'I've got no time' excuse. It isn't good enough. It's a poor excuse to stay lazy. You've got to set aside the time to exercise, or it just won't happen. When you exercise for 20 minutes, three times per week, you'll be exercising for one hour out of a possible 168 hours. That's doable, isn't it?"

"I guess so," I mumbled.

Mrs Moffet reached out her hand to shake on it. Instinctively, I committed myself.

"One hour a week is a great way to start out. Especially when your body isn't used to exercise! It's wise to gradually build up your level of fitness and stamina. Exercise three times a week and take rest days in between to allow your muscles to recuperate. Work up to exercising for 20 minutes daily."

She must've seen the dismay on my face.

Stretch it out

"Don't panic! The fitter you get, the easier exercise becomes. Next, let me introduce you to a truly delightful and excellent form of passive exercise: Stretching! It's simple to do. And the healing effects are amazing."

"What's so great about it?"

"Well, for one thing, stretching requires you to look within. You see, you have to get in tune with your body so that you're able to feel how far and for how long you can hold a stretch. It's a fantastic way to raise your body consciousness. It's also a fabulous way to work out tension, and it's relaxing and revitalizing."

"My wife does yoga and Pilates," I told her.

"You should join her, Sweetie," she replied, tapping my leg. "I highly recommend you learn these disciplines. They'll help you to stretch your muscles, tone your body, improve fitness, and develop your concentration, focus, posture and breathing. This'll help to heal your body. Do it! The results will amaze you."

"I can't even touch my toes without bending my knees," I groaned. "It hurts."

"The more you exercise and stretch, the more you'll come to enjoy it," Mrs Moffet assured me. "Stretching also massages your internal organs – especially your organs of elimination, like your kidneys, bladder and liver. As we discussed earlier today, it's very important to cleanse these organs on a healing journey. Now you try," she commanded sweetly.

Flatties

"Stand up, bend over, and touch your toes."

"I don't have that kind of relationship with my feet. Can I just wave?" I replied.

She giggled. "Put your hands flat on the floor, look at your navel, push your knees back and breathe comfortably for one minute. I call these Flatties."

I did my best to do as I was told. It wasn't half bad.

"Now, stand up, put your hands on your hips, and look at the roof above your head for 30 seconds. Arch your back, if you can. This exercise is useful to undo the tension created by a forward stretch."

Once again, I obeyed.

Pointies

"Now try Pointies. They're super easy: Bend over, touch the floor with pointed fingertips, look at the horizon, straighten your back, push your knees back and breathe comfortably for one minute."

Hangies

Next, we tried Hangies. She told me to stand up, put my hands together above my head, straighten my arms, look at my hands for 30 seconds and arch my back. Then she told me to bend over again, lock my knees, hold my elbows, hang forward and breathe comfortably for one minute. I'm pretty sure she made up these names. Lastly, she got me to stand up, raise my hands above my head, as if worshipping, look at the roof, and arch my back for 30 seconds. The whole routine only took five minutes or so, and I liked it!

"I can't emphasize enough how important it is for you to stretch and keep your organs of elimination active on a healing journey," she said. "You can assist the process by deeply massaging yourself on the surface of your body, where these organs are found. I do this while stretching, showering, bathing, sitting and standing. This reminds me, you really should establish a habit of drinking a glass of water immediately after urinating. This'll ensure that your body is hydrated and that your kidneys, liver and bladder are active all day long. As a rule of thumb, if your urine is yellow, you're not drinking enough water. Don't wait until you're thirsty to drink water. That's too late! When your urine is clear, then you're on the right track. Got it?"

"Yup."

"You don't just have to drink water. There are many excellent herbal teas on the market that are great for detoxifying your system. Green tea is especially good for you. Get some and drink it regularly!"

My notepad was full. "Phew, I've used my last sheet of paper," I said, flipping through the pages.

She reached out, took my notepad, and turned it over. "There's still a little space left," she replied, tapping the back cover.

I laughed. "Alright then, let's fill it, shall we? I know you've some wonderful piece of advice to give me that I'd never in a million years think of myself.

She giggled like a little girl with a secret. "Have you ever wondered why some people wake up in the morning with breath that smells like Gandhi's flip-flops?"

I roared with laughter. "Tell me."

Brush your tongue

"Your tongue is also an organ of elimination. It's the excess toxins and impurities that your body manages to expel overnight that cause the bad odour. Bad breath is a sure sign that you're putting too many toxins into your body. The good news is that if you eat natural foods, your breath won't stink. It's very important that you brush your tongue with your toothbrush every day."

"How come?" I asked.

"To help rid your body of unwanted waste, of course!" she replied. "Do it. You won't regret it. Your friends will appreciate it, too!"

We laughed together.

"I'm very pleased the two of you are getting along so well," said a voice from behind us.

"Henry Jones!" I cried out, spinning around to see his broad smile. He gleamed like a bright, shiny, new car in sunlight.

"Wow, you look fantastic!" Mrs Moffet exclaimed.

"Thank you," he responded politely. "I feel fantastic, too. How do you feel, my friend?"

My eyes filled with tears. I couldn't find the words to express my gratitude to Henry Jones and Mrs Moffet. We shared the last of the herbal tea and laughed about the day's mishaps. We didn't see Lucy again that day. Just as well – we didn't need another incident. I had wanted to apologize to her for my appalling behavior, but that would have to wait for another time.

"Unfortunately, we need to be leaving now, Mrs Moffet. Thank you. It was a glorious day of purification," said Henry Jones.

"Would you like to stay for supper?" she asked.

"I'm afraid we'll have to take a rain check, my dear. I've another surprise in store for him." He winked, and she nodded. I wondered what else Henry Jones had up his sleeve for me.

CHAPTER 14

FOOD MAKETH THE MAN

I was gobsmacked to discover that Henry Jones had arranged for us to have supper with my estranged daughter. We shared a meal at my favorite restaurant and it was lovely to see her again. I could tell that she was anxious about spending time with me, but on this occasion, I surprised her. I didn't get drunk, abuse the waiters or cause a scene. I ordered a light salad; drank an imported herbal-fusion tea and listened intently to her every word. She was as pensive as a color-blind bomb disposal technician. We all knew why. One snip of the wrong wire could bring the house down. Yes, I'd set this precedent. My family had experienced it far too many times before not to be weary of me. The old me.

However, I parked my ego-mind and took my true-self for a test drive. Henry Jones was my co-pilot. He did a wonderful job of defusing the tension between us. He cracked jokes and told interesting stories about faraway places. We didn't talk about work, sickness, or money. My usual points of debate were set aside, and I didn't rant or rave. Neither did I dominate the conversation with my inflated opinions, sharp criticisms or harsh judgments. For once, I was more interested in my daughter; her studies; her plans; views; likes and tastes. She spoke cautiously, and I accepted everything she told me without prejudice.

Towards the end of the evening, I reached out to cover her hand with mine. Instinctively, she pulled away from me. I knew I deserved it, but it still hurt. Luckily Henry Jones was there to save us. He quickly initiated a new conversation about changing weather patterns. My daughter was, after all, studying to be a climatologist. In the past, I had seen little value in anything to do with the environment. Consequently, we hadn't spoken much since our last big fight about her career choice. Fortunately, I didn't make the same mistake that night at the restaurant. I listened with new ears. She told us about climate change and its impact on humanity and the planet. Her conviction and passion stunned me. I saw myself in her, but luckily, she had her mother's elegance and grace. I was proud of her, and I told her so. Faced with a compliment from me, she didn't know what to do with herself. She then told me that she had been dating a Scandinavian man for over a year. What hurt most was that they'd just returned from a getaway trip to our beach cottage with my wife. It took everything I had to not fall into sullen silence.

"Just breathe deeply, just breathe deeply," I could hear Mrs Moffet telling me. My daughter knew I'd been cut deep by that news. I saw it in her eyes. There was a mixture of pity, sorrow, anger and revenge in them. A strange combination, I know, but our past was complicated and wrought with emotional pain.

I pushed through it, gently. Each time I spoke, Henry Jones would nod his head ever so slightly and smile. He was guiding me, and I gladly followed his lead. At the end of the evening, we said our goodbyes in the car park. I thanked my daughter for spending time with me, and I really meant it. She held back.

Love conquers all

I walked towards Henry's rattletrap with a heavy heart. She was my little girl and I'd lost her, too. No, I'd pushed her away from me, along with the rest of my family. My years of belligerence and ill temper had taken their toll. The lump in my throat ached unbearably. I cast a final look across the car park to where she was standing by her jeep. Our eyes connected. Everything I wanted to say to her was discharged in a split second. I wanted to fall to my knees and beg her for forgiveness. I wanted to hold her in my arms and tell her I loved her. I wanted to heal our relationship and keep her close to me forever. It felt as though my heart was about to burst. The intensity was just too much for me to bear.

I looked away to stop myself from dying inside. That's when it happened. I heard the sweetest sound ring out. A sound so fine and pure, it shattered me to the core.

"Daddy!" she called.

I glanced up to see her running towards me. My feet took flight, and we met somewhere in the middle in a tight, inseparable embrace. "I'm so sorry, my child. Please forgive me, for everything. I love you, so much," I cried out. "Daddy, I've missed you," she wept.

Our world stood still. We were transported to another realm. It was a strange and fantastic place where love and forgiveness become one. I hugged her tighter than I've ever done before. I knew deep down in the bottom of my heart I'd never let her go again. Never, ever!

She asked me if I'd like to meet Joerg, her boyfriend, and she told me of their plans to marry in the Fall. I said yes, of course. Riding home with Henry Jones, I chattered like an excited monkey. I was elated. I'd experienced the true power of my true-self, and a miracle had manifested right in front of my eyes. I was totally converted to this new way of thinking. The night's outcome had won me over. Henry Jones was right all along. Love conquers all things. I felt energetic, creative, alive and full of possibility – exactly as he said I'd feel when my true-self was in charge of my life. I was in a state of consciousness that allowed me to be in harmony with the universe, which made me feel safe, secure and loved.

No doubt about it, that was another turning point for me. I was no longer 'along for the ride' on my healing journey with Henry Jones. I was in the driving seat now. He'd shown me how to grip the steering wheel of my true-self, and I'd felt the healing power under the hood of my thoughts, feelings and actions. Yes, I was in charge of my recovery now. I was on the path to perfect health, and I was going to push the pedal to the metal.

I spent that night at Henry Jones's apartment. It was a three-room flat in the middle of the city. The rooms were sparsely furnished, and I got the feeling that he was moving out. There were several cardboard boxes stacked one on top of the other in the entrance hall. He offered no explanation for the disorder, and I made no inquiry. Henry Jones had told me of his plans to relocate to an island in the near future, but I didn't want to think about it, nor discuss his departure. What would I do without him? I wondered for a terrible second, but then pushed the idea aside.

I got up early the next morning and deliberately made as much noise as possible, in the hope of waking Henry Jones. I ran the bath water full blast, banged cupboard doors, stomped my feet and even smashed pots and pans together in the kitchen. My ruckus worked. It wasn't long before we were working again.

"If you're serious about wanting to heal your body, then I've got a simple exercise for you to do right now," Henry Jones said sternly, sipping his early morning cup of herbal tea. I got the feeling he was testing me.

"What is it?" I asked in a daredevil tone.

Embrace the naked truth

He nodded somberly. "Stand totally naked in front of a full-length mirror and stare at your body. But don't just sneak a peek for a few seconds. Stop and have a good, long look. Stare at yourself from all angles: Front, back and sides. Focus on the shape of your figure and how it makes you feel. Okay?"

"Right now?" I exclaimed.

"Yes. Right now!"

"In front of you?"

"No. Do it in the privacy of your bedroom or bathroom. This exercise is for your eyes only."

I must say, I was relieved to hear it. Nudity and intimacy were a major problem for me. I didn't need to stand naked in front of a mirror to know that I was disgusted by my body. I was out of shape, and I knew it. I didn't want anyone to see me naked, especially not Henry Jones! I didn't even parade naked in front of my wife.

I skedaddled to the bathroom and removed all my clothes, as instructed. I stared hard at my naked body. Just as I expected, the bathroom mirror was unforgiving and cruel. Clearly, I wasn't young and athletic anymore. I'd traded my six-pack for a barrel a long, long time ago. I looked flabby and old. I tried to flex my muscles like a bodybuilder, but that made me look even more ridiculous and pathetic. I settled for wobbling my gut with my fingers. It wasn't a pretty sight. I scowled at myself in the mirror. How did I feel? Ashamed of myself. A big part of me wanted to quit the exercise after a minute or two, but I didn't. I forced myself to do exactly what Henry Jones had told me to do. I studied my naked body from all angles, and it made me feel sick to my stomach! Demoralized and depressed, I eventually got dressed and joined Henry Jones in the dining room. The storm cloud above my head followed me.

"Answer these two questions honestly," he said upon my return. "What did you think of your body? And, how did your reflection make you feel?"

"Not good," I mumbled begrudgingly.

He could tell I was unhappy. "Thank you for doing this exercise, my friend," he replied softly. "It's great to see that you're now fully committed to your healing journey."

"What was the point of that exercise?" I snapped back at him.

"Well, for one, this exercise reveals the relationship between your mind and body. It exposes how you think and feel about the magnificent vessel that transports you through life."

I scoffed. "You wouldn't call my body a magnificent vessel if you'd just seen me naked."

He ignored my remark. "Do you realize that trillions of body cells work perfectly together in your body each and every second of your life? What you see in the mirror is actually a marvelous, mind-boggling, biological miracle. Professor Kaufman already told you that, didn't she?"

I shrugged. He continued: "I'm guessing you focused on your perceived imperfections instead of your natural biological perfection. Correct?"

There was no guesswork involved. He had me pegged. "Correct. I only saw my faults and imperfections," I admitted. "My body isn't in good shape anymore."

He was quick to respond. "I can tell you this, my friend: If you're unhappy or dissatisfied with the condition and shape of your body, then you're making a big mistake! Your body is perfect just the way it is. It's responded perfectly to your diet and exercise program. I've told you this before. You can't blame your body for being out of shape or sick. It's not guilty in any way, shape or form. Don't be duped. The truth is: Your ego-mind is the cause of your unhappiness and dissatisfaction. It's solely responsible for the condition of your body. I've already taught you about cause and effect. In this case, the cause of your physical problems is your ego-mind. The effects of the life choices you have made are manifested in your body. So, if you think about it, the mirror actually reflects the state of your mind, not just the physical condition of your body. Make sense?"

It did make sense to me. Perfect sense! As long as I persecuted my body, my ego-mind got away scot-free.

"You're suggesting I love my body and sort my mind out, aren't you?"

"Exactly!" he trumpeted. "Your natural body is beautiful. It's a wonder of creation, despite what you may have done to it."

I really needed to hear that message. Up until then, I had it all wrong. I blamed my body for my misery and suffering. It took the full brunt of my self-loathing and self-deprecation. My ego-mind had run amok with my life and my poor body was the whipping boy. This must stop immediately, I thought to myself.

Henry Jones continued: "Michelangelo said the angel he sculpted was trapped inside the rock, and he merely released it. This is you, my friend. You're Michelangelo's angel. Your natural body is waiting to be discovered inside of you."

Unleash your natural body

"So how do I release it?" I asked without much thought.

"Isn't it obvious? You can only bring out the natural shape of your body by eating natural foods. It's that simple! Junk food will give you a junk body. What you put in is what you get out, my friend. But don't be ruled by your ideas of a good body. Too many people make the mistake of comparing themselves to fashion models and Hollywood stars. That's just crazy! Your body is genetically different in umpteen million different ways! You are you. You're not an underwear model or a celebrity who can afford to spend hours in the gym with personal trainers each day. Your top priority should be to strive towards being fit, healthy and strong. So what if you're not in ideal shape today. You can be soon enough. Accept responsibility for your diet and exercise program and you'll soon strut in front of the mirror with confidence and pride."

I liked the sound of that. It made me feel better. The mirror exercise had exposed a hidden truth: I didn't just have a health problem, I had a relationship problem. I treated my body badly. I abused it. It suddenly occurred to me that if my body was a person, I'd be liable for grievous bodily harm. And then I realized that my body is a person – the most important person in the world to me – me! That hit me like a ton of bricks, too.

"Oh boy, I really need to heal my relationship with my body, don't I?" I announced with newfound conviction.

"Precisely!" he hollered back. "If you don't start paying more attention to your body, treating it properly and showing some consideration towards it, you're going to lose it. And you don't want that to happen, do you?"

"No, sir. I definitely don't want that to happen," I replied. I could relate to this concept very easily. Once again, an image of my wife popped into my head.

Heal your relationship with your body

"Good. In that case, let's examine how you can heal your relationship with your body. The first thing you need to know is how your body works. That is basic logic. If your car breaks down, you can't fix it unless you know how it works. Agreed?"

"Yes, but I usually take it to a mechanic," I replied, trying to be clever.

Henry Jones frowned. "Don't make me beat this drum again. We've already discussed this point. There's a distinct difference between reactive and proactive behavior. Most people respond reactively when they experience physical discomfort or disease. They absolve themselves of the responsibility of self-healing. They race off to the pharmacy or doctor for quick-fix drugs. While they wait for the medication to suppress their symptoms, they wallow in self-pity and allow themselves to be the victim of their disease. They don't fight for their recovery. Instead, they focus on their weaknesses, lack of strength, pain and discomfort. This kind of reactive thinking fuels a feeling of helplessness and inadequacy. As a result, they spend their time worrying about their condition, instead of doing something about it. They forget that worry will accomplish nothing. Let me give it to you straight. Reactive behavior is restrictive. It causes the ability to change to wither and die." He reached out and crunched his fist into a tight ball. His knuckles turned white and his fist shook under the pressure of his grip. My eyes widened, and I heard myself gulp. Suddenly, his hand opened.

"Proactive behavior, on the other hand, effects positive change. When you're proactive, you're creative, resourceful and solution-orientated. Above all else, you accept your response-ability. Did you get that? Response-ability. There's a lot that you can do to positively influence your healing process. When you think and act proactively, you empower yourself."

Choose to be proactive

"Unlike reactive behavior, proactive behavior is expansive. When you're proactive, you develop your personal inner strength and grow stronger as a person. Your individual outlook becomes more positive, and you feel better about yourself. Naturally, this attitude assists your healing process, speeds up recovery and ultimately restores your body to perfect health."

Henry Jones took a deep breath and let it out slowly. "Let's pick up from where we got derailed, shall we? In short, you need to know how your body works so that you can take the right actions to fix it. This is what I'd like to focus on this morning. I'm going to teach you exactly how your body works. You'll be amazed at how few people know this information. They go through their lives without understanding the basic mechanics of their bodies. Eventually, when their bodies break down because of misuse and abuse, they don't know how to fix themselves, and depend on medical mechanics who charge them an arm and a leg."

The importance of diet

"Let's continue your healing journey by discussing your diet. Your body's efficiency is largely determined by what you put into it. I think it's important enough to tell you right from the start that your diet plays an extremely important role in your recovery. It's critical to understand that everything you put into your stomach – every sip, every morsel – affects the chemical universe inside your body. This triggers a chain reaction. Your body's internal reaction to what you consume determines how you feel physically, mentally, emotionally and spiritually. In other words, what you eat and drink affects your experience of life."

If anyone else had told me this, I would've thought they were exaggerating. But Henry Jones was in a league of his own. I'd learned to trust him completely.

He continued. "When I was growing up, nobody explained to me what food I should eat, when I should eat it, or why I should eat it. Like most people, I was told to eat whatever was on my plate, and to be grateful for it. Sound familiar?"

"It sure does," I replied. "I must've heard my father say those exact words a thousand times."

"I bet millions of people have experienced the same thing. As a result, I rated food by how good I thought it tasted, and I developed a habit of consuming the food I enjoyed. I must admit, as an adult, my diet was entirely ruled by my taste buds. Sure, I'd heard fruit and vegetables were good for me, but I lived on man-made food because it accommodated my lifestyle. Like you, when I was hungry, I scoffed down a burger and chips with lots of tangy sauce, followed by a fizzy drink. How come, you ask? Because it tasted great, and I always felt full afterwards. That was my goal!"

"That's hard to believe coming from you, Henry Jones," I remarked.

"Oh yes. Fruit and vegetables weren't an option for me, I'm sad to say. I didn't think twice about my diet. I honestly thought I was healthy. Then I learned the hard way that ignorance is no excuse for not obeying the law: The Natural Law, that is! And were the penalties severe, or what? I was shocked to discover that you can get the death penalty for not eating properly. It's that serious!"

I felt a shiver run down my spine.

"Now that I know better, it scares me to think how many people eat man-made junk food as an integral part of their diet. They also consume alcohol; tobacco; drugs; preservatives; refined sugars; caffeine; processed foods and goodness knows what else. It's tragic how some people disregard their bodies. They mistakenly think they're healthy because they're not yet sick. But take it from me: You can only be healthy if you eat healthily. You'll eventually pay a price for poor eating. I'm telling you this again so that you don't forget to put it in our book. Keep repeating it, over and over. Some people need to hear a message a few times before it finally sinks in. Disregard for your body results in sickness, pain and premature death. I can't spell it out for you any clearer than that. Got it?"

"Got it," I said, underlining my notes multiple times.

"You should tell our readers that if they're not already eating a healthy diet, they've got to change their ways. The right way to go is the natural way. Eating natural foods is the only way to enjoy radiant health and vitality every day for the rest of their lives. I highly recommend a whole-foods, plant-based diet, especially on a healing journey. Did you get that?"

I wasn't sure if Henry Jones was dictating to me for his book or talking to me directly, for his words pricked my conscience. I'd only been eating healthily for a week. Truth be told, hearing him talk about hamburgers, fries and fizzy drinks had made me yearn for fast food. My stomach rumbled. I could've easily devoured a greasy breakfast from the joint on the corner. The fruit salad I'd eaten for breakfast hadn't touched sides.

"What can I do to break the habit of unhealthy eating?" I asked.

"Feed your body natural food five times a day," he replied swiftly. "Eat abundantly! This will ensure your system is full of nutrients, vitamins and minerals. These essential elements are abundant in fresh fruit and delicious vegetables. Trust me, when you give your body what it needs to restore, rebuild and rejuvenate itself, you won't crave unhealthy food."

I wondered if Henry Jones had psychic abilities. He read me like a book and I felt my cheeks flush.

"I usually eat three big meals each day, and I still get hungry," I told him.

"Do you know what your problem is? You've been eating too much dead food," he told me.

"Huh?" I didn't know what he was talking about.

"Hold on a second," Henry Jones said, scratching in his big, brown envelope. I knew what to expect. "Read this," he commanded at the end of his search.

> *Cooked food is dead food. Live food is raw food.*

I read it, and then tucked it away safely in the pouch of my notepad.

"Please explain," I said.

"You need to become familiar with a remarkable little entity called an enzyme."

I raised an eyebrow in curiosity. "Go on," I encouraged him.

"Essentially, enzymes are your body's labour force. These microscopic protein molecules are involved in every single activity and process in your body."

"But what do they do?" I interrupted him impatiently.

He leaned towards me. "Enzymes digest the food you eat. They break it down into its simplest building materials. They literally help to build your body. This is the reason why enzymes are so important to you when you're unhealthy or sick. Enzymes help to build your body. There's something else you should know, too: Illness undoubtedly manifests in the human body because of a lack of enzymes."

I scribbled this fact down in my new notepad and underlined it twice. "Go on."

Go raw

"Here's where it gets interesting. Listen up. Raw foods contain their own digestive enzymes."

"What are you saying Henry Jones?"

"I'm saying raw food breaks itself down in your stomach."

"Raw food naturally contains all the enzymes needed to digest it?"

"That's right," he replied swiftly. "Can you see where I'm going with this? Heat destroys enzymes in food."

It took a while for this statement to sink in. "If that is the case, how does your body digest cooked food?"

"That's an excellent question. Your body has to manufacture enzymes or provide them to you from the precious reserves with which you were born."

"What does that mean?"

Henry Jones replied sharply. "Your body has to repair its enzyme level, or else your metabolism will slow down and you'll lack energy. Remember, your body needs energy to heal itself, so you don't want that to happen! This is especially pertinent for the elderly. It's entirely possible to exhaust your enzyme reserves over a lifetime of eating cooked food. As a result, the body doesn't digest food properly. This excess waste rots in the colon, which produces toxins that poison the bloodstream. Semi-digested nutrients also carry toxins into the body. Together, these toxins impair your body's ability to heal itself. But wait, there's more. Enzymes also play a very important role in your body's immune system. They have a powerful influence on your defence mechanism. The more enzymes you have in your body, the stronger your immune system will be."

He rattled on, but I never heard word. I was studying the notes I'd just scrawled.

"So, let me get this straight," I blurted once I'd figured it out. "Raw food is live food because it's full of living enzymes, and cooked food is dead food because heat kills enzymes. My body needs enzymes to heal, so I should eat food that digests itself. In other words … I mustn't eat cooked food on my healing journey. I must eat raw food." The penny dropped. It made perfect sense. Henry Jones was right. If you want to fix something that's broken, you need to know how it works. Understanding exactly how your body works at a biological level is critical if you want to heal it naturally.

Vitamins and minerals

"I think he's got it!" Henry Jones yelled playfully, looking upwards. "Now you're ready to learn about vitamins and minerals."

Henry Jones was already two steps ahead of me. "Hold on a second. What's the connection between live food and vitamins and minerals?"

"Isn't it obvious? Live food is a rich source of vitamins and minerals." He slapped my leg surprisingly hard. I rubbed away the sting. "Sorry about that," he said. "Vitamins and minerals are amazing! You don't need to know all there is to know about vitamins and minerals. Even a basic understanding will revolutionize your life. Let's discuss vitamins first. They are vital. Simply put: Your body can't sustain itself without vitamins. They're essential to health, growth, vitality and well-being. Vitamins also help to build the molecular structures of your body, energize your metabolism and convert carbohydrates and fats into much-needed energy."

"Phew!" I heard myself breathe.

"You may be interested to know that most vitamins are not produced by your body. They must be consumed by eating organic food, or by taking supplements."

"Do you mean vitamin pills?"

"Yes. But I must say, I have reservations about supplements. There are many dubious pill manufacturers out there. Who knows what actually goes into their products? Your body was designed to take vitamins in small doses from natural foods. When you overload on unnatural doses – one pill or more – your body uses what it needs and discards the rest as toxic waste. That's like trying to pour 500 gallons of fuel into a 15-gallon tank. You ain't gonna go faster, nor further. You're just gonna waste a lot of fuel!" he said, slipping into a cowboy-like drawl. "Make sense?"

I laughed. "It sure does, pardner," I replied, tipping an imaginary hat.

"Besides, you can't live on vitamin supplements. You must eat! The secret is to eat the right food. I promise you this: All the vitamins that you'll ever need are found in fresh fruit and vegetables. The quality of man-made products may be questionable, but the quality of Mother Nature's products is not!"

He had a good point. "Okay, you've convinced me. I'll eat lots more fruit and raw vegetables," I promised.

He looked chuffed. "While we're on the subject: These three tips will help your body tremendously. Write them down."

I obeyed.

Don't soak fruit or vegetables.
Whenever possible, leave on the peels or skins.
Always try to eat them raw and fresh.

"Remember that when you're sick, your internal system is under stress. As a result, your body is robbed of essential nutrients; your glands and organs are unable to function properly; cells are destroyed; and poisonous toxins are probably rife in your bloodstream. It's vital for you to eat appropriately on a healing journey in order to supply your body with all the vitamins it needs to restore your body to perfect health. Got it?"

"Yes, I've got it now," I replied, tapping my notepad with my pen.

"Very good! Now let's discuss minerals. They're essential too. Did you know that vitamins can't function without minerals?

"No, I didn't. Why not?"

"Because vitamins and minerals work together. They make and break the chemical compounds in your body. You see, minerals act as catalysts. They enable electrical activity to take place in your body, which allows nutrients, like vitamins, enzymes, proteins and carbohydrates, to perform their tasks. Minerals are literally the 'spark of life'. They help to store and distribute water in your body, and they also help to facilitate the chemical reactions that occur in your body and brain every second of your life. They're essential for the forming of your bones and blood, and the maintenance of your body cells."

"That's astonishing!" I remarked.

"That's not all," he replied. "Minerals can also affect your mood. They provide you with energy, youthfulness and mental alertness. Believe it or not, a grumpy, belligerent, short-tempered individual can become happy and loving by taking the right minerals."

"You're kidding, right?"

"Nope. This is no joke," he replied with a stern expression on his face.

"I should probably get some minerals, huh?" I half-jested.

He chuckled. "That's probably a good idea. In this case, before you go shopping, you should know there are six main minerals: Zinc; phosphorus, calcium; iodine; iron and magnesium. However, 18 minerals are required to maintain your body functions. Interestingly, your body can't manufacture a single mineral. Plants absorb minerals from the Earth, and we eat plants. Fruit and vegetables are the primary source of minerals for mankind. Come on," he suddenly said, leaping to his feet. "It's a gorgeous day outside. Let's go for a walk!"

"A walk!" I exclaimed in horror. I never exercised on impulse.

"Yes. Put on your hiking shoes and we'll drive down to the park. There's a lovely trail that winds up through the forest, then down the valley to the sea."

"But we're working now!" I cried, pointing to the papers and books scattered across the desk in front of us.

"We can continue our discussion en route," he replied, brushing aside my protest.

"Let's go now."

CHAPTER 15

A WALK IN THE PARK

Sure enough, I soon found myself walking in the park with Henry Jones. He set a brisk pace for a man of his age, and I struggled to keep up with him. It was a gorgeous day, without a cloud in the sky. The forest bed was dry and dusty and leaves and twigs crunched beneath our feet. Henry Jones skipped from rock to rock, like a little boy on a great adventure. I trudged behind him, stopping from time to time to catch my breath. Tall trees lined the pathway on either side. They stretched on for as far as my eyes could see.

"How much further are we going to walk?" I wheezed, my hands firmly planted on my knees.

"We'll hike down to the coast," he replied cheerfully.

"What?" I yelled. "That's got to be miles from here."

He laughed loudly. "It's not that far."

"Not for you, maybe! But for me, it's bloody miles." I gasped. "I'm sick. Remember?"

"The exercise will do you good," he told me.

I grimaced. Not because we still had far to walk, but because it suddenly occurred to me that we'd left the Land Rover behind us and we weren't on a circular walk. "How are we going to get back to the car?" I shrieked like a girl with a spider on her dress.

"Ah! I have a plan," he assured me. The mischievous twinkle in his eye confirmed it. I didn't ask for details. I feared his answer. Anything was possible with Henry Jones. He took off, and I had no choice but to follow him.

"Let's continue with our discussion," he said.

It was the perfect antidote to fatigue. We soon became embroiled in conversation, and I completely forgot about the physical exertion of the walk. Looking back on it, that was another important life-lesson. Keeping your mind active is a fantastic way to disconnect from the physical discomfort of strenuous exercise. By focusing on issues that stimulate your thinking processes, you don't have the mental capacity to be concerned about the strain on your body.

The building blocks for survival

"Your body needs six vital nutrients to survive: Vitamins, minerals, proteins, fats, carbohydrates and water. These nutrients are necessary for energy; cell growth; restoration; regeneration; organ function; food utilisation and immunity. They're divided into two categories: Micronutrients and macronutrients."

"What's the difference?" I panted, trying to keep up with him.

"Micronutrients are vitamins and minerals. They don't directly provide you with energy, but they do release it from macronutrients like proteins, carbohydrates and fats. It's very important for you to know how micronutrients and macronutrients work."

I needed a rest. My heart was racing and I was short of breath. "Let's take a short break, shall we?" I suggested, staggering towards a nearby bench. He agreed, much to my delight.

Henry Jones plonked himself down next to me. "We've already discussed vitamins and minerals. But let's not stop here. Let's go the whole hog and examine macronutrients a little more closely."

"Sure thing," I huffed, pulling my notebook from my pocket. Anything for a break.

Amino acids

My attempt to buy more time to recuperate was transparent. He grinned and then obliged me. "Let's start with protein. Your body needs protein to survive. More specifically, your body needs the building blocks of protein, called amino acids. When you consume protein, your body naturally breaks it down into amino acids, which assist your body to synthesize protein and use it effectively. Of the 22 known amino acids, nine are essential. Hence, they're called essential amino acids. Your body can't manufacture the nine essential amino acids, but it does produce the others, naturally. You must obtain the essential amino acids by eating the correct food."

Protein

"Isn't there some debate about protein?" I inquired.

"Yes, there's a popular perception that people who don't eat meat are prone to suffer from protein deficiency. Rubbish! Let me set the record straight. First of all, protein isn't built in the body by eating protein. If you think animal protein becomes human protein in our bodies, you're wrong. Protein is built from amino acids in food. Not necessarily meat. In fact, animals can't form the nine essential amino acids. They're either directly or indirectly dependent on the plant kingdom for these nutrients. They either eat plants, or they eat animals that eat plants. The same goes for you, too. You don't have to eat meat. If you eat vegetables, fruits, nuts, sprouts and seeds regularly, you'll receive all the amino acids necessary for your body to build the protein it needs.

"The fact of the matter is that we need much less protein than we're led to believe. The recommended daily amount is only 56g per day. And, just to be on the safe side, the RDA is double the actual amount needed. Eat any more than that in a day and it will just be discarded as waste. In their book, *Fit For Life*, Harvey and Marilyn Diamond present a pretty strong case against the need to eat meat. For instance: Some people eat meat because they think it gives them strength. That, too, is nonsense. As the Diamonds point out, some of the most powerful animals in the world don't eat meat: Oxen, donkeys, mules, camels and elephants have been used to haul huge loads since civilization began, but you don't see those animals eating meat, do you?"

"No. Definitely not."

"Meat takes 10 to 20 times longer to digest in your system. What does this mean? It means you burn 10 to 20 times more energy trying to digest it. That is energy that could've been used to help your body heal itself."

"Are you trying to convince me to become a vegetarian?" I asked suspiciously.

"No! Not at all. I realize that some people like meat. It's one of their vices. I am, however, strongly recommending that you don't eat meat while you're on a healing journey. And if you must eat meat, catch it and kill it yourself. That will dampen your enthusiasm. You see, there is an enormous gap between the animal and the packaged meat we buy in supermarkets. This gap is filled with unspeakable cruelty and perversion of nature. But don't just take my word for it. Albert Einstein was a very smart guy. Agreed?"

"Sure thing."

"Well, he said this: 'Nothing will benefit human health and increase the chances for survival of life on Earth as much as the evolution to a vegetarian diet.'"

Carbohydrates

"Let's move on to carbohydrates. They're made up of carbon, oxygen and hydrogen. Hence the name: Carb-o-hydrates."

"What do they do?"

"Carbohydrates provide your body with energy. As they pass through your digestive system, they're broken down into glucose – your brain and body's primary fuel."

"Tell me more."

"Well, I can tell you that carbohydrates are divided into two categories: Simple carbohydrates and complex carbohydrates."

"What's the difference?"

"Simple carbohydrates are found in enriched flour, such as refined breads, pastas, honey and sugary foods. They provide calories, but few nutrients." Just then, Henry Jones reached out, grabbed the scruff of my neck and pulled me close towards him. "Avoid refined sugar at all costs," he growled.

"How come?" I stammered.

"Refined sugar offers you no nutritional value. When you consume sweets, fizzy drinks, chocolates, cakes and cookies, the refined sugar is absorbed into your body very quickly. This spikes your insulin levels, which can result in hyperactivity, aggression and irritability, followed by tiredness, apathy and even depression. If you don't believe me, watch children who've had too much sugar. They go crazy, right?"

"They sure do," I said, remembering my own daughter after a sugar binge.

"It makes me so angry when I hear parents complaining that their children are out of control while allowing them to consume refined sugars. Does the problem lie with their children? Nope. It's their diet. Cut out refined sugars and the change in the children's behavior will be almost immediate."

"I'll spread the word," I promised him.

"Good," he said, straightening my collar. "We'll get back to the evils of refined sugar when I teach you about vices later on. For now, though, let's move on to complex carbohydrates. You need energy when you're sick, right?"

"Right."

"Then you need to consume complex carbohydrates, like wholegrain breads, starchy vegetables and beans. They have fibre as well as valuable amounts of vitamins and minerals. Your body naturally breaks down complex carbohydrates into simple sugars, which are then used to supply your system with energy. This conversion process happens gradually, and your blood sugar level remains stable. This is what you need most to heal your body – the good, natural energy that you get from complex carbohydrates, not the false energy rush you get from refined sugar. Okay?"

"Okay, okay!" I said. "I've got it. No more sugar."

"Excellent. Sugar is a killer, and you don't want it in your body. It may taste sweet and delicious, but it destroys human health."

"What's next?" I asked, flipping the page of my notepad.

Fats

"Fats. Let's talk about fats. They play a vital role in your body."

"What do they do?"

"They're essential for maintaining nerve endings, cell membranes and hormones. There are two categories of fats: Saturated fats and unsaturated fats. You get saturated fats from eating meat, and unsaturated fats from eating plants. Saturated fats tend to raise cholesterol levels and have been linked to heart disease, cancer and strokes. Stay away from them. There have never been any reports of a vegetable and fruit diet causing any kind of disease."

I jotted down his advice as fast as I could.

"I hope you're beginning to realize the importance of eating healthily. If not, perhaps you'll be convinced when you understand the process of food digestion in your body. Let's have some fun, shall we?" Henry Jones said.

"What do you have in mind?" I asked, enjoying the break from the hike.

"Well, it's sort of a guided meditation. I'd like you to pretend that you missed your last meal. Imagine you're feeling very hungry. Your stomach is rumbling and your mouth is watering. Can you do that?"

"Yes, easily," I answered. I was feeling kind of peckish. It was nearly lunchtime, after all.

"Good. Now, I'd like you to imagine that you're just about to put a delicious spoonful of your favorite food into your mouth. Can you picture it?"

"Ah huh! It smells divine. Hmmm, yummy!" I joshed, closing my eyes.

He smiled. "This is probably a good time for me to tell you that there's a special enzyme in saliva that starts to break starches down into simple sugars. When saliva builds in your mouth, your body begins the process of breaking down food into its smallest chemical components so that they can be absorbed into your system. Do this now: Swirl your tongue around in your mouth. Can you feel the saliva building up?"

"Yes."

"Excellent. Now, put an imaginary spoonful of food into your mouth and start to chew it. Feel your jaw moving up and down. This mastication breaks the food down further. It's very important to chew your food thoroughly because it helps to release more nutrients, so they're absorbed into your bloodstream more quickly. I'd like you to imagine the food slowly turning into a fine paste."

"It's bursting with flavor – a true taste sensation," I teased.

He chuckled. "Next, move this delicious mouthful of food to the back of your throat and swallow. Under normal circumstances, your attention would most likely be focused on scooping up the next mouthful on to your spoon, right? But, for this exercise, feel the food sliding down your oesophagus towards your stomach. This part of your digestive track has a series of valves that cleverly prevent food from coming back up. It also stages the release of the proper enzymes at exactly the right time. Can you feel the muscles in your digestive track constricting and relaxing? This action 'milks' the nutrients and propels the food to your stomach. In anticipation, place your hand over your lower ribs. Done? Good. Your stomach is now directly behind your hand. It's not in your belly, as most people believe. To digest this mouthful further, your stomach produces a concoction of gastric juices, mostly consisting of enzymes and acids. For the next three to five hours, your gastric juices will continue to split this once-mouthful of food into smaller and simpler chemical fragments. You can drive to the mall, watch a movie, visit the hairdresser and by the time you get back home, the remains of your mouthful of food will only just be moving into your small intestine. All this time, your stomach has been working for you. Please bear in mind that if you'd swallowed greasy, oily, fleshy food, your stomach would have to work much longer and harder, producing more acids and enzymes, and using more vital energy."

Henry Jones wiped an insect from his arm. It buzzed around our heads and then disappeared into the forest. He continued: "You're not going to like this: Undigested food is often forced into the small and large intestine by the next meal. As a result, the digestive tract doesn't function properly, and undigested foodstuff rots in the colon. As Mrs Moffet already told you, this is the cause of most infections and many diseases."

"Yuck!" I remarked.

"I know, right?" he said, pulling a nasty face. "Hopefully, by the time your food moves into your small intestine, it has been broken down properly. It's in your small intestine that most of the digestive process occurs. Nutrients are absorbed in your small intestine."

"I didn't know that," I commented.

He appeared shocked. "Your body needs nutrients to function and heal itself. Don't you think it's important to know how to get more nutrients into your body when you're sick?"

"I do now," I responded.

"I've got another interesting piece of information for you: Your small intestine is approximately 22ft long! Unlike your stomach, which is an acid environment, your small intestine is alkaline. It's important to have an alkaline environment in your small intestine as this aids digestion and absorption. As your food/paste mixes with the alkaline bile, pancreatic juice and secretions from your intestinal walls, it becomes semi-liquid. When all the nutrients have been removed, this watery substance is passed into your large intestine, or colon. For the next 12 to 14 hours, your colon will store this substance while dehydrating it. Your colon absorbs mostly water. The indigestible substance that's left behind mixes with bacteria, expelled impurities, toxins and other waste materials and is finally discharged as faeces."

"I'm not that hungry anymore," I joked.

Your diet determines your health

He chuckled heartily, and then continued: "Keep in mind that your body was designed to process and digest natural foods. They pass through your system with normal, natural effort and without complication! But, when you eat unnatural, synthetic, processed, chemically altered junk food, your body receives very few nutrients and works considerably harder to try to break down those foreign substances. When you eat badly, you're damaging your system in a horrible way. You must understand your body is a fragile chemical universe that's governed by natural laws. When you mess with it by putting man-made junk food into it, you create chemical mayhem that requires millions upon millions of processes to remedy. Over a prolonged period of time, this chaos will manifest as a physical disturbance in your body – in other words, you'll get sick. Now, make a fist and stare at it for a minute or two. Pay particular attention to its size. That's the size of your stomach! Now I ask you, how can you possibly fit a cheese burger, fries and a double thick milkshake into that small space? Over-eating is seriously bad for your health."

Avoid overeating

I stared at my fist. I'd usually eat three times that amount in a meal. Henry Jones saw the horror in my eyes.

"If you usually eat to achieve a full, stodgy, bloated feeling, then you're making a grave mistake. Overeating places your system under tremendous stress. As a result, your body lacks energy and your immune system suffers. Once again, when you overeat, the excess food forces the contents of your stomach into your small intestines, whether it's been properly digested or not. The food that your body is unable to process causes constipation and, as you now know, it ultimately rots in your colon."

"That's not good!" I remarked.

"But wait, it gets worse," he told me. "Excess food is also stored as fat. Overeating is the main reason why so many people are overweight. Consumers in the USA spend over $15 billion on weight-loss programs, diets and supplements each year. All this money could be saved if people ate according to the size of their stomachs. So, if you've got unwanted fat on your body, it's because you've been eating more food than your body can digest. By eating smaller meals – the size of your fist – more regularly, you'll gradually lose the fat – and keep it off!"

"Five small meals a day, right?" I added.

"Yes, you've got it. That's an excellent way to lose weight. There are other advantages, too. Small meals are easier to digest because your stomach has room to produce gastric juices, and the muscles surrounding your stomach can move freely. You'll also find that you don't get hungry eating small meals more often, so you won't overeat. On top of this, regular eating keeps your body supplied with essential nutrients. It boosts your metabolism, so your whole system works better."

"I usually eat big meals to give me the energy I need to get through my long work days," I told him.

"You'll be surprised how little energy your body actually needs to function effectively. You can eat half as much as you do and your body will still have energy to spare – especially when you eat nutritious food! The key word here is 'nutritious'. When you eat food that lacks essential nutrients, your body sends messages to your brain demanding more food. You end up overworking your system while depriving it of the very nutrients it so desperately needs to keep up with your heavy workload. This leads to an abyss of suffering, and there's only one way to escape it."

Get back on nature's track

"You've got to change your eating habits. Turn your diet around and get back on nature's track. When you do this, your body will begin to repair the damage and restore itself to perfect health, naturally. The less energy your body spends processing bad food, the more energy you'll have to heal your body. Make sense?"

It really did. Henry Jones made it easy for me to understand how the human body worked. He had used simple logic and reason to convince me to change my diet.

"Do this now," he suddenly demanded: "Close your eyes, put your right hand on your heart and your left hand on your belly. Take a deep breath and make a promise to your colon that you will no longer take it for granted. From now on, you'll do your best to make life easier for your whole digestive tract by eating natural, healthy foods."

"Are you serious?" I asked, looking around uncomfortably.

"Yes. I am. Do it now. No one can see you."

I hesitated.

"Come on, do it. Take your healing seriously."

Oh, what the heck, I thought. I actually did it, and I will never forget it. The promise I made to myself had a profound impact on me. When you make a promise to someone, your conscience reminds you to keep it. A verbal promise to yourself is no different.

"Now try this," he instructed the moment I was done: "Block your ears with your thumbs; your nostrils with your index fingers and squeeze your lips together between your other fingers. Take a deep breath and listen."

I did as he asked and was amazed. Truly amazed!

"Believe it or not: That's the sound of your internal engine at work. You can hear it humming 24/7/365. And, like all engines, it needs the right fuel for optimal performance. We've already spoken about putting junk food into the tank of your car, so what would you say if I told you there's a very simple way to eat that will give you loads more energy, help your body to detoxify itself tremendously and boost your internal healing processes?

"I'd be interested!" I replied quickly.

"Excellent. But first, answer these simple questions while we walk." He leaped off the bench like a panther and started pacing down the path. I had no choice but to follow him.

"Do you ever eat egg and toast, or cereal and milk, or oats and milk for breakfast? What about cheese and bread, or pasta and cheese sauce, or fish and rice for lunch? Tell me: Do you ever eat steak and chips, or chicken and potatoes for supper? Hmmmm?"

He knew I did. "Guilty as charged, your honour," I called after him, lifting my hands in the air, as if to surrender for the second time that day.

"Those food combinations sound pretty normal, don't they? I bet you know people who eat like that all the time. Now let me ask this: Have you ever seen a lion eating a zebra while taking mouthfuls of grass, or a giraffe eating leaves from a tree and then swooping down for a swig of milk from a nearby buffalo?"

"Nope." That sounded ridiculous.

"No way, right? Animals don't eat more than one food group at a time. I guess Mother Nature must've told them about the principle of food combining."

"Pardon."

Food combining

"The principle of food combining," he shouted back over his shoulder. "Your stomach isn't designed to digest more than one concentrated food at the same time."

"What's a concentrated food?" I asked, breaking into a short jog to keep up.

"A concentrated food is any food that's not a fruit or vegetable, my friend."

"I didn't know that," I told him, tripping over a concealed root. I stumbled forward and caught myself just in time to prevent a calamitous fall. I did, however, bump my head on a low branch.

I rubbed my head vigorously. Henry Jones waited for me to recover. "Well, if you didn't know that, then there's a pretty good chance you won't know this either: Your body processes proteins and carbohydrates differently. Proteins require an acid juice to break them down into amino acids. Pepsin is the protein-digesting enzyme, and it's activated by hydrochloric acid. Starch, on the other hand, requires an alkaline juice to break it down into simple sugars. Ptyalin is the enzyme in saliva that breaks down starch. So, when you eat proteins and starches together, your stomach produces both acid and alkaline juices. Naturally, these juices neutralize each other. The bottom line is that your body needs to secrete more digestive juices, which are once again neutralized. Do you see the problem? In case the light bulb hasn't gone on yet, let me make it quite clear: This reaction retards and prevents digestion. Consequently, your body needs to burn extra energy. On top of this, the undigested food is invariably pushed into your intestines where it begins to rot."

Eat one concentrated food at a time

Henry Jones's preacher voice was in full cry. I scampered after him as he raged on. "Get this straight: Protein putrefies and carbohydrate ferments in your colon. Even worse, these reactions generate toxic acids, such as alcohol, ammonia and acetic acid, which are even stronger than vinegar. All of these acids are poisonous. They go straight into your bloodstream, causing allergies, flatulence, cramps, indigestion, mucous, headaches, fatigue and worse!" he cried.

"So, I should eat one concentrated food at a time?"

"Precisely!" he yelled, hoisting himself over a fallen tree that blocked our path. My attempt was far less gracious. I rolled over it and got stuck. I hugged and straddled the log, my legs dangling on either side. For a moment I seriously considered calling for help, but Henry Jones pushed on at a brisk pace.

"Eat one concentrated food at a time, with lots of vegetables or salad. Why? Because that's the way your body was designed to work by the Creator himself! Why deviate from the Master Plan? I promise you, my friend, practise proper food-combining and you'll enable your internal engine to break food down fully and all the vital nutrients to be absorbed and used. Do this, and you'll have more energy for detoxification, which will boost your immune system. You need this on your healing journey!"

"Okay, okay," I conceded, flopping on to all fours on the other side of the log. "I'll practise proper food combining from now on."

"Good. Good," he replied, stopping for me to catch up. "You'll see that it works. And it works splendidly!"

"I will. I really will," I assured him.

Care for your immune system

"Excellent. Now I want to discuss your body's immune system. This is your body's internal protection mechanism and your greatest ally against infection, sickness and disease. It works around the clock to defend your body against millions and millions of bacteria, viruses, parasites, microbes and toxins. That's quite a job. These nasty critters want nothing more than to invade, consume and destroy your body."

"Are they really that bad?" I asked.

"If you think I'm exaggerating, consider what happens when you die. Within hours of your immune system shutting down, your body is invaded by these critters. Without your immune system to attack and destroy them, they literally dismantle your body cell by cell, until all that's left within a few weeks is a skeleton. That should give you some idea of the importance and power of your immune system while you're alive."

I couldn't argue with that.

"Your body does everything possible to remain in tip-top shape on the inside. And it does so with military precision! Seriously! Your immune system is on guard 24/7/365."

"Where do the nasty critters come from?" I asked.

He spun around on his heels. "The biggest threats to the fragile chemical universe inside your body come from foreign substances from the outside. As you know, you must eat, drink and breathe to stay alive, so foreign substances are constantly entering your body. Agreed?"

I saluted.

"Your body has set up a powerful defence mechanism to warn and protect itself in the event that these foreign substances are harmful to you. But, this system isn't infallible. Like any army, it becomes tired when overworked, and it can stop functioning effectively. This is when you're vulnerable to attack from viruses, bacteria and disease. Your enemies are called antigens. These are any substances that elicit an immune response – from a virus to a splinter. In the event that antigens enter your body, your immune system's first line of defence is found in your blood. Think of your white blood cells as being your body's army. This is an outstanding metaphor to use, because this army is complete with generals, killer soldiers, special-forces, spies and cleaners."

"What?" I exclaimed, bending over like a linebacker to catch my breath.

"Oh yes," he replied abruptly. "Think back to the last time you got a splinter in your finger. The wounded area became swollen on the outside, and a red circle developed around it. Right? I bet it felt hot and painful, too."

I was about to answer him but then I realized it was another one of his rhetorical questions.

He pressed on: "If you didn't dig out the splinter with a needle, chances are it was pushed out, together with puss, after a few days. In a week or two, your finger healed completely. Look at your finger now. There's absolutely no trace of a wound, is there? Every cell has regenerated perfectly, hasn't it? That was your external experience of the healing process. Now, let's examine your internal experience. When you understand what happens inside your body, then you'll begin to appreciate the sheer genius of your immune system."

"Go on and take your time," I begged him. My chest wheezed.

He was off: "Your immune system has an astonishing range of responses to attacks from outside the body. It can even change defence strategies to optimize its response to unwanted intrusions. To simplify things: The 'spies' in your blood let the 'generals' know there's an invasion. The generals are in charge, naturally. They are called T-Cells."

"How come?"

"Because, after being born in your bone marrow, your white blood cells are sent to your thymus gland to learn how to become expert warriors. There are three types of T-Cells: The T4, T8 and Killer Cells. Your T4 cells are the warmongers, and T8 cells are the peacekeepers. Both play an equally important role in commanding the army."

I had a brain wave. "Wait a moment," I yelled. "I need to get this all down." I pulled my notepad and pen from my pocket and Henry Jones stopped in his tracks.

"Ready? On receiving word of the invading splinter, your generals then deploy the army to defend your body."

"How does that work?" I inquired, taking a seat on a nearby rock to write. My plan to rest worked.

"Here's the drill: Your immune system responds in phases. Phase one: More blood is needed in the trouble spot, so that your white blood cells can get to the area to begin their operation. This explains why the wounded area becomes swollen. Phase two: The first troops on the battlefield are called small eaters. They surround and contain the area to prevent germs from the splinter spreading to the rest of your body."

"That's the red circle?" I asked.

"Yes, my friend," he replied. "Now, let's proceed to phase three. Next on the scene comes the artillery. They're called big eaters. These warriors are armed with heaters, which they switch on to kill germs. This explains the hot, painful sensation. If the area becomes infected and you get feverish, then you know the battle is heating up. High temperatures are just big eaters in action."

"Got it," I said, switching to shorthand.

"Phase four: In the heat of the battle, killer cells swoop in to destroy strategic targets. The fighting is fierce. Both sides take casualties. What you call puss is actually dead white blood cells and germs."

I grimaced.

He kept going: "Your immune system's attack is relentless. It fights as if your life depends on it. Actually, it does. If it fails, you die! Fortunately for you, most times, it wins."

"Then what?"

"When the war has been won, the T8 generals call off the troops, and cleaners are sent in to clear the battlefield."

"That's neat," I whispered to myself.

He grinned. "The really neat thing is that your white blood cells never stop fighting for you. Never! They're on standby and patrol constantly. Your immune system is there to protect you and to preserve your health. But, as I've already told you, it must be in a good condition. This involves eating nutritious food and getting enough rest and recreation. What do you think happens to an army that's forced to fight day in and day out for decades without the proper support?"

I flipped back to my notes and read: "It stops functioning effectively."

"So, what makes you think that it's okay to treat your immune system any differently? An overworked, unsupported immune system becomes slow, unresponsive, depressed, exhausted, weak and ineffective. Not surprisingly, many crucial battles are lost. This is when disease triumphs in the body!"

I could tell he was deadly serious. The idea of my immune system failing terrified me. I really didn't want millions and millions of bacteria, viruses, parasites and microbes eating away at my rotting flesh in a grave. I suddenly felt very uncomfortable. "Let's keep walking," I suggested, surprising myself.

"Before we move on, I must tell you about antibodies." I took my seat and pulled out my notepad. "Let's say a virus like measles gets into your system. As usual, your spies inform the generals. They in turn commission a group of white blood cells to go to military school to learn how to defeat this new enemy. This is commonly referred to as the window period. Once these special forces are fully trained, they're deployed to destroy the measles. Having won the battle, these measles antibodies stay in your body for the rest of your life and make sure you don't get measles again. How amazing is that?"

"Isn't this how vaccines work?" I asked curiously.

"Yes. This is exactly how vaccinations work. Let's take measles as an example. A small dose of measles is injected into the body. As a result, the wounded area becomes swollen, red and hot. White blood cells are sent to become measles antibodies, which then kill the virus. If the body is exposed to measles in the future, the window period isn't necessary, so the antibodies can destroy the virus before sickness takes hold. Now that's what I call biological genius," he said proudly, tapping his chest.

I nodded enthusiastically. "Wow! That's impressive. I must admit, I didn't really know how my immune system worked until now. Thank you."

"It's my pleasure," he replied, giving a quick bow. I clapped loudly. He'd earned it.

"So, what happens to the destroyed virus?" I asked. "Where does it go?"

"Ah! That's a great question. This leads us to your glands, lymphatic system and liver. Let's discuss your glands on the way, he said, pointing to the path. "You have glands throughout your body. The more obvious glands are found in your neck, armpits and groin. Inside your glands are big eaters. They work like vacuum cleaners. They suck up antigens, like infections, toxins, viruses and waste. This is why your glands swell up when you're sick."

"I wondered why my glands had been swollen," I remarked. "Where do the antigens go when the glands are full?"

Your amazing lymph system

"Your glands empty into your lymph vessels. Heard of them?"

"Nope," I responded.

"Just like you have blood vessels running throughout your body, you also have lymph vessels. These systems are intertwined. Your lymph vessels are responsible for transporting the agents of your immune system."

"How do they do that?"

"Lymph is an alkaline fluid that flows in the lymphatic vessels. It bathes tissues and organs in a protective covering."

"What does it look like?"

"It's usually clear, transparent and colorless. This fluid carries the destroyed antigens to your liver."

"How is the fluid pumped through the vessels?" I asked, ducking under a low-hanging branch.

"That's another good question. Your heart pumps blood through your body, but your lymph system doesn't have a pump. It relies on your muscles to press against the vessels, pushing the lymph through your body. This is another reason why massage, stretching and exercise are so important: They help to drain your lymph system."

"So, this walk is actually draining my lymph system?"

"Exactly!"

"Where does the lymph go?"

"Next stop is your liver – a highly underrated organ. Your liver is one of your body's primary filtering systems. Everything that enters your body – food and liquid – passes through your liver. It separates the good stuff from the bad. The good is sent to your heart for distribution to the rest of your body, and the bad stuff is sent to your intestines, kidneys and bladder for disposal."

"So, you're saying the liver processes whatever your body doesn't want or need, then gets rid of it?"

"Precisely! Viruses; bacteria; dead body cells; toxins; medication; alcohol – whatever! Your liver is the filter."

"Can it get blocked?"

"Oh yes. If the waste piles up continuously, the liver can become blocked. As a result, the lymph can't release its load, so the glands swell. Plus, the liver can't process all the junk, so it's pumped to the heart, which then distributes it throughout the system. Consequently, the blood is heavier, so the heart must work much harder, causing high blood pressure and fatigue. So, if you get tired easily, you now know why!"

"I've got high blood pressure," I told him.

"Are you surprised?

"Not anymore."

Henry Jones was content to let me lead the way. The shoreline was in sight now. We were almost there. I was pleased that the hike was nearly over and that I'd made it to the end. It was another boost of accomplishment, and my self-confidence spiked. But, Henry Jones had more to say about the liver.

"Sometimes, when the liver is blocked, the junk is pushed through the skin. This explains most skin problems, such as sores, pimples and rashes. If you know someone with bad skin, tell them to stop rubbing on cream and start cleaning out their liver."

I immediately thought of Lucy from Shanghai. I bet her liver was blocked, too. The idea of helping her had popped into my mind. That thought would stay with me.

"How can we clean our livers?"

"I'll give you a great liver cleanser now," he replied. "It's very simple but extremely effective. Take a whole lemon, peel included; liquidize it into a pulp; add one tablespoon of olive oil and a half a glass of water. Blend it and drink it."

"How often?"

"One glass a day for three days will do the trick. But if you've been very sick, drink two glasses a day for a week. I strongly recommend you repeat this process every two or three months for the rest of your life!"

"Are there any side-effects?"

"Your urine might turn dark yellow, or even brown, but don't worry about it. That's just your liver releasing all the junk. Just drink lots of water – more than usual. Don't stop drinking water until your urine becomes clear. When your urine becomes clear, your liver is clean. Later on, I'll teach you another way to deep-clean your liver that will change your life forever."

As he spoke these words, we stumbled across a man-made staircase that led down to the beach. Our hike was over. I was very pleased with myself, and grateful to Henry Jones, too – for both the hike and the precious information he'd shared with me. We sank into silence as we strolled, side-by-side, along the coastline towards the buildings in the distance.

It wasn't a far walk back to civilization. I secretly hoped Henry Jones's rattletrap Land Rover would be waiting for us in the carpark at the beachfront. I scanned the vehicles in vain. "Okay, so what's next?" I said, thrusting my hands on my hips.

CHAPTER 16

A BIG BOWL OF QUANTUM SOUP

"We're off to Juju Banks."

"What's a Juju Banks?" I asked suspiciously.

He howled with laughter. "Not what. Who? Juju Banks is a person. His studio is over there." Henry Jones pointed to a small office block above a string of trendy beach cafés.

"Is he expecting us?" I inquired, disbelievingly.

"Yes, after lunch. We'll grab a quick salad at one of these restaurants first. The one in the middle makes a pretty mean hot mustard and honey salad with avocado, roasted almonds and peppadews."

My mouth watered instantly. I was surprised. A cheeseburger, fries and a milkshake never entered my head.

"You'll need an open mind when you meet Juju," he advised me.

"Why?" I responded, feeling a little panicked.

He grinned back at me. "Juju heals with his hands."

I crinkled my brow. "You're kidding, right?"

"Nope. Juju and I are going to show you how to nurture yourself with touch."

I couldn't hide my skepticism.

"Let me ask you: What's the first thing you did when you bumped your head on that branch earlier?" Henry Jones asked.

"I rubbed it!"

"And, what's the first thing you do when you kick your toe?"

"I hold it!"

"And, what do you do when you have a wound?"

"I cover it with my hand!"

"Do you think this impulse is just a coincidence? It's instinctive, isn't it?"

"Yup, I guess so."

Healing hands

"Have you ever stopped to wonder if your hands can heal?"

"No, I haven't. Well, not until now. Our hands would need to transfer energy in order to heal. Is this possible?"

"Well, the ancient healers believed it is. They used their hands to help heal people all the time. In fact, hands were used as a primary healing tool. Ancient healers said they felt a connection between the body and their hands. They couldn't always see it, but they were certain they could feel an exchange of energy between themselves and their patients. They became quite adept at explaining this phenomenon and developed specialist practices to heal people by using their hands to shift the energy in their patients' bodies. Understanding how and why these practices work will motivate you to apply them to yourself on your healing journey."

I stared at him blankly. I wasn't sure what to make of what he had told me. I was keen to heal my body, but I didn't want to get flaky about it.

"Convince me," I said.

"I'd prefer to let modern science do it for me," he replied with a big smile on his face.

We'd reached the restaurant and pushed our way through the crowd to an open table under an umbrella on the sidewalk. Henry Jones pulled out a chair and insisted I sit on it.

"What are you up to now, Henry Jones?" I asked.

"I'm going to give you the royal treatment!" he replied with a twinkle in his eye. "You're about to discover a new kingdom in a different realm."

I didn't know how to respond to that. He twiddled his fingers like a wizard conjuring a spell. He seated himself and leaned towards me. "I can't wait to tell you more, but first we need to have a conversation about the mechanics of the universe. Just wait until you realize the power in your hands. You're going to flip. Your mind will boggle when I tell you about quantum physics."

He snapped his fingers to get the attention of the waiter.

I was sure Henry Jones was losing it. He couldn't contain his excitement. He suddenly launched himself forward. "Relative physics explores the external universe and spans into outer space. Quantum physics, on the other hand, explores the subatomic universe and investigates inner space. I took you to meet Dr Sahib so that you could experience outer space and learn about relative physics. Today, however, is the day we're going to explore quantum energy and inner space. This is where it starts to get fascinating. We're going to discuss the universe, and you, at a molecular level."

"Shoot," I said.

Everything is made up of energy

"The very first thing you need to know is this: By studying atoms over the past few decades, quantum scientists have come to realize that everything in existence is made up of energy."

"Everything?"

"Yes, everything! Even your body is made up of particles of energy and forms part of one, great energy field. Have you heard of Fritjof Capra?"

My thoughts jumped a track. "Who?"

"Fritjof Capra. The author of *The Tao Of Physics!*" he declared, like I was supposed to know who he was.

He then proceeded to recite this passage, word for word, theatrically.

"The exploration of the subatomic world in the 20th century has revealed the intrinsically dynamic nature of matter. It has shown that the constituents of atoms, the subatomic particles, are dynamic patterns that don't exist as isolated entities, but as integral parts of an inseparable network of interactions. These interactions involve a ceaseless flow of energy manifesting itself as the exchange of particles; a dynamic interplay in which particles are created and destroyed without end in a continual variation of energy patterns. The particle interactions give rise to the stable structures that build up the material world, which again don't remain static, but oscillate in rhythmic movements. The whole universe is thus engaged in endless activity; in a continual cosmic 'dance of energy'."

The Bohemian-looking waiter who'd been standing beside us the whole time replied: "Whoa, dude. That was righteous!" He reached out and they pumped fists.

I sat forward. "I must admit, that sounded pretty impressive."

Henry Jones kept the hits coming: "Dr Deepak Chopra puts it like this: 'Although your body may appear to be a solid form, it's actually an intricate web of interconnected particles of energy that interact with themselves and everything else through the inexplicable, inseparable interconnectedness of all things.'"

"Wow!" exclaimed our waiter. "That's beautiful, man"

I turned to him. The only thing I could think to say was: "Do you know George-the-Surfer?" Where that question came from I'll never know. The obvious connection was their lingo, but that doesn't explain why I chose to ask that particular question at that precise moment. Then, the strangest thing happened.

"Yo bro, George is the bomb, man," the waiter swaggered. He stepped back and snapped his fingers like a rapper on MTV."

"You know George?" I exclaimed.

"The health boffin, right? The waiter asked.

"Yes"

"Sure, who doesn't, man? That dude chases gnarly waves," the waiter said. "You definitely don't want to get him started on pharmaceutical companies though. That's a big mistake. He goes ballistic."

Like George-the-Surfer, our waiter drifted off momentarily. I cleared my throat to get his attention. He responded promptly: "Can I recommend the mustard and honey salad?" he said.

I couldn't believe it. I thought I was in the twilight zone. The more things came together, the less I knew what was going on.

We are made of energy

For once, Henry Jones was insensitive to my confusion. He kept ploughing on: "Now, let's take this explanation a step further. Not only are you composed of energy, but you also have energy running through you. This concept is not new to mankind. For many thousands of years, Chinese healers referred to 'chi', or life energy, flowing through the body in channels, or meridians. This flow of energy sustains life in your body."

"I feel you, bro," the waiter said, tapping his heart with his right fist. Henry Jones copied him.

"Get this: when you're healthy, this 'life energy' flows unimpeded through your body, sustaining health and inner harmony. However, when the 'life energy' in your body becomes congested or blocked, it stagnates causing discomfort and disease. By placing your hands on to your body, the energy flowing from your hands gradually dissolves and dissipates these energy blocks, restoring the natural flow, and subsequently returning your body to health."

"Righteous!" the waiter remarked. I was momentarily captivated by the tattoo on his upper arm: A green, two-headed dragon emerged from a purple egg. Fire spewed from its mouth. It gave me the willies. "Two mustard and honey salads?" the waiter inquired suddenly.

"Yes, yes," I cried, waving him away.

But Henry Jones used his index finger to pull the waiter closer. "It's true. Your hands are powerful healing forces. They're a great source of healing energy," he whispered to him.

The waiter gave a thumbs-up sign and went on his way.

Healing is in your hands

Without the waiter present, Henry Jones turned to me. "Laying your hands on your body to heal yourself is very powerful and extremely effective. All you need to do is place your hands on to your body in a variety of predetermined positions for several minutes at a time, with the intention to heal yourself. That's it!"

I was still wrapping my head around this concept, and Henry Jones was already giving me instructions.

"It's best to set aside specific times for a proper, thorough treatment. But you can also treat yourself whenever you feel the need. It's very easy to do. Simply place your hands on your body with the intention to heal yourself, and you will immediately begin to heal your body. You will."

"But how does it work?" I asked loudly. The patrons around us gave me disapproving looks.

"What does it matter?" Henry Jones replied. "You don't have to know how electricity works to benefit from it, do you?"

"I guess not," I groaned, but his answer didn't satisfy me.

"Perhaps you should experience it for yourself. Do this right now: Close your eyes and put your hands together in front of your chest for a minute." We were surrounded by people and I suddenly felt very self-conscious. Henry Jones opened one eye after a minute had passed. It seemed like an hour to me.

"Finished yet?"

"I can't do that here," I moaned. "We're in a public place, for Pete's sake."

Henry Jones looked around. "Why not? Who cares?"

"I care," I cried. "I don't want to look like an idiot in front of all these people."

"Did I look like an idiot?" he asked. "Did the people around us point at me and laugh?" I scanned the faces around us. Admittedly, nobody had even noticed us. I felt a bit foolish.

"Forgive me," I said. "My ego got in the way of your lesson." I took a deep breath, closed my eyes, and connected my hands together in front of my chest. I did it exactly as he'd instructed me.

After 30 seconds had passed, Henry Jones spoke up. "I bet you are conscious of the place where your hands touch. Right?"

I nodded.

"Good. In that case, let's crank it up a notch. I'd like you to interpret the sensation of touch as healing energy. Tune into the healing energy in your hands. Focus on the feeling."

I took all the time I needed to fully experience what Henry Jones was talking about.

"Done?"

I opened my eyes and slowly dropped my hands to the table. I have to say, it wasn't difficult for me to imagine my hands had healing power. I felt something, too: A warmth and comfort flowing through my fingers.

"Amazing, isn't it? Within a minute, you mustered healing energy into your hands. I know you felt it. It's subtle at first, but it grows stronger and stronger over time. The more you practise this technique, the more powerful and effective it becomes. When you use your hands with the intention to heal, they become powerful forces of healing. The best part is, you can make this connection and use this energy to heal your body anytime you like."

"Have you got any more tricks in your bag?" I asked him.

"I've got plenty more, my friend. But I'll leave some of them for Juju Banks to show you. Let's enjoy our meal now. You'll meet Juju Banks soon enough."

CHAPTER 17

THE HEALING HANDS OF JUJU BANKS

Our food was soon served, and it was surprisingly delicious. Halfway through the meal, I felt like ordering a bottle of white wine, so I sipped a glass of cold tap water instead. It certainly wasn't easy to break old habits, but I was realizing that it was possible. Henry Jones kept me entertained with funny stories about places he'd visited, people he'd met and things he'd done. Time flew by.

After lunch, I met Juju Banks. Of all the strange and interesting people I'd already met through Henry Jones, Juju Banks was the most unforgettable. A tall, muscular man, as black as the Ace of Spades, Juju had big, round googly eyes that sparkled hypnotically. But his most distinguishing feature wasn't his eyes; his Jamaican accent; his deep, raspy voice; nor the massive Afro that crowned his head – it was his laugh. He made a strange wheezing sound as he sucked in air, and then let out a loud guffaw that exploded from his gut. He laughed so hard that his body buckled over, and his shoulders shook as if he was dancing. This was accompanied by a peculiar yet distinctive hissing sound – much like an angry goose or territorial cat. One thing was sure, Juju Banks loves to laugh. Everything seemed to amuse him.

Juju Banks and Henry Jones were incorrigible. They had clearly been good friends for a long time. I could tell by their easy banter and exchange of old jokes. It wasn't long, however, before we started discussing more serious matters, like healing with your hands. On this subject, Juju Banks was an expert. His knowledge of quantum physics and the human body was unrivalled. Even Henry Jones listened intently when Juju Banks spoke. His deep voice filled his words with power and authority.

I felt particularly weak and vulnerable as I lay on the massage table in the treatment room next to his office while the two of them leaned over me. One consolation was that I was fully dressed – except for my shoes. To make matters worse, there was a small hole in my left sock and the tip of my toe stuck out of it. I can't explain why, but I was so conscious of it. I really hoped Henry Jones and Juju Banks hadn't noticed it, but they had.

Juju Banks stared down at me, commanding my full attention. "Every atom is composed of energy, mon, and it's da nature of energy ta be in constant motion. Dis means, as da energy confined in da atom swirls around, it constantly bombards da atom walls and a limited amount of energy is able ta escape. Amazingly, dis liberated energy retains an affinity to da bulk of da energy inside da atom. Da result is dat dis liberated energy doesn't drift off into space, but instead it 'angs around da atom and forms an etheric field. Dis means, everyting in our known universe 'as an etheric field, because everyting in existence is made of atoms." This fact amused him greatly. He roared with laughter.

"Did I tell you he would expand your mind, or what?" Henry Jones whispered excitedly.

"Dat's troo. Dat's veery, veery troo too," Juju replied. "Yer brain processes billions of pieces of information every second. Wat ya see, and wat yer brain sees are not da same ting. Ya actually see much more dan yer eyes tell you. Wen ya meet people, yer naked eye is able ta perceive der physical form, but yer mind picks up and reads da 'vibes' of dat person. Dat's why ya feel comfortable wid one person and extremely uncomfortable wid anada person." This, too, earned a hearty laugh.

I turned to Henry Jones. "Did I miss the punch line here?"

He laughed, too. "All Juju is saying is that you have the ability to read the energy that surrounds and interpenetrates the body. With practice, you can tune your mind into these subtle energies and begin to consciously work with them."

"Dat's troo. Dat's veery, veery troo! We're standing on da verge of a 'ole, new but very old approach to 'ealth care 'ere, mon." Juju's shoulders shook violently from hysterical convulsions.

"Huh?"

We all have energy fields

"Let me explain," Henry Jones suggested to Juju. "For many thousands of years, mystics and spiritual healers referred to the aura of the human body, and they worked with this energy field to heal people. Modern-day scientists, however, required hard evidence before the etheric body could be taken seriously. Fortunately for us, technology has advanced rapidly in the past few decades and marvelous, new scientific equipment has been invented to detect electromagnetic energy fields."

Juju butted in. "Today, da doctors use an electrocardiogram – an ECG – to measure da electrical current of yer 'eart, an electroencephalogram – an EEG – to measure da electrical current in yer brain, and a super-conducting quantum interference device – a SQUID – to measure da electromagnetic field around yer body."

"You can even have your aura photographed using Kirlian photography," Henry Jones added.

"Do ya still need more proof of dis mysterious energy field?" Juju asked me in a slow, deep voice. I was speechless. All I could do was stare at them, hovering over me.

"'e needs more proof," Juju told Henry Jones.

"Okay, then. Over the years, numerous experiments have been conducted that conclusively prove the existence of an electromagnetic field. In 1939, Dr Burr and Dr Northrop at Yale University were able to determine the health of a fully-grown plant by studying the energy field of the plant seed. In 1957, Dr Leonard Ravitz at William and Mary University showed that the human electromagnetic energy field fluctuates with a person's state of mind. They noted that disturbances in mental or psychological stability affected the electromagnetic field and caused psychosomatic symptoms. In 1979, Dr Becker of Upstate Medical School in New York found that the electrical field of the body changed shape and strength with physiological and psychological changes.

"This quote by Aart Jurriaanse in his book called *Bridges* summarizes these findings perfectly: 'The etheric field forms the intangible framework on which the physical body is constructed. It constitutes the mainstay of all physical existence, not only surrounding but also minutely interpenetrating and supporting the tangible body. The real underlying cause for many ailments is to be found in the inharmonious condition of the etheric body.

Similarly, restoration in the etheric field will automatically result in physical recovery.'"

An odd silence fell over us. They just stood there, soaking it in. I lay on the massage table, motionless.

After some time had passed, Henry Jones spoke: "To begin to understand how to use energy to heal yourself, you must accept that our physical world isn't made up of solid concrete objects, but rather a swirling, fluid world of radiating energy. And, when you consciously work with this invisible energy field, you can use it to heal. Make no mistake, when you lay your hands on or near to your body with the intention of healing yourself, you direct energy towards achieving a specific objective."

"I tink it's time for ya ta try dis short exercise," Juju said. His Jamaican accent was so strong, I struggled to understand his English. "Da objective is ta test yer internal consciousness."

Gosh, I hope I have one! I thought to myself. But, as I was soon to find out, we all have an internal consciousness. The exercise would prove it.

"Close yer eyes and focus yer attention towards da little toe dats peeking out of da 'ole in yer left sock, mon. Allow yer mind ta dwell in dat area of yer body for a moment. Now, shift yer mind into da same toe on da oda foot. Wat does it feel like? Does it feel any different ta yer oda toe? Wriggle dem about ta feel if der is a difference. Wat does dat feel like?"

I did as I was told, but before I could respond to Juju's questions, he started up again: "Ya now exercising yer internal consciousness," he said and laughed heartily.

Focusing your internal consciousness

"You can use your internal consciousness to focus on any part of your body," Henry Jones added. "Amazingly, you can tune into your internal consciousness in two or more places at the same time. Focus your attention simultaneously on the toes of your left and right foot. Feel how your mind can access both places at the same time."

I did, and it could.

"Take a minute to connect with a few other places in your body right now. Learning to explore and interpret your internal world is an important part of self-healing," Henry Jones told me.

"Dat's troo. Dat's veery, veery troo," Juju responded.

I closed my eyes and sent my mind to my foot, knee, belly, chest, head and arms. A connection was made instantly with whatever part of my body I decided to focus on. "It works! It really, really works," I assured them.

"We know, mon. Dats why we told ya ta try it. Now, do dis quick exercise. Close yer eyes, rub yer 'ands together for tirty seconds, and den push da tips of yer index fingers togeda. I want ya ta focus on creating a force of 'ealing energy in yer fingertips. After tirty seconds, put da tips of yer fingers onto da area wer ya generally feel discomfort in yer body."

"Go on, give it a go," Henry Jones said, egging me on. Once again, I did what they asked.

"Ya 'ave ta use yer mind ta imagine 'ealing energy pouring out through yer fingers into yer body. Dis is 'ow ta conjure up da 'ealing force within ya, mon."

"Feels pretty good, doesn't it?" Henry Jones commented.

"What does?" I exclaimed.

"Practising your intention to heal your body," he replied.

All I felt was the touch of my fingers. I'd hoped to feel a powerful, electric jolt penetrate my body and nuke the disease. I half-expected to see bright lights beaming out of my fingers, like the Jedi swords in *Star Wars*. Apparently, hands-on-healing doesn't work like that. I definitely wasn't on the same page as them.

"Are you absolutely sure this works?" I had to ask.

Bursts of healing

"Of course, mon. It works fine. Ya kan genuinely 'arness da 'ealing energy in yer 'ands and use it ta 'eal yer body," Juju said, rubbing his hands together. "Let me show ya anada simple technique. I call it Bursts of 'ealing. Close yer eyes now. Make da connection wid yer internal consciousness. 'Old yer hands directly over yer 'eart ta charge dem. Tune in ta da 'ealing energy. Wen ya become conscious of it, ya give it energy. Energy flows wer attention goes, mon. Wen ya feel yer 'ands are fully charged, put dem directly on da area of yer body dat requires 'ealing for one, full minute. Stay in da moment."

I did as he asked. That was the first time in my life that I'd tried to heal myself with my hands. It felt a bit awkward at first, but their encouragement and acknowledgement made it easier to do.

"Ya kan do dis exercise as often as ya like. But wen ya do it, know dis ta be troo: Every time ya do it, ya 'elping to 'eal yer body."

Lay on hands

"I'll now give ya a few key pointers ta make 'ands-on-'ealing even more powerful. Firstly, wen ya lay yer 'ands on yer body, always be aware of yer thoughts. Ya must become conscious of da ideas, intuitions or inspirations dat spring in ta yer mind. Dees impulses are often keys ta unlocking da cause of yer condition. Secondly, be aware of yer feelings. Ya must question and evaluate yer emotions. Try ta identify da circumstances dat caused ya ta feel da way ya do. Ask yourself: 'Wat people were involved in dat situation? Wat lessons did I learn? 'ow 'as it changed my behavior? Are dees emotions still relevant in my life, or 'ave I outgrown dem?' It's essential ta process 'ow ya feel, mon. By peeling back da layers of yer emotions, ya will eventually come ta da core of yer disturbance."

All this time, Juju pressed his hands gently down on my body in different places. It was as if he was searching for something with his fingertips. I could feel strange physical sensations under his hands, and I told him so.

"Good, good," he sang in his deep, throaty voice. "Even dough 'ands-on 'ealing works at an unconscious level, ya kan usually feel a variety of strange sensations, such as warmth, cool, tingling, shivers, flushes, vibrations or waves flowing across yer body. Most of dees sensations feel pretty good. In fact, it's not uncommon for der sooding effect ta put patients into a deep, peaceful sleep."

"I don't feel sleepy," I replied curtly. I definitely wasn't about to nod off.

Henry Jones placed his hands gently over my feet and kept them there. "You may find this healing technique stirs up old emotions or memories that are hurtful or distressing. If this happens to you, try to understand that this reaction is happening to you because the healing process is taking effect. These thoughts and emotions need to surface so that you can process them and heal. Sure, this may be relatively unpleasant at the time, but it's ultimately good for you to release the old, stored-up memories that are clogging up your mind and causing blockages in your system."

"I'd still like to know how it works," I nagged.

Juju pacified me "Wen 'ands are placed on da body widda intention ta 'eal, a channel is created dat enables energy ta flow between da 'ealer and da patient. Dis energy comes from widin and it's limitless. It's a 'ealing power, for sure, mon," he told me.

Henry Jones followed suit: "This exchange of energy has the ability to restore depleted energy levels in your body cells, which strengthens your immune system and speeds up the healing process."

"And dis also provides ya wid a deep sense of peace, comfort and relaxation, mon," Juju drawled. His voice was hypnotic. I felt the tension in my body melting away.

"Another good reason to regularly practise hands-on-healing is that you start to develop a conscious awareness of the relationship between your inner-self and your body. This is a vital step in your healing process," Henry Jones added.

"Dat's so troo, mon. Wen yer external world unites wid yer internal world, 'oleness and balance is restored," Juju remarked.

"You need this," Henry Jones said softly.

I lay there, trying to tune into my thoughts and feelings. No, I didn't feel lightning bolts zapping through my body. Nor did I have any profound, life-changing realizations. I did, however, feel something. It was ever so slight, but it was definitely present. There was a connection between my mind and their hands. My internal consciousness ran through me to where their hands rested on my body. This inner awareness seemed to pull the energy through my body. I tried to explain to them how I was feeling inside. They listened carefully. When I was done, Juju responded by saying: "Da more ya practice 'ands-on-'ealing, da more ya will become aware of da energy flowing troo yer body. Dis 'appens for two good reasons, mon. Firstly, yer self-awareness increases, which 'eightens yer sensitivity. Secondly, energy gradually builds in yer body through concentrated periods of self-treatment or treatment performed by an 'ealer."

"How often should one do this treatment?" I asked.

"Treating yerself daily is da best way to increase energy build-up," Juju replied, pressing his fingertips under my rib cage. "With practice, one can learn ta 'arness dis energy and direct it wer ya want it ta go in da body."

"Is there a routine to follow, or are the hand movements random?"

"Dat's a veery good question, mon. It's best ta work down da body, from da 'ead to da toes."

"There are seven basic hand positions," Henry Jones piped up. "You should hold each position for two to five minutes, depending on your strength and the intensity with which you wish to treat yourself. You can leave your hands in a position for longer, but this doesn't necessarily mean that the treatment will be more effective. The key is this: Follow your intuition. If you suddenly feel the urge to move on to the next position, then do so."

"And if ya don't, wait until ya dooooooo," Juju said, snorting with laughter.

Listen to your body

"Learning to listen to your body intuition is very important," Henry Jones said, picking up from where he left off. "You've got to learn to trust yourself on a healing journey."

I glared at the area on my body that was giving me grief and thought of all the pain and suffering that I'd endured. My hands felt hot.

"Wat do ya feel?" Juju asked.

My emotions were easy to peg. "Anger and resentment," I replied.

"No, no, no, mon," he said and laughed so hard his shaking shoulders jiggled the massage table. I was being serious, so I didn't get the joke.

"Please explain what's so funny," I retorted.

He gathered himself. "Ya 'ave it all wrong. Der is no point in tryin' ta nurture yer body while ya feelin' anger or resentment towards it. Dat just won't work!" He started laughing again.

I turned to Henry Jones for some kind of support, but he wasn't much help. "You wouldn't get cross with a child for being sick, would you?" he asked.

"Of course not!"

Juju jumped in. "Many people make da mistake of resenting, or feeling anger towards, or even 'ating, da part of der body dat is sick. Dis may be a normal reaction, but it's entirely wrong. If ya suffering from disease, den da part of yer body wer da symptoms are manifesting themselves is functioning perfectly ta let ya know dat ya need ta 'eal yer body, and yer life. Ya need ta accept and acknowledge da sickness in ya, not persecute it. Da part of yer body dat is sick isn't da cause of yer problem. It's merely da part of ya dat elected ta bring da problem ta yer attention."

"What are you saying to me?"

Juju leaned over me and said in a deep, low voice: "Don't shoot da messenger, mon! Ya need ta tink of dat part of yer body as a sick child. Ya need ta nurture it back ta 'ealth. Ya need ta give it kind thoughts and love."

"But how do I do this?" I cried.

315

Think positive, healing thoughts

"Use yer internal consciousness ta carry positive, 'ealing thoughts ta da problem area in yer body, and surround dat part of ya wid love. Do dis, and ya will soon feel da troo power of da 'ealing energy widin ya."

"Loving thoughts are the key here, my friend," Henry Jones said, closing his eyes and changing his hold on my feet.

"Why are you both smiling?" I asked, feeling unsettled.

Juju answered. "Smiles are infectious, but in a good way. Dey spread well-being, peace, 'armony and 'appiness." Another hearty laugh followed.

"Smiles are also disarming," Henry Jones added. "They break down personal barriers and get past phoney projections."

"Dat's troo. Dat's veery, veery troo! Ya can prove dis to yerself. Da next time ya pull up ta a traffic light, give dat person sitting in da car beside ya a big smile and observe der reaction. I bet dey will smile back at ya, and den ya will both be left wid a feeling dat ya communicated wid each other on a deeper level."

"Why are you telling me this?" I exclaimed. So, maybe I was in a state of panic. I'd just had two grown men resting their hands on my body while I lay sprawled on a massage table in a room above the restaurant where I'd just dined for lunch. They hung over me with big grins on their faces. I felt like a missionary about to be eaten by cannibals.

"Believe it or not, you can communicate with your body in exactly the same way. Your eyes are connected to your autonomic nervous system, which – as you now know – is divided into two parts: Your sympathetic and parasympathetic nervous systems. Let's briefly discuss your sympathetic nervous system, again. It controls your fight or flight reaction. This is your most guttural or instinctive response."

"I think I'm feeling it now," I replied. Juju thought that was very funny. Henry Jones not as much.

He continued: "Let me give you an example: When someone jumps out of the dark and gives you a fright, you instantly react to what you see by screaming, hitting and running, right? In that moment, every nerve, muscle, tissue and organ responds automatically. You don't think about it. You just do it. Yeah?"

"Yeah, yeah!"

"On the other hand, your parasympathetic nervous system permits your body to rest and feel secure. It generates calm, loving feelings in you, and inspires similar feelings in others. Most importantly, it activates homeostasis."

"That's my body's ability to regulate and repair itself. Right?"

"Yes. What a good memory you have! When you smile through your eyes, your mind and body automatically enter a state of relaxation. They are freed of tension and are allowed to focus on harmonizing with their internal and external environment. When you smile through your eyes you help your body to heal itself."

"Try smiling through yer eyes now. Give it a go, mon!" Juju instructed me.

I did my best, but I don't think my attempt was very convincing.

Juju nudged me along. "Try smiling troo yer eyes at yer internal organs."

"By smiling through your eyes, you send a message to your body that says: 'Everything is okay, take it easy, I'm your friend and I love you.'"

My trust in Henry Jones was being tested. My head was racing and I couldn't stop it. Just breathe, I told myself.

Juju leaned over me again. His googly eyes looked more googly than ever. "Let go of da tension in yer body, mon. Let yer mind go. Don't be trying ta rationalize dis experience. Wen ya set yer mind ta it, ya can let da smile in yer eyes flow down into every organ in yer body, especially ta wer ya need it most."

Henry Jones shook my feet. He got my attention. "Don't battle against your disease and don't fight this experience. Accept it. Welcome the message it's sending you right now. Acknowledge it. Listen to what we're telling you, my friend. Lay your healing hands on your body, and then send that area a smile through your eyes."

"Dis 'ealing technique works wonders," Juju said. "Give it a chance, mon."

"You do want to heal your body, don't you?" Henry Jones asked me for the umpteenth time.

"Yes, I do," I replied, mustering conviction in my voice. I couldn't figure out why this exercise was so difficult for me. Perhaps it was because I needed hard facts. Perhaps my ego wouldn't allow me to be vulnerable. Perhaps I was afraid of change. I'll never know the exact reason why I struggled so much. But, I was about to have the breakthrough I needed to move forward on my healing journey.

The first hand position

Henry Jones led the way: "Lay your healing hands on your beautiful body now. Inhale deeply and place your hands over your temples. This is the first hand position that you need to do when treating yourself. Touch your middle fingers to the crown of your head. Imagine a circuit of healing energy flowing through your arms, hands and head. Create a mental image of your brain between your hands. It is the most complex organism in the universe. It consists of billions of brain cells working together in absolute perfect harmony. Your brain is literally alive with activity. Each thought triggers an electrochemical impulse that fires from one synapse to the next at speeds in excess of 105 miles per hour. Everything you perceive results in an explosion of millions of perfectly synchronized processes that are beyond imagining. As you feel your hands over your temples, visualize millions of minute energy particles dancing with renewed vitality. Imagine your brain is being revitalized, rejuvenated and restored. While you do this, remind yourself that in order to heal your body, you must first heal your mind."

Juju butted in: "Dis particular 'and position is great for relieving worry, anxiety, stress and depression. Especially wen dey are caused by sickness or disease!"

I felt myself slipping deeper into a state of relaxation.

Henry Jones's voice was soft and soothing: "Your brain is divided into two hemispheres: The left and right hemisphere. Your left hemisphere is your logical side; your right hemisphere is your creative side. This being said: When you reason, rationalize and analyze, then you're using your left brain. And when you're intuitive, creative and imaginative, then you're using your right brain. When your left brain accepts information to be true, then it allows your right brain to create without thinking it's just fantasy. When this happens, your whole brain begins to work for you. You're probably asking yourself: Why is he telling me this? Because it's essential for your logical mind to accept that you have healing hands. Only then can your creative mind bring healing into your reality. Get it?"

"I think so," I breathed.

"Surrender yer skeptical nature, mon, and let yerself believe dat yer whole brain is benefiting from da magical touch of yer 'ealing 'ands. If ya get wat I'm saying ta ya now, let me 'ear ya say: 'I know dat perfect health is restored ta my body now.'"

I repeated his words.

318

The second hand position

"Good, good," Juju drawled. "Okay, now take a deep breath and, as ya exhale slowly, slide yer cupped hands over yer eyes ta da second position. Rest yer hands lightly on yer face wid yer closed fingers, covering yer brow. Try not ta touch yer eyelids. Dis sensation is distracting."

I complied.

Henry Jones took the lead again: "Smile through your eyes. It may help to have a slight smile on your face. As we've discussed before, smiling is calming, soothing and relaxing. You're now pouring vital energy into your eyes, nose, sinuses, jaws and teeth. This position also stimulates your pituitary and pineal glands. As you settle into this position, you should automatically feel a shift in your state of awareness. You'll probably become more conscious of your inner world."

My hands brought darkness to my eyes. It pushed me into a deeper state of relaxation. I nodded. Speech was beyond me.

"You may be experiencing heat in your hands. They naturally regulate themselves through heat and cold. If you can feel heat, think of it as vital healing energy flowing into your body. Breathe this warm, healing energy into your lungs and imagine your blood distributing it throughout your body. If your hands start to lose their heat, that's a sign to move on to the next step."

My hands were on fire. I let them linger in that position for quite a while before I was ready to move on.

How can this technique heal me? It's so simple. Could it really work? I wondered.

Henry Jones was on to me: "I want you to accept that there are remarkable forces at work in nature. Forces that are beyond human understanding or comprehension! Believe me, my friend. By doing this exercise, you're employing the magical and mystical forces of the universe. They will heal you."

"Dat's troo. Dat's veery, veery troo," Juju sang.

"Isn't that what you want most?" Henry Jones asked again.

"Yes, it is."

"Den repeat da following mantra, mon: 'I see my body restored ta perfect 'ealth'."

I repeated it and sunk deeper into relaxation. There was no doubt about it. I was starting to unwind. I used my internal consciousness to find the tension in my body and release it. My breathing slowed and I was beginning to calm down.

The third hand position

"Good, good," Juju chanted. "Now, take a deep breath, den release da air from yer lungs and slowly slide yer 'ands ta da back of yer 'ead. Dis is da tird position."

It was an easy instruction to follow. I knew exactly what to do. I moved my hands from my eyes and placed them behind my head in the third position. Henry Jones was quick to adjust my positioning.

"Place your left hand under your right hand at the base of your skull. This area controls the nervous system for your entire body. Millions of messages race between your brain and your body. In this position, your hands are covering the station where these microscopic travellers embark and disembark from their body/mind journeys."

"Ya may tink dis is silly, but try ta imagine dat ya standing on dis station, wishing dem well on der travels. Make sure der cases are packed wid 'ealing energy, mon. Remind dem ta tell every cell dey see dat yer committed to 'ealing yerself, naturally."

The more I loosened up, the more vivid my imagination became.

"This area on your body absorbs a tremendous amount of energy. Feel it flowing up and down your spine, fuelling your entire body. People often fold their hands behind their heads when they feel in control, don't they? So, send this message to your body. Let it know that you're taking control of your healing. Muster the strength that this proactive behavior provides you, and then direct it to that part of your body that requires healing. Feel your personal power surrounding that area. You're now healing your body at a subatomic level. Yes, you're manifesting a miracle from the creative forces of the universe."

"Believe it," Juju said. "Repeat after me: Every single cell in my body is restored ta perfect 'ealth."

I said it without hesitation, and without the Jamaican accent.

The fourth hand position

"Now, take another deep breath. Ya about ta move yer internal 'ealing energy to da next part of yer body. Dis is da forth position. As ya exhale, slide yer 'ands to da front of ya neck, so dat yer wrists touch in front of yer Adam's apple."

"Your jaw should rest on the inside of your hands, below your little fingers. Your fingers run towards the back of your neck," Henry Jones added. "But don't press hard on your throat. Your hands should rest lightly on the surface of your skin. This is a good time to contemplate the things you say and don't say."

"Tell me sumting," Juju breathed huskily. "Do ya keep yer emotions bottled up inside of ya? Do ya bite yer tongue when people upset ya? Have ya ever felt a lump in yer throat dat has prevented ya from sharing yer feelings?"

I didn't even try to answer him. I knew his questions were rhetorical.

He continued: "Don't feel alone. Most people fail ta express der emotions properly. Instead of saying 'ow dey feel, dey store da emotions deep inside. Sometimes dey push dem so deep down dat dey try ta bury dem for good." He leaned over, putting his face close to mine. "Dis isn't good, mon!"

Henry Jones eased the tension by saying in a gentle voice: "You know by now, my friend, that if those emotions aren't released, they'll eventually manifest as a physical disturbance in your body, such as sickness, disease or pain."

Juju cut in. "Do yerself a favor, mon! Always speak yer truth. Every single time dat ya don't speak yer truth, it 'as a negative effect on yer physiological system. And dis in turn 'as an effect upon yer life!"

I suddenly thought about the lies I'd told. The string of awful excuses I made up so that I could do whatever I wanted to do, regardless of others. All of a sudden, I felt guilt and shame fall over me, like a dark shadow. My discomfort level rose steadily.

"As you lay your healing hands on your throat, visualize all those blockages that prevent you from sharing your feelings, ideas and truths dissolving and being removed. When you practise this specific hand position regularly, it reminds you to speak your truth all the time, no matter what!" Henry Jones said.

"Let's shake tings up a bit, shall we 'enry?" Juju said. Henry Jones gave a nod of consent and then discharged one of his broadest smiles.

Juju wasted no time. "To further activate yer throat, mon, try 'umming or chanting ta yerself."

I hoped I'd heard wrong, but they were being serious.

"Don't knock it til ya tried it, mon," Juju bellowed over me. "I'm going ta share a few powerful, primordial sounds wid ya. I want ya ta use dem. Dey will bring ya great comfort. Eyrie! Dey work, mon. And dey are great fun, too!" His googly eyes bulged even more. I can't pinpoint the source of my trepidation. I guess I associated chanting with monks, hippies, stoners, and New-Agers. It just wasn't my thing.

"Here ya go, mon. Follow my instructions carefully. Always start by taking a deep breath troo yer nostrils. Den, practice chanting da words 'aah', 'ohm' and 'rah'. Ya can also chant da vowels, A, E, I, O, U."

"It's okay," Henry Jones interjected, squeezing my toes reassuringly. "You should try it."

"Try ta say dees words or sounds from yer stomach, rather dan from yer throat. Chant da word for as long as possible. Wen ya draw short of breath, put yer lips togeda and complete da word by 'umming. Like this ..."

Juju proceeded to demonstrate, making the sound I was expected to copy.

Henry Jones offered a slither of advice. "This technique is more effective if you open your throat and hum into your nasal passages. You know you're doing it right when the resonance makes your head feel like it's vibrating."

"Jah mon, dat's an awesum feelin'. Ya 'ave got ta try it for yerself," Juju insisted.

Lying on the massage table, I felt very self-conscious. The sheer absurdity of the situation was freaking me out. But, I started chanting. No one I knew would have believed it. Not my colleagues at work, nor my estranged family. I have to say that it wasn't half bad. Chanting forced me to control my breathing and to concentrate on the sound I was making in my throat. It helped me to stay focused. Much to my surprise, that exercise made my scalp tingle. I actually enjoyed it.

Juju kept going: "Wen ya feel da vibrations raising yer energy, direct dis energy to da area on yer body dat requires 'ealing. Dat's wen it really works!"

I tried that, too. I imagined the vibrations in my skull flowing through my body to my problem area. My internal consciousness definitely made the connection. I liked the idea that I was sending healing energy to my body. As 'left-field' as it seemed, at least I was doing something to heal myself, and that was empowering.

Juju's voice thundered above me. "Dis technique is veery, veery powerful, mon. Don't underestimate it for a second. If ya feel it, repeat aloud: 'Wid dees sounds, my body is restored ta perfect 'ealth'."

Before I even thought to answer him, I heard the words coming from my mouth.

Henry Jones squeezed my toes.

The fifth hand position

"We're making great progress," Juju told us. "Now, let's get to da 'eart of da matter. Take a deep breath and slide yer 'ands down ta yer chest."

I shifted into the fifth position.

Henry Jones took over. "Take a few more gulps of air. It's important to breathe deeply – especially in this position! Become conscious of your chest rising and falling. Inhale slowly through your nose. Feel the oxygen flowing down your throat, filling your chest to capacity. Drink in the air. Then, blow the air out through your mouth and let your chest fall naturally.

"As you lay your hands over your heart area, become aware of your capacity to love and to be loved in return. Hold that thought. Keep it in your mind, and then let your internal consciousness carry this message to your body; especially to the areas where you most need healing!"

For some reason, I struggled with that. Love was a complex issue for me. I wanted to be loved, but I didn't know how to love in return. I had an appalling track record.

Juju picked up on it. "If ya feel stuck, ask yerself: 'Did I lose my 'eart ta a loved one? 'Ave sad experiences caused me ta close my 'eart? 'Ave I cut myself off from da rest of da world emotionally?' If so, did ya really tink dat would protect ya? Or 'elp ya! Let us look at dis situation objectively for a minute. Instead of releasin' all dat 'urt, ya locked it up inside of ya. Instead of dealin' wid it, ya carry it around wid ya on yer back, like an old, shabby coat dat ya choose ta wear every day. Now ask yerself, mon: Dus dat make sense? Dus it? Reelly?"

I shook my head from side to side. Juju had more to dish out. "Sure, ya may 'ave successfully deadened da emotional pain, but 'avent ya also deadened all of yer emotions? Be 'onest wid yerself. Do ya ever feel dat ya not as 'appy as ya could be? Do ya ever suppress yer excitement or sorrow? Do ya struggle ta completely surrender yerself to da emotion?"

I attempted to nod, but the best I could do was roll my head up and down the massage table. I was afraid that if Juju Banks kept going for much longer, I'd start bawling. I'd been well-primed for this exercise. Henry Jones had been planting this message in my head since the day we'd met. It was only now beginning to germinate.

"Oh dear, mon. Dis isn't good for ya. Wen ya try ta master yer emotions by locking dem up in yer 'eart, ya imprison yerself from experiencing life ta its fullest. Dis is crazy, mon. Yer feelings make yer life a rich and rewarding experience."

At that statement, he chuckled like a hyena on helium. I didn't get the feeling that Juju was laughing at me, but rather, at the simplicity of this truth.

"So, 'ere's our message ta ya: Don't be afraid ta live yer life ta its fullest potential. Open yer 'eart and let yer emotions flow. 'Appy or sad, good or bad! Let da feelin' flooooow."

I tried the same line I fired at Henry Jones when we had a similar conversation. "But you can't always expect life to be a bed of roses."

"No, ya can't!" But ya can expect yerself ta grow from negative experiences and emotions. 'Ow ya grow is up ta ya. If ya open yer 'eart and release yer feelings, ya will 'eal quickly and grow tall. But, if ya close yer 'eart, ya will never 'eal and ya will become twisted, distorted and bent." He mangled his big hands together. "Ya may even wither and die!" Juju growled in a deep, fearsome, prophetic voice that gave me the willies. He found immense humor in the terror on my face and his great guffaw roared above me.

Once JuJu's laughter had died down, Henry Jones stepped in to restore order. "Do you remember how your lungs work."

I nodded.

"Excellent. I'd like you to imagine healing energy flowing from your hands through your chest into your heart, and then into your lungs. Picture your heart and lungs pumping healing energy throughout your system. Connect your internal consciousness to your blood circulation system, and visualize it carrying healing energy to your entire body."

I did as I was asked. It took a few minutes to establish a comfortable rhythm, but it was a surprisingly easy exercise to do. The combination of breath, meditation and concentration captivated me.

"As discussed previously, the Chinese believe in a life-energy called chi. Picture this chi flowing through your bloodstream, bringing vital energy and life to your body. Imagine it in your bloodstream, washing away blockages and impurities that may be clogging your system. As these blockages are swept away, your whole system begins to function harmoniously."

The smile on my face widened. Noting it, Juju Banks said, "Repeat dis, 'In my 'art I know dat my body is restored to perfect health'."

I did.

"Alright den, now it's time ta center yerself. We're going ta teach ya 'ow ta generate strength and power," Juju said.

"Sounds good," I breathed slowly.

The sixth hand position

"Take a deep breath and exhale," Henry Jones instructed. "Then, without breaking contact with your body, slowly slide your hands down to your solar plexus. This is the sixth position."

They waited for me to complete the movement. "Next, take another deep breath and imagine your stomach is a beach ball filling with air. When it feels as though your stomach is filled to capacity, hold your breath for a moment, and then use your stomach muscles to force the air out of your body. It's important to control your breathing using your stomach muscles. It's this control that gives you strength. Work it. After a few minutes, you'll literally feel the strength that emanates from this part of your body. Yes, you can draw energy and strength into your body through your solar plexus. People who study martial arts use this technique to increase their strength and power. You've seen them chop through stacks of bricks and perform seemingly impossible feats of strength? This technique gives them the power to do that."

"Da converse is also troo, mon," JuJu interjected. "Ya can also lose energy from yer solar plexus. Let me give ya an example. It feels like ya've been punched in da gut wen ya get bad news, doesn't it? Ya left feeling weak, vulnerable and sensitive. Right mon?"

"I just wanted to fold over into the foetal position and cry when I found out that I was sick," I told him.

Juju carried on speaking as if I hadn't said a word. "It's veery important dat ya safeguard yer solar plexus from losing energy wen ya sick. Dat's why we're goin' ta show ya 'ow ta do dis."

He gave Henry Jones a nod, who nodded back in return and took over the teaching.

"Focus on your breathing, my friend, but this time I'd like you to imagine that you're inhaling and exhaling through your solar plexus. Try to keep this in mind: When you were in your mother's womb, around her navel point, you absorbed nutrients, expelled impurities and breathed through the umbilical cord that was attached to your navel. Each breath circulated through your body by flowing from your navel; down your perineum; up your spine to the top of your head; then through your tongue; down the front of your chest to your navel again. Chinese Taoists believe the navel is the starting point of the flow of primordial life energy, or chi. They say it remains the strongest point of energy storage and circulation.

"Keeping your hands on your solar plexus, imagine that you're breathing in through your navel. Inhale slowly and imagine that your breath travels down to your perineum – the base of your spine – then up your spine and into your head. Next, turn your tongue upside down and slide it towards the back of the roof of your mouth. Right at the back, you should feel a hole or small crater. Taoists refer to this hole as the 'heavenly pool'. Place the underside of your tongue into this heavenly pool and hold it in this position. As you breathe out through your nose – your mouth is closed – imagine your breath flowing down the front of your chest and out through your navel. Do this technique for a couple of minutes and you'll be amazed by the sensations that you experience. Try it now. Dip your tongue into your heavenly pool, then inhale up your spine and exhale down the front of your chest to create an energy circuit."

"Go on," Juju drawled. "Yer tongue closes da energy circuit in yer body and da current is den able ta flow troo ya."

"Your tongue may tingle or buzz with electric-like shocks, and you may even get a metallic taste in your mouth. This is your chi energy," Henry Jones said. "When you get your Chi circulating through your body in this manner, you can direct it to the parts of your body that you want to heal. This is how you can help to heal your body. Focus your attention on the needy area, and smile through your eyes at it."

"Dat's 'ow simple it is," Juju purred. "Now repeat after me. 'I 'arness my personal power ta restore my body ta perfect 'ealth.'"

These mantras had a strange effect on me. They provided me with a sense of closure. I felt better for saying them. I don't know how they worked – they just did!

The seventh hand position

"To do the seventh position, move your hands down to your pelvic region."

"Just below yer belly button," Juju interjected.

"Once again, change position by taking a deep breath and sliding your hands over your body as you exhale. After learning about the digestion process in your body today, it should be easy for you to imagine how the small and large intestines process your last meal and dispose of toxins and other waste materials."

"It will be," I replied.

"Apply it den!" Juju chanted.

Henry Jones added: "This is a good time to reflect on your past experiences. Let your digestive process be an example to you. In other words: Keep the good and release the bad. As you inhale, draw all things positive into your life, and, as you exhale, release all things negative."

"That's it?" I asked.

"That's it!" he replied.

A few minutes passed, then Juju raised his hand: "Repeat after me," he whispered, uncharacteristically. "I release sickness and pain and restore my body ta perfect 'ealth."

Scooping

After hearing me say those words aloud, Juju instructed me to climb off the massage table and sit on the edge of a chair. Feeling shaky, I obeyed.

"Now den, straighten yer spine. Make sure yer weight is on yer sittin' bones. Ya can find a delicate place of balance by rockin' back and forth ever so slightly. Ya shud always sit in dis position ta do scoopin'."

"Scooping?" I exclaimed. "What's that?"

"It's a veery powerful 'ealing technique, mon. To grasp da motion of dis technique, it may 'elp ya ta imagine dat ya scoopin' water out of a canoe. Place yer 'ands on ta yer body, and den slide dem togeda, scoopin' up da disease and trowin' it awaaaay," he sang in a very low voice.

He demonstrated how it should be done. I copied him.

"Repeat this exercise all over your body, especially in areas of discomfort or pain," Henry Jones said.

"Show 'im 'ow ta do pushing, 'enry," Juju said.

Pushing

"Place your hands directly on to the afflicted part your body so that the tips of your thumbs and forefingers touch each other, forming the shape of a triangle. Take a really deep breath and constrict the muscles in your body, as if you were constipated. Imagine pushing the disease out through the center of the triangle. Try to muster up as much internal force as possible, being careful not to strain yourself. Use your internal consciousness to help you push from the inside of your body."

Squeezing

"Now, I'll show you squeezin'," Juju said, stepping forward. "Place yer thumbs and forefingers on eeda side of da afflicted area. Taking a deep breath, slowly exhale and squeeze da disease out yer body. Let yer fingers run along da surface of yer skin until dey come togeda, den repeat dis exercise."

I got it first time.

"Dis one's a quick learner, 'enry. I'm goin' to teach 'im kneadin', too."

Kneading

"Dis movement is just like kneadin' dough. It stretches and relaxes yer muscles and skin, improves circulation, brings fresh blood and nutrients to da area and 'elps da absorption and elimination of waste materials. It's greeeat!" Juju said, giving a thumbs-up. "Place yer 'ands flat onto yer skin directly above da afflicted area. Press down wid da palm of one 'and den gently grasp da flesh or skin between yer fingers and thumb, and push it tawards da oda. Let go of da flesh, grasp it wid yer oda 'and, and repeat dis movement back tawards da oda side. Ya will soon establish a natural rhythm of squeezing and releasing yer flesh or skin with alternate 'ands."

I tried it, and it felt pretty good.

Henry Jones gave me some pointers: "Try varying the effect by changing the speed and depth of kneading. It's best to make the work slow and deep, as well as fast and shallow. But don't let the physical exercise dominate the mental exercise. It's very important that you concentrate on working the disease out of your body. Working with your hands should be a mental exercise, too."

"Dat's troo. Dat's veery, veery troo!" Juju remarked.

Chopping

"Try chopping," Henry Jones suggested. "Gently strike your skin with the side of your hands, instantly pulling your hands back for the next alternating stroke. Work very quickly. This brisk, percussion movement is highly effective for improving circulation and stimulating your muscles and skin. But don't cause yourself any discomfort. Imagine that you're chopping up the disease, thereby destroying it. Every so often, scoop away the imaginary waste material and start chopping again."

Pressure

"Pressure works, too," Juju said, taking over. "Try dis: Place da pads of yer tumbs on eeda side of da afflicted area and gradually apply pressure by leanin' on dem. Press down for a few seconds, den slowly release and glide ta da next point of pressure. Deep, direct pressure is extremely helpful for releasing tension. As ya press down with your thumbs, imagine the disease surfacin', and then occasionally wipe it away with ya 'and."

I was getting the hang of it now. These hand movements were easy to do. Henry Jones and Juju Banks looked pleased with my progress.

"Shud we tell 'im, 'enry?" Juju suddenly asked.

"Only if you think he's ready," Henry Jones replied.

"I tink 'es ready, mon." Juju looked very excited. He rubbed his hands together with delight. "'Ave ya seen da movie *Edward Scissorhands*?"

"Er, yes," I answered cautiously.

Psychic surgery

"Dis technique reminds me of dat strange and powerful film. It's called psychic surgery," he replied, laughing like an evil mastermind with plans to conquer the world. He leaned back and spoke slowly: "Imagine dat ya extendin' yer fingers by several inches. Grip one finger at a time widda fingers of yer opposite 'and, and den slide yer fingers over dat finger towards da tip and beyond. Wen ya 'ave completed 'extending' each of yer fingers in dis way, pretend dat ya slowly digging dem into yer body and removing the disease."

It sounded very strange indeed. I glanced towards Henry Jones. He had a stern expression on his face. "Psychic surgery is extremely effective on your internal organs. When you've finished 'operating' on yourself, don't forget to push in your fingers. To do this, simply imagine that the opposite hand is sliding the imaginary finger extensions back into place."

He smiled reassuringly at me. Our session was coming to an end. A sense of accomplishment was written all over Henry Jones's face. "To close your hands-on-healing sequence, always rest your hands at your sides with your palms facing upwards. Relax in this position for a couple of minutes."

Juju was determined to have the last word. "In da eye of yer mind, imagine dat yer 'ole body is surrounded by a womb of love, and know dat ya receivin' everyting ya need in dis moment ta restore, rejuvenate and 'eal yer body."

Henry Jones wasn't to be outdone: "Imagine an umbilical cord connecting you to the universe, or a Higher Power. Breathe through the imaginary umbilical cord, drawing in new vitality as you inhale, and expelling impurities and negative thoughts as you exhale."

Juju playfully pushed him aside. "Don't forget ta dip yer tongue into da 'eavenly pool at da back of da roof of yer mouth, and circulate yer bree-ding."

Henry Jones chuckled. "As you inhale, draw the healing energy up your spine and into your head, then exhale and let the energy flow down your front."

"Smile inwardly, mon," Juju called over his shoulder, and then broke out in laughter.

With that they high-fived each other and left the room. I was left alone for a brief second, before Henry Jones popped his head back into the room and said: "Drifting off to sleep at this point isn't uncommon. Have beautiful, colorful dreams, okay?"

It'd been a long, eventful day. I was physically and mentally exhausted. I rolled back on to the massage table, where I could stretch out. My eyes closed. I tried to recall all the lessons I'd learned that day. There were a lot of them to remember.

Henry Jones had taught me to take action. He'd told me it was my responsibility to be proactive instead of reactive. We'd examined two areas where I could be proactive: Nourishment (food) and nurturing (touch). In food, we discussed why we should eat live food (uncooked) instead of dead food (cooked). I'd learned about enzymes and the importance they play in restoring health. We took a closer look at vitamins, minerals, proteins, carbohydrates and fats, and subsequently discovered why it's in our best interests to eat healthily.

With touch, we'd explored the scientific research that proves we have an electromagnetic energy field. I was also shown seven positions to lay my hands on my body in order to heal myself. I was given a series of practical healing techniques that work with this subtle energy. I tried to remember their names: Scooping; pushing; squeezing, kneading; chopping; pressure and psychic surgery. Henry Jones said that applying these techniques would give me more energy and vitality. He said I would feel the difference physically, mentally, emotionally and spiritually.

I drifted off soon after.

PART 3

SPIRITUAL HEALING

CHAPTER 18

THE PLANE TRUTH

A lot of exciting things happened to me in the days and weeks that followed my first appointment with Juju Banks. Henry Jones and I established a daily regimen of healing exercises intermingled with impassioned work sessions. We ploughed our way through his big, brown envelope and slowly crafted his book. There was never a dull moment. Each day was jam-packed with interesting things to do and talk about. Henry Jones kept me on my toes all day. We lost hours, perhaps days, discussing the extraordinary healers he'd met in different countries around the world, and experimenting with the amazing modalities they use to restore health and happiness in their patients. I had the time of my life.

I'd learned more about myself, and the true meaning of life during that time than I'd ever done before. Every day brought new revelations. The healing techniques that I discovered, worked. I could see and feel the results manifesting in my body. I used the Workbook he gave me, each and every day. I scored myself, too – and set goals! As time passed, my quest for health and wellness gathered momentum, and my newfound conviction in my healing journey grew from strength to strength.

My relationship with Henry Jones grew stronger too. He became the father-figure I'd never had, and I felt safe, protected and loved. I trusted him with my private thoughts and felt safe to freely share my most intimate feelings with him. His responses never let me down. We laughed, cried, divulged secrets, and challenged each other. There was very little we didn't do together: We debated; walked; talked; worked; wrote; edited; entertained;

ran; stretched; prepared food; and cleaned together. I never got tired of his company. When we took time out from each other to enjoy personal space or run errands, I missed him. It wasn't some infatuation or superficial bromance. It was my first, true friendship. At last, I'd found someone who saw me for who I really was, not what I'd become, or who I pretended to be. Most importantly, he encouraged me to be myself – my true-self.

The weeks slipped by. We invited Prof Kaufman and Dr Sahib to have dinner with us one evening, which proved to be interesting, to say the least. George-the-Surfer helped me to catch my first wave. Kevin occasionally cracked my spine and popped my joints, which reset the bone structure of my body.

I met Joerg, my daughter's fiancé, and yes, once again, I behaved myself. It turned out that he was a health nut too, so we had lots to talk about – although I tried to do most of the listening. I liked him, and I think he liked the new me, too. My daughter seemed happy with the outcome of our meeting. She kissed me goodbye and hugged me twice. Thinking about it still brings a lump to my throat. My new approach to life offered instant benefits. Each new activity made me feel even better.

Henry Jones's influence on me was undeniable. He made me want to be a better person, to live to my fullest potential, and to love and be loved in return. He became my cherished mentor, and I made sure to follow his advice to the letter.

Each night, before going to bed, I'd write in my Workbook and Notebook. My Notebook was my healing journal, and I loved reviewing it. I also made sure I knew exactly what healing techniques and exercises I was going to do the next day. I always wrote about my experiences. My Workbook and Notebook became increasingly important to me over time, just as Henry Jones had predicted.

I can say with pride that my diet was immaculate. I'd begun consuming a whole-foods, plant-based diet, eating mostly fruits, nuts, legumes, salads and vegetables, which I interspersed with short fasts. I only drank water and herbal tea. The secret to success on a whole-foods, plant-based diet, I soon discovered, is to know how to prepare your food. That is all-important. Fortunately for me, Henry Jones taught me a few, great recipes for snacks and meals. Before I met him, I'd never prepared my own food, but Henry Jones taught me that food preparation was a big part of the program. It's important to take responsibility for feeding yourself properly. That means working out a daily menu, selecting the right produce from the store, preparing it, cooking it and even cleaning up after yourself. Yes, I did dishes too! Happily! Putting in that amount of effort is guaranteed to produce positive results.

My energy levels went up, my sinuses cleared, my constipation disappeared, and I slipped up a few notches on my belt. My confidence in my new, healthy lifestyle grew as the benefits kept coming. I was truly amazed at how quickly my body had responded to a whole-foods, plant-based diet. I had both seen and felt dramatic results in a few weeks. I became certain of it: Eating predominantly fruit and vegetables is Mother Nature's optimum eating plan for us humans. Our bodies love a whole-foods, plant-based diet, and when fruit and vegetables are prepared properly, our taste buds love them, too.

I also began making smoothies every day. My sunrise mix was my favorite smoothie of the day. Carrots, papaya, avocado and almonds blended into a thick, sludgy mix. I call it The Mrs Moffet. I used to be addicted to coffee, but the idea of drinking strong, sweet, black coffee early in the morning eventually didn't appeal to me at all. Drinking a healthy smoothie first thing in the morning somehow set a precedent for the rest of my day. It put me on the right trajectory. Henry Jones also insisted that I plan my meals a day in advance and keep a record of everything I ate and drank. He made me list the ingredients of each meal in my Workbook, so I knew exactly what I ingested each day. This practice soon became a habit.

I also got into the habit of visiting healing practitioners, which I enjoyed immensely. Needless to say, I became a regular customer of both Mrs Moffet and Juju Banks. The more I visited them, the more progress I made. I have realized that healers are not miracle workers and that they don't have magic wands that instantly heal you. It's a process, and you must go through it. It takes several visits for them to shift the energy in your body and repair the damage you've done to yourself over years. Of course, Henry Jones asked me to write about each of my treatments, and to describe the impact they had on me physically, emotionally, and mentally. I also had to prioritize them, so that I could plan to do the most impactful treatments more regularly on my healing journey. He got me to record my dominant thoughts each day in my Workbook, as well as personal realizations, breakthroughs and inspirations. I also had to describe how I felt physically each day and write down any physical sensations in my body. This exercise helped me to tune into my body, which raised my body consciousness to new heights.

However, what I didn't enjoy was recording any indulgence of my vices, or any activities that compromised my healing journey. But Henry Jones insisted that I do it. Those hand-written confessions glared at me menacingly from my notes. They tarnished my Workbook. I eventually cut out my vices completely because I didn't want to spoil my record.

Henry Jones was two steps ahead of me and two steps behind me all the way. He'd many tricks up his sleeve and they all worked like magic. He helped me to design a 'Happy Plan' and a 'Be Plan', which aren't more complicated than creating a list of things that make you happy and doing at least one of them every day, and planning in advance how you want to 'be' each day. It really worked for me. Thinking about the day ahead and pre-programming my behavior to meet my needs was extremely effective.

I had to meet my insufferable boss, once or twice, for business matters. That's when I preprogrammed myself to be tolerant and patient with him. I discovered how to handle situations that usually pressed my buttons. I planned to "be" the best person I could "be" each day. This simple technique radically transformed my behavior. I became proactive rather than reactive, and I was truly amazed by the results. My life became more pleasant. I experienced much less confrontation and stress, and I subsequently became calmer and more centered.

Henry Jones also encouraged me to have Me Time. This quickly became my favorite part of the day. This involved making time each day to deliberately raise my self-awareness. I did small, seemingly innocuous activities, like picking flowers, watching the Sun set, and pampering myself, but I did them with the explicit intention of connecting with myself – my true-self. Walking barefoot on the grass for 10 minutes a day became one of my favorite things to do. Don't knock it until you've tried it. This can be really powerful, especially when you combine it with other healing techniques.

I'd walk barefoot on the grass and repeat affirmations. Each morning, Henry Jones gave me a new healing affirmation to learn and recite. I enjoyed those mantras immensely. Saying them over and over helped to convince me they were actually true. I started to believe them because I heard myself saying them repeatedly. Their message sunk in.

Each and every day, he would ensure I spent five minutes visualizing my healing and future health; five minutes reflecting on my day and past, and five minutes meditating on all the things for which I could be grateful in my life. He also made me write down one Blessing that I received each day. This forced me to look for blessings in my life. To my amazement, they started to appear – more and more.

The fun part of each day was scoring myself. Henry Jones designed a simple scorecard and got me to award myself points each day for doing the things that promoted my healing. I had to be totally honest with myself. The maximum I could score each day was 100 points. When I did everything that I planned to do in order to heal my body, I had a True-Day. I found myself wanting to get high scores and feeling very disappointed in myself when my score dropped. Together, we calculated the total points I earned each week, and tracked all the points I'd earned on my healing journey. You guessed it: The points were linked to specific goals and rewards that we'd put in place at the start of my healing journey. I found myself striving to reach those milestones. Every goal I achieved was celebrated with a small reward, and that drove me towards the next target.

All in all, I was having great fun on my healing journey, but I was still sick. Some days weren't so great. My symptoms flared up and the afflicted part of my body was sore. Some days I spent in bed; some days I regressed mentally; some days I wanted to drown my sorrows in a bottle of whiskey; some days I just wanted to shrivel up in a ball and die – despite everything that I'd learned about the ego-mind. Physical symptoms feel pretty damn real when you're sick. Working towards wellness isn't the same as being better. Enlightenment doesn't happen in a blinding flash. It's a process, too. I'm human after all. Fortunately, I had Henry Jones at my side. He nursed me when I needed care, lifted my spirits when I was low, and yes, kicked my arse when I needed a good arse-kicking, too.

Overall, however, when I gauged my thoughts, feelings and actions, I knew that I was better for it. Looking back at the man who had first had a conversation with Henry Jones on a park bench not that long before, I was in a different league. He'd given me a crash course in human health and healing. The knowledge and wisdom I'd accumulated in a matter of weeks had forever changed my outlook on disease, recovery, wellness and life in general. We'd covered physical and mental healing in depth. Only spiritual and emotional healing remained. Did that mean I was half-way through my healing journey? Of course not! Putting your finger on a map at the midway mark between your departure point and final destination doesn't mean you're halfway there. I still had a long way to go – several thousand miles, as it turned out.

The day I started my spiritual healing process, Henry Jones walked into the kitchen while I was preparing breakfast and casually asked: "Got a passport?"

I froze. "Why?"

"I've just arranged for us to meet a special friend of mine in India."

"India?" I exclaimed.

"Yes, I can't wait for you to meet him."

"Who?"

"My swami."

"Swami? Sounds like a Greek fast food," I remarked.

"Not shwarma, silly. Swami!"

"What's a swami?"

"An Indian holy man."

I raised a questioning eyebrow.

"The word 'swami' means master. It means striving for the mastery over one's conditioned mind; over one's mental patterns and habits; and over one's fickle personality – all of which refer to striving for mastery over one's ego-mind. You'll learn a lot from him, and you'll like him, too."

"Is that his full-time job?"

"I suppose you can say that. But he doesn't do it for money. He put aside worldly interests long ago. He pursues a life of truth-seeking, enlightenment and serving others. As a swami, this renunciation makes him akin to a monk, except that he doesn't serve an organization or institution. Self-discipline is the key to his lifestyle."

That went straight over my head. "What religion does he practice?"

"He doesn't. Although most swamis are linked via their teacher and guru to ancient India and the ancient Vedic teachings, they wouldn't claim allegiance to any particular group or religion because they believe beyond all of these religions that there's one indivisible reality, truth or God who is recognized by various names in different cultures. And here lies a very important point: My friend has dedicated his life, one could say, to the Absolute Truth, beyond the different forms of religions."

The concept of swamis was buried deep in the recesses of my mind. I knew why, too. "Hold on a second. I think I've seen them on television. Aren't those the guys who wear orange bandages wrapped around their bodies?"

He laughed. "Yes, it's customary for swamis to wear orange/saffron clothes. Some people say the orange clothes are a reminder of the fire of knowledge that burns away wrong knowledge; and the fire of hardship that burns away desire and attachment to worldly goods."

"So, they're like spiritual bums? I asked callously.

Henry Jones took offence. "Definitely not! Bums offer little value to society. They do nothing but take, lie, cheat and steal. Swamis, on the other hand, live with total integrity, for the good of all. Swamis strive to master their own conditioning and go beyond the differences of the phenomenal world, while striving to become instruments and servants of the Divine. Their goal is ultimately to merge with the Highest, the Absolute, the Great Spirit, or whatever name you call God. I'd hardly call someone who practises that sort of spiritual lifestyle a bum, would you?"

"No," I mumbled apologetically. Henry Jones was mad as a snake, I wanted to make peace fast. "So, how do swamis serve other people?"

Henry Jones uncoiled. "In practical terms, swamis ask questions nobody else asks. They teach us to look beyond the apparent, and they encourage self-inquiry and reflection. They support those who endeavour to look for a higher purpose in life; they build bridges between people, dogmas and religions; and rekindle respect and love. They don't distinguish between East and West; one race from another; or one religion from another. They are citizens of the Earth."

I suddenly felt ashamed of my ignorance and prejudice. It had been wrong of me to cast aspersions based on the few snippets I'd seen on TV. "I'm sorry for my outburst," I muttered.

"That's okay, my friend. I know you meant no harm. It's normal for the ego-mind to be judgmental, skeptical, distrustful and suspicious. That is why I want you to meet my friend. He has a wonderful way of teaching people to be more conscious of their true-selves. This, by the way, is the primary objective of spiritual healing: To raise your level of self-awareness, so that you feel more in tune with your true-self, and to make your internal and external world more connected."

"And he's going to teach me all of this in India?"

"Yes, we have one session with him."

"Just one?"

"That's more than enough time together. I've asked him to show you how to heal your body through meditation. He knows powerful meditation techniques to clear, clean and unblock your body's energy centers. If this doesn't raise your self-awareness, nothing will. I promise you, meeting Swami G will be a real spirituality booster!"

"Swami G?" I exclaimed.

"Swami Gurudevananda Satyarthi, but he permits foreigners to call him Swami G."

I suddenly recalled Henry Jones telling me I'd meet Swami G. That seemed like ages ago.

"I've never been to India."

"Well, start packing your bags. With a bit of luck, we'll be there in a week."

I felt a flit of excitement. This was totally unexpected, even from Henry Jones. I liked traveling abroad. It brought out a sense of adventure in me. All of a sudden, my healing journey had taken a new direction. I was off to India to learn about spiritual healing from Swami G. How exciting!

The days that followed were filled with great anticipation and agitation. We had to organize emergency visas, which was a nail-biting exercise. They very nearly didn't come through in time for our flight. I'm not sure what strings were pulled, but our travel agent literally handed the paperwork to us at the airport. Sure enough, despite the anxiety, Henry Jones and I found ourselves aboard a fight to Delhi in less than a week.

I clutched the armrest of my seat during take-off. "India, here we come," I yelled to Henry Jones above the roar of the engines.

"There's no going back now," he replied, rubbing my leg affectionately. "Well done. I'm proud of you."

"For what?"

"For the manner in which you've embraced your healing journey. You've really thrown yourself into it."

"I'm totally committed to healing my body," I told him.

"I can see that," he replied, reaching for the inflight magazine. He took one look at the glamorous cover and put it right back. "The mental and physical healing processes are behind us; only spiritual and emotional healing lie ahead. If you keep this up, you'll be well again before you know it. It's now time to awaken your spirit. You'll be thrilled to know that this process is going to make you feel even better."

"How come?"

"Because your spirit has tremendous healing power. Seriously! When you connect with your spirit, you connect with an internal force that has an astonishing ability to heal your body."

"So, what do you think Swami G is going to teach me about spiritual healing?"

"He'll teach you how to align yourself with the creative energy of the universe, and to become a co-creator of your future reality. Swami G will teach you how to tap into the healing energy within you."

"Through meditation?"

"Uh-huh, meditation is the key. Swami G will show you how to use meditation to remove the blockages that have been holding you back. You'll be astounded at how easily you'll change your life for the better when you clear out destructive behavioral patterns. If you don't do this, you'll stay locked in an endless cycle of despair."

"I don't want that!" I gulped.

"Let me warn you in advance, India is a strange place, filled with many strange things. Everything you see, smell, taste, hear and touch will be foreign to you. Unless you keep an open mind and go with the flow, the vastness of it could overwhelm you. I assure you, your ego-mind will try to analyze, rationalize, evaluate and judge your actions and experience during the week ahead of us. Especially the process Swami G will teach you!"

"Is spiritual healing really such a biggie?"

"Yes, it is! It's amazing and extremely powerful, but it's not that easy to comprehend. You see, physical healing can be authenticated through technology and science, while mental healing is mostly common sense. Spiritual and emotional healing, however, require faith."

"Didn't you once tell me faith is manufactured through repetition?"

"Yes, exactly! That's why the information he shares with you will be familiar to you. You'll probably recognize most of the content because we've already discussed it. The reason I previously gave you the basics of spiritual healing is so you can listen without prejudice."

Henry Jones ripped open the plastic bag containing a blanket and wrapped it around his body. I did the same. He placed a sleeping mask on his forehead. I knew I had to say something quickly, or he would try to sleep. I wasn't ready for bed yet – I was too excited.

"I must admit that I'm a bit nervous about all of this spiritual healing stuff," I said.

Henry Jones chuckled. "Don't worry, my friend. Spiritual healing has nothing to do with ideologies, organizations or institutions. I may ask you to visit a few ancient temples with me in the days before our appointment, but I won't ask you to worship in them, or make you go to church, mosque or shul on your healing journey. Like I told you in the cabin, your spirit has nothing to do with any man-made religion, and it certainly can't be boxed into a dogma of any kind. The only place you're going to search for your spirit is within you."

I fiddled with the knobs above my head for a while.

"What is spirit?"

He stroked his chin thoughtfully. "Spirit, by its very nature, is difficult to define. Like I told you when we sat together on the bench in the hospital courtyard, I like to describe it as the life force that connects and binds your mind and body together. Does that make sense?"

"Kinda."

"Spirit lies deep within you. It's the essence of your true-self, and as such, it's pure and eternal. It's fully present in each and every one of us, all the time. No matter what we do, spirit doesn't leave us until we die. Even then, it's actually the mind and body that die, and spirit lives on. But let's not get into that now. We can leave that discussion for another time."

I suddenly recalled something Henry Jones told me in the cabin. "*We are spiritual beings having a human experience, not human beings having a spiritual experience.*" The truth was, I hadn't given my soul much consideration before. My soul had been asleep. I secretly hoped Swami G would give me a proper wake-up call. Henry Jones had been gently nudging me out of spiritual slumber, but I felt I needed a cold bucket of holy water to be thrown in my face.

"To deny your spirit is to deny the very essence of life. If you don't know what I'm talking about, then I strongly suggest that you sit on top of a mountain, or watch the Sun set, or walk on a beach, or camp out in the woods. Experiences like these will stir your soul from slumber. In those moments, you'll be reminded of the Great Spirit in everything – including yourself!"

"I do remember you telling me that too many people make the mistake of thinking that to become spiritual means becoming religious. You said, *'Awakening your spirituality means becoming conscious of yourself'*."

"Precisely! This is the great universal journey of the soul," he replied.

The journey to the soul starts with self-awareness

"But where does the journey start?"

"Self-awareness. The first step on the path of spirituality is self-awareness," he told me. "Your number one goal in life should be to strive towards becoming conscious of yourself. When you become conscious of what you think, say and do, you'll realize that you have the power of choice. Making the right choices is the key to successful living. This is your greatest responsibility. Each choice you make is a creative act of spiritual power for which you're accountable. Try as you may, you can't escape consequence. In spiritual terms, it's called karma."

"You mean: You reap what you sow. That sort of thing?"

"Exactly! What goes around comes around. I bet that rings a bell, right?"

"It sure does."

"I thought so. Karma is simply the spiritual version of the universal Law of Cause and Effect. When you begin to understand and accept this fact, you'll realize the true power of choice. I know Swami G is going to have this conversation with you, too."

"I don't know if this uplifts me or terrifies me," I confessed.

He smiled.

I tried to explain my feelings: "Realizing you have the power of choice goes hand-in-hand with realizing you're also responsible for how you use it. I'm not accustomed to this mental alertness. I barge my way through life like a bull in a china shop."

"You already know the difference between right and wrong. Agreed?"

"Hmmm, you're referring to my conscience again, aren't you?"

"Yes, but what drives your conscience?"

"What do you mean?"

"I mean, what invisible force guides your sense of right and wrong?"

"I give up."

"It's the spirit within you. At the core of your being, you're aware of your spiritual qualities. They're your inner-guide. Believe it or not, they govern the happiness of your life and the healthiness of your body. You see, your 'soul' purpose in life should be to achieve spiritual fulfilment, and you can only do this by applying spiritual qualities to your life."

"Such as?"

"Love; beauty; harmony; justice; wholeness; perfection; peace; power and service. Just hearing those words lifts your spirit, doesn't it?"

"I guess so."

"What about: Honour; integrity; dignity; trust; loyalty; patience; understanding; forgiveness; compassion and truthfulness?"

"Yeah, they make me feel good, too." I said, recalling our time together in the cabin.

"When you think and act with those qualities in mind, you're being a spiritual person. It's that simple! When you do that, you naturally follow your inner guidance. Your spirit leads you. That is the only way to discover your life purpose. Your spirit always steers you towards your life purpose, just as a compass always points north."

"Life purpose? What's that about?"

Find your life purpose

"In spiritual terms, your life purpose is also called your dharma. That is the reason you were born. It's the path you're meant to follow; the life you're meant to live."

"You mean your destiny, don't you?"

"No, not quite. Your destiny refers to your end destination, whilst your dharma refers to your spiritual journey."

I processed my thoughts. I needed more answers.

"So, how do we know if we're following our dharma?"

Henry Jones adjusted his position. "When you follow your dharma, the universe seems to orchestrate itself around you. Everything happens synchronistically and purposefully, because you're in harmony with yourself and the universe. This naturally gives you peace of mind about your future and allows you to experience true pleasure. Plus, all the signs will be there."

"What signs?"

"Well, for one thing, your body won't be sick. Sickness is caused by your ego-mind. Your spirit only manifests through your true-self, and it will never make you sick." He dimmed the cabin light.

"Never?"

"Never! Healthy mind, healthy body. That's how it works!"

I folded my arms in a huff. "There's no way I'm on my dharmic path. I'm sick, I haven't been practising spiritual qualities daily, and there's no way on Earth that my life purpose is to work myself to death for a boss I despise," I grumbled.

"So, why do you do it?"

"I need to support my family, and my boss demands I work long hours. This leaves me with very little time for much else," I replied through clenched teeth.

"Sounds to me like you're blaming others for your choices," he replied. "You're 100% responsible for the choices you make. Accept that! If you're not on your dharmic path, it's because you've allowed yourself to be led astray by your ego-mind." He closed his eyes and pretended to sleep.

That upset me. "That's unfair," I retorted. "I've worked really hard to build my career and establish myself so that I can provide for my family. What's wrong with that?"

"You tell me," he replied.

That upset me even more. I knew he was scratching at the surface of a hidden truth, but I couldn't put my finger on it.

Listen to the signs

"No, you tell me," I demanded.

"What do the signs say about your life?"

That was a sucker punch. It hit me square on the jaw, and my resistance toppled like a felled tree.

"Oh God, I'm a basket case, aren't I?" I groaned.

Henry Jones took out the inflight magazine again and began flipping through it, too fast to read. He spoke in a monotone: "Don't beat yourself up. You're not alone. In this modern age, most people neglect their spiritual aspect. They mistakenly think their hope of happiness in the future is linked to their success in the physical world. Consequently, they spend all of their time pursuing personal ambition and acquiring possessions. They fail to realize that their desires and expectations of the material world are manufactured by their ego-mind. This preoccupation is their ego-mind's way of keeping control of their lives. So, to cope with the complexities of their reality, people then create layers of personality. These layers are like masks that each individual learns to wear for specific occasions. There are masks for work; masks for family; masks for friends; masks for church, etc. Each mask is merely a projection of personality. More importantly, none of them are the real person. Don't forget: Your personality is a construct of your ego-mind. Over time, you've constructed an image of yourself in your mind. This is what you project to others in the hope that you'll convince them it's who you really are. This is the great game of the mind. So then, let me ask you directly: Is the real you buried beneath the person you've become? If so, let me remind you one more time: Your mind is meant to be the servant of your spirit."

I grew frustrated. "Why doesn't my spirit take bloody charge then?"

"Your spirit has no need to assert its superiority. It's eternal and in no rush. When you choose to let your ego-mind run your life, your spirit merely waits patiently for you to learn the life-lessons you need to learn. But, be warned: Any imbalance between your mind and spirit will cause you suffering or pain. If the imbalance is great, then suffering can be severe. Sickness and pain are sure to follow. Illness is merely the depletion of your internal power, or spirit. It's a sign that your ego-mind is ruling the roost. When something goes wrong with your body, your spirit is telling you it's time to find your way back home. The spirit is never wrong. You will return to spirit. It can be in this lifetime, or in the hereafter. The choice is yours."

"I don't want to die," I whispered in a panicked voice.

"We must all pass on. But, if you want to restore your body to perfect health, then you must accept there is an imbalance in your life. This acceptance is where healing begins. Over the past few weeks I've shown you how to rejuvenate your body and open your mind. Now we need to awaken your spirit to complete the next stage of your healing journey."

"But what does it mean to awaken your spirit?"

Awakening your spirit

"Spirit is the eternal flame that burns inside of you. It's the source of light on your dharmic path. As you reconnect with your spirit, your inner flame grows stronger, and you begin to see the world more clearly, through the eyes of your true-self. I should warn you, as you bring yourself back into a balanced state, your outlook on life may change. What matters to you most today may be very different tomorrow. You see, your ego-mind's constant 'head trip' creates frenetic energy that surrounds you like a murky cloud. This prevents you from seeing your daily life experiences with the clarity of spiritual perception. Your ego-mind makes you afraid, worried, critical, judgmental, opinionated and self-righteous. It never allows you to see the full picture, so you live a half-life. It's only when you let go of this narrow point of view that you can truly embrace the expansiveness of your consciousness and experience the fullness, abundance, and joy of life."

I panicked. "I'm afraid to let go of what I've got. It's all I know." I replied, close to tears. "Please, tell me how I'm supposed to do this?"

"Be true to yourself," he replied. "Spirituality is measured by genuineness."

"But, there'll be consequences to any actions I take," I protested.

He shrugged. "So what? Live your truth and let the cards fall where they may."

"That's easy for you to say," I snapped back. "When our time together comes to an end, I've got to go back to the real world."

"Really?"

"Yes, really! My work is stressful; my boss is uncompromising; my position is replaceable; my overheads are high; my debt is real; my body is sick; and my marriage is on the rocks. In fact, my life sucks!"

"How does this make you feel?"

"Pretty shitty, actually!"

Make feel-good choices

"Then it's wrong for you," he replied offhandedly. "Spirit wants you to move towards the things in life that make you feel good."

"But I can't just put an end to the things in life that make me feel bad!" I cried.

"Sure, you can. Don't be afraid to do what is best for you, my friend. Stand up for what you really want in life. It's your birthright to express your thoughts and feelings through action. Make choices that make you feel good. Don't do things that make you feel bad. Be an individual – that is the roadmap to your true-self."

I sat back in a huff. "Let's change the subject," I fumed.

"Why?"

"The direction of this conversation is making me feel uncomfortable. I don't want to talk about making changes to my life just because I feel bad." I heard how ridiculous I sounded as the words left my mouth.

"You should talk more about what you want from life, and less about what you don't want. Listen to yourself. Are you speaking with your true voice? Is what you're saying what you want most for your life, or are you just ranting from your ego-mind?"

We create our own realities

That knocked me for six! I became aware of my true voice. I finally understood that every time we speak, we're either expressing our ego-minds or our true-selves. We're responsible for creating our reality through our words. We talk ourselves into it. That profound realization hardly had time to sink in before Henry Jones jumped on to his next point.

"Finding your true voice is spiritually significant because it requires self-awareness, which is an attribute of your true-self. So, the instant you practise self-awareness, you connect with your true-self and, as a result, harmony and balance are restored to your life. Remember, you must bring physical, mental, emotional and spiritual balance back into your life in order to heal your body. To be spiritually balanced, you must speak your truth. You'll never be spiritually balanced or fulfilled if you live a lie. How can you ever expect to follow your dharma if you don't speak up about what you do and don't want for your life? What do you think is going to happen? Do you expect mystical forces to carry you there without any instruction from you? Sorry, but it doesn't work like that. What you say is what you get."

I mulled this over for a minute or two before responding. "You have a good point. If I don't make myself happy and healthy, who will?"

Our minds affect our health

"Precisely! Now, let me tell you something else: If you don't lead the life you want, you'll make yourself sick. The purpose of life is to enjoy it! Our most basic animal instinct is to move towards what gives us pleasure and away from what gives us pain. When you consciously and deliberately move towards what causes you pain every day, something is wrong with you. If you live a life you don't want, you have a sick mind. A sick mind means a sick body! You'd be shocked to know how many people don't realize that physical conditions are related to mental, emotional and spiritual conditions. How many times must I tell you? Your state of health is a manifestation of your emotional, mental and spiritual state of mind. In other words, any physical disturbance in your body is the result of a mental, emotional or spiritual disturbance. Over the past several years, scientific breakthroughs in the field of psycho-neuro-immunology, or PNI, have proven the effect that 'mind states' have upon the body's immune system. Clinical studies have shown unequivocal impairment of immunity and other body functions in times of stress. Mounting evidence also reveals significant correlations between the state of a person's mind, the development of 'disease states', and the maintenance of health. Of late, exciting advances have been made in the understanding of this phenomenon."

"Hold on a minute, I've got to write this down," I said.

Henry Jones reached up, switched on the overhead light above my head and adjusted the knob so it shone on my page.

"As you already know, quantum physicists acknowledge the existence of the electromagnetic field around the human body. But what you may not know is that this energy field contains and reflects each person's thought energy. It stores information about their internal and external experiences and is charged with their positive and negative emotions. More than this, these forces influence the physical condition of the body. So, when you get sick, you can find the cause of your problem in your mental, emotional or spiritual 'mind state'. We remove it by dealing with the real issue. I'm going to recite an extract from one of my favorite books. I want you to close your eyes and open your ears. It could change your life forever. In his book *Bridges*, Aart Jurriaanse puts it like this: "In one most important aspect medical science has so far unconsciously been badly handicapped. It has remained unaware of the etheric body, which forms the intangible framework on which the physical body is constructed, and which therefore plays an important role in the maintenance of its health. No wonder that physicians, notwithstanding their extensive knowledge of the physical aspects, have in the past so often been sorely puzzled by inexplicable features of disease, and by the unaccountable reactions their patients who for no explainable reasons might show either improvement or deterioration. Little did they realize that the real underlying cause for many complaints was to be found in the inharmonious condition of the etheric body. With the existence of the etheric body now becoming an accepted fact, medicine is standing on the verge of a totally new approach to disease and treatment. As yet there are, however, only a few who fully recognize the full extent of the implications of this so-called 'electromagnetic field', and that it constitutes the mainstay of all physical existence, not only surrounding but also minutely interpenetrating and supporting the tangible body.""

His recital was flawless. It almost took my breath away. I'd never heard anything like it. I wondered: Could it be true? Was this really how disease manifests in the body? Could this lead me to the cause of my problem?

As you feel, so you become

"So, let me get this straight: Our physical bodies have an electromagnetic field surrounding them, and this field somehow records whatever we think, feel and experience, and whenever we put out negative thoughts, emotions and actions, it causes a disturbance in this field, this etheric body, and we become sick."

"Bingo! I want you to take a moment to think of a situation in your life that made you very, very sad. As this memory is processed through your biological system, you may notice a physiological response. Your whole body feels sad, right? That is because when you experience emotions, your body creates chemicals called neuropeptides."

"Neuropeptides! I've never heard of them, either."

"Oh, they exist alright. One might say neuropeptides are simply thoughts converted into matter."

"What do they do?"

"They reside in your body and interact with your body cells and tissues. Through this process, your emotions become you at a molecular level."

"So, our emotions are actually encoded into our bodies?"

"Precisely, yes. This energy pulsates into your electromagnetic field. Believe it or not, you're constantly in communication with everything around you in this system."

"How?"

"That's another good question. I love your inquisitive mind. Your energy field connects your internal universe to your external universe through energy centers called chakra points."

Chakras

Huh?" I exclaimed. I couldn't hide my skepticism.

"I see that look in your eye," he said. "I must admit, I was skeptical at first, too, but I changed my tune when I found out that millions of people around the world know about chakra points and work with them daily to improve their health and quality of life. This universal knowledge will irrevocably change your outlook on health and healing. Chakra points are swirling, cone-shaped vortices of energy that exist in your energy field. Without them, you wouldn't, and couldn't, exist!"

"No kidding?" An air hostess pushed past us with a trolley. I rejected her offer of a damp towel. Henry Jones graciously accepted, although he didn't use it.

"I'm serious," he replied, making strange circular motions with his hands, near his tummy and head. "They filter energy throughout your system and supply you with the vitality you need to sustain life. Their functions are to absorb, transform and transmit energy into your central nervous system, your endocrine glands and your bloodstream, to nourish your body."

"Where are they?" I asked patting my body like a man searching for his wallet.

"Imagine a vertical flow of energy pulsating up and down your spinal cord. On this line, you have seven major chakra points. They start at the base of your spine and end at your crown. These seven power centers regulate the flow of your life energy. You'll learn more about this from Swami G, so I don't want to reveal too much now!"

"No, don't stop here! I'm curious to know more."

"Well, alright then, if you insist." Henry Jones said, lifting his chair into an upright position. I immediately did the same.

"The literal translation from the ancient Sanskrit means 'wheels of light', because when they're healthy, each of your chakra points is an open, moving, oscillating, vibrating and shimmering vortex of energy that spins in the front and back of your body."

"I can't see them," I remarked, studying my body.

"Just because you can't see them with the naked eye doesn't mean they're not there. The human aura is well-documented, thanks to modern-day inventions. You may, however, be interested to know that many people have trained their eyes to see chakra points, and they use this remarkable skill to determine whether a person's life energy is free-flowing or blocked. Pay attention now. It's your thoughts, attitudes and emotions that determine whether your chakra points are open or blocked. Every thought and feeling passes through one or more of your chakras. That is how your internal universe communicates with your external universe. More importantly, each of your seven chakra points has its own specific function in maintaining the health of your physical body, as well as your emotional, mental and spiritual life. Each chakra point relates to specific organs in your body, and processes specific aspects of your life."

I scratched my head. I could tell this information was hugely significant, but I struggled to fully comprehend what I was hearing.

"Why is this so important?" I spluttered.

"It's important to know how the chakra system works because when you get sick, or feel pain, you can identify the likely cause of your condition by associating the problem area to the corresponding chakra point. That's extremely powerful, don't you think?"

I grappled with this game-changing concept. This was the first time we'd discussed how to identify the cause of disease. Up until then, we'd attributed disease to poor diet, wrong living habits and emotional blockages. Now, it seemed Henry Jones was revealing a way to pinpoint the actual cause of physical disturbances in the body. If I'd drawn the right conclusion, this was big!

"I need to know how the chakra system works," I commanded hastily.

Your external situation reflects your internal situation

"Each chakra point is like a projector lamp, and your reality is the screen. In other words, your external situation reflects your internal situation. When your internal universe gets stuck in destructive thought patterns or emotions, your chakra points become blocked and spin sluggishly, making certain aspects of your life or physical body feel the same way, or worse. It's also possible to overwork a specific chakra point by overworking a specific pattern of thought or emotion. As a result, your chakra points spin too fast and become overactive. This causes an imbalance on various levels. When your chakra points are unbalanced or malfunction, you feel disorientated, uncomfortable and lethargic, or worse. My message is this: Dysfunctional chakra points can result in sickness, disease and pain. If you wish to enjoy optimum health, you should strive to achieve a well-balanced chakra system. When your chakra points work at optimal levels, you'll feel fit, healthy and harmonious in every aspect of your life. These chakra points are then referred to as 'balanced' and 'open'. Got it?"

"I think so."

"I can't wait for you to hear exactly what each chakra point does for your body, but I'm afraid you'll have to wait until you meet Swami G. I'll leave that privilege to him."

"Oh no, you can't leave me hanging like this!" I cried.

He slid his seat back into the recline position and pulled his sleeping mask over his eyes.

"You're seriously going to go to sleep now? You're going to leave me sitting on the edge of my seat? That's so cruel!"

He chuckled. "I promised you an adventure, didn't I?" With that, he rolled his head to the side and slipped into silence.

I wanted to go and find Swami G right there and then, but, I was sitting at 36 000 ft in the air. Oh well, I thought. At least I'm headed in the right direction.

CHAPTER 19

TEA WITH SWAMI G

We arrived in Delhi the next morning. After disembarking and collecting our luggage, we caught a ride into the city. It wasn't like arriving in London, New York, or Switzerland, or any other place I'd visited. India is something else entirely.

"You're either going to love India or hate it," Henry Jones said, looking fondly out the window of our open-air cab. No, it wasn't a convertible. It was a mobile bucket on wheels with storage facilities for baggage on the roof, back and sides.

"Love it or hate it, you say," I repeated under my breath.

"That seems to be the norm. Personally, I love it," he replied with a broad grin. "Indian society represents one of the most varied and complex ancient civilizations in the world. Its astounding diversity of religions, languages, and cultures is unique and unparalleled." His voice trailed off, as if he were in a trance.

There was a lot to take in. Delhi writhed like an angry snake. Henry Jones sighed deeply and finished his thoughts. "In my opinion, 5 000 years of history have nourished the growth of a great civilization. There are six major religions: Hinduism, Islam, Sikhism, Christianity, Buddhism, and Zoroastrianism; two major language families: Aryan and Dravidian; 18 official languages and innumerable dialects and tribal languages; three racial strains: Aryan, Dravidian, and Proto-Australoid; and over 4 000 castes, all hierarchically ranked, endogamous, and occupational. It's truly amazing!"

He may as well have been speaking Greek to me. All I knew for sure was that the road we were traveling was insanely busy and riddled with potholes. I'd never seen anything like it. Cars, scooters, animals, bicycles and pedestrians all seemed to have right of way. Hooters blasted, engines roared, people yelled and machines moaned. It was a strange, mystical, organized chaos. I wound down the only working window, but rolled it back up as quickly as possible. My nose couldn't handle the smell. The city smelled like dirty socks rolled in sewage.

"Jeez, I've never seen so many people," I remarked, but Henry Jones was lost in thought. I nudged him and pointed out the window. "I said that I've never seen so many people," I shouted above the noise.

"Ah yes! There are a billion plus people living in India – one sixth of the world's population," he yelled back.

"It looks like most of them stay in Delhi," I replied, half-joking.

Just then, the cab driver swerved violently to one side, avoiding another cab by inches. My head cracked against the window frame. He leaned out of the window and started shouting at the cab driver who had cut in front of us. No, he wasn't blasting him for nearly pushing us off the road – they appeared to know each other. They exchanged the universal thumbs-up sign at breakneck speed and then veered apart. That's when I noticed an enormous cow in the middle of the road in front of us. It just stood there, like a life-sized statue mounted on a roundabout. I assumed our driver hadn't seen it, and impulsively dived for the steering wheel to save our lives. The cab driver yanked on the wheel at the last second, and we missed the beast by a hair. Was the driver grateful to me? No, I don't think so. He rattled off a string of heated sentences in a language I didn't understand.

"This is crazy," I yelled.

"What?" Henry Jones shouted back.

"Never mind." I waved off any attempt to communicate and sat back in my seat, resolving to stare out of the window instead. I soon lost myself in the swirling masses of people and began to feel more insignificant than I'd ever felt before. Delhi hungrily consumed my identity. I felt as important and unique as a drop of water in the Ganges. I could tell that Henry Jones was thrilled to be back in India. He couldn't stop smiling, and his excitement was infectious: The diversity; colors; classes; architecture and people all boggled my mind.

I was amazed at how quickly I got used to the commotion. Within an hour or two, the hullabaloo seemed normal. How we found our hotel in the underbelly of the city, I'll never know. It was tucked away among millions of little buildings heaped together in an interconnected, urbanized mass that was Delhi. It was a quaint establishment: Very rudimentary, but functional. The staff members were extremely helpful. I'm still not sure if they were genuinely the best hosts in the world, or if their warmth and servitude was a well-mastered ploy to get their hands deeper into our pockets. I didn't mind either way.

After booking in and dropping our bags in our room, we went in search of food. We saw lots of strange things to eat, but nothing that grabbed our fancy. Of course, there were the usual big brand fast food joints, but we wouldn't touch any of those. Eventually, with help from an entourage of youth, we found a place that served healthy food. It looked less dodgy than the rest. I'm sure there's an opulent, lavish, rich side to Delhi, but we didn't see it. Henry Jones insisted we took the budget option – not because we were penny-conscious, but to experience how most Indians lived. We each paid our own way, but we both got more than we paid for. A small neon sign blinked on and off above the entrance, enticing us to indulge in the buffet of spicy delicacies that festooned the serving table.

Swami G could only meet with us towards the end of the week. Apparently, he had ceremonies to attend, so we had time to kill. Henry Jones took it upon himself to drag me to some of the popular tourist spots and to some of his favorite locations, which only locals and regular visitors would have known about. I enjoyed those best of all. They weren't the most striking or exceptional places, but they did bring out a great joy in Henry Jones. It was lovely to see his vitality and enthusiasm for life. I especially admired the way he engaged with everyone we met as though they were kindred spirits. He invited them to join us whenever possible. We were hardly ever alone. It was the perfect antidote to the intensity of my healing journey and our great assignment together. Being in India was mind-expanding and refreshing.

The last three days of our trip, preceding our appointment with Swami G, were spent at his ashram. It was an experience I'll never forget. I'd never been to an ashram before, so I didn't have any idea what to expect. Henry Jones said it was better that way.

After taking another flight and negotiating a price with a cab driver, we once again found ourselves in the back of a taxi van, rumbling up a mountain road lined with blooming flowers and banana trees. After 20 minutes or so, we turned down a dirt driveway, and suddenly we were at the front gate to the ashram. It was all so surreal.

The ashram we visited is set in acres of tropical splendor in the foothills of the Western Ghats. The natural beauty of the forested surroundings, and the cool green coconut tree groves and colorful flower-filled views offer an ideal atmosphere for the practice of yoga and meditation. The ashram program covered classical yoga techniques, taught in a warm and friendly environment by highly-qualified teachers. Their objective was to instil in guests a deep awareness of the spiritual essence of life – or at least, that's what the brochure said.

We met many spiritual travellers from around the world. Several of them had come to the ashram in search of physical healing. Yes, they were sick, too. I avoided them, although I'm not sure why. The ashram offers medical consultations with the resident doctor, Ayurveda oil massage, and other treatments to guests. I didn't use any of those services either. I was there in search of wellness, and I didn't feel like digging up my sickness and disease. Instead, I did a lot of thinking, reading, listening, sleeping and some meditation. We hiked in the mountains, washed our own clothes, cleaned our room, prepared our meals, and ate scrumptious home-cooked Indian food.

Henry Jones and I shared a non-airconditioned twin room with a private bathroom that had cold water only. The furnishings were sparse. We were given a mattress to sleep on, two bed sheets, a pillow, a pillowcase, and a mosquito net. That was it!

We wore loose, comfortable clothing we had bought at a market in Delhi. Henry Jones said we would need them for asana yoga. I'd never taken yoga classes before, but I loved them. I never thought stretching my body would feel so good. I'm proud to say, I became an enthusiast. I made sure I was the first person to arrive for class so that I could get a mat closest to the teacher. One time, we arrived late for class after a long hike and were told politely that latecomers weren't allowed to enter the class. Punctuality is important in an ashram. I made sure that never happened again.

On the morning we met Swami G, I woke up with butterflies in my stomach. I was both excited and anxious. I shared breakfast with a guest, who described Swami G as one of the greatest saints of modern times. He was apparently the spiritual strength behind several ashrams; he trained many exceptional disciples in yoga and Vedanta; and he synthesized the ancient wisdom of yoga into basic principles that could be easily incorporated into a more modern lifestyle, providing the foundation for healthy living. In the ashram, he was like a celebrity on a film set, or the CEO on rounds in a large corporation. Everybody knew who he was, and there was a constant buzz about him. It's not that people put him on a pedestal, but they did revere him. Not every ashram visitor got to meet him. When I told the other guests that we had an appointment with Swami G, they all wanted to know how we had organized it. What had I done? What was my secret? Why had he agreed to see us? I didn't know the answers myself. All I knew was that Henry Jones had organized for me to meet his friend in India. I didn't even know how well they knew each other. When I asked Henry Jones how he had met Swami G, he'd simply replied: "It's a long story."

Minutes before we were due to meet Swami G, Henry Jones stopped me in the hallway. He took me by the arms and said in his most tender voice: "Before we go in to meet my friend, I'd like to ask you a question."

"Sure, anything. What is it?"

"If you plant a seed, will it grow?"

I thought about it for a split second. "Probably not."

"How come?"

"It needs water and sunlight to germinate. Right?"

"Exactly!" he replied, patting and squeezing my arms like a proud father. I raised my eyebrows. "What's your point?"

He inhaled deeply. "Since we first met, I've been planting many seeds inside your head. I believe they have fallen into fertile soil. In the next few hours, Swami G will sprinkle them with water and sunlight, and you'll be given the opportunity to grow. Most of what you'll hear, you've heard before, but he'll undoubtedly give you this information from a spiritual perspective. I presented these concepts to you from an intellectual perspective, but today will be a practical session. Listen without prejudice. Don't be afraid to try new things. Learning new things makes us grow."

I nodded. "I'll keep it in mind, and in my heart," I assured him.

With that said, we were ushered into a large, empty meditation room. In its center, a small table with a teapot and three cups was neatly placed beside three mats and some pillows. At first, I didn't see the old man in the corner, standing on his head. I nearly jumped out of my skin when I realized he was there.

"I'm sorry I startled you," he said, still on his head. "Please take a seat on the mats. I was just about to have some tea. Would you care to join me?" With that, he rolled over on to his feet and emerged upright with a smile on his face.

And that's how I met Swami G. It certainly wasn't the ceremonious introduction I'd imagined. I stood there like a lump of wet cement while he embraced Henry Jones. I could tell they shared a deep bond.

"And who is this Young One?" he asked in a velvet tone. Serenity, joy and peace hung like musical notes on his words. He was fluent in the Queen's English – probably because of India's colonial past. Of course, though, his accent was strong. Swami G had a profoundly peaceful presence. It oozed from him. His serenity flowed into his environment, saturating all who shared his space. I guess a lifetime of yoga, meditation, and an immaculate diet will give that to you. I couldn't detect an ounce of spiritual arrogance about him. He had a friendly disposition and I liked him immediately.

"This is my friend," Henry Jones announced with a huge grin on his face. "The one I've been telling you about."

I shuffled forward, like a man with his feet tied together.

He greeted me warmly. "Come, sit down. Let us share some tea together. We make fantastic tea in India. Many people tell me our tea is the best in the world. Please allow me to pour you a cuppa."

"Okay," I mumbled. "Thank you."

"You're most welcome. I trust our humble accommodation and facilities have met your needs?"

"Uh yeah, they're fine. Better than fine actually. They're fantastic!"

"Fantastic," he cried, taking a seat on the mat. His legs folded like a pretzel. "That is my favorite word in the English language. It has an explosive quality, don't you think? Whenever I hear it, say it, or see it, I feel fireworks in my belly. Fantastic, fantastic! It's just so, well, fantastic!"

I cracked a smile. He pronounced it 'fun-taas-tick'. His face beamed with enthusiasm and joy. Much like Henry Jones! The pair were clearly kindred spirits. They looked like brothers: One Indian and one Caucasian.

"We're very grateful to be here," Henry Jones said, taking a seat beside his friend.

"At my ripe, old age, I'm grateful to be here, too," he joked. "Come, Young One, sit beside me on this mat, or pull up a pillow if you think it'll make you more comfortable."

I didn't take a pillow. I probably should've, but I didn't. I guess I wanted to be like Swami G and Henry Jones. They sat on mats, so I did, too, but there was no way my ankles could rest on my upper thighs. That was where I drew the line.

"Tea?"

"Please, thank you," I spluttered.

He zapped me with swami speak. "It's my great pleasure to serve you. Ultimately, we walk this path of spirituality alone, but with love, support and commune with other spiritually-minded souls, our veiled hidden potentials and unconscious inhibiting weaknesses can be seen, so that true inner growth can be actualized."

I felt cross-eyed and bit my tongue; afraid that if I spoke, chimpanzee noises would come screaming from my throat, revealing the apparent status of my spiritual evolution.

"Thank you for the tea," I said awkwardly, accepting the cup he handed to me. I blew on the tea and took a sip. He waited to see my reaction.

"It's delicious," I responded, evidently bringing him even more joy.

"Isn't it delicious, Henry?" I said, prompting him to say something. I needed to be rescued.

He didn't take the bait. He sniffed the contents of his cup and took a moment to take in the aroma.

"Ah! It's very good indeed, but a different blend from yesterday, if I'm not mistaken?"

"Yes, well-spotted Henry. It's a different blend from an entirely different region of India," Swami G answered.

"Yesterday?" I whispered to Henry Jones.

"Uh-huh! Swami G and I met yesterday to catch up on old times and to prepare for today."

They just sat there, smiling, staring at me expectantly. I was at a loss for words.

"You look good for your age," I blurted, regretting it immediately. What was I thinking?

"Thank you for the compliment. How do you see yourself?" he replied with eyes that twinkled like sparklers. Perhaps it was nerves that set off my answer. I launched into a long description of the mirror exercise that Henry Jones made me do on the day I had met Juju Banks. I explained my reaction in great detail and the lesson I had learned.

361

Swami G listened intently, his eyes closed. So intently in fact that at one point I wondered if he'd slipped off to sleep. Finally, once I'd run out of things to say and a long minute of deafening silence had passed, he responded: "It's a fun-taas-tick question, isn't it? Who do you see when you look into the mirror? When you do this exercise again, try not to just look at the physical you. Fix your awareness into your own eyes; your own inner-self. Who is there behind the physical form? What is that person like? How does that person feel, think, act, and experience life? Then go a little further: How does it feel to truly look into yourself? Are you scared, embarrassed, angry, disgusted or confused? Or do you feel calm, loving, and gentle? Those are the true aspects of ourselves that the mirror reflects, but we don't always allow ourselves to see them. We are blinded by the fun-taas-tick physical reflection that we see shining back at us. Our inner truths are concealed behind the projection of our reality. Isn't that so?"

His words resonated with me. In that moment, all I could do was move my head up and down. My mouth hung open.

He continued: "The good news is that the long journey of spirituality is about revealing these inner truths, not only about ourselves, but of the world we see around us, too. In yoga, we teach that what we see in the world is a projection of our own self. The world we see before us is a collaborative creation of the human experience: 'The good, the bad, and the ugly', as they say. Yet, what we see and experience in this world is a direct result of our projections. What we're searching for is a modification of who we are internally. To be honest with ourselves about who we are is an essential prerequisite for understanding what we're looking for. What we're looking for can only be found if it is a part of reality. Otherwise, we're likely to be disappointed."

Instinctively, I patted myself down in search of my notepad, but there was no place to keep it in my flowing Indian garb. I felt lost, naked and exposed. There was only little ol' me, sitting cross-legged on the floor with Henry Jones and Swami G. My fidgeting distracted them. They waited for me to settle down before carrying on.

Appeased, Swami G spoke: "What is it that you're looking for, Young One?" he asked, taking a loud slurp of his tea and then smacking his lips together.

"I'm sick and I want to heal my body," I wasted no time telling him.

"And when you're honest with yourself, Young One, what are the internal modifications that you feel you must make to your life in order to heal your body?"

I frowned. "There's no short answer to your question, I'm afraid, and I know our time with you is limited. We need to leave your ashram today to catch a connecting flight to the international airport, because we're flying home this evening," I told him, tapping my wristwatch.

Swami G looked at me with great bemusement in his eyes. "Perhaps, this is part of your problem," he said, offering no further explanation. He slurped his tea, and then studied a tea leaf that swirled on the surface, waiting patiently for it to absorb enough liquid to finally sink. This, too, appeared to bring him immense joy. Oddly, Henry Jones did exactly the same thing every time a tea leaf floated in his tea.

"I haven't had the time to explore my internal world," I suddenly blurted out. "My work is demanding, I've a family, I've been sick, and I …" As I said it, I knew they were all just lame excuses. There was no conviction behind my words. I didn't even finish my sentence. I instantly realized that ignorance was my biggest problem. I was oblivious to the true meaning of life prior to meeting Henry Jones, and my priorities were all wrong. In his presence, I really wanted to be someone else; someone better and wiser. I could feel my ego-mind throttling me. Its grip on my throat tightened, strangling my words.

"Perhaps, now that you're waiting for wellness to return to your body, you have the time you need to explore your inner world, to unveil your hidden potential, and to become conscious of inhibiting weaknesses, so that true inner growth can be actualized. Perhaps this is the great gift of your sickness, Young One. The physical disturbance in your body has borrowed your wellness for a while, but it might just return it to you with a brand-new understanding of life, wrapped up in a higher consciousness, bound by a shiny red ribbon that is your true-self. Wouldn't that be a fun-taas-tick present to receive from such an unwanted guest in your house?" He moved his hands up and down his body, and then placed them on his knees with his palms facing upwards.

I couldn't argue with that.

"You're right, Swami G. I do have the time now. Please show me what to do." Finally, I had said something sensible.

Swami G looked thrilled. "Fun-taas-tick!" Let's get started straightaway. First of all, we'd like to show you a neat trick. It's a simple technique that lets us tune into our internal energy. Today, we're going to work with our chakra points, which is all about working with our internal energy."

"Okay, let's go for it. I'm keen to learn as much as I can from you."

"Oh gracious me!" he responded. "I can only show you the basic techniques. The really good stuff you'll have to learn through practice."

I should've expected him to say something like that. "Fine, let's begin with the basics," I said, spurring him on.

"Tell me, you do know what chakra points are, don't you?" Swami G asked me, looking to Henry Jones for confirmation.

"Of course I do," I said confidently, winking at Henry Jones. He shook his head ever so slightly, but disapprovingly, nonetheless. "Actually, I just found out about the chakra system a few days ago," I admitted.

Swami G brushed my foolishness aside. Clearly, I hadn't yet learned the importance of being genuine. That lesson was to come soon enough. First, I had to learn how to meditate.

Meditation is key

"Today, we're going to discuss the basics of meditation for a very good reason. It is the key to accessing our internal world and working with chakra energy. Let us give you just a little taste of it right now. Alright, Young One?"

"Okay, I'm ready and willing," I assured him.

He took a slurp of tea. "Fun-taas-tick! If you can't sit on the floor with your legs crossed comfortably, then you can sit on a pillow or chair. But, don't lie down! We can only lie down when we're accomplished meditators, or if we're very, very sick."

I shuffled around to make myself comfortable. We faced inwards, the three of us in a triangular formation, our knees almost touching. Henry Jones and Swami G put their hands on their knees, facing upwards. I copied them.

Swami G began: "We are about to share our Rock-Tree meditation with you. Close your eyes, breathe deeply, and focus inwardly. In your mind's eye, visualize Planet Earth hurtling through time and space. Picture it as a very big rock, many thousands of miles in diameter, moving at tremendous speed. Get a sense of it. Now, see yourself as a tiny speck sitting on this rock. Feel the weight of your body on the ground. Can you feel gravity pulling you to Earth? Fan-taas-tick! Next, use your imagination to push out a root from the base of your spine into the Earth. Create a mental image of the root making its way deep into the ground, pushing through layer upon layer of soil and rock. The Earth is filled with vital minerals and nutrients. With each inhalation, draw this natural energy into your body through the imaginary root. Do this a couple of times and establish a rhythm that's comfortable for you. When you feel ready to move on, feel this energy rising up through your torso. Imagine that your torso is the trunk of a mighty tree. As you inhale, pull this energy up through this mighty trunk, up through your body, to the core of your being, in your stomach area. Repeat this mental exercise a few times, until you're accustomed to the feeling of energy rising from the Earth, through the root, and through your body. With each inhalation, draw the energy up through your body to your core area, as you did before. Then pull the energy up through your body towards your head."

I didn't hold back. I was all in.

He continued: "Imagine big branches bursting out the top of your head. As you exhale, pull the energy into these branches with your breath. Repeat this a few times; each time seeing them divide and multiply into smaller and smaller branches, until they eventually become twigs and leaves. One more time, as you inhale, draw Earth energy through the root, into the trunk of your body, and then pull the energy through your body, towards your head, into the branches, into the twigs and leaves, and beyond, into the universe surrounding you. As you exhale, release this energy into the atmosphere around you. Once you feel comfortable, imagine warm, golden sunlight shimmering on the leaves. Get a sense of it. In this space, you're now connected to your internal energy and the universal energy that surrounds you."

We sat there in silence, unable to move. It felt as though I'd been hypnotized. It was the closest I'd ever come to an out-of-body experience. My consciousness and body had detached from one another, or so it seemed. Henry Jones was right: I was in a totally new realm, and I liked it.

"Was that fun, or what?" Henry Jones whispered to me after a while.

"Did you notice how easy it was for you to imagine energy running through your body?" Swami G asked me.

I had to admit, it was really easy.

He grinned victoriously. "At a level of consciousness, this thought energy became 'real'. Yes, when we imagined it, we actually created it. More than this, Young One, the moment we create energy with our minds, our inner-self can tune into it. When we make that connection, we can use this unlimited energy resource to heal our bodies. How? By working with our chakra points through meditation! Am I making sense to you?"

"Sure. It sounds simple enough," I replied with unintentional sarcasm in my voice. "So, what's next? When do we start learning about chakra points?"

"Right now," Swami G said with a grin. "Right now."

CHAPTER 20

DISCOVERING MY CHAKRAS

Swami G rocked back and forth a few times before he spoke. He seemed so content that I envied his calmness. He took another sip of tea. "Fun-taas-tick. Now we can begin."

The root chakra

"The entry point to our internal energy system is found at the base of our torso. It's commonly referred to as our root chakra, and it's pivotal to our overall well-being. It's primary function is to process the thoughts and feelings that relate to the basic fundamentals of our lives. In other words, Young One, it deals with our survival and security in the world."

"I'm sorry to butt in, but how do I know if my root chakra is working properly?"

"To enjoy a healthy root chakra, we need to have structure, stability, order, security and patience in our lives. These aspects enable us to maintain a balanced life. This will only happen when these aspects manifest in our lives. Without them, we have no foundation on which to build a solid future – one that we can depend on."

"How can I bring these aspects into my life?" I asked.

"Unless we have structure, stability, security, order and patience in our thinking, Young One, they will not be manifest in our lives," he replied. "If our thoughts are unstable, our life circumstances will be unstable. When our thinking stabilizes, our life circumstances will stabilize, too. It's that simple! This goes for the other aspects of our root chakra, too. People often make the mistake of thinking their thoughts will change when their reality changes, but it doesn't work like that. I'll say it again: Our external world reflects our internal world. This means we must first change our internal world before we can expect our external world to change."

His sing-song Indian accent made it sound so simple and poetic. I tried to fathom this wisdom, but my brain failed me. All I could think to ask was: "So, where's my root chakra?"

He pointed it out. "We find our root chakra at the base of our spine, at our coccyx, or tailbone. It's called the root chakra because it's the root of our energy system. An open, healthy root chakra enables us to be rooted in reality, while a closed, blocked root chakra causes us to disconnect from it. On the physical level, if we have problems with our spinal column, rectum, legs, bones, feet and immune system, or anything in the vicinity of our root chakra, we most likely have to deal with issues relating to our root chakra. See how this works?"

"Yes, but how does it become blocked?"

"Our early years have a powerful influence on the development of our root chakra. If we receive love, nurturing and proper nourishment during our childhood, then our root chakra flourishes. A stable, secure, structured and ordered environment makes for a healthy root chakra. This lays the foundation for our future strengths – the foundation of a balanced life with emotional and mental well-being. But, if our past didn't measure up to our expectations, or society's expectations, then we may find ourselves always chasing our ideals, dreams, visions and fantasies to make up for it." He wagged his finger. "Don't get me wrong, Young One, it's good for us to have desires and goals, but they mustn't compromise our basic physical needs in the here and now. If your basic physical needs aren't being met currently, then there's something wrong. This means your root chakra is dysfunctional and you must strive to bring structure, stability, security, order and patience back into your life. That is the only way to restore balance."

"Is that it?"

"No, Young One. It also becomes blocked when we disconnect from the fundamentals of human existence and lose touch with reality."

"How does that happen?"

"It happens when we spend too much time in our head … When we're so busy scheming, making plans and chasing personal ambitions and dreams that we neglect the fundamentals that we need to keep our life intact in the 'real' world."

"Sometimes, when we live with our head in the clouds, our feet don't touch the ground. Do you know what I mean?" Henry Jones interjected.

I shrugged my shoulders. Swami G leaned towards me. "Let me warn you, Young One: We always come plummeting back down to Earth."

"How come?" I asked.

"Because we need strong, solid foundations to support our fun-taas-tick dreams for the future! We simply can't build a healthy life for ourselves on an unhealthy base. This is the reason our root chakra is so important. It grounds us on the material plane. Grounding is crucial because it gets us out of our head and puts us back in touch with reality. Grounding reconnects us with our inner being, which brings back awareness of our body. Grounding teaches us to take care of ourselves and respect our needs. When we're grounded, we know our body's limitations. We become aware of what we need to keep balance and harmony in our lives at the most basic level. This is essential for our health and happiness."

I felt a piercing pang of guilt. I'd spent too much time in my head. I'd lost my connection with my body, and I'd stopped caring for myself properly on a physical level. Until I met Henry Jones, I'd lost my grip on reality completely. My career was suffering; my marriage was on the rocks; my daughter hardly spoke to me; and I had pretended to be someone else. I had spent a lot of my time worrying about the fundamentals of my life. In fact, I was worried sick. "So, what must I do to create a stable base?" I asked.

Swami G had the answer instantly: "To create a stable base, we've got to look after ourselves by providing for our basic, physical needs, such as nourishing our body, nurturing ourselves, and providing for our well-being. On an emotional level, we should try to build strong relationships with our family, friends and broader society. We depend on people for our basic needs, whether we like it or not. Everything we know, we learned from observing, studying and listening to the people around us. We developed our most basic belief systems through these interactions over the course of our lives. People taught us norms and customs, right from wrong, and good from bad. Isn't that so?"

"I suppose so."

"If you doubt it, cut yourself off from other people for a while. You'll soon see that you feel isolated and alone when your actions go against the norms of society. Feeling excluded or rejected isn't good for any of us. It causes us to lose energy. This is unhealthy for us, Young One. Remember, energy depletion weakens our immune system and results in disease. To maintain health, we must endeavour to maintain societal values. This being said, there are times when it may be necessary to look past what we've been taught, to deeper levels of truth. Everything isn't always as it seems. But let me caution you here: This process can be quite painful. We may encounter great resistance from others. When we go against the norm, we open ourselves to rejection, failure, abandonment, loss of order and ridicule. But push on, Young One. Our spirit grows in these moments of transformation."

The sacral chakra

"Spiritual transformation is one of life's great accomplishments," Henry Jones said. "This leads us neatly to your sacral chakra."

"My what?"

"Your sacral chakra."

"Where's that?"

"You'll find it about three fingers below your naval."

"What does it do?"

Swami G answered me: "The primary function of our sacral chakra is to process the thoughts and feelings that relate to our sense of well-being. This is determined by our experience of pleasure, or lack thereof. The aspects of our life that relate to pleasure are sexuality and physical desires. These are connected to morality and creativity. Unfortunately, in this modern world, our sense of well-being is also determined by our prosperity, or lack thereof. The aspects of our life that relate to prosperity are work and career, which are connected to money and power."

"So, whenever I deal with anything that relates to my pleasure or prosperity in the physical world, my sacral chakra is at work. Is that correct?" I asked.

"Quite correct, Young One. Knowing this, we should take great care not to overwork our sacral chakra. Let me explain: The condition of this energy center is affected by our need to control our physical world. This is a common problem in these modern times in which consumerism is given such a high priority. Keeping up with the Joneses isn't easy to do, as you probably know. Through this obsession, we put undue pressure on ourselves to succeed, which is unhealthy for our sacral chakra. It's even unhealthier for us when we fail to meet our self-imposed expectations. When we overwork our sacral chakra, it stops functioning properly, or becomes blocked and dysfunctional!"

"What are the signs?" I had to ask.

"We fear losing control, for one thing. In response to this fear, we hold on to our material desires more tightly and we struggle to let things go. We also worry a lot about money and the things we don't have. We may end up denying ourselves the things in life that bring us pleasure – not just the things that cost money – even the simple things that don't cost a cent. We may also feel envious, resentful and bitter, and we'll probably do things that compromise our physical well-being. These could include ingesting harmful substances and denying ourselves the pleasure of exercising and stretching our bodies. At a physical level, we'll experience problems with our sexual organs; large intestine; appendix; kidneys; bladder; pelvis; hips; gonads; pancreas; spleen; eliminative system; reproductive system and muscular system."

I couldn't help grimacing. "How can I unblock my sacral chakra?" I inquired.

"If we want to unblock our sacral chakra, we must realize that we live in an abundant universe. There's an abundance of everything around us, Young One. Nature is full and plentiful, and we can achieve whatever we set our minds to. There's no need to struggle. We should take a lesson from nature: The grass doesn't struggle to grow and the leaves don't struggle to fall."

Henry Jones piped up: "There's an Egyptian proverb that says: 'A man can go through his life charging towards his dreams like a raging beast, but this will not change his destiny.'"

Swami G thought this very funny. He laughed so hard, it brought a tear to his eye.

"I guess the point you're trying to make is: I should take it easy?" I said.

"Exactly!" Henry Jones exclaimed. "We don't need to have everything we want. That approach to life is a breeding ground for selfishness and greed. What we have in life isn't more important than what we give. Those two aspects are connected. They must go hand-in-hand if we are to be healthy."

"You've lost me."

"Allow me," said Swami G. "We live in a universe that flows. There's a constant cycle of giving and receiving. To receive, we must give, and to give, we must receive. If we hold on to things too tightly, we break the cycle of giving and receiving, and subsequently we stop the natural flow of the universe. Like water, energy becomes stagnant when it stops flowing. That is sure to block our sacral chakra, eventually manifesting as disease in our bodies."

"So, you're saying I should open my sacral chakra by giving back. Do you mean donating money to charity?"

Swami G thought this was funny, too. "Yes, that can be a part of it, too, but I was actually referring to giving of yourself – your true-self. You see, on an emotional level, our sacral chakra manages our emotional life and our need for relationships, which makes sense if you think about it, because our emotions and relationships directly affect our well-being. This gives us a significant clue about the health of someone's sacral chakra. Individuals with blocked sacral chakras seldom honour the people around them. They are takers, not givers. They don't respect other people's feelings because they can't feel the emotional effect they have on them. Why do you think this is so?"

"Perhaps the reason we don't feel other people's emotions is because we're disconnected from our own?" I heard myself confess.

Swami G frowned for the first time. "It's not so much that these folks are detached from their emotions, or that they control their emotions, or that they don't have emotions. That's not it at all! The fact is, Young One, there's a definite blockage that's preventing them from experiencing their emotions fully. Period."

I hung my head low. They could've been talking about me. I wasn't sure what to say without revealing my guilty conscience. Fortunately, Henry Jones interjected: "Consider these scenarios," he said. "One: A group of people are laughing with joy, but one person just smiles along. Have you noticed that before? It may even be that that person is pretending to smile, when in fact they're looking on with bemused amazement. Why? Because they simply can't access that kind of joy, so they can't experience it. Here's another one for you: There's the person who doesn't shed a single tear at the funeral of a loved one, even though they're terribly sad. It's not that they don't want to cry, but rather that they literally can't find it in themselves to cry. These emotional blockages stem from blockages in the sacral chakra. You can bet your bottom dollar on it!"

"You see, Young One, when our sacral chakra is open, we can experience the abundance of life in its richest and fullest sense. This means experiencing our emotions completely. There's a time for laughter and a time for tears. Sure, we can keep our emotional self as rigid as a stick, but our life will be dull. Who wants that?"

"Not me. So how do I unblock my sacral chakra?"

"That's a fun-taas-tick question!" Swami G said, wobbling his head. "We must break out of this behavioral pattern. It's a bad habit, that's all."

Henry Jones jumped in again: "Remember, people cling to habits to stop the flow of change. Hah! Is this an exercise in futility, or what? As Swami G said: 'We live in a universe that flows,' so they may as well try to hold back the hands of time."

"I think my sacral chakra is blocked," I suddenly blurted out.

"Oh dear! This is distressing news indeed," Swami G remarked. "Chances are, if you have a blocked sacral chakra, your well-being was compromised at some point in your past. Here's what you can do to fix this problem: Think back to those occasions when life wasn't a pleasure for you. Think of the people in your life at that time and how they made you feel. If you feel hurt, anger, resentment, bitterness, blame or disappointment, you need to work on letting go of those negative feelings. If you don't, your sacral chakra will stay blocked, and your outlook on life will always be distorted. You don't want that for yourself, do you?"

"No. Definitely not! Please tell me exactly how to let go of those negative feelings."

"I'm happy to oblige you. First of all, it's important to realize that our relationships with others serve to make us more conscious of ourselves. People reflect us. Every single person we meet reflects a different aspect of ourselves. People show us what we like and don't like. They reveal our strengths and weaknesses, our good and bad, our values and principles. When we like someone, it's usually an aspect of ourselves that we like in them. And when we don't like someone, it's usually an aspect of ourselves that we don't like in them. That is why our relationships can help us to learn and grow, if we let them."

"You've lost me."

"Oh, gracious me! I'll try to make it even easier for you to understand. We should regard our transgressors as teachers, because they help to shape us, and they give us the chance to practice tolerance, patience and forgiveness. Everyone plays a role in our life experience. They're all actors in our story. We should try to accept them for who they are and the role they play in our precious life, whether it's good or bad."

"Does this help to open one's sacral chakra?"

"Oh yes. Quite right! To open our sacral chakra, we must learn how to interact consciously with others. Tell him how to do this, Henry," Swami G instructed whilst reaching for another sip of tea.

"We should always look for the value that people bring to our lives. Try to find the good in them or the lesson we learn from them," he replied.

"What a fun-taas-tick answer!" Swami G exclaimed, wobbling his head more intensely. "You see, Young One, there is a constructive lesson in every human encounter. Even in the negative encounters with people who upset and hurt us."

I thought about my boss, the owner of the publishing company for which I worked. We had a strained relationship, to say the least. He was a real dick. He made me look like a pussycat. Our personalities just clashed and we fought often. I'd been thinking about him a lot. He employed me because I was good at my job, and I had made him a lot of money. I worked for him because he paid me well, and I'd built my career in his company. Quitting at my age wasn't necessarily the smartest idea, even though I hated my work environment.

"What are we supposed to do if we're in a destructive relationship?" I heard myself ask.

"Oh, gracious me, that's not good," Swami G answered back. "When we find ourselves stuck in negative relationships that compromise our individuality, values or morals, we should break away from those people as soon as humanly possible. Negative relationships make us sick. We should learn our lesson and move on, for the sake of our health and quality of life."

Henry Jones spoke, too. "It's important to honour our personal identities and to establish our personal boundaries. When we know what we will and won't accept from others, we can build relationships that satisfy our emotional, mental, spiritual and physical needs."

That news didn't come easily to me. I knew exactly what it meant, but acting on it would be a different story altogether. My job defined me. It was the source of my power. I'd worked my way to the very top of the corporate ladder. What would I be without my title? Who would employ me? What if I couldn't find another job? I wondered.

Henry Jones tuned into my dismay. My awful relationship with my boss had come up several times in the past few weeks. It was a source of my discontent, no doubt. Should I quit my job? Was it time to tell my boss to take his stressful job and shove it? What would I do for money? I wondered, rubbing my tummy. Fortunately, they didn't give me much time to dwell on this issue.

The solar plexus chakra

"Bad news feels like a kick in the gut, doesn't it?"

"Yes."

"Why is this?"

"Um, perhaps there's an energy center in that region of our body?" I guessed.

"You're quite correct, Young One. Our solar plexus chakra is found in the center of our torso, just below our ribs," Swami G told me.

"It's about four fingers width above our navel," Henry Jones added.

Swami G continued: "Before you ask me what it does, I'll tell you. The primary function of our solar plexus chakra is to process the thoughts and feelings that relate to our personal power. The aspects that relate to our personal power are determination, commitment, persistence, discipline and will. How we practice these aspects depends on our self-esteem. One might say the condition of our solar plexus chakra depends on our self-esteem, too. When we have a good self-esteem, we naturally have the courage to follow our inner convictions and face life's challenges. It gives us the strength of character we need to stand up for ourselves, for our ideas and our beliefs. We find it easy to accept responsibility for ourselves and we have the confidence to take risks.

"On the other hand, a low self-esteem is a sure sign of a problem. When our solar plexus chakra is blocked or dysfunctional, we fear rejection and criticism, and this drives our inhibition, because we're afraid of looking foolish or 'inferior' in front of others. On a physical level, our solar plexus chakra affects our digestive system; stomach; adrenals; upper intestines; gallbladder; liver and pancreas."

"How will I know if my solar plexus is dysfunctional, too?"

"You can test the health of your solar plexus chakra by answering these three, simple questions. How do you feel about yourself? Do you like yourself? Do you lovingly accept your physical self – your appearance and your body?"

I didn't need to answer him. The answers were written on my face.

"If you answered 'No' to any of these questions, then you should work on opening your solar plexus chakra. Don't worry, Young One, we can teach you how to do this."

"Pay attention!" Henry Jones instructed, nudging my leg.

"I am," I assured him.

"To open our solar plexus chakra, we must work on raising our self-esteem. The key is to look at all of our good attributes."

"I'm struggling to see past my failings at the moment," I admitted.

"We can dwell on our weaknesses or focus on our strengths. The choice is ours," Swami G replied with a smile.

"I've been a bad person for years," I confessed.

"You're not a bad person, Young One. We are all capable of being bad and good. We have two distinct sides to us. Our ego-mind, as Henry calls it, is always bad, and our true-self is always good. When you start to behave as your true-self, you'll feel good and your self-esteem will improve. I guarantee it!"

"Anything else?"

"Yes, we can also shift our focus from the external world to our internal world. When we look within, Young One, we become conscious of our personal power. This is a spiritual passage. Choosing to develop a good self-esteem is the same as choosing to enhance our spiritual power."

"How do I do this?" I inquired, sipping my tea.

"That's another fun-taas-tick question. Let me give you a few hot tips to heal the solar plexus chakra. I hope you can remember all of them. They are fun-taas-tick! Do you think you'll be able to remember them?"

"Yes, I'm sure."

"Okay then, here we go: To heal our solar plexus chakra, we must focus on our strengths and not our perceived weaknesses. We should also establish our own identity; exercise our personal authority when challenged; practice standing up for ourselves daily; go with our gut feel; maintain our principles, and act on our personal ambitions. I also recommend repeating this mantra every day for as long as it takes to internalize it: 'To my own self be true'."

I made a mental note of his sound advice.

"Okay, that about covers the basic characteristics of our solar plexus chakra. Let's move up, shall we?" Henry Jones suggested.

"Don't you mean, move on?" I asked.

"Nope, I mean up," he replied, running his hand from his root chakra up towards his head. That's when I realized chakra points run sequentially.

"Ah! I get it now," I said, mimicking Henry Jones's hand movement. Swami G did the same thing. For no apparent reason, we all started laughing.

"Okay, now tell me, Young One: Was there ever a time in your life when you were so overcome with grief and sadness that it felt as if your heart was broken?"

"Sure. Who hasn't experienced heartache?"

The heart chakra

"Yes, we've all experienced these emotions at some point. But why do our hearts ache? Why not our brains? It's because our heart chakra is in the middle of our chest. Its primary function is to process our thoughts and feelings related to love. The aspects of love associated with our heart chakra are compassion, forgiveness, peace, harmony and brotherhood."

I put my hand on my chest and inhaled deeply.

"Our heart chakra mediates between our body and spirit. It plays a key role mediating between our physical and spiritual worlds. When it's open, we're able to love both ourselves and humanity. We feel connected to our fellow man and have a sense of 'oneness', Young One. This affinity to people enables us to be loving, compassionate and forgiving. These qualities are the ultimate expression of our spiritual nature."

Henry Jones added: "When our hearts are filled with love, we naturally practice the qualities of love. But this love shouldn't be confused with the conventional idea of love, which is manufactured by the ego-mind. The love that stems from our heart is warm and true. It extends beyond sentimental romance and passion. It's governed by spirit, rather than emotions. So, instead of being ruled by our feelings, this love puts us in touch with them."

Swami G clapped excitedly. "This leads me to my next point. When our heart chakra is open, we naturally and spontaneously use our emotions appropriately. We're able to experience them to their fullest without becoming irrational or unbalanced. Our thoughts are also non-judgmental, non-critical and non-cynical. As such, we're able to love all of mankind. But, most importantly, we're able to practise true 'unconditional love', which is divine. Unfortunately, when there's no unconditional love in our heart, we become hard-hearted, our spirit is suppressed, and our ego-mind rules us. In this state, it becomes increasingly difficult for us to love and to be loved in return. On the other hand, we naturally become soft-hearted when our heart is filled with unconditional love. Then our spirit's liberated, and our true-self flourishes. In this state, it becomes increasingly easy for us to love and to be loved. Do you see how this works?"

"I think so," I stammered.

"We're telling you that spiritual awakening occurs through your heart. We must open our hearts to love in order to evolve spiritually."

I had a problem. "I'm afraid of rejection," I declared honestly.

Henry Jones shook his head from one side to the other. "No, no, no! Don't be afraid of being rejected, hurt, disappointed or betrayed any longer. It's time to let go of your ego-mind's past perceptions."

Swami G leaned towards me: "Open the door to your heart and let love in. Love everything: Love life, love nature, love God, love others, and most of all, love yourself."

"Love yourself," Henry Jones repeated.

"To love yourself means to be conscious of yourself. That is the great spiritual passage of life. We must first love ourselves before we can truly love others. But this doesn't happen by accident. We must make it so. To love ourselves we need to make time for self-discovery, Young One. Self-exploration is a divine quest. Knowing ourselves is a divine right. No matter how busy our schedules may be, we must make a point of getting to know ourselves – our true-selves. We must ask: What really makes me happy? Knowing the answer to this simple question is vital to our well-being. We can't be true to ourselves, or happy, unless we've defined who we truly are and what we enjoy doing. Sound reasonable?"

"Yes, it does. But I'd like to ask you a question about someone else, if that's okay. It's about my wife. She constantly compromises herself and her own happiness for others. She gives and gives and gives, and she lets people take advantage of her all the time. Is this really better than pursuing your own happiness above all?"

Swami G gave me the full answer in two parts. "Firstly," he said, "the only happiness that one must pursue is the long-standing happiness of the true-self. We should never pursue the fleeting happiness of the ego-mind, Young One. It will only lead to heartache in the future. Got it?"

"Got it," I said.

"Fun-taas-tick! Secondly, people who compromise themselves, their true-selves, forego what's good for them at the expense of their individuality and personal happiness. That isn't good. Each time they compromise themselves, their ego-mind records this indiscretion as self-deprivation. In response to this, negative emotions are constantly triggered and suppressed. They add up over time, eventually blocking the heart chakra. Sadly, this loss of energy results in jealously, bitterness, anger, resentment and an inability to forgive. These people literally become heartsick because these negative qualities have no love in them."

"Are you saying a heartsick person simply doesn't have love in their heart?" I exclaimed. Did that explain why my wife no longer had love in her heart for me? I wondered.

"That's exactly what I'm saying," Swami G replied. "But don't be fooled, Young One. They're victims of their ego-minds, too. Excessive self-sacrifice is an ego trip in another form. Ego isn't just about thinking you're fun-taas-tick and always putting your mind's desires first. It can also be self-sacrificing, self-pitying, self-loathing, self-destructing, and even self-mutilating. Oh yes, Young One, the ego-mind will do anything and be anything to keep a person from living as their true-self."

"So, what should I advise my wife to do?"

"Well, for one thing, you should encourage her to reconnect with her true-self before she gets sick, too. You see, people who give away too much of themselves deplete their spiritual energy. That makes them susceptible to illness. Like I've already told you, don't be taken in by their apparent good-heartedness. They're sufferers of their own ego-minds. The reason they preoccupy themselves with giving is so that they don't have to deal with their personal issues on their spiritual path. Is that a healthy way to live? No! Definitely not! If you know anyone who is guilty of this, gently advise them to stop it at once. They must stop living for others and start living for themselves."

"But she's just not selfish," I told him.

"Putting one's self first shouldn't be confused with being selfish. When we listen to our heart, we can't be selfish because the very nature of heart energy is completely selfless."

"She cares for others too much to put herself first," I tried to explain.

"She should stop that behavior, too."

"I don't think she'll ever be able to stop caring for others. It's in her nature," I replied.

"Oh, gracious me! You've got me all wrong, Young One. That's not what I'm saying at all. Please don't think that by putting ourselves first, we have to stop caring for others. If we truly want to care for others, we should start by caring for ourselves. It's easier to give from a full cup than from an empty one. For this reason alone, nurturing one's self and addressing one's true personal needs is spiritually important. Our spirit knows that the more we care for ourselves, the fuller our cup will be, and the easier it'll be for us to care for others. We'll have the energy we need to care wholeheartedly."

"That goes for you, too," Henry Jones interjected, placing his hand gently on my leg. "How can you expect to care for others when you're lying flat on your back? That just won't do, my friend. Get your personal strength back by caring for yourself first. Then you'll truly be able to care for your wife and the others in your life."

"I'm not sure she'll let me," I said, taking a swig of cold tea to stop myself from bawling. "I haven't cared for her properly in years. I've been emotionally distant and detached from our marriage. I have never shared my heart with her. I kept all of my emotions bottled up inside of me. How can I open up to her now, Swami G?"

"If you want to heal your body, you've got to get to the heart of your problem. You need to identify your old emotional wounds and open them up. Take one issue at a time. Get into it; speak about it; write about it; shout about it; and act it out. Just make sure you do whatever it takes to let the emotions out. You must pour out your heart to her, Young One."

"That will help to open my heart chakra?"

"Definitely! I absolutely guarantee it. Unless you bring your painful memories to the surface and deal with them, you'll not truly heal your body, your marriage or your life. The only way to heal painful memories is by releasing the old, negative emotions that are stored in your body."

"How do I know which painful memories to focus on?" I asked.

"More often than not, painful memories relate to negative experiences with people. The sad truth is: People can cause great psychological damage to each other, often without even knowing it. You may be harbouring deep resentment towards someone who is totally oblivious of your feelings. These unresolved emotions could be making you sick. If you were exposed to any kind of abuse, you're most likely harbouring damaged emotional patterns, which are affecting your heart chakra. I'll say it again: You must deal with these emotions by confronting these issues, no matter how painful or scary."

Swami G slurped his tea.

"We all have emotional issues from our past with which we've not properly dealt. There's a wounded child in all of us, Young One. Oh yes, we take on the wounded child syndrome whenever we don't express hurtful feelings. You know what I'm talking about, don't you? Think back to the times in your life when you just couldn't express or deal with your emotions, so you bottled them up inside. Take a minute to reflect on your painful memories."

Swami G was being serious. He slipped into silence. We sat pondering our pasts. It didn't take long before I started thinking about my ex-fiancée and her influence on my relationship with my wife. Henry Jones had planted the seed in the cabin. He'd shown me the reason for my lack of commitment, jealously and emotional distance. I knew my wife deserved better. My thoughts then skipped to my estranged father and our embattled relationship. The fact that he's dead didn't kill the way I felt about him. My awful boss elbowed his way into my thoughts, too. I couldn't suppress the rage that welled up inside of me. Henry Jones and I had touched on each issue in the cabin. I knew I had unresolved issues that I'd carried with me most of my life. Those emotional burdens weighed me down. My heart began to ache.

"I'm going to say it again, and again, and again, until you can recite the words yourself: You must confront these issues and deal with the negative emotions once and for all. That's the only way to find out for sure what's making you sick, my friend," Henry Jones declared.

I knew they were right. "What can I do to heal my broken heart?" I suddenly cried out.

Swami G rescued me. "Ask yourself: What good came of it? What did I learn? Now that you can see the big picture, look for the positive outcomes. It makes forgiveness easier. The key here is love. With love in our heart, we can heal our bodies. Love has the power to heal because it gives us the strength to forgive. Forgiveness is an act of love through which healing is manifest. Trust me, Young One, there's no better way to release the negative emotions that are stored in our body. We simply must forgive our transgressors in order to heal our body. When we forgive, we naturally bring back power into our life, and we need this power to heal our body. The spiritual power of heart energy is its ability to forgive. This is divine. Without love in our heart, our physical body will struggle to heal itself. We can't forgive and we can't love when our heart chakra is blocked with negative thoughts and emotions. However, we naturally find the strength to forgive when we open our heart chakra, and by doing so, we open ourselves for healing. Make sense?"

It was starting to make sense to me. I'd heard these words before. It was all coming back to me now. But I don't think I had previously been ready to hear the message in these words. I'd just started my healing journey back then. Heck, I'd just found out about my ego-mind and true-self. I was still so green.

But so much had happened since. I'd spent weeks with Henry Jones, working on his book about healing, listening to his stories, meeting his friends. I'd come a long way on my healing journey. I wasn't the same person anymore.

"I bet you're going to tell me to forgive myself, too, huh?" I remarked, dispatching an affectionate glance towards Henry Jones.

"Ah! You've surfaced another great truth, Young One. Before we can forgive others, we must first forgive ourselves. No one is perfect. We all make mistakes. As the old saying goes: 'To err is human.' But, the most important thing we can do is learn from our mistakes and move on. Believe me: The biggest mistake we can make is holding on to the mistakes we think we've made in our past. Let them go! Try to see it like this: Our mistakes help to shape our destiny. They should lead us to self-discovery. No matter what road leads us to self-discovery, the journey is worth it."

"Henry Jones has told me this repeatedly since we met," I said.

"Well, I can't say I'm surprised. You're lucky to have him in your life, Young One. I hope you tell him that all the time."

Henry Jones blushed. My cheeks flushed, too. The truth was, I hadn't genuinely expressed my gratitude to him at all. I'd said 'thank you' once or twice, but I hadn't genuinely told him how much he meant to me, or how grateful I was to him for spending so much time with me, or for teaching me how to heal my body. We had a deal. That was how I saw it. He'd help me on my healing journey and I'd help him to write and publish his book. But what started out as a business transaction of sorts had morphed into something else entirely. Henry Jones had become my friend; my confidante; my mentor; my motivator; my cook; my gym partner; my transport; my host; my all. Why hadn't I expressed my sincerest gratitude to him? Why hadn't I told him how much I appreciated him? What was stopping me from letting him know how I truly felt about him? I wondered.

The throat chakra

"Now, let's move on to the throat chakra. Tell me, Young One, do you ever feel a lump in your throat when you're feeling emotional or sad?"

"Yes, I feel one right now."

"Oh, gracious me! That's the throat chakra. We find it at our throat area, just below our Adam's apple. The primary function of this chakra is to process the thoughts and feelings that relate to the way we express ourselves in the world. I'm talking about our personal communication. The aspects of communication associated with our throat chakra are honesty, integrity, genuineness, sharing and openness. These qualities relate to how we express our power of choice and will."

"I've never had a problem expressing my opinions …?" I stated in a clear voice. I wanted to finish my thought but Swami G did it for me.

"Yes, but can you express your feelings? Are you honest about how you feel in your relationships? When our throat chakra is open, we can communicate our ideas, thoughts and feelings freely, both verbally and in writing. We find it easy to talk openly and honestly to people on all levels, rich or poor, smart or simple, young or old. The key word here is honestly. Our throat chakra connects us to our inner voice, so we find it easy to speak our truth when it's open. Finding our voice is spiritually significant. Do you want to know why?"

"Yes, please."

Henry Jones piped up: "When we put our thoughts and feelings into words, we harness the creative energy within us. By expressing ourselves, we help to manifest our reality. As we speak, we bring things into being. Make no mistake about it: What we say is what we get."

"It's true, what Henry says," Swami G confirmed. "There is power in the spoken word. Communication is the means whereby consciousness extends itself from one place to another. Invisible, sometimes even inaudible, communication is the connecting principle that makes life possible."

"So, if you want to heal your body, you've got to talk yourself into it," said Henry Jones.

"Are you referring to affirmations?"

"Yes, precisely! You should say affirmations daily. Humming, chanting and singing also work wonders. They help to open the throat chakra, sending auditory vibrations through our system, which in turn gets our internal energy flowing. Of course, the opposite is also true. If we want to heal our bodies, then we've also got to talk our way out of it. We must open up and share our feelings to resolve past and present conflict. Get it?"

"I think so. Henry and I have discussed this topic. He also told me that there is power in the spoken word. He advised me to share my feelings and to speak my truth," I admitted.

Henry Jones nudged our conversation along: "Tell him how to open the throat chakra, Swami G."

"Of course!" he replied with his hands pressed together. "To open our throat chakra, we must learn to constructively express our emotions. Did you notice I said 'constructively'? Many people mistakenly think the only way to deal with conflict is through conflict. They choose to fight fire with fire. Instead of calmly discussing problems to find solutions, they become aggressive, confrontational, angry and upset. Do you know what I mean?"

I admitted that I did this too.

"Oh, gracious me! This isn't good for you, Young One. By losing control of our emotions, we do more damage than good. Invariably, we say things we don't mean, and later on, we regret our words and actions. Regret isn't a garment we want to wear," Swami G told me. "Regret is bound by a lack of understanding and unforgiveness. Regret leaves us in emotional tatters."

Henry Jones couldn't resist chipping in. "Remember, my friend, how we react is always a choice we make. For this reason, our throat chakra is closely associated with our power of choice. Keep in mind that there are always consequences to how we choose to express our thoughts and feelings. As they say, what goes around comes around."

"There are two, mischievous culprits that we need to watch out for," Swami G announced. "They are anger and fear. Before we express ourselves, we should always ask: 'What is motivating my choice?' If it's anger or fear, then our ego-mind, as Henry would say, is driving our choice. When we catch ourselves doing this, Young One, we should stop it immediately and ask ourselves: 'How can I respond from a place of love and peace?' Practising this technique is an excellent way to open the throat chakra."

"This isn't always easy. Sometimes people make us angry, or threaten us, or challenge our livelihood. Isn't it a natural response to defend ourselves in these situations?" I turned to Henry Jones for support. "Do you remember we discussed this issue when we were having breakfast in the restaurant on the way to the cabin? I told you that people piss me off sometimes, remember?"

I didn't get the support I'd hoped for.

"Yes, I recall our conversation clearly, and I'll give you the same answer today as I did back then, because nothing has changed. When your true-self is present, you choose loving and positive thoughts, regardless of your life circumstances."

Swami G clapped his hands together enthusiastically, like a child receiving a present. "Fun-taas-tick! You see, Young One, when our throat chakra is blocked, our ego-mind tricks us into believing that we don't have a choice. But this isn't true at all. We should not let it deceive us! We always have a choice. Our power of choice is a divine right. The Great Spirit wants us to do what is right, to follow our hearts and to lead full and meaningful lives. Oh yes, the Great Spirit in us always wants to respond from a place of love and peace because it emanates from a place of love and peace, and it wants us to move towards a place of love and peace, so that we can ultimately return to a place of love and peace. This, too, is a spiritual passage, and a part of the great circle of life. Where do we find love and peace? We receive them from the Great Spirit through our true-selves, and we return love and peace to the world through our true-selves. This great, eternal philosophy connects us to the flow of the universe and makes us whole. It isn't very complicated at all. The bottom line is this: We may think we have no choice, but actually we do. Deep down in our hearts, we always know the right thing to do for our lives."

"Then why don't we always do it?" I protested.

"Because our ego-mind tricks us into being afraid!" Henry Jones said, as if it was obvious.

"Afraid of what?"

"Rejection, criticism and abandonment, mostly."

"Oh, gracious me! That isn't good," Swami G declared. "When we fear rejection or criticism, we're prone to making the wrong choices. We've a tendency to go with the flow, even if we don't truly agree with its direction. If we are guilty of this behavior, then we're most likely also prone to lying. Yes, lying! You know the kind I mean. The little white lies people tell each other to supposedly smooth things over. I should warn you: We never get away with it. We're always accountable to our spiritual karma. It's much better for us to speak our truth. If we don't speak our truth in order to avoid conflict, we'll undoubtedly block our throat chakra and it'll become dysfunctional. We'll most likely develop inner frustration and anger. This silent child will rage in us, until eventually this spiritual disturbance manifests as disease. We don't want that, do we?"

I shook my head. "So, what else can we do to open our throat chakra?"

"We must listen to our inner voice and express it gently. Our throat chakra is the key, Young One. It facilitates inner voice communication between our head and our heart, our ego-mind and our true-self. It lies between our heart and our head for good reason, you know. Did you think this was merely a coincidence?"

Henry Jones had some good advice of his own. "Think of your throat chakra as a filter. When you speak from your ego-mind, it becomes blocked and dysfunctional, but when you speak from your true-self, it opens and functions well."

"Pretty simple," I admitted. "In the cabin you told me to seek silence, center myself, and look within to hear my inner truth."

"Fun-taas-tick advice," Swami G exclaimed, applauding his friend. "Follow it. When we practise this technique and we hear what our heart is telling us, then it's our spiritual responsibility to express it. We shouldn't let the little voice in our head tell us otherwise, or we'll compromise our true-selves. We must use our willpower to communicate our thoughts and feelings to others. When we want to open our throat chakra, we should answer these questions. Who controls my willpower? What or who do I give up my willpower for? Knowing the answers to these questions helps us to evolve spiritually. I say this because when we become conscious of the power we give away, it's much easier for us to reclaim it. Spiritual power is all about reclaiming personal power."

"Giving up our personal power is unhealthy for us, my friend." Henry Jones said. "By its very nature, it's self-destructive."

"Oh, gracious me! This, too, isn't good," Swami G remarked again, wagging his finger. "If we want to heal our body, we must break the destructive cycles in our life. The only way to break destructive cycles in our life is by choice. Oh yes, it's our spiritual responsibility to make the right life choices and communicate them to others. This vocalization is tremendously important, Young One. Do this, and we reclaim our personal power."

"Okay, I've got it now. Thank you."

"Fun-taas-tick!" Swami G declared, refilling his teacup gleefully.

"We still have a lot of ground to cover. Should we move on to the next chakra point?" Henry Jones suggested.

"No, wait one moment please," Swami G responded. "I'm not finished yet. I've another fun-taas-tick practice to share with you. This is a real knock-out: A great way to reclaim our personal power and open our throat chakra is through confession. When we confess our sins, we liberate our fears, purge our guilt and rid ourselves of negatives memories. Said another way, confession reclaims the spirit from the consequences of our choices. This is powerful stuff!"

"But I'm not Catholic," I exclaimed unthinkingly.

They both chortled. "You don't have to be a Catholic to practise confession, Young One. You can confess all of your sins and innermost fears to a total stranger, friend or family member, if you must. Just share your whole sob story. Get all those heartfelt issues off your chest. Afterwards you'll feel much better. Trust me. So much so, that you'll wish you did it years ago. Try it. Okay?"

"Okay," I replied. I remembered Henry Jones suggesting confession in the cabin too. It's one of many ways to connect with your true-self. Back then, I didn't know about chakra points. He obviously did. How did he resist spilling the beans? I wondered for a fleeting second.

The brow chakra

"Okay, now I'm ready to move on, Henry," Swami G said. "Let's discuss the brow chakra."

"Let me guess. It's found in the center of our forehead?"

"You're quite correct, Young One. Well done. The brow chakra is a powerful energy center. Its primary function is to process the thoughts and feelings that are related to our intuition. The aspects of intuition associated to our brow chakra are discernment, wisdom, insight, imagination and the sixth sense. These aspects relate to clairvoyance, or vision beyond ordinary sight, as well as our ability to visualize and manifest. The mystics say: 'The flame of our spirit shines through our brow chakra.'"

"I'm not exactly sure what that means, but it sounds nice," I replied, rubbing my forehead.

"You've heard about the third eye?" Henry Jones asked me.

I nodded. "Yes, but I don't know what that means either."

Swami G made a tut-tut sound. "According to Wikipedia, the third eye is a mystical and esoteric concept referring to a speculative invisible eye, which provides perception beyond ordinary sight. It's the gate that leads to inner realms and spaces of higher consciousness."

I did a double-take. "Did he just say Wikipedia?" I whispered to Henry Jones, who looked more surprised than me.

"What? Do you think I haven't heard of the Internet?" Swami G said, hiding behind his teacup. "Don't panic! I haven't been surfing the web in my spare time. An American tourist printed it out for me so that I can explain it to foreigners in a manner they will understand. Tell me, did it help you? Do you have a better idea of what we're talking about now?"

"I think I do."

"Fun-taas-tick! Even though most of us can't see it with the naked eye, I can assure you, our third eye is as real as the nose on our face. To get a sense of it, close your eyes and move your index finger in tiny circles near to the center of your forehead."

"Give it a go," Henry Jones suggested.

I tried it.

"Can you feel a strange sensation at your brow?"

I could.

"What do you think is causing it?"

"My brow chakra?" I offered.

"Precisely," replied Henry Jones.

Swami G grinned. "When our brow chakra is open, we can 'see' the celestial love that encompasses everything around us, and we can recognize this love reflecting within ourselves. We also enjoy a high emotional intelligence and strong mental reasoning abilities. This is most useful, especially when it comes to maintaining health. At a glance, we're able to determine what works for us and what doesn't; what's good for us; what isn't good for us; what we should do and what we shouldn't do. And, most importantly, we see the importance of applying it to our lives. Oh yes, Young One, when our brow chakra is open, we naturally do what is best for us in the long run. In other words, what's best for our true-self. Subsequently, we strive to protect and nurture all life, not just our own. We understand that our well-being is directly dependent on the well-being of others and the immediate world around us. This practice requires the spiritual act of discernment."

"Discernment?" I questioned.

"Discernment is our ability to determine the value and quality of a certain subject, practice, person or event – particularly our ability to go past the mere perception of something and to make detailed judgments about that thing. A discerning individual is considered to possess wisdom and be of good judgment; especially when regarding subject matter often overlooked by others," Swami G explained.

"Why is this relevant?"

"Oh, gracious me! I can't begin to tell you how essential it is for us to practice discernment in our daily lives. We must be discerning about our thoughts, words and deeds all the time; every second of every minute; every minute of every hour; every hour of every day; and every day of our life until we return to the Great Spirit."

"It really is that important," Henry Jones contributed.

"Can you give me a practical example?" The pragmatic side of me needed to know.

"We should be discerning about the food we eat; the people with whom we associate; our exercise program; our meditations; our spare time – pretty much everything!" Swami G replied.

"You make it all sound so easy," I said, frowning.

Henry Jones was quick to respond: "A healthy brow chakra gives us the power of discernment, so these things come naturally to us. I'm sure of this, too: People who neglect themselves or abuse their bodies don't have open brow chakras. They haven't been discerning about the food they eat; the people with whom they associate; their exercise program; their meditations; or their spare time. I'm not judging them. I'm merely pointing out that it's wise to practice discernment!"

"Ah! Wisdom," Swami G said loudly, poking the air above his head with his finger. "This is by far the most essential aspect of the brow chakra."

"I'd love to hear your description of wisdom too, Swami G." He had a way with words, and I knew his explanation would be useful in our book.

He obliged me. "Wisdom is fun-taas-tick! It really is. Listen closely: Wisdom is a habit or disposition to thinking and acting with the highest degree of adequacy under any given circumstance. This implies a possession, or seeking of knowledge, of the given circumstances, and this involves an understanding of people, things, events and situations, and the willingness, and the ability, to apply perceptions, judgments and actions in keeping with an understanding of what is the right course of actions."

Swami G's eyes twinkled more mischievously than ever before. "Oh yes, this explanation comes directly from this Wikipedia too. Isn't it fun-taas-tick what you can find on this Internet? It goes on to say – and let me get this right – 'Wisdom often requires control of one's emotional reactions, so that universal principles, values, reason and knowledge prevail to determine one's actions. In short, wisdom is a disposition to find the truth coupled with an optimum judgment as to right actions.' This could've been written by a swami, don't you think?" He chuckled until his shoulders shook like Juju Banks.

"It sounds complicated," I said.

"It doesn't have to be," Henry Jones replied. "It's not rocket science! At a basic level, we receive wisdom through our life experiences. For instance:

If we eat something that disagrees with our bodies, we feel poorly, so we make that connection and we don't eat it again. It's simple. But for people with blocked brow chakras, it doesn't work like that. Some people love to drink coffee, even though it makes them anxious. Some people eat dairy products even through it blocks their sinuses. Some people eat lots of sugar, even though they are overweight. Some people drink too much alcohol even though it makes them act stupid or become aggressive."

"Shouldn't this be common sense?" I asked.

"No, my friend, you're missing the point here. Not applying common sense, especially when it's good for you, is unwise. Said another way, it shows a lack of wisdom. You see, we often intuitively know what's best for us, but we do the complete opposite. This inability to tune into our abstract intuition is another sign of a blocked brow chakra."

"This is quite correct. An open brow chakra does enable us to develop abstract intuition," Swami G said.

"What's that?"

"Oh, gracious me! Abstract intuition is fun-taas-tick! Tell him more, Henry."

"It's an attribute that enables us to arrive at a concept or conclusion without going through a logical process."

"Wikipedia?"

"No. That's 100% Henry Jones," Henry Jones said, polishing his knuckles on his chest. "Let me try to give you an example. You can stand in front of a buffet table and identify the foods to avoid just by looking at them. You don't know the ingredients, but something inside you tells you to pass. Here's another one: You're invited to attend an event, but you decline the offer because you intuitively know there'll be substance abuse and you don't want to partake in it. This sixth sense of what is good or bad for us is a powerful internal guidance mechanism. When our brow chakra is open, we're aware of it, and can tune into it to steer us in the right direction. In short, when our brow chakra is open, we become self-conscious and we can act on it. This is a spiritual breakthrough. Most people don't get to this level of self-awareness. How many people do you know who are concerned about their weight or health, but can't stop eating junk food? Plenty, right? Need I say more?"

"It's crystal clear now. Thank you. So, how can I unblock my brow chakra?"

Swami G opted to answer: "To open the brow chakra, we must look for the difference between truth and illusion."

"How can I tell them apart?"

"Don't look outside for what is real. Rather, look within."

I frowned even harder.

"You should try this approach to life, Young One: Shift your awareness to your internal dialogue. Detach from yourself and observe your thoughts and feelings. By practising this technique, you'll learn to 'watch' your thinking before you act. In other words: Become conscious of yourself."

"This wasn't my thing either, until I met Henry Jones," I confessed.

"An unwillingness to look within is yet another sign of a blocked brow chakra," Swami G said. "If you had to guess why anyone wouldn't want to look within, what would you guess?"

I shrugged.

"Fear," Swami G sang.

"Of what?"

"Truth," Henry Jones answered.

"Please explain."

"Sometimes we refuse to accept our inner truth, even though it's glaringly obvious to everyone else. In these cases, the ego-mind is always in control. Always! Let me give you an example. Some people are homosexual. Their sexual preference is obvious to all, but they don't 'come out' because they're afraid of the consequences conjured up by their ego-minds."

It was a good example. I had a colleague who got married in an attempt to show his family and friends he wasn't gay, but it was futile. He was clearly gay and divorce was inevitable. I had my own issues to deal with, and Swami G was on to me: "Tell me, Young One, are you avoiding facing the truth in some aspect of your life? Are your internal alarm bells ringing, but you're just not answering?"

I nodded sheepishly.

"Do you do this often?"

I did not stop nodding.

"Do you ever experience anxiety, mood swings, irritability, depression or insomnia?"

"Yup!"

"What about headaches, especially in the center of your brow?"

"Uh-huh?"

"Oh, gracious me! These are sure signs that your brow chakra is blocked and dysfunctional. Is there a better way for you to live? You bet! Unblock your brow chakra and discover it for yourself."

"Tell him what else we can do to unblock our brow chakra," Henry Jones chimed.

Swami G pressed his hands together. "Our imagination is a powerful tool for unblocking our brow chakra. We can develop it, you know. It's like a muscle. The more we use it, the more powerful it becomes."

"Are you referring to visualization?"

"Oh yes, it's fun-taas-tick, too!"

"Henry Jones taught me this technique in the cabin."

"Good job, Henry! Well done." Swami G turned to me. "I should give you a word of caution here: If I were you, Young One, I would stop watching so much television. Television does nothing for your imagination. In fact, it probably destroys it. Instead of being glued to that box, you should read a book, write a novel, draw a picture, invent a widget, or make something with your own hands. The important thing is to trigger your imagination. Visualize, fantasize and dream! That is the ticket to a healthy, spinning brow chakra."

"You should imagine yourself well, since you want to create this reality," Henry Jones suggested, giving me a play punch on the arm.

"I'll let you in on a secret," Swami G whispered. "To make our imagination an even more powerful reality-making tool, we should employ all of our senses. We shouldn't just create pictures in our minds, Young One. We should go deeper, and ask ourselves: What do I see? What do I hear? What do I smell? What do I taste? What do I feel? When we imagine in fine detail, we stimulate our brow chakra, and it functions better and projects our internal world into our external world faster and brighter. What we imagine, we will manifest. This includes healing our body!"

"Ooh, that reminds me, what organs does your brow chakra affect, Swami G?" Henry Jones asked.

Swami G slapped his forehead. "The brain; pituitary and pineal gland; ears; eyes; nose; and central nervous system."

I found myself rubbing my forehead again, hoping to open my third eye. No, the flame of my spirit didn't come shining through, but I felt better for doing it. It gave me hope, and I liked it.

"So, what's next?"

The crown chakra

"Ah, that's the spirit, Young One. Keep pushing on. We're nearly there. Six down and one to go! Last, but not least, let's discuss your crown chakra," Swami G said, patting the top of his head. "You will find it …"

"… on top of your head," I said, finishing his sentence.

He chuckled. "You're quite correct, Young One. You'll be pleased to know that our crown chakra is the gateway to our soul and our direct connection to spirit. Its primary function is to process our thoughts and feelings that relate to our spirituality. The aspects of spirituality that are associated to our crown chakra are devotion; inspiration; mystical connections; creativity; beauty; spiritual insight and vision."

I listened carefully.

"When our crown chakra is open, we're connected to our spiritual nature, so we naturally integrate spiritual principles into our life, and as spiritually-centered people, we seek a connection with the Divine in everything we do. This practice draws us closer to the Higher Power, the Absolute Truth, the Great Spirit, that governs all existence."

As he said these words, he lifted his hands like an evangelical preacher and looked upwards. Unfortunately, his words of wisdom were wasted on me. I didn't fully understand what he was talking about. I'd always had an estranged relationship with God. The closest I'd come to finding God was during my three-day vision quest.

"I used to be atheist until recently," I confessed, shrugging my shoulders.

Swami G's face filled with compassion. He looked genuinely saddened by my comment. Then he did a peculiar thing. He reached out and fluffed up my hair. He didn't pat my head or run his fingers through my hair. No, he fluffed it, like he was messing it up. When I was a kid, I had a weird uncle who would mess up my hair every time he saw me. He committed suicide, I think, and no one had fluffed my hair since. I just stared at Swami G. My fringe flopped forward. I didn't dare straighten it. He never explained his actions to me. After a while, he broke the awkward silence with a real humdinger: "Do you fear death?"

I looked around anxiously. "Sure, who doesn't?"

It suddenly occurred to me that I was talking to a Swami, a holy man. Why would he fear death?

He brushed my question aside like an old woman sweeps a dead mouse from her kitchen. "Another sure sign that one's crown chakra is blocked is a fear of death. This is brought on by an estrangement from God. I can tell you this, Young One: A blocked crown chakra makes us feel cut off from our spirituality and disconnected from the Great Spirit. This is unhealthy for us. We must be connected to the Divine creative energy within us, or we can't co-create our reality. This is obviously a problem if we want to create a reality in which we enjoy radiant health and vitality every day for the rest of our lives. Wouldn't you agree?"

"Yes, I agree."

"Fun-taas-tick! True creativity comes from the Divine. When our crown chakra is open, we're able to see Divine beauty in everything, and we become aware of our ability to create beauty around us. This is a fun-taas-tick gift from the Great Spirit. When we indulge in this practice, the life experiences we create for ourselves are filled with love, regardless of our personal circumstances. When others persecute us, we feel great compassion. When times are dark, we trust that light will follow. This is a fun-taas-tick approach to life, wouldn't you agree?"

"I guess so."

"You guess so?" Henry Jones exclaimed. "What does your inner wisdom tell you?"

I shrugged.

Swami G spoke softly. "Don't worry, Young One, we can show you how to tap into the vast reservoirs of universal wisdom within you by opening your crown chakra. This is a source of tremendous power, and therefore tremendously important. Make no mistake about it: Wisdom is essential for healing to take place. Tell him why, Henry."

"You need to be wise about the choices you make and the actions you take," Henry Jones announced.

"That was a fun-taas-tick answer, Henry," Swami G trumpeted and then turned to face me. "It's our inner wisdom that lets us know we're loved by the Great Spirit. The Great Spirit resides in us. We're a reflection of God. We're made in His image, so He must love us. It's totally absurd to think otherwise. Be wise, Young One. It's wisdom that gives us the power to honour the Great Spirit in us. Tell him how we do this, Henry."

"By loving ourselves," he replied.

"We're not talking about a superficial love that inspires us to spoil ourselves with nice things. Or vanity, either. We're talking about a deep and profound love that emanates from the very core of our being. Come closer to me," Swami G instructed in an even softer voice. I shuffled closer.

"What I'm about to tell you is the most important piece of information that you'll hear from me. This knowledge is by far the most important, significant and powerful wisdom that we'll share with you." He leaned in towards me while wobbling his head. "We have Godliness in us, Young One, and our body is a temple. When we treat our body badly, we dishonour the Godliness in us. When we treat others badly, we disrespect the Godliness in them."

He sat back and let me chew on it. Once or twice, I opened my mouth to speak, but decided it was best to keep it shut. Henry Jones and Swami G sat quietly with their eyes closed. I did my best to process his statement. I thought of all the people whom I'd insulted, belittled, humiliated and abused over the years. It made me nauseous. No wonder I was sick.

Swami G was kind enough not to prolong my torture. He opened one eye and said: "Tell me, do you feel lonely, even when you're surrounded by people?"

I could barely nod, never mind talk.

He spoke in a low voice. "If we can't see the Godliness in ourselves, we'll not see it in others. When our crown chakra is open, we don't think of ourselves as being separate from our fellow man. We realize that the separateness we once felt is just a preoccupation of our ego-mind. Instead, we're able to tune into the interconnectedness of all things. We feel a sense of oneness with our fellow man, the universe, and the Great Spirit. This enables us to experience inner peace. Please, tell me why you think peace is so important on a healing journey?" Swami G looked at me expectantly, but I still couldn't talk. My mind was completely blank. I turned to Henry Jones for help.

He mouthed one word "Dis-ease."

My dam wall broke and the memories came flooding back. We'd discussed dis-ease in the car ride to the cabin, and we must've spoken about the importance of peace on a healing journey at least a hundred times since then. I'd been reciting the affirmations Henry Jones had given me every day. I suddenly recalled Henry Jones's exact words: 'When your mind returns to a natural, peaceful, loving state, your body will soon follow.' I managed to recite this sentence despite the enormous lump in my throat.

"Fun-taas-tick answer, Young One. This is the reason it's so important to open our crown chakra. There's a vast reservoir of healing energy available to you. Your spirituality is the key to accessing it. You must find your inner peace in order to find your spirituality. Find your spirituality, and you will find your healing."

With that, my inner resistance crumbled. I knew the time had come to end the conflict that raged inside of me. I'd been at war with the world around me for far too long. I needed peace of mind. More than anything else, I wanted my body to return to a natural, peaceful, loving state. My sickness had brought me to this point. I learned by the sword, and I was grateful for it. But, it was time to let go of the struggle. At last, the battle was coming to an end. Yes, I gave in. I surrendered to the process.

"You're right. That's exactly what I need. Please help me," I groaned, wiping a single tear from my cheek.

Swami G rubbed my back in big, round circles without saying a word. He waited patiently for me to collect myself. I fought back the tears. Only when he thought I was ready for more did he continue. "To open our crown chakra, we must start living in the present moment. When we become conscious of the here and now, we discover a new spiritual freedom."

"Freedom," I muttered under my breath, shaking my head. The concept eluded me. I was stuck with a sick body, tied up in remorse, clinging to my job, and hanging on to Henry Jones as though my life depended on it. What freedom did I have?

In that moment, Swami G gave me the best advice of my life. "You should find your life purpose," he said.

This was an 'aha' moment for me. The light bulb went on. I knew instantly that was what I'd been missing all along. I worked hard for a boss I didn't like, publishing books that offered no value, blaming the world for my lot in life. I'd become a mean, grumpy bastard because my life had no purpose. I wasn't following my heart. I knew it, and all of a sudden, I was absolutely convinced that was a big part of my problem. My proof lay in the fact that since I'd met Henry Jones I'd been following my heart. I really believed the book we were writing together would add tremendous value to its readers. I'd discovered my life's purpose. A broad smile broke on my face, like the Sun appears from behind a storm cloud. This realization changed everything!

Henry Jones and Swami G were unaware of my breakthrough. They couldn't see the tears streaming down my cheeks. Their eyes were closed, looking within. I guess they didn't hear my panting either. They pressed on.

396

"Our crown chakra flourishes when we're devoted to our life purpose. Devotion is essential, Young One. We can't achieve anything substantial and significant without devotion to its attainment."

"This is especially true when it comes to healing your body," Henry Jones added. "You must be devoted to your healing journey. Devotion is a healing force. The more you practise it, the stronger it gets. Take meditation and prayer, for example. It's essential to make time to meditate and pray each day. When you set aside time to meditate and pray, you develop precognition. Precognition is a sense of knowingness about your future. If you want to know that you will heal your body, meditate or pray each day. Devotion is the key here. To further express your devotion, you should write down your meditations and prayers. There is no better way to define them. That's why I gave you a Notebook. Use it, okay?"

I promised.

Swami G stepped in. "Fun-taas-tick. I only have one final piece of advice for you: To open your crown chakra, find a medium that allows you to be creative. Seriously, if you seek spiritual healing, then you absolutely must find a way to release your creativity. Creativity is a spiritual force. Why do you think we call God the ultimate Creator? It doesn't really matter how you express your creativity. You can paint, draw, sing, perform, write – just be open to whatever wants to be expressed through you. Who cares what it looks like, or sounds like? Just do it. As you begin to create, you release the creative energy within you. This is the same energy that helps you to create the reality you desire. To create a healthy, healed body, you must harness it and use it. Then it will work for you."

"What part of our body is affected by our crown chakra?" Henry Jones prompted.

"Oh, gracious me, I nearly forgot to tell you this essential information. My humblest apologies. Our crown chakra affects our central nervous system, muscular system and skin. So, if we have problems in any of these areas on our bodies, then we should work on opening this chakra point."

And with that, we were done. Yes, we'd systematically worked through all seven chakra points, and it'd been a fantastic learning experience. Honestly, I could've left the session right there and then, and my trip to India would've been worth it. But Henry Jones and Swami G were only getting started. The best was yet to come.

CHAPTER 21

FINDING MYSELF IN THE LAST PLACE I LOOKED

Much to my delight, Henry Jones suggested we take a comfort break. Swami G agreed. We'd been sitting cross-legged for a while and had drunk a lot of tea. I came back feeling refreshed and energized, ready for the next stage of my lesson.

Henry Jones stepped up to the crease first. "Okay, before we move on, let's recap the key points, to ensure you've understood the basics of spiritual healing."

"Shoot."

"How do you know if one or more of your chakra points is malfunctioning or blocked?" Henry Jones asked me.

"There are four, telltale signs. First of all, you'll have a problem with your physical health in a particular area of your body."

They nodded wildly.

"You may also feel off-center, unhinged, or out of balance mentally." Their eyes widened expectantly.

"You realize you have emotional issues from your past that you haven't released yet."

"And?"

"You're not always conscious of yourself – your true-self."

"By Jove, he's got it!" Henry Jones exclaimed ecstatically. I'm surprised they didn't jump up and dance in circles. Their attention and praise overwhelmed me. I felt my cheeks blush.

"You must keep in mind two polar principles. On the one hand, when your chakra points are healthy, they allow energy to flow freely through your body, which subsequently vitalizes and nourishes your internal system. On the other hand, when your chakra points become blocked or unbalanced, they prevent energy from flowing freely through your system, which subsequently causes illness."

"That has sunk in," I assured them.

"Excellent! Tell us, how can understanding the basic functions of your seven chakra points help you to identify the cause of your physical problem?"

I cleared my throat. "Each chakra point influences specific parts of our body, so by associating the area of our physical problem to the corresponding chakra point, we can identify the probable emotional, mental or spiritual problem that is causing the physical disturbance in our body. When we know which chakra point needs attention, we can start healing the problem directly at the source of energy. Right?"

"Precisely!" Henry Jones exclaimed. "The key to healing yourself lies in unblocking your body's internal energy system. Unless you sort out your chakra system, you will not get better. To heal yourself naturally, holistically and permanently, you must clear blockages in your chakra system."

"You can count on it."

"Good. Now that you've a basic understanding of the functions of your chakra points, your next step is to learn how to apply this knowledge to heal your body."

"Sounds great. I'm ready, let's go!" I replied enthusiastically.

Henry Jones paused for a moment to stare directly into my eyes, as if searching my soul. I didn't flinch, nor bat an eyelid. Satisfied that he'd seen in me whatever he was looking for, he gave Swami G a stern nod.

Search for harmony

"If you wish to restore your body to perfect health and bring true wellness into your life, then you should embark on a relentless search for harmony," Swami G said with a quirky grin.

"Harmony and healing reside in the same place. Where you find one, you will find the other."

"It's true," Henry Jones declared before I could answer. "Mental, emotional, spiritual and physical harmony creates the perfect environment for healing to occur. You need this."

"Okay, so how do I find harmony?" I asked impulsively.

"Meditate!" Swami G yelled out. I nearly jumped out of my skin. I'd grown accustomed to his calm and soothing voice. His outburst was totally unexpected.

"Trying to find harmony without meditation is like trying to swim without water. You can do your best, but you won't get very far."

While they chuckled, I put two and two together. "Meditation is essential because harmony exists within us, right?"

"Eureka!" Swami G shrieked excitedly. "Meditation allows one to look within, and harmony is found within. Ta-dah! If you look, you will find."

"I hope so," I remarked. "I'm afraid my stressful work situation knocked the harmony out of me years ago."

"Harmony is a quality of spirit, so it never leaves you. Even when you're stressed out to the maximum, harmony is within you, Young One, waiting to be restored."

"And, the best way to restore harmony is to balance your chakra points through meditation," Henry Jones was quick to add. "When all your chakras are whirling, open, bright and clean, your energy system is balanced and you feel harmonious. When even one chakra point is malfunctioning or blocked, your energy system is unbalanced, and you feel …"

"Inharmonious," I said, finishing his sentence. They looked bowled over.

"So, what should you do to heal your body, smarty-pants?" Henry Jones quipped.

"My goal should be to raise all my energy centers to the same heightened level of functioning."

"And what's the best way to do that?"

"Through meditation," I said with confidence.

"Exactly! Meditation is the medicine of natural healing. There's no better tonic for your soul. Each dose leads us further down the pathway of spiritual healing."

"So, when you say: Become conscious of yourself and look within, you're actually saying that I should become spiritual and meditate?" I asked.

"That's right. You hit the nail on the head," Henry Jones replied. "I remember being very apprehensive about attending a meditation class for the first time. I wasn't at all sure of what to expect. My Christian upbringing had told me that meditation was evil. I was told to pray, not meditate."

"Why did you go?" I asked, seeking to understand his motivation.

"I guess I went because I was searching for something inside me. Thank goodness I did, because meditation helped me to find it. That first meditation class was a real game-changer."

"So, what happened?"

"We sat in a circle. I immediately noticed that the room was filled with perfectly ordinary people from all walks of life. Many of them had a palpable peace about them. Their eyes were calm and clear. I couldn't quite put my finger on it at the time, but they had a deep spiritual quality that I admired very much. Five minutes into the class and I had completely forgotten my concerns about being lured into a weird cult. The process was slap-your-forehead-simple! All I learned to do was breathe deeply while focusing inward. That's it! But, what I discovered changed my life. I'm not exaggerating! It can change yours, too."

"Interested?" Swami G asked me, lifting his bushy eyebrows up and down. His eyes twinkled.

I nodded enthusiastically.

"Great! Then let us tell you more about meditation right now," he said in a tantalizing manner.

"Go ahead."

Why you should meditate

Swami G dived in. "If you want to get better, listen up. On a healing journey, meditation is an absolute must! The benefits of meditating are fun-taas-tick. Trust me. Meditation is calming and soothing. It's a subtle, passive exercise that positively affects our whole being. It's astonishingly good for us; easy to do; free; and only takes a few minutes a day. And, it makes us feel great afterwards!" He paused to inhale deeply. The smile on his face grew bigger. I lingered on his words, eagerly anticipating his next line. "Wait. There's more to it. I can go on and on. Believe me. Meditation also keeps us positive and proactive; it gives us inner strength; it connects us directly to the healing energy within us; it's brilliant for helping us to deal with discomfort and pain; and it enables our mind and body to relax so that our higher Divine self can communicate with us on a conscious level. It may be soft and seldom at first, but I assure you, Young One, over time, you'll experience powerful moments of consciousness."

"How long will this take?"

"Be patient. Don't expect cosmic fireworks immediately. If that's what you're thinking, then you've got the wrong idea. It's highly unlikely that you'll get it first time. Meditation gradually introduces you to profound internal peace and harmony. You can't rush into it. It takes regular practice to find the bliss you seek. Oh sure, you'll feel relaxed and uplifted after your first session, but it goes much, much deeper than that. There exists an abundance of harmony and bliss within you. It's an unlimited reserve of healing energy. You can dive into it whenever you wish, and swim around like a child in a paddling pool on a hot summer's day for as long as you wish. No one can blow the whistle and tell you to get out of the pool," he chuckled heartily. "Try it. You'll be surprised at how quickly you'll cotton on to it. Stay committed and you'll become progressively more in tune with yourself. Keep an open mind and you'll discover something new each and every time you meditate."

"How often must I meditate?" I asked.

"You should get into the habit of meditating daily, Young One. Meditation is a discipline. It's better to meditate for 5 minutes a day than 20 minutes every other day," Swami G replied.

"Urgh!" Something about the word 'discipline' repelled me.

"That's your ego-mind gagging on the idea of giving up control," Henry Jones said. "Your ego-mind won't enjoy being disciplined at all when you first start meditating. Push through it!"

Swami G sent a mischievous look my way, while wagging his finger. "I must warn you, however, meditation is very catchy. When you get into it, you'll most likely do it for the rest of your life."

"He's not kidding," Henry Jones interjected. "There's something about altering the state of our consciousness that we humans find highly addictive. I think it's because we enter into the spiritual realms of the Divine when we alter our consciousness."

Swami G had his own ideas: "I think it's because we return to Source, to the Ultimate Truth, to the Great Spirit, and this is our deepest, intrinsic longing and desire."

"Is this desire for an altered state of consciousness the reason some people take drugs?" I asked curiously.

"Yes, but people who take drugs only think they have a 'spiritual' experience. I can assure you, taking drugs does not, and will never, put you in touch with anything that's Divine. Doing drugs is just a chemical experience. That's all. The only way to truly connect with the Divine is the natural way. Nothing beats a natural high! If you don't believe me, ask anyone in rehab whose life has been destroyed by drugs," Henry Jones snapped.

I must've hit a nerve. He looked mad as a snake.

Swami G folded over into a body position that would've snapped my hamstrings. He made it look easy.

Henry Jones collected himself. "So, drugs aside, you need to know how to alter your state of consciousness naturally. It's time for you to learn how to connect with the Divine within you."

Swami G swooped in: "You're about to discover a fun-taas-tick meditation to clean, clear, heal and balance your chakra points. More than that, this exercise will lead your mind to wells of tranquil healing energy, where you can bathe in spiritual ecstasy for as long as you like."

He pretended to do breaststroke, then backstroke. I knew I needed to experience this for myself. There could never be a better time or place for it. After all, I was with a genuine swami, in an ashram in India.

"Tell me more, please."

Swami G was happy to indulge me. "The objective of this chakra meditation is to connect your conscious mind to your internal energy system. When you become conscious of your internal universe, you make a connection to your true-self. This in turn unleashes the healing energy within you. It's this flow of energy that removes blockages from your chakra points."

"How often must I do this meditation?"

"Daily. It's that important. Especially on a healing journey!"

"For how long?"

"Once you've become familiar with this technique and you've cleansed and aligned your chakra points, you'll no longer have to follow the whole process in each session. With a little practice, you'll be able to send energy to your chakra points in seconds. Like topping up your battery with power surges. For instance, if ever you need to stand up for yourself, you can boost your personal power by sending energy to your solar plexus chakra. If you need to speak your truth, you can send energy to your throat chakra. In the instant you send energy to your energy centers, you connect your mind to your spirit. When you make time to meditate properly, you bathe your mind in spirit. That is first prize!"

I had to stretch my legs. They were cramping. Even with a pillow under my bum, I found it difficult to sit on the floor for a long period of time. I had pins and needles! Henry Jones and Swami G looked very comfortable and relaxed. I needed to practise more to be like them.

Henry Jones was sensitive to my discomfort. He tried to help me out of my predicament with some good advice: "If you find that your level of physical discomfort is distracting you from concentrating on your meditation, feel free to change position or wriggle your limbs. It also helps to curl and release your toes. But if you are in a group, try not to be a distraction to others."

I tried curling my toes. The relief was instant. Henry Jones, my hero!

"Be aware that your ego-mind will use this initial discomfort to trick you into losing focus. It doesn't want to give up control of anything – especially not to your true-self! Your ego-mind likes to watch TV. It likes to go out for burgers and chips. It likes to worry about stuff. Simply put: It likes constant stimulation and instant gratification. At the mere thought of meditating, you can almost hear your ego-mind throwing a tantrum!"

Henry Jones wasn't done yet. "Yes, your ego-mind is going to resist you meditating, especially when you're sick. As you know, when you're not feeling well, you're generally not in a good mood, and tend to feel sorry for yourself. In this state, your ego-mind tends to be uncooperative. Be prepared. When you first sit still and focus inward, your ego-mind is going to try to distract you. It'll come up with wayward ideas, flashes of inspiration, things to do, perturbing thoughts, erotic fantasies, whatever! Just ignore it! Focus on your breathing. Your ego-mind will eventually tire and give in to your true-self. When your true-self decides that it's time to sit cross-legged, breathe deeply and meditate, there's not a darn thing your ego-mind can do to stop you."

"Because my true-self is the ultimate ruler of my life!"

"Precisely. Now, to fully comprehend and appreciate this chakra healing meditation, you must experience it yourself. We're about to show you how to cleanse and align your chakra points through meditation. That is why we travelled to India. Are you ready now?" Henry Jones teased.

Cleanse and align your chakras

"I've never been readier for anything in my life."

"The basic principles are very simple. You can lie down on your back, or sit in a comfortable position in a private, sacred space."

Swami G was in a deep, meditative state. Then, all of a sudden, he spoke: "Sitting is better. Health permitting, of course! It may help you to keep your eyes closed, too, Young One."

"How come?"

"This shuts out distractions, and allows you to focus inward," Swami G advised without opening his eyes or making the slightest movement.

"Thank you, both of you," I said gratefully.

"Okay. Let's try it now," Swami G suggested.

I took a deep breath and closed my eyes.

Swami G led the way. "Become conscious of the weight of your body resting against the ground. Allow yourself to feel safe and relaxed. Straighten your spine. Slightly lift your sternum and your chin. Drop your shoulders and arms. Breathe slowly and deeply. Feel your chest rising and falling with every breath."

It suddenly became obvious to me that Swami G had taught Henry Jones to meditate. I recognized the words and the tone.

Swami G continued: "The secret doorway to inner peace and harmony is your breath. As you inhale, fill your lungs completely. Take in as much oxygen as you need to feel satisfied. If you can, gently hold your breath for a second or two before expelling the carbon dioxide from your lungs. This technique slows your breathing down, which calms you naturally. It also gives you more control over your breathing and improves concentration."

I tried it. It worked.

"When you must exhale, do so by gently blowing out the air between your lips. Try exhaling with a little more force than usual. As you breathe out, scan your body for tension and try to release it. Start at your toes. Can you relax them more? When they feel totally relaxed and heavy, move your attention to your ankles, then work your way up through your knees, thighs, stomach, chest, arms, hands, and finally your head. When you become good at this relaxation technique, you can achieve the same result by visualizing waves of energy flowing across your body. After some practice, you'll no longer need to consciously put yourself into a relaxed state of mind. You'll slip in to it like a comfy, old slipper."

That remark brought a smile to my face. I enjoyed Swami G's colloquialisms. I opened my eyes to gaze at him in wonder.

"Exhale completely before taking a new breath. Do this and you'll feel yourself gradually sinking into a deeper and deeper state of relaxation."

I was on my way.

"As a beginner, you may find your thoughts run away with you. That's okay! You probably needed to release this thought energy in order to relax fully. So, whenever you catch your mind wandering, simply return to focusing on your breathing."

I thought about what he said.

He paused while I scrambled to find the concentration I'd lost. How did he know? How can I stop myself from drifting off? Will he catch me out again? I wondered.

He continued: "There are many different types of meditation. All of them are good for you. Today, however, we want to share our two favorites with you. These are: Emptying your mind and guided meditation," Swami G said, pressing his hands together in the prayer position.

"We chose them because they go hand-in-hand on a healing journey," Henry Jones added. "One prepares you for the other."

"I'm not sure I follow," I replied.

"When your mind is clear, you have a blank canvas on which to paint the guided meditation," Swami G told me. "The first part is a bit tricky," he remarked, and then chuckled harder. Once the amusement wore off, he continued: "The first technique is self-explanatory. It focuses on clearing the mind of all thought. In a busy world filled with busy minds, it's easy to understand why this meditation is so popular. It brings relief."

"Can you imagine how peaceful you'd feel if you switched off the little voice in your head?" Henry Jones asked me.

Swami G took the gap: "I can assure you of this: It's fun-taas-tick to take a vacation from yourself, Young One. Five minutes seems like a summer holiday. Genuinely!"

"That sounds nice," I replied.

"It's much better than nice. It's blissful, Young One," he assured me. "Say, I've a fun-taas-tick idea. Why don't you give it a go right now? Stop what you're doing for a moment and clear your head. Go on. Try it"

I batted my eyelids. Panic set in. My vulnerability induced hysterical laughter in both of them. "I'm just kidding," Swami G chortled. I breathed a sigh of relief too soon.

"My friend, you'll soon discover that emptying your mind isn't that easy to do. Yes, for me too. I must admit, I tried this method when I first started meditating, but I wasn't any good at it. If your mind is anything like mine, then it's very busy. I'm constantly thinking. I can't help it. The little voice in my head always has something to say. Since I'm playing open cards here, I don't mind telling you that I still struggle to clear my mind, even after plenty of practice. I have to spend quite a while releasing my thoughts before I'm able to find true inner peace," Henry Jones admitted.

"It helps to focus your attention on the core of your being in your solar plexus, Young One. The mystics call this 'the seat of your soul'," Swami G advised.

This exercise, as it so happens, was easier explained than done.

Henry Jones put his hand on my leg. "It takes some people many years of regular practice to clear their minds through meditation. But, no matter how long it takes, you should strive towards it. The reward is definitely worth the effort."

"What kind of reward are you talking about?"

"You have to experience it for yourself."

"Can you give me a hint?"

"When you get it right, you'll discover pure bliss."

"It's fun-taas-tick!" Swami G declared, touching his index finger and thumb.

"Since this meditation will take a lifetime to perfect, and all we have is the present moment, I recommended we move on to guided meditations," Henry Jones suggested, sounding like a facilitator. "We want to manage our time with you carefully, Swami G."

He bowed his head. Henry Jones returned the gesture. I bowed, too. Swami G warmed his throat by making a humming sound. "This is a fun-taas-tick way to get into meditation. The technique is very easy to master. You'll get the hang of it in two flicks of a lamb's tail."

Henry Jones and I exchanged a quizzical look. It was an odd expression for a Swami.

"All you need to do is use your imagination. Using your imagination is like letting your mind out to play," he said with a big smile on his face.

"Keeping your mind occupied is much easier than emptying it," Henry Jones explained.

Swami G chuckled knowingly. "Henry is right. Our minds thrive on creativity. They're capable of calling up and projecting an infinite number of fun-taas-tick mental images. Your imagination can see multitudes of colors, shapes, sizes, patterns, objects and designs from varied angles and unlimited perspectives, instantly."

"Wow! I hadn't thought of it like that."

"We simply can't afford to take our imaginations for granted, Young One. Our imagination is the most powerful tool we can use to connect with our inner selves in order to create our reality."

"And to heal our bodies," Henry Jones inserted. "You should revere it."

"Okay, I'm convinced. Where do we start?"

Swami G applauded. "A skilled facilitator takes you on a journey of the mind using mental imagery. All you have to do is listen carefully to the words and let your imagination follow the story."

"Like the Rock-Tree exercise we did earlier?"

"Precisely! That was easy enough, wasn't it?"

"Sure. No problem."

"Do you remember listening to bedtime stories as a child? Can you recall how vivid your imagination used to be?"

I nodded enthusiastically.

"I can't say I'm surprised, Young One. Children have fun-taas-tick imaginations. This makes them very good at following guided meditations. You should be like a child. Imagine anything is possible and believe it."

"What do we do first?"

"You need to find your private sanctuary," Swami G told me.

"Eh?"

"We all have a private sanctuary to go to when we meditate," he replied. "This unique 'mental environment' is the most private place on Earth for you. Only you can access it."

"How come?"

"Because the only way to get there is through your imagination, Young One."

"Oh, so it doesn't really exist?"

"Oh, it exists in another realm alright! And you're about to discover it for yourself."

"It's imperative that you find this place if you want to heal your body. It is where harmony and healing reside," Henry Jones added.

Swami G agreed with him. "Quite right! It's also a place of comfort, security, safety, peace and tranquility. But the really great thing about it is that once you've been there, you can always find your way back. You can visit it as often as you like, and access is free. Come on, Young One. Let's go in search of your private sanctuary right now, shall we?"

Henry Jones and Swami G effortlessly shuffled into a meditation pose. I tried to copy them, but my legs couldn't cross as theirs did. I fell over backwards.

"I guess it takes years of practice," I mumbled awkwardly.

"You can start by sitting normally," Swami G replied with a grin. "The important thing is to be comfortable."

I sat cross-legged on the floor with a cushion under my bum. They waited for me to settle before continuing with the meditation exercise.

He began: "As you're sitting there, relax your body using the techniques you've already learned. Breathe deeply. When you feel completely relaxed, raise your hand and I'll begin."

When I was ready, I gave him the sign.

"Fun-taas-tick. Now, listen to my voice, and allow your mind to picture my words. I'll pause for a breath between each sentence. That will give you the time to fully absorb the content. Focus on this process completely, from start to finish.

"Imagine you're walking through a rolling meadow on a cool summer's day. The grass beneath your feet is green and lush. The meadow stretches out in front of you for as far as your eyes can see. There's a bright-blue sky above your head. It's dappled with white, fluffy clouds. A cool breeze brushes against your skin. The air is fresh. You're feeling very happy and very relaxed. Now look ahead of you. In the distance, you will see a small wall. It runs along the horizon, from the far left to the far right. There is no way around it, but there is a small gateway directly in front of you. Make your way towards it. As you get to the gateway, you notice seven steps leading down the other side.

"Stand on the first step and get a sense of the landscape around you. Here, make a connection to the physical world. It helps to imagine the feeling of your feet pressing against the step. Your interaction with the physical world confirms you exist on Earth at this time. Your presence is a glorious manifestation of your existence, your being, your consciousness. Allow yourself to feel the joy that comes from being alive. Let it bubble up from within you." Swami G's voice was calm and soothing. His strong Indian accent was gentle on my ears. It had a warm and inviting tone.

"When you feel ready, stand on the second step and get a sense of your well-being. Here, let yourself dwell on the good things in your life. Think of all the things in your life for which you can be grateful. Put a smile on your face. It will help you to find pleasure in your existence, your being, your consciousness.

"When you're ready, stand on the third step. Here, as you inhale, imagine you are drawing in energy from the universe. Let it fill you. This energy makes you feel powerful and strong. Clench your stomach muscles and focus on the feeling you get in your core. This helps you to tune in to your inner strength. You can use your personal power to control your thoughts and feelings. This enables you to express your individuality. You have the power to be who you truly are. Claim it."

We sat in silence for a few minutes. Swami G was in no rush. His breathing was deep and constant. I picked up his rhythm. My chest expanded to its fullest. I felt it ache from the influx of air. I let the air out, slipping deeper into the meditation with each exhale.

"When you're ready, stand on the fourth step. Here, allow yourself to feel full of love. Feel it flowing from your heart, into your body, and into everything around you. Let your existence, your being, and your consciousness be entirely saturated with love. Tune in to the peace and harmony within you. Try to relax your body and calm yourself even more. In this state of love, allow yourself to feel great compassion for all living things. Send compassion and love in to the universe and know that you will receive love in return."

At that point, I got pins and needles in my left leg. I had to stretch it. My body ached, even with a soft pillow under me. I shuffled around like a man with ants in his pants. Henry Jones and Swami G didn't move a muscle. I admired them.

"When you're ready, stand on the fifth step. Here, open the channel of communication between your internal world and your external world by humming. Loosen your voice by making this sound: 'Aaah!'"

Henry Jones let out a long sound. I felt obliged to go after him. I gave it my best shot. I didn't hold back at all. I heard my voice carry through the room.

"Very good! Now, imagine this sound connects you to the universe. Try to get a sense of oneness. There is an inseparable interconnectedness between all things. Accept and embrace this feeling now.

"When you're ready, stand on the sixth step. Here, try to look at the world through your third eye in the centre of your brow. Use your internal consciousness to connect with this spot. Imagine you are tuning in to your intuition. Allow this sixth sense to give you a feeling of your future. Your future is what you make it. You can make of it what you will. Your life choices are yours alone. Do you know what is right for you and what is wrong for you? Try to connect with your power of discernment and let it guide you. Dwell on your new-found spiritual principles. This will connect you to your higher self and all will be well. Try to feel this wellness now."

My head rushed. A strange giddiness came over me, and I felt a peculiar sensation on my brow. It felt as though I was frowning, but I wasn't. I got the urge to rub my forehead, but I was too self-conscious to move. My eyebrows raised themselves involuntarily instead.

"When you're ready, stand on the seventh step. Here, become aware of the beauty within you and your ability to create beauty around you. This raises your self-awareness. You have the god-given power to create the reality you desire for yourself and your loved ones by projecting beautiful thoughts and feelings into the universe through meditation. Look within. Try to get a sense of your true spiritual nature. Imagine you are becoming one with yourself and everything around you." Swami G let several minutes of silence slip by before he continued.

"You have now entered a state of super consciousness. You're in a deep state of relaxation, and you feel connected to your spirit. Look through your mind's eye. Directly in front of you is a small garden. It's very beautiful – a true wonder of nature. A stream trickles nearby. The sun's rays filter down through the trees and shine on to a patch of lush green grass. Make your way into the brightest spot and sit down. Get a sense of your surroundings. Allow your imagination to explore the space around you. Through your mind's eye, picture the garden in great detail. See all the shapes and colors. As your garden reveals itself to you, make a point of remembering it. Take your time. Allow yourself to feel safe and secure. You're in your private sanctuary."

I was truly amazed. Everything Swami G and Henry Jones told me was true. I could see a garden. It did exist in my consciousness, and it was every bit as beautiful as they said it would be. I felt extremely satisfied. This was why I'd flown halfway across the world. I was searching for a place of inner stillness and tranquility; a place where peace and harmony were palpable. A place of healing. In that moment, I knew I'd found it.

Several more minutes passed before Swami G spoke: "When you're ready to leave, bless this spot. Give thanks for the special time you shared with yourself, then make your way up the stairs and back across the meadow to where you started. It's not necessary to meditate on each stair as you leave, but it's important to leave your private sanctuary and return to your starting point. If you stop meditating without making the return journey from your private sanctuary, you may feel incomplete, unfulfilled and disoriented afterwards. Also, when you return to your private sanctuary in the future, you may feel the sanctity of it has been compromised in some way. You don't want anything to rob you of the joy that this experience offers you. When you reach your starting point and you feel the meditation is over, open your eyes."

Henry Jones was the first to speak. "Was that enjoyable, or what?"

"It certainly was a rush," I breathed, slowly coming to my senses. "Thank you."

"You're welcome," he replied humbly. "Now, go and drink some water and return to us. We want to teach you a fun-taas-tick meditation technique that'll bring your chakra points back into balance and restore them to perfect health," Swami G said.

I gulped down a whole glass of water without taking a breath, refilled it and drank another glass. I was exceptionally thirsty. It felt good to stretch my legs, too. When I re-entered the room, Swami G had folded himself into a position that would make most contortionists blush. "Come sit down beside me, Young One," he instructed, patting my pillow. I appreciated his warm hospitality and told him so.

"It's my sincerest pleasure," he responded, unravelling himself. I took a seat between them and then looked up expectantly. Swami G rubbed his hands together. "You're about to learn how to heal your body by healing your chakra points. You should practise this technique at least once a day during your spiritual healing program, as Henry said. After successfully completing your healing journey, we recommend you do it regularly to keep your chakra system functioning optimally. Okay?"

"Okay," I promised.

"Fun-taas-tick. You travelled such a long way to get here and we don't want you to go away disappointed. We'll show you the technique shortly, but before we get into it, let us run through a few fundamentals. First of all, your breathing should be constant, slow, deep and rhythmical. Don't force it. Just fall into a natural breathing pattern that's comfortable for you. Secondly, it's essential to feel secure, grounded and relaxed before you begin working on your chakras, while also being in an elevated, or heightened, state of consciousness. I suggest you go back to your private sanctuary. You know how to get there now. Follow the path that has been created in your mind. It'll lead you back to your private sanctuary."

"I'd like to add a few more points here," Henry Jones called out. "One: Make sure you've enough time to complete the meditation process. You don't want to be interrupted, yeah? Two: The basic steps are repeated for each chakra point. We'll show you the steps now, but you should learn the sequence by heart, so that you can keep the meditation flowing when you're alone. Three: Each chakra point has its own color. You'll have to memorize the colors of the chakras, because they play a key role in this chakra meditation. Four: When you do this exercise for the first time, it's important to set aside enough time to do the whole meditation, starting at your root chakra and ending at your crown chakra. The full meditation takes 30 to 60 minutes to complete. You must be committed to doing the whole process, or you shouldn't start it at all."

"I'm totally committed to finishing this process now," I declared.

Henry Jones started up again: "Just so we're clear, today we'll run through the full chakra cleansing meditation, but in our book, you should advise the readers to meditate on one chakra point a day for seven days, before they do the full meditation. This approach will provide them with a deeper understanding of each chakra point and give them a chance to prepare their answers to the questions that relate to each chakra point. That way, they can meditate on their prepared answers during the full meditation. Got it?"

"I won't forget," I assured him.

"Good. Once you've done the full meditation, you can meditate on one chakra point at a time in a session, for about 10 to 20 minutes. That's easy enough, isn't it?"

I nodded.

Clear and balance your chakras

"Okay then, Young One, take a deep breath. You're about to learn how to clean, clear and balance your chakra points." Swami G clapped his hands together. "Let's take a few minutes to find our way back to our private sanctuary. Sit peacefully, correct your posture, close your eyes, breathe comfortably, and relax your body."

After some time had passed, Swami G began. "We always start by treating our root chakra, because it's the base of our energy system. Then we work upwards to our crown chakra. Take a deep breath. As you inhale, bring your attention to your root chakra. Imagine a glowing, red ball of energy spinning around and around at the base of your spine. Feel the energy growing stronger as you focus on it. Can you see and feel it?"

I nodded.

"Fun-taas-tick. When you're ready, slide your tongue into the heavenly pool on the roof of your mouth. Take another deep breath through your nose. As you do so, slowly draw the energy from the red ball up your spine towards your head, on the backside of your body. Fill your head with the energy from your root chakra until you can't inhale anymore air. Then, as you exhale, imagine this energy flowing down the front of your body towards the base of your spine. With each new breath, simply allow your internal consciousness to move up your back, along your spine, and then down your front towards your root chakra, until it reconnects with the red ball of energy. Each time you complete a cycle, the energy grows stronger and more powerful. Keep repeating this breathing exercise until you 'feel' the intensity of the energy inside the ball reach its maximum. Trust yourself: You'll know when you're at that point."

Swami G let a few minutes pass. I imagined the red ball of energy at the base of my spine.

"Now that the red ball of energy is at its maximum intensity and power, allow your internal consciousness to settle inside it. Try to become one with this red ball of energy. Once you're comfortably centered inside the glowing, spinning ball, feel yourself opening like a flower. In your mind's eye, picture the petals slowly opening in your mind's eye. As you do this, imagine the energy spiraling outwards from the center of the open, red ball. As it spirals outwards, allow your consciousness to expand past your body, through the aura that surrounds you, and outwards into the universe."

Swami G's voice was soft and melodic. His words were calming and soothing. "Now, let us take this exercise to the next level. Imagine a red mist emanating from the spinning, open, red ball of energy. Picture it in your mind's eye. See the red mist pouring out of the ball of energy, filling the space around you. Do you see this mist now?" Swami G asked.

It looked like someone had plugged a smoke machine into my imagination and flicked the switch.

"Yes," Henry Jones and I chanted together.

"Fun-taas-tick! Once the red mist is thick, begin to think about the issues in your life that relate to your root chakra. Ponder the answers to these important questions: Am I happy with my physical world? (What can I do to make myself even happier with my physical world?) Am I happy with my body? (What can I do to make myself even happier with my body?) Am I stable and secure? (What can I do to feel even more stable and secure?) Do I have enough structure, stability and order in my life? (What can I do to have even more structure, security and order in my life?) Am I impatient in certain areas of my life? (Where do I need even more patience in my life?) Don't project your answers. Rather, allow them to emerge. Don't try to influence them either. Just let them be. Observe your answers, as if you were watching someone else's mind. Pay attention to how you feel physically, emotionally and mentally. The areas that need your attention will come to you."

Several minutes passed. Unfortunately, it wasn't enough time for me to think about my answers to all of his questions. I knew I'd have to do this exercise over again. On my own, I could give myself all the time I needed to answer the questions properly. Even so, some answers came to me in a blinding flash. I didn't have to think about them. They just popped out.

"Next, imagine your answers to these questions clinging to the red mist around you. It absorbs all your thoughts and feelings about these issues. Feel how they weigh the mist down. When you're done, use your hands to slowly begin scooping all the red mist into a new energy ball, as if you were making a snowball of red mist. The mist wants you to collect it. It comes to you effortlessly. When you've gathered all the red mist, hold the new ball of energy between your hands. Allow your fingertips and wrists to connect. In your mind's eye, be sure you have gathered all the red mist, including all of your related thoughts and feelings. The space around you is clear. Then, focus all your attention on the new ball of red energy. Intensify your concentration until it feels like the new ball can't hold any more energy. In this moment, imagine that it instantly turns into a bright, white ball of energy. This light is so brilliant that it shines through your fingers and illuminates the space around you. This light is pure."

I saw it clearly in my imagination.

"Now, slowly and purposefully, lower your hands towards your root chakra, until your wrists rest against your body. Take a deep breath, and then slide your wrists apart, keeping your fingertips together. Imagine that you're inserting the new ball filled with brilliant, white light energy into the first ball of red energy. As you do so, they become one. The ball of white light energy doesn't replace the ball of red energy; it purifies it. Can you see how it glows red more luminously?"

I could barely nod.

"Fun-taas-tick! Now, we need to vitalize your body with this new, pure energy by repeating the breathing cycle. Bring your attention to your root chakra. Begin breathing in and out from it. As you inhale, feel the energy at the base of your spine growing stronger. As the energy grows stronger, visualize it as a bright, glowing ball of cleansed red energy. Imagine it spinning in a counter-clockwise direction. When you're ready, place your tongue into your heavenly pool and then draw the energy up your spine and into your head with each breath. As you exhale, allow your consciousness to move down your front, until it becomes centered in the glowing ball of cleansed, red energy. Repeat this exercise several times. Do it, over and over, until you feel the intensity and power of the energy inside the ball reach its maximum. You'll know when you have arrived at this point. Once there, let yourself become one with the cleansed, red ball of energy. Allow your internal consciousness to settle inside it. Once you're comfortably centered inside the glowing, spinning ball, feel yourself closing like a flower. In your mind's eye, picture the petals folding back into the tightest bud. Your root chakra has been cleared and cleansed," Swami G said.

He let us stay in the moment for a minute or two. "That's fun-taas-tick work. Well done, Young One."

"Thank you," I whispered too softly for him to hear. Perhaps I was talking to a higher power. Heaven knows. I've never felt so close to God. The hairs on the back of my neck stood on end and my body tingled.

Swami G started up once more. "When you're ready, Young One, we can move to the next energy center and repeat the same exercise. Only this time, we'll change the color of the energy ball and the mist to suit the corresponding chakra point. Obviously, we'll also focus our attention on the new energy center and meditate on the corresponding questions. We'll do this meditation, over and over, until we've treated all seven chakras. Okay?"

"Okay, I'm ready."

We proceeded to repeat the exact same process, word for word. All that changed were the colors and the questions.

We visualized an orange sacral chakra and asked these questions: Is my life filled with pleasure? (What can I do to have even more pleasure in my life?) Do I feel the abundance of the universe? (What can I do to feel the abundance of the universe even more?) Am I experiencing total well-being? (What can I do to experience even more well-being?).

We visualized a yellow solar plexus chakra and asked these questions: What is my gut telling me? (Where can I listen to my gut even more?) Am I using all my willpower to manifest my goals? (Where can I use willpower to manifest my goals even more?) Do I give up my personal power? If so, to whom and why? (What can I do to reclaim my personal power even more?)

We visualized a green heart chakra and asked these questions: Do I love unconditionally? (Where can I practice unconditional love even more?) Am I compassionate, affectionate, kind and caring? (Where can I be even more compassionate, affectionate, kind and caring?) Is my heart open? (What can I do to open my heart even more?)

We visualized a turquoise throat chakra and asked these questions: Am I having trouble being heard? (What can I do to be even more heard?) Am I speaking my truth? (What can I do to speak my truth even more?) Am I honest with others and myself? (What can I do to be even more honest with myself and others?)

We visualized an indigo brow chakra and asked these questions: Am I hearing the still, silent voice of intuition? (How can I listen to my intuition even more?) Do I need to liberate myself from delusion? (What can I do to liberate myself from delusion even more?) Can I see the connecting patterns in my life? (Where can I see the connecting patterns in my life even more?) What is the real meaning of things? (How can I understand the real meaning of things even more?)

We visualized a brilliant-violet crown chakra and asked these questions: Can I see beyond birth and death? (How can I see beyond birth and death even more?) Who am I? (How can I understand 'who am I' even more?) Am I fulfilling my destiny right now? (What can I do to fulfil my destiny even more?) Am I contributing to the evolution of humanity right now? (How can I contribute to the evolution of humanity even more?) Where do I need to apply wisdom in my life? (What can I do to apply wisdom in my life even more?) Do I feel my connection with the whole of the universe? (What can I do to feel my connection with the universe even more?)

Once we'd finished all seven chakra points, Swami G said: "Now, sit still for a minute or two. Let your mind rest and focus on your breathing. You don't want to rush to the end of this exercise, or you may feel unfulfilled afterwards. Take your time, relax fully, and allow yourself to soak up the experience."

I focused on my chest rising and falling, because my buttocks and legs were completely numb. I needed to stretch my legs badly. It'd been a lengthy session. I wasn't used to sitting cross-legged on the floor for such a long time.

"We're now going to close the chakra cleansing meditation," Swami G said. "This particular closing exercise is directly related to healing. It only takes a minute."

I inhaled deeply.

"Imagine that an angel is pouring a chalice filled with golden, healing energy into your crown chakra. As it fills up, the energy spills over into your brow chakra, then your throat chakra, then your heart, solar plexus, sacral and root chakras. Allow yourself to feel a smooth, languid sensation as this healing energy courses freely through each chakra point. By now, all your energy centers are full. They should be coupled together through the influx of golden, healing, light energy. Repeat to yourself, aloud or silently: 'I feel completely refreshed, calm and peaceful. I am full of vitality and energy.'"

I thought we were done but Swami G had one more card to play. "This last step is quick and easy, too. We're going to show you how to balance your chakra points. Listen carefully, Young One. Imagine two more balls of light energy – one deep in the core of the Earth, and the other directly above your head in outer space. Next, imagine there's a silver thread connecting these two balls of light energy. You're suspended on this silver thread. Picture it running from outer space down into your crown chakra, down the center of your body, linking your energy centers, and out your root chakra to the core of the Earth. Feel how this line separates the left from the right; the feminine from the masculine; the past from the future. Let your mind explore both sides. Rest here for a while. When enough time has passed, imagine that the silver thread is pulled tight. As it becomes taut, feel your chakra points aligning."

As he said these words, my spine straightened and I felt myself coming into alignment. It was an odd sensation. Something in me shifted. I know imagination is a mental thing, but I genuinely had a physical response. Swami G sensed it.

"Don't be surprised if you catch yourself correcting your posture. This experience seems real. Make the adjustment and allow yourself to stay

418

suspended on this silver thread until you feel it's time to end your meditation. Hang in there, as you say in the West."

We sat in silence for several minutes. I felt extremely calm and relaxed, almost blissful. My breathing was slow and rhythmical. I don't think I'd ever experienced such deep serenity, either before or since. I could've lingered there all day long, but Swami G lifted us out of it.

"Now I'll show you how to end this meditation. Take another deep breath and let it out by saying: 'Aaaah'. Then, in your mind's eye, snip the silver thread above and below your body. You'll feel yourself drifting back to your private sanctuary. It helps to ground yourself by focusing on the weight of your body against the floor. When you've settled down sufficiently and you feel ready to leave your private sanctuary, bless this special place and then make your way up the stairs and back to your point of departure. When you're ready, open your eyes."

I followed his instruction and then blinked a few times. The first thing that came into focus was my wristwatch – more specifically, the time on my wristwatch. I suddenly realized that we had to be at the airport in less than an hour. If we didn't leave immediately, we'd never make it. As much as I had loved the company of Swami G, and enjoyed the meditation, I knew we had to hustle. I caught Henry Jones's attention by flashing my eyes towards my wrist watch.

"What?" he mouthed.

Swami G's eyes were closed. I thought it would be disrespectful to disturb him. The best I could do was imitate a flying bird and tap my wrist. He got it.

"You may feel a bit queasy or light-headed after this meditation exercise, so don't stand up too quickly. Take your time coming back into yourself," Swami G said calmly.

"Okay."

"I also suggest you relax afterwards. As a rule of thumb, I recommend you take it easy for as long as you were meditating. Just do simple things, nothing too strenuous or complex."

"Alright."

"Anything else?" Henry Jones asked. I glared at him, careful not to lose more time.

"It's a good idea to drink lots of water. And, if you feel hungry, only eat natural foods."

"Is that it?"

"No, there's a teensy-weensy bit more. If you have experienced any personal realizations or breakthroughs, write them down."

"Your Workbook is perfect for that," Henry Jones whispered to me.

I tapped my watch frantically. Swami G didn't take notice. "If it occurred to you to do something positive and constructive for yourself or someone else, you should do it as soon as possible. Don't procrastinate putting good ideas into action."

"Speaking of which, we really must be on our way, Swami G. We're flying back home today," Henry Jones informed him.

"Oh, gracious me, I'm very sorry for taking up so much of your time. I've enjoyed meeting you immensely. You're most welcome to leave now and return whenever you wish," Swami G said humbly.

"Thank you, thank you," we replied in unison, standing to our feet.

"Go in peace," Swami G told us, folding his hands into the prayer position one last time. "Go in peace, my friend," Henry Jones told him.

We shuffled out of the room backwards, facing him, bowing repeatedly as we left. Exiting the room, we scampered down the hallway excitedly. We'd less than an hour to get to the airport or we'd miss our flight to Delhi.

"Was that a power session, or what?" Henry Jones whispered loudly. "Yeah, I feel terrific," I replied breathlessly.

"Can you imagine the positive impact this daily meditation will have on you and your body?"

I couldn't. I was absolutely convinced, however, that practising these techniques regularly would raise my self-awareness to a new level, and that I'd become increasingly alert and aware of my thoughts, feelings and actions. I knew I'd meditate in future – not just on my healing journey, but for as long as I lived.

The next hour passed by in a blur of crazed activity, hurried along by a local group of supporters. They helped us to pack our clothes; carry our bags; say our goodbyes; catch a taxi; navigate the traffic; shout at pedestrians; and check-in our baggage. Henry Jones gave them the last of the rupees from his pocket and they looked very satisfied. They waved us goodbye like we were emigrating family members. It was strange, since we hardly knew them.

"Come visit us again," they sang merrily as Henry Jones and I made our way through customs.

"I'll be back," I shouted spontaneously, much to my own astonishment. Perhaps I'd return to the ashram with my wife someday. I'd bring her to India, if she'd let me. I guess India does that to you. Slowly and surely, it casts its spell on you. Without you noticing it, her many hypnotic charms draw you in and sweep you away.

We caught the connecting flight to the international airport in the nick of time. I slept like a baby on that flight. A few hours later, on the plane ride home, I had time to reflect on my thoughts and to summarize the extraordinary experience I'd shared with Henry Jones and Swami G in India. It had been quite a trip. I'd experienced the power of spiritual healing, and yet another notebook was crammed with precious information. I turned the pages, one by one. There was a lot to take in.

"What did you learn?" Henry Jones asked me, pointing to my notepad.

I took a deep breath and replied: "Well, I learned that the primary objective of the spiritual healing process is to demystify spirituality and to make us conscious of our spiritual nature. We defined spirit and explored ways to awaken spirituality. We looked at the spiritual conflict between the ego-mind and the true-self, and its effect on our health. I learned that the etheric body, which houses our thoughts and feelings, is the framework of our physical body. With this in mind, we briefly examined the role emotions play in causing disease through blocked energy centers called chakra points. I learned that when our chakras are open, we are healthy, and when they're blocked, we are sick. We studied their individual functions and you taught me to identify the cause of physical problems by associating them to the corresponding chakra point. That was a real eye-opener. After that, we went on to talk about meditation, and Swami G taught me a powerful meditation technique to clear, cleanse and balance my chakra points. All in all: I was made conscious of my spiritual nature and shown how I can heal my body through my spirituality." I closed my notepad and tucked it away safely. "Awesome stuff!" I finally said.

"I promised you a spirituality booster, didn't I?" Henry Jones remarked, reclining his seat.

"You sure did, Henry Jones. You sure did."

"What do you think was your most valuable lesson?"

I had to think about my answer for a while. "I'd never have pegged myself as being a spiritual person before this trip. But, things have changed. I've changed. I now understand that awakening your spirituality means becoming conscious of yourself. That's it in a nutshell. You don't need fancy churches, ancient rituals or ordained priests. You just need to be aware of your thoughts, feelings and actions. You need to live in the moment and follow your true-self."

"And how is this new-found wisdom going to change your life?"

I knew the answer to that question. "Well, for one thing, I've decided to quit my job!"

"What?" he exclaimed, bolting upright.

"Yup. It's over. Life's too short and precious to waste. I won't be ruled by my ego-mind any longer. I'm going to follow my heart now."

"What are you going to do?" he cried.

"Well, I hate my job, but I love the publishing industry. I've always fantasized about starting my own business, but I never had the courage to do it. So, brace yourself, I'm going to start a company that publishes books that offer real value to their readers – books that change lives. Books that matter! How would you like to be my first client, Henry Jones?"

His beautiful smile broadened. "I'd be honoured. Where do I sign up?"

We didn't have a contract to sign, but we shook on it. It was a done deal.

I wasn't through yet. There was something else I had to do. Something that had been a long time coming. I turned to him: "Henry, I'd like to thank you from the very bottom of my heart for helping me to heal my body. The time that I've spent with you has been the best time of my life. I'm so grateful to have you in my life. You've saved me from myself, and I'd be lost without you. I love you, Henry Jones. I love you, like a brother, a father, a best friend, with all my heart."

Both of our eyes filled with tears. He placed his hand on my leg and squeezed it. "You're welcome," he said. I started bawling. I didn't care about the strange looks we got from the other passengers. All I cared about was living in the moment and living my life to its fullest potential.

"So, all things considered, I'd say your spiritual healing process has been a great success, wouldn't you?" he asked, leaning back into his seat and pulling the sleeping mask over his eyes. Only the grin on his face remained visible.

"Oh, gracious me, I can tell you this: It was fun-taas-tick," I said imitating Swami G.

We laughed til it hurt.

PART 4

EMOTIONAL HEALING

CHAPTER 22

GETTING UNSTUCK WITH HENRY'S HEALING STANCES

It's a funny thing, traveling abroad. When you're away, you get to experience a totally different world. For a while, the people and places you see are so real. But, once you return home, all you have left of the trip are some souvenirs, a compressed folder of digital photos, and your memories. Reality is rendered to a single, obscure truth: The only world that's real to you is your own. A week later, India was just a set of thoughts in my head. I found myself right back in the thick of things with Henry Jones and his book; my soon-to-be ex-boss; my broken marriage; my body and my healing journey.

On the face of it, my external world had not changed. My 'realities' were just as real as the day we left for Delhi. But, under the surface, my internal world had shifted irrevocably. I knew it would only be a matter of time before my external world shifted, too. I had made a point of integrating chakra meditations into my daily schedule, and of writing down the answers to the questions Swami G suggested I ask myself for each chakra point. I took my time to answer each one properly. I did that exercise as if it was the most important thing in my world. I simply made the time to do it.

Swami G was right. Using your imagination to visualize what you want most for your life is much better than preoccupying your mind with external stimuli that don't do anything for your future reality, such as television. I had new goals to achieve and a new world to create for my family and myself.

My Workbook became more than a daily log. It transformed into my plan of action, my roadmap for the future and the canvas for my dreams.

If all of us spent as much time working on ourselves, our true-selves, as we do watching television, I'm pretty sure our world would be a much better place. What stops us? Why don't we use our time to improve our quality of life? What holds us back from living the lives we most want for ourselves? Of course, there's only one answer to these questions. The ego-mind.

I had been pondering all of these issues when Henry Jones walked into the dining room with two steaming bowls of porridge.

"What are you writing about?" he asked, gently placing one of the bowls on the table in front of me.

"The porridge smells delicious. Thank you, Henry." I said, sniffing the aroma through one nostril at a time. I couldn't believe how my sinuses had cleared up since I started eating a whole-foods, plant-based diet. My sense of smell and taste had improved dramatically, too.

"It's a great pleasure," he replied smiling. "What's on your mind?"

"I've been reflecting on the healing processes that we've completed together."

"Three down, one to go," he replied, nodding encouragingly.

"Emotional healing, right?"

"Yes, my favorite. Trust me, the knowledge and wisdom you'll receive in this stage of your healing journey will make everything else seem like kindergarten."

"You must be joking!" I said disbelievingly.

"Nope. Not at all. I promise you: It's in another realm altogether."

My heart skipped a beat. What had Henry Jones in store for me? How would this final process change my life? Would it be the one to heal my body once and for all? I wondered.

"I'm looking forward to it. Bring it on. I'm ready to go the distance." I told him.

He smiled broadly. "That's the spirit. I'm thrilled you're so committed to this program. A healing journey is a sure-fire test of character. It takes real guts to get this far on a healing journey. Many people don't find the courage to change their ways. They try it for a while, but eventually give in to their ego-mind and quit their journey. But not you, my friend, you've shown extraordinary devotion towards healing yourself, and you will be rewarded for it. Believe it!"

"The things is, I'm a believer now," I told Henry Jones with a confident grin that was almost as big as the smile on his face.

"Good. By taking action to restore your body to perfect health naturally, you not only express your divine right to be your own healer, but you employ God's own healing remedy. Through devotion to the natural laws, you will be healed. You will," Henry Jones affirmed.

I flipped my notepad around and showed him the statement I'd doodled across the front cover. It said: "Natural healing leads to perfect health."

"Boy-oh-boy, you've changed!" Henry Jones exclaimed. "Well, we're in the home stretch now, my friend. You'll have all the knowledge you need to heal your body once you've completed the upcoming emotional healing process. All of your effort is about to pay off. You'll soon know exactly how to release the emotional blockages that are making you sick. But, I must warn you in advance: emotional healing isn't easy to do. The theory behind it isn't a walk in the park either. I've seen grown-ups cry like babies. It really works, but it requires total commitment."

"I'm committed," I assured him.

"Come on then. Grab your jacket. I want us to take a trip before sunrise," he instructed.

"Do I need my passport?" I joked.

"Not this time," he chuckled.

"Where are we off to now?" I asked, leaping to my feet.

"The beach."

Sure enough, 20 minutes later, we were standing on the dunes as the Sun came up. No, it wasn't a spectacular sunrise; there was no golden light rippling playfully along the crashing waves, nor pastel pink and blue clouds streaking across the expansive sky. It was just another ordinary day – but something truly extraordinary was about to happen.

The 10 healing stances

"Today I'm going to teach you 10 healing stances that will unlock incredible healing power within you," Henry Jones said. "You see, sickness and disease are a result of 'stuckness'. I've told you before: When energy becomes stagnant in the body, it causes illness. This is why movement is so important on your healing journey. You've got to get the energy flowing in your physical body, so that it can release the blockages in your mental, spiritual and emotional body. When you move your physical body with intention, your etheric body shifts, too."

I was intrigued. I recalled Henry Jones telling me movement was a way to restore homeostasis in the body, but we hadn't explored the concept further.

"Go on," I pleaded.

He grinned broadly. "I've designed a powerful healing technique that connects your physical body to your emotions. When you make this connection – consciously and deliberately – you evoke powerful healing forces at will. Don't underestimate the significance of this healing technique. It's truly transformative."

The hairs on my neck prickled. Perhaps my chills came from the morning breeze that blew across the beach, but I think it was the way Henry Jones spoke those words. Despite his grin, he was as serious as a heart attack.

"Are you ready to do them right now?" Henry Jones asked.

"Ready, willing and able," I responded.

Reflect

"Great, let's get started. The first stance is called Reflect. It's super-easy to do: Stand tall with your hands on your hips. Close your eyes and reflect on your life. Visualize snippets of your childhood, teenage years and adult years. Think of places you visited, people you met, and things you've done. But don't judge or criticize your memories. Just observe them, as if you were watching someone else's life. Accept whatever mental images come to you. Don't try to push any of them away. Also, don't dwell on one particular memory for too long. Move on. It is important to reflect on your whole life in just a few minutes. Try it now. You may be surprised at the memories that come up."

Henry Jones was right. It was easy. Flashes of my past sprung up, almost as though I was watching a three-minute promotional video of my life, beginning on the day I was born, right up to that moment on the beach.

He continued: "When you've done this healing exercise several times, you can then reflect on specific themes, such as places; people; emotions; experiences and outcomes. Most importantly, ponder on the questions: Who am I? What matters to me? What shaped me? What are my most powerful memories, and why?"

After a few minutes had passed, he instructed me to open my eyes, and to 'shake it off' by kicking my legs, flicking my arms and dusting myself off. It must have looked like a great, big spider had dropped into my shirt and I was frantically trying to rid myself of it. I immediately thought of the Huntsman spider we had seen in the cabin. My animated response pleased Henry Jones immensely.

"Now, take one, big step forward, so that you're in a new space. This is important. You must move to another spot. This exercise is about movement, after all," he told me.

"No problem," I replied, taking a massive leap forward.

Reach

"The second position is called Reach. It's a chance for you to express how you strive to find the answers to life's biggest questions. Ask yourself: What is the meaning of life? Why am I here? What is my higher purpose? Keep one foot on the ground in the same place and take a big step with the other foot. Reach forward as far as possible. Really stretch your body to the maximum, from the tips of your fingers to your toes. Pretend you're in a hot desert and there's a bottle of cold water just out of reach in front of you. You have to use your last bit of energy to stretch out as far as possible to grab it. It's important that you put emotion into this stance. Allow yourself to feel the frustration, exasperation, aggravation and desperation of reaching for the answers you seek in life. The more feeling you put into these reaches, the better the exercise will work for you. It helps to grunt from your gut to express yourself fully."

I did as I was instructed, and groaned loudly. Henry Jones clapped even louder.

"Fun-taas-tick! That's great work! When you feel exhausted from one stretch, stand up and then stretch in the opposite direction. You must reach out in four different directions – front, back, left and right."

Once I'd finished my four stretches, he got me to 'shake it off' again, and then take another big step forward.

Realization

"The next stance is called Realization. As you now know, you have two, distinct sides to you – your ego-mind and your true-self. I'd like you to express these two aspects of yourself now. Start by turning to your left hand side and allow yourself to completely be your ego-mind. Feel all your anxieties, doubts, insecurities, fears, worries, stresses and disappointments. Immerse yourself in resentment, anger and bitterness. Allow these negative feelings to saturate your whole being. Let your body, face and hands express how you're feeling. When people do this exercise, they usually twist or contort their bodies. They crunch up into a ball and pull painful expressions on their faces. Try it now. Really sink into these negative feelings. Push down, as if you were very constipated. Imagine that pushing down on your body makes the negative feelings ooze out of your skin. It's good to make noises, such as moaning and groaning. Feel the pain. Squeeze your body until it's not possible to feel the emotions of your ego-mind any more intensely than you do in this moment."

I was shocked at how easily I could demonstrate the emotions of my ego-mind. My body buckled and I writhed slowly. I didn't enjoy the exercise, but I could feel the power of it. It was overwhelming and scary.

"When you're done, shake it off, and then turn 180 degrees to face in the opposite direction. In this position, I'd like you to express your true-self. Stand comfortably and relax completely. There is no reason to struggle or strain. Your true-self is cool, calm and collected. In this stance, allow yourself to feel love, compassion, harmony and peace. Let these feelings saturate the core of your being. It helps to smile through your eyes and to smile inwardly."

I felt comfortable swaying from side to side with my arms outstretched. I was amazed at how quickly I had changed from my ego-mind to my true-self. The dramatic shift in my physical appearance and state of mind was unmistakable. He let me linger in that position for a few minutes, although I could've held it for hours.

"When you are done, shake it off, and take another big step forward," Henry Jones said, nudging me along.

Roar

"The next position is called Roar. Stand with your feet a bit wider than shoulder-width apart. Bend your knees slightly and sink into your seat. Clench your fists at your sides and flex your muscles, as if you're a powerful warrior about to fight for your life."

I'd always admired the All Blacks – the New Zealand rugby team – who do the haka to intimidate their opponents. The haka is an ancient Māori war dance that is traditionally used on the battlefield. It's a fierce display of the tribe's pride, strength and unity. Actions include violent foot-stamping, tongue protrusions and rhythmic body slapping to accompany a loud chant. I did it all, and Henry Jones showered me with praise.

"You must be strong to be your true-self. It takes might to do what is ultimately best for you all the time. This stance gives you the rare chance to muster your inner strength and express your personal power to its fullest. Don't hold back. Connect with your inner warrior. When you can't flex your muscles any longer, let out a mighty ROAR. This is not a roar of anger or rage, but of power and purpose."

He didn't have to ask me twice. I let out a mighty roar, like a fearsome lion. The blood vessels in my brow nearly burst. Henry Jones stumbled backwards. His animation amused and inspired me.

Repent

"When you are done, shake it off, and take another big step forward. The next stance is Repent. Kneel with one knee on the ground and bow your head. Putting your elbow on your knee helps you to keep your balance," he told me. "Imagine that you're bowing before a great king, or your Maker. This is your chance to repent for all the wrong choices you've made, and all your wrong-doings while your ego-mind ruled your thoughts, actions and feelings. It helps to think or say: 'I am sorry,' over and over again. Forgiveness is healing. This stance is very powerful and truly transformative when you genuinely feel sorry."

I immediately thought of my wife and daughter. My ego-mind had run amok in our relationship and ruined our family. I had a lot of bad behavior for which to apologize. I bowed my head in shame and heard myself saying: "I am sorry, I am sorry," until tears rolled down my cheeks.

Release

Henry Jones brought me out of it. "When you're done, stand up, shake it off, and take another big step forward. The next stance is called Release. It's essential to 'let go'. Using your whole body, find a way to express the word 'release'. Some people act as if they are throwing something away with great force; some act as though they're frantically scooping water out of a boat; while others act like they're releasing doves in to the sky. The important thing is to move your body. Act out this movement to its fullest. Keep performing this 'release' action until you intuitively know you've let go of the negative feelings that you've been harboring in your body and mind."

I imagined that I was wearing a dirty, tattered coat. I took it off and threw it away.

Receive

"Outstanding," Henry Jones remarked. "Now, shake it off and take another big step forward. The next position is called Receive. Stand with your feet shoulder-width apart, lift your arms slightly and open your hands. Some people feel more comfortable with their hands together in front of them, like a beggar, or a child receiving a gift. It doesn't really matter how you choose to express yourself – the important thing is to imagine you're receiving everything you need and desire. This is your chance to receive your healing; to find what you're looking for; and to get what you want most for yourself and your loved ones. It's essential to feel gratitude during this stance. Allow it to permeate the core of your being."

I imagined two shafts of light beaming out from the palms of my hand. The universe poured blessings into my hands through these beams of light. It felt really good to receive them.

Rejoice

"When you're done, shake it off, and take a big step forward. The next stance is called Rejoice. Lift your arms in to the air, as if you're worshipping a Higher Power. Put a smile on your face and rejoice. Feel happiness, excitement and joy. Allow yourself to feel the ecstasy that flows from receiving everything you desire most for yourself and your loved ones. Drench yourself in jubilation. Bathe yourself in this celebration. Shower in the blessings that flow to you. If you feel like dancing, do it. The important thing is to express yourself to the fullest."

My body swayed from side to side until my feet sprung into a shuffle and I started to dance. That really did feel fun-taas-tick!

Rest

"When you're done, shake it off, take another big step forward and sit down on the ground. The next stance is called Rest. Sit with your legs crossed and your eyes closed. Touch your thumbs and index fingers together, as if you're meditating. Completely relax your body and mind. When you're calm, replay the sequence of healing stances in your mind. Run through each position: From Reflection to Rest. Don't try to feel the emotions of each position. Just observe yourself in each stance and feel content. Don't judge or criticize, or analyze and rationalize – just be. Breathe slowly and deeply."

I recalled the 10 healing stances and couldn't hide the smile on my face. Several minutes passed and I was in a state of bliss.

Recharge

"When you're done, stand up, shake it off, and take another big step forward. The final stance is called Recharge. It's simple to do. Stand up, and then run on the spot as fast as you can for as long as you can. Try to get your blood pumping. Imagine this exercise is recharging your energy levels. When you've exhausted yourself, stop running, put your hands over your heart, close your eyes, and focus your attention on your heartbeat until it eventually stops racing."

It only took a minute and I was pooped. I collapsed to the floor, put my hand on my belly, and howled like a wolf. Henry Jones joined me.

"That was incredible," I yelled at the top of my voice. "I'll definitely do that exercise again."

"I recommend that you do it three or four times a week on a healing journey. The more you practise it, the more powerful it becomes," he said.

I got it. I really did! "Thinking becomes doing, doing becomes feeling, feeling becomes being," I told him. "These 10 healing stances will help me to 'be healed', won't they?"

Henry Jones grinned from ear to ear. "You're going to take to your emotional healing process like a duck to water," he said slapping my leg with pride.

I wondered if it was a good time to tell him I'd swiped Dwayne the Duck, and I'd been bathing with him every day since we'd left the cabin in the mountains. But I decided it was 'poultry' and let it go. We spoke for an hour or so and then went for a long walk along the beach. Juju Banks joined us for brunch and we spoke about the contents of Henry Jones's book until noon.

"What's next?" I asked him.

Henry Jones's smile faded and was replaced by a pained expression.

I gulped involuntarily. What did he have in store for me next? I wondered.

CHAPTER 23

STUCK IN A VICE GRIP

"We're off to the mall!" Henry Jones announced.

"What?" I exclaimed. That was the last place in the world I thought Henry Jones would ever want to go.

"You heard me. Let's go to the very busy shopping mall in the center of the city."

"Why on Earth do you want to visit the mall?" I cried, pulling on my jacket.

"You'll see soon enough!"

About a half hour later, we were sitting in the middle of the fast food and entertainment section of the busiest mall in town. It was packed. People literally crammed into every nook and cranny. There were all different shapes and sizes, races and religions, colors and creeds.

"This is a strange place to bring me," I said, somewhat apprehensively.

"It's the perfect place for us to talk about emotional healing," he replied. I didn't get it. We'd done lots of exciting things together, but we had never been to a shopping mall! I was curious.

"Okay, spill the beans. Why are we here?" I had to ask him, while pushing an empty hamburger box off our table. Tomato sauce smeared on to the back of my hand. I wiped it off with an unused napkin I had taken from a nearby table.

He grinned. "Today's the day I'm going to introduce you to emotional healing, so sit tight because I've got a ton of mind-boggling information to share with you."

"But why bring me to the mall?' I asked him again, flagging a waiter to wipe the grime from our table. "And why sit in this particular spot?"

"Be patient, my friend. Within the next hour or so, you'll understand why I brought you here."

I still wasn't happy. "Let's get on with it then," I moaned.

"What would you like to know first?" he replied, smiling at a group of children with snotty noses sucking on milkshakes next to us.

"Tell me your agenda."

He leaned forward. "Okay, then. In your emotional healing process, you'll discover how to manage your emotions properly so that you can enjoy a rich and full life, free of sickness and disease. Plus, you'll learn how to raise your emotional intelligence so that you can accurately identify your own feelings, identify the feelings of others and solve problems involving emotional issues. I'm also going to introduce you to a very good friend of mine, Sister Simone. She'll show you a powerful breakthrough technique to identify and release emotional blockages from your past, which could be the cause of your physical problem. Trust me: By letting go of the negative feelings that are blocking the natural flow of energy in your body, you'll start to feel better instantly. The results of this emotional healing therapy session are nothing short of miraculous!"

"Let's do it. I'm keen to meet Sister Simone right now."

"Before you meet her, I need to teach you how to release your emotional energy from the unhealthy vices that keep you trapped in your ego-mind. This first step is essential on your emotional healing journey. When you break your emotional attachments to vices that are harmful to your body, you free up your emotional energy to work on healing your body, mind and spirit."

I sat back down in a hurry. "What are you talking about?"

"Well, vices are things we do habitually that are bad for us. As William Shakespeare wrote in *King Lear*: 'The gods are just, and of our pleasant vices, make instruments to plague us.'"

"I know what vices are, Henry. But what did you mean about 'releasing our emotional attachments to vices'?"

"All your vices are driven by emotional deficiency, and it's your wayward desire to fill this emotional gap that triggers your vice. You know what I'm talking about, don't you? You've had a bad day at the office, so you pour yourself a stiff drink when you get home. Your relationship breaks up, so you go on a sugar binge. If you need companionship, you meet someone for a cup of coffee. Want a quick break from stress, you have a cigarette. Sound familiar?"

I was too busy chewing on my lip to answer him back.

Fill the gap and break the vice

"If you want to break the habit of your harmful vices, you must fill the emotional gap in your life. There's no other way to do it. Willpower will only get you so far. The emotional need must be met, too, or your ego-mind will just find another substitute to fill the gap. Be warned, my friend, breaking the habit of harmful vices isn't easy to do. Certain vices are physically addictive because of their chemical composition, but the real problem is that they're all emotionally addictive."

"What kind of vices are we talking about?"

"There are many kinds of vices and they're all bad for you. Make no mistake about it. Over time, clever marketing campaigns have tricked us into believing common vices are socially acceptable, or even good for us. In fact, they are extremely harmful to our bodies and lives. These products may give you instant gratification, but the long-term effects are very, very detrimental to your well-being. Let's examine the side-effects of a few, common vices, shall we?"

"Where do we start?"

Henry Jones leaned back and put up his hand to signal the waiter. "This may take some time. Fancy a cup of tea or coffee?" he asked me casually.

"Sure. I'll have a cappuccino if we have the time," I answered him.

"What do you prefer?"

"Coffee. I definitely drink more coffee than tea. Especially at work!"

"How often?"

"Phew, I can have a few cups a day, easily."

"Two mineral waters, please," Henry Jones said to the waiter. That's when it hit me: I'd spent weeks with Henry Jones and he'd never offered or served me coffee. I should've guessed what he was up to. He leaned in towards me. "I'll tell you something, my friend: If you drink tea or coffee daily, you're most likely addicted to it."

"Addicted? Isn't that a bit strong?"

Curb the coffee

"No. It's not! Caffeine is a drug! You should avoid it like the plague!"

"But I enjoy the buzz I get from caffeine," I told him. "It gives me a rush of energy, especially in the morning."

"Many people do," he replied. "That's probably because they don't understand what's causing it."

"We're about to have a strong and heated debate, aren't we?" I jested.

"Yes, coffee causes a latte problems," he punned. "You see, that sensation is your body's way of warning you that something is attacking your central nervous system. The 'buzz' is caused by an induced release of stored sugar in your liver, which puts stress on your endocrine system. That isn't good for you."

"Jeez, sometimes I have up to five cups a day," I confessed. "The technical name for a pot of coffee at work is break fluid."

He cringed. "The *British Medical Journal* says five cups of coffee a day gives you a 50% greater chance of having a heart attack." I cringed. "Tests have proven that four to five cups of coffee a day causes birth defects in animals, and high doses cause lab animals to go into convulsions and die. Did you know 10g of caffeine could kill you?"

"No, I didn't."

"Did you know the active chemicals in caffeine cause prostate problems, bladder cancer, lower urinary tract cancer, anal itching, high cholesterol and hypertensive heart disease?"

"No."

"Well, it's all true. Look at that," he said, pointing to a pregnant lady drinking coffee a few tables down from us. "Did you know studies conducted at John Hopkins University have proven that caffeine interferes with DNA replication?"

"No."

"This is just one of the reasons why the Center For Science advises pregnant women to stay off coffee. I'll tell you another thing: If you want to heal your body, then you should avoid drinking tea and coffee, because caffeine increases cravings for sugar; wastes Vitamin B and washes out potassium, which promotes fatigue, and inhibits iron absorption. Iron promotes resistance to disease and depletes zinc, which accelerates healing."

"I didn't know this either."

"Well, now you do. Stay away from any substance with caffeine in it. It poisons your system. The dosage may be small, but you're still poisoning your body. Hear what I'm telling you, my friend: Tea and coffee are a vice. You've got to give them up."

"What about herbal teas?"

"Herbal teas are okay for you because they don't contain caffeine. You want to avoid caffeine. Let's not overlook the fact that most people enjoy drinking tea and coffee with one or more teaspoons of sugar. That's where even more damage is done!"

Avoid the sugar trap

"Why? What's wrong with sugar?"

Henry Jones looked up at me, shaking his head from side to side. "In my opinion, refined sugar is the greatest evil of our times," he said solemnly. "At the beginning of the last century, the average person consumed about 5 pounds of sugar per year. There was virtually no cancer, heart disease or other degenerative diseases. A hundred years later, the average person in developed countries consumes approximately 175 pounds of sugar per year. Today, cancer and heart disease kill one out of three people."

"There's no way I eat that much sugar," I told him.

"You'd better take a deep breath, my friend. I'm about to give you a good reason to have an anxiety attack," he replied. "You're most likely eating way too much sugar without even knowing it. It's estimated that a staggering 135 million tons of sugar are produced in 121 countries per year, and two thirds of this production is added to manufactured food products. Sugar is the number one food additive. We consume 10 times more sugar than we do of all the other 2 600 or so food additives put together. You'd be shocked to discover how many processed food products from supermarkets contain sugar. For instance: Did you know that a tablespoon of ketchup contains a full teaspoon of sugar?"

I shook my head in disbelief.

"You'll also find sugar in most breads; cereals; processed meats; sauces; dressings; biscuits; juices; soups; jams; canned fruits; canned vegetables and all artificial sweeteners. I strongly recommend you get into the habit of studying the labels on packaging. Look out for anything ending in 'ose', which indicates the presence of sugar – sucrose; fructose; glucose; maltose and lactose. You want to stay away from these additives. They may taste sweet and delicious on your tongue, but they offer your body no nutritional value. In fact, eating sugar actually depletes your body of nutrients. Yes, that's right! It depletes vitamins, minerals and even enzymes. There are literally hundreds of reasons why refined sugar is harmful to you."

"Such as?"

"Sugar suppresses your immune system; upsets your body's mineral balance; lowers your enzymes' ability to function; induces cell death; has a deteriorating effect on your endocrine system; and is the number one enemy of your bowel movements. Sugar can promote tooth decay; an acidic stomach; an elevation of harmful cholesterol; raised adrenaline levels; aging; weight gain; obesity; glucose intolerance; and weakened defences against bacterial infection. It also contributes to diabetes; osteoporosis; gastric cancer; cancer of the breasts, ovaries, prostrate, rectum and gallbladder. Wait, there's more! Sugar can cause hormonal imbalances; hypertension; anxiety; headaches; migraines; depression; hypoglycemia; cardiovascular disease; copper deficiency; chromium deficiency; food allergies; eczema; damage to capillaries; damage to your pancreas; kidney damage; free radical formation in the bloodstream; high blood pressure in obese people; loss of tissue elasticity and function; emphysema; cataracts and a decrease in insulin sensitivity. The list goes on: Sugar can also increase bacterial fermentation in your colon; fluid retention; systolic blood pressure; total cholesterol; the amount of fat in your liver; kidney size; and blood platelet adhesiveness, which increases your risk of blood clots and strokes. There are probably many more medical reasons why sugar is bad for you, but I think you get the point. Don't you?"

My mouth hung open. It took me a moment to collect my thoughts. "I'd no idea that excess sugar consumption could be so devastating to the human body. After hearing what you've just told me, we have to be insane to eat or drink it."

He nodded knowingly. "You've got to cut out sugar, my friend. Especially when you're sick! When you put sugar into your system, it quickly increases your blood glucose levels. In response, your pancreas secretes insulin to drop your blood-sugar levels.

"These rapid fluctuations of your blood-sugar levels put enormous stress on your body, which is very unhealthy for you. As your insulin levels spike, it inhibits the release of growth hormones, which in turn depresses your immune system. The root of all disease is at a cellular and molecular level, and more often than not insulin is going to have its hand in it."

"How does it depress my immune system?"

"Your body's white blood cells need to accumulate vitamin C to eliminate viruses and bacteria. The problem is that glucose and vitamin C have very similar chemical structures, so they're mistaken for each other. When your sugar levels go up, there's more glucose around, so less vitamin C makes it into your cells. As a result, 1 teaspoon of sugar slows your immune system down to a crawl for 24 hours."

"So, when I was drinking a few cups of coffee per day with 2 teaspoons of sugar in each cup, I was really pummelling my immune system."

"You can't do that to yourself anymore, my friend. You've got to stop hurting yourself like that."

"Thanks a lot. I really mean it. I didn't know the damage I was doing to my body."

"If that shocked you, I must tell you something else that will knock you flat. Cancer's preferred fuel is glucose. Yes, it's a fact. Sugar feeds cancer. Cancer patients must do their utmost best to control the supply of glucose to their bodies. Cutting out sugar slows the growth of cancer and enables the immune system to catch up to the disease."

"I should put that in our book," I said.

"Yes, you really should. Many of our readers will probably have cancer because this dreadful disease is so prolific in these modern times."

"Consider it done. So, what can we recommend using instead of sugar?"

"Use natural sweeteners, including pure maple syrup, molasses, dehydrated cane sugar juice, or raw unfiltered honey. You should also warn our readers that giving up sugar won't be easy. Sugar is an addictive substance. Try not eating sweets or chocolates for a month and then you'll see what I'm talking about."

"Let's move on," I suggested.

Avoid fizzy drinks

"Believe it or not, fizzy drinks are another vice. Millions and millions of people around the world are addicted to soft drinks. Get this: In some developing countries, it's easier to find some global brands than it is to find clean drinking water."

"That's scandalous," I remarked.

"Have you got any idea how bad they are for you?"

"No, not exactly."

"Besides water, the biggest single ingredient in soft drinks is, you guessed it, sugar. A single can contains 40–50g. You'd have to eat two large packets of oranges to get that much natural sugar in your system. Fizzy drinks are also laced with artificial flavorants, colorants and sweeteners. Those substances are killers! To add insult to injury, cola manufacturers add caffeine to their products. They do it for one reason, and one reason only – to get you addicted to it."

I was shocked. "It's disgusting that they're allowed to get away with it," I said bitterly.

"Recent studies presented to the World Health Organization have likened the effects of drinking soft drinks to a heroin rush. Like heroin, sugary foods trigger a release of dopamine, a mood-enhancing chemical, in the brain. Both become addictive because of the 'feel good' factor they induce. When these triggers are removed, the withdrawal symptoms include mood swings, excessive thirst, fatigue, the shakes, faintness and headaches. This is much the same as nicotine, morphine and heroin withdrawal! Research indicates that people living in the UK and USA drink an average of two fizzy cans per day. The scariest research suggests that a child consumes about 200 liters of fizzy drink every year."

"Holy crap!" I exclaimed.

"The consequences on the human system are severe. Let's start where fizzy drinks enter your body. The high level of sugar reacts with bacteria in plaque, which causes tooth decay, while the acidity causes erosion. Although this is a serious problem worldwide, rotting teeth are the least of your worries. Fizzy drinks are implicated as the cause of some cancers. For example: Researchers have found that the number of people with cancer of the gullet, the area between the throat and stomach, has dramatically increased with fizzy drink consumption. Diabetes is another hot contender. The World Health Organization also attributes the alarming rise of obesity to fizzy drinks. Somebody who drinks one can a day could put on 15 pounds over a year. The *Journal of the American Medical Association* says the problem may be that the drinks fail to make people feel full, despite being loaded with calories, posing a serious health risk. These are just some of the reasons that many health organizations around the world are lobbying to ban fizzy drinks. I couldn't agree with them more."

I grimaced.

Henry Jones continued: "Here's my motto: If it comes in a can, bottle or box, don't drink it. If you want to heal your body, stay away from sugar-sweetened colas, lemonade and fruit drinks. Instead, drink lots of clean, fresh water, or freshly squeezed fruit or vegetable juice. If you like, you can flavor chilled herbal teas with lemon juice, orange juice or honey. That sounds delicious, doesn't it?"

"Hmmmm, I think I'll stick to water and vegetable juices. What other vices are there?"

Henry Jones immediately pointed to a woman lighting a cigarette beside us.

Stop smoking

"Smoking?" I questioned.

"Yes, definitely smoking! Tell me, why did you start smoking?" Henry Jones suddenly asked.

"I saw an advert of a wealthy man with a cigar in his mouth and a glass of expensive whiskey in his hand, and I aspired to be like him."

"Advertising sure is powerful, isn't it?" He remarked. "It's absurd how a good marketing campaign can make us want to buy products that can kill us."

"Okay, this is one vice that I already know is bad for me," I said defensively.

"No, smoking isn't just bad for you. It's probably the worst thing you can do to your body. Tobacco smoke is a lethal cocktail of toxic chemicals. There are over 100 poisons in every cigarette. The British government recently released information verifying that cigarettes contain deadly poisons, including chemicals used to make paint stripper, toilet cleaner, lighter fuel, mothballs, rocket fuel, as well as the poison used in gas chambers. Do you really want that disgusting stuff in your body? Do you?"

I was too ashamed to answer.

"I dare you to reread my notes that explain how your lungs filter oxygen into your body, and then imagine the damage caused by these tars and poisons as they build up in the capillaries in your lungs. Tell me, have you noticed that heavy smokers have a grey, dull, lifeless complexion?"

"Yes, I have."

"Have you ever wondered why?"

"No."

"Smoking starves the skin of nutrients, which damages skin more than anything else. It's quite ironic when you think about it. Like you, people start smoking to supposedly improve their self-image, but a bad skin wreaks havoc on one's self-image. So, smoking actually works against the reason they do it in the first place. This raises another important point. The ego-mind seeks instant gratification, whereas the true-self seeks long-term benefit. Smokers are clearly ruled by their ego-minds."

"That makes sense," I agreed.

"Smoking will kill you. Read the box. The manufacturers are now forced to print it in black and white. And if you doubt it, take a look at an x-ray of a smoker's lungs. A smoker's lungs are literally black from the tar! This starves the whole body of oxygen and as you know, oxygen is the elixir of life."

As he said it, I watched the woman sitting beside us suck a lung full of cigarette smoke and blow it out her mouth and nose. It wasn't pretty! Henry Jones caught my glance. Together we watched as the last remnants of the smoke dribbled from the sides of her mouth while she spoke.

"Need I say more?" he said.

"Nope. I get your point. We can move on, please."

"I'm afraid not," he replied. "I've got more to say. The most infamous chemical in cigarettes is nicotine. This poisonous drug is said to be even more addictive than heroin or cocaine. That's why many smokers choose to die a horrible, painful death rather than give up smoking. They're hopelessly addicted to nicotine. The *Journal of the American Medical Association* reported that in the year 2000, tobacco was responsible for 435 000 deaths in the US. That's 18.1% of all fatalities, making it the number one killer in the USA. Heck, tobacco is so bad even passive smoking is extremely harmful to you. Inhaling drifting tobacco smoke kills more people each year than motor accidents, crime, drugs and even Aids. It's estimated that over 40 000 people die from heart and blood vessel disease caused by other people's smoke each year in the US alone.

"I knew smoking was bad, but I had no idea it was that bad!" I had to admit.

He leaned back and put his hands behind his head. "If you smoke, you're in grave danger. Since you want to heal your body, you should know this, too: Every time you inhale on a cigarette it destroys about 25mg of vitamin C. You need Vitamin C because it helps to prevent bacterial infections and accelerates healing. If you've had surgery, or if you're scheduled for surgery, you need to quit smoking now. Smokers take 10 times longer to heal than non-smokers."

I suddenly remembered how much I had wanted to go home and smoke a cigar on the day I left the hospital with Henry Jones. It made me wince. I had smoked a packet of cigarettes a day when I was younger. The thought of it made me cringe. How much damage had I done to myself? I wondered.

Henry Jones studied the woman beside us with great compassion. She puffed away, oblivious to the harm she was doing to herself. I scanned the crowd. Since it was an 'open' area, there were smokers everywhere. My heart sank with sorrow.

Henry Jones sighed. "If I had to give you a list of all the negative effects of smoking, it would be too long to publish in our book. Top of the list however are lung cancer; throat cancer; cardiovascular and pulmonary disorders; high blood pressure and high cholesterol. There's no doubt about it my friend, smoking destroys human health. It's a killer."

"We should find another place to sit," I suggested, standing up.

"Not today," Henry Jones replied. "Today I want us to observe the masses. I want to immerse us in the everyday experience of millions and millions of people, so that you fully realize the importance of the book we're writing together. Please, take a seat. I want to ask you another simple question."

"Okay," I mumbled begrudgingly, sitting back down.

"If you saw a bottle marked poison, would you drink it?"

"Of course not!"

"Not even a little swig?"

"Nope. No chance."

Avoid alcohol

"So, how come you drink alcohol? Don't you know that alcohol is a poisonous drug, too?"

I knew we'd get to this vice eventually. It was just a matter of time. Impulsively, I wanted to defend my whiskey drinking. I'd been doing it for years and years, and I'd grown accustomed to it.

"Surely, a shot of alcohol isn't that bad for you?" I suggested, my voice trembling.

He glared at me. "Don't kid yourself, my friend. Small doses wreak havoc on your system, and high doses will kill you. Alcohol is poison, pure and simple. But it's not just the alcohol you should be worried about. The chemicals that are put into all alcoholic beverages are extremely toxic. Add to this toxic mixes, like soft drinks, which disguise the horrible taste, and you're pouring a slow-killing concoction down your throat every time you consume alcohol. Big alcohol companies have spent billions of dollars convincing people that good times and their products go together. Think celebrations, think alcohol. Think success, think alcohol. Think stress, think alcohol. You've got to hand it to them: They've done a marvelous job of tricking the masses into spending fortunes on their evil products. It's almost inconceivable that they can so successfully market a foul-tasting product that's extremely harmful to the human body.

"Young people actually aspire to drink alcohol. It has become a modern-day rite of passage. They can't wait to reach the legal drinking age. They associate it with growing up. How spiritually retarded is a society in which this can happen? No, no, no! Alcohol is bad. It makes no difference what you drink: Wine, beer and spirits are all unhealthy for your body. When you say: 'Cheers', it really is to your health. The World Health Organization conducted a study on the Global Burden of Disease. The study established that alcohol is the third most important risk factor, after smoking, for ill-health and premature death. It's estimated to be 9.2% of the disease burden."

"That's scandalous!"

"But wait, there's more: One in 16 hospital admittances are alcohol-related. Take a second to think about this statistic and try to comprehend the actual cost to society of alcohol consumption. It's astronomical!"

"We could probably end hunger if that money was used to feed the world's poor," I commented.

"Well put," he said loudly. "The more you drink, the greater your risk of harm. Drinking alcohol daily can cause organ damage, especially to your liver, kidneys and bladder. It's proven to cause 20% of cancer of the oesophagus, as well as liver cancer and cirrhosis of the liver. Alcohol destroys brain cells; dehydrates cells; depletes the body of vitamins B1, B2, B6, B12; and forms destructive free radicals. It also prevents absorption and proper storage of ingested vitamins. Appalled yet?"

"Actually, I am."

"On top of this, it's extremely difficult for your body to process alcoholic beverages, because alcohol is unnatural. Nothing else is absorbed through your stomach walls but alcohol. When you drink alcohol, it infiltrates your blood stream, which distributes toxic poisons to your entire body. These poisons are capable of rupturing veins. If you don't believe me, look closely at the face of a heavy drinker and you'll be able to see that the tiny blood capillaries under the skin have burst."

"My father's face was riddled with burst blood vessels," I said scornfully. Just the thought of his bulbous, red nose made my stomach turn.

He pointed to the pregnant woman again. "Did you know that alcohol is one of a few substances that can pass through the placenta? It's true. Babies of heavy drinkers are often born with brain damage or deformities, because alcohol eats away at the foetus – especially the facial features, like the nose and ears. This problem is so common that the medical fraternity have given it a name: Foetal Alcohol Syndrome. How much more proof do you need that the human body isn't designed to cope with alcohol?"

"None." I almost begged him to stop.

He threw his hands in the air. "Take my advice: Avoid alcohol. Especially when you're sick!"

"Why specifically when you're sick?" I had to ask.

"Alcohol depletes chlorine, which helps your liver to eliminate poisons and drugs from your body, like medicine. It also depletes folic acid, which acts as an analgesic for pain and protects against intestinal parasites. When folic acid is deficient, so are your antibodies. You absolutely must increase folic acid when fighting illness. It also depletes niacin, which promotes a healthy digestive system and increases circulation. It depletes magnesium, which is important for converting blood sugar to energy, which you need when you're sick to heal your body. It also depletes zinc, which accelerates the healing of wounds. Last but not least, alcohol is full of sugar. I can run through the harmful effects of sugar again …"

"No, thank you! I've got it. Alcohol, fizzy drinks, caffeine and cigarettes are harmful vices." I put my hands in the air, as if to surrender. "Please, let's move on."

Refuse refined wheat

"Alright. Let's discuss grain."

"Isn't grain good for you?" I inquired, only too happy to change the subject.

"Let's just say this: If you walked into a wheat field and plucked a handful of kernels, they would be 100% whole-grain, just as God intended them to be. In their natural state, grains of wheat are jam-packed with life-giving, energy-giving nutrients. However, most of the nutritive elements, over 23 natural vitamins and minerals, including the bran and the fibre, are situated in the outer layers of the grain. Unfortunately, most of the wheat products you buy from supermarkets are made from processed or refined flour. When wheat or any other grain is 'refined', the outer layers are removed, which renders the grain hopelessly deficient in nutritional value and fibre."

"I didn't realize this."

"Wait. It gets worse. The refinement process also removes the wheat germ, which stores the essence of the natural goodness of grain, over 30 vitamins and minerals, plus natural oils. So, to make up for it, manufacturers put back synthetic vitamins and then have the audacity to label their products as 'enriched' or 'fortified'. Do they take us for stupid, or what?"

"Actually, I do feel stupid, right now," I said.

Henry Jones grunted. "I could go on to tell you about how manufacturers bleach refined flour with more chemicals, so that it looks white and pure, but I don't want to bore you with the details. I'm sure you catch my drift, right? The glue-paste that's left over doesn't do you any good. The fact is: Refined flour is bad for you."

"But why?" I asked. "Our readers need to know."

"White, refined flour is a simple carbohydrate. When you eat it, your body converts it to sugar very quickly. This stimulates your pancreas to produce excess insulin, which signals your liver to produce cholesterol. Your body must then work extra hard to get rid of the excess sugar from your bloodstream. Because this process is so unnatural, the body usually over-compensates, which leaves you with low sugar levels. As a result, you lack energy. I've already told you that the rapid fluctuations of your blood sugar levels put your body under severe stress. If you do this to yourself regularly, it's possible that the system that controls your blood sugar levels can break down, causing you to become diabetic."

"Jeez, that doesn't sound good. Does it?" I remarked, my eyes glued on a couple sitting opposite who were sinking their teeth into giant hamburger buns.

"I'm not done yet, my friend. I can go on, and on, and on! Refined flour has been known to cause constipation, food allergies, increased cholesterol, dermatitis, fatigue, muscle weakness and an impaired immune system. The bottom line is this: It's best for you just to refuse refined foods! Don't you agree?"

Ditch dairy

"I do," I said. "And what about dairy? Should I avoid dairy, too?" I asked with a sense of trepidation.

"Take a close look at nature and you'll soon realize that milk is meant for weaning young mammals. Once weaned, they never go back to the teat, do they?"

"No, I guess not!"

"Here's another thing: You don't ever see a bull dropping down to drink from a cow, do you?"

"Nope!"

"And, have you ever seen monkeys drink milk from giraffes, or dogs drink milk from cats?"

"Never!"

"So, why do human beings drink milk from cows?"

I didn't have an answer for him.

"Are we biologically different from every other mammal created by Mother Nature?"

"But I thought milk was good for you? I clearly remember seeing adverts that encourage mothers to give their children milk," I replied.

Henry Jones rolled his eyes. "Those adverts are funded by people who profit from milk sales, my friend. Milk is meant for calves, not humans! The problem is: Your body needs two enzymes to break down milk: Renin and lactase. Unfortunately, it stops making these enzymes by the time you're three. There's also an element in cow's milk and human milk called casein. The big difference between them is that there's 300 times more casein in cow's milk. Casein is used as the base element in wood glue."

"Oh-oh!"

"Cows have four stomachs. They can break this casein down, but, inside your body, this goo covers your organs in sticky mucous, which is extremely difficult to break down and dispose of. Also, because of forced mass production, udders become septic and produce a puss-like substance, so farmers pump cows full of powerful antibiotics. If you add this to the pasteurizing and homogenizing processes that follow, there's very little natural quality left in milk."

"What about cheese? I like cheese," I blurted.

He sighed. "Dairy products, such as cheese, ice-cream, milk, butter and yoghurt, contribute significant amounts of cholesterol and fat to your diet, which can increase your risk of chronic diseases. High on the list are cardiovascular disease, breathing problems such as asthma and sinusitis, and many more degenerative diseases caused by mucous."

"Yuck!" I exclaimed.

"This mucous is a major problem. People, especially children, with constantly blocked or running noses are most likely consuming dairy and/or sugar. The body can't cope with the amount of toxins, so it expels them wherever possible. An overflowing nose is a sure sign of overflowing toxic waste."

"That's enough!" I moaned. I was ready to go home.

"Sadly not. There are more harmful vices to avoid."

I grimaced. "Such as?

Ditch the drugs

"Narcotics! You're a responsible adult, so I really shouldn't have to explain to you how bad drugs are for our mind, body and soul. All I will say is this: If you do drugs, clean out! If you can't, get over your ego and seek professional help immediately! Your life and quality of life are at stake. That's all there is to it!"

"What else?"

Deal with overeating

"Overeating is also a vice, and it poses a serious health risk. If you eat for a full, stodgy feeling, you're most likely compensating for a lack of emotional fulfilment in your life. Try cutting back on your food and you'll be surprised at how quickly you'll find the energy you need to raise your emotional energy."

"I suppose fast food is a vice too, huh?" I asked, looking around me in sheer horror.

Avoid fast food

"It's a travesty, but fast food has become quite normal in our society. Poor dietary habits are built into our way of life. Right? If you choose convenience instead of nutritional value, then you need to develop an emotional attachment to the real value of food. How? By developing a sense of gratitude for natural, wholesome food! And you can only do this when you begin to understand and respect the needs of your body. When you eat junk food, like fast food and fizzy drinks, you make yourself sad. Genuinely!

The amino acids in these foods travel directly to your brain and stimulate the production of a chemical called acetylcholine, which makes you feel negative emotions. On the other hand, when you eat fruit and vegetables, the amino acids stimulate the production of dopamine, which makes you feel positive emotions. In other words, a whole-foods, plant-based diet makes you feel good. Is Mother Nature smart, or what?"

Say no to sauces

"You should also avoid condiments and sauces, my friend. They may make your food taste good, but they're bad for your body and they pervert your taste buds. Make no mistake: these man-made concoctions are jam-packed with toxic chemicals, flavorants, colorants and preservatives. They're also usually loaded with sugar. Eating sauces is a temporary fix to make junk food taste good. I say 'fix' because they're physically and emotionally addictive, too. Try cutting them out of your diet and you'll be shocked at how many negative emotions emerge. You'll feel deprived, cheated, miserable, unenthusiastic, depressed, quick-tempered and irritable, but your taste buds will rejuvenate over time, and you'll be able to truly appreciate how delicious natural food is."

My brain was numb. Henry Jones had beaten me into submission. "What else?" I groaned.

Let go of meat

"Meat is a vice too."

"Meat?"

"Sure. A vice is something that's bad for you if done in excess and you can't give up. Right? If you don't think of meat as being a vice, try giving it up. I know it's a controversial health subject and opinions differ, but I've already shared my point of view with you. I regard meat as bad for you, animals and our planet. If everyone switched to a whole-foods, plant-based diet, we could end world hunger."

"What? How come?"

"Because most maize crops are used for feeding livestock through intensive farming methods. If this maize went to feed humans instead, there would be no more hungry people in the world. Feeding cattle maize is completely unnatural. Cattle are meant to eat grass, not maize. It's no secret that the demand for meat, created by global fast food chains, is the biggest reason why

449

we're cutting down the rain forests at such a rapid rate. Major agricultural corporates need this land to grow food and rear livestock. Around 150 billion animals are slaughtered each year worldwide. In the United States alone, around nine billion animals are slaughtered every year. This includes about 150 million cattle, bison, sheep, hogs, and goats, and nine billion chickens, turkeys, and ducks. Slaughtering animals on such a large scale poses significant logistical problems, as you can imagine. Most often, animals are driven for hundreds of miles to slaughterhouses in conditions that result in injuries and death en route. There has been strong criticism of the methods of transport, preparation, herding, and killing within some abattoirs. Investigations by animal welfare and animal rights groups have indicated that in some cases, animals are skinned or gutted while alive and conscious. Never in the history of the planet has this cruelty to animals been so prolific."

"That's really disgusting!" I declared. The sight of so many out-of-shape people munching burgers around us suddenly made me nauseous. My stomach churned.

Get exercising

"Here's another vice for you to consider: A lack of exercise. Yes, laziness is a vice. Over the last 100 years, our modern lifestyle has systematically engineered physical activity out of our daily lives. We do very little physical labour compared to people who lived a century ago. We drive cars, catch taxis and ride trains and planes. We don't walk as much or work as hard as we used to work. The less we exercise, the less we want to exercise, so we become unfit and lazy! Some people don't even think about exercising! Some people try it, but they get tired quickly and quit."

"So, what's the solution?"

"There's only one way to get fit, my friend. Get off your lazy bum and do some exercise. You've got to get your heart rate up for 20 minutes every day. What's your favorite exercise?"

"Chewing."

He didn't appreciate my humor. "You've got to exercise!"

"But it hurts," I protested. I was stiff and sore from all the exercise that Henry Jones and Mrs Moffet had made me do.

"Push through the pain until it becomes a pleasure."

I knew I wouldn't win this conversation. "Anything else?

Stress less

He shrugged. "Stress is a vice, and some people are addicted to it."

"Explain."

"Stress is simply your body's response to change," he said. "When your life circumstances evolve in a way that makes it difficult for you to cope mentally, physically, spiritually or emotionally, you become stressed. This phenomenon has reached epidemic proportions in the modern world. Millions of people constantly push themselves to the limits because they are addicted to the adrenaline created by stressful situations. They literally become stress junkies. Some people do extreme sports; some people become workaholics; and some people just invent one small reason after the next to stress out. The problem with this addiction is that, even though they develop stress stamina, it eventually manifests somewhere in the body as disease. Yes, stress makes people sick. Very sick!"

"But how can we avoid it?"

"I can give you a list of simple yet effective tips to reduce stress and calm down."

"Go for it. I'm all ears." I needed to hear something positive.

He counted them down on his fingers. "Learn how to manage your emotions better; whenever possible, avoid stressful situations and people; learn to accept the things you can't change; talk out your troubles; look for the good in life instead of the bad; exercise regularly; stretch your body to help you release tension; meditate daily; and above all else, avoid harmful vices!"

I won't lie. In that moment, I became stressed. Stressed beyond measure. I looked around in absolute horror. We were surrounded by hundreds of people stuffing their faces with junk food, sucking on soft drinks, knocking back beers, puffing on cigarettes and jabbering their unconscious heads off. It was awful! I realized why Henry Jones brought me to the mall. He wanted me to see how millions and millions of people live their daily lives. The scales weren't lifted from my eyes, they were ripped off.

"Jeez, Henry, these really are the killing fields, aren't they?" I said, looking around me.

He didn't answer me. We sat in total silence for a long time, studying the people around us. It was a sad and tragic sight. The worst part was that most of them appeared to be happy. They laughed and smiled and chatted and flirted.

"I guess ignorance is bliss," I eventually declared.

Henry Jones narrowed his eyes and said in a deep and solemn voice: "Ignorance is only bliss until the hammer falls. Then it becomes a living hell, or worse – a death sentence. For the last time, don't be duped by vices. They are nothing more than bad habits employed by your ego-mind to keep control of your life. When you give in to your vices, you always do so at the expense of your true-self. They rob you of your life's true potential and keep you trapped in habitual cycles of despair. You must sever yourself from your vices, my friend. Don't try to wean yourself off your vices. Don't allow yourself any slack at all. Setting timelines for kicking bad habits is all well and good when you're fit as a fiddle, but when you're sick, you don't have time to pussyfoot around. Cut yourself loose immediately."

"I hear you, Henry. Please tell me how to do it!" I almost grabbed him by the collar and shook him in desperation.

Henry Jones spoke slowly and carefully: "It starts with self-awareness, my friend. Sit down with a notepad or computer and make a list of all your vices. Writing them down brings them into your awareness."

"Is that it?"

"There's more. Once you have your list of vices, write down the names of the people who usually practise them with you, as well as the places where you do them."

"How come?"

"You've got to steer clear of temptation. Don't visit places that you associate with your vices, or you'll find yourself in situations that may lead you astray. Trust me: Severing yourself from harmful vices is hard enough without having to watch others indulging in them. Use your common sense. If you usually pop into a bar on your way home from work, don't! If you're invited to a wild party, decline the offer. If you usually buy cigarettes or cigars from the tobacconist on the corner, stay away from it. Get it?"

"Sure."

"Secondly, avoid instigators. Again, use your common sense. If you usually smoke cigars with a particular friend who has a strong personality, don't visit him or invite him over to your house. If you know people who like to drink alcohol, avoid them. If you have friends who are lazy, distance yourself from them. What you want to do is find other interesting things to do with nice people who won't tempt you with harmful vices."

"Are you saying that I must never ever again partake in any of my vices?" I felt panicked.

He sighed. "Yes. You won't regret it in the long run."

Abstain

"The ego-mind gets the better of many people and tricks them into thinking that life will be dull without the occasional, delectable vice. It convinces them that it's okay to 'revel in their humanness' from time to time. Perhaps there's some truth in that belief. But be warned: Indulging in your vices is a very slippery slope. I know this to be true. I've seen how people slowly but surely slip back into their old vices once they recover their wellness. This is the reason I favor abstinence. There's purity in it. But the choice is ultimately yours to make. If you want to heal your body, you must put your body's needs first. It's best to go cold turkey."

"Cold turkey!" I exclaimed.

"Yes. The fastest, quickest, surest way to eliminate unwanted vices, like sugar, alcohol, meat, nicotine and caffeine addiction, is to go cold turkey. Just say: 'No!'"

"That's easier said than done. Bad habits are hard to break. The mind and body struggle to adjust to abrupt change," I protested in vain.

He shrugged once more. "What choice do you have? Remember, your primary objective isn't to kick the habit, but rather to get well as fast as you can."

He'd a good point. In fact, it was irrefutable. Who wouldn't give up their vices to be well again?

"You're right. You're right! We'd have to be crazy to choose our vices over wellness, wouldn't we?" I mumbled. He didn't reply. Instead, he steepled his fingers on the table-top and waited patiently for my thoughts to settle.

Keep busy

"How did you do it?" I eventually inquired.

"I found the best way to go cold turkey was to keep myself busy. That made all the difference in the world. I didn't have time for my vices because my schedule was filled. Keeping yourself busy is more than a suggestion: It's an instruction!"

"I'd like to follow your lead, Henry Jones. What did you do, exactly?"

"I started practising healing techniques. Lots and lots of healing techniques! I made sure that my days were jam-packed with activities and people who could help me to heal my body. That's how my healing journey started. I didn't plan to do it. I found myself on a healing journey after months and months of keeping myself busy with practising healing techniques and visiting healing practitioners."

"I'm amazed you found the way on your own," I commented. "I'd be lost without you."

Seek help

He pondered my statement for a moment. "We must encourage our readers to get professional help, if necessary. Sometimes support from friends, family and colleagues just doesn't cut it. If they are seriously addicted to their vices, they must seek help from qualified professionals and attend support groups. There is no need to feel ashamed. Shame comes from not seeking help."

"What else?"

Note your mistakes

"Record your indiscretions."

I knew why he made this suggestion. I'd been recording my indiscretions in my Workbook and I know how seeing them in print had plagued my conscience.

"You'll be amazed at how quickly you forget how you indulged in your vices. It's almost as if your ego-mind erases your memory on purpose, to hide the evidence. But, when you write down your misdoings, they serve as a permanent record. Don't be surprised if you find yourself avoiding vices on your healing journey because you don't want to see them logged in your Workbook. Vice entries are blemishes that stay in your Workbook forever."

Replace bad habits with good ones

He was on to me. Henry Jones grinned. "Your main aim is to cut out your vices. If you feel the urge to indulge, find positive replacements. Cutting out vices will leave a void in your life. You need to replace bad habits with good ones. For instance: If you usually have a sundowner after work, get into the habit of making a fruit or veggie juice instead."

"Whiskey or carrot juice, huh?" I joked.

"The secret is to put lots of effort, passion and creativity into the positive replacement so that the process stimulates and satisfies you. Imagine handing your wife a tall glass of crushed ice, blended with watermelon and mint, served with a cocktail umbrella."

I was sold instantly. He had me on the mention of my wife. The drink sounded delicious, too. Together, the experience was irresistible. I cursed the countless times I had got home from work pickled and poured myself a double whiskey before flopping in front of the TV without even saying hello. I swallowed hard to suppress my surging emotions.

Reward yourself

"I suppose you're going to recommend I reward myself for cutting out my vices, eh?"

"You bet. I suggest you set up a series of targets in the weeks and months ahead, and then reward yourself as you hit them, one by one. For example: If you don't drink caffeine or alcohol for a week, treat yourself to a desired music CD. If you don't want to spend money, plan to do something you really enjoy that doesn't cost money, like watching a sunset, or picking flowers, or camping under the stars. This will give you something to strive for. Trust me: It's very important to reward yourself for your small successes on a healing journey, but it's essential to reward yourself for cutting out vices. Now," Henry Jones said: "Should we blow this pop-stand and make our way to Sister Simone's convent?"

I practically leapt to my feet. I couldn't get out of there fast enough.

"Wait for me," Henry Jones yelled as we skedaddled to the car.

"Catch me if you can," I yelled back. But, I wasn't slowing down, and I wasn't going back!

CHAPTER 24

LIFE AIN'T A BED OF ROSES

The mall had been a miserable, wonderful learning experience. Seeing all those people, either consciously or unconsciously, gorging on their vices was sickening to me. Henry Jones had given me precious insights into the harmful effects of common vices, all of which I was guilty of doing on a regular basis. I'd never be the same again. Not much was said in the car ride to the convent. I felt sad, demoralized and depressed. As we turned into the convent I thought to myself: Something is definitely wrong with our society. We've lost our humanity. We've sold our souls for the 'convenience' of the modern-day lifestyle. We've swallowed all the lies and deceit, hook, line and sinker.

"You okay?" Henry Jones asked.

"I was thinking about our experience at the mall."

"What about it?"

"How stupid and gullible we are. We don't think for ourselves. We're just like sheep."

"What do you mean?"

"Our masters feed us unnatural and inappropriate food to fatten us up for a commercial killing. We stand around bleating and baaing, oblivious to the fact that we're being bred for slaughter."

"Phew, that's a morbid thought," Henry Jones gasped.

"I wonder if people would continue stuffing their faces with junk food if they rolled a few cancer patients into the fast food section at the malls each day."

"Oh dear, I can tell you're in a dark place. Perhaps we should go for walk in the convent gardens to cheer you up before we go to see Sister Simone. She's a shy bird and I wouldn't want you to frighten her."

"Good idea," I said, climbing out of the Land Rover.

"There's a lovely rose garden at the bottom of the grounds. Let's sit there for a while."

"Lead the way," I replied, trying to smile.

The rose garden was lovely. There was a small, wooden bench tucked beneath a round, gabled archway at the opposite side of the garden. We made our way towards it, through a maze of pathways and flower beds. The fragrance of the flowers was heavy and strong. Henry Jones stopped to smell the roses. I pushed on. After taking some time to admire a statue of Mother Mary in the center of the garden, he joined me on the bench.

"I'm sorry," I said as he sat down beside me.

"For what?"

"My outburst."

"That's quite alright," he replied. "As I recall, the last time we had a conversation on a park bench, you weren't able to express your emotions at all."

That brought a quick smile to my face.

"That's what I call progress," Henry Jones remarked.

I loved spending time with Henry Jones, and I knew our time together was coming to an end. His wife was waiting for him on a faraway island and he'd be leaving me all too soon.

I cleared my throat. "You said you'd put me back in touch with my emotions, and you've evidently succeeded."

"Good. I'm very pleased. They're meant to be your internal guidance system. They exist to serve you."

At that exact moment, either through coincidence or some strange twist of fate, a fresh breeze blew through the rose garden. I felt its coolness brush over my skin. It seemed to be a sign.

"When you feel emotion, it's always because a basic human need is either filled or unfilled. When your needs are met, your emotions are positive. When your needs are unmet, your emotions are negative. Believe it or not: Your life's direction is determined by this very simple, yet extremely complex, emotional steering mechanism."

"Please elaborate."

"To put it simply, your emotions make you move towards what gives you pleasure and away from what causes you pain. This basic principle determines every aspect of your life. It governs your interaction with the world around you. Your emotional response to life determines who you become, what you do, how you do it, why you do it, and even when you do it."

"So, your emotions not only steer you through life, but they actually determine the outcome of it?" I inquired.

"That's precisely what I'm saying, my friend. Stop and think about this: The quality of your life isn't determined by what you know – it's determined by what you feel." He paused, allowing this statement to sink in. "Agreed?"

"I guess so."

He sat back and folded his arms. I can tell you're struggling to wrap your head around this concept. It may help you to distinguish between knowledge and spirit."

Your emotions are the key

"Eh?" I was befuddled.

He chuckled. "Knowledge is connected to the mind, whereas spirit is connected to emotions. In other words, what you know is connected to your ego-mind, and what you feel is connected to your true-self. For this reason, a person can be incredibly knowledgeable but unhappy, and a person can be blissfully happy without knowing very much. The key to your true-self is your emotions. They determine your quality of life because they determine your connectedness to your true-self."

The light went on in my head. It suddenly made perfect sense. I sat back and folded my arms, too. The delighted expression on my face said it all. He chuckled harder.

"There's another reason it's critical for you to tune into your emotions. They alert the people around you to how you're feeling. Emotions are brilliant at capturing people's attention." He turned to me: "Have you ever experienced the reaction that occurs when someone walks into a room crying? It's a showstopper, right?"

I saw my mother crying often. I stopped biting down on my lip when it hurt too much. "Yes, it's a showstopper alright."

Henry Jones nodded knowingly. "Emotions definitely help us to communicate. They amplify the message we're trying to put across. Without making a connection to our emotions, our words are impotent. You can put this to the test by trying to say angry words with a big smile on your face. You can't, can you?"

"I suppose not."

"Of course not!" he cried. "Emotions are pure and honest. We can't fake them. Not really. We can pretend to be happy or sad, but deep down we know the truth of how we feel. We can also try to hide our emotions and suppress them, but this doesn't work either."

Emotions should be shared

"Emotions are meant to be shared, not bottled up inside. If we don't tell people how we're feeling, our emotions build up inside of us until we feel like we'll burst. It's a natural human response. Sharing our emotions is essential to our quality of life because they help us to feel understood, cared about and acknowledged. We all need this to feel fulfilled."

"This is probably the reason why I felt unfulfilled for so long," I admitted.

"Did you feel isolated and alone, too?" he asked without mercy.

"Yes, I did."

"I'm not surprised. You see, our feelings unite us."

"They do?"

"Sure. It's entirely possible to share an emotional experience with someone you don't know, or don't even like, for that matter! Have you ever watched a sporting event with a mixed crowd of people? You instantly forget your differences when your team scores, don't you? In that moment, you unconsciously let your emotions override your prejudices. Before you know it, you find yourself jumping up and down with joy, hugging complete strangers, yeah?"

"I've done that plenty of times," I admitted.

"Our emotions help us to make conscious and subconscious decisions all the time. Ask advertising executives and they'll tell you that people make buying decisions based on their emotions. They can rattle off the features and advantages of their products until they're blue in the face, but it's the emotional benefits that clinch the deal! Without emotions we wouldn't be able to make the simplest decisions. We wouldn't know how we feel about our choices. Make sense?"

"I think so."

"Perhaps it'll become clearer when you learn how to understand your emotional-self properly."

"How do I do this?"

He raised his hand so that he could count down on his fingers. "You need to be familiar with these five terms: Emotional literacy, emotional honesty, emotional awareness, emotional intelligence, and EQ."

"I'm lost," I confessed.

Emotional literacy

"Let's kick off with emotional literacy. This just means being able to label feelings with specific 'feeling words'. These are words that can explain the emotion instantly."

"Can you give me an example?"

"Sure. Let's take a quick trip down memory lane, shall we? Before you started your healing journey, do you remember feeling unfulfilled, dissatisfied, confused, frustrated, afraid, pessimistic, discouraged, hopeless, insecure, unaware, unmotivated, tense, needy, nervous, worried, useless, inadequate, empty, powerless, weak, helpless, resentful, bitter, isolated, lonely, disconnected, unlovable or undesirable?"

"Uh huh."

"And now, would you say that your healing journey has made you feel more optimistic, encouraged, enthusiastic, energetic, confident, motivated, focused, independent, worthy, deserving, proud, excited, happy, aware, safe, secure, supported, peaceful, comfortable, relaxed, satisfied, fulfilled and lovable."

"Definitely!"

"That's wonderful news. Defining your feelings accurately is very important. It helps you to understand the real issue or problem! How many times have you said: 'I'm angry'?"

"Plenty."

"Fine. Now consider this: Although that was an expression of emotion, it didn't help you, or anyone else, to understand which emotional need was unmet."

"You've lost me gain."

"The whole point of expressing emotions is to find ways to make you feel better. If you said: 'I feel neglected,' or 'I feel disrespected,' then you, and the person with whom you shared your feelings, could focus on the real problem to find a solution. Hence, your capacity for emotional literacy enables you to discuss emotions and communicate your feelings clearly and directly. Does that make sense to you now?"

The penny dropped. "Yes, emotional literacy is the ability to understand, interpret and articulate emotions. Right?"

Emotional honesty

"Yes. Now, let's discuss emotional honesty."

"Wait. Does emotional honesty mean expressing your true feelings?" I guessed.

"Bingo!" he yelled. "But don't let this concept fool you. The name may be easy to interpret, but it's not always easy to do. You see, we're conditioned from a young age to suppress our true feelings. The root of the problem lies in the fact that most parents and teachers treat children as if their emotional needs are identical. This is a big mistake!"

"What do you mean?"

"Simply this: We're all very different. Our emotional and psychological needs are not the same. Some individuals need close interpersonal relationships, while others need lots of space. Some individuals are naturally secure within themselves, and others need plenty of reassurance. You get the picture?"

"Yes, but what's the problem?"

"Well, if we're treated as though all of our emotional needs are identical, then it's obvious that some of our needs won't be met. When this happens, a young, developing ego-mind will always grab the opportunity to fill this gap with negative behavior or harmful vices. I bet you've heard this one before: 'Don't mind him, he's just looking for attention!'"

"I have, come to think of it. I've a nephew who throws tantrums and demands sweets and toys in order to be pacified. I just thought he was a spoilt brat who needs a darn good hiding. It never occurred to me that he probably doesn't get much attention from his parents. They both have booming professional careers, and he spends most of his time at school or with his au pairs."

"Poor kid! It certainly sounds like he's misunderstood. Most likely, his response to his unmet emotional needs is being inaccurately interpreted as misbehavior. In response, he'll almost certainly be reprimanded or punished by others, so that he's 'put back into his place' alongside everyone else. In the years ahead, however, he could develop an unconscious, internal belief system that expressing his emotions is wrong. He could learn to associate his outbursts with pain and rejection, and subsequently suppress his natural instinct to share his true feelings. Of course, he could also swing the other way. His outbursts could become a conditioned response and he'll never grow out of them. There are millions, perhaps billions, of people of all ages who act up when their emotional needs are not met. They immediately look for attention to alert people to their unmet emotional needs."

"I should spend more quality time with my nephew. He's obviously a lot like me. There's no way I had my emotional needs met by my parents. As you know, my father was an emotionally and physically abusive drunk, and my poor mother was a wreck most the time because she lived with him. I don't want my nephew to grow up making the same mistakes as me."

"What mistakes?"

I shrugged. "I bury my true feelings deep inside me. So deep, in fact, I don't think I can be emotionally honest with myself."

"You'll be surprised," Henry Jones replied. "It's easy when you know where to start."

"Tell me, please."

Emotional awareness

"Emotional honesty starts with emotional awareness. To really know oneself requires that we know how we feel in all of life's situations. This means becoming conscious of how we feel in the present moment. Our innate capacity for self-awareness enables us to be aware of our own feelings and the feeling of others as they're occurring. Emotional awareness is all about becoming conscious of feelings in yourself, and others. This is a spiritual passage. As you strive to become more conscious of your emotions, you naturally become more conscious of yourself, which is our definition of spirituality. Isn't it?"

"It sounds good, but how do I do this practically?"

"You need to ask yourself: 'How does this situation make me feel?' And your answer can't be 'good' or 'bad'! You've got to use feeling words to fully understand your range of emotions. Life isn't just good or bad, happy or sad. It's much wider and richer and fuller. It's essential to be aware of your full range of emotions. Why? Because these feelings determine the depth and quality of your life!"

"So, you're saying if we don't tune into our true feelings, we miss out on the richness and fullness of our lives?"

462

"Exactly! When we become more aware of our true feelings, we're more likely to find our own individual happiness. Remember the Law of Attraction: We attract what we think and what we feel. Our feelings fuel the creative process. So, when we're aware of our true feelings, we can use them to steer our lives. At a high level, the principle works like this: If our thoughts make us feel bad, we must change our thinking to the outcome that makes us feel good. This is how we create the reality we want for ourselves. At a deeper level, the more information we can consider, the more we have to go on; the more control we have over the creative process and our future. Think of emotional literacy, honesty and awareness as stabilizers. They ensure that our lives aren't just good or bad. They keep us on an even keel as we sail towards our future dreams."

I slapped my forehead. "I totally get it now. Blocking our true emotions stops our emotional guidance system, which in turn prevents us from creating the reality we truly desire through the law of attraction. That's why emotional awareness is so crucial. It doesn't just tell us how we're feeling, it also tells us what reality we're bringing towards ourselves."

"Ta dah! You nailed it. Well done, my friend," Henry Jones cried out. "With this wisdom, you'll find your relationships with people will improve, too. Tuning into your emotional awareness also sharpens your ability to perceive and identify emotions in others. Without emotional awareness, people can end up hitting each other out of sheer frustration. Do you know what I mean?"

"Yup, I've smacked a few people in my day, I'm ashamed to say. I should've met you years ago, Henry. My whole life could've been different."

He chuckled. "It's never too late to raise your emotional intelligence, my friend."

Emotional intelligence

"Explain."

"Emotional intelligence is simply your ability to accurately identify your own feelings, to identify the feelings of others, and to solve problems involving emotional issues."

"Are you born with it, like mental intelligence?"

"No, not exactly! Some people are lucky. They're naturally sensitive to their emotions and the emotions of others, but these people are few and far between. For most of us, our emotional intelligence is determined by our upbringing and life circumstances. Unfortunately for us, this learning process seldom happens in a constructive, premeditated and deliberate way. We learn how to manage our emotions inadvertently by observing others."

Henry Jones leaned over, picked up a pebble and tossed it into the pool at the feet of the statue of Mother Mary. "We develop a high or low emotional intelligence depending on our experience of others. Emotional intelligence, therefore, follows a simple and obvious logic. If we grow up with people who have low emotional intelligence, we'll most likely develop a low emotional intelligence. With a low emotional intelligence, we struggle to cope emotionally with the challenges of everyday life. This produces negative feelings, which attracts more negative experiences, and so on. As a result, people with low emotional intelligence become prone to sickness and disease due to constant emotional stress. On the other hand, people who grow up engaging with others who have high emotional intelligence naturally learn to manage their emotions properly, which enables them to cope emotionally with life. This makes them feel good, which attracts more good things, which enables them to enjoy long-term health and happiness."

"So, in a nutshell, it's the ability to identify, assess, and control the emotions of oneself, of others, and of groups. Right?"

Henry Jones responded with two thumbs up.

"So then, what's EQ?"

EQ

"Ah! Your emotional quotient is a relative measure of how well you developed your emotional intelligence."

"I probably have a low EQ," I mumbled. "I don't handle anything to do with emotions very well."

Henry Jones sighed sympathetically. "The good news is: You can do something about it."

"Really?"

"Ah huh. It's easy to raise your EQ. Go out and buy one or two books about EQ. Read them from cover to cover, twice. I'm not kidding. You really should explore this new life science. Learn all you can and put the theory into practise. Do this, my friend, and your whole life will change."

"Is EQ really that important?"

"You'd better believe it. You'll be amazed at how much more harmonious your life will be when you improve your EQ. It's the difference between chalk and cheese. You'll see results fast. As your EQ develops, you'll become more aware of yourself as an emotional being. That'll enable you to take more responsibility for your own emotions and happiness; turn negative emotions into positive learning experiences and growing opportunities; and help others identify and benefit from their emotions. You'll naturally begin to incorporate your feelings into analysis, reasoning, problem-solving and decision-making. Your feelings will increasingly guide your thinking and actions in a positive and constructive manner. Understanding EQ is the roadmap to happiness, harmony and health."

"I'm feeling emotional right now," I remarked, half-jokingly.

He saw the humor in it. "Good. Let them out. Laugh, cry, scream or shout. Do as you feel you must. Emotions are best expressed."

A pained expression appeared on my face. "That's not what my parents taught me. I got belted for expressing my emotions. And then, if I dared cry, I got thrashed again."

Henry Jones winced. He reached out and gently squeezed my leg. "So, I take it you've heard the expression: 'Cowboys don't cry'?"

"Yes, often."

"I can't say I'm surprised. Whenever I hear someone say: 'Cowboys don't cry,' I want to finish their sentence by adding: 'Instead, they bottle things up inside and eventually get sick and die.'"

I chuckled. I'm not sure why.

Invalidating emotions

"It makes me furious when I hear people invalidating the emotions of others. This is one of the most harmful things that we can do to each other, and we do it all the time!"

"What do you mean 'invalidating emotions'?"

He turned sharply towards me. "Invalidating someone's emotions simply means trying to talk them out of their feelings. I must warn you: This is a very destructive and hurtful practice. It always stems from the ego-mind, and people have become experts at it."

"I can't say I've noticed it," I replied.

He looked shocked. "It's really important for you to know all the ways that emotions can be invalidated. When you're aware of them, you can watch out for them. Of course, you can also stop yourself from invalidating the emotions of others."

Did I unintentionally victimize others? Was I that cruel? How did I hurt them? I wondered.

"Can you give me a few examples?" I asked, wracking my brains.

"Oh, my goodness! There are loads of ways that people invalidate each other's emotions. You'd better take out your notepad again. The list is that long."

"Go on then."

"You asked for it," he said, placing his hands behind his head. "Let's kick off with the one I detest most: Ordering others to feel differently about themselves. I'll bet you a million bucks you've heard or given these orders before: 'Don't cry'; 'Don't be sad'; 'Don't worry'; 'Don't be so sensitive'; 'Cheer up'; 'Stop taking everything so personally'; 'Stop being so emotional'. I could go on, but you get my point."

I grimaced. I had barked those statements thousands of times.

"Then you're probably guilty of this one, too: Ordering others to behave differently. Do these instructions sound familiar? 'Grow up'; 'Wise up'; 'Lighten up'; 'Give it a rest'; 'Do it like this'; 'Don't do it like that'; 'Say this'; 'Don't say that'; 'Sort yourself out'; 'Cut it out'; 'Stop complaining'; and 'Stop whining'?"

He raised his eyebrows. I nodded slowly. "Yes, I've said them, too."

"What about this one: Ordering others to look differently. You know: 'Don't look like that'; 'Don't make that face'; 'Don't look so down/serious/ pleased with yourself'; 'Don't wear that'."

I was hit by pangs of guilt. I'd said those words to my wife more often than I cared to remember. "Okay, I get it now. We can move on."

"Oh no, I'm afraid we can't!" he replied, shaking his head from side to side. "We're only just scratching the surface. There are many more ways to invalidate emotions, and I need you to be aware of all of them. How many times have you heard or said these words: 'You shouldn't let it bother you'; 'You shouldn't worry so much'; 'You should feel ashamed of yourself'; 'You should just forget about it'; 'You should just drop it'; 'You should feel guilty'; 'You should be furious'; 'You should be thankful that'?"

"Too many to count," I answered, nibbling nervously on my top lip.

"What about this one: Minimizing other's feelings. That's when you say or hear things like: 'It's not that bad'; 'You're just acting'; 'You can't be serious'; 'You must be kidding'; 'You're just being difficult'; 'You're exaggerating'; 'You're making a big deal out of nothing'; 'You're blowing this way out of proportion'; and 'It's not worth getting that upset over'. You know what I'm talking about, don't you?"

"Sadly, I do."

"Have you ever noticed how some people try using reason to beat you down? They do their best to brow beat you with statements like: 'Let's stick to the facts'; 'There's no reason to get upset'; 'You're not being rational'; 'But if you really think about it ...'"

"Guilty as charged."

"Then there's debating with others. I bet you've heard or said: 'I don't *always* do that. It's not *that* bad.'"

I threw my hands in the air in surrender, but Henry Jones showed no mercy. He was in 'tough-love' gear, and he wasn't slowing down.

"Here's one that drives me crazy: Turning things around. People say: 'You always make it about you'; 'Why don't you look at yourself?'; 'What's wrong with you?'; 'I may have done that, but you ...'"

Of course, I had to admit that I'd probably used those words in every argument ever.

Henry Jones was like a kid in a candy store. "Ooh, ooh! I've got another one: Trying to isolate others. I'm pretty sure this won't be the first time you've heard these expressions: 'You're the only one who feels that way,' and 'It doesn't bother anyone else, so why should it bother you?'"

I was about to answer, but I didn't get the chance.

"Here's another corker for you: Trying to get others to question themselves. Be honest: How often have you heard these questions: 'What's the matter with you?'; 'What's your problem?'; 'Why are you making such a big deal about it?'; 'Why can't you just get over it?'; 'Why do you always have to ...?'; 'What's wrong with you?'; 'Can't you take a joke?'; 'How can you let a little thing like that bother you?'; 'Don't you think you're being a bit dramatic?'; 'Do you really think that crying about it will help anything?'"

I spoke to my wife like that all the time. Hearing Henry Jones hammer out those questions struck a chord in me. I felt very uncomfortable. I hadn't realized how easy it was to invalidate people's emotions. I'd bulldozed my way through life without a second thought for the impact I had on people's feelings. No wonder my days were filled with conflict, arguments and fights.

Henry Jones was on a roll and there was no stopping him. "Then there's trying to make others feel guilty by saying things like: 'I tried to help you, but ...'; 'After everything I've done for you ...'; 'At least I ...'; 'At least you ...'

And how about this one: Judging and labeling others. People say things like: 'You're a cry-baby'; 'You're too sensitive'; 'You're over-reacting'; 'You're way too emotional'; 'You've got a problem'; 'You need to get your head examined'; 'You're impossible to talk to'; and 'You're impossible/hopeless/useless/stupid, etc.' These responses are a dead giveaway that the ego-mind is in charge. The true-self would never be so condescending. Judging and labeling is simply venting. These expressions only put you down. If you're having a conversation with someone who starts judging and labeling you, then you should end it immediately and walk away. You can't reason with an ego-mind. It doesn't seek truth. Truth is a virtue of one's true-self."

I kept my big mouth shut, and listened.

"Denying the perception of others is another one to look out for. You'll often hear people saying things like: 'But I do respect your feelings'; 'But I do listen to you'; 'That's ridiculous'; 'I was just joking'; 'That's not what I meant'; 'You've got it all wrong'; 'I don't do that'; 'You're making it up'; and 'You're just being paranoid'. That person is trying to override your feelings with their point of view. This is a sure sign that you're not connecting emotionally or communicating effectively."

He was talking about me. I knew it. I did all these things. I invalidated people's emotions all the time. His words penetrated my thick hide and pierced my heart.

"Are you done yet?"

"Not yet. There's a few more to go."

"I don't think I can handle much more," I moaned, flipping to another clean page of my notebook.

"Defending the other person. When this one comes up, you'll hear things like: 'I'm sure they didn't mean it like that'; 'You just took it wrong'; 'Maybe they were just having a bad day'; 'They wouldn't say that'. Another popular one is negating, denial and confusion. People say things like: 'Now you know that isn't true'; 'You don't really mean that'; 'You're just in one of your moods'; and 'You'll feel differently tomorrow'."

"Yup, I've said those too," I remarked.

He grinned ever so slightly. "How about this one: Sarcasm and mocking. People say things like: 'Do you think the whole world revolves around you?'; 'You're just perfect, aren't you?'; 'Oh, poor baby, did I hurt your feelings?' and 'Did you get out on the wrong side of bed?'"

I thumped my notepad with my pen. "Thank goodness this isn't a test. I'd be failing miserably," I confessed.

Henry Jones drove his point home: "You should also watch out for people who like laying guilt trips. They're easy to spot. You'll hear them saying things like: 'Don't you ever think of anyone but yourself?'; 'What about me?'; and 'Have you ever stopped to consider my feelings?'"

I clearly remembered yelling all of those sentences at my wife while in a drunken state. They weren't pleasant memories. A cold shiver ran down my spine. "Is that it? I really, really don't think I can bear anymore."

"We're nearly done. Hang in there. I realize this isn't easy listening, but there are a few more ways to invalidate emotions that you must know about. How else can you watch out for them?"

"Okay, okay. Fire away, if you must."

"Good. Here's one: Philosophizing or using clichés. You've probably heard people say: 'Time heals all wounds'; 'Every cloud has a silver lining'; 'When you're older you'll understand'; 'You're just going through a phase'."

"I used to talk like that to my daughter all the time," I admitted.

"And, when you had family fights, did you make the mistake of talking about someone so they can hear it? That's when you say stuff like: 'He/she is impossible to talk to. You can't say anything to him or her.' Talking over someone is hurtful and cruel. It makes them feel small and irrelevant."

I flinched. I'd done that to my daughter too. I slumped into my seat.

Henry Jones's salvo finally came to an end. "Showing intolerance is the last one on my list. This method of emotional invalidation is probably the cruellest of them all. It's meant to belittle and demean. It's horrible to hear people say things like: 'This is getting really pathetic'; 'I'm sick of hearing about it'; 'This is boring'; and 'I'm so over you'. Have you heard these words before?"

"Yes, from my own lips," I mumbled. I felt mortified. I was an emotional ignoramus. No wonder my life was in a mess. I'd battered and bruised everyone in my world.

I studied the long list of things we do and say to invalidate the emotions of others. I read each sentence, line after line, and realized that we invalidate people's emotions when we discard; reject; dismiss; ignore; judge; mock; tease or diminish their feelings.

To validate means to acknowledge and accept. To invalidate means to deny and reject.

Deny and Reject. I wrote down those two little monstrous words in my notepad and drew circles around them. They leaped off the page and smacked me straight between the eyes. How awful it is to deny and reject the way people feel. This invalidates much more than just their emotions. It invalidates their very existence. Ultimately, we are how we feel.

I shared my insights with Henry Jones, who agreed wholeheartedly. "When we reject someone's emotions, we're rejecting the essence of their reality and belittling their existence. Not only does this behavior make people feel bad, but it's extremely damaging to them emotionally, mentally, spiritually and physically. It breaks down their self-confidence and lowers their self-worth. In short: Invalidation distances a person from their true-self. Why would anyone want to be so cruel?"

"I don't want to do this anymore," I blurted. "I really don't! How do I stop it?"

He served a fastball back into my court. "You've got to learn how to validate people's emotions. Honestly, this'll bring you a lifetime of healthy, happy, harmonious human relationships."

How to validate others' emotions

"It's quite simple, actually. The first step to validating someone's emotions is accepting unconditionally how that person is feeling. Listen to what they're saying without reacting to how their emotions make you feel. By doing so, you'll make it safe for them to share their feelings with you. Try it. You'll be surprised at how positively people will respond to you. The simple act of listening encourages people to open up and share their inner truth with you. It makes them feel heard, acknowledged, understood and accepted. This is what we all want most. Agreed?"

"Yes, I do. Go on."

"Once you've accepted their feelings, try to understand them. It's not very hard to do. Just listen. People always try to explain why they feel the way they do. Give them the chance to open up. If you let them, they'll help you to understand their emotions."

"Let me see if I've got this straight," I replied, studying my notes. "All I have to do is allow people to finish talking, listen carefully, and try to see things from their side. Is that it?"

"Yup! It really is that simple."

"But what if they're wrong, or I disagree with them?"

"Whether you think they're right or wrong isn't the point, my friend. The point is: That's how they're feeling in the moment. That's all that matters to them! So, let them feel it to the fullest."

"But doesn't that antagonize the situation?"

"Oh no!" he exclaimed, shaking his head from side to side. "Not at all! Once people have fully expressed and released their emotions, they go away." He paused, and then let out an amused chuckle. "I mean, the emotions go away, not the people. Trust me on this: No one wants to feel bad. They'll jump at the chance to unload painful emotions. It's cathartic for them to get all that stuff off their chest. Let them speak it out and you'll find they'll feel much better afterwards."

I tried to comprehend what Henry Jones was telling me, but I was stuck in a groove that had been deeply etched by my ego-mind over many years.

"But what about my feelings? I have emotions, too," I bellowed, beating my chest.

His answer disarmed me. "First of all, you'll find that people will listen more openly to your feelings once you've helped them work through their emotions first. Secondly, I strongly advise you to look to the source of your emotions. Your true-self only produces positive emotions, and your ego-mind only produces negative emotions. If you feel the need to be defensive; confrontational; argumentative; angry; vengeful; spiteful or hurtful, then your ego-mind is in the driving seat, and you should change drivers immediately. Conversely, if you feel the need to be understanding; accepting; empathetic; sympathetic; caring; compassionate and kind, then you're functioning from your true-self, and your responses will be appreciated."

"It's not that easy to snap out of negative emotions during an argument or fight," I retorted with less emotion in my voice.

"Yes, it is," he replied even more calmly. "When your responses indicate that you're reacting from your ego-mind, there's only one thing for you to do: Quietly and humbly thank the person for making you aware that your actions have been coming from the wrong source and assure them that you'll look at their side of things from the perspective of your true-self. Believe me, this answer is powerful enough to neutralize every human conflict on Earth."

I sat back and weighed up our conversation. It wasn't easy for me to accept this advice. I had a confrontational personality. I didn't spare people's feelings. I put my feelings first. I, I, I. I could tell my ego-mind was trying to defend its existence. I could feel it trying to control me. As my self-awareness was growing stronger on my healing journey, my ego-mind was becoming more transparent. I was increasingly able to see myself acting from my ego-mind, as if I was looking in on myself. It wasn't an outer body experience – it was an inner body experience. From that new vantage point, I could see the need to change drivers. It was time for the observer to step up. Eventually, I spoke. "And this approach works without fail?"

"Oh yes. I find that applying the techniques I've just given you helps me avoid conflict, arguments, debates and fights. I'm pretty certain that if you applied the same techniques, you'd get the same results. Just imagine: You could eliminate all emotional conflict for the rest of your life. Doesn't that sound better than scrapping all the time?"

"You make it sound so easy," I scoffed.

He leaned forward, looking back at me. "When you nurture people's feelings, you bring out the best in them. It's that simple!"

"Yes, but some people's problems are their own doing. They need to be set straight," I replied curtly.

"Hear me carefully," Henry Jones said in a controlled voice. "If you listen with the intention of problem-solving, then your ego-mind is in the driving seat. The instant you start to analyze, rationalize, judge or reason, then a red flag should go up. That's when it's best to stop yourself, take a deep breath, and go back to being a sounding board." I was about to comment, but he silenced me by raising his hand.

"You can't solve an emotional problem or heal an emotional wound with logic and reason. You can't! Trying to intellectualize people's feelings is invalidation at its very worst."

"I'm guilty of this," I admitted before he had time to stop me.

"Men usually are. Read the book called *Men are from Mars And Women are from Venus* by Allan Grey and you'll understand that men mistakenly think they're helping by looking for solutions. They dispense advice instead of letting people express their emotions unreservedly. Silly buggers."

"I still can't see why this is so wrong?" I mumbled defiantly.

"Well, firstly, you shouldn't give advice unless people ask for it. Secondly, people will only turn to you for advice when they trust you with their emotions."

"How can I get people to trust me with their emotions?" Secretly, I hoped his answer might help me win back my wife.

"There are just two things you need to do in order for people to trust you with their emotions. When people are expressing negative emotions, steadily encourage them to feel better about themselves, and when they're expressing positive emotions, steadily reinforce their feelings."

"That's it?"

"Yup, that's it. This simple formula works wonders. This is what people want and need most when they share their emotions with you. They don't need judgement, analysis, ridicule or rejection. They want and need reassurance. Nothing fancy, just plain old-fashioned reassurance! Try it next time. You'll be amazed at how effectively it works."

As difficult as this lesson was for me to grasp, I knew in my gut that I had no choice. My old approach brought only conflict and misery. It certainly didn't win me any friends or a happy marriage.

Right there, in that moment, I decided to try it. What the heck, I thought. I've got nothing to lose and everything to gain. I made a conscious choice, and it felt good. I threw my hands up and started to laugh, much to Henry Jones's surprise.

"Are you okay?" he quizzed with a grin on his face.

"I am now," I replied, laughing even louder. The tension of the day slipped from my shoulders. The relief brought tears to my eyes. It felt great to let go. My shoulders shook with convulsions of laughter that came from my gut. Henry Jones soon caught my giggles, and the two of us sat side-by-side on the bench in the rose garden and laughed our heads off. It was perhaps the silliest, most joyful moment of my life. I had started laughing because I'd realized how stupid I'd been to let my feelings dominate the feelings of others, but I'd no idea why I laughed so hard in the end. Perhaps we laughed for the sake of laughing. Perhaps we laughed at the simplicity of truth. Perhaps we laughed to soak up one more great moment together before our paths parted ways forever. Whatever the reason, it was blissful, and I'll cherish the memory, always.

CHAPTER 25

DIGGING DEEP

We had another 30 minutes to kill before we were scheduled to meet Sister Simone. I told Henry Jones about my decision to put the feelings of others first. That pleased him immensely. He told me about the massive difference that practice had made to his life over the years, and he shared more tips on how to be sensitive towards people's feelings. I guess it was inevitable, but we found our way back to discussing the importance of emotional healing and powerful techniques to do it.

"The secret to emotional healing is finding the root of your problem," he told me.

"How do I do this?" I asked enthusiastically.

"To find the painful memory that's making you sick, you have to peel away the layers of negative emotion that have built up inside of you over time."

"I'm confused. Where do the layers come from?"

"Oh, that's easy. Negative feelings, unless dealt with properly, spawn more negative feelings. Unresolved negative feelings can and do sink into deeper layers of your psyche as time passes. Each new negative emotion becomes another layer."

"Can you give me an example?"

"Sure, I can. Let's say your colleague gets the promotion you think that you deserved more. How would this make you feel?"

"Shocked!" I blurted out arrogantly.

He brushed my ego-mind aside. "Yes, shock might be your initial response, but as time goes by you may start to experience a range of different emotions.

Let's run through a hypothetical sequence, shall we?" He lifted his hand and started counting down on his fingers. "Shock could be followed by feelings of disbelief; denial; betrayal; hurt; anger; spite; resentment; bitterness; hate and even loathing. Right?"

"I guess so."

"Good. Now, here's where the wheels start to spin. In order to manage your professional relationship with your colleague, who is now your new boss, you'll probably suppress those feelings. To save face with your colleagues, you might act like the new situation doesn't bother you. Heck, you may do such a good job that you even trick yourself into believing that response is true. But it's not, is it? Indifference is just the tip of the iceberg. It sits on top of all the other negative feelings that are buried deeper and deeper inside of you. Make sense?"

All I could do was nod. As fate would have it, I had had that exact experience in my youth.

"Excellent. I'm pleased you understand how this principle works. These emotional layers are little more than layers of perception, or misperception, created by your ego-mind to obscure your true-self. You have to remove those layers, one by one, to find the hurtful memory that's holding you back. You need to release it."

"Okay, so how do I remove these layers?"

"You've got to peel them away, one by one, like an onion."

"Peel them away?"

"Yes. You must work through them, layer by layer. We're going to discuss this in a lot more detail later on, but now we need to talk about some killer emotions. Why? Because these negative feelings are the cause of most sickness and disease. Trust me, my friend, it's very important that you're aware of them, and that you know how to deal with them properly so that you can restore harmony and balance to your life. Otherwise, you won't find your healing. Understand?"

I didn't like the sound of that. Not one little bit. "Okay, let's get on with it. Where do we start?"

Disappointment

"Tell me, have you ever heard the expression: 'I'm sick with disappointment?'"

"Sure. Who hasn't?"

"But where does this expression come from? How come it's known throughout the world?"

I hadn't thought about it before. Was it really that obvious? Do we all know that disappointment makes us sick? I wondered. I let the word sink into my psyche: Disappointment. The more I thought about it, the worse I began to feel. Old memories loomed from the depths of my mind, like eerie shadows creeping out of dark alleyways. My chest tightened and my breath became heavy.

"Go on, tell me. Please."

"No matter where you live in the world, disappointment can creep into your mind, churn you up inside, twist you inside out, grind you down, and even drive you into your grave. Disappointment is extremely powerful and destructive. Make no mistake: Disappointment will take as much of you as it can get. I'm not exaggerating. Disappointment will take over your whole life, if you let it."

Henry Jones's words suddenly detonated the time-bomb I'd been sitting on for years. I could relate to his words 100%. I was terribly disappointed in my parents. Once again, I told Henry Jones about my past. He listened carefully to my story, as though he were hearing it for the first time. When I was done, he sighed deeply and then said in a slow and steady voice: "Yep, that's how it is. You'll feel disappointed when your self-imposed expectations or demands about how you think the world should be, or how you think others should act, are unmet."

That blunt, simple explanation summed up all my problems. That was the kernel of it.

"Oh my God! This is why I've been so miserable, isn't it? I carry this disappointment in me, and I project it on to everyone around me, don't I? I set expectations that are almost impossible for people to achieve, so that I can feed my disappointment when they fail to reach my standards. Isn't that so?" I blurted.

He gazed across the rose garden without saying a word. A faint smile appeared on his lips. I dived into a long and passionate explanation of my negative feelings. I told him yet again how badly my father treated my mother and I, and what an awful person he had been to almost everyone he met.

"You must be careful of disappointment, my friend," he responded. "The feeling is easy to harbour because it feels justified. That is how it tricks you. No matter how justified your disappointment feels, at the end of the day,

476

disappointment leads to sadness, disillusionment, frustration and depression – all of which can make you judgemental, disapproving, critical and angry. Those negative emotions are a downward spiral that end in sickness and disease."

I flopped forward and put my head in my hands. "I'm so stupid. Jeez, I feel so bad right now."

He nodded empathetically. "I'm pleased you no longer underestimate the destructive power of disappointment. This negative emotion can affect you emotionally, mentally, spiritually and physically. If you're not careful, it can destroy you and your relationships."

I started to hyperventilate. "What should I do now?"

"You may not like my advice. It's usually not what people who suffer from disappointment want to hear."

"I'm a big boy. I think I can handle it," I groaned.

"Don't make such a big deal of it. Life is full of disappointments. The sooner you accept that fact, the better. Holding on to disappointment is like sucking a slow poison pill. If you want to heal your body and stay healthy, you've got to learn how to overcome disappointment once and for all."

"How do I do that?" I cried. "Where do I start?"

"Begin by checking to see if your expectations are unrealistic. Answer this question: Did you create a false reality based on your own expectations? If so, don't be surprised when you feel disillusioned because the illusions you created in your mind don't materialize. Illusions will always let you down. It's their nature."

"What do I do if I've created an unrealistic expectation?"

"You should try to see the situation from the perspective of the person you feel has disappointed you. Listen to their side of things. You may find they've been trying to tell you that they can't, or don't want to, play a role in your illusion. The ego-mind is fantastic at setting people up to fail. It creates expectations or fantasies that give it reason to run amok in your life. These illusions are manufactured by your ego-mind as a ploy to preoccupy your thoughts in order to gain control of your life. Once in control, your ego-mind will unleash all kinds of negative feelings to lead you away from your true-self."

I slipped into another moment of silence as I tried to apply that wisdom to my childhood. My parents didn't meet my expectations, but my feelings felt justified. I was just a child, and they had abused me and neglected me.

They were in the wrong, not me. Without giving Henry Jones the context of my thoughts, I suddenly blurted out: "I wanted a father who was sober and who looked after me and loved me," I spewed. "Surely, those expectations were not unrealistic?"

"They're totally unrealistic if your father is an abusive drunk," Henry Jones replied, as cool as a cucumber. "It's wiser to look at reality the way it really is, and not how you want it to be."

"It wasn't my fault. My parents disappointed me," I protested.

"Oh no! You've got it all wrong, my friend. Disappointment is always self-inflicted. You do it to yourself!"

"But…"

"No buts," he replied, waving his finger from side to side. "It's unfair of you to try to make someone else responsible for your disappointment. The simple truth is: You chose to be disappointed, rather than to be understanding and accepting. Hear me carefully now: It's wiser to accept responsibility for your actions and choices than to lay guilt trips on others. Be careful about laying guilt trips when you feel disappointed. They are a favorite vice of the ego-mind. It's the thing we do when we emotionally manipulate others by trying to make them feel guilty about disappointing us. This practice stems from the ego-mind and it does great harm. If your intention is to make someone feel guilty, ashamed, inadequate or unworthy, then you must question your motive. Ask yourself: Why am I making this person feel bad? Am I defending my misguided feelings? What do I stand to gain from laying blame? Beware: Guilt does long-term damage to self-esteem, which often manifests as disease. You don't want to bring sickness down upon anyone, do you?"

A cold shudder ran down my spine. My estranged mother was sickly. She'd been ill with emphysema for many years. I never forgave her for not leaving my father, and I'd blamed her for my unhappy childhood. Even so, I didn't like the idea that I could be responsible for her poor health.

"So, you're saying I should just accept the situation?"

"Yes, that's exactly what I'm saying. Accept the situation for what it is. Accepting reality dissolves disappointment. You don't want to hold on to disappointment. Trust me: Holding on to disappointment makes you resentful. That isn't good for you. It is a grave mistake."

Resentment

I felt my insides shift instantly. It was like I had changed into a lower gear. The hairs on the back of my neck prickled and I heard myself growl.

Perhaps it was a painful groan. I felt it curdle in my gut. Just hearing the word: 'Resentment' triggered an involuntary response. I instinctively knew that resentment had a grip on me.

I turned to my notes for help. The words I'd scrawled just minutes earlier were waiting there to release me. I stopped, took a breath, and tried to listen from my true-self.

"Go ahead. Tell me, what makes us resentful?"

"There are tons of reasons we feel resentful," Henry Jones exclaimed, dramatically throwing his hands into the air again. A frightened bird took flight from the rose garden. It startled both of us and brought on a brief round of chuckles. He continued: "Where should I start? You'll feel resentful when someone deprives you of your physical and psychological needs; tries to tell you what to do, what you need, or how to run your life; how they think you should feel or act; lie to you; accuse you falsely; act superior to you; persecute you; discriminate against you; judge you; belittle you; ignore you; invalidate you; underestimate you; shout at you or insult you."

"That's a pretty long list of wrongdoings," I remarked. "It's almost impossible to go through life without experiencing them at some stage or another."

"Precisely! These circumstances rear their ugly heads all too often. That's why you must be prepared to handle them. If not, you'll become resentful towards the people involved, and you don't want to carry resentment. This negative emotion leads to anger; spite; hurtfulness; bitterness; nastiness; sarcasm and vengefulness. Be warned, these negative feelings eat away at you like a cancer. They get into your system and fester, and ferment, and mutate, and multiply, which turns you bitter and makes you sick! If you're holding on to resentment, then you'd better listen closely to what I'm about to tell you."

I sat up and paid attention.

He leaned towards me: "You've got to release resentment. That is your responsibility. No one can take it away from you. You must give it up," he declared, poking his finger into my chest.

I rubbed the spot to sooth the pain. "But how?"

"First of all, focus on the role you might've played in creating the situation. Laying blame on someone else only gives away your personal power. It's important to identify your contribution to the problem. That way, you can accept responsibility for your actions and choices. Instead of blaming someone else, you can begin to focus your attention on your personal learning, growth and development."

"But what if I wasn't to blame?"

He narrowed his eyes at me. "If you honestly feel that you didn't contribute to the problem in any way and there wasn't anything you could've done about the situation, then you only have one real challenge to face: You must accept reality for what it is and come to terms with it," he said in a sage-like voice. "Accepting reality releases resentment."

"But how? How do I accept reality?" I cried from my ego-mind.

"Look for the good in all things," he told me. "Focus on the positive outcomes only. Do this, and you won't be disappointed."

For some reason, I felt agitated inside. "What's next?"

Anger

"Anger!"

"You don't have to tell me what makes people angry. I've got this one covered," I told him. "My list is as long as my arm. Do you want to hear it?"

"Why not?" Henry Jones replied, amused.

"Here goes: I feel angry when someone disrespects me; disobeys me; insults me; cheats me; pressures me; ignores me; rejects me; steals from me; neglects me; betrays me; violates me; mocks me; hurts me; harms someone or something I care for; or is cruel to a defenceless creature. Oh yes, and when someone invalidates my emotions. I'm sure there are others, but those are definitely my hot buttons."

Henry Jones laughed heartily. "Phew, that's a lot of anger to contend with."

"My wife says I'm an angry man," I remarked with a shaky chuckle. "If only she could see me now. I've changed in the past few weeks. I really have."

"You'll be pleased to know that anger isn't all bad. It's an intense emotion with many uses. Some of them are positive. For instance: If you see someone being cruel to a defenceless animal, your anger may prompt you to defend the creature. The sudden rush of emotion gives you the energy to take immediate action. But what you need to watch out for is prolonged anger and repressed anger. Prolonged anger comes from not getting over it, while repressed anger comes from not giving in to it. Both are very unhealthy for you."

"In what way?"

"Well, among other things, they can cause high blood pressure; heart attacks; hypertension; muscle and respiratory problems; metabolism changes; and strokes. That's all bad!"

"No kidding!" I gasped. "How do we deal with anger?"

"You nailed it," he replied. "You've got to deal with anger – you can't suppress it. That means that you need to process it. You see, anger is never your primary feeling. You always feel something else first. The next time you feel yourself getting angry ask yourself: Why am I getting angry? What is my primary feeling? What need do I have that's not being met? That'll help you to identify your unmet emotional need.

"Next, express how you felt before the primary emotion progressed to anger. Say it aloud. For instance: 'I feel humiliated, or disrespected, or betrayed.' This technique enables you to deal with the real issue. It's important to address and resolve the real issue. Anger fades over time, but the real issue behind the anger can linger for a lifetime. You don't want that to happen to you. Stored negative emotions can make you bitter and twisted, which leads me neatly to the next negative emotion that I want to discuss with you. This is a nasty piece of work. It sinks deep into your psyche and hangs around for ages."

"What is it?"

"Bitterness."

Bitterness

"What's the cause of bitterness?"

"You'll feel bitterness when you allow yourself to totally depend on, or count on, expectations that are then unmet. As a result, you feel betrayed, deceived, let down, dissatisfied, disenchanted or thwarted."

"What's the difference between bitterness and disappointment?"

"The negative feelings that stem from bitterness are more intense and powerful than disappointment. You could say that bitterness is what happens when you take disappointment to the extreme. It's a killer! It imbeds itself deep into your psyche and it's not easy to let go. You become imprisoned by your past perceptions, which you now know is an attribute of your ego-mind. I must caution you: Bitterness towards others is another poison pill that you, yourself, take. Your negative feelings can be so overwhelming that they prevent you from seeing peaceful solutions, even if they're staring you in the face. You can get so caught up in them that they override your ability to apply logic and reason. Even though you know that certain memories are painful for you, you desperately cling to them. That makes no sense at all. Why would you hold on to things that cause you pain?"

481

"Perhaps you don't know how to let them go," I offered.

"I don't think so. It's not hard to do."

"Go on, then. Tell me."

"To overcome bitterness, you must turn the negative experience into a positive learning opportunity. If you don't, you'll never grow out of it. If you do, your initial disappointment can lead to wisdom."

"What else can I do?"

"Let your true-self search for understanding and acceptance. No matter how hard it is for you to do, try to learn more about the person or people who embittered you. Discovering more about them may help you to understand their motives, and subsequently explain their actions. Trust me on this: It's much easier to forgive with knowledge and insight in your favor."

"Forgiveness is essential too, huh?"

"Bingo!"

"I made some excellent notes on forgiveness when we were in the cabin. I've literally read them scores of times since then."

"Good. I'm pleased to hear it. In that case, you'll probably recall me saying: 'Forgiveness is the key to letting go of negative emotions.' I'll say it again: Emotional healing is all about releasing the negative emotions that are stored in your body. This is essential to do in order to heal yourself. Storing negative emotions is bad for you. Plain and simple!"

"Are there any signs that one can look out for?"

"Sure. There are several. The first one that springs to mind is feeling destructive towards yourself, others and objects, over a long period of time. That's a dead giveaway. You feel destructive when you're angry with yourself, or with someone else, or with something else. Usually, the need to be destructive is a physical urge. You may want to smash, punch or throw something! Do you ever feel like this?"

"You bet I do," I replied. "Come to think of it, I haven't felt destructive in the past few weeks, ever since I started my healing journey. I used to smash stuff all the time. My favorite thing to do was to smash plates on the floor. I'm not proud of it, but I once smashed every single piece of the crockery set my father gave my mother on their 20th wedding anniversary. He got drunk and insulted her cooking during lunch and I completely lost the plot. I just saw red. It was the only time I ever challenged my father. It happened the day before I left for the marines. I threw the plates at him like frisbees, and he ran for his life. I chased him out the house and down the street, and then I returned to the dining room blinded by rage and broke the rest of the set on the floor. Of course, my father claimed not to remember the incident and, to protect me, my mother told him she had accidently dropped the set while putting it away after doing the dishes. He repaid her kindness to me by smashing her top lip with his fist. The bastard.”

Henry Jones consoled me with words of kindness. He reminded me of the higher virtues of my true-self and encouraged me to forgive and forget. I told him I would try my best to apply his wisdom.

“When you next feel destructive, ask yourself: Who or what do I really want to destroy? Is it a person, a relationship, a life situation, or myself? Why do I want to destroy it? What are the consequences of destroying it? What will destroying it achieve? You’ll be surprised at how the answers to these questions will calm you down.

“If that doesn’t work for you, try putting your energy into constructive activities that produce positive outcomes. For instance: Clean the house; wash your car; cut the lawn; fix something broken.”

“That’s a great help. Thank you.”

Hopelessness and discouragement

“It’s my pleasure,” Henry Jones replied. “Since you’re taking notes, you can also write down hopelessness and discouragement. These two negative emotions go hand-in-hand. They’re like evil twins. You’ll be astounded at how many people get sick because they feel overwhelmed by a sense of hopelessness or discouragement.”

“Why do some people feel that way?”

“They have no source of encouragement and hope in their lives. It’s that simple!”

“So, what advice would you give them?”

“I’d say use your common sense. Search for things that give you hope and encouragement, but don’t expect some external stimuli to come along and save you. You’ll only be opening yourself up for disappointment. The best place to find a constant source of hope and encouragement is within you. Focus your attention on encouraging truths about yourself and the future you desire for yourself.”

“But what if you have a low self-esteem?”

“There’s only one answer to your question, my friend. You must do what-ever it takes to put positive, optimistic and inspirational information into your subconscious mind. Do that by employing the mind-programming techniques that I've already taught you."

"You mean visualization and affirmation techniques?"

"Precisely! You can also read inspirational books; watch uplifting movies; visit fun people; or serve your community. These activities will lift your spirit, guaranteed!"

"What happens to people who feel hopeless and discouraged but don't practice mind-programming techniques?"

"If one isn't careful, negative emotions can escalate into depression."

"Please don't tell me we're going to discuss depression now," I moaned. "I really, really don't think I can handle any more negative emotions right now."

Depression

"I'm afraid we have to discuss it, my friend. Depression is nasty. Ask anyone who suffers from depression and I'm sure they'll agree that it's soul-destroying."

"What causes depression?"

"We become depressed when we feel discouraged; hopeless; lonely; isolated; misunderstood; overwhelmed; attacked; invalidated or unsupported. Depression is also a secondary emotion. It usually follows primary negative emotions, which accumulate and escalate until they become overwhelming. Once depression sets in, it triggers more negative feelings, so the individual spirals down into further depression. There are no limits to depression. It can even lead to death through sickness or suicide."

"What's the best way to deal with depression?"

"There are a number of ways. Personally, I think it's best to identify and deal with the primary emotions one at a time. If you feel lonely, seek company. If you feel uninspired, find goals. If you feel unproductive, do something. The key is to take action. You can't think your way out of depression. You've got to work your way out of it. Busy people are seldom depressed. They simply don't have time for it."

"What else?"

"Well, you can cure depression by serving others. It gives you something wholesome to do. It's a well-known fact: Helping others is uplifting and it makes you feel valued. Giving back to your community also makes you feel more connected to others. When you work closely with people who are less fortunate than yourself, you begin to appreciate your life. It's an excellent tonic. Appreciation leads to gratitude, and gratitude is the single, most powerful antidote for depression. Genuinely! I once treated a woman who suffered from severe depression by making her count her blessings every morning and every night. She still does it, and she is no longer depressed."

"That makes perfect sense. Gratitude is an attribute of your true-self, so it would be impossible to be depressed if you were living from your true-self. Wouldn't it?" I asked.

"Yes, naturally. However, depression is a very complex emotional state, and it can be related to psychological disorders. If none of these methods work, then one really should seek professional help."

"Is that it? Are we done yet?"

"Not quite. We've got time for one last comprehension test. I'd like you to recall the techniques we discussed to let go of fear and guilt during your mental healing process. Can you remember the key points?"

"I think so," I replied. "I should accept the things I can't change, change the things I can, and pray for the wisdom to know the difference."

"Bravo!" he cried, clapping his hands.

Just then, a nun emerged from behind the tall hedge that separated the rose garden from the main building of the convent. I immediately knew it was Sister Simone. I could tell by the expression of delight on Henry Jones's face. We watched her meander down the pathway towards us, her hands held behind her back. The first distinct feature I noticed about Sister Simone was her thin smile. Her lips seemed to tuck under her teeth. She was short and slender; I guessed in her late 40s, perhaps younger.

Sister Simone's gaunt cheeks, high protruding cheek-bones, sharp beak and beady eyes bestowed upon her a rather unfortunate avian quality. At first glance, I felt somewhat disappointed. You see, I'd imagined someone bubbly and attractive, like Mrs Moffet, steering me through my emotional healing session. Silly me! I should have known better. My first lesson would be not to judge a book by its cover. Appearances can be deceiving. In fact, Sister Simone was the perfect match for me, as I'd soon discover.

CHAPTER 26

A SESSION WITH SISTER SIMONE

"I thought I'd find you here," Sister Simone said in a no-nonsense tone. Both Henry Jones and I leaped to our feet like naughty schoolboys who'd been caught smoking behind the bicycle-shed. I couldn't help noticing that he didn't hug her, as was his custom with friends. Instead, he took her hand, as if leading her to dance.

Having introduced me, I straightaway expressed my gratitude to her for making time to teach me about emotional healing. Her eyes darted from side to side, like a goshawk searching for a little mouse in long grass. They flickered with a fierce intelligence. She struggled to make eye contact with me. I couldn't tell if she was cripplingly shy or deliberately avoiding any kind of intimacy. Henry Jones had described her to me as a frail bird, but despite her chilly exterior and impish demeanor, I could tell there was a fire in her belly.

She invited us to accompany her to her office. On the way, Henry Jones proceeded to inform her about our day's activities and our discussions in the rose garden. She walked with her hands behind her back once more and listened attentively. I studied her closely. Sister Simone was unlike his other friends. All of the others had big, outgoing personalities and seemed larger than life. She, on the other hand, was most definitely introverted and would slip through life unnoticed by all but bullies. Her cool disposition wasn't what I would've expected from a practitioner of emotional healing. The paradox intrigued me.

We'd hardly entered her office when she got down to business. "Okay, now that you know a bit more about the negative emotions that can and do cause disease, let's discuss in detail how emotions are stored in your body cells," she said seriously.

I rubbed my hands together. "I'm ready. Let's do it!" I said enthusiastically.

She almost grinned. Almost. "Today, we're going to teach you the real nitty-gritty of healing. Yes sirree, you're going to learn the ultimate secret of self-healing," she told me.

"You need this," Henry Jones piped. "You can clean out your body, change your attitude and meditate on your chakra points all you like, but it's only when you let go of the negative emotions stored in your body cells that your real healing can begin."

She nodded in agreement and her face softened slightly. "When you let go of your emotional blockages, it releases healing on all levels," she said, arranging three chairs to face inwards in the center of her office.

"Take a seat," she instructed.

We obeyed. I looked around the small, cosy room, scanning the photographs on the walls and the strange objects on the bookshelves and side tables. Clearly, she'd travelled to many faraway places. She also had an interesting obsession with elephants, judging by the little statues that festooned her shelves.

Henry Jones got us going: "Everything you've learned, everything you've read, and everything you've practised to date has prepared you for what we're about to reveal to you. Up to this point on your healing journey, all I've been doing is laying the groundwork for your healing. Now it's crunch time. You're about to discover how you can heal your body, once and for all. The time has come for the magic to begin, my friend."

Sister Simone's eyes twinkled. She was in cahoots with Henry Jones, I could tell. They had it all figured out.

"Tell me, have you read any of Dr Deepak Chopra's books?" Sister Simone asked suddenly.

"Not yet, but I plan to," I replied. "Henry's been raving about him for weeks."

She cracked a smile. "We're both great fans. You'll be, too, when you learn more about his work."

"What makes him so special?" I asked curiously.

"Well, he's a thought-leader on the human healing process. His deep insight and knowledge of the human mind, body and spirit, combined with his enigmatic charm, eloquence and prose, have earned him a reputation as one of the top 10 most influential men on the planet in the field of health and healing," she stated. She offered me some cashew nuts from a glass jar shaped like an elephant.

"That's impressive!" I agreed, popping a handful of nuts into my mouth.

"His work is particularly useful if you're looking for scientific and biological facts to support the idea that you can heal your body. If this is your objective, I strongly recommend you buy all of his books on healing and read them 10 times each," she commanded.

Henry Jones cupped his mouth with one hand and pointed at her with the other. "She's a Chopraholic," he jested.

"I am," she agreed, crunching down on some nuts. "Read his book *Quantum Healing*, and I've no doubt that you'll be, too. That book convinced me that a single body cell contains formidable intelligence and healing power. I've read it so many times that I can recite passages word for word. He shares my fascination with body cells. They are phenomenal," she exclaimed, chipping away at the nuts with her front teeth. She really did look like a bird. I half-expected her to peck the nuts from the bowl with her beak. "Everything about them is mind-boggling."

"Did you know there are over 50 trillion cells in your body?" Henry Jones asked me.

"That's staggering!"

"I know, right?" she chirped. "Try to imagine how tiny they must be. It's beyond human comprehension."

"Funny, that's similar to what Dr Sahib said about the universe," I commented to Henry Jones.

"I bet he did," she responded.

"You know him?"

"Of course! He's a dear friend of ours. We've a lot in common."

"How so?"

"Our worlds are inextricably linked. He studies relative physics while I have a doctorate in quantum physics."

"Aren't you a nun?" I asked suddenly.

"I became a nun after my studies," she said and left it at that.

"Right, let's talk more about body cells. Did I mention how amazing they are? Contained within the outer membrane, or cell wall, of each cell is a mind-boggling mixture of water and swirling chemicals. At the core of each body cell is a nucleus that safeguards your DNA. This is the very essence of you."

"You may be interested to learn that there's only a one percent difference between your DNA and that of a gorilla," Henry Jones sported.

"Gosh! That doesn't leave much margin for error, does it?" I replied. I turned to Sister Simone. "So, what exactly do body cells do?" I mumbled through a mouthful of cashews.

"We've not yet begun to fathom all the functions of body cells, but already these microscopic entities fill volumes of medical journals. If we knew all their capabilities, we'd most likely solve the riddle of life and the mystery of the universe," she sighed deeply. "At the very least we're certain of this: Cells are capable of formidable intelligence, as evidenced by the infinite number of functions they execute each and every second of our lives."

"Dr Chopra talks about a delicate web of intelligence that binds the body together," Henry Jones remarked, trying to take the bowl of nuts from me. I shielded it beneath my forearm.

Sister Simone was beginning to thaw. She beckoned me to come closer to her. "Part of this intelligence is devoted to healing," she breathed.

"It is?"

"You bet," Henry Jones exclaimed. "As we've discussed, a blood cell knows exactly where to go and what to do in order to heal a cut. It travels to the exact location and forms a clot – completely, spontaneously and without guesswork."

Sister Simone shuffled closer to me, like a parrot on a pole.

"You've met Juju, right? He works with body energy. Where do you think this energy comes from? It comes from your body cells. They're the key to your healing. Yes sirree, there's a powerful, inextricable, inseparable, inter-connectedness between your body cells, inner intelligence and healing. That's a fact."

Henry Jones added: "Since there's intelligence in every single body cell, and your body is made up of cells, we can deduce there's intelligence present everywhere in your body. Make sense?"

"Uh huh."

"Good. You should also know this fact: Your own inner intelligence is far superior to anything we can try to substitute from the outside, like medicine. Your body naturally manufactures more healing chemicals than a fully stocked, man-made pharmacy. It knows exactly which healing chemicals to manufacture for which virus, bacteria or disease," Sister Simone said.

"Hey, that's exactly what George-the-Surfer told me," I cried.

"You know George-the-Surfer, too? Wow, you do get around, don't you?" Sister Simone smiled affectionately at Henry Jones. He responded by explaining our deal: I'd help him to publish his book and he'd help me to heal my body.

"Well then, in that case, make sure to tell your readers that the intelligence in our cells is more important than the actual matter of our body. Without it, the matter would be undirected, formless and chaotic," Sister Simone said.

Henry Jones was quick to insert another quote from their favorite author: "Dr Chopra says: 'Intelligence makes the difference between a house designed by an architect and a pile of bricks.'"

"It is an absolute corker, isn't it?" Sister Simone replied enthusiastically. Their theatrics made our conversation interesting and fun.

I interjected: "So, let me see if I've got this straight. The concoction of water and chemicals that comprise our body cells contain an infinite intelligence that has the ability to heal our body?"

"That's it in a nutshell," she replied. "Now let me tell you something else that's truly remarkable: Ninety eight percent of the atoms in your body today won't be in your body in one year's time. I hope you understand what I'm trying to tell you?" she said.

"Let me explain this to you," Henry Jones interjected. "Dr Chopra describes it perfectly when he compares the body to a house made of bricks. He says, 'Each year the bricks are systematically removed and replaced with new bricks, but the house stays exactly the same.'"

"You're in top form today, Henry. That's the third quote from Deepak in five minutes," she remarked playfully.

"Three to me. Zero to you," he replied cajolingly.

She turned to me and whispered: "He thinks he's fancy with his one-liners. Just wait until I bring out the big guns. Then we'll see who knows Deepak best."

I enjoyed their banter. They made it easy for me to relax and settle into the process. The more I heard, the more I craved their knowledge, insights and wisdom. I couldn't stop myself from asking a million questions.

"Do our body cells regenerate at the same speed?"

"No. They regenerate at different speeds. For instance, your skeleton regenerates every 3 months; your skin every month; your liver every 6 weeks; your stomach lining every 4 days; and your eyeballs every 24 hours."

"Hold on a second. I'm confused. How come people with poor eyesight still need to wear glasses if they have brand new eyeballs every 24 hours? And, why do people with stomach cancer suffer from the disease for years when their stomach cells regenerate within days?"

"Why indeed?" she replied, narrowing her beady eyes. "That is the million-dollar question, isn't it?"

"So, what's the answer?" I pleaded.

"A cell's memory is able to outlive the cell itself."

"Say what?"

The blueprint

"Each dying body cell transfers information to the new cell replacing it."

"That means memory is more permanent than matter," Henry Jones added.

"Are you saying disease is merely a memory?"

"Precisely! It's the memory of disease that's passed on to the new cell. This suggests there's one original blueprint of your body – the architect's plan. Chopra's words, not mine."

"More importantly, where is this blueprint stored, and how can one access it?" Sister Simone asked.

"Wait a minute. Why is this important?" I blurted.

"Isn't it obvious?" Henry Jones remarked. "When you can access the blueprint and interrupt the memories, you can heal your body."

I blinked twice. Could this be true? Is it possible? Can one learn this healing technique? I wondered. Both Henry Jones and Sister Simone sat back in their chairs and folded their arms at the same time. They waited for me to mull it over. The significance of the concept suddenly dawned on me.

"Oh, my goodness! If I can access my body's blueprint and interrupt the memories that are making me sick, I can heal my body," I exclaimed.

"That's exactly what I just said," Henry Jones replied with a great, big grin on his face.

"So how do I access my blueprint?" I yelled.

"Your blueprint lies in your etheric body, which houses your emotional body and it's the mainstay of your physical body," he replied, moving his hands through the air around himself.

Sister Simone raised her hand to speak. "Your body is just the place your memory calls home. I believe Deepak says: 'A cell is a memory that has built some matter around itself, forming a specific pattern.' This pattern is your body, and the blueprint of the pattern lies in the etheric field. Right now, however, it's very important that you comprehend what we're sharing with you before we move on. We're suggesting that you fully embrace this extraordinary notion: Your body is made out of cells, but it's equally right to say it's made out of your experiences and memories. I believe these are Deepak's words, too." She tapped Henry Jones's knee. "That's two to me, four to you," she notified him playfully.

She turned her attention back to me: "When you grasp this big idea, you'll realize that your disease resides in your memories, which merely reflect in your body cells."

Henry Jones jumped in. "Your emotions create neuropeptides that reside in your body and interact with your body cells and tissues. You can say that your body is made up of your emotions at a molecular level."

"You told me this on the plane ride to India. Didn't you?" I recalled.

Sister Simone gasped: "Don't tell me you went to see Swami G, too?"

"We did, actually."

"Oh, gracious me! That's fun-taas-tick," she drawled in an excellent Indian accent. We laughed knowingly. I felt the tension pop. In that precious moment, Sister Simone and I became friends, I could tell.

"Now then, one more time. What happens when we interrupt the memories in our body cells?"

"We can heal our bodies."

"Yes, yes!" Sister Simone twittered excitedly. "We can heal our bodies permanently."

"Do you know how to do this? How long does the process take? Have we got time to do it right now?" I asked.

She laughed. "Yes, we can. All you need is an open mind. The duration depends entirely on you, and yes, we have time to do it now."

"Right now?"

"Yes. We're nearly done giving you the information you need to under-stand why and how the process works. There are just a few more things you need to know before we can proceed to your treatment. Hang in there, we're almost done," she assured me. "I've some important news for you that will most probably make you very excited. You must promise to contain yourself when you hear this absolute truth."

"I promise. Go on, then."

Let go of memories and heal your body

She spoke slowly and clearly: "The instant you let go of the old emotions stored in your body cells, your body spontaneously and automatically begins to regenerate healthy cells."

"Instantly?"

"Yes, instantly!"

"Is that awesome, or what?" piped up Henry Jones.

"So, what must I do to let go of the sick memories stored in my body cells?" I practically shouted. I knew in my gut that I was close to finding the ultimate answer to my top question: How can I heal my body?

Sister Simone sharpened her hawk-like stare. I felt her beady eyes pierce through me. My ego-mind scampered for cover like a frightened white mouse. She chose her words carefully and spoke in a calm and calculated voice: "To let go of the memory stored in your cells, you've to get in touch with the part of you that recorded the memory in the first place."

"What exactly do you mean?" I cried.

Sister Simone knew I was on the verge of a life-changing discovery. Savoring the moment, she topped up the elephant bowl with more cashew nuts. I watched her every move. She filled the bowl to the brim, scooped up a handful, and then sat back and began popping them into her mouth one at a time. I was totally transfixed. My anticipation was unbearable.

"Oh, come on. I'm dying over here," I moaned.

Rewrite the program

"If you were writing code for a software program and you unintentionally made an error that resulted in a glitch that compromised the usability of the program, what would you have to do to fix the problem?"

I batted my eyelids. "I'd have to work my way back to the cause of the problem and correct it."

"Yes, you would," she replied, dicing the nuts with her front teeth again.

"That is exactly how emotional healing works, too. The only way to fix a problem is to go back into the past and undo the error."

"But I can't go back in time," I exclaimed, realizing instantly that this could be incorrect. Can I?"

"Yes, you can. We'll show you how to do this in a minute. But first, we need to explain how your body cells communicate."

"I already know," I replied smugly. "I studied biology at school twenty years ago."

She smiled sweetly. "I bet they taught you that your body communicates via electrical impulses through the central nervous system. Am I correct?"

"Yes, on both counts."

Henry Jones shook his head from side to side. Sister Simone went on to explain how it really works. "Today that understanding is considered old-school, thanks to the discovery of a new class of minute chemicals, called neurotransmitters."

"Neuro-what?" I exclaimed.

"Neurotransmitters." Henry Jones said, annunciating the vowels.

"What do they do?"

"They act as 'communicator molecules' in your body."

Henry Jones couldn't contain his excitement. "They enable your cells to communicate by racing to and from your brain, telling every organ inside you about your emotions, desires, memories, intuitions and dreams," he said quickly.

"How do they do that?" I asked Sister Simone specifically.

Her eyes flickered with excitement. "They transmit nerve impulses, through which the neurons in your brain constantly talk to the rest of your body."

"Let me get this straight: Whatever I think and feel is communicated to each and every cell in my whole body."

"Precisely!" yelled Henry Jones.

"But how does this work?" I needed to know.

"You tell him," Henry Jones instructed Sister Simone. "He needs to know."

"The outer membrane of your body cells is covered with sticky receptors that attach themselves to molecules using an extremely sophisticated Velcro-like system. These receptors are not fixed to your cell walls. They look like lily pads that stem from the depth of the cell. Their roots are attached to the cell's nucleus. This is where your DNA sits. It constantly produces new receptors and sends them to the surface to receive potentially infinite amounts of messages. Each new piece of information produces new receptors, each with a specific purpose. Once a cell grabs on to a message-carrying molecule, your inner intelligence transfers the information from the molecule to the host cell, and then to all the other cells in your body. All of this happens in an instant, almost at the speed of light."

Sister Simone's fingers danced across her body. She appeared amazed and awestruck by the exchange of information she imagined taking place under her skin. I sat motionless and silent.

"Right now, in this moment, our bodies are fluently communicating incalculable messages through our entire systems. We can't begin to fathom the complexity, intricacy and sophistication of this communication network. The language of the body is beyond our human comprehension. It's of Divine origin."

A thoughtful, reverend silence prevailed. I didn't dare utter a single word, for fear of ruining it. Henry Jones was first to gather his senses. He cleared his throat before speaking in a crackly voice: "Researchers have also discovered neurotransmitters and neuropeptides on cells in the immune system, as well as on other organs, like the intestines, kidneys, stomach and heart."

"What's the significance of that?" I asked, finding something to say.

"This means that these messenger molecules don't just reside in your brain, my friend. They float in your bloodstream, giving them free access to every other cell in your body."

"This is how your brain freely circulates intelligence throughout your body's inner space." Sister Simone added. "It also means your organs can 'think', in the sense that they can produce the identical neuropeptides found in your brain. These breakthroughs lead the way for brain researchers to talk about the 'bodymind', which is a new buzzword that suggests your mind is present throughout your body in each and every cell."

"That's a bit farfetched, isn't it?" I asked.

"That's what I first thought, too, but then I learned about an amazing experiment conducted by leading brain researchers. They found a way to photograph a thought's tracks in 3D, like a hologram."

"How on Earth did they do that?" I inquired.

"It's quite amazing, actually. They injected glucose into the bloodstream. The carbon molecules of the glucose had been tagged with radioscopes."

"Why glucose?"

"Glucose is the brain's sole food. It uses glucose much faster than ordinary tissues."

"I still don't get it."

"You will in a second. Let me explain. When the injected glucose reaches the brain, its marker molecules can be picked out as the brain uses them, and thus pictured on a monitor – much the same way that a CAT scan is produced."

"So?"

"So, this experiment enables us to see the new chemical patterns that are triggered by your thoughts, emotions and memories. More importantly, by taking a full-length portrait of the body, scientists observed whole body changes at the same time, due to the cascade of neurotransmitters and messenger molecules."

"What does this prove?" Henry Jones asked me.

"Go on, tell me," I said.

"When you think of a painful memory, your whole body thinks of a painful memory."

"What?" I exclaimed. "Is that true?"

"Yes sirree, it sure is. This fascinating development led the way to a whole, new field of study."

"What's that?"

"How cells communicate chemically."

"Eh?"

"Let me illustrate my point. If you sit on a needle, you instantly and spontaneously react by leaping out of your chair. Right? But why? The answer is simple. Your entire molecular system erupts, thanks to the messenger molecules. This is a major breakthrough in our understanding of how the body actually works. Many years ago, researchers tracked the electrical impulses as they ran up and down the central nervous system, much like a telegraph wire. That's why you were taught this information in your biology class. But these new chemical-based messenger molecules appear to function differently. Instead of the message being passed from one molecule to the next, they all get the message instantly."

I shook my head vigorously. "Say what? I can't believe what I'm hearing."

"Well, it's true."

I shuffled anxiously in my seat. "I'm afraid we're going to have to take baby steps if you want me to wrap my head around this stuff."

"Take your time. We know this information can be perplexing when you first hear it," Henry Jones suggested kindly.

"Thank you," I responded, taking a deep breath. "Let me know if I've got this right so far: My body is made up of cells that store all my memories and emotions, and they can communicate instantly with each other. So, when I release the hurtful memory that's making me sick, I can heal my body permanently. Is that about it?"

"He summed it up pretty good, don't you think?" Henry Jones asked Sister Simone.

"I'd say he knocked that one out of the ball park," she replied with a wink.

"Something is still puzzling me," I confessed. "How do I know which one of my 50 trillion body cells contains the memory that's making me sick?"

Sister Simone adjusted her habit. "You're not looking for one specific cell. Everything about you – your genetic programming and your life experiences – are encoded and recorded in every single body cell in your bodymind. Deepak puts it like this: 'There's no single messenger molecule – each one is a strand in the body's web of intelligence. Touch one strand and the whole web trembles.' That's three quotes," she reminded Henry Jones.

"That's pure poetry!" he remarked.

"Isn't it?" Sister Simone replied, smiling as much as her thin lips would allow.

Henry Jones pretended to nudge Sister Simone in the ribs. "Now that he's got his head around Chopra, do you think we should introduce him to Talbot?"

"I think he's ready," she sported.

"Who is Talbot?" I inquired curiously with a measure of trepidation in my voice.

"Michael Talbot wrote a groundbreaking book called *The Holographic Universe*. Have you heard of it?" she asked.

"Nope."

"Well then, you'd better brace yourself, my friend. We're about to blow your freakin' mind."

CHAPTER 27

BLOWING MY MIND

"Hold on tight. Things are about to get a little strange," Henry Jones giggled.

Sister Simone sang an eerie tune and wiggled her fingers playfully. I thought I recognized it from a sci-fi movie sound track. She was no longer the stoic nun I'd met earlier. Sister Simone had transformed into a radiant emotional being right in front of my eyes. She couldn't wait to share her knowledge, and I was eager to learn it.

"Do yourself a big favor. When you go shopping for Deepak Chopra's books, slip Michael Talbot's book into your basket, too. It'll radically change your perception of the universe and everything in it!"

"Why is this necessary?"

"If you want to heal your body, especially if you have a life-threatening disease, then you must change your view of reality."

Change your view on reality

"And Talbot's book will do this for me?"

"Yes sirree. I guarantee his concepts will irrevocably transform your understanding of the physical structure of your body, the universe and reality," she assured me.

"Michael Talbot's insights inadvertently paved the way for a whole new approach to healing," Henry Jones added.

"How did they do that?"

"To answer your question, we'll have to take you back in time a bit so that you have some context to Talbot's concepts."

"Lead the way," I told them.

Subatomic particles

"In 1982, a physicist by the name of Alain Aspect discovered that sub-atomic particles are able to instantaneously communicate with each other, regardless of the distance separating them."

"Are you serious?"

"Yes sirree. It makes absolutely no difference whether they're one meter apart or a million kilometers apart. Somehow, under certain circumstances, a particle always seems to know what the other is doing. What makes this experiment so important is that it suggests subatomic particles can communicate with each other faster than the speed of light, which Einstein said was impossible."

"So, what gives?"

"You'll get the picture when you understand more about holograms," Sister Simone replied.

"Holograms? Seriously?"

"You bet. Holograms are everything!" she answered with a peculiar giggle in her voice.

"Why don't you shed some light on the matter for him, right now?" Henry Jones suggested.

"Yes, please do," I begged.

Understanding holograms

"Alright then. A hologram is a three-dimensional photograph that's created using lasers. If we wanted to make a hologram of you, we'd start by shining a laser beam at your physical form. Next, we'd bounce a second laser beam off the reflected light of the first. The resulting interference pattern – the area where the two laser beams co-mingle – would be captured on film. When the film is developed, it'd look like a meaningless swirl of light and dark lines, but as soon as the developed film is illuminated by another laser beam, a 3D image of you would appear."

"Amazing, huh?" Henry Jones exclaimed.

"I guess so," I mumbled, scratching my head. I couldn't quite see where they were going with this topic. Fortunately, my confusion was short-lived.

"Now, here's where it gets even more intriguing," she said. "If we took a pair of scissors and cut the piece of holographic film of you in half, then illuminated the halves with a laser, each half would contain the entire image of you. We could repeat this exercise over and over again, but each piece of film will always be found to contain a smaller but intact version of your original image."

"That is the nature of holograms. Every piece contains the whole. In other words: All the information possessed by the whole is in every part."

"Is this making sense to you?" Sister Simone asked gently.

"Yup. Sort of."

"That's good enough," Henry Jones said, rubbing his hands together excitedly. "Let's tell him about Bohm's work. I've been waiting for this moment for weeks and I just can't wait any longer."

Bohm's breakthroughs

"That's an excellent idea. If you enjoyed learning about body cells, you're going to love this. University of London physicist David Bohm, a protégé of Einstein's and one of the world's most respected quantum physicists, didn't buy the idea of subatomic particles being able to communicate by sending mysterious signals back and forth. He had other ideas. He believed the reason subatomic particles can remain in contact with one another, regardless of the distance separating them, is because their separateness is an illusion. He argued: 'At some deeper level of reality, such particles are not individual entities, but are actually extensions of the same fundamental something.'"

"Tell him about the fish. Tell him about the fish," Henry Jones prompted.

"Okay, then. Bohm provides this explanation to laymen: Imagine an aquarium containing a fish. Imagine also that you're unable to see the aquarium directly and that your knowledge about it and what it contains comes from two television cameras: One directed at the aquarium's front and the other directed at its side. As you stare at the two television monitors, you might assume that the fish on each of the screens are separate entities. After all, the cameras are set at different angles, so each of the images will be slightly different. But, as you continue to watch the two fish, you'll eventually become aware that there's a certain relationship between them. When one turns, the other also makes a slightly different but corresponding turn; when one faces the front, the other always faces toward the side. If you remain unaware of the full scope of the situation, you might even conclude that the fish are communicating with one another. That clearly is not the case. You follow?"

Before I could answer, Sister Simone continued: "Bohm goes on to say that the apparent faster-than-light connection between subatomic particles is really telling us that there's a deeper level of reality we're not privy to: A more complex dimension beyond our own. He states: 'We view objects such as subatomic particles as separate from one another because we are seeing only a portion of their reality. Such particles are not separate parts, but facets of a deeper and more underlying unity that's ultimately holographic and indivisible.'"

"Do you get it? Has the penny dropped yet? Can you see where we're going with this now?" Henry Jones fired.

"Give him a chance, Henry. This isn't an easy concept to grasp," she said.

"He's a very quick learner," he retorted. "He'll take to the implicate order like a duck to water."

"Implicate order?" An image of Dwayne the Duck popped into my head. It was followed by a flashback of the spider and the fake snake. I shuddered violently.

The implicate order

"Yes. Bohm calls this reality the implicate order," Sister Simone told me.

"Implicate means 'enfolded' or 'hidden'," Henry Jones added.

"Within the implicate order everything is connected. In theory, any individual element could reveal information about every other element in the universe. Simply put: Everything is enfolded into everything. Got it?"

"Yes, I get the principle, but what's the relevance?"

Henry Jones laughed loudly. "Stay with us! Everything you're currently learning is relevant to your upcoming emotional healing therapy session."

"I know, Henry. I trust you completely. I just wish I could see the big picture, that's all."

"You will. Let's push on," Sister Simone said. "Now that you know a bit more about Michael and David's work, let's go back and address the issue of going back in time to heal yourself from the degenerative memories that are stored in your body cells. You only think you can't go back in time if you believe you live in a linear, secular universe. What you're about to discover will smash that paradigm into tiny, little pieces," Sister Simone chimed.

"I want to tell him. I want to tell him!" Henry Jones shouted. "Our physical reality comprises subatomic particles, and since everything enfolds into everything, we can assume the universe is itself a projection, a hologram."

501

The holographic universe

"Why is this important?"

Sister Simone was quickest off the mark. "The notion of a holographic universe irrevocably changes our understanding of time and space. Talbot says, 'In a universe where nothing is truly separate from anything else, concepts like location break down, so time and three dimensional space, like the images of the fish on the TV monitors, also have to be viewed as projections of this deeper order.'"

Henry Jones slapped his hand on my leg. "This means reality, at its deeper level, is a sort of 'super-hologram' in which the past, present, and future all exist simultaneously."

Sister Simone picked up where she left off. "This is the reason why subatomic particles that have once interacted can instantaneously respond to each other's motions thousands of years later when they're light-years apart."

Suddenly, Henry Jones did the strangest thing. He squeezed my leg hard, just above the knee. This sent shock waves up my leg.

He spoke sternly. "I want you to take a mental note of what Sister Simone has just told you. Mark it in your mind as Green Flag One. Get an image of this flag in your mind now. You'll know why when she does the cellular healing technique with you at the end of this session."

I didn't have a clue what he was talking about, but I did it anyway.

The super-hologram

Sister Simone pushed on. "In theory, this super-hologram contains every subatomic particle that has been created, or ever will be created."

"This is Green Flag Two," he interjected.

"Okay," I stammered.

She resumed: "Talbot describes the super-hologram as 'a sort of cosmic storehouse of All That Is.' Said another way: Each subatomic particle potentially holds all the information of the universe – a microcosm of the macrocosm! Now you can understand why we say there's an inseparable interconnectedness between all things. Bohm agrees. He said, 'If the apparent separateness of subatomic particles is illusory, it means that at a deeper level of reality all things in the universe are infinitely interconnected.' This means the atoms in your brain are connected to the atoms in your body, which are connected to the atoms in the chair you're sitting on, which are connected to the atoms in everything you see around you. At a subatomic level, we're all connected to everything – the grass on the ground, the leaves in the trees, the stars in the sky, and even each other. Ultimately, all of nature is a seamless web."

"Perhaps this is what the poet William Blake meant when he wrote: 'To see the world in a grain of sand, and a heaven in a wild flower, hold infinity in the palm of your hand,'" I suggested.

"That's lovely," Sister Simone remarked. "Yes, that's probably exactly what he meant."

"If it's true that everything in the universe is holographic, then our bodies are holograms too, right?" I offered.

Your holographic body

"You're absolutely right!" Sister Simon exclaimed. "In fact, the nature of a hologram can be seen in the cellular structure of all living bodies. Scientific research has demonstrated that every cell contains a copy of the master DNA blueprint, with enough information to make an entire body from scratch. Cloning is proof of this. It's no secret that scientists have successfully cloned sheep and other creatures. Yes, sirree, it's now entirely possible to take an immune cell and, given the right conditions, produce an identical copy of the body, or a million identical copies, for that matter."

"Your body was constructed in much the same way, my friend. Do you remember what Prof Kaufmann told you? Every cell in your body grew out of one single cell that duplicated itself."

"Now, it's time to bring out the big guns," she sported. "Deepak says: 'Everything you can do – think, speak, act – builds on a capacity programmed into that one original molecule, which duplicates itself. Even though an immune cell becomes an immune cell, it still has all the infinite possibilities of the DNA. The only difference between an immune cell and a brain cell is that their DNA has selected to emphasize certain aspects of its total knowledge and suppress others.'"

"Don't forget to tell him about our holographic brains too," Henry Jones piped.

Your holographic brain

She nodded. You should also read Stanislav Grof's book, *The Holotropic Mind*. You'll discover overwhelming evidence to suggest that our brains function like holograms, too."

"Our brains?"

"Yes, our brains. I had my doubts, too, until I read about a series of experiments conducted by pioneering brain researcher Karl Lashley in the 1920s. He wanted to determine how and where memories are stored in the brain. So, he taught rats to navigate complex mazes. Then he surgically removed different parts of their brains. He hoped that the rats would forget how to do the tasks he'd taught them prior to surgery and he'd be able to identify the part of the brain where memories are stored."

"That sounds logical enough. What were the results?"

"To Lashley's utter amazement, he discovered that no matter which part of the brain he removed, the rats never lost their memory. Memory appeared to be dispersed throughout the brain. These experiments left Lashley, and many other researchers that followed him, scratching their heads. That is, until Stanford neurophysiologist Karl Pribram was introduced to holography. After extensive research, Pribram postulated that memories are not stored in the brain's neurons, as previously thought, but rather in patterns of nerve impulses that crisscross the entire brain – pretty much like the patterns of laser light that crisscross the entire area of a piece of film containing a holographic image. Like a hologram, your brain mathematically constructs your objective reality by interpreting frequencies that are ultimately projections from another dimension, a deeper order of existence that's beyond both space and time. In effect, your consciousness uses your brain to convert frequencies from the implicate order – the hidden – to the explicate order – the external or visible – much like the laser beam that shines through the holographic film to interpret the patterns of a hologram."

"If you need more proof that your brain functions like a hologram, consider this: A fragment of a hologram contains all the information possessed by the whole. So, too, can one fragment of the brain remember the contents of the brain as a whole. Also, your brain processes a myriad of different frequencies through your five senses. It decodes these frequencies to construct the seemingly concrete reality that surrounds you. Similarly, an illuminated piece of holographic film decodes a meaningless blur of swirling light into a coherent image. And lastly, a hologram can store many billions of bits of information and recall them instantly, much like the brain," Henry Jones concluded.

"That's true," Sister Simone affirmed. "The brain is a hologram enfolded in a holographic universe. If Pribram is right, and there's no evidence to prove that he's not, then he's given humanity a major reality check. You see, by putting together Bohm's theory of a holographic universe and Pribram's holographic model of the brain, we're presented with a whole, new understanding of reality. This view is referred to as 'the holographic paradigm'."

The holographic paradigm

"As you may know, paradigms are your models of perception. They're formed by how you perceive, understand and interpret the world around you. But, as Talbot points out: 'If the concreteness of the world is but a secondary reality and what is 'there' is actually a holographic blur of frequencies, and if the brain is also a hologram and only selects some of the frequencies out of this blur and mathematically transforms them into sensory perceptions, what becomes of objective reality?'"

"There's only one correct answer – it ceases to exist!" Henry Jones declared.

I ran my fingers through my hair. They were starting to freak me out. I wanted to know how to heal my body, and they were telling me reality didn't exist. Where were they going with this? Did this mean my sickness wasn't real? Were my symptoms just an illusion? I wondered.

Henry Jones read the perplexed look on my face. "You may think that you're a physical being moving through a physical world, but this is just an illusion. Talbot writes, 'We're really receivers floating through a kaleidoscopic sea of frequency, and what we extract from this sea and transmogrify into physical reality is but one channel from many extracted out of the super-hologram.' He goes on to say, 'Your brain is capable of seeing the whole picture, but it's obscured by your limited and unclear perceptions of the universal hologram.'"

Sister Simone applauded. I clapped too. They deserved it. But, I was struggling to join the dots. "So, what does this all mean?"

Your brain is a decoder

"It means you may think that your brain is processing your reality, but in actual fact your reality is streamed through your brain by your consciousness. I don't mean to quote Chopra, Bohm and Talbot all day long, but these guys are on to something big. Really big! Talbot explains: 'Each brain is like a decoder that is tuned to a different state or frequency of consciousness. In much the same way, the interference patterns of more than one hologram can be preserved on the same film by using various different angles of projection of the laser beams. A different hologram appears depending on the direction and frequency of the beam that you send through the film. So, if applied to the brain, consciousness literally becomes the co-creator of the reality portrayed depending upon its angle of perception.' This is ground-breaking stuff!"

"I still don't get it," I cried.

"It's simple," Sister Simone told me calmly. "The brain is like a super-cosmic television set. It broadcasts the life streamed to it through consciousness. That's right. Your brain merely decodes the frequency of the channel of consciousness that broadcasts your life. You can say that your life is the ultimate reality TV show, running 24/7/365 until you die."

"If this is so, the body is an antenna, right?"

Your body is an antenna

"Yes sirree. You've got it. Suffice to say, the clarity of your reception depends on the condition of your body. Think about it: The cells in your body primarily function as transmitters. They're designed to communicate with your brain and with all the other cells in your body. Each and every second of your life, your body cells process your experience by transmitting messages to each other and to your brain. When your cells are weak, due to poor nutrition and toxic interference, your whole life experience is compromised. You must understand this: Your internal universe then interprets the messages it receives and communicates this information to your external universe. Simply put: Your life experience is an expression of consciousness. You literally create your reality. You're the director, producer and star of your own show. The quality of your show is determined by the quality of the messages you receive. Make sense?"

"I think so. You're telling me my reality is broadcast from my consciousness, right? And what's broadcast from my consciousness is received by the cells in my body and then transmitted into the world around me, which I experience as my reality."

"Bingo. Now you've got it. So, why are we sharing this with you?"

"I hope it's going to help me heal my body?" I replied.

"Oh, it will. We can guarantee it. Sit closer, you'll find this fascinating."

The illusion of sickness

"The holographic paradigm radically transforms our understanding of medicine and the healing process. In a secular paradigm, we've a tendency to think of sickness and disease as being very real aspects of our physical bodies. When we're sick, our minds constantly worry about our physical condition – as if the mind and the body are detached from each other. This is entirely wrong! If you can accept that the concreteness of reality that you see around you is just a holographic illusion, then you can't say your brain produces consciousness because it's actually consciousness that creates the appearance of the brain."

"And the body and everything else around us we interpret as physical. This suggests that sickness and disease aren't afflictions cast at random upon the innocent, but rather, they're illusions created through each individual's consciousness," Henry Jones stated boldly.

Sister Simone leaned towards me. Her eyes filled with tears of compassion. "The apparent physical structure of your body is just a holographic projection of your consciousness. When you accept this, it becomes clear that you're much more responsible for your health than current medical wisdom allows."

I felt the weight of her words on my shoulders. I had all the proof I needed to convict myself. I felt the blood drain from my face.

Healing your consciousness

"Don't look so glum," she said softly. "This is meant to be good news for you. You can now use this knowledge to your advantage. What do you think causes miraculous remissions of disease? I'll tell you. They're due to changes in consciousness. When there's a change in consciousness, it effects a change in the hologram of the body. This is the great secret of self-healing."

The lights suddenly went on. "I get it now. I really do. I've got to heal my consciousness to heal my body."

"Precisely. That's what I've been telling you since our conversation in the hospital courtyard."

"But how do I do this?"

Henry Jones howled with laughter. "You're already doing it. You've been doing it since the day we met, and you accepted responsibility for healing yourself. Why do you think I've been encouraging you to learn and apply so many healing techniques to your body?"

"To be honest, I thought they were physical healing processes. I never realized they were healing my consciousness, too."

"Don't you get it? They are all acts of consciousness. Meditation, diet, sleep, rest, exercise, stretching, breathwork, positive emotions, movement, healing techniques – they are all expressions of consciousness. You've been shifting your consciousness. Consider who you were before you started your healing journey with me. Consider who you are today. Tell me, are you feeling better physically, mentally, spiritually and emotionally?"

"I feel better and stronger and healthier than I have in years," I admitted.

"Well then, keep practising these healing techniques. They're healing your body because they're healing your consciousness, not the other way around."

Holographic healing

"In particular, visualization works so well because, in the holographic domain of thought, images are ultimately as real as reality. In the implicate order, as in the brain, imagination and reality are indistinguishable. The holographic model explains why your bodymind can't tell the difference between the neural holograms your brain uses to experience reality and the ones it conjures up while imagining reality. I'd like you to keep this principle in mind. It's another Green Flag, and you don't want to forget it. Once again, your bodymind can't tell the difference between what is real and what is imagined. This amazing phenomenon provides you with an extraordinary ability to influence your health, control your physical form and heal your body."

"Please explain."

"It's simple. You can tell your body what to do by using images in your mind, and your bodymind will react and respond as if the images are 'real'. Try this: Visualize an imaginary screen in your mind. On it, imagine the disease shrinking. Imagine your body's natural immune system destroying the disease. When you hold these images in your mind, your body responds accordingly."

"It's a fact," Sister Simone said in agreement. "Images held in your mind can and will ultimately manifest as realities in your life. Do you realize how powerful this is?"

"I do. I really, really do."

"The key here is intention," Sister Simone said.

The power of intention

"Yes sirree, every action starts as an intention in the implicate order. Intention is extremely powerful because it's the spark of creation."

Henry Jones explained further: "The real beauty of all the physical healing techniques you've learned is that they are powerful expressions of your intention to heal your body. When you give yourself a salt glow or hot fomentation, you start to bring the reality of your healing into being through intention alone. You literally draw it from the implicate order to the explicate order. This is the magic and power of it."

"What's the difference between intention and imagination?" I asked.

"Oh boy! There's a quantum leap between intention and imagination," Sister Simone said. "The big difference is this: The imagination is already the creation of the form. Your imagination already has the intention and the germs of all the movements needed to carry it out. I can give you proof, if you like."

"Okay."

"Alright, let's talk about the placebo effect."

The placebo effect

"Basically, if patients are given a dummy drug, usually a sugar-coated pill, and told that it's a powerful painkiller, many of them report feeling much less pain, even after traumatic surgery."

"That's astounding!" I gasped.

"Experiments have been done where patients with life-threatening illnesses have been told a placebo is 'a new, wonder drug' and their symptoms have disappeared completely. In some cases, when patients were informed that it was just a placebo, the disease promptly returned. The opposite is also true. There's an actual term called 'nocebo', which occurs when a doctor gives a patient a viable drug but expresses their disbelief in the drug having any positive effects. Needless to say, it doesn't!"

"Now that's freaky."

"It's only freaky if you don't know that the bodymind can't tell the difference between what is real and what is imagined, and responds accordingly. This is another key principle to remember for your emotional healing therapy session. Mark it with another Green Flag so that you can remember it."

Sister Simone said: "In his book called *Health and Healing*, Andrew Weil states that the entire history of medicine may simply be the history of the placebo. He isn't the first scholar to say that, either!"

Henry Jones powered ahead: "The bottom line is this: If your mind believes you will get better, you will! The instant you imagine yourself getting better, your body begins to respond on a physiological level. The worst thing you can do is buy into the illusion that you're sick. When you worry about your poor health, you're creating it!

"There are many stories about people who have lived with tumors in their bodies for years. When they're eventually diagnosed with cancer, they die within months. Why is that? Because they feed the disease with attention. Similarly, there are stories about people who have been told that they're fine when they're actually not, and they've gone home and recovered. There are also many accounts of people who've cured themselves from diseases, such as cancer, by laughing at funny movies, or drinking grape juice, or eating raw food, or taking other medicinal substitutes."

"I once read about a woman who was diagnosed with cancer, but she refused treatment because she was too busy raising her children to get sick. She recovered completely!" Sister Simone told me.

"Do you still need more proof that the mind masters the body? If so, read Anthony Robbins' book called *Unlimited Power*. In it, he refers to someone with multiple personality disorder who was diabetic while one personality, and perfectly healthy as the other personality. Now ask yourself: How is it possible that the same body can have and not have a disease?" I wasn't sure if this was a rhetorical question. We just stared at each other. "Well?"

This was my cue. "I guess the one personality believed she was sick so her body produced the disease, and the other personality believed she was well, so her body produced health," I replied.

"So, then, what does this tell you?" Sister Simone asked me.

"It tells me I can heal my body using any technique, if I believe in it strongly enough."

"That's correct," she said.

I sighed. "I don't mean to be a party pooper, but my symptoms feel so real. It's hard to accept my sickness is just an illusion and that I can overcome it simply by 'believing in healing techniques'."

"Actually, this is the only challenge that you need to overcome in order to heal your body, my friend," Henry Jones replied empathetically.

Sister Simone was franker: "Sickness and disease only seem real when you view them from the explicate order. When you view them from the implicate order, you realize they're just a blur of frequencies streamed through your brain by your consciousness."

Let go of the illusion

"I know this might be difficult for you to swallow, especially when the symptoms of your disease seem so real. Believe me: I know what it feels like to experience suffering and pain. As you know, I got to a point when I couldn't sit with my legs crossed. Why? Because my bladder was so swollen, I thought it was going to explode. The pain was unbearable. Eventually, it became such a big part of me that it seemed to permeate my whole being and I could no longer tell where the pain was coming from. The pain consumed me, and I was consumed by it.

"When I first read that my suffering and pain was an illusion, I wanted to punch the author. But, the more I thought about it and began to understand the science behind it, the more it made sense to me. When I thought of my physical problem as an illusion, I was able to break its hold over me. My situation was no longer permanent. It was just an illusion, and illusions fade away. That thinking gave me tremendous strength. I kept repeating to myself: 'This too shall pass. This too shall pass.' And it worked, too! If you want to heal your body, it's absolutely essential for you to understand and accept that you merely need to let go of an illusion. You created it, so you can let it go."

"This is powerful stuff. It puts the ball in your court entirely. Many people pray to God to take away their illness, but holographically speaking, God would reply: 'It's not for me to take it away, but for you to release it.'"

"But they seem so real," I groaned once more.

Henry Jones chuckled. "Albert Einstein said: 'Reality is merely an illusion, albeit a very persistent one.'"

"He was a smart guy, so it must be true," I conceded.

Sister Simone rolled her lips under her teeth. "Let me make this point crystal clear: Sickness and disease are illusions. Period."

"But why do they persist?" I complained.

"They're created by consciousness to express the imbalance between the body, mind and spirit. You can only release them by overcoming the life-lessons they have to teach you."

"What about children? How come they get sick, too?"

Why children get sick

"In the case of young children, I believe the life-lessons are meant for those closest to them, or linked to karma, or to that soul's life-lesson!"

511

"We shouldn't make the mistake of underestimating the power of a child's psyche, either!" Sister Simone commented. "'There is no chance event in a holographic universe,' Pribram said. 'Even random events would have to be seen as based on holographic principles and therefore determined.' In the holographic model, everything that happens to you has an underlying symmetry with the universe, and everything in reality must be seen as a metaphor. Got it?"

I was about to reply, but Henry Jones stretched out his arms and said loudly: "Everything happens for a reason. Everything!"

Change your future

Sister Simone was hot on his heels. "Your life's path has synchronistically led you to this moment for a specific reason. The time has come for you to give up your linear, secular understanding of a reality governed entirely by physical laws to embrace a new, dynamic holographic reality that's ultimately governed by consciousness. Look around you. Look at your life. What you perceive to be reality is really a blank canvas on which you can create anything you wish. In a holographic universe, there are no limits to the extent to which we can alter the fabric of reality."

"You can make magic happen when you set your mind to it," he interjected.

"Yes sirree. That's true. By setting your mind to healing your body, you orchestrate everything in the universe around that objective. It makes no difference whether you have the flu or a life-threatening illness – you can heal your body in record time when you deal with the problem at a molecular, cellular level. Ultimately, everything occurs at a molecular, cellular level, including healing."

"The only trick you need to learn is how to get into the fabric of reality in order to alter it."

"And you're going to show me how to do this?"

"Yes, we're going to take a trip into the implicate order. It's time for us to teach you how to get into the Healing Zone."

"The Healing Zone?"

"Come closer to me," Sister Simone commanded, curling her finger repeatedly. I leaned towards her. "Boo!" she shouted loudly. I nearly jumped out of my seat.

"What just happened to you?" Henry Jones asked.

Super-positioning

"I nearly peed in my pants?" I said, pulling myself together.

They chuckled like a pair of hyenas. "You just experienced your most primal response. Fight or flight. You only had two, instinctive choices. You could've leaped backwards or lashed out to defend yourself."

"What's your point?" I growled, my heart still pounding.

"Simply this: Cause and effect is obvious in our physical world. Matter stays within set rules. For every visible action, there's a reaction. Consequences are predictable in the physical world."

"I still don't get it."

"Let's explore what just happened inside your body. The fright triggered the emotion of fear, which turned into neuropeptides that communicated the message to your bodymind. Instead of the message being passed from one molecule to the next, they all got the message instantly – all 50 trillion of them! Deepak says: 'The message is conveyed so perfectly that literally every single body cell learns of your fear and joins in.' As a result, your brain instantaneously sent signals to your adrenal glands, which released adrenaline. This caused your heart to pound, which elevated your blood pressure and caused a chain reaction throughout your whole system. On the surface, this reaction seems simple enough, but let's back up to the point where the thought of fear, which is non-matter, turned into the neuropeptide, which is matter. How and where does this happen?"

"I haven't a clue."

"Let's work it out together, shall we?"

The origin of neuropeptides

"We know that a neuropeptide isn't a thought. It's the chemical messenger molecule. They appear to be connected, but there's no visible connection between the non-material and the material. So, where does it come from?"

"I really have no idea?" I confessed.

"We must assume there is some hidden transformation happening that turns a thought into a molecule. But where does that hidden process take place?"

I shrugged helplessly. "Tell me."

"I wish I could. Sadly, not even the best minds in the world can answer that question yet. We simply don't know. It remains a mystery. Dr Chopra refers to it as 'the zone'. Some people call it 'the gap'. Personally, I like to refer to this hidden realm as the Healing Zone, because this is where we can go to heal our bodies."

The Healing Zone

"If you want to release old, negative emotions that are trapped in your body cells, then you've got to find your way to the Healing Zone. If you want to heal your body, that is where you need to go. If you want to change your consciousness and shift your reality, then you must visit the Healing Zone. Is this clear?"

"Yes, but where is this place?" I breathed.

"It doesn't exist in any particular time or space," he said. "It's merely the place where we go to turn thought into molecules, consciousness into matter, and intention into reality."

This all sounded delightfully mysterious. A zillion questions bombarded my brain. "What happens inside this place?" I asked.

"Well, we don't exactly know what happens in the Healing Zone, but it appears that mind and matter cooperate with miraculous consequences. By getting into the Healing Zone, you can instantaneously change the physical reality of your body."

"How does it work?"

"I wish I could tell you, my friend. All I know is that the Healing Zone appears to hold the original blueprint of everything in the universe, including your body. Each time you enter the Healing Zone, you return to the source of intelligence within you. When you access it, all the distortions of disease can be dissolved and removed instantly."

This sounded incredible. "Go on. Don't stop now. What else?"

Henry Jones breathed slowly and spoke steadily. "Imagine your body as a complex building designed by a Master Architect Builder. You're the owner of the building and you allow a lousy tenant, your ego-mind, to move in. It decides to renovate the space, even though it's not an architect or builder. In comparison to the Master Architect Builder, your ego-mind would have the building skills of a toothbrush salesman. Instead of using the natural materials recommended by the Master Architect Builder, your ego-mind decides to use cheaper, nastier, man-made products. It quickly discards the original blueprints because it wants to be in control of the whole project. It starts to pile bricks on top of each other in the hope of creating the mansion it has in mind. From time to time, professionals may try to caution the ego-mind that the physical structure will cave in eventually, but it refuses to listen to their advice. Then, one day, the inevitable happens. Certain parts give in, and the whole building threatens to come crashing down. As the owner, wouldn't it be wonderful if you could evict this tenant, erase the misdoings, and return the condition of your building to the exact specifications of the original blueprints of the Master Architect Builder? I'm not saying you can go back in time and space to start over again, but rather to instantly have your house go back to the way it was intended by the Master Architect Builder before your ego-mind took occupation. Sound too good to be true?"

"Yes, it does."

"But what if it wasn't? We're going to show you how to get into 'the gap'. When you get to your Healing Zone, you'll experience a fundamental transformation that goes deeper than your organs, tissues, cells, and even your DNA. You'll communicate directly with the intelligence that resides at the source of your body's existence in time and space. In that moment, you'll experience pure healing bliss. I promise."

If anyone else on Planet Earth had said that to me, I would've taken it with a pinch of salt, but I trusted Henry Jones.

You're no stranger to the gap

"You probably don't know it, but you're no stranger to this place," Sister Simone told me. "The gap occurs in a fraction of a second between each instance of thought in your stream of consciousness. You're literally blinking on and off very, very quickly, in much the same way that a photographic role of still shots creates the illusion of a moving reality when played through a projector. As you blink on and off, the memories in your cells are transferred from the old to the new. And, if you could just get into the gap to release the memory that's distorting your picture of health, you would reappear instantly in perfect physical form."

"Is this the only access route to the gap?"

"No, we also slip into the gap just before we fall asleep, dream and wake up, too. In fact, every time there is a shift in our state of consciousness, we slip into it. It appears to be an integral part of our grand design. For some unknown reason, it's essential for us to visit it constantly, if only for a split second. The trick you need to learn is how to consciously get into the gap."

"Where do I sign up?"

The invisible field

"Right here. But first, we must finish preparing you for this remarkable journey inward. You need to be aware of the space between all things: The invisible field of absolute intelligence. Take a careful look at the notepad in your hands. You may think you have a firm grip on it, but in terms of quantum physics, there are galaxies of space between your fingers and the paper. All atoms are more than 99.99% empty space. So, the image you see is actually what Deepak calls 'a faint shadow line' between the carbon atoms of the notepad; the hydrogen atoms of the air; and the solid atoms of your body cells. In truth, what you perceive as reality is mostly comprised of 'nothingness'," Sister Simone said.

"The fabric of this 'nothingness' is supreme intelligence. It holds all of reality together in an invisible field," Henry Jones added.

"You tap into this invisible field every time you have a thought, emotion, desire or memory. As your brain fires, the neurological impulses are literally created or recreated from 'nowhere'. Think about it. Remember what happened when I gave you a fright? The brain cells that fired in that moment no longer exist, so when you recall the experience you're literally drawing the memory from nowhere."

I chewed on my bottom lip. "This concept is vaguely familiar to me. Why is that?"

"This invisible field is well-known in science. It's a common understanding that atoms exist as particles in the form of matter, as well as waves in the form of pure potentiality. Similarly, a photon is a form of light as well as a light wave. Both arise from a hidden field. Dr Chopra states: 'The reason they can both exist in one reality is that they pre-exist as mere possibilities in the quantum field – the invisible field.'"

Unified Field Theory

Sister Simone raised her hand to speak. "Albert Einstein spent a large portion of his life trying to identify a formula that would explain what has become known as Unified Field Theory. In essence, he was so convinced that there was one unifying field that he strived to identify one theory that would unite all the forces in creation. Unfortunately, he didn't succeed before his death. Quite possibly, he failed because he looked for answers externally, rather than internally. Everything we perceive about the physical world is processed through consciousness. Since consciousness is simply awareness, it's feasible to assume that an awareness of a unified field of intelligence would come forward through a state of consciousness."

States of consciousness

"Excuse me?"

She sighed. "Here goes: We have three states of consciousness: Waking, dreaming and sleeping (or dreamless sleep). Everything we know about our existence comes from our subjective experience of these three states. Got it?"

"Uh-huh."

"Good. All three of these states exist in our consciousness. So, if there is a unified field, then it will most likely be discovered through an additional state of consciousness. Right?"

"Agreed."

"Okay. In 1975, Dr Robert Keith Wallace of the University of California in Los Angeles wrote a thesis titled: *The Physiological Effects of Transcendental Meditation*. That thesis was of great significance. Why? He proved the existence of a fourth state of consciousness that is only accessible through meditation. After many years of dedicated research, Wallace was able to quantify the human body's physiological response to meditation. Through a series of measurements, he proved that meditation affects the heart rate, breathing pattern, brain waves and even metabolic rate. His thesis established that people who meditate enter a heightened state of awareness that is an entirely new state of consciousness. So, if you think meditation is just a way to relax, then you're grossly underestimating the potential of this awesome mental exercise. When you meditate, you bring yourself to the point of transformation between 'reality' and the 'unified field of absolute intelligence' – the verge of the Healing Zone. Are you beginning to see how valuable this information is to you?"

"Yes. You're saying meditation can consciously lead me to the Healing Zone."

"That's exactly what we're saying," Henry Jones exclaimed. "You should know that Wallace also says the biggest obstacles to achieving the fourth state of consciousness are what he calls 'the negative elements in man', or 'our inner enemies'. In other words, our vices."

Sister Simone added: "It's only by giving up our vices that we can become eligible for higher states of consciousness. Our minds and bodies must be clear and pure in order for us to experience true healing bliss."

The blueprint of your body

"The only way to cure a disease is to promote the cure from within. To do this, you have to enter the Healing Zone. This is the only way to return to the source of intelligence within you – to your internal unified field. There, at the source, you can access the original blueprint of your body. In that moment, every molecule of your being quivers with the pure potentiality of your existence. They spontaneously become open and receptive to receiving communication streamed to them through the fourth state of consciousness. You can literally talk to your body cells. And, as one of them gets the message, they all instantly get the message and respond accordingly. As you can imagine, this is a truly remarkable experience!"

Peak experiences

Henry Jones added: "Renowned psychologist Abraham Maslow called these moments 'peak experiences'. He said, 'These moments were pure, positive happiness, when all doubts; fears; inhibitions; tensions and weaknesses were left behind. Now self-consciousness was lost. All separateness and distance from the world disappeared.'"

"Even Albert Einstein visited the Healing Zone!" Henry Jones cried. "Einstein said: 'One feels free from one's own identification with human limitation. At such moments one imagines that one stands on some spot of a small planet gazing in amazement at the cold and yet profoundly moving beauty of the eternal, the unfathomable. Life and death flow into one, and there's neither evolution nor destiny, only Being.'"

"I must warn you, however," Sister Simone said sincerely. "Being in the Healing Zone is bliss, but getting there can be a different story."

The nowhere zone

"You see, sometimes there's a black void before the bliss, and you must pass through it. I can tell you from personal experience, giving up your construct of reality and passing through to the hidden world where intelligence is supreme can be extremely distressing. You need to first let go of everything your ego-mind believes is real. This isn't always easy to do!

"My first trip to the Healing Zone was extremely challenging. After a half-hour of hypnotic regression, I was in a state of deep meditation. I'd drifted back to a particular hurtful experience in my past. I had issues with a troubled relationship that I hadn't dealt with properly. I could hear my therapist asking me to share my feelings with the person I had in my mind, but for some inexplicable reason I couldn't understand what she was saying. I could hear the words, but I couldn't get their meaning. I kept asking her to repeat her instruction, but each time I heard it, my internal dialogue shut down. Intellectually, I understood what she was asking me to do, but I didn't understand it emotionally. You see, as a teenager I swore that I'd never allow myself to feel hurt again. I've a vivid memory of commanding the reflection in my bedroom mirror to sever from my emotional self. I buried anger and resentment deep inside. In its place, I consciously and deliberately welcomed stoicism."

"What happened next?"

"Well, needless to say, for a long time I was stuck in a black void where I felt only apathy and indifference. It took close on three hours to break through the barriers that I'd built up inside me. When I eventually did break down, I was shocked to discover how much negative emotion was stored inside me. Once I'd finally worked through the layers of emotions and the void of indifference, I slipped into a state of pure bliss. In those precious moments, I felt delightful physical sensations running through my body. At best I can describe them as mild, electric tingles coursing through my veins. My head, heart and hands were the source of the palpitations that ran throughout my body. I felt the bodymind connection, and, like I said, I genuinely began to experience pure, healing bliss. At the time, I was reading a book written by Dr Chopra wherein he said: 'As you enter the state of bliss, waves of consciousness well up from the field of intelligence, cross the gap and are infused into every body cell. This is the body's own awakening'. I could relate to that 100%. This was exactly what I felt in this moment."

"That's an incredible story," I remarked enviously.

Bliss

"Deepak talks about this bliss often. He describes it as the vibration intelligence sends into the world. He says it bridges mind and matter," Sister Simone added. "He goes on to say: 'Your mind talks to your DNA through bliss. When your mind sends signals, your DNA receives them through the sensation of bliss. Bliss is the carrier signal. So, when you do your emotional healing therapy session and you feel bliss, you know that you've entered the gap, the Healing Zone. The bliss you feel is your body receiving healing messages from the invisible field where your original blueprint is stored.'"

"But first, you have to work your way through the layers of emotions that are stored in your cells. Clogged emotions make it difficult for us to reach bliss," Henry Jones reminded me.

Emotional healing therapy

"Okay, are you ready for your emotional healing therapy session?" Sister Simone asked cheerfully. "Trust us. It will take you into the Healing Zone to find your healing."

"Let's do it right now," I cried out. "Now, now, now!"

CHAPTER 28

SEVEN FLAGS TO FLY

"Where do we start?" I asked excitedly.

"We'll go over the key principles first," Sister Simone stated. "There are seven of them. They'll all be familiar to you because we've spent the afternoon discussing them."

"Here's where the green flags become relevant," Henry Jones interjected with a wink.

"Ah!"

Her eyes gleamed. "Did you think we'd forgotten?"

The first flag

"The first flag reminds us that in a super-hologram, the past, present and future all exist simultaneously," Sister Simone said. "Moreover, subatomic particles in the super-hologram can communicate with each other. It's a proven fact: Subatomic particles that have interacted can instantaneously respond to each other's motions thousands of years later when they're light-years apart."

"So, if you still think you live in a solid, physical universe where time is linear, forget it!" Henry Jones contributed.

"That's good advice. Life is much more than we know it to be," she said. "The general consensus is: We are born, we move on, and we die, but that's just our perception based on our subjective experience. From the perspective of a holographic universe, time and space are relative. This means, at this exact moment, you exist as a child in another space and time. We all do."

"And we're all connected to our other selves?"

"Yes, we are one and the same."

"Your inner child is merely the remnants of your other self."

"And this is relevant because …?"

"The objective of the upcoming session is to take your consciousness back to a time in your life when you experienced emotional distress, so that you can make peace with yourself."

My heart skipped a beat. I knew I had unresolved emotional issues from my past, and those experiences were still influencing my personality and affecting my behavior. I suddenly understood my objective perfectly. I had to interrupt the communication between the younger me and the current me. I had to somehow change the messages encoded in the emotions that were recorded in my body cells. The first flag had been hoisted.

The second flag

"The second flag reminds us that the super-hologram contains every subatomic particle that has been created or will ever be created. This is an important concept to grasp. It suggests your whole life is a series of events that have already been recorded, past and future."

"How can the future be recorded if it hasn't happened yet?"

Sister Simone pressed her hands together, as if in prayer. "The fact that you haven't experienced your future yet is irrelevant. Everything that can possibly happen in the future exists in a state of pure potentiality."

"Even a future in which you're well," Henry Jones said, nudging my side.

"Really?" I gasped.

"Yes, yes, yes! You can manifest this future for yourself. A healthy, happy, healed you already exists in a state of pure potentiality. It does! All you need to do is make a connection to that future state," Sister Simone replied.

Henry Jones jumped in: "Try to wrap your head around this concept: The universe is actually a multiverse wherein everything that can exist does exist. Everything you desire for yourself exists in a state of pure potentiality, and it's waiting for you to connect with it in order for you to bring it into your reality."

"So, what's the secret? How do I connect with it?"

"You do it through your consciousness."

"My consciousness?" I exclaimed.

"Yes. Consciousness is governed by thought, which in turn governs pure potentiality," she explained.

"So, you're telling me our reality is determined by what we stream though our consciousness?" I summarized.

"Yes, exactly!"

"In other words, what we think about, we bring about?"

"You've got it now!" Sister Simone declared.

A cold shiver suddenly ran down my spine. I thought back to the months and months and months of 'sick thoughts' I'd streamed through my consciousness. I got the fact that I'd been creating the reality in which I was sick. I'd attached my past-experience to my present-self to my future state. I carried the sickness with me into the future. I instantly realized the importance of changing the thoughts and feelings I streamed through my consciousness. My future health or sickness is a choice I alone have the power to make. I make it in the present moment every time I think and feel. That revelation rocked my world.

The third flag

"The third flag is there to remind you that every cell in your body grew out of a single cell that came into existence in the instant of your conception. This means your very first memory is of you being a single cell inside your mother's womb. In that state you embodied the original, perfect blueprint of your body. You were in a state of perfect health." Sister Simone paused to take a breath.

"Go on," I ordered impatiently.

"If you want to reconnect with the perfect blueprint of your body, then you've got to get back inside that original cell. You need to get back to your mother's womb."

Henry Jones put his hand on my shoulder. "She's right, my friend. If you want to get into a single cell to release old emotions, the womb is the place to do it."

I knew this was big. They were showing me the gateway to my healing. My heart began to pound in my chest. I was nearly there. My healing journey with Henry Jones had brought me to this crucial point in time and space.

"Please tell me that you're going to show me how to get back into the womb right now."

They nodded simultaneously.

"You bet we are. We're going to show you how to use meditation and visualization to regress back into the womb and to connect with the original blueprint of your body," Sister Simone told me earnestly.

My hands trembled with excitement. I knew what that meant. The significance of it overwhelmed me. I figured if I could reconnect with the original blueprint of my body, I could reconnect with my health and I would be healed.

"Tell him about the fourth flag," Henry Jones suggested to Sister Simone.

The fourth flag

She turned to me. "This one is a game-changer. The fourth flag reminds us that our bodymind can't tell the difference between the neural holograms our brains use to experience reality and the ones they conjure up while imagining reality. In other words, when you think of past and future experiences, the neurological impulses in your brain fire in the same way as when you perceive your current reality."

"This means your memories and desires appear real to your bodymind. You may think you've put hurtful memories behind you, but they're alive and present in your mind and body," Henry Jones said.

The fifth flag

Sister Simone pushed on. "The fifth flag reminds us that images held in our minds can, and will, ultimately manifest as reality in our lives. I seriously urge you to imprint this statement deep into your brain so that you never forget it. It's that important!"

"You do realize the significance of it, don't you?" Henry Jones asked me.

"Yes. It means when I visualize healing at a cellular level, my body must respond accordingly." As I said it, I suddenly realized what I'd just said. It didn't just hit me. It knocked me for a six. "Geez, this is huge!" I gasped.

The sixth flag

The sixth flag is about to be hoisted," he sported. "This flag reminds us that messages are not passed from one molecule to the next inside your body. They all get the message instantly – all 50 trillion of them. So, when you release the negative emotions stored in a single cell, they're released throughout your entire body."

"What?" I cried.

524

"That's not all," she responded. "Once the negative distortion has been dissolved and removed, your body then automatically and spontaneously regenerates healthy cells. In other words, your body begins to heal, naturally!"

"Amazing!"

The seventh flag

Henry Jones threw his hands in the air. "If you think that's amazing, you're going to get a real kick out of this. The seventh flag reminds us that healing occurs in a state of bliss. If you want to heal your body, you must put yourself into a state of bliss. Clogged emotions and vices make it difficult for you to reach bliss. You must cut out your vices and peel away the layers of your emotions, one by one, until eventually there are no negative emotions between you and bliss. Only then can you enter the Healing Zone. We were inspired by the pioneering work of Brandon Bays in this field. You should really get a copy of her book, *The Journey*."

I tingled all over. "Just show me what to do."

Sister Simone smiled. "The objective of the upcoming emotional healing therapy session is to allow yourself to fully experience each of the emotional layers within you. It's important to thoroughly immerse yourself in each emotion. Remember, you're in a consequence-free environment, so don't be afraid to let them out. Okay?"

"I've always been quite cagey with my emotions," I admitted. "But today I won't hold back. I want to get the most out of this session."

"Great. The path forward is clear. There are seven, sequential steps in a session: Reconnaissance; Regression; Recall; Re-enactment; Release; Re-program and Rejoice."

"They all start with R?"

"Well spotted. Yes, hopefully this'll help you to remember them," Henry Jones answered. "Like the Rs in the 10 healing stances." He nudged me.

Sister Simone stepped in. "I'd like to run through these steps with you before we apply them in your session. The objective of the first step, Reconnaissance, is to establish the condition of specific body cells. We do that through guided meditation. The second step, Regression, takes you on a trip down memory lane. The third step, Recall, is designed to identify and retrieve a particular memory."

"The memory that's making me sick?"

"Not necessarily. It can also be a memory that's holding you back from reaching your full potential. If it surfaces, then it's for good reason. You must deal with it, once and for all. You may have to do this process multiple times before you find all the painful memories that plague your past. You see, in order to construct the illusion that you're sick, your ego-mind has stacked your suppressed emotions inside of you like a house of cards. You won't necessarily know which card is the one that's making you sick. You may need to remove a few cards before you bring the house down. Make sense?"

I gave a single nod.

"Good. The fourth step, Re-enactment, involves re-enacting the memory. It's essential to relive the memory. You must re-experience it. This unblocks the suppressed emotions. All of them. You must take as much time as you need on this step to fully express yourself."

Henry Jones jumped in. "The fifth step, Release, refers to forgiving yourself and others. We can't proceed to the sixth step, until you've passed through forgiveness. Deal?"

"Deal."

"Excellent. The sixth step, Reprogram, is your chance to change your perception of your past experience. This enables you to replace the negative feelings created by your ego-mind with the positive, healthy feelings produced by your true-self. The seventh step, Rejoice, is where you celebrate the release of negative memories. You should feel lighter and happier when you reach this final step. Most people do."

"I can't wait to get there," I stated optimistically.

"By following these seven steps, you'll experience a powerful emotional healing therapy session. It will lead you to the heart of your problem. I guarantee it. I'm thrilled for you, because you're just about to learn exactly how you can release the negative emotions stored in your cells and heal your body. I mean it!"

"That's what I want most," I declared.

Sister Simone felt the need to insert a word of caution: "This process can also be quite traumatic. You must make sure that you're totally prepared for it."

"How does one prepare for it?" I asked, choosing to rather be safe than sorry.

"That's a good question. There's a pre-process checklist. Let's run through it quickly."

"Should I take notes?"

"You can, if you like. That may help you to remember them in the future."

"Okay, fire away."

"First of all, it's important to be in a safe place. You must be able to do the process in peace. You don't want to be disturbed in any way, so it's essential to set aside adequate time to complete the process without being interrupted."

"How long does it take to do?"

"The process can take anywhere from one to three hours to complete. You'll also need time to recover after the process. Emotional healing can be hectic. It can leave you mentally, emotionally, spiritually and even physically exhausted."

"How long does it take to recover?"

"As a rule-of-thumb, you need to remain in a quiet, meditative state for as long as it took for you to complete the process. However, you'll probably feel its effects days, weeks and months later."

"Do you need a partner?"

"No. You can put yourself through this process, but it's a thousand times more effective if you do it with the help of someone else. I strongly suggest you identify a suitable partner to guide you through it. Choose someone you can trust with your emotions. It's very important that you feel comfortable enough to release your emotions completely. If there's even the slightest possibility that your emotional issues are connected to your partner, then choose someone else. Doing the process with a complete stranger would be better than doing it with someone with whom you have suppressed emotions. If you can't find the ideal partner, I'd like to recommend you select someone who has counselling experience, such as a minister, teacher or social worker. Trust your intuition to choose the right person. If it feels right, then it is right. Make sure that you and your partner study the process beforehand. Their understanding of the process is actually more important than your own."

Henry Jones leaned towards me and whispered: "It would help tremendously if both parties read our book, once it's published." He winked and then nudged me again.

"At the very least, they should have a basic understanding of the key principles – the seven flags – and know the sequence of the process. You don't want to be unclear about what steps to take next or you'll break the continuity of the process. Continuity is important if you want your emotions to flow freely. Lastly, it's imperative that you develop the right mental attitude towards the process."

"Please explain."

"You should go into the process willingly and enthusiastically. This is crucial! The process will only work for you if you're totally committed to it. You must, however, commit with your heart, not your head. Don't try to rationalize or analyze your feelings. Allow yourself to experience them for what they are; feel them to their fullest; and don't hold anything back," she advised me.

Henry Jones dispensed some good advice, too. "You've got to completely surrender yourself to the process. Embrace it for what it truly is – an extraordinary opportunity for you to open yourself up and empty out all your old, negative emotions. This is your chance to let them go. Just trust the process. It works. It will liberate you, if you let it!"

"Okay, I'm convinced. Now let me see if I got all the points down correctly: Find a safe place, set aside adequate time, identify a suitable partner, study the process beforehand and develop the right attitude."

"That's it. You nailed it. Now, let's move on. We need to paint some mental pictures in your mind," Henry Jones said. "Let's start by discussing the womb again. It's a very special place. As Dr Kaufmann described it: 'Inside the womb, you felt totally safe and secure. It was the perfect place for you. Every single biological function worked towards sustaining your life and nurturing your development.' Remember?"

"Yes, that does sound familiar."

Henry Jones cleared his throat. "I'll never forget the time my family and I visited an exhibition at the Natural Science Museum in London. I was just a boy, but I remember it as though it was yesterday. One of the rooms had been transformed into an identical replica of the womb, only much bigger. The exhibition was enormously popular, and my parents insisted we see it. There were long queues of people waiting to get inside. It was only when we got into the womb that I understood the attraction. The shape, color, temperature and sound of the mother's heartbeat was so soothing and comforting that once inside, people didn't want to leave. We were only given a few minutes inside the womb before we were ushered out to make room for the next group of people. Even so, the experience was powerful enough to create a vivid memory in my mind."

"How did being in the room make you feel, Henry?" Sister Simone inquired with the tone of a school teacher.

"I remember feeling comfortable, safe, secure, relaxed, at ease, content and warm. I also had a sense of being nurtured, loved and protected. It was quite extraordinary."

"That makes perfect sense to me," Sister Simone commented. "Those are exactly the feelings that I associate with being inside the womb. Some people also use words like 'evolving'; 'expanding' and 'growing' to describe the sensations they feel inside the womb during the guided meditation. Now, let's talk about body cells again. Do you remember blowing bubbles as a child?"

"Sure."

"Can you get an image of them in your mind right now? Picture them, perfectly round and clear, drifting through time and space."

Sister Simone didn't need to ask me twice. In fact, she'd hardly finished her sentence and I had bubbles floating around in my imagination. I reached out and pretended to pop one.

She giggled. "Now let me ask you this: Were you ever lucky enough to see two bubbles fly into each other? As they connected, they merged into one, right?"

"Right."

"Did you ever see your refection on a bubble wall?"

"I think so."

"What about a rainbow of colors glistening on the surface of a bubble? Of course, you did!"

Henry Jones joined in. "What do you think it would be like to be inside a bubble looking out? Think about it. Reality would be perceived as an image screened on the bubble wall, wouldn't it?"

"I imagine so," I stammered as I tried to fathom this odd perspective.

"Fun-taas-tick!" Sister Simone said, playfully wobbling her head. "I'd like you to recall these images when we do the session and the guided meditation takes you into your original body cell."

Henry Jones tossed some more spice into the pot. "The qualities that we'd like you to associate with being inside a body cell are: Spaciousness; depth; wonder; magic; purpose; omnipotence and universal energy. Got it?"

"Yup! This is child's play," I remarked glibly.

"Okay then, since we're painting mental pictures in your mind, let's discuss the colors of emotion. Have you ever heard any of these expressions: Red with anger; green with envy; yellow with cowardice?"

I nodded.

"I'm sure you have! For some reason, people have always associated emotion with color. Accepting this phenomenon will come in handy for you when we do the process."

"How come?"

"Well, it's sometimes easier for suppressed emotions to emerge as colors before the actual feeling arises, especially when the emotions have been buried deep inside for a long time!"

"Psychiatrists use a similar technique to draw out emotions when they ask patients to interpret ink splodges or squiggles. For instance: If a patient has suppressed anger towards a parent because of abuse but they can't express it, then they'll see a cruel father beating a frightened child in the meaningless pattern on a sheet of paper. You follow?"

"Yes."

"It's as if the human psyche will take advantage of any opportunity to release suppressed emotions. So, if you're struggling to feel an emotion during the process, look out for colors that appear on the inside of the cell wall. Behind each color is an emotion."

"What do I do if I see a color?"

"Allow yourself to absorb it completely. In your mind, you'll get to a point when the color is at its fullest. The blue can't become bluer; the yellow can't become yellower; and the black can't become blacker. When your psyche has been saturated by it, then you can begin to interpret the emotion. This is the time to ask yourself: 'How does this color make me feel?'"

"And what do I do when I start to feel an emotion?"

"Allow yourself to feel it completely. Don't analyze it – just accept it. Let it saturate your psyche thoroughly. Beyond this point is a state of mental nothingness. When you reach this state, then the emotion is fully present and you can pass through it to the next color or emotion."

"What do the various colors mean?"

"Any color can represent any emotion, but over the years I've observed some common interpretations. For example: Black is often associated with hate, loathing and depression; Purple is used to express resentment, bitterness and frustration; Red represents anger, rage, pain and hurt; Green is envy and jealousy; yellow is fear; mustard is deep fear; and blue is cold, indifference and depression."

"Gosh, how many colors can you see in a session?" I exclaimed in horror.

"That depends entirely on how many layers of emotions are locked up inside you. Some people have only a few layers to get through, while others have many. Regardless of how many layers need to be peeled back, you must keep working through them until the cell wall becomes clear. You can only see the mental images of your memories reflected on the cell wall when it's clear. Often white is the last color, which symbolizes the inner purity that lies beneath all the emotional layers."

"Is that the final step?"

"Nope. Not quite! You must get to the Healing Zone."

"How do I get there?"

"At one stage during the guided meditation, you'll pass through the clear cell wall into the unified field on the other side. This is the space between your body cells. A word of caution here: This crossing over is difficult for some people. They get stuck in a Nowhere Zone. You may have experienced this headspace before. For instance, do you remember sitting on top of a tall slide, or a high wall, or a bicycle, about to push off for the first time? If so, then you'll most likely know what I'm talking about when I say: 'in the Nowhere Zone.' You don't want to go backwards, but you don't want to go forward either. The result is that you stay stuck in the moment until you either let go of your fear or succumb to it. Make sense?"

"Uh-huh."

"It's not easy to let go of your perception of reality to embrace the unknown. As the ego-mind clings desperately to its existence, it kicks up powerful emotions."

"Such as …?"

The feelings that you can associate with being in the Nowhere Zone are fear, apprehension, doubt, numbness and indifference."

"How can I overcome these emotions?"

"Just trust the process and allow yourself to push through the Nowhere Zone. You won't regret it. The reward is definitely worth it."

"That's an understatement," Henry Jones piped. "Once you push past the Nowhere Zone, you'll slip into a state of bliss!"

Sister Simone fervently agreed. "People sometimes feel physical sensations running through their bodies, such as tingles or electric shivers. The other feelings that you can associate with being in the state of bliss are oneness; wholeness; expansiveness; joy; love; peace; harmony; ecstasy; elation; freedom; eternity and closeness to God or a Higher Power."

"I like the sound of that," I admitted.

Henry Jones continued: "Remember the chart on Professor Kaufmann's wall? Inside the womb, it looked like you were floating around in a fluid-filled bubble, holding a balloon, which was actually a yolk sack that would supply you with vital nutrients until the placenta was fully developed. Well, there's a stage in the process when you're asked to reach out for this 'Resource Sack' to assist you to handle a situation better."

"How will it do that?"

"It gives you the wisdom of hindsight. This is a wonderful gift. I bet with hindsight you'd react differently to many of your past experiences."

"Sure. Who wouldn't?"

"Precisely. It's an exact science, and that is what makes this stage in the process so powerful and important."

"Is there anything else, Henry?" Sister Simone asked.

"No, I don't think we've left anything out. You're good to go," he replied, rubbing his hands together.

My palms started to sweat.

"In that case, please be so kind as to leave us alone now, Henry. This needs to be a private session," Sister Simone said respectfully.

"Of course," he replied, practically jumping to his feet. He grabbed his car keys from the nearby table and made for the door.

"Henry!" I called after him. He stopped and turned around. His head cocked characteristically to one side to hear what I had to say. But, I couldn't speak. There was so much I wanted to tell him in that moment, but the words eluded me. We just stared at each other.

Is it possible to express enough gratitude to someone who changes your life forever? Are there words so deep and meaningful that they can compensate someone for giving you the keys to enlightenment? If there are such rare and precious words, I couldn't find them in that moment. Hopefully my tearful eyes told the full story.

His beautiful grin broadened. "Good luck, my friend. I look forward to seeing you on the other side," he said, leaving the room with a wave.

CHAPTER 29

GRANDMA, THE BIG BAD WOLF, AND THE CUPBOARD

"I'm lucky to have met Henry Jones," I told Sister Simone. "That man changed my life."

She smiled. "That's not the first time I've heard those words. He's helped many, many people to restore their bodies to perfect health. That is his mantra, isn't it?"

"I hear it all day long."

She chortled, pushed Henry's chair to one side and rearranged our seats. I stood awkwardly to one side as she placed them side by side, in the center of her office. She turned them slightly inwards, but not so much that they faced each other. "Come sit down beside me," she said, tapping one of the seats. She placed a notepad and two pens on the small table beside her. "Are you ready to start your emotional healing therapy session?"

"I've never been readier for anything in my whole life," I replied.

"Good. This process is performed in a state of meditation; the fourth state of consciousness."

"Naturally," I replied, drumming my knees apprehensively.

"Can I assume Henry has taught you how to enter a state of meditation?"

"Yes. Swami G, too."

She nodded approvingly. "What sequence did they show you?"

"They told me to sit peacefully in a quiet place, in the correct posture, close my eyes and breathe in a slow and rhythmical manner. Then, they told me to totally relax my body, and travel to my private sanctuary. Here,

533

I usually do a few breathing cycles up my back and down my front, whilst putting my tongue in the Heavenly Pool to connect my internal energy. The basics, you know."

"Excellent. I can tell you've had an excellent schooling. Okay then, before we begin the process, I'd like you to do as they suggested for a couple of minutes so that you feel relaxed and comfortable. After that, all you need to do is follow my lead and you'll sail through the process. Let's begin. Close your eyes, slow your breathing down and relax your body. Listen to my voice. I'm going to ask you questions and invite you to repeat what I say. Your participation is essential. Take all the time you need to respond to my questions and instructions. You don't want to rush this process. Okay?"

I nodded. She slipped into silence. I used the time to my full advantage. My only mental distraction was speculating about my body's physiological response to meditating. Like Dr Robert Keith Wallace, I tried to gauge my heart rate, breathing pattern, brain waves and even metabolic rate. I wondered if I was entering a heightened state of awareness, an entirely new state of consciousness.

After some time had passed, Sister Simone spoke softly and gently. "When you're ready to begin the process, let me know by raising your right hand, as if you were pledging to tell the truth in a court of law."

I did as she asked.

"Good. Now, extend your left arm so that I can hold your hand. As our hands connected, she asked me to raise my right arm again and say: "Together, in this moment, we open ourselves to love, wisdom and truth. It is our intention to induce emotional healing for the highest good of all concerned."

Once I'd repeated it, she took a deep breath and replied: "With these words, I access my true-self so that I may serve this unique individual with integrity and love, from my heart and soul. So be it." A minute or so passed by. I guessed she was absorbing the moment. Then she proceeded to say: "When you're ready to move on to step one, raise your right hand and say: 'I'm ready and willing to take the next step in my healing process now.'"

I obliged her request.

"Good," she said. "Then let's proceed. As you're sitting there, become aware of the fullness of your being. Right now, your internal consciousness is calling out to you. Explore your inner-being and notice feelings or physical sensations that emerge into your consciousness from within your body. Is there a particular place in your body that's drawing your attention now? Take your time. Let me know when the particular place in your body has revealed itself to you by raising your right hand and saying, 'I'm aware of the place in my body that's calling to me now.'"

My internal consciousness immediately connected with the pain in my body that constantly reminded me I was sick: That annoying place that perpetually plagued my mind. I let her know that I was aware of it.

"Very good. Now, as you exhale, feel yourself slowly submerging into the ocean of your body cells. Allow the current of your internal consciousness to carry you to the place in your body that's calling for you now. Get a sense of the journey as you're traveling through your body to this place. Become aware of the images that are passing through your mind. Notice any changes that occur in color or temperature as you're nearing the place that's calling to you. Let me know when you're there by raising your right hand and saying: 'I have arrived at the place that's calling to me now.'"

I allowed myself to sink into my system. In my mind's eye, I saw red and imagined heat. I was surprised at how quickly I arrived at the spot. It was as though I knew exactly where to go. I repeated the sentence.

"Excellent, now look around you. There's one distressed body cell that's transmitting the signal to which you're responding. You'll know it when you see it. You'll feel it communicating with you. You may hear it humming or see lights flashing as the chemical messages are broadcast to you. Don't expect or visualize this body cell to be anything in particular, just allow it to 'be' on its own terms. Let me know that you can see it by raising your right hand and saying, 'I can see the body cell that's calling to me now.'"

Sure enough, my imagination created a cluster of cells and I felt myself wading through them like jelly. One cell stood out from the rest. "I really can see the body cell that's calling to me now," I told her.

"Good. Now, move towards it, until you can almost touch it. Expand your energy field and try to feel the presence of the distressed body cell. Get a sense of its vibration now. You're beginning to resonate on the same frequency as this distressed body cell. It's as though you're becoming one with the body cell now. When you're ready, slowly and steadily push through the cell wall until you're inside the distressed body cell completely. Let me know when you've merged with the body cell by raising your right hand and repeating: 'I'm inside the distressed body cell now.'"

I'd seen enough sci-fi movies to give me the mental imagery I needed to perform this. I imagined stretching out my arms and pushing my hands into the cell. I felt around on the inside of the cell before stepping into it. I let her know that I was ready to proceed.

"Good, now look around the inside of this distressed body cell. Get a sense of your surroundings. Stay sensitive to the message that's being communicated to you. And, in your own words, describe what you see, smell, hear, taste and feel."

Sister Simone allowed me to describe my experience in detail. I told her about the colors that appeared on the cell walls and the stench of stale milk that filled my nostrils. She didn't influence my experience in any way. She merely listened. I described the metallic taste in my mouth and the stickiness. When I fell into silence, she prompted me. "And what can you hear?"

"I can hear a droning sound," I replied. "It has a deep, mechanical vibration."

She accepted everything I told her graciously. "Very good," she replied. "Now, connect with your deepest intuition and tell me what the distressed body cell is communicating to you. What is it telling you? How is it making you feel? What is the message that you're receiving right now?"

I tried to tune into the cell, but nothing came to me. She waited patiently. Eventually she spoke up: "You can identify with the message. You can understand the message. You can trust the message because it's your very own nature."

I imagined myself standing with my arms outstretched and fingers splayed, in the center of the cell. After a few deep breaths, the message emerged.

"It's angry and frustrated. It wants to explode, and destroy the universe," I heard myself saying. This lit my fuse. I went on to describe all that I felt. She let me speak until I had nothing left to say. Once I'd finished, she continued with the process.

"Thank you. Now, understanding that you live in a holographic universe where the past, present and future all exist simultaneously, leave the distressed body cell and travel through space and time back to when you were a single cell in the womb. Let me know when you've arrived inside the womb by raising your right hand and repeating: 'I'm inside my original body cell now.'"

I followed her instruction. "Good. Inside the womb, you're feeling totally safe and secure. It's the perfect place for you to be. Every single biological function works towards sustaining your life and nurturing your development.

536

In the instant you connect with the original blueprint of your body, you'll become perfectly whole and perfectly healthy. Get a sense of this now."

I pictured myself inside the womb and tried to get a sense of what I felt. The muscles in my cheeks relaxed. I informed Sister Simone that a deep peace had come over me.

"Excellent. You've successfully taken your first step towards healing your emotional body. When you're ready to move on to step two, raise your right hand and say, 'I'm ready and willing to take the next step in my healing process now.'"

I repeated the line.

"Good, then let's proceed. Knowing that once two subatomic particles have interacted, they can instantaneously respond to each other's motions, even though they're separated by time and space, allow yourself to make a connection between the distressed body cell you visited and the original body cell in the safety and sanctity of the womb. Get a sense of the disparity between them right now. If you can feel the difference, repeat after me, 'Yes, I can feel the difference between these cells now.'"

The difference was obvious. In one state, I was peaceful. In the other, I was clearly disturbed. "Oh yes, I can feel the difference between these cells now," I told her.

"Excellent. Now, tune into the communication between these two cells as they establish what has changed between them and why. Get a sense of what occurred to create this disparity."

I did as she asked, and soon realized the process had surfaced a curious paradox within me. I'd started out perfect and whole, but I'd allowed my life experiences to make me angry and frustrated. Henry Jones's training had prepared me well for this process. That was clear!

She continued: "Let your mind drift through time and space to the origin of these new feelings. Is an experience coming to mind yet?"

"No," I replied.

"Okay, then. Now, from within the safety and sanctity of the womb, absorb the most dominant feeling of the distressed body cell into the original body cell with each new breath." She gave me a chance to inhale and exhale a few times. "As you do this, the dominant color of the distressed cell will start to appear on the walls of the original body cell. Attach the feeling to the color and focus your attention on it. This will help you to transfer the feeling to the original body cell. Let me know when you can see this color by raising your right hand and repeating, 'I can see the color, name it, emerging now.'"

As I inhaled, I clearly saw the color appearing on the original cell wall. "Yes, I can see the color red emerging now."

"Excellent, now use your mind to sharpen the color. You'll notice that as you're sharpening the color, the feeling behind it is also intensifying. As the feeling gets stronger, allow yourself to absorb it completely. Don't let your ego-mind try to analyze or rationalize it. Just accept the feeling for what it is. Let it saturate you to the very core of your being. Feel it at its fullest. Let me know when you have immersed yourself in the feeling by raising your right hand and saying: 'I'm feeling, state the emotion, now.'"

"I'm feeling angry now," I told her.

"Good, well done. Now, look at the color. Is it at its fullest, or can you still sharpen it?"

I put all my attention on the red color that I saw in my imagination. The color genuinely seemed to brighten. I kept at it.

"As the color sharpens, the feeling will intensify. Take your time to feel the feeling to its fullest. Let me know when you have immersed yourself in the feeling by raising your right hand and saying, 'I'm feeling anger to its fullest now.'"

It was easy to do. "I'm feeling anger to its fullest now," I said through clenched teeth.

"Good. Now that this color is at its fullest and you've experienced the emotion completely, you're passing through a brief state of nothingness, from which a new color is beginning to emerge on the wall of the original body cell. Bring it into being by focusing your attention on it. Let me know when you can see this new color by raising your right hand and repeating: 'I can see the color, name it, emerging now.'"

I was amazed when red gave way to purple. My hand shot up and I repeated Sister Simone's line.

"Excellent. Now, use your mind to sharpen this color. You'll notice that as you're sharpening the color, a new feeling is starting to emerge. As the feeling gets stronger, allow yourself to absorb it completely. Let it saturate you to the very core of your being so that you can feel it at its fullest. Let me know when you've immersed yourself in the feeling by raising your right hand and saying: 'I'm feeling, state the emotion, now.'"

I couldn't find the feeling behind the purple. The anger persisted. After some time had passed, Sister Simone nudged me along. "You can identify with this feeling. You can understand this feeling. You can trust this feeling because it's your very own nature," she said.

As she said it, I felt a wave of hatred crash over me. "Hatred. I feel hatred, okay?" I cried out. My eyes opened, and I turned to her for support.

"That's fine. Well done. Now, look at the color. Is it at its fullest, or can you still sharpen the color with your mind?"

I closed my eyes and slipped back into the process. In seconds, the color sharpened and the hatred intensified. It scared me. I felt evil, poisoned and rotten.

"Take your time to feel the feeling to its fullest. Let me know when you've immersed yourself in the feeling by raising your right hand and saying: 'I'm feeling hatred to its fullest now.'"

And so it went on. The colors and feelings kept coming. We worked our way through bitterness, resentment and disappointment. No, I didn't have to explain why I felt these emotions, I just had to feel them to their fullest.

Sister Simone was wonderful. She kept her cool and encouraged me onwards. Her voice was kind and compassionate. She took long pauses in between her sentences, and I could tell that she occasionally wrote in her notepad. Finally, no more negative feelings emerged, and the cell wall became clear.

"Excellent. You've successfully taken the second step towards healing your emotional body," she told me. "When you're ready to move on to step three, raise your right hand and say: 'I'm ready and willing to take the next step in my healing process now.'"

I didn't hesitate.

"Good, then let's proceed," she responded. "Now, accepting that somewhere in your memory are the experiences that are causing you to feel these negative emotions, and knowing that inside the womb you can hear noises, recognize voices, feel vibrations and identify with emotions, cast your mind back to the point in time and space when these feelings first emerged. Ask yourself: What memory is springing to mind? Which of my memories represents my suffering and pain? Whose voices am I hearing? What emotional experience am I recalling? Let me know when you've identified this memory by raising your right hand and saying: 'Yes, I'm recalling the memory behind these feelings now.'"

Waves of bad memories came flooding back to me. The years of abuse, rejection, and neglect had left their marks on me. My mind sifted through them all. "I don't know which one to choose. There are too many," I bawled.

"You can identify this memory. You can recall this memory. You can trust this memory to emerge because it wants to be recalled," she said ever so gently.

I waded through them in my mind, much the same way I waded through my body cells in search of the one that stood out at the beginning of the process. I had a buffet of misery to gorge on. I had hundreds, perhaps thousands, of memories of my drunken, abusive, embarrassing father to choose from, but none of them stuck. To my great surprise, my grandmother emerged from behind them all. She looked guilty, and anxious, and scared.

No, this can't be, I thought to myself. I had been absolutely convinced it was my father that I needed to process. After all, he was to blame for my ruined childhood and dysfunctional personality. I even tried to attach myself to images of beatings that I'd taken from him, but that didn't help.

"Shooo, settle down. It's okay. You're in a safe place," Sister Simone whispered, gently rocking my shoulder. I suddenly became aware of the groaning in my throat. I'd been thrashing about and moaning. Obviously, I didn't want to face this memory. Something deep inside of me was shielding me from it. No matter how hard I tried to reject it, and avoid it, my grandmother dominated my mind. In the end, she overcame me and I raised my right hand.

"Yes, I'm recalling the memory behind these feelings now," I said.

"Good. Now, allow yourself to witness this experience from within the safety and sanctity of the womb. See the memory. It's being screened on the wall of the original body cell in front of you."

My thoughts momentarily drifted back to when Henry Jones asked me if I'd ever seen reflections on a bubble. This helped me to see the memory reflecting on the cell wall. It was blurred, like the lines on holographic film that Sister Simone had spoken about earlier.

"Take note of the details," she suggested. "How old are you? What are the circumstances? Who is involved? Take a few minutes to recall the memory fully. Let me know when you're ready to describe the experience to me by raising your right hand and saying: 'I'm ready to recall this memory now.'"

This was probably the hardest thing I've ever had to do in my life. At the time, I couldn't understand why I had this overwhelming sensation that if I spoke I'd die. It was very peculiar, and very terrifying.

"You can unlock this memory. You can share how this memory makes you feel. You can relive this memory because it wants to reveal itself," Sister Simone said.

I couldn't hold back any longer. Once again, my dam wall broke. I described the memory my subconscious mind had screened on the wall of my original cell. I was just a boy. My grandmother was babysitting me while my parents were out. Lost in my own world, I'd made a crayon drawing of my family. My mother was praying on her knees. My father was falling backwards through the air. I was flying towards him, like superman, with my arm stretched out in front of me to punch him. I suppose I intended for no one to see it, but my grandmother took it from me and showed it to my father upon his return. No, it wasn't the severe beating I got that stood out in my mind. It was my grandmother's words afterwards that hurt most. "You deserved it, you little demon," she said. "You don't belong in this family. You belong in hell."

"Thank you for sharing this memory with me." That's all Sister Simone said. She didn't discuss the incident with me in anyway. It's not that my story had no impact on her, or that she wasn't interested, or that she didn't care. She felt deeply for me. I could hear it in her voice. You see, the process is about releasing memories. That's it! It's not about analysis, or discussion, or judgment. Realizing this made me feel less vulnerable, safer, sheltered. This helped me to open up, let go, release. "You've successfully taken your third step towards healing your emotional body. When you're ready to move on to step four, raise your right hand and say: 'I'm ready and willing to take the next step in my healing process now.'"

"I'm not ready yet," I admitted. "I need a moment to gather myself, please."

She got up, poured a glass of water, and handed it to me, along with some tissues. I took a few sips and blew my nose. Done, we settled back into a state of meditation.

"When you feel that you're ready to proceed to step four, raise your right hand and say, 'I'm ready and willing to take the next step now,'" she said in due course. I was all set to move on and I told her so.

"Good, then let's proceed. Now, knowing that your bodymind can't tell the difference between the neural holograms your brain uses to experience reality and the ones it conjures up while imagining reality, do you accept that by re-enacting this memory, you're actually reliving it at a level of consciousness, which will reflect in your body and mind now?"

"I do," I replied.

"Excellent. Now, look at the memory reflecting on the cell wall. At the time this memory was recorded, you evidently suppressed the emotions you're feeling now. They've been stored inside your body cells all this time, longing to be set free. Are you at last ready and willing to release these feelings now?"

"I am," I blurted. "I really want to let them go."

"Very well then. In this moment, allow yourself to be the younger you in your memory. Get a sense of how the memory made you feel. At that point in time and space, you didn't get the chance to express how you felt for whatever reason. Accepting that you're now safe and secure in the sanctity of the womb, tell your grandmother how you're feeling and why. Embracing this opportunity wholeheartedly, what do you want to say to your grandmother now that you didn't say before? Express the emotions you couldn't express at the time."

"Are you serious?" I asked with one eye open.

"Yes sirree."

"You want me to act like I was eleven years old?"

"Yes."

Even though I felt very awkward and self-conscious, I closed my eyes, stepped into the role, and let my grandmother have it. Yes, I did! I told her exactly how I felt. I must admit, it felt good to get all that stuff off my chest. I didn't hold anything back.

"Excellent. Now, knowing your grandmother's personality for what it was, what would she reply to you?"

"She would probably tell me that my opinion doesn't matter, that I'm nothing, and that no one is interested in what I have to say."

"And how does this make you feel?"

"Unworthy. Rejected. Unloved."

"And how does this make you feel?" she asked once more.

"Hurt. Defiant. Angry," I replied after giving it some thought.

"Anything else?"

"Nope." I couldn't get past anger.

"Tell me, what would your ego-mind say to your grandmother in response to her words?"

She'd hardly finished her sentence and I unloaded another round of insults and accusations. As I spoke, I realized that this experience was in fact a turning point in my life. It destroyed my youthful innocence and severed my intrinsic belief that family provided love and shelter. I took on the notion that I was bad and came from hell. From then on, I became a terror. I made darn sure nobody ever put me down again. She condemned me to a lifetime of conflict, rage and isolation. Thinking about it inflamed my personal power. I felt a dark hero rising within me. My jaws clenched as tight as my fists and my chest heaved.

"Do you have any other feelings towards your grandmother that you think should be heard before we move on?"

"No, I'm done with her," I moaned.

"Well done," Sister Simone replied, rubbing my back until the emotions passed. "Now, from the bottom of your heart, how did you want your grandmother to respond to you in this situation?"

"I wanted her to see my picture and protect me, and my mother, from my father. I wanted her to tell me that I was a good boy, brave and strong, and that she loved me. I wanted her..." I couldn't speak any further because I broke down.

She waited for my sobbing to ease, and then said: "Now, what would your true-self have said to your grandmother in that moment?"

I sighed deeply. I had to consciously change drivers in my head. I knew what my true-self would say, but it took a while before I found my voice. Eventually I spoke my mind: "Grandmother, I accept you for who you are. I understand that you must've had a difficult upbringing to make you the person you've become. I know that you have your own life-lessons to learn and I hope that you find peace and happiness."

"Now, if your grandmother responded to you from her true-self, what would she say to you now?"

I repeated all the things I truly wanted to hear.

"Thank you. You've successfully taken your fourth step towards healing your emotional body. When you're ready to move on to step five, raise your right hand and say: 'I'm ready and willing to take the next step in my healing process now.'" I did as she asked.

"Good, then let's proceed. Look around the inside of the womb. There's a balloon-shaped sack floating nearby. Can you see it yet?"

"Yes, I can."

"Excellent. Now, knowing that this sack nurtures and sustains your personal growth and development, slowly reach out and take hold of it now. Inside this sack, the older you has made available all the resources the younger you needs to cope with this experience. When you have it in the palm of your hand, you'll start to feel the wisdom of hindsight filling your being. Do you have it now?"

"Uh-huh."

"Good. Now, tell me: What would your older, wiser self say to your younger self?"

I pictured myself having a conversation with my younger self, as if I was talking into a mirror – except the reflection I saw wasn't my usual face; it was me as a boy; and it wasn't a mirror, it was the cell wall.

"You're going to be okay. Trust me for I am you. When you get older, you'll realize that you're not a bad person. You're capable of being loving and kind, despite your circumstances. There's no need to act superior to everyone you meet in the future. You don't have to fight your way through life. This behavior will only make you unhappy and sick. You're fundamentally a good person with a lot to offer the world. You're brave and strong, and it's not your fault for the way you were treated growing up. You're worthy of love and acceptance. You'll turn out to be a great success in life because you'll find the wisdom to learn and grow from this experience. You're most definitely going to be okay."

"Good, now please repeat after me: 'I allow the values of my true-self to come forth now.'"

I repeated the sentence.

"Thank you. Now, responding from your true-self, can you totally accept that your grandmother's personality was merely a product of her conditioning, and that she was merely acting from her ego-mind at the time?"

"I can. I really can."

"Good for you. And, can you also accept that her words and actions, no matter how inappropriate or wrongful, played a necessary role in helping you to learn the life-lessons you needed to learn, in accordance with the life path you chose to fulfil your destiny?"

"Yes."

"So then, would you say that you're ready and willing to completely forgive your grandmother from the very bottom of your heart right now?"

I paused to think. I didn't know much about my grandmother's life. I still don't. I don't know why she became the person she did. All I could remember about her was that she was a mean-spirited person who smelled of ointment, kept a droopy fag in her mouth, and was found dead in her flat when her corpse started to smell. I suddenly felt great pity for her. Even though she was mean to me and probably worse to my father when he was a boy, I knew it wasn't my place to judge her.

"I am," I said.

"Thank you. Then, speaking from your true-self, let your grandmother know that you wholeheartedly forgive her now."

I held an image of her in my mind and said sincerely: "I forgive you grandmother from the very bottom of my heart." There was no more to it than that. I said it and it was done.

"Excellent. Now, responding from your true-self, can you totally accept that your inner child was merely a product of your conditioning, and the younger you was responding to your life experiences as best you could through your ego-mind at the time?"

"Yes, I can."

"Good for you. And, can you also accept that your decision to suppress your emotions played a necessary role in helping you to learn the life-lessons you needed to learn, in accordance with the life path you chose to fulfil your destiny?"

"Yes."

"So then, would you say that you're ready and willing to completely forgive the younger you from the very bottom of your heart right now?"

"Yes, I am."

"Good. Now then, speaking from your true-self, let the younger you know that you wholeheartedly forgive him now."

I did as she requested, and it felt great.

"Thank you. You've successfully taken the fifth step towards healing your emotional body. When you're ready to move on to step six, raise your right hand and say, 'I'm ready and willing to take the next step in my healing process now.'"

I took a moment to revel in the feeling that surfaced as a result of forgiving my younger self. I felt lighter, happier, liberated. I explained how I was feeling to Sister Simone, and she looked pleased.

"Good, then let's proceed. Now that you've completely forgiven your grandmother as well as yourself, slowly reach out and rest your hands on the inside of the cell wall. As you do so, the younger you, reflecting on the cell wall in front of you, mirrors your actions. You're now facing each other, and your hands are pressed together, separated only by the thin cell wall. Can you see this now?

"Yes, I can."

"Good. Now, look lovingly at yourself, smile and repeat after me, 'I'm grateful to you for always being there for me,'" Sister Simone said. I repeated her sentence. Then she proceeded to say the following lines, pausing for me to repeat what she'd said after each sentence.

"Thank you for releasing those suppressed emotions … You have removed a great burden from me … I know I will not feel the pain and anguish of those emotions in future … Now I am free to receive love unconditionally … Peace and harmony are restored within me … I am whole … I am healed … I am loved."

It felt amazing to forgive myself and to release the younger me from the role it had played in my life. In that precious moment, I realized that I had, in fact, grown up. I wasn't a frightened little boy any more. My grandmother may have been a mean woman and my father an abusive drunk, but my wife and my daughter were soft and gentle creatures. It was unnecessary for me to be a terror with them and act superior to everyone else I met. It was time to let the younger me go. Sister Simone knew it.

"Now, I'd like you to get ready to step through the cell wall into your younger self, so that you become one with the implicate order. Are you ready to take this important step now?"

As much as I wanted to take the next step, I couldn't. Something was holding me back. I felt afraid, uncertain, anxious. "I can't. I'm stuck," I moaned.

"The transition from the original cell, the material, through the cell wall into the unified field, the non-material, requires you to pass briefly through a void. This void is stronger than the state of nothingness that you experienced transitioning between each of the colors earlier. It's often described as a black hole, an abyss, a vacuum, emptiness or nothingness. It's normal to feel fear; despair; trepidation; indifference; apathy; boredom and numbness. Sometimes individuals get stuck in it. Understand that your ego-mind is simply afraid to let go of the feelings that have served it for so long. I can assure you, the void is just a thin veil of darkness separating you from your healing. It, too, is just an illusion. I encourage you to trust the process. Don't be afraid. Feel the void to its fullest. You can embrace this feeling. You can transcend this feeling. You can pass through this feeling into your very own cosmic nature."

I appreciated her words of encouragement.

"I can, I can, I can," I repeated to myself.

She pressed on. "When you feel the void to its fullest, take a deep breath, and as you exhale, step through the cell wall, allowing yourself to merge with your younger self. As you become one, you'll feel the painful memory and all else dissolving into nothingness. Allow yourself to pass freely into this nothingness now."

I guess the growing smile on my face let her know I was through to the other side.

"Good. Now, as you move into this nothingness, let your core essence expand into the vast, expansive realms of the unknown. Allow your awareness to extend into the eternal space that's unfolding on all sides of you right now. Let me know when you're in this state of nothingness by nodding your head."

I literally felt myself dissolving into what I imagined to be the implicate order. In this state, the younger me faded away. I was content to see him go, and he was content to leave. I described what I saw and felt to Sister Simone. "That's wonderful," Sister Simone said softly. "Here resides the essence of who you are, beyond time and beyond space. In this place, you simply are. There's no need, there's no sickness, and there's no pain. There's only divine love, wisdom and truth. Allow your essence to radiate strongly and steadily into this boundless place. Let go of all you know and just be. You're free to bathe in bliss now."

She paused for a few minutes, and then said: "Repeat after me: Here resides the essence of who I am, beyond time, beyond space. This is where divine healing energy is found in abundance. I am in the Healing Zone now."

She paused for a few more minutes. In that space and time, I felt bliss, pure bliss. My hands tingled and the hairs on the back of my neck stood up. I genuinely felt as though I'd left my body and been transported into another realm. The imagination truly is a powerful tool for healing. In that moment, I discovered something magical that happens when the imagination and emotion and spirit become one. The feeling is out of this world.

"I feel so blissful right now," I breathed.

"Good, very good. Now, knowing that images held in your mind ultimately manifest as realities in your body, I'd like you to hold an image of your original body cell in your mind. Picture it as the perfect blueprint of your healthy body. Do this now." She let another minute or so pass by before she spoke again. "When you're ready, let me know that you can feel the divine healing energy restoring your body back to the original blueprint by saying: 'I invite the divine healing energy to restore my body to perfect health right now.'"

I said it and I meant it with all my heart.

"Excellent. Now, when you're ready, slowly step back through the cell wall, so that you're back inside your original body cell. Let me know that you're back inside the cell by saying: 'I'm back inside my original body cell.'" It wasn't easy leaving the Healing Zone. I could've lingered there for eternity. Eventually, I stepped back through the cell wall that I so clearly saw in my mind's eye.

Sister Simone was pleased to hear it. "Good. Now, knowing that your body cells can communicate instantly with each other, allow this message of healing to be communicated to every cell in your body. Imagine messenger molecules instantly broadcasting this information to every single cell in your body. Get a sense of this now. Know that from this moment forth, your body is automatically and spontaneously regenerating healthy cells as your healing begins. Know it. Believe it. Live it. When you're ready to accept your healing completely, take a deep, new breath, and exhale saying: 'I welcome this divine healing energy into my body and life now.'"

I repeated her line with a big smile on my face.

"Good. Now, knowing that by releasing the negative emotions stored in a single cell, the negative distortions are dissolved and removed throughout your entire body. Look around the inside of the original body cell. Get a sense of your surroundings. What has changed? How do you feel? What is the message that you're receiving right now?"

I answered back immediately. "The cell is healthy. The cell is healthy."

"You can identify with the message. You can understand the message. You can trust the message because it's your very own nature," she stated with joy in her voice.

I went on to describe the inside of my original body cell in more detail. She listened attentively and then said: "Thank you. Now, understanding that you live in a holographic universe where the past, present and future all exist simultaneously, leave the original body cell and travel through space and time back to the first body cell you visited at the start of the process. Let me know when you've arrived by raising your right hand and repeating: 'I am inside the body cell now.'"

I followed her instruction. "Good. Now, once again, look around the inside of the body cell. Get a sense of your surroundings. What has changed? How do you feel? What is the message that you're receiving right now?"

I explored the body cell in my mind's eye. It wasn't red, angry, or smelly. It was normal. I burst into tears. "The cell is healthy. It really is healthy," I cried.

"Excellent," she replied tearfully too. "You've successfully taken your sixth step towards healing your emotional body. When you're ready to move on to step seven, raise your right hand and say: 'I'm ready and willing to take the next step in my healing process now.'"

Needless to say, that didn't happen for a while. I needed a few minutes to express the jubilation I felt. At one point, I'm pretty sure I lifted Sister Simone off her feet, swung her around in circles and kissed her forehead repeatedly. She laughed loudly. I wanted to run and find Henry Jones and tell him all about my mind-blowing experience, but she insisted we weren't finished yet. After much hullabaloo, I took my seat once more.

"Good, now that you've settled down, let's proceed," she said, squaring up her habit. "I'd like you to take a deep breath. As you exhale, feel yourself submerging once again into the ocean of your body cells. Allow the current of your internal consciousness to carry you through your whole body and back into your head. Get a sense of the journey as you're traveling through your body. Imagine that you're receiving a hero's welcome and your body cells are lining your internal pathways, singing and rejoicing at your triumph. Let me know when you're there by raising your right hand and saying: 'My mission is complete. I've arrived back inside my head, safe and sound.'"

I sang it.

"Excellent. You've done magnificently well," Sister Simone said. "We're nearly done. Now, in closing, think back to the memory you recalled and the feelings you once suppressed. When I ask you, 'And what of this anger?' what answer comes to you?"

"It's gone," I replied, as if streamed through my true-self from the state of bliss.

"What then is your reply when I ask you: 'And what of this hatred?'"

"It's gone."

"And what of this bitterness?"

"It's gone, too."

"And what of this disappointment?"

"All gone."

"And what of this resentment?"

"It's all gone. All of it."

"And what of this …?" She proceeded to drill through each one of my emotions.

"Seriously. They are all gone. I'm rid of them."

She looked content. "Thank you. Accepting your answers, please repeat after me: 'I'm rejoicing right now because I don't feel these negative emotions anymore. Instead, I'm filled with understanding, forgiveness and love.'"

The words flowed off my tongue.

"Thank you," she responded. "Now, let me know that your healing has begun by raising your right hand and saying: 'From deep within the cells of my body, I know that my healing is beginning now.'"

I obeyed her instruction happily.

She reached out and touched my shoulder. In the sweetest voice, she said: "Thank you for allowing me to witness your remarkable healing process. I honour the light and love within you and I'm grateful to have shared this time and space with you. May light and love shine through you always. So be it."

My eyes filled with tears. Never before in my life had I experienced such tenderness. Her kindness overwhelmed me. "What can I say to you? What can I say to you?" I moaned with my head in my hands.

She grinned. "If you feel so inclined, please repeat after me: 'Thank you, Sister Simone, for witnessing my remarkable healing process. I honour the light and love within you. I'm grateful to have shared this time and space with you. May light and love shine through you always. So be it.'"

It was my pleasure to oblige her. With that, my emotional healing therapy session was complete. When we were ready, we both slowly emerged from the meditation. Suffice to say, I was elated. "Thank you so, so, so much," I cried.

She narrowed her beady eyes at me. "It was my pleasure. You must come back and see me again sometime soon. There may be other memories that require healing. Alternatively, I'll give you a script to follow, so that you can repeat this emotional healing therapy session on your own, or with someone else."

I nodded. "Can anyone do this process with me?"

"Pretty much! But you must choose a partner who you can trust with your emotions and innermost secrets. You don't want anything you say to be held against you. For this reason, as I said before, it's sometimes better to do the process with a stranger, especially a professional, like a priest, a doctor, or a healing practitioner. Obviously, it can't be just anyone off the street. You must try to find someone who is good, kind, and considerate."

"I think I'll visit you again," I said, flattering her like a smitten schoolboy.

"Well, you know where to find me," she said.

"I'd love to write about it in our book," I suggested.

"Fun-taas-tick!" she exclaimed, wobbling her head like Swami G. That got a giggle out of me.

"I'm sure Henry won't mind," she replied. "He developed the process, and he seems determined to share his wisdom with the world before we lose him for good to a faraway island."

Hearing these words struck panic in me. "Henry!" I exclaimed. "I must tell him about my experience. I need to dash."

"Off you go then," she replied, opening the door. I bolted up the pathway, past the rose garden to the car park. Sure enough, Henry Jones was waiting for me.

"Oh, my goodness! Was that a power session, or what?" I roared, as I jumped into the Land Rover.

"Did you find what you were looking for?" Henry Jones asked.

"Did I? Boy-oh-boy, it was incredible!"

"I'm pleased for you, my friend. I really am," he replied in a warm and affectionate tone. I slumped into the seat and rubbed my eyelids in big, round circles. It'd been quite a day and I was exhausted. I felt like a big bowl of butternut soup, a bath, and my bed.

"It's important to get lots of good rest after an emotional healing therapy session. Let's get you home as soon as possible," he advised.

I sighed deeply. "That sounds great. Thank you."

He turned on the ignition, and the vehicle sprung into life. Soon, we were whizzing down the highway on our way back to his apartment. "Let's wrap up what you learned today, okay?" he suggested.

"Alright then," I replied with a big yawn, reaching for my notepad.

"Go for it," he said, turning on some soft classical music.

"Here goes: Firstly, I learned 10 powerful healing stances that connect the physical body to emotions, which help people to become 'unstuck' by combining movement and intention. They are Reflect; Reach; Realisation; Roar; Repent; Release; Receive; Rejoice; Rest and Recharge. Next, our primary objective was to identify the role emotions play in our lives, and to determine the influence they have on our health. I learned that old, negative emotions are stored in our body cells and subsequently cause sickness and disease. Next, we explored our emotional attachments to physical vices, so that I could learn how to free up my natural emotional energy. We examined the harmful effects of caffeine, sugar, nicotine, alcohol, refined foods and dairy. Not to mention narcotics, over-eating, fast foods, condiments, stress and a lack of exercise. You then shared with me the secret of severing harmful vices and gave me hot tips to kick nasty habits."

"Go on."

"With vices behind us, we moved on to emotional management. Here we got stuck into emotional literacy, honesty, awareness, intelligence and EQ. We went over the reasons why we most likely have emotional blockages, and then we examined the negative emotions that make us sick. To understand how emotions are stored in our body cells, we took a closer look at how cells function, with specific emphasis on their ability to regenerate and communicate. This led us to the fascinating holographic nature of the universe, the brain, the body and even body cells."

"What did you learn from this conversation?"

"Well, I discovered that sickness and disease are merely illusions. In order to release them, I learned about a mysterious gap between thought and matter where miracles occur."

"What else?"

"Lastly, I was shown an amazing technique to get into the Healing Zone, so that I can heal my body, once and for all."

"Hooray!" he yelled, flooring the gas pedal. "You're definitely on your way now, my friend. It's easy sailing from here onwards."

"Thank you, once again, Henry Jones. You've changed my life," I drooled, as the rocking car carried me off to sleep.

CHAPTER 30

THE JOURNEY'S END

We got back to Henry Jones's apartment and I crashed for a few more hours. I was beat after my session with Sister Simone and slept like a baby. Much to my surprise, I awoke to a raucous noise. Voices and laughter bubbled up from the balcony. It sounded like a party. I got up, washed my face, and went to see what the commotion was all about.

"Ah! There he is. Bloody hell, we thought you were comatose," Dr Sahib bellowed. I was partially blinded by the festoon of glowing candles that had been placed on every available surface. The balcony shimmered resplendently. Slowly, the crowd came into focus. I couldn't believe my eyes. They were all there: Professor Kaufmann; Dr Sahib and his assistant; George-the-Surfer and his girlfriend, Shirley; Mrs Moffet; Kevin the Chiropractor; the crazy intern, Lucy; Juju Banks; and even Sister Simone. All of them!"

"What on Earth …?" I spluttered.

"Join us," Henry Jones said warmly.

"A toast to your health," Dr Sahib announced to everyone as I entered the room. A mighty "Cheers!" resounded across the balcony. I was overwhelmed by their presence. If this was a surprise party, it was a good one. I had had no clue.

"Give us your best description of the human body?" George-the-Surfer instructed in a gruff voice. I gathered this had been the topic of debate before my arrival.

Mrs Moffet got the game going again. "I said the body is a miraculous self-healing mechanism."

"I said the body is just a pile of biological goop without the bone structure," Kevin added.

"I said it's biological engineering at its best," Professor Kaufmann stated with her strong German accent.

Sister Simone didn't want to be left out. "Well, I said it's a magnificent mutated cell."

"What do you think?" Shirley asked. Her lips never moved because her smile was so big.

"The human body is a battery-operated transmitter," I replied glibly. There was stunned silence. My mechanical answer clearly didn't gel with their organic orientations. Luckily, Dr Sahib thought this was an excellent answer, and he roared his applause.

"I rest my bloody case," he shouted, and they all started laughing.

"Why did you say that?" Henry Jones asked inquisitively, turning the spotlight back on me.

I sat down beside Shirley, poured myself a cup of ice-cold mint water, and took a sip. "Of late, I've come to believe our souls are fractals of the soul of God. Their purpose is to experience life and to communicate this experience back to the Source of all things."

"So, you think the body is a transportation vehicle for the soul?" Mrs Moffet inquired.

"Yes, I do. I'll say it again: The body transports the soul through life while the cells record and transmit the experience."

"Why is da body a battery den?" Juju Banks asked with a wink.

"Well, it takes energy to propel us through the physical world and to keep the transmitters broadcasting. This energy is produced by the body and stored in the cells. They're no different to the cells of a battery in that they must be fully charged to produce optimum energy and power. The energy we use, we lose."

"Yes, but how do we lose our power?" Dr Sahib's timid assistant squeaked.

"We use up energy when we think, feel and act. This is the reason why it's essential for us to recharge our battery daily."

"How do we do recharge our battery?" he asked again, showing a keen interest in the subject.

"Rest, meditation, regular exercise and proper diet," I told him. "They are essential for true wellness. You see, we attract and manifest our reality by the thoughts, feelings and actions we project into the universe. The energy we put out is the reality we get back."

"Explain, please."

"Energy vibrates and pulsates at different frequencies. There are higher frequencies and lower frequencies. Everything we desire for our lives and the lives of others that is wholesome and good has a high frequency because it comes from our higher selves – our true-selves. Everything we fear or worry about has a low frequency because it comes from our ego-minds – our lower selves. When our energy is low, we transmit low frequencies, which attracts what we don't want. When we raise the energy levels in our body cells, we begin to transmit higher frequencies, which attracts what we most want."

"Preach on," George-the-Surfer hollered, high-fiving Henry Jones.

"When our cells are fully charged, we shine brightly, and our projection is strong and clear. The stronger we project our thoughts, feelings and actions, the quicker we can attract what we desire into our lives. In short, when our energy is high, our ability to manifest is high, and when our energy is low, our ability to manifest is low. Make sense?"

I'd left the assistant behind. "Rest, meditation, regular exercise and proper diet," he muttered. "Which one is the most important?"

"They're all essential, like I said. But if I had to pick one, it would be diet."

"Why da diet mon?" JuJu Banks queried.

"Food is our primary source of energy. There are high-energy foods and low-energy foods. When we consume low-energy foods, our body energy is low, and therefore our energy level is low. In this state, we simply don't have the energy we need to do the things that raise our energy level, so we stay stuck in low energy."

"I believe this is called the mediocrity trap," Dr Sahib commented loudly.

"And we should try to avoid it at all costs," I said, finishing his sentence.

"What would you suggest I do?" the assistant asked with surprising tenacity.

"For one thing, only eat food that Mother Nature made for you."

"What? Yu no eat so much fatty-boom-boom burgers no more?" Lucy shrieked. I almost didn't recognize her. The colored streaks in her hair had washed out and her fringe was tied into a tight bun on top of her head. She looked much better without the studs and piercings in her face. Her eyes and skin were much clearer, too. Actually, Lucy looked great!

"Good on you, mate," George-the-Surfer remarked and then he whispered to the assistant: "Man-made food will deplete your energy, not replenish it."

"You want your energy to be on a high frequency," I told him. This earned me a fist pump from Henry Jones and George-the-Surfer.

"This very simple wisdom is the great secret to health, well-being and abundance. It's the key to your health, happiness and dreams," I told him.

"Wow, how do you know so much stuff?" the assistant gasped.

I had to stop myself from chuckling. "I learned it all from them," I said, proudly pointing at the people around the table.

"I've just been diagnosed with sugar diabetes," the assistant confessed unexpectedly. I felt the tension shift in the room. Henry Jones and his friends had conspired to heal him. I could tell that he was oblivious of their plan. His confusion reminded me of me just 40 days and 40 nights ago.

"Well, it seems you've come to the right place," I mused.

They all jumped in. "You can activate an incredible healing force within you, my friend. All you need to do is give your body what it needs to repair itself and restore true wellness," Henry Jones said, leading the charge.

George-the-Surfer caught the next wave in. "Exactly, dude! Cut out man-made, toxic waste-forming junk food, and feed yourself God's own products – fruit and vegetables," he evangelized to the converted.

"There is formidable healing energy in your body cells," Sister Simone chimed in.

"Yeah, man. You just need to look within, bro. Everything lies within you," George-the-Surfer said.

And that's how the night progressed into the early hours of the morning. The constant stream of good conversation and laughter never waned.

Dr Sahib and George-the-Surfer were the last to leave. I went to bed soon after that. Even though it'd been a long day, I had the presence of mind to write in my Workbook and Notebook for the last time. I flipped through the pages and recalled my journey. It provided me with a daily record of my thoughts, feelings and actions. I tallied my scores and counted my True-Days. All in all, I'd experienced a life-changing event. In just 40 days and 40 nights, I'd transformed into a whole, new person. I fell asleep thinking about the wonderful and weird experiences I'd enjoyed with Henry Jones and his merry band of healers. Needless to say, I had pleasant dreams.

When I got up the next day, Henry Jones was gone. That wasn't unusual. He often left early to do his own thing, but this time was different. Intuitively,

I knew he hadn't popped down to the grocer for carrots or juice, or sneaked in a sunrise walk, or gone to the early-bird yoga class. This time I knew he was gone for good. My heart sank. I called out his name several times on the off-chance that my gut feeling was wrong. But it wasn't.

My awful suspicion was confirmed when I saw an envelope propped up against a polished apple on the dining room table. It had my name written on it. I approached it pensively. Lifting it carefully between two fingers, I pulled it towards me. My knees buckled, and I sank slowly into the nearest seat. It took a while before I mustered the courage to open it. Perched on the edge of my seat, I started to read his final words to me. This is what he wrote:

My dear friend,

The past 40 days and 40 nights have been a real blast. Thank you so much for spending time with me. It's been great fun sharing the first stage of your healing journey with you. I enjoyed getting to know who you truly are. Since our conversation on a park bench, you've grown in leaps and bounds. We're all extremely proud of you.

Our time together has unfortunately come to an end. From now on, you're on your own. (Don't panic! You're going to be okay!) My friends and I have shown you exactly how to restore your body to perfect health by bringing your mind, body and spirit back into balance, naturally.

You've rejuvenated your body, refreshed your mind, awakened your spirit and freed your emotions. Well done. This is a remarkable accomplishment in such a short time. You're off to a great start. I strongly urge you to stay on your healing program and follow a whole-foods, plant-based diet. Keep practising the healing techniques we've shown you and you will become whole, healed, and at one with yourself.

I promise you this: The results of treating yourself naturally are nothing short of miraculous. You will restore your body to perfect health and enjoy radiant health and vitality every day for the rest of your life. Be your true-self and you will discover true wellness.

The secret is to live one True-Day at a time. If ever you need guidance, turn to the big, brown envelope. It contains all the information you need to heal your body. The material is yours to do with as you please. I trust you'll find a novel way to write it. Please develop the Workbook that accompanies the notes, for this I believe will be our true gift to humanity. Good luck with your new publishing business venture. I hope it brings you great success. Please never forget that you're a good person who is deserving of love, health and happiness. With all my heart, I wish this for you.

Be true to yourself, always.

Your friend,
Henry Jones

P.S. I have one more Post-it for you to read when you finally figure out what is missing in your life.

This letter was written on the back of a crumpled leaflet that had been pressed out. I turned it over and saw that it was the same promotional leaflet that I'd read in the waiting room the day before I met Henry Jones. I recognized it immediately. I also recognized Henry Jones's telephone number.

I wondered who had retrieved it from the bin and given it back to Henry Jones. I had my suspicions that Sister Lillian and Henry Jones were in cahoots. I bet they had conspired to put that leaflet on the coffee table in front of me. I pictured them watching my response from a concealed spot in the waiting room. That brought a smile to my face.

Having reread the leaflet, I tipped the envelope upside down and the carefully folded Post-it note fell into my open hand. I tucked it into my pocket for safekeeping. That was it. Our journey together was over, and I was gutted. I folded my head into my arms and cried bucketloads. I'd probably have lamented like this for days, had it not been for the cry of a distinct voice from behind me.

"Yu no sit there clying like liddle girl, troublemaker!" Lucy announced as she entered the room. "Yu man up."

"What in heaven's name …?" I gasped. "What are you doing here?"

"I live here now. Yu sit in my loom."

I couldn't understand a word she said. "Pardon?" I cried.

She marched over to me, stood at ease in military fashion in front of me, and planted her hands firmly on her hips. "I yor loomate!" she shrieked. "I yor loomate!"

"Loo-mate?" I muttered to myself.

558

"Yes, I loomate. I live here now. You no sit here in my loom and cly like liddle girl. Is Lucy house now, too."

That's when the lightbulb went on in my head. "Ah, roommate!"

"Dats what I say, loomate, loomate."

"But how?" I stammered.

"Yor friend say I live here now, while I intern with Mrs Moffet."

"Henry said you could stay in his apartment?" I asked again.

"Dats what I say now. You deaf or what, mister? Perhaps yu hit yor head on table when you crash house, huh? I think so, too."

I should mention that her whole face was plastered with green goop. It looked like she'd been apple diving in a bowl of guacamole. "You're going to live here with me?" I asked, annunciating each word.

"I know, Dumbo. Dat's what I say?" She turned and stomped away yelling to herself in Chinese.

"Stop," I yelled. "Give me a second to wrap my head around this whole situation. You're saying Henry Jones gave you permission to stay here, in this apartment, with me, while you finish your internship with Mrs Moffet? Is that correct?"

She stomped back across to me and assumed the same position. "You pay attention now. I only say dis one more time. I yor loomate, I yor loomate, I yor loomate."

"But I live here," I protested, beating my chest.

"Yu no live here long time. Yu go back where yu belong. Yu go back home."

Yes, I'd come to an understanding with Henry Jones that I could stay in his apartment while I finished the book. I needed some time to find my feet after separating from my wife, too. I was glad to have a place to land, and was already settling in. But, hearing Lucy say the words: "Yu go back where yu belong. Yu go back home," changed everything for me. I knew instantly where I needed to be: Home. It hit me like a 10-pound hammer on my forehead. "I must win my wife back," I suddenly declared, like a coal miner who had struck gold.

"Yu no win wife back when yu sit here clying like liddle girl. Yu go get her back with flowers and big presents now."

A sudden reality check set in. "But she doesn't want me back?" I moaned.

"How yu know dis? Yu sit here clying like liddle girl. Yu no out there with flowers and big presents. Do dis den yu see," she cried, apparently very frustrated.

"It's not that simple, Lucy," I tried to explain. "I never treated her well. I think I've lost her."

"Yu bad ass, huh?"

"Yes, I bad ass," I admitted.

"No, yu got it all long. Yu no bad ass, mister. Yu dumb ass. Yu no treat lady like lady, yu lose lady. Lucky for yu, ladies got short memory. No matter how dumb ass man be, flowers with big presents make all better."

She made me laugh loudly.

"No joking now. Yu go find happy ending. Yu deserve it."

"Do you really think I deserve it?" I quizzed.

"Sure. Yu not so bad guy. I know what you did."

"Excuse me?"

"Yu no fool me. Yu not so tough guy, mister. Mrs Moffet tell me it was yu. It was yu," she shrieked, pointing at me accusingly.

"What?"

"Yu know what I'm talking about now. I know what yu did."

"I'm sorry?" I said, although I knew she was on to me.

"Yu paid for me to have full treatment every day from Mrs Moffet for three months. Yu give money to make me look like beautiful lady when I go back China," she said pretending to flick her hair back like a supermodel. Some goop cometed off her cheek and splashed on to the wall beside her.

"That was meant to be our secret," I hollered.

"Mrs Moffet tell me ele-ting." She sang in her heavy Chinese accent. "So, yu no fool me, mister. Yu not so big tough guy now. Yu nice guy now."

"Thank you, Lucy," I said blushing.

"But nice guy no sit here clying like liddle girl. Nice guy go buy flowers and big presents. Yu go now."

"What if she doesn't love me anymore?" I asked.

"She no know yu. She know old fatso. Yu different now. Yu go give her flowers and big presents now. Yu win back her love. Yu see."

Such simple advice, but it knocked me for a six. I'd been sitting around licking my wounds and feeling ashamed and rejected for months, but I hadn't done anything to fight for my wife's love. I'd made no effort to sweep her off her feet; nor had I developed a plan of action to win her back permanently.

I realized I had to fight to get my wife back with the same diligence and tenacity as I'd applied to my healing program with Henry Jones. I needed to commit myself to healing my relationship, as much as I was committed to my new, healthy, holistic lifestyle. This was my most heartfelt desire. I was absolutely certain that I wanted to spend the rest of my life loving her like I knew she needed to be loved.

Lucy was quite correct. I'd been sitting around blubbering like a little girl when I should've been buying my wife flowers and big presents. Of course, the biggest gift I could give her was the gift I'd received from my sickness – a brand-new understanding of life, wrapped up in a higher consciousness, bound by a shiny red ribbon of my true-self. It was time for me to step up. This idea mainlined youth back into my blood. I felt it coursing through my veins, renewing my energy. I jumped to my feet and grabbed Lucy by the arms. "I'm going to get her back," I declared in a hero's voice.

"Good. Yu go light now. Yu take train. It go super faster."

"I can't leave right now. I must plan my strategy. I've got to get my approach right," I said bashfully, trying to find my swagger.

She hesitated for a split second. "Okay, den yu go tomorrow."

Lucy had dropped another bombshell on me. My ticking clock stopped, recalibrated and then her words went off like an explosion in my head. I could go tomorrow. There was nothing stopping me from reaching out to my wife but me. She may reject me, yes, but at least I'd have tried to win her back. I had nothing to lose because I'd already lost her. But I did have everything to gain.

"Okay, I'll do it. I'll arrange to meet her," I trumpeted bravely.

"Yu no break promise to me now, or yu get piece of me later, okay? Lucy still kung fu your arse, mister nice guy," she barked.

Her challenging tone was hilarious. I broke into a chuckle and an image of Henry Jones popped into my mind. What strange plan did he have up his sleeve when he paired me with Lucy? This was no coincidence, that was for sure. I imagined him chuckling to himself on the plane ride home to his wife, as he revelled in his reasons for bringing us together. No doubt, my reaction to finding out Lucy was my new 'loomate' would've amused him tremendously. The perplexed look on my face must've been priceless. What could I do? I just had to accept the situation and trust him.

"He's gone," I groaned, twisting his letter in my hands.

"Who gone where?" Lucy asked, looking around.

"Henry Jones has gone back to his family," I explained.

Once again, she didn't hesitate for a second in answering me. "He smart guy. Yu be like him, too. Yu go back home to yor family now. Okay?" she said. I detected a sense of encouragement buried beneath the fierceness in her voice.

"I'll arrange to meet my wife tomorrow," I told her softly. "Today I'm going to miss my friend, Henry Jones."

"Okay, but no more clying, okay?" she scowled, shaking her finger at me. "Yu can miss yor friend, but yu don't have to cly like a liddle girl. I'm yor loomate now. Yu no cly like liddle girl in Lucy new house. Okay?" With that, she stomped away. I thought we were done, but she stopped in her tracks, spun around as if on ice, stomped back over to me and planted a big, fat kiss on my cheek, along with half a bucket of green goop.

"Dats for giving Mrs Moffet money to make Lucy beautiful lady when go back China."

"It's my pleasure, Lucy," I purred, feeling good. She'd tamed the tiger in me.

"Yu no get no special favors, though. Yu wash yor own dishes, too. Lucy intern, not maid. Okay?" she shrieked for the final time.

Lucy left the room. I sat there and read Henry Jones's letter a few more times. I knew I'd miss him dearly. I spent the rest of the day listening to his classical music and collating his notes. No, I can't describe my mood as melancholic. I had romance on my mind! Sure, I was heartsore to lose him, but I felt young again. I was a man on a mission to get his family back together again.

Tomorrow

When the next day came, I found myself waiting anxiously for my wife in my car at the beach. No, I hadn't arranged to meet her. My daughter tipped me off that she was planning to walk the dogs at that beach in the morning – and I was there! I'd been waiting for two hours. With nothing else to do, I scratched around the car for something to read. All I could find, besides the Post-it note in my top pocket, was a crumpled piece of writing paper with a message scrawled in Henry Jones's handwriting:

> *"One of the most sublime experiences we can ever have is to wake up feeling healthy after we have been sick."* – Rabbi Harold Kushner

Coincidently, I once went to a doctor who had that exact sentence blown up, framed and hung on the waiting room wall. I'd scowled at it in my misery. At that precise moment my wife's car pulled into the car park. My thoughts came to a grinding halt. Time stood still. I hadn't felt this way since I reconnected with my daughter in the car park of my favorite restaurant. Her vehicle cruised by and pulled into a vacant space on the opposite side of the lot. Impulsively, I sunk into my seat so that I couldn't be seen. Fixing my eyes on the rearview mirror, I watched the car door open and saw her climb out. My heart skipped a beat. Unleashed, the mutts scampered down to the shore. She strolled after them, oblivious to my presence.

I needed a minute to pull myself together. Just breathe deeply, just breathe deeply, I told myself. It's now or never, I thought, plucking up the courage to speak to her. It's not easy facing up to your past mistakes. I owed my wife a massive apology for years of neglect, indifference and emotional abuse. How would she respond to me? Would she let me spend the rest of my life making it up to her? Would she tell me to take a hike? There was only one way to find out.

I ran after her. Icy-cold waves splashed against my ankles as I tore through the shoreline. I'd come a long way since plodding through the icy-cold waves on the beach with George-the-Surfer's girlfriend, Shirley, on my first day with Henry Jones. That seemed like a lifetime ago. Back then, I was sick, scared, and confused. Now, I felt fit, strong, and healthy. Yes, I was still on my healing journey, but I was on the pathway to perfect health. I was living one True-Day at a time. Each new day was an opportunity for me to honour all that I'd learned from my friend. I was determined to make him proud of me. I was committed to loving myself, my true-self, and to being loving to everyone and everything around me – especially my wife and daughter.

The dogs spotted me first. They raced towards me as fast as their tiny legs could carry them. They jumped up and down, exuberantly licking my hands and face. Evidently, they bore no grudges, even though I hadn't loved them properly either. Seeing me, my wife stopped in her tracks and stood her ground. I settled the dogs and then walked slowly towards her, trembling with anticipation. My heart pounded in my chest. Would she give me a chance to show her how much I had changed?

"You look … wonderful," she said in amazement. I was 25 pounds lighter, but, it wasn't about me. It was about her. I was ecstatic to see her again.

"So do you," I replied from the very bottom of my heart. We stared at each other for what felt like eternity. I had so much to say to her, but I couldn't speak. The truth was, in that moment I could hardly even breathe. I needed her like I needed my next breath.

"I'm going to take the dogs for a walk. Would you like to join me?" she asked. I could tell that she feared rejection. The vulnerability in her eyes was unmistakeable. She would never have to worry about that again. That was the old me.

"Yes," I replied, as though my life depended on it. "Yes, please."

We strolled along the beach, finding our feet. The dogs yapped excitedly around us. I imagined Professor Kaufmann, Dr Sahib, George-the-Surfer, Shirley, Mrs Moffet, Kevin the Chiropractor, Lucy, JuJu Banks, Swami G and Sister Simone dancing in circles behind us. Occasionally, I looked over my shoulder to see if their footprints left a trail on the beach behind us. I also scanned the horizon, hoping to catch a glimpse of Henry Jones in the distance, watching over me from afar. But alas, besides the mutts, there were only two sets of footprints in the sand. We were on our own from here onwards. Well, not entirely alone. They'd always be with me, deep inside my heart. Henry Jones, wherever he was, took pride of place. He'd left an indelible mark on my life. It was his legacy that I was about to share with the world. You see, I'd almost finished writing our book. There was one thing left to do. Acting on his final instruction, I pulled the last Post-it note from my pocket and read it. This is what it said:

> *It's good to have an end to journey towards, but it's the journey that matters in the end.*

I tucked it away in my notepad for safekeeping one last time. With that done, I turned to my wife and said in a soft and gentle voice: "Would you like me to share with you my miraculous healing journey with Henry Jones?"

PAY IT FORWARD

If you read *The Healing Chronicles of Henry Jones* and derived true value from it, please pay it forward by recommending this book to three people and write a short, positive reference on our website or digital distribution channels. You have the power to influence others. Use it to help us get Henry Jones's important message to the world.

If you read this book without paying for it or receiving it as a gift, please be true to Henry Jones's message and honour the value you received from it by purchasing a copy of *The Healing Chronicles of Henry Jones* online. Your contribution will help us to reach more people and make a greater difference in the world for the highest good of all.

ABOUT THE AUTHOR

Peter Shrimpton was diagnosed with cancer at the age of 33. Many visits to medical practitioners and hospital left him feeling helpless and afraid. As a victim of disease, he was told to depend entirely on his treatment and medication to get well again (and just hope for the best).

Searching for answers, he read volumes of medical journals and spent many long, dry hours researching the latest drugs that modern medicine had to offer. Nothing he read brought him closer to understanding the cause of his problem, nor healing his body. But then Peter discovered natural healing, and a whole, new, exciting world of opportunity opened to him.

He consumed every self-help book that he could find on the subject and started practising natural healing techniques. As he immersed himself in this fascinating approach to wellness, he made key notes from the scores of inspirational books he read, and the people he met, and began writing about his experiences.

After restoring his body to perfect health, he volunteered in a local hospital for two years, where he got to share his new-found knowledge and experience with sick people. Finding great value in the notes he liberally distributed, patients frequently suggested he write a book. Most of the books he read specialized in a field of healing, but he couldn't find one that showed readers exactly how to heal themselves holistically: physically, mentally, emotionally and spiritually. Preferring novels to self-help books, he was finally persuaded to write a story that can genuinely help people heal themselves, naturally, holistically and permanently.

His book, *The Healing Chronicles of Henry Jones*, was written for people who are sick, but it is relevant to everyone in this modern world. His writing style is colloquial and easy-to-read, so complex issues are made slap-your-forehead-simple for ordinary folk with no medical background.

After writing *The Healing Chronicles of Henry Jones* Peter set out to develop a healing program that would enable people to apply what they learn from his book. He took his years of research and practical experience and developed the *Henry Jones Workbook* and *Handbook*, and produced the *Jumpstart Healing Program*. He founded The Henry Jones Wellness Institute in Cape Town, South Africa, and embarked on a mission to help people heal themselves through his exclusive books, programs, classes, seminars and retreats.

If you need to heal your body, the Henry Jones book series will provide you with a complete, natural and holistic self-healing kit that is very easy to use, and extremely effective. It is our sincerest wish that you embark on this healing journey and experience firsthand how it helps you to heal your body and brings true wellness into your life. It worked for Peter and many others, and it will work for you too.

Printed in Great Britain
by Amazon